Get the eBook FREE!

(PDF, ePub, Kindle, and liveBook all included)

We believe that once you buy a book from us, you should be able to read it in any format we have available. To get electronic versions of this book at no additional cost to you, purchase and then register this book at the Manning website.

Go to https://www.manning.com/freebook and follow the instructions to complete your pBook registration.

That's it!
Thanks from Manning!

Microservice APIs

Microservice APIs

USING PYTHON, FLASK, FASTAPI, OPENAPI AND MORE

JOSÉ HARO PERALTA

SHELTER ISLAND

For online information and ordering of this and other Manning books, please visit www.manning.com. The publisher offers discounts on this book when ordered in quantity. For more information, please contact

Special Sales Department
Manning Publications Co.
20 Baldwin Road
PO Box 761
Shelter Island, NY 11964
Email: orders@manning.com

Manning Publications Co.
20 Baldwin Road
PO Box 761
Shelter Island, NY 11964

Development editor: Marina Michaels
Technical development editor: Nick Watts
Review editor: Mihaela Batinić
Production editor: Andy Marinkovich
Copy editor: Michele Mitchell
Proofreader: Katie Tennant
Technical proofreader: Al Krinker
Typesetter: Dennis Dalinnik
Cover designer: Marija Tudor

ISBN: 9781617298417
Printed in the United States of America

To Jiwon, without whose constant support and encouragement I wouldn't have been able to write this book, and to Ivy, that boundless spark of joy that makes everything I do worth it.

brief contents

contents

preface

APIs and microservices have taken the software industry by storm. Under the pressure of increasing software complexity and the need to scale, more and more organizations are migrating from monolithic to microservices architecture. O'Reilly's "Microservices Adoption in 2020" report found that 77% of respondents had adopted microservices, a trend that is expected to continue growing in the coming years.

Using microservices poses the challenge of driving service integrations through APIs. According to Nordic APIs, 90% of developers work with APIs and they spend 30% of their time building APIs.[1] The growth of the API economy has transformed the way we build applications. Today, it's more and more common to build products and services that are delivered entirely over APIs, such as Twilio and Stripe. Even traditional sectors like banking and insurance are finding new lines of business by opening their APIs and integrating within the Open Banking ecosystem. The wide availability of API-first products means that we can focus on our core business capabilities when building our own applications, while using external APIs to handle common tasks such as authenticating users and sending emails.

It's exciting to be part of this growing ecosystem. However, before we embrace microservices and APIs, we need to know how to architect microservices, how to design APIs, how to define an API strategy, how to make sure we deliver reliable integrations, how to choose a deployment model, and how to protect our systems. In my

[1] J. Simpson, "20 Impressive API Economy Statistics" (https://nordicapis.com/20-impressive-api-economy-statistics/ [accessed May 26, 2022]).

experience, most organizations struggle with one or more of these questions, and a recent report by IBM found that 31% of businesses haven't adopted microservices due to lack of internal expertise.[2] Equally, Postman's 2022 State of the API Report found that 14% of respondents experience API integration failures 11%–25% of the time (http://mng.bz/Xa9v), and according to Salt Security, 94% of organizations experienced API security incidents in 2022.[3]

Many books address the problems mentioned in the previous paragraph, but they typically do it from a highly specific point of view: some focus on architecture, others on APIs, and yet others on security. I felt there's a gap for a book that brings all these questions together and addresses them with a practical approach: essentially, a book that can get an average developer up and running quickly with the best practices, principles, and patterns for designing and building microservice APIs. I wrote this book with that goal in mind.

Over the past years, I've had the opportunity to work with different clients helping them to architect microservices and deliver API integrations. Working on those projects gave me a vantage view into the major hurdles that development teams face when working with microservices and APIs. As it turns out, both technologies are deceivingly simple. A well-designed API is easy to navigate and consume, while well-architected microservices boost developer productivity and are easily scalable. On the other side of the spectrum, badly designed APIs are error prone and difficult to use, and badly architected microservices result in so-called distributed monoliths.

The obvious questions arise: How do you design good APIs? And how do you architect loosely coupled microservices? This book will help you answer these questions and more. You'll also get your hands dirty building APIs and services, and you'll learn how to secure them, test them, and deploy them. The methods, patterns, and principles that I teach in this book are the outcome of many years of trials and experimentation, and I'm very excited about sharing them with you. I hope you find this book a valuable resource in your journey towards becoming a better software developer and architect.

---

[2] "Microservices in the enterprise, 2021: Real benefits, worth the challenges," (https://www.ibm.com/downloads/cas/OQG4AJAM [accessed 26th May 2022]).

[3] Salt Security, "State of API Security Q3 2022", p. 4 (https://content.salt.security/state-api-report.html).

acknowledgments

Writing this book has been one of the most fascinating journeys in my career, and I couldn't have done it without the help and support of my family and an amazing team of colleagues. The book is dedicated to my wonderful wife, Jiwon, without whose constant encouragement and understanding I wouldn't have been able to complete this book, and to our daughter, Ivy, who made sure I never had a dull moment in my schedule.

I have benefited enormously from the people who contributed ideas for the book, helped me better understand the tools and protocols I use in it, and provided feedback on various chapters and drafts. Special thanks go to Dmitry Dygalo, Kelvin Meeks, Sebastián Ramírez Montaño, Chris Richardson, Jean Yang, Gajendra Deshpande, Oscar Islas, Mehdi Medjaoui, Ben Hutton, Andrej Baranovskij, Alex Mystridis, Roope Hakulinen, Steve Ardagh-Walter, Kathrin Björkelund, Thomas Dean, Marco Antonio Sanz, Vincent Vandenborne, and the amazing maintainers of Ariadne at Mirumee.

Since 2020, I've presented drafts and ideas from the book at various conferences, including EuroPython, PyCon India, API World, API Specifications Conference, and various podcasts and meetups. I want to thank everyone who attended my presentations and gave me valuable feedback. I also want to thank the attendants to my workshops at microapis.io for their thoughtful comments on the book.

I want to thank my acquisitions editor, Andy Waldron. Andy did a brilliant job helping me get my book proposal in good shape and keeping the book focused on relevant topics. He also supported me tirelessly to promote the book and helped me to reach a wider audience.

The book you now have in your hands is readable and understandable thanks to the invaluable work of my editor, Marina Michaels, who went far and beyond to help me write a better book. She did an outstanding job helping me improve my writing style, and keeping me on track and motivated.

I want to thank my technical editor, Nick Watts, who rightly pointed out many inaccuracies and always challenged me to provide better explanations and illustrations, and my technical proofreader, Al Krinker, who diligently checked all the code listings and the GitHub repository for this book, making sure the code is correct and executes without issues.

I also want to thank the rest of the Manning team who was involved in the production of this book, including Candace Gillhoolley, Gloria Lukos, Stjepan Jureković, Christopher Kaufmann, Radmila Ercegovac, Mihaela Batinić, Ana Romac, Aira Dučić, Melissa Ice, Eleonor Gardner, Breckyn Ely, Paul Wells, Andy Marinkovich, Katie Tennant, Michele Mitchell, Sam Wood, Paul Spratley, Nick Nason, and Rebecca Rinehart. Thanks also go to Marjan Bace for betting on me and giving this book a chance.

While working on this book, I had the opportunity to receive detailed and outstanding feedback from the most amazing group of reviewers, including Alain Lompo, Björn Neuhaus, Bryan Miller, Clifford Thurber, David Paccoud, Debmalya Jash, Gaurav Sood, George Haines, Glenn Leo Swonk, Hartmut Palm, Ikechukwu Okonkwo, Jan Pieter Herweijer, Joey Smith, Juan Jimenez, Justin Baur, Krzysztof Kamyczek, Manish Jain, Marcus Young, Mathijs Affourtit, Matthieu Evrin, Michael Bright, Michael Rybintsev, Michal Rutka, Miguel Montalvo, Ninoslav Cerkez, Pierre-Michel Ansel, Rafael Aiquel, Robert Kulagowski, Rodney Weis, Sambasiva Andaluri, Satej Kumar Sahu, Simeon Leyzerzon, Steven K Makunzva, Stuart Woodward, Stuti Verma, and William Jamir Silva. I credit them all with much of the good content that made its way into the book.

Since the book went into MEAP, I've been blessed by the words of encouragement and feedback that many of my readers sent me through various channels, such as LinkedIn and Twitter. I was also lucky to converse with a brilliant community of readers who actively participated in the book's forum in Manning's liveBook platform. I'm heartily grateful to all of you.

This book wouldn't have been possible without the tireless work of thousands of open source contributors who created and maintain the amazing libraries that I use in this book. I'm very thankful to all of you, and I hope my book helps to make your amazing work more visible.

Finally, thank you, the reader, for acquiring a copy of my book. I can only hope that you find this book useful and informative and that you enjoy reading it as much as I enjoyed writing it. I love to hear from my readers, and I'd be delighted if you share your thoughts on the book with me.

about this book

The goal of this book is to teach you how to build microservices and drive their integrations using APIs. You'll learn to design a microservices platform and to build REST and GraphQL APIs to enable communication between microservices. You'll also learn to test and validate your microservice APIs, to secure them, and to deploy and operate them in the cloud.

Who should read this book?

This book is helpful for software developers who work with microservices and APIs. The book uses a very practical approach, and nearly every chapter illustrates the explanations with full coding examples. Therefore, hands-on developers who work directly with microservice APIs will find the book's contents valuable.

The coding examples are in Python; however, knowledge of the language isn't necessary to be able to follow along with them. Before introducing new code, every concept is explained thoroughly.

The book contains a lot of emphasis on design strategies, best practices, and development workflows, and therefore it's also useful for CTOs, architects, and VPs of engineering who need to decide whether microservices are the right architectural solution for them, or who need to choose between different API strategies and how to make the integrations work.

How this book is organized: A roadmap

The book is divided into four sections with a total of 14 chapters.

Part 1 introduces the concepts of microservices and APIs, shows how to build a simple API, and explains how to design a microservices platform:

- Chapter 1 introduces the main concepts of the book: microservices and APIs. It explains how microservices differ from monolithic architecture, and when it makes sense to use monoliths versus microservices. It also explains what APIs are and how they help us drive integrations between microservices.
- Chapter 2 offers a step-by-step guide for implementing APIs using Python's popular FastAPI framework. You'll learn to read an API specification and understand its requirements. You'll also learn to build APIs in gradual steps, and how to test your data validation models.
- Chapter 3 explains how to design a microservices platform. It introduces three fundamental microservice design principles, and it explains how to decompose a system into microservices, using decomposition by business capability and decomposition by subdomains.

Part 2 explains how to design, document, and build REST APIs, and how to build a microservice:

- Chapter 4 explains the design principles of REST APIs. It introduces the six constraints of REST architecture and the Richardson Maturity Model, and then moves on to explain how we leverage the HTTP protocol to design well-structured and highly expressive REST APIs.
- Chapter 5 explains how to document a REST API using the OpenAPI specification standard. You'll learn the basics of JSON Schema syntax, how to define endpoints, how to model your data, and how to refactor your documentation with reusable schemas.
- Chapter 6 explains how to build REST APIs using two popular Python frameworks: FastAPI and Flask. You'll learn about the differences between the two frameworks, but you'll also learn how the principles and patterns for building APIs remain the same and transcend the implementation details of any technical stack.
- Chapter 7 explains fundamental principles and patterns for building microservices. It introduces the concept of hexagonal architecture, and it explains how to enforce loose coupling between the layers of an application. It also explains how to implement database models using SQLAlchemy and how to manage database migrations using Alembic.

Part 3 explains how to design, consume, and build GraphQL APIs:

- Chapter 8 explains how to design GraphQL APIs and how the Schema Definition Language works. It introduces GraphQL's built-in types, and it explains how to define custom types. You'll learn how to create relationships between types, and how to define queries and mutations.

- Chapter 9 explains how to consume GraphQL APIs. You'll learn to run a mock server and how to explore GraphQL documentation using GraphiQL. You'll learn to run queries and mutations against a GraphQL server and how to parametrize your operations.
- Chapter 10 explains how to build GraphQL APIs using Python's Ariadne framework. You'll learn to leverage the API documentation to automatically load data validation models, and also to implement resolvers for custom types, queries, and mutations.

Part 4 explains how to test, secure, and deploy your microservice APIs:

- Chapter 11 explains how to add authentication and authorization to your APIs using standard protocols such as OpenID Connect (OIDC) and Open Authorization (OAuth) 2.1. You'll learn how to produce and validate JSON Web Tokens (JWTs) and how to create an authorization middleware for your APIs.
- Chapter 12 explains how to test and validate your APIs. You'll learn what property-based testing is and how to use it to test your APIs, and you'll also learn to use API testing automation frameworks like Dredd and schemathesis.
- Chapter 13 explains how to Dockerize your microservice APIs, how to run them locally using Docker Compose, and how to publish your Docker builds to AWS Elastic Container Registry (ECR).
- Chapter 14 explains how to deploy your microservice APIs to AWS using Kubernetes. You'll learn to create and operate a Kubernetes cluster using AWS EKS, how to launch an Aurora serverless database into a secure network, how to inject application configuration securely using envelope encryption, and how to set up your services to operate at scale.

All chapters have a common theme: building components of a fictitious, on-demand coffee delivery platform called CoffeeMesh. We introduce CoffeeMesh in chapter 1, and in chapter 3, we break the platform down into microservices. Therefore, I recommend reading chapters 1 and 3 to get a better understanding of the examples introduced in later chapters. Otherwise, every part of the book is fairly independent, and each chapter is pretty self-contained. For example, if you want to learn how to design and build REST APIs, you can jump straight to part 2, and if your interest lies with GraphQL APIs, you can focus on part 3. Equally, if you want to learn to add authentication and authorization to your APIs, you can jump straight into chapter 11, or if you want to learn how to test APIs, you can go directly to chapter 12.

There're some cross-references between chapters: for example, chapter 12 references the API implementations from parts 2 and 3, but if you're comfortable building APIs, you should be able to skip directly to chapter 12. The same is true for the other chapters in part 4.

About the code

This book contains many examples of source code both in numbered listings and in line with normal text. In both cases, source code is formatted in a `fixed-width font like this` to separate it from ordinary text. Sometimes code is also **`in bold`** to highlight code that has changed from previous steps in the chapter, such as when a new feature adds to an existing line of code.

In many cases, the original source code has been reformatted; we've added line breaks and reworked indentation to accommodate the available page space in the book. In some cases, even this was not enough, and listings include line-continuation markers (➥). Additionally, comments in the source code have often been removed from the listings when the code is described in the text. Code annotations accompany many of the listings, highlighting important concepts.

Except for chapters 1, 3, and 4, every chapter of the book is full of coding examples that illustrate every new concept and pattern introduced to the reader. Most of the coding examples are in Python, except in chapters 5, 8, and 9, which focus on API design, and therefore contain examples in OpenAPI/JSON Schema (chapter 5) and the Schema Definition Language (chapters 8 and 9). All the code is thoroughly explained, and therefore it should be accessible to all readers, including those who don't know Python.

You can get executable snippets of code from the liveBook (online) version of this book at https://livebook.manning.com/book/microservice-apis. The complete code for the examples in the book is available for download from the Manning website at www.manning.com, and from a GitHub repository dedicated to this book at: https://github.com/abunuwas/microservice-apis. Every chapter has a corresponding folder in the GitHub repo, such as ch02 for chapter 2. Unless otherwise specified, all file references in each chapter are relative to their corresponding folder in GitHub. For example, in chapter 2, orders/app.py refers to the ch02/orders/app.py file in GitHub.

The GitHub repository for this book shows the final state of the code in every chapter. Some chapters show how to build features progressively, in iterative steps. In those cases, the version of the code you'll find on GitHub matches the final version of the code in the chapter.

The Python code examples in the book have been tested with Python 3.10, although any version of Python upwards of 3.7 should work just the same. The code and the commands that I use throughout the book have been tested on a Mac machine, but they should work without problems on Windows and Linux as well. If you work on Windows, I recommend you use a POSIX-compatible terminal, such as Cygwin.

I've used Pipenv to manage dependencies in every chapter. In each chapter's folder, you'll find Pipfile and Pipfile.lock files that describe the exact dependencies that I used to run the code examples. To avoid problems running the code, I recommend you download those files at the start of every chapter, and install the dependencies from them.

liveBook discussion forum

Purchase of *Microservice APIs* includes free access to liveBook, Manning's online reading platform. Using liveBook's exclusive discussion features, you can attach comments to the book globally or to specific sections or paragraphs. It's a snap to make notes for yourself, ask and answer technical questions, and receive help from the author and other users. To access the forum, go to https://livebook.manning.com/book/microservice-apis/discussion. You can also learn more about Manning's forums and the rules of conduct at https://livebook.manning.com/discussion.

Manning's commitment to our readers is to provide a venue where a meaningful dialogue between individual readers and between readers and the author can take place. It is not a commitment to any specific amount of participation on the part of the author, whose contribution to the forum remains voluntary (and unpaid). We suggest you try asking him some challenging questions lest his interest stray! The forum and the archives of previous discussions will be accessible from the publisher's website for as long as the book is in print.

Other online resources

If you want to learn more about microservice APIs, you can check out my blog, https://microapis.io/blog, which contains additional resources that complement the lessons of this book. On the same website, I also keep an up-to-date list of workshops and seminars that I organize frequently, which also complement this book.

about the author

José Haro Peralta is a software and architecture consultant. With over 10 years of experience, José has helped organizations big and small to build complex systems, architect microservice platforms, and deliver API integrations. He's also the founder of microapis.io, a company that provides software consulting and training services. Recognized as a thought leader in the fields of cloud computing, DevOps, and software automation, José speaks regularly at international conferences and frequently organizes public workshops and seminars.

about the cover illustration

The figure on the cover of *Microservice APIs* is captioned "L'invalide," or "The Disabled," and depicts a wounded French soldier who was a resident at the Hôtel national des Invalides, or National House of the Disabled. This image is taken from a collection by Jacques Grasset de Saint-Sauveur, published in 1797. Each illustration is finely drawn and colored by hand.

In those days, it was easy to identify where people lived and what their trade or station in life was just by their dress. Manning celebrates the inventiveness and initiative of the computer business with book covers based on the rich diversity of regional culture centuries ago, brought back to life by pictures from collections such as this one.

Part 1

Introducing Microservice APIs

Microservices are an architectural style in which components of a system are designed as standalone and independently deployable applications. The concept of microservices has been around since the early 2000s, and since the 2010s it has gained in popularity. Nowadays, microservices are a popular choice for building modern websites. As you'll learn in chapter 1, microservices allow you to leverage the power of distributed applications, scale components more easily, and release faster.

However, for all their benefits, microservices also come with challenges of their own. They bring a substantial infrastructure overhead, and they're more difficult to monitor, operate, and trace. When working with microservices, the first challenge is to get their design right, and in chapter 3 you'll learn several principles and strategies that will help you build robust microservices.

Microservices collaborate through APIs, and in this book, you'll learn to design and build REST and GraphQL APIs for your microservices. Chapter 2 gives you a taste of building a REST API, and in the second part of this book, you'll learn additional patterns and principles to build robust REST APIs. The most challenging aspect of working with APIs is ensuring that both the API client and the API server follow the API specification, and in chapter 1 you'll learn about documentation-driven development and the importance of starting the API journey with a good and well-documented design.

The first part of this book teaches you foundational patterns and principles for building microservices and driving their integrations with APIs. In the rest of this book, we build on top of the concepts introduced here, and you'll learn how to build robust APIs, how to test them, how to protect them, and how to deploy your microservice APIs to the cloud. Our intrepid journey is just about to begin!

1 What are microservice APIs?

This chapter covers

- What microservices are and how they compare with monolithic applications
- What web APIs are and how they help us drive integrations between microservices
- The most important challenges of developing and operating microservices

This chapter defines the most important concepts in this book: microservices and APIs. Microservices are an architectural style in which components of a system are designed as independently deployable services, and APIs are the interfaces that allow us to interact with those services. We will see the defining features of microservices architecture and how they compare with monolithic applications. Monolithic applications are structured around a single code base and deployed in a single build.

We'll discuss the benefits and the disadvantages of microservices architecture. The last part of this chapter talks about the most important challenges that we face when designing, implementing, and operating microservices. This discussion is not to deter you from embracing microservices, but so that you can make an informed decision about whether microservices are the right choice of architecture for you.

1.1 What are microservices?

In this section, we define what microservices architecture is, and we analyze how microservices compare with monolithic applications. We'll look into the benefits and challenges of each architectural pattern. Finally, we'll also take a brief look at the historical developments that led to the emergence of modern microservices architecture.

1.1.1 Defining microservices

So, what are microservices? Microservices can be defined in different ways, and, depending on which aspect of microservices architecture we want to emphasize, authors provide slightly different yet related definitions of the term. Sam Newman, one of the most influential authors in the field of microservices, provides a minimal definition: "Microservices are small, autonomous services that work together."[1]

This definition emphasizes the fact that microservices are applications that run independently of each other yet can collaborate in the performance of their tasks. The definition also emphasizes that microservices are "small." In this context, "small" doesn't refer to the size of the microservices' code base, but to the idea that microservices are applications with a narrow and well-defined scope, following the Single Responsibility Principle of doing one thing and doing it well.

A seminal article written by James Lewis and Martin Fowler provides a more detailed definition. They define microservices as an architectural style with "an approach to developing a single application as a suite of small services, each running in its own process and communicating with lightweight mechanisms, often an HTTP resource API" (https://martinfowler.com/articles/microservices.html). This definition emphasizes the autonomy of the services by stating that they run in independent processes. Lewis and Fowler also highlight that microservices have a narrow scope of responsibilities by saying that they are "small," and they explicitly describe how microservices communicate through lightweight protocols, such as HTTP.

> **DEFINITION** A *microservice* is an architectural style in which components of a system are designed as independently deployable services. Microservices are designed around well-defined business subdomains, and they talk to each other using lightweight protocols, such as HTTP.

From the previous definitions, we can see that microservices can be defined as an architectural style in which services are components that perform a small and clearly defined set of related functions. As you can see in figure 1.1, this definition means that a microservice is designed and built around a specific business subdomain, for example, processing payments, sending emails, or handling orders from a customer.

Microservices are deployed as independent processes, typically running in independent environments, and expose their capabilities through well-defined interfaces. In this book, you will learn to design and build microservices that expose their capabilities

[1] Sam Newman, *Building Microservices* (O'Reilly, 2015), p. 2.

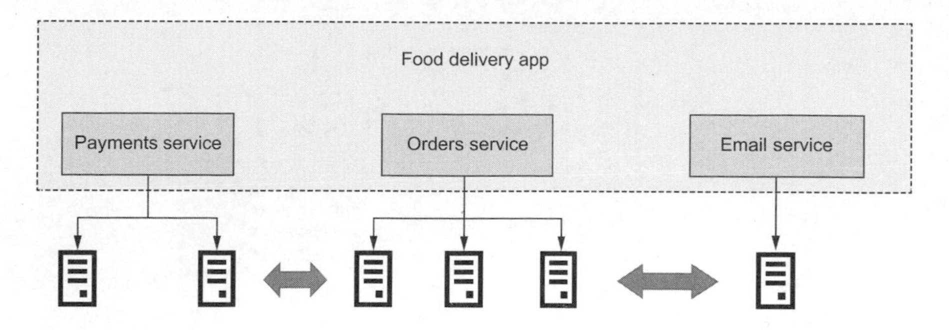

Figure 1.1 In microservices architecture, every service implements a specific business subdomain and is deployed as an independent component that runs in its own process.

through web APIs, though other types of interfaces are also possible, such as messaging queues.[2]

1.1.2 Microservices vs. monoliths

Now that we know what microservices are, let's see how they compare with the monolithic application pattern. In contrast with microservices, a monolith is a system where all functionality is deployed together as a single build and runs in the same process. For example, figure 1.2 shows a food delivery application with four services: a payments service, an orders service, a delivery service, and a customer support service. Since the application is implemented as a monolith, all functionality is deployed together. We can run multiple instances of a monolithic application and have them run in parallel for redundancy and scalability purposes, but it's still the whole application running in each process.

> **DEFINITION** A *monolith* is an architectural pattern in which the whole application is deployed as a single build.

In some situations, the monolith is the right choice of architecture. For example, we'd use a monolith when our code base is small and it isn't expected to grow very large.[3] Monoliths also come with advantages. First, having the whole implementation in the same code base makes it easier to access data and logic from different subdomains. And because everything runs within the same process, it is easy to trace errors through the application: you only need to place a few breakpoints in different parts of your code, and you will get a detailed picture of what happens when something goes wrong. Besides, because all the code falls within the scope of the same project, you

[2] For a comprehensive view of the different interfaces that can be used to enable communication between microservices, see Chris Richardson, *Microservices Patterns* (Manning, 2019).

[3] For a thorough analysis of strategic architectural decisions around monoliths and microservices, see Vernon, Vaughn and Tomasz Jaskula, *Strategic Monoliths and Microservices* (Addison-Wesley, 2021).

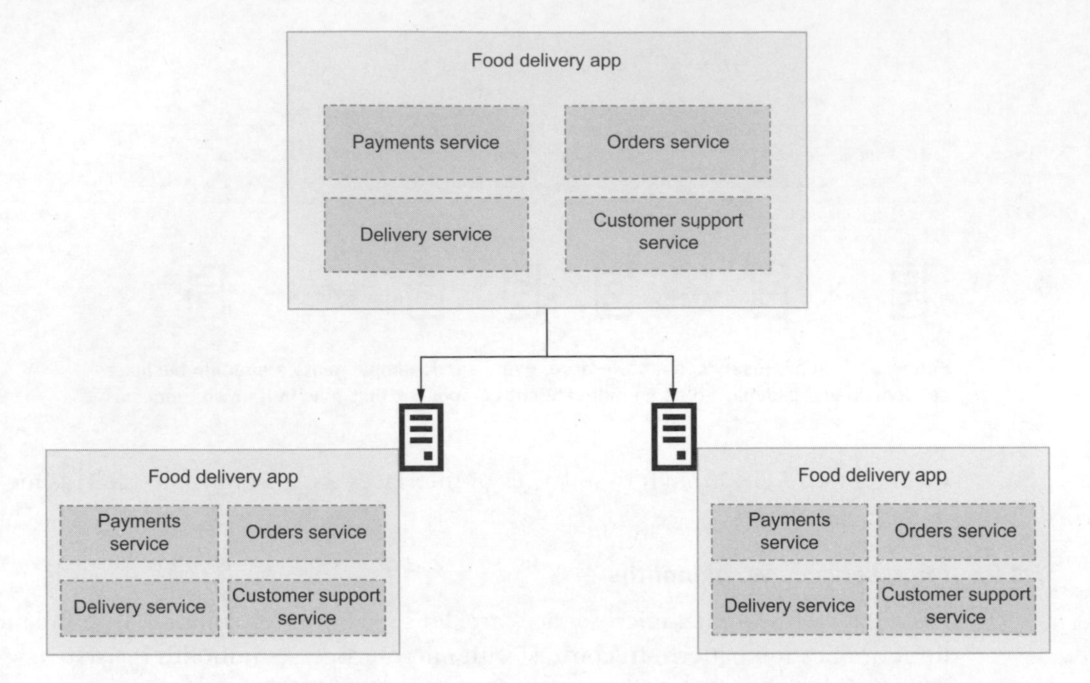

Figure 1.2 In a monolithic application, all functionality is deployed together as a single build to each server.

can leverage the productivity features of your favorite development editor when consuming functionality from a different subdomain.

However, as the application grows and becomes more complex, this type of architecture shows limitations. This happens when the code base grows to a point where it becomes difficult to manage, and when finding your way through the code becomes arduous. Additionally, being able to reuse code from other subdomains within the same project often leads to tight coupling among components. Tight coupling happens when a component depends on the implementation details of another piece of code.

The bigger the monolith, the longer it takes to test it. Every part of the monolith must be tested, and as we add new features to it, the test suite grows larger. Consequently, deployments become slower and encourage developers to pile up changes within the same release, which makes releases more challenging. Because many changes are released together, if a new bug is introduced in the release, it is often difficult to spot the specific change that caused the bug and roll it back. And because the whole application runs within the same process, when you scale the resources for one component, you are scaling for the whole application. Long story short, code changes become increasingly risky and deployments become more difficult to manage. How can microservices help us address these issues?

Microservices address some of the issues associated with monolithic applications by enforcing strict boundaries separating components. When you implement an application using microservices, each microservice runs in a different process, often in different servers or virtual machines, and can have a completely different deployment model. As a matter of fact, they can be written in completely different programming languages (that does not mean they should!).

Because microservices contain smaller code bases than a monolith, and because their logic is self-contained and defined within the scope of a specific business subdomain, it is easier to test them, and their test suites run faster. Because they do not have dependencies with other components of the platform at the code level (except perhaps for some shared libraries), their code is clearer, and it is easier to refactor them. This means the code can get better over time and become more maintainable. Consequently, we can make small changes to the code and release more often. Smaller releases are more controllable, and if we spot a bug, the releases are easier to roll back. I'd like to emphasize that microservices are not a panacea. As we will see in section 1.3, microservices also have limitations and bring challenges of their own.

Now that we know what microservices are and how they compare with monolithic applications, let's take a step back and see what developments led to the emergence of this type of architecture.

1.1.3 Microservices today and how we got here

In many ways, microservices are not new.[4] Companies were implementing and deploying components as independent applications well before the concept of microservices became popular. They just did not call it microservices. Werner Vogels, CTO of Amazon, explains how Amazon started to experiment with this type of architecture in the early 2000s. By that time, the code base for the Amazon website had grown into a complex system without a clear architectural pattern, where making new releases and scaling the system had become serious pain points. To combat these issues, they decided to look for independent pieces of logic within the code and separate them out into independently deployable components, with an API in front of them. As part of this process, they also identified the data that belongs to those components and made sure that other parts of the system could not access the data except through an API. They called this new type of architecture *service-oriented architecture* (https://vimeo.com/29719577). Netflix also pioneered this type of architectural style at scale, and they referred to it as "fine-grained Service Oriented Architecture."[5]

---

[4] For a more comprehensive analysis of the history of microservices architecture and its precursors, see Nicola Dragoni et al, "Microservices: Yesterday, Today, and Tomorrow," *Present and Ulterior Software Engineering* (Springer, 2017), pp. 195–216.

[5] Allen Wang and Sudhir Tonse, "Announcing Ribbon: Tying the Netflix Mid-Tier Services Together," *Netflix Technology Blog*, January 18, 2013, https://netflixtechblog.com/announcing-ribbon-tying-the-netflix-mid-tier-services-together-a89346910a62. For an excellent discussion of the difference between service-oriented architecture (SOA) and microservices architecture, see Richardson, *Microservices Patterns*, pp. 13–14.

The term *microservice* grew in popularity in the early 2010s to describe this type of architecture. For example, James Lewis used this concept in a presentation at the 33rd Degree conference in Krakow in 2012, under the title "Micro-Services—Java, the Unix way" (https://vimeo.com/74452550). In 2014 the concept was consolidated with a paper written by Martin Fowler and James Lewis about the architectural features of microservices (https://martinfowler.com/articles/microservices.html), as well as the publication of Newman's influential book *Building Microservices*.

Today, microservices are a widely used architectural style. Most companies in which technology plays an important role are already using microservices or moving toward its adoption. It is also common for startups to begin implementing their platform using a microservices approach. However, microservices are not for everyone, and although they bring substantial benefits, as we have shown, they also carry considerable challenges, as we will see in section 1.3.

1.2 What are web APIs?

In this section, we will explain web APIs. You will learn that a web API is a specific instance of the more general concept of an application programming interface (API). It is important to understand that an API is just a layer on top of an application, and that there are different types of interfaces. For this reason, we will begin this section by defining what an API is, and then we will move on to explaining how APIs help us drive integrations between microservices.

1.2.1 What is an API?

An API is an interface that allows us to programmatically interact with an application. Programmatic interfaces are those we can use from our code or from the terminal, as opposed to graphic interfaces, in which we use a user interface to interact with the application. There are multiple types of application interfaces, such as command-line interfaces (CLIs; interfaces that allow you to use an application from a terminal), desktop UI interfaces, web UI interfaces, or web API interfaces. As you can see in figure 1.3, an application can have one or more of these interfaces.

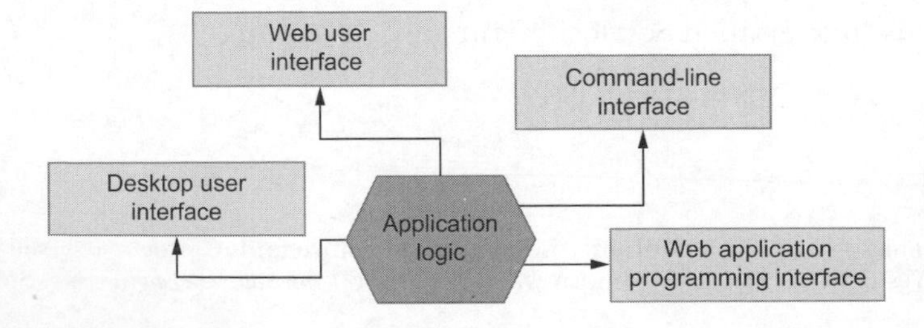

Figure 1.3 An application can have multiple interfaces, such as a web API, a CLI, a web UI, and a desktop UI.

To illustrate this idea, think of the popular client URL (cURL). cURL is a CLI to the `libcurl` library. `libcurl` implements functionality that allows us to interact with URLs, while cURL exposes those capabilities through a CLI. For example, we can use cURL to send a GET request to a URL:

```
$ curl -L http://www.google.com
```

We can also use cURL with the `-o` option in order to download the contents of a URL to a file:

```
$ curl -O http://www.gnu.org/software/gettext/manual/gettext.html
```

The `libcurl` library sits behind the cURL CLI, and nothing prevents us from accessing it directly through the source code (if you are curious, you can pull it from Github: https://github.com/curl/curl) and building additional types of interfaces for this application.

1.2.2 What is a web API?

Now that we understand what an API is, we will explain the defining features of a web API. A web API is an API that uses the Hypertext Transfer Protocol (HTTP) protocol to transport data. HTTP is the communication protocol that underpins the internet, and it allows us to exchange different kinds of media types, such as text, images, video, and JSON, over a network. HTTP uses the concept of a Uniform Resource Locator (i.e., URL) to locate resources on the internet, and it has features that can be leveraged by API technologies to enhance the interaction with the server, such as request methods (e.g., GET, POST, PUT) and HTTP headers. Web APIs are implemented using technologies such as SOAP, REST, GraphQL, gRPC, and others that are discussed in more detail in appendix A.

1.2.3 How do APIs help us drive microservices integrations?

Microservices communicate with each other using APIs, and therefore APIs represent the interfaces to our microservices. APIs are documented using standard protocols. The API documentation tells us exactly what we need to do to interact with the microservice and what kind of responses we can expect from it. The better the API documentation, the clearer it is for the API consumer how the API works. In that sense, as you can see in figure 1.4, API documentation represents a contract between services:

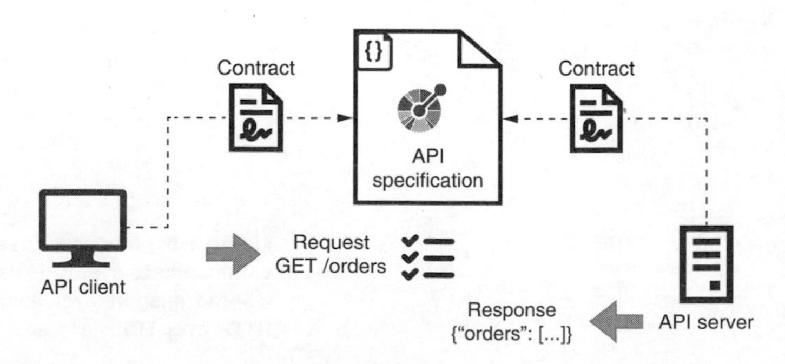

Figure 1.4 API specifications represent a contract between the API server and the API client. As long as both the client and the server follow the specification, the API integration will work.

as long as both the client and the server follow the API documentation, communication will work as expected.

Fowler and Lewis popularized the idea that the best strategy for integrating microservices is by exposing *smart endpoints* and communicating through *dumb pipes* (https://martinfowler.com/articles/microservices.html). This idea is inspired by the design principles of Unix systems, which establish that

- A system should be made up of small, independent components that do only one thing.
- The output for every component should be designed in such a way that it can easily become the input for another component.

Unix programs communicate with each other using pipelines, which are simple mechanisms for passing messages from one application to another. To illustrate this process, think of the following chain of commands, which you can run from the terminal of a Unix-based machine (e.g., a Mac or Linux computer):

```
$ history | less
```

The `history` command shows you the list of all commands you have run using your Bash profile. The list of commands can be long, so you may want to paginate `history`'s output using the `less` command. To pass data from one command to the another, use the pipe character (|), which instructs the shell to capture the output from the `history` command and pipe it as the input of the `less` command. We say that this type of pipe is "dumb" because its only job is passing messages from one process to another. As you can see in figure 1.5, web APIs exchange data through HTTP. The data transport layer knows nothing about the specific API protocol we are using, and therefore it represents our "dumb pipe," while the API itself contains all the necessary logic to process the data.

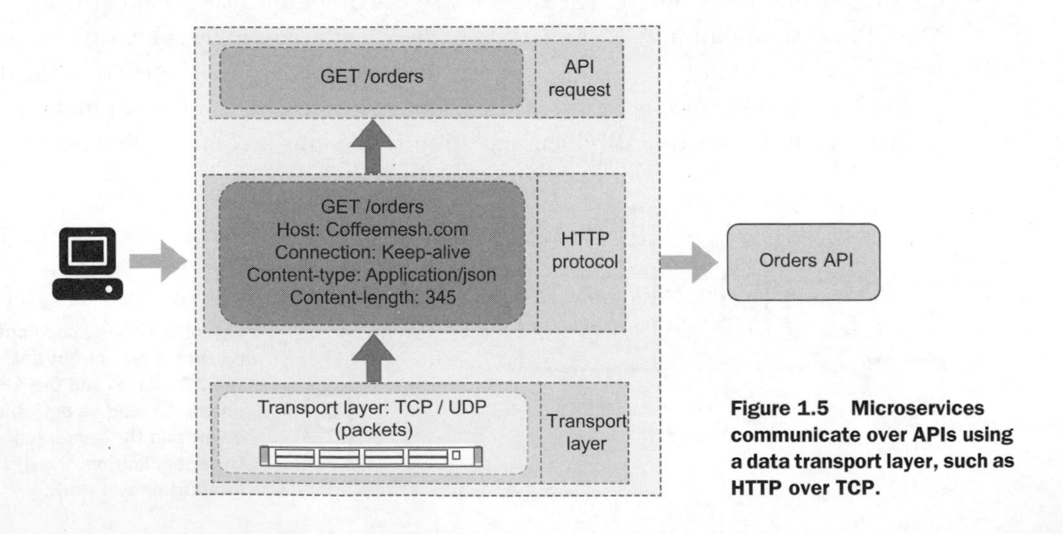

Figure 1.5 Microservices communicate over APIs using a data transport layer, such as HTTP over TCP.

APIs must be stable, and behind them you can change the internal implementations of any service provided they comply with the API documentation. This means that the consumer of an API must be able to continue calling the API in the exact way as before, and it must get the same responses. This leads to another important concept in microservices architecture: *replaceability*.[6] The idea is that you should be able to completely replace the code base that lies behind an endpoint, yet the endpoint, and therefore communication across services, will still work. Now that we understand what APIs are and how they help us drive integrations between services, let's look at the most important challenges posed by microservices.

1.3 Challenges of microservices architecture

As we saw in section 1.1.2, microservices bring substantial benefits. However, they also come with significant challenges. In this section, we discuss the most important challenges that microservices pose, which we classify into five main categories:

- Effective service decomposition
- Microservices integration tests
- Handling service unavailability
- Tracing distributed transactions
- Increased operational complexity and infrastructure overhead

All the problems and difficulties that we discuss in this section can be addressed with specific patterns and strategies, some of which we detail over the course of this book. You'll also find references to other resources that deal with these issues in depth. The idea here is to make you aware that microservices are not a magical cure for all the problems that monolithic applications present.

1.3.1 Effective service decomposition

One of the most important challenges when designing microservices is service decomposition. We must break down a platform into loosely coupled yet sufficiently independent components with clearly defined boundaries. You can tell whether you have unreasonable coupling between your services if you find yourself changing one service whenever you change another service. In such situations, either the contract between services is not resilient, or there are enough dependencies between both components to justify merging them. Failing to break down a system into independent microservices can result in what Chris Richardson, author of *Microservices Patterns*, calls a *distributed monolith*, a situation where you combine all the problems of monolithic architectures with all the problems of microservices, without enjoying the benefits of any of them. In chapter 3, you'll learn useful design patterns and service decomposition strategies that will help you break down a system into microservices.

[6] Newman, *Building Microservices*, pp. 7–8.

1.3.2 Microservices integration tests

In section 1.1.2, we said that microservices are usually easier to test, and that their test suites generally run faster. Microservices integration tests, however, can be significantly more difficult to run, especially in cases where a single transaction involves collaboration among several microservices. When your whole application runs within the same process, it is fairly easy to test the integration between different components, and most of it will simply require well-written unit tests. In a microservices context, to test the integration among multiple services you need to be able to run all of them with a setup similar to your production environment.

You can use different strategies to test microservices integrations. The first step is making sure that each service has a well-documented and correctly implemented API. You can test the API implementation against the API specification using tools like Dredd and Schemathesis, as you'll learn in chapter 12. You must also ensure that the API client is consuming the API exactly as dictated by the API documentation. You can write unit tests for the API client using the API documentation to generate mocked responses from the service.[7] Finally, none of these tests will be sufficient without a full-blown end-to-end test that runs the actual microservices making calls to each other.

1.3.3 Handling service unavailability

We have to make sure that our applications are resilient in the face of service unavailability, connections and request timeouts, erroring requests, and so on. For example, when we place an order through a food delivery application such as Uber Eats, Delivery Hero, or Deliveroo, a chain of requests between services unfolds to process and deliver the order, and any of those requests can fail at any point. Let's take a high-level view of the process that takes place when a user places an order (see figure 1.6 for an illustration of the chain of requests):

1. A customer places an order and pays for it. The order is placed using the orders service, and to process the payment, the orders service works together with the payments service.
2. If payment is successful, the orders service makes a request to the kitchen service to schedule the order for production.
3. Once the order has been produced, the kitchen service makes a request to the delivery service to schedule the delivery.

In this complex chain of requests, if one of the services involved fails to respond as expected, it can trigger a cascading error through the platform that leaves the order unprocessed or in an inconsistent state. For this reason, it is important to design

[7] To learn more about API development workflows and how to use API mock servers to build the client, check out my presentation "API Development Workflows for Successful Integrations," Manning API Conference, August 3, 2021, https://youtu.be/SUKqmEX_uwg.

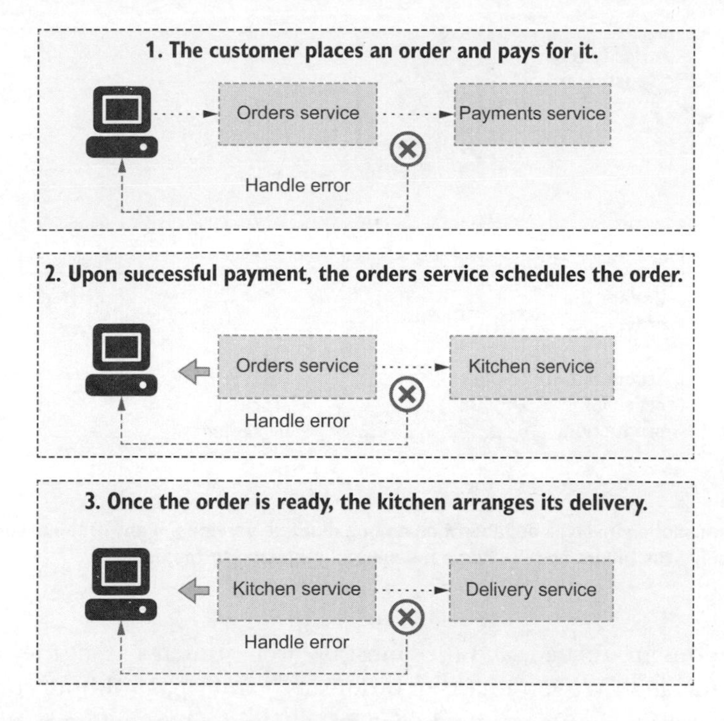

Figure 1.6 Microservices must be resilient to events such as service unavailability, request timeouts, and processing errors from other services and either retry the requests or come back to the user with a meaningful response.

microservices so that they can deal reliably with failing endpoints. Our end-to-end tests should consider these scenarios and test the behavior of our services in those situations.

1.3.4 Tracing distributed transactions

Collaborating services must sometimes handle distributed transactions. Distributed transactions are those that require the collaboration of two or more services. For example, in a food delivery application, we want to keep track of the existing stock of ingredients so that our catalogue can accurately reflect product availability. When a user places an order, we want to update the stock of ingredients to reflect the new availability. Specifically, we want to update the stock of ingredients once the payment has been successfully processed. As you can see in figure 1.7, the successful processing of an order involves the following actions:

1. Process the payment.
2. If payment is successful, update the order's status to indicate that it's in progress.
3. Interface with the kitchen service to schedule the order for production.
4. Update the stock of ingredients to reflect their current availability.

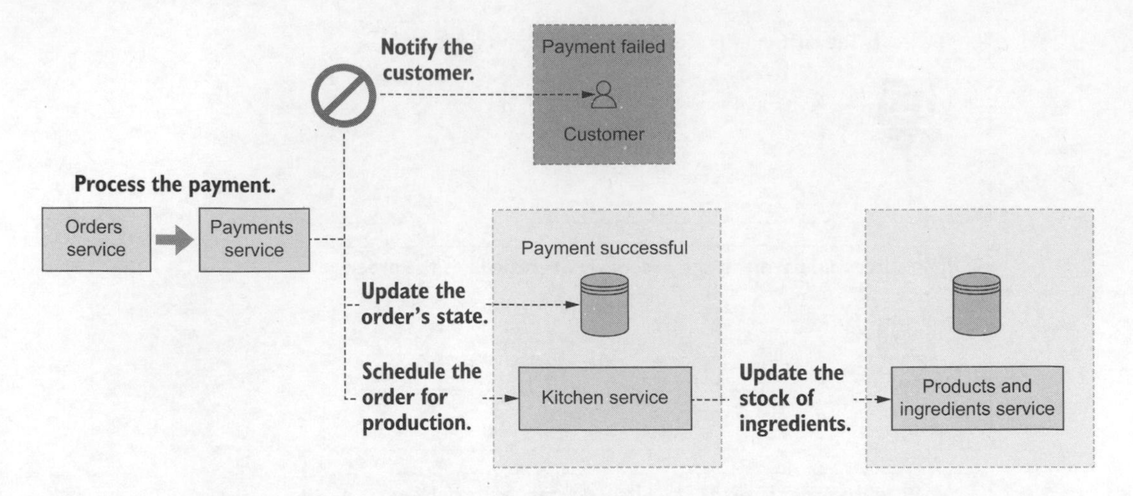

Figure 1.7 A distributed transaction involves collaboration among multiple services. If any of these services fails, we must be able to handle the failure and provide a meaningful response to the user.

All of these operations are related, and they must be orchestrated so that they either all succeed or fail together. We can't have an order successfully paid without correctly updating its status, and we shouldn't schedule its production if payment fails. We may want to update the availability of the ingredients at the time of making the order, and if payment fails later on, we want to make sure we rollback the update. If all these actions happen within the same process, managing the flow is straightforward, but with microservices we must manage the outcomes of various processes. When using microservices, the challenge is ensuring that we have a robust communication process among services so that we know exactly what kind of error happens when it does, and we take appropriate measures in response to it.

In the case of services that work collaboratively to serve certain requests, you also must be able to trace the cycle of the request as it goes across the different services to be able to spot errors during the transaction. To gain visibility of distributed transactions, you'll need to set up distributed logging and tracing for your microservices. You can learn more about this topic from Jamie Riedesel's *Software Telemetry* (Manning, 2021).

1.3.5 Increased operational complexity and infrastructure overhead

Another important challenge that comes with microservices is the increased operational complexity and operational overhead they add to your platform. When the whole backend of your website runs within a single application build, you only need to deploy and monitor one process. When you have a dozen microservices, every service must be configured, deployed, and managed. And this includes not only the provisioning of servers to deploy the services, but also log aggregation streams, monitoring systems, alerts, self-recovery mechanisms, and so on. As you'll learn in chapter 3, every service owns its own database, which means they also require multiple database setups with all the features needed to operate at scale. And it is not unusual that a new deployment changes the endpoint for a microservice, whether it's the IP, the base URL, or a specific path within a generic URL, which means its consumers must be notified of the changes.

When Amazon first started their journey toward a microservices architecture, they discovered that development teams would spend about 70% of their time managing infrastructure (https://vimeo.com/29719577 at 07:53). This is a very real risk that you face if you do not adopt best practices for infrastructure automation from the beginning. And even if you do, you are likely to spend a significant amount of time developing custom tooling to manage your services effectively and efficiently.

1.4 Introducing documentation-driven development

As we explained in section 1.2.3, the success of an API integration depends on good API documentation, and in this section, we introduce an API development workflow that puts documentation at the forefront of API development. As you can see in figure 1.8, documentation-driven development is an approach to building APIs that works in three stages:

1. You design and document the API.
2. You build the API client and the API server following the documentation.
3. You test both the API client and the API server against the documentation.

Let's dive into each of these points. The first step involves designing and documenting the specification. We build APIs for others to consume, so before we build the API, we must produce an API design that meets the needs of our API clients. Just as we involve users when we design an application's user interface (UI), we must also engage with our API consumers when we design the API.

Good API design delivers good developer experience, while good API documentation helps to deliver successful API integrations. What is API documentation? API documentation is a description of the API following a standard interface description language (IDL), such as OpenAPI for REST APIs and the Schema Definition Language (SDL) for GraphQL APIs. Standard IDLs have ecosystems of tools and frameworks that make it easier to build, test, and visualize our APIs, and therefore it's worth investing time in studying them. In this book, you'll learn to document your APIs with OpenAPI (chapter 5) and the SDL (chapter 8).

Once we have produced a documented API design, we move on to the second stage, which consists of building the API server and the API client against the API documentation. In chapters 2 and 6, you'll learn to analyze the requirements of an OpenAPI specification and to build an API application against them, and in chapter 10, we'll apply the same approach to GraphQL APIs. API client developers can

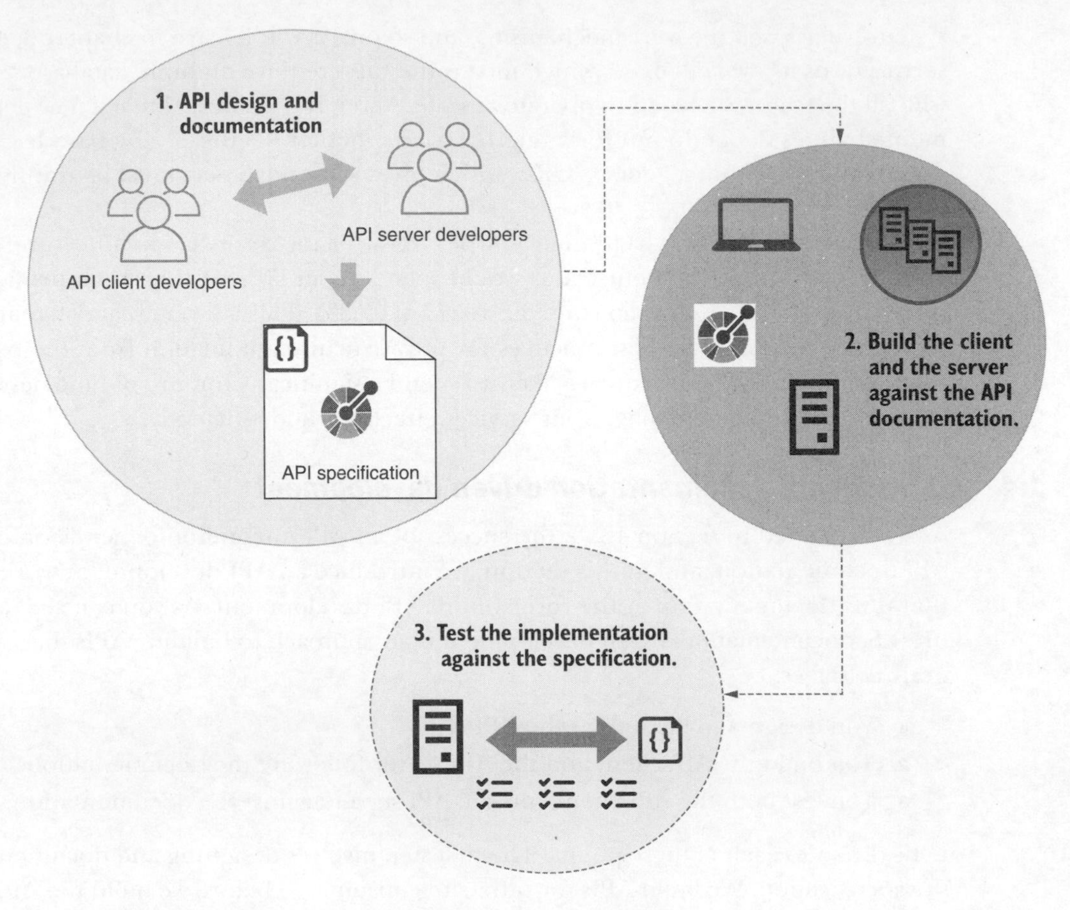

Figure 1.8 Documentation-driven development works in three stages: design and document, implement, and validate.

also leverage the API documentation to run API mock servers and test their code against them.[8]

The final stage involves testing our implementation against the API documentation. In chapter 12, you'll learn to use automated API testing tools such as Dredd and Schemathesis, which can generate a solid battery of tests for your API. Running Dredd and Schemathesis in combination with your application unit test suite will give you confidence that your API implementation works as it should. You should run these tests in your continuous integration server to make sure you don't release any code that breaks the contract with the API documentation.

[8] To learn how API server and client developers can leverage API documentation in their software development process, check out my talk "Leveraging API Documentation to Deliver Reliable API Integrations," API Specifications Conference, September 28–29, 2021, https://youtu.be/kAWvM-CVcnw.

By putting API documentation at the forefront of the development process, documentation-driven development helps you avoid one of the most common problems API developers face: disagreements between the client and the server development teams about how the API should work. In the absence of robust API documentation, developers often need to guess on implementation details of the API. In such cases, the API rarely succeeds its first integration test. Although documentation-driven development won't give a 100% guarantee that your API integrations will work, it will significantly reduce the risk of API integration failure.

1.5 Introducing the CoffeeMesh application

To illustrate the concepts and ideas that we explain throughout this book, we'll build components of an application called CoffeeMesh. CoffeeMesh is a fictitious application that allows customers to order coffee in any location, at any time. The CoffeeMesh platform consists of a collection of microservices that implement different capabilities, such as processing orders and scheduling deliveries. We'll undertake a formal analysis and design of the CoffeeMesh platform in chapter 3. To give you a taste of the kinds of things you'll learn in this book, we'll begin implementing the API of CoffeeMesh's orders service in chapter 2. Before we close this chapter, I'd like to dedicate a section to explaining what you'll learn from this book.

1.6 Who this book is for and what you will learn

To make the most out of this book, you should be familiar with the basics of web development. The code examples in the book are in Python, so a basic understanding of Python is beneficial but not necessary to be able to follow along with them. You do not need to have knowledge of web APIs or microservices, as we will explain these technologies in depth. It is useful if you are familiar with the model-view-controller (MVC) pattern for web development or its variants, such as the model-template-view (MTV) pattern implemented by Python's popular Django framework. We will draw comparisons with these patterns from time to time to illustrate certain concepts. Basic familiarity with Docker and cloud computing will be useful to get through the chapters about deployments, but I'll do my best to explain every concept in detail.

This book shows you how to develop API-driven microservices with Python through a hands-on approach. You will learn

- Service decomposition strategies for designing microservice architectures
- How to design REST APIs and how to document them using the OpenAPI specification
- How to build REST APIs in Python using popular frameworks like FastAPI and Flask
- How to design and consume GraphQL APIs and how to build them using Python's Ariadne framework
- How to test your APIs using property-based testing and API testing frameworks such as Dredd and Schemathesis

- Useful design patterns to achieve loose coupling in your microservices
- How to add authentication and authorization to your APIs using Open Authorization (OAuth) and OpenID Connect (OIDC)
- How to deploy your microservices using Docker and Kubernetes to AWS

By the end of this book, you will be familiar with the benefits that microservices architectures bring for web applications as well as the challenges and difficulties that come with them. You will know how to integrate microservices using APIs, you will know how to build and document those APIs using standards and best practices, and you will be prepared to define the domain of an API with clear application boundaries. Finally, you'll also know how to test, deploy, and secure your microservice APIs.

Summary

- Microservices are an architectural pattern in which components of a system are designed and built as independently deployed services. This results in smaller and more maintainable code bases and allows services to be optimized and scaled independently of each other.
- Monoliths are an architectural pattern in which whole applications are deployed in a single build and run in the same process. This makes the application easier to deploy and monitor, but it also makes deployments more challenging when the code base grows large.
- Applications can have multiple types of interfaces, such as UIs, CLIs, and APIs. An API is an interface that allows us to interact with an application programmatically from our code or terminal.
- A web API is an API that runs on a web server and uses HTTP for data transport. We use web APIs to expose service capabilities through the internet.
- Microservices talk to each other using smart endpoints and "dumb pipes." A dumb pipe is a pipe that simply transfers data from one component to another. A great example of a dumb pipe for microservices is HTTP, which exchanges data between the API client and the API server without knowing anything about the API protocol being used. Therefore, web APIs are a great technology for driving integrations between microservices.
- Despite their benefits, microservices also bring the following challenges:
  - *Effective service decomposition*—We must design services with clear boundaries around specific subdomains; otherwise, we risk building a "distributed monolith."
  - *Microservice integration tests*—Running integration tests for all microservices is challenging, but we can reduce the risk of integration failures by ensuring APIs are correctly implemented.
  - *Handling service unavailability*—Collaborating services are vulnerable to service unavailability, request timeouts, and processing errors, and therefore must be able to handle those scenarios.

  - *Tracing distributed transactions*—Tracing errors across multiple services is challenging and requires software telemetry tools that allow you to centralize logs, enable API visibility, and trace requests across services.
  - *Increased operational complexity and infrastructure overhead*—Each microservice requires its own infrastructure provisioning, including servers, monitoring systems, and alerts, so you need to invest additional efforts in infrastructure automation.
- Documentation-driven development is an API development workflow that works in three stages:
  - Design and document the API.
  - Build the API against the documentation.
  - Test the API against the documentation.

  By putting API documentation at the forefront of the development process, documentation-driven development helps you avoid many common problems that API developers face and therefore reduce the chances of API integration failure.

2 A basic API implementation

This chapter covers

- Reading and understanding the requirements of an API specification
- Structuring our application into a data layer, an application layer, and an interface layer
- Implementing API endpoints using FastAPI
- Implementing data validation models (schemas) using pydantic
- Testing the API using a Swagger UI

In this chapter, we implement the API for the orders service, which is one of the microservices of the CoffeeMesh website, the project we introduced in section 1.5. CoffeeMesh is an application that makes and delivers coffee on demand at any time, wherever you are. The orders service allows customers to place orders with CoffeeMesh. As we implement the orders API, you will get an early look into the concepts and processes that we dissect in more detail throughout this book. The code for this chapter is available under the ch02 folder of the GitHub repository provided with this book.

2.1 Introducing the orders API specification

Let's begin by analyzing the requirements of the orders API. Using the orders API, we can place orders, update them, retrieve their details, or cancel them. The orders API specification is available in a file named ch02/oas.yaml in the GitHub repository for this book. OAS stands for *OpenAPI specification*, which is a standard format for documenting REST APIs. In chapter 5, you'll learn to document your APIs using OpenAPI. As you can see in figure 2.1, the API specification describes a REST API with four main URL paths:

- `/orders`—Allows us to retrieve lists of orders (GET) and create orders (POST).
- `/orders/{order_id}`—Allows us to retrieve the details of a specific order (GET), to update an order (PUT), and to delete an order (DELETE).
- `/orders/{order_id}/cancel`—Allows us to cancel an order (POST).
- `/orders/{order_id}/pay`—Allows us to pay for an order (POST).

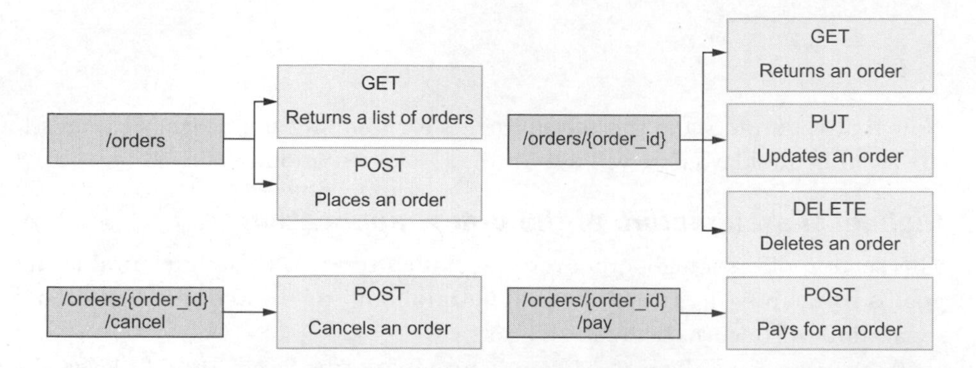

Figure 2.1 The orders API exposes seven endpoints structured around four URL paths. Each endpoint implements different capabilities, such as placing and cancelling an order.

In addition to documenting the API endpoints, the specification also includes data models that tell us what the data exchanged over those endpoints looks like. In OpenAPI, we call those models *schemas*, and you can find them within the components section of the orders API specification. Schemas tell us what properties must be included in a payload and what their types are.

For example, the `OrderItemSchema` schema specifies that the `product` and the `size` properties are required, but the `quantity` property is optional. When the `quantity` property is missing from the payload, the default value is `1`. Our API implementation must therefore enforce the presence of the `product` and the `size` properties in the payload before we try to create the order.

Listing 2.1 Specification for `OrderItemSchema`

```
# file: oas.yaml

OrderItemSchema:
  type: object
  required:
    - product
    - size
  properties:
    product:
      type: string
    size:
      type: string
      enum:
        - small
        - medium
        - big
    quantity:
      type: integer
      default: 1
      minimum: 1
```

Now that we understand the requirements for building the orders API, let's look at the architectural layout we will use for the implementation.

2.2 High-level architecture of the orders application

This section offers a high-level overview of the orders API's architectural layout. Our goal is to identify the layers of the application and to enforce clear boundaries and separation of concerns between all layers.

As you can see in figure 2.2, we organize into three layers: the API layer, the business layer, and the data layer.

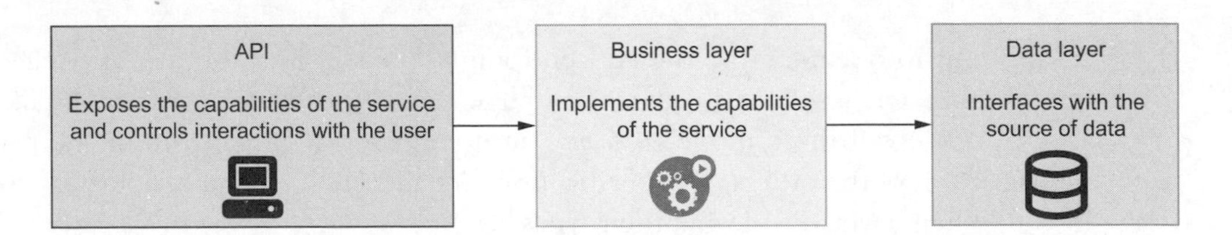

Figure 2.2 To enforce separation of concerns among the different components of our service, we structure our code around three layers: the data layer knows how to interface with the source of data; the business layer implements the service's capabilities; and the interface layer implements the service's API.

This way of structuring the application is an adaptation of the three-tier architecture pattern, which structures applications into a data layer, a business layer, and a presentation layer. As you can see in figure 2.3, the data layer is the part of the application

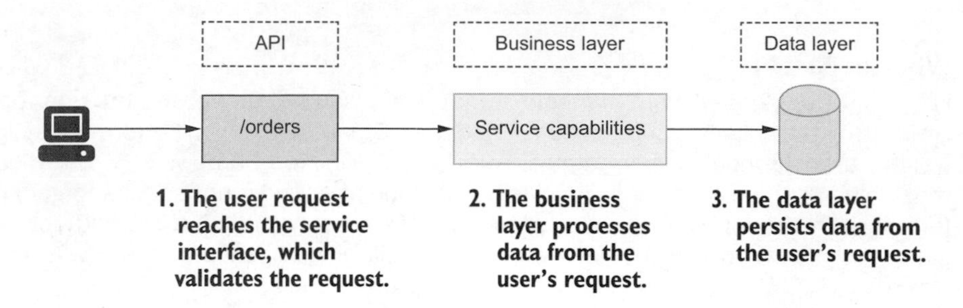

Figure 2.3 When a user request reaches the orders service, it's first validated by the interface layer. Then the interface layer interfaces with the business layer to process the request. After processing, the data layer persists the data contained in the request.

that knows how to persist data so that we can retrieve it later. The data layer implements the data models required for interfacing with our source of data. For example, if our persistent storage is an SQL database, the models in the data layer will represent the tables in the database, often with the help of an object relational mapper (ORM) framework.

The business layer implements our service's capabilities. It controls the interactions between the API layer and the data layer. For the orders service, it's the part that knows what to do to place, cancel, or pay for an order.

The API layer of a service is different from the business layer. The business layer implements the capabilities of a service, while the API layer is an adapter on top of the application logic that exposes the service's capabilities to its consumers. Figure 2.2 illustrates this relationship among the layers of a service, while figure 2.3 illustrates how a user request is processed by each layer.

The API layer is an adapter on top of the business layer. Its most important job is validating incoming requests and returning the expected responses. The API layer communicates with the business layer, passing the data sent by the user, so that resources can be processed and persisted in the server. The API layer is equivalent to the presentation layer in three-tier architecture. Now that we know how we are going to structure our application, let's jump straight into the code!

2.3 *Implementing the API endpoints*

In this section, you will learn to implement the API layer of the orders service. I'll show you how to break down the implementation of the API into progressive steps. In the first step, we produce a minimal implementation of the endpoints with mock responses. In the following sections of this chapter, we enhance the implementation by adding data validation and dynamic responses. You'll also learn about the FastAPI library and how you can use it to build a web API.

What is FastAPI?

FastAPI (https://github.com/tiangolo/fastapi) is a web API framework built on top of Starlette (https://github.com/encode/starlette). Starlette is a high-performance, lightweight, asynchronous server gateway interface (ASGI) web framework, which means that we can implement our services as a collection of asynchronous tasks to gain performance in our applications. In addition, FastAPI uses pydantic (https://github.com/samuelcolvin/pydantic/) for data validation. The following figure illustrates how all these different technologies fit together.

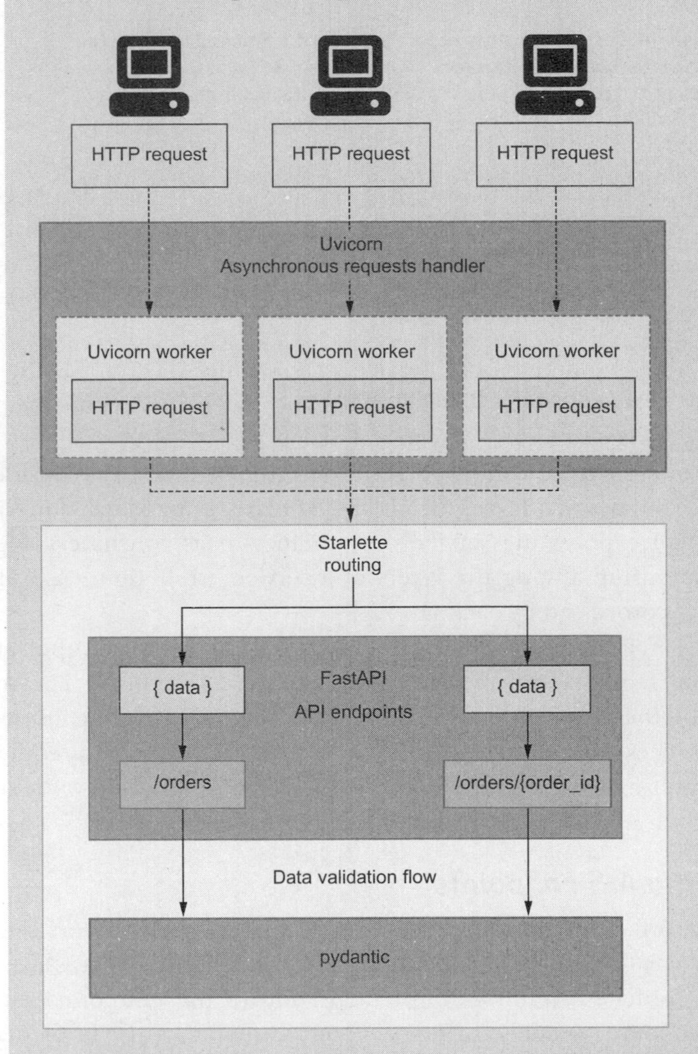

Uvicorn (https://github.com/encode/uvicorn) is an asynchronous web server commonly used to run Starlette applications. Uvicorn handles HTTP requests and passes them on to Starlette, which functions within your application to call when a request arrives in the server. FastAPI is built on top of Starlette, and it enhances Starlette's routes with data validation and API documentation functionality.

Before we start implementing the API, we need to set up our environment for this project. Create a folder named ch02 and move into it using the `cd` command in your terminal. We'll use Pipenv to install and manage our dependencies.

> **About dependencies**
>
> If you want to make sure you use the same dependencies that I used when writing this book, you can fetch the ch02/Pipfile and ch02/Pipfile.lock files from the GitHub repository for this book and run `pipenv install`.
>
> `Pipfile` describes the environment that we wish to create with Pipenv. Among other things, `Pipfile` contains the version of Python that must be used to create the environment and the URLs of the PyPi repositories that must be used to pull the dependencies. Pipenv also makes it easier to keep production dependencies separate from development dependencies by providing specific installation flags for each set. For example, to install `pytest` we run `pipenv install pytest --dev`. Pipenv also exposes commands that allow us to easily manage our virtual environments, such as `pipenv shell` to activate the virtual environment or `pipenv --rm` to delete the virtual environment.

Pipenv is a dependency management tool for Python that guarantees that the same versions of our dependencies are installed in different environments. In other words, Pipenv makes it possible to create environments in a deterministic way. To accomplish that, Pipenv uses a file called Pipfile.lock, which contains a description of the exact package versions that were installed.

Listing 2.2 Creating a virtual environment and installing dependencies with `pipenv`

```
$ pipenv --three                         # Create a virtual environment using pipenv and setting the runtime to Python 3.

$ pipenv install fastapi uvicorn         # Install FastAPI and Uvicorn.

$ pipenv shell                           # Activate the virtual environment.
```

Now that our dependencies are installed, let's build the API. First, copy the API specification under ch02/oas.yaml in the GitHub repository for this book in the ch02 folder we created earlier. Then create a subfolder named orders, which will contain our API implementation. Within the orders folder, create a file called app.py. Create another subfolder called orders/api, and within that folder create a file called orders/api/api.py. At this point, the project structure should look like this:

```
.
├── Pipfile
├── Pipfile.lock
├── oas.yaml
└── orders
    ├── api
    │   └── api.py
    └── app.py
```

Listing 2.3 shows how to create an instance of the FastAPI application in file orders/app.py. The instance of the `FastAPI` class from FastAPI is an object that represents the API we are implementing. It provides *decorators* (functions that add additional functionality to a function or class) that allow us to register our view functions.[1]

Listing 2.3 Creating an instance of the FastAPI application

```
# file: orders/app.py

from fastapi import FastAPI

app = FastAPI(debug=True)

from orders.api import api
```

We create an instance of the FastAPI class. This object represents our API application. (annotates `app = FastAPI(debug=True)`)

We import the api module so that our view functions can be registered at load time. (annotates `from orders.api import api`)

Listing 2.4 shows a minimal implementation of our API endpoints. The code goes within the orders/api/api.py file. We declare a static `order` object, and we return the same data in all the endpoints except the DELETE `/orders/{order_id}` endpoint, which returns an empty response. Later, we'll change the implementation to use a dynamic list of orders. FastAPI decorators transform the data we return in every function into an HTTP response; they also map our functions to a specific URL in our server. By default, FastAPI includes 200 (OK) status codes in our responses, but we can override this behavior by using the `status_code` parameter in the routes decorators, like we do in the POST `/orders` and in the DELETE `/orders/{order_id}` endpoints.

Listing 2.4 Minimal implementation of the orders API

```
# file: orders/api/api.py

from datetime import datetime
from uuid import UUID

from starlette.responses import Response
from starlette import status

from orders.app import app

order = {
    'id': 'ff0f1355-e821-4178-9567-550dec27a373',
    'status': "delivered",
    'created': datetime.utcnow(),
    'order': [
        {
            'product': 'cappuccino',
            'size': 'medium',
            'quantity': 1
        }
```

We define an order object to return in our responses. (annotates `order = {`)

[1] For a classic explanation of the decorator pattern, see Erich Gamma et al., *Design Patterns* (Addison-Wesley, 1995), pp. 175–184. For a more Pythonic introduction to decorators, see Luciano Ramalho, *Fluent Python* (O'Reilly, 2015), pp. 189–222.

```
    ]
}

@app.get('/orders')
def get_orders():
    return {'orders': [orders]}

@app.post('/orders', status_code=status.HTTP_201_CREATED)
def create_order():
    return order

@app.get('/orders/{order_id}')
def get_order(order_id: UUID):
    return order

@app.put('/orders/{order_id}')
def update_order(order_id: UUID):
    return order

@app.delete('/orders/{order_id}', status_code=status.HTTP_204_NO_CONTENT)
def delete_order(order_id: UUID):
    return Response(status_code=HTTPStatus.NO_CONTENT.value)

@app.post('/orders/{order_id}/cancel')
def cancel_order(order_id: UUID):
    return order

@app.post('/orders/{order_id}/pay')
def pay_order(order_id: UUID):
    return order
```

We register a GET endpoint for the /orders URL path.

We specify that the response's status code is 201 (Created).

We define URL parameters, such as order_id, within curly brackets.

We capture the URL parameter as a function argument.

We use HTTPStatus.NO_CONTENT.value to return an empty response.

FastAPI exposes decorators named after HTTP methods, such as `get()` and `post()`. We use these decorators to register our API endpoints. FastAPI's decorators take at least one argument, which is the URL path we want to register.

Our view functions can take any number of parameters. If the name of the parameter matches the name of a URL path parameter, FastAPI passes the path parameter from the URL to our view function on invocation. For example, as you can see in figure 2.4, the URL `/orders/{order_id}` defines a path parameter named `order_id`, and accordingly our view functions registered for that URL path take an argument named `order_id`. If a user navigates to the URL /orders/53e80ed2-b9d6-4c3b-b549-258aaaef9533, our view functions will be called with the `order_id` parameter set to `53e80ed2-b9d6-4c3b-b549-258aaaef9533`. FastAPI allows us to specify the type and format of the URL path parameter by using type hints. In listing 2.4, we specify that `order_id`'s type is a *universally unique identifier* (UUID). FastAPI will invalidate any calls in which `order_id` doesn't follow that format.

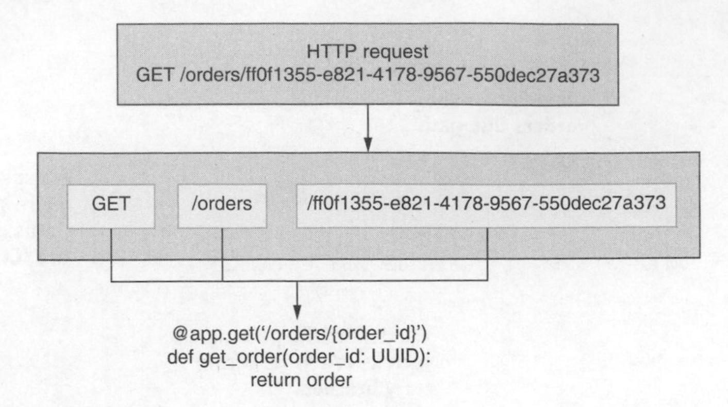

Figure 2.4 FastAPI knows how to map a request to the right function, and it passes any relevant parameters from the request to the function. In this illustration, a GET request on the `/orders/{order_id}` endpoint with `order_id` set to `ff0f1355-e821-4178-9567-550dec27a373` is passed to the `get_order()` function.

FastAPI responses include a 200 (OK) status code by default, but we can change this behavior by setting the `status_code` parameter in the endpoints' decorators. In listing 2.4, we set `status_code` to 201 (Created) in the POST `/orders` endpoint, and to 204 (No Content) in the DELETE `/orders/{order_id}` endpoint. For a detailed explanation of status codes, see section 4.6 in chapter 4.

You can now run the app to get a feeling of what the API looks like by executing the following command from the top-level orders directory:

```
$ uvicorn orders.app:app --reload
```

This command loads the server with hot reloading enabled. *Hot reloading* restarts your server whenever you make changes to your files. Visit the http://127.0.0.1:8000/docs URL in a browser and you will see an interactive display of the API documentation generated by FastAPI from our code (see figure 2.5 for an illustration). This visualization is called Swagger UI, and it's one of the most popular ways of visualizing REST APIs. Another popular visualization is Redoc, which is also supported by FastAPI under the http://127.0.0.1:8000/redoc URL.

If you click on any of the endpoints represented in the Swagger UI, you will see additional documentation about the endpoint. You will also see a Try it Out button, which gives you the opportunity to test the endpoint directly from this UI. Click that button, then click Execute, and you will get the hardcoded response we included in our endpoints (see figure 2.6 for an illustration).

Now that we have the basic skeleton of our API, we'll move on to implementing validators for our incoming payloads and our outgoing responses. The next section walks you through the steps needed to accomplish that.

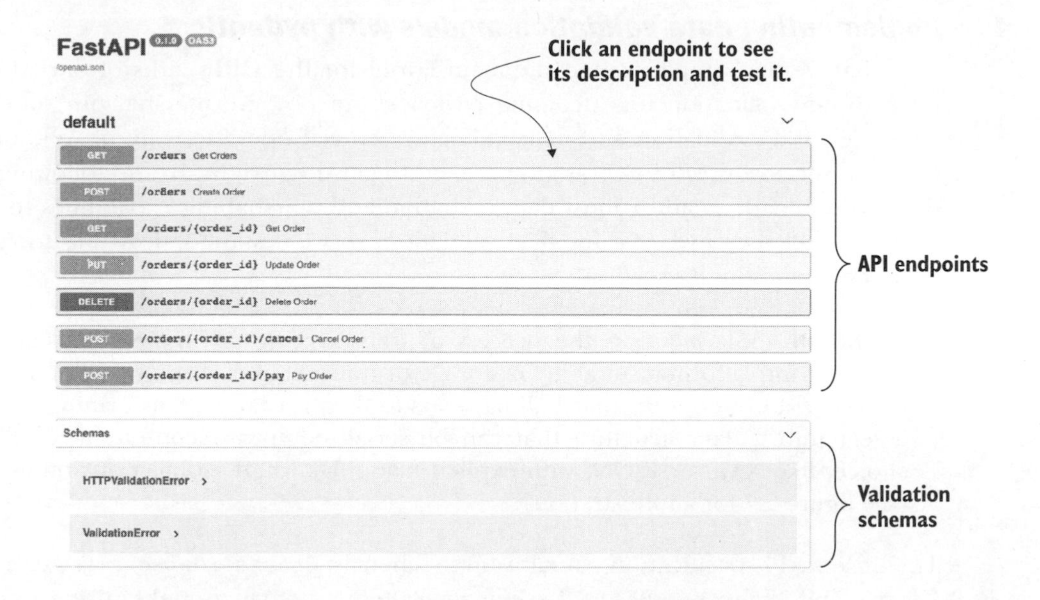

Figure 2.5 View of the Swagger UI dynamically generated by FastAPI from our code. We can use this view to test the implementation of our endpoints.

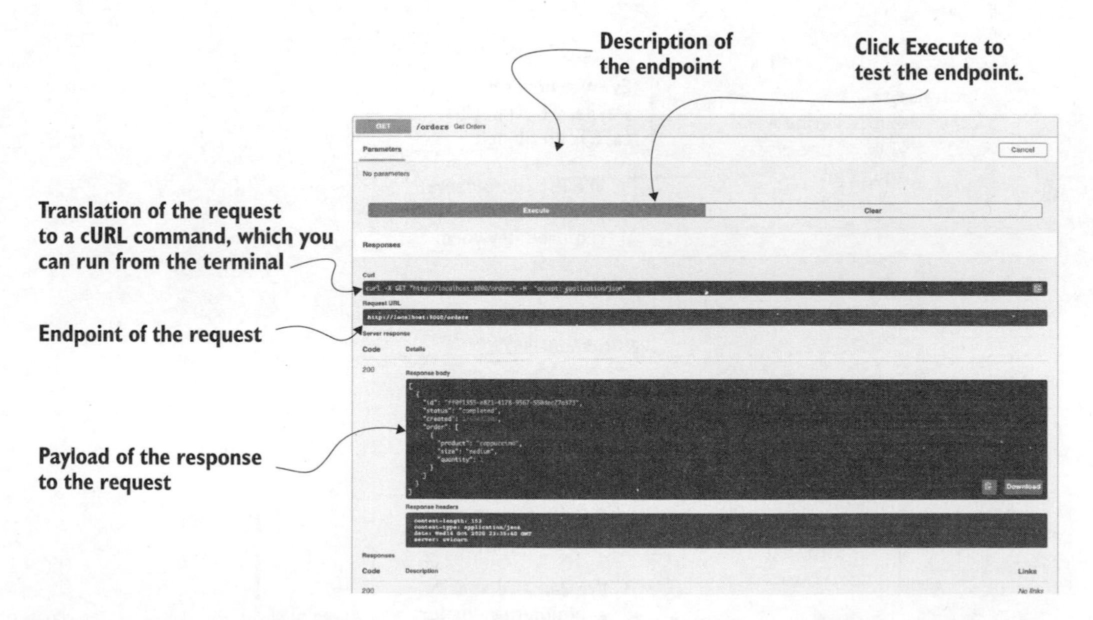

Figure 2.6 To test an endpoint, click it to expand it. You'll see a Try it Out button on the top-right corner of the endpoint's description. Click that button, and then click the Execute button. This triggers a request to the server, and you'll be able to see the response.

2.4 Implementing data validation models with pydantic

Now that we have implemented the main layout for the URL paths of our API, we need to add validation for incoming payloads and how we marshal our outgoing responses. Data validation and marshalling are crucial operations in an API, and to deliver a successful API integration, we need to get them right. In the following sections, you'll learn to add robust data validation and marshalling capabilities to your APIs. FastAPI uses pydantic for data validation, so we'll start by learning to create pydantic models in this section.

> **DEFINITION** *Marshalling* is the process of transforming an in-memory data structure into a format suitable for storage or transmission over a network. In the context of web APIs, marshalling refers to the process of transforming an object into a data structure that can be serialized into a content type of choice, like XML or JSON, with explicit mappings for the object attributes (see figure 2.7 for an illustration).

The orders API specification contains three schemas: `CreateOrderSchema`, `GetOrderSchema`, and `OrderItemSchema`. Let's analyze these schemas to make sure we understand how we need to implement our validation models.

Listing 2.5 Specification for the orders API schemas

```
# file: oas.yaml

components:
  schemas:
    OrderItemSchema:
      type: object            <- Every schema has a type, which in this case is an object.
      required:               <- We list compulsory properties under the required keyword.
        - product
        - size
      properties:             <- We list object properties under the properties keyword.
        product:
          type: string
        size:
          type: string
          enum:               <- We constrain the values of a property using an enumeration.
            - small
            - medium
            - big
        quantity:
          type: integer
          default: 1          <- Attributes can have a default value.
          minimum: 1          <- We can also specify a minimum value for a property.

    CreateOrderSchema:
      type: object
      required:
        - order
```

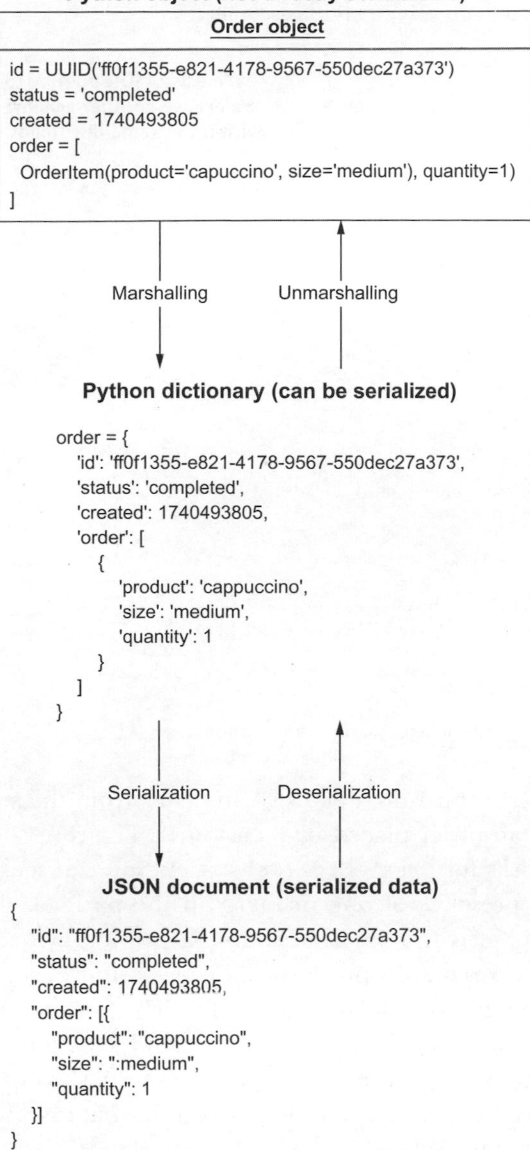
Python object (not directly serializable)
Order object
id = UUID('ff0f1355-e821-4178-9567-550dec27a373')
status = 'completed'
created = 1740493805
order = [
OrderItem(product='capuccino', size='medium'), quantity=1)
]
Marshalling
Unmarshalling
Python dictionary (can be serialized)
order = {
'id': 'ff0f1355-e821-4178-9567-550dec27a373',
'status': 'completed',
'created': 1740493805,
'order': [
{
'product': 'cappuccino',
'size': 'medium',
'quantity': 1
}
]
}
Serialization
Deserialization
JSON document (serialized data)
{
"id": "ff0f1355-e821-4178-9567-550dec27a373",
"status": "completed",
"created": 1740493805,
"order": [{
"product": "cappuccino",
"size": ":medium",
"quantity": 1
}]
}

Figure 2.7 To build a response payload from a Python object, we first marshal the object into a serializable data structure, with explicit mapping of attributes between the object and the new structure. Deserializing the payload gives us back an object identical to the one we serialized.

```
      properties:
        order:
          type: array
          items:
            $ref: '#/components/schemas/OrderItemSchema'

    GetOrderSchema:
      type: object
      required:
        - order
        - id
        - created
        - status
      properties:
        id:
          type: string
          format: uuid
        created:
          type: string
          format: date-time
        status:
          type: string
          enum:
            - created
            - progress
            - cancelled
            - dispatched
            - delivered
        order:
          type: array
          items:
            $ref: '#/components/schemas/OrderItemSchema'
```

We specify the type of the items in the array using the items keyword.

We use a JSON pointer to reference another schema within the same document.

We use `GetOrderSchema` when we return the details of an order from the server and `CreateOrderSchema` to validate an order placed by a customer. Figure 2.8 illustrates how the data validation flow works for `CreateOrderSchema`. As you can see, `CreateOrderSchema` only requires the presence of one property in the payload: the `order` property, which is an array of objects whose specification is defined by `OrderItemSchema`. `OrderItemSchema` has two required properties, `product` and `size`, and one optional property, `quantity`, which has a default value of `1`. This means that, when processing a request payload, we must check that the `product` and `size` properties are present in the payload and that they have the right type. Figure 2.8 shows what happens when the `quantity` property is missing from the payload. In that case, we set the property to its default value of `1` in the server.

Now that we understand our API schemas, it's time to implement them. Create a new file called orders/api/schemas.py. This file will contain our pydantic models. Listing 2.6 shows how we implement `CreateOrderSchema`, `GetOrderSchema`, and `OrderItemSchema` using pydantic. The code in listing 2.6 goes in the orders/api/schemas.py module. We define every schema as a class that inherits from pydantic's `BaseModel` class, and we specify the type of every attribute using Python type hints. For attributes

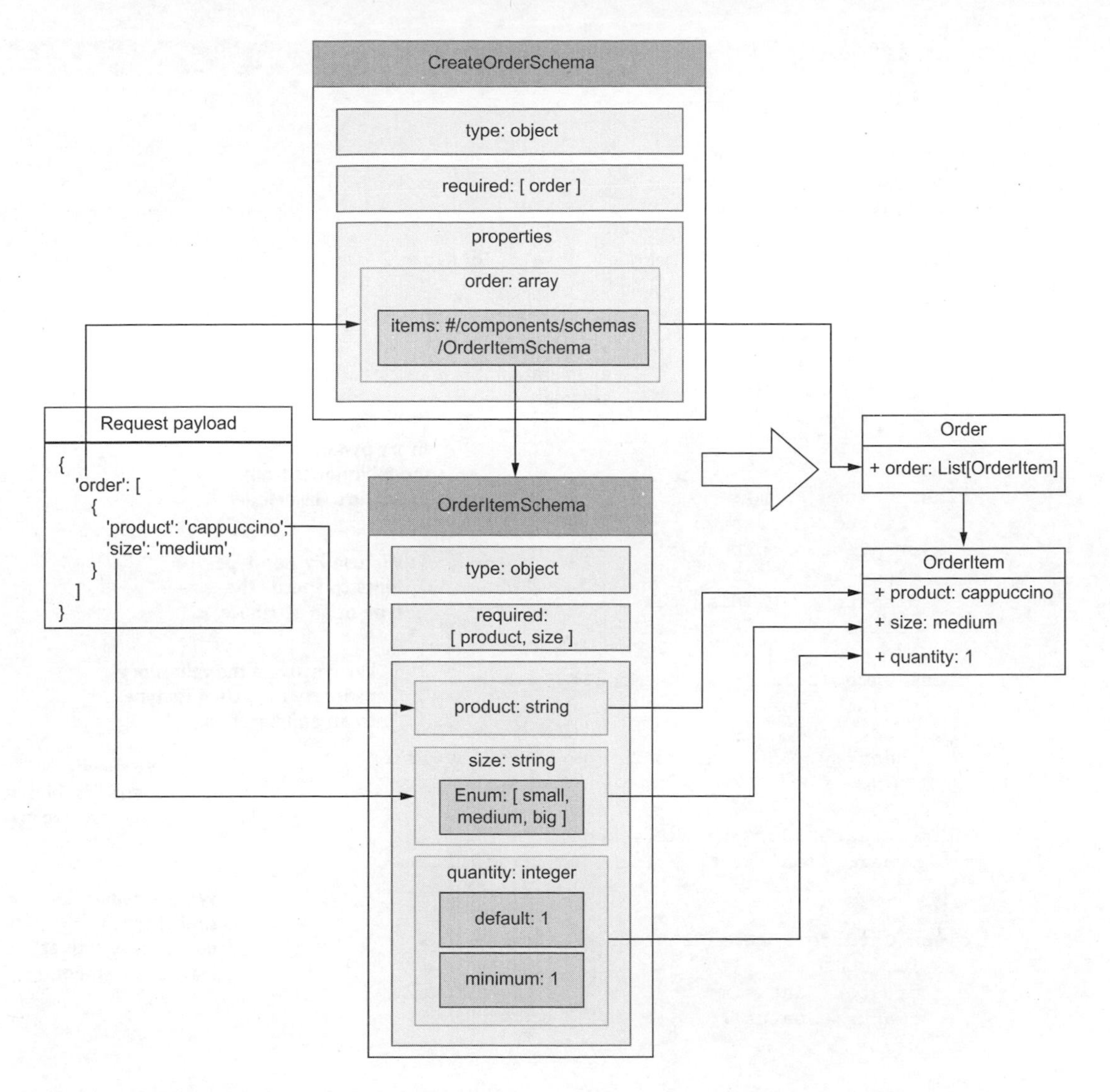

Figure 2.8 Data validation flow for request payloads against the `CreateOrderSchema` model. The diagram shows how each property of the request payload is validated against the properties defined in the schema and how we build an object from the resulting validation.

that can only take on a limited selection of values, we define an enumeration class. In this case, we define enumerations for the `size` and `status` properties. We set the type of `OrderItemSchema`'s `quantity` property to pydantic's `conint` type, which enforces integer values. We also specify that `quantity` is an optional property and that its values should be equal or greater than 1, and we give it a default value of 1. Finally, we use pydantic's `conlist` type to define `CreateOrderSchema`'s `order` property as a list with at least one element.

Listing 2.6 Implementation of the validation models using pydantic

```
# file: orders/api/schemas.py

from enum import Enum
from typing import List
from uuid import UUID

from pydantic import BaseModel, Field, conlist, conint


class Size(Enum):                                           <-- We declare an enumeration schema.
    small = 'small'
    medium = 'medium'
    big = 'big'


class Status(Enum):
    created = 'created'
    progress = 'progress'
    cancelled = 'cancelled'
    dispatched = 'dispatched'
    delivered = 'delivered'

class OrderItemSchema(BaseModel):                           <-- Every pydantic model inherits from pydantic's BaseModel.
    product: str                                            <-- We use Python-type hints to specify the type of an attribute.
    size: Size                                              <-- We constrain the values of a property by setting its type to an enumeration.
    quantity: Optional[conint(ge=1, strict=True)] = 1       <-- We specify quantity's minimum value, and we give it a default.


class CreateOrderSchema(BaseModel):
    order:  conlist(OrderItemSchema, min_items=1)           <-- We use pydantic's conlist type to define a list with at least one element.


class GetOrderSchema(CreateOrderSchema):
    id: UUID
    created: datetime
    status: Status


class GetOrdersSchema(BaseModel):
    orders: List[GetOrderSchema]
```

Now that our validation models are implemented, in the following sections we'll link them with the API to validate and marshal payloads.

2.5 Validating request payloads with pydantic

In this section, we use the models we implemented in section 2.4 to validate request payloads. How do we access request payloads within our view functions? We intercept request payloads by declaring them as a parameter of the view function, and to validate them we set their type to the relevant pydantic model.

Listing 2.7 Hooking validation models up with the API endpoints

```
# file: orders/api/api.py

from uuid import UUID

from starlette.responses import Response
from starlette import status

from orders.app import app
from orders.api.schemas import CreateOrderSchema    <-- We import the pydantic models so that we can use them for validation.

...


@app.post('/orders', status_code=status.HTTP_201_CREATED)
def create_order(order_details: CreateOrderSchema):    <-- We intercept a payload by declaring it as a parameter in our function, and we use type hints to validate it.
    return order


@app.get('/orders/{order_id}')
def get_order(order_id: UUID):
    return order


@app.put('/orders/{order_id}')
def update_order(order_id: UUID, order_details: CreateOrderSchema):
    return order

...
```

If you kept the application running, the changes are loaded automatically by the server, so you just need to refresh the browser to update the UI. If you click the POST endpoint of the /orders URL path, you'll see that the UI now gives you an example of the payload expected by the server. Now, if you try editing the payload to remove any of the required fields, for example, the `product` field, and you send it to the server, you'll get the following error message:

```
{
  "detail": [
    {
      "loc": [
        "body",
        "order",
        0,
        "product"
      ],
      "msg": "field required",
      "type": "value_error.missing"
    }
  ]
}
```

FastAPI generates an error message that points to where in the payload the error is found. The error message uses a JSON pointer to indicate where the problem is. A JSON pointer is a syntax that allows you to represent the path to a specific value within a JSON document. If this is the first time you've encountered JSON pointers, think of them as a different way of representing dictionary syntax and index notation in Python. For example, the error message `"loc: /body/order/0/product"` is roughly equivalent to the following notation in Python: `loc['body']['order'][0]['product']`. Figure 2.9 shows you how to interpret the JSON pointer from the error message to identify the source of the problem in the payload.

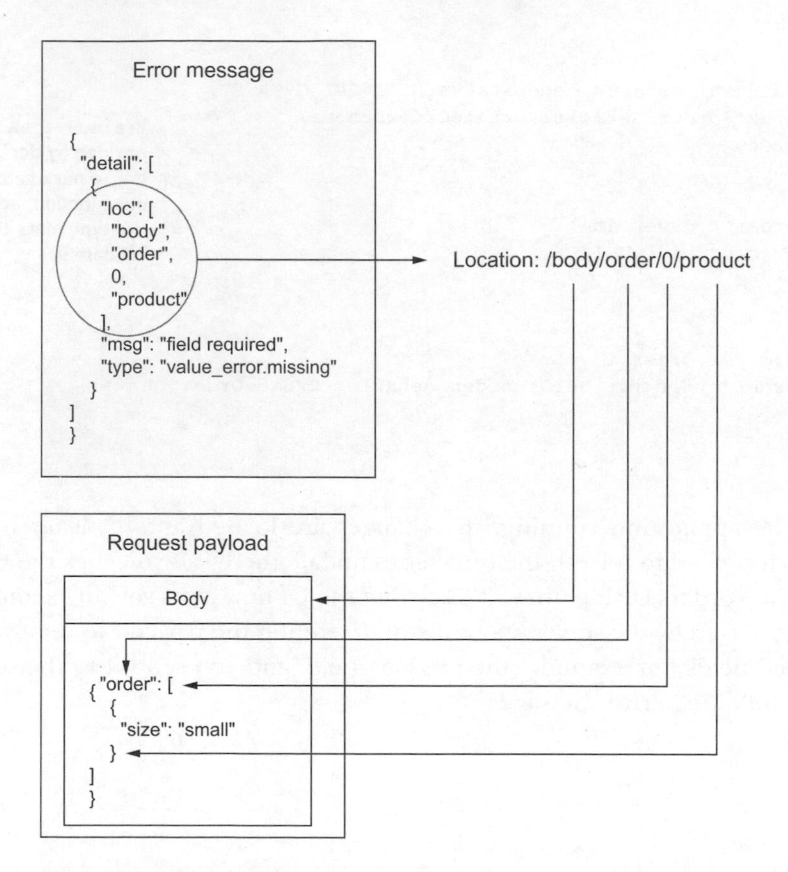

Figure 2.9 When a request fails due a malformed payload, we get a response with an error message. The error message uses a JSON pointer to tell us where the error is. In this case, the error message says that the property `/body/order/0/product` is missing from the payload.

You can also change the payload so that, instead of missing a required property, it contains an illegal value for the `size` property:

```
{
  "order": [
    {
      "product": "string",
      "size": "somethingelse"
    }
  ]
}
```

In this case, you'll also get an informative error with the following message: `"value is not a valid enumeration member; permitted: 'small', 'medium', 'big'"`. What happens if we make a typo in the payload? For example, imagine a client sent the following payload to the server:

```
{
  "order": [
    {
      "product": "string",
      "size": "small",
      "quantit": 5
    }
  ]
}
```

In this case, FastAPI assumes that the `quantity` property is missing and that the client wishes to set its value to `1`. This result could lead to confusion between the client and the server, and in such cases invalidating payloads with illegal properties helps us make the API integration more reliable. In chapter 6, you'll learn to handle those situations.

One edge case with optional properties, such as `OrderItemSchema`'s `quantity`, is that pydantic assumes they're nullable and therefore will accept payloads with `quantity` set to `null`. For example, if we send the following payload to the POST `/orders` endpoint, our server will accept it:

```
{
  "order": [
    {
      "product": "string",
      "size": "small",
      "quantity": null
    }
  ]
}
```

In terms of API integrations, optional isn't quite the same as nullable: a property can be optional because it has a default value, but that doesn't mean it can be `null`. To enforce the right behavior in pydantic, we need to include an additional validation rule that prevents users from setting the value of `quantity` to `null`. We use pydantic's `validator()` decorator to define additional validation rules for our models.

Listing 2.8 Including additional validation rules for pydantic models

```
# file: orders/api/schemas.py

from datetime import datetime
from enum import Enum
from typing import List, Optional
from uuid import UUID

from pydantic import BaseModel, conint, validator

...


class OrderItemSchema(BaseModel):
    product: str
    size: Size
    quantity: Optional[conint(ge=1, strict=True)] = 1

    @validator('quantity')
    def quantity_non_nullable(cls, value):
        assert value is not None, 'quantity may not be None'
        return value
...
```

Now that we know how to test our API implementation using a Swagger UI, let's see how we use pydantic to validate and serialize our API responses.

2.6 Marshalling and validating response payloads with pydantic

In this section, we'll use the pydantic models implemented in section 2.4 to marshal and validate the response payloads of our API. Malformed payloads are one of the most common causes of API integration failures, so this step is crucial to deliver a robust API. For example, the schema for the response payload of the POST `/orders` endpoint is `GetOrderSchema`, which requires the presence of the `id`, `created`, `status`, and `order` fields. API clients will expect the presence of all these fields in the response payload and will raise errors if any of the fields is missing or comes in the wrong type or format.

> **NOTE** Malformed response payloads are a common source of API integration failures. You can avoid this problem by validating your response payloads before they leave the server. In FastAPI, this is easily done by setting the `response_model` parameter of a route decorator.

Listing 2.9 shows how we use pydantic models to validate the responses from the GET `/orders` and the POST `/orders` endpoints. As you can see, we set the `response_model` parameter to a pydantic model in FastAPI's route decorators. We follow the same approach to validate responses from all the other endpoints except the DELETE `/orders/{order_id}` endpoint, which returns an empty response. Feel free to check out the code in the GitHub repository for this book for the full implementation.

Listing 2.9 Hooking validation models for responses in the API endpoints

```
# file: orders/api/api.py

from uuid import UUID

from starlette.responses import Response
from starlette import status

from orders.app import app
from orders.api.schemas import (
    GetOrderSchema,
    CreateOrderSchema,
    GetOrdersSchema,
)

...

@app.get('/orders', response_model=GetOrdersSchema)
def get_orders():
    return [
        order
    ]


@app.post(
    '/orders',
    status_code=status.HTTP_201_CREATED,
    response_model=GetOrderSchema,
)

def create_order(order_details: CreateOrderSchema):
    return order
```

Now that we have response models, FastAPI will raise an error if a required property is missing from a response payload. It will also remove any properties that are not part of the schema, and it will try to cast each property into the right type. Let's see this behavior at work.

In a browser, visit the http://127.0.0.1:8000/docs URL to load the Swagger UI for our API. Then head over to the GET `/orders` endpoint and send a request. You'll get the order that we hardcoded at the top of the orders/api/api.py file. Let's make some modifications to that payload to see how FastAPI handles them. To begin, let's add an additional property called `updated`:

```
# orders/api/api.py
...

order = {
    'id': 'ff0f1355-e821-4178-9567-550dec27a373',
    'status': 'delivered',
    'created': datetime.utcnow(),
    'updated': datetime.utcnow(),
```

```
    'order': [
        {
            'product': 'cappuccino',
            'size': 'medium',
            'quantity': 1
        }
    ]
}

...
```

If we call the GET `/orders` endpoint again, we'll get the same response we obtained before, without the `updated` property since it isn't part of the `GetOrderSchema` model:

```
[
  {
    "order": [
      {
        "product": "cappuccino",
        "size": "medium",
        "quantity": 1
      }
    ],
    "id": "ff0f1355-e821-4178-9567-550dec27a373",
    "created": datetime.utcnow(),
    "status": "delivered"
  }
]
```

Let's now remove the `created` property from the order payload and call the GET `/orders` endpoint again:

```
# orders/api/api.py
...

order = {
    'id': 'ff0f1355-e821-4178-9567-550dec27a373',
    'status': "delivered",
    'updated': datetime.utcnow(),
    'order': [
        {
            'product': 'cappuccino',
            'size': 'medium',
            'quantity': 1
        }
    ]
}
```

This time, FastAPI raises a server error telling us that the required `created` property is missing from the payload:

```
pydantic.error_wrappers.ValidationError: 1 validation error for GetOrderSchema
response -> 0 -> created
  field required (type=value_error.missing)
```

Let's now change the value of the `created` property to a random string and run another request against the GET `/orders` endpoint:

```
# orders/api/api.py
...

order = {
    'id': 'ff0f1355-e821-4178-9567-550dec27a373',
    'status': "delivered",
    'created': 'asdf',
    'updated': 1740493905,
    'order': [
        {
            'product': 'cappuccino',
            'size': 'medium',
            'quantity': 1
        }
    ]
}

...
```

In this case, FastAPI raises a helpful error:

```
pydantic.error_wrappers.ValidationError: 1 validation error for GetOrderSchema
response -> 0 -> created
  value is not a valid integer (type=type_error.integer)
```

Our responses are being correctly validated and marshalled. Let's now add a simple state management mechanism for the application so that we can place orders and change their state through the API.

2.7 Adding an in-memory list of orders to the API

So far, our API implementation has returned the same response object. Let's change that by adding a simple in-memory collection of orders to manage the state of the application. To keep the implementation simple, we'll represent the collection of orders as a Python list. We'll manage the list within the view functions of the API layer. In chapter 7, you'll learn useful patterns to add a robust controller and data persistence layers to the application.

Listing 2.10 shows the changes required for the view functions under api.py to manage the in-memory list of orders in our view functions. The changes in listing 2.9 go into the orders/api/api.py file. We represent the collection of orders as a Python list, and we assign it to the variable `ORDERS`. To keep it simple, we store the details of every order as a dictionary, and we update them by changing their properties in the dictionary.

Listing 2.10 Managing the application's state with an in-memory list

```
# file: orders/api/api.py

import time
import uuid
```

```
from datetime import datetime
from uuid import UUID

from fastapi import HTTPException
from starlette.responses import Response
from starlette import status

from orders.app import app
from orders.api.schemas import GetOrderSchema, CreateOrderSchema

ORDERS = []    <-- We represent our in-memory list of orders as a Python list.

@app.get('/orders', response_model=GetOrdersSchema)
def get_orders():
    return ORDERS    <-- To return the list of orders, we simply return the ORDERS list.

@app.post(
    '/orders',
    status_code=status.HTTP_201_CREATED,
    response_model=GetOrderSchema,
)
def create_order(order_details: CreateOrderSchema):
    order = order_details.dict()    <-- We transform every order into a dictionary.
    order['id'] = uuid.uuid4()    <-- We enrich the order object with server-side attributes, such as the ID.
    order['created'] = datetime.utcnow()
    order['status'] = 'created'
    ORDERS.append(order)    <-- To create the order, we add it to the list.
    return order    <-- After appending the order to the list, we return it.

@app.get('/orders/{order_id}', response_model=GetOrderSchema)
def get_order(order_id: UUID):
    for order in ORDERS:    <-- To find an order by ID, we iterate the ORDERS list and check their IDs.
        if order['id'] == order_id:
            return order
    raise HTTPException(    <-- If an order isn't found, we raise an HTTPException with status_code set to 404 to return a 404 response.
        status_code=404, detail=f'Order with ID {order_id} not found'
    )

@app.put('/orders/{order_id}', response_model=GetOrderSchema)
def update_order(order_id: UUID, order_details: CreateOrderSchema):
    for order in ORDERS:
        if order['id'] == order_id:
            order.update(order_details.dict())
            return order
    raise HTTPException(
        status_code=404, detail=f'Order with ID {order_id} not found'
    )
```

```
@app.delete(
    '/orders/{order_id}',
    status_code=status.HTTP_204_NO_CONTENT,
    response_class=Response,
)
def delete_order(order_id: UUID):
    for index, order in enumerate(ORDERS):      <-- We order from the list using
        if order['id'] == order_id:                 the list.pop() method.
            ORDERS.pop(index)
            return Response(status_code=HTTPStatus.NO_CONTENT.value)
    raise HTTPException(
        status_code=404, detail=f'Order with ID {order_id} not found'
    )


@app.post('/orders/{order_id}/cancel', response_model=GetOrderSchema)
def cancel_order(order_id: UUID):
    for order in ORDERS:
        if order['id'] == order_id:
            order['status'] = 'cancelled'
            return order
    raise HTTPException(
        status_code=404, detail=f'Order with ID {order_id} not found'
    )


@app.post('/orders/{order_id}/pay', response_model=GetOrderSchema)
def pay_order(order_id: UUID):
    for order in ORDERS:
        if order['id'] == order_id:
            order['status'] = 'progress'
            return order
    raise HTTPException(
        status_code=404, detail=f'Order with ID {order_id} not found'
    )
```

If you play around with the POST `/orders` endpoint, you'll be able to create new orders, and using their IDs you'll be able to update them by hitting the PUT `/orders/{order_id}` endpoint. In every endpoint under the `/orders/{order_id}` URL path, we check whether the order requested by the API client exists, and if it doesn't we return a 404 (Not Found) response with a helpful message.

We are now able to use the orders API to create orders, update them, pay for them, cancel them, and get their details. You have implemented a fully working web API for a microservice application! You've become familiar with a bunch of new libraries to build web APIs, and you've seen how to add robust data validation to your APIs. You've also learned to put it all together and run it with success. Hopefully, this chapter has sparked your interest and excitement about designing and building microservices exposing web APIs. In the coming chapters, we'll delve deeper into these topics, and you'll learn to build and deliver robust and secure microservice API integrations.

Summary

- To structure microservices into modular layers, we use an adaptation of the three-tier architecture pattern:
  - A data layer that knows how to interface with the source of data
  - A business layer that implements the capabilities of the service
  - An interface or presentation layer that exposes the capabilities of the service through an API
- FastAPI is a popular framework for building web APIs. It's highly performant, and it has a rich ecosystem of libraries that make it easier to build APIs.
- FastAPI uses pydantic, a popular data validation library for Python. Pydantic uses type hints to create validation rules, which results in clean and easy-to-understand models.
- FastAPI generates a Swagger UI dynamically from our code. A Swagger UI is a popular interactive visualization UI for APIs. Using the Swagger UI, we can easily test if our implementation is correct.

3 Designing microservices

This chapter covers

- Principles of microservices design
- Service decomposition by business capability
- Service decomposition by subdomain

When we design a microservices platform, the first questions we face are, "How do you break down a system into microservices? How do you decide where a service ends and another one starts?" In other words, how do you define the boundaries between microservices? In this chapter, you'll learn to answer these questions and how to evaluate the quality of a microservices architecture by applying a set of design principles.

The process of breaking down a system into microservices is called *service decomposition*. Service decomposition is a fundamental step in the design of our microservices since it helps us define applications with clear boundaries, well-defined scopes, and explicit responsibilities. A well-designed microservices architecture is essential to reduce the risk of a distributed monolith. In this chapter, you'll learn two service decomposition strategies: decomposition by business capability and decomposition by subdomains. We'll see how these methods work and use a practical example to learn to apply them. Before we delve into service decomposition strategies, we introduce the project that will guide our examples throughout this chapter and the rest of the book: CoffeeMesh.

3.1 Introducing CoffeeMesh

CoffeeMesh is a fictitious company that allows customers to order all sorts of products derived from coffee, including beverages and pastries. CoffeeMesh has one mission: to make and deliver the best coffee in the world on demand to its customers, no matter where they are or when they place their order. The production factories owned by CoffeeMesh form a dense network, a mesh of coffee production units that spans several countries. Coffee production is fully automated, and deliveries are carried out by an unmanned fleet of drones operating 24/7.

When a customer places an order through the CoffeeMesh website, the ordered items are produced on demand. An algorithm determines which factory is the most suitable place to produce each item based on available stock, the number of pending orders the factory is taking care of, and distance to the customer. Once the items are produced, they're immediately dispatched to the customer. It's part of CoffeeMesh's mission statement that the customer receives each item fresh and hot.

Now that we have an example to work with, let's see how we design the microservices architecture for the CoffeeMesh platform. Before we learn to apply service decomposition strategies for microservices, the next section teaches you three principles that will guide our designs.

3.2 Microservices design principles

What makes a well-designed microservice? As we established in chapter 1, microservices are designed around well-defined business subdomains, they have clearly defined application boundaries, and they communicate with each other through lightweight protocols. What does this mean in practice? In this section, we explore three design principles that help us test whether our microservices are correctly designed:

- Database-per-service principle
- Loose coupling principle
- Single Responsibility Principle (SRP)

Following these principles will help you avoid the risk of building a distributed monolith. In the following sections, we evaluate our architectural design against these principles, and they help us spot errors in the design.

3.2.1 Database-per-service principle

The database-per-service principle states that each microservice owns a specific set of the data, and no other service should have access to such data except through an API. Despite this pattern's name, it does not mean that each microservice should be connected to a completely different database. It could be different tables in an SQL database or different collections in a NoSQL database. The point of this pattern is to ensure that the data owned by a specific service is not accessed directly by another service.

Figure 3.1 shows how microservices share their data. In the illustration, the orders service calculates the price of a customer order. To calculate the price, the orders service needs the price of each item in the order, which is available in the Products database. It also needs to know whether the user has an applicable discount, which can be checked in the Users database. However, instead of accessing both databases directly, the orders service requests this data from the products and users services.

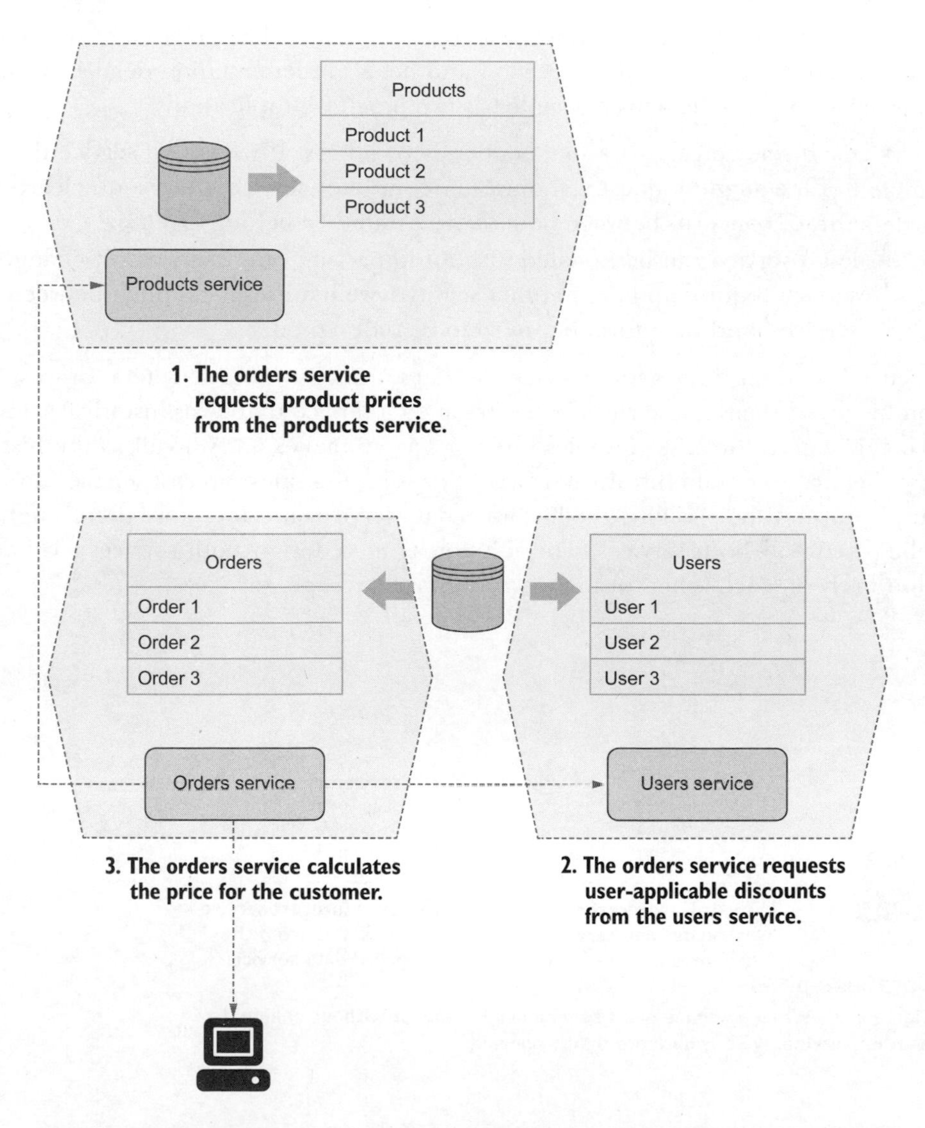

Figure 3.1 Each microservice has its own database, and access to another service's data happens through an API.

Why is this principle important? Encapsulating data access behind a service allows us to design our data models for optimal access for the service. It also allows us to make changes to the database without breaking another service's code. If the orders service in figure 3.1 had direct access to the Products database, schema changes in that database would require updates to both the products and orders services. We'd be coupling the orders service's code to the Products database, and therefore we'd be breaking the loose coupling principle, which we discuss in the next section.

3.2.2 Loose coupling principle

Loose coupling states that we must design services with clear separation of concerns. Loosely coupled services don't rely on another's implementation details. What does this mean in practice? This principle has two practical implications:

- Each service can work independently of others. If we have a service that can't fulfill a single request without calling another service, there's no clear separation of concerns between both services and they belong together.
- Each service can be updated without impacting other services. If changes to a service require updates to other services, we have tight coupling between those services, and therefore they need to be redesigned.

Figure 3.2 shows a sales forecast service that knows how to calculate a forecast based on historical data. It also shows a historical data service that owns historical sales data. To calculate a forecast, the sales forecast service makes an API call to the historical data service to obtain historical data. In this case, the sales forecast service can't serve any request without calling the historical data service, and therefore there's tight coupling between both services. The solution is to redesign both services so that they don't rely on each other, or to merge them into a single service.

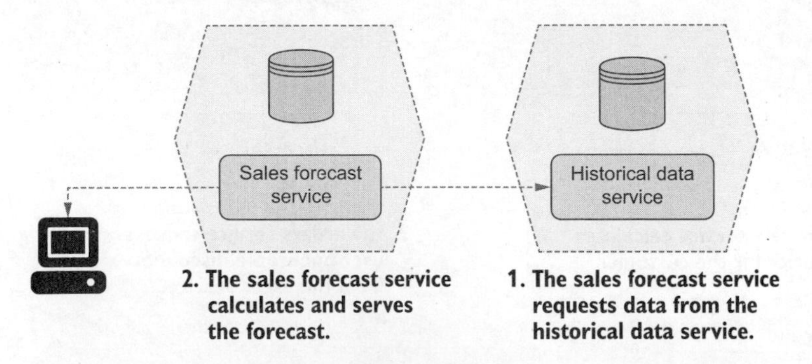
Sales forecast service
Historical data service
2. The sales forecast service calculates and serves the forecast.
1. The sales forecast service requests data from the historical data service.

Figure 3.2 When a service can't serve a single request without calling another service, we say both are tightly coupled.

3.2.3 Single Responsibility Principle

The SRP states that we must design components with few responsibilities, and ideally with only one responsibility. When applied to the microservices architecture design, this means we should strive for the design of services around a single business capability or subdomain. In the following sections, you'll learn how to decompose services by business capability and by subdomain. If you follow any of those methods, you'll be able to design microservices that follow the SRP.

3.3 Service decomposition by business capability

When using decomposition by business capability, we look into the activities a business performs and how the business organizes itself to undertake them. We then design microservices that mirror the organizational structure of the business. For example, if the business has a customer management team, we build a customer management service; if the business has a claims management team, we build a claims management service; for a kitchen team, we build the corresponding kitchen service; and so on. For businesses that are structured around products, we may have a microservice per product. For example, a company that makes pet food may have a team dedicated to dog food, another team dedicated to cat food, another team dedicated to turtle food, and so on. In this scenario, we build microservices for each of these teams.

As you can see in figure 3.3, decomposition by business capability generally results in an architecture that maps every business team to a microservice. Let's see how we apply this approach to the CoffeeMesh platform.

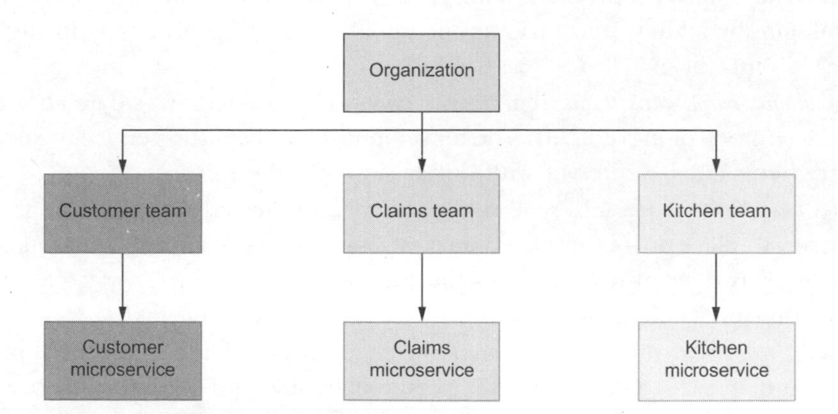

Figure 3.3 Using service decomposition by business capability, we reflect the structure of the business in our microservices architecture.

3.3.1 Analyzing the business structure of CoffeeMesh

To apply decomposition by business capability, we need to analyze the structure and organization of the business. Let's do this analysis for CoffeeMesh. Through the CoffeeMesh website, customers can order different types of coffee-related products out of a catalogue managed by the products team, who is in charge of creating new products. The availability of products and ingredients depends on the CoffeeMesh stock of ingredients at the time of the order, which is looked after by the inventory team.

A sales team is dedicated to improving the experience of ordering products through the CoffeeMesh website. Their goal is to maximize sales and ensure customers are happy with their experience and wish to come back. A finance team makes sure that the company is profitable and looks after the financial infrastructure required to process customer payments and return their money when they cancel an order.

Once a user places an order, the kitchen picks up its details to commence production. Kitchen work is fully automated, and a dedicated team of engineers and chefs called the kitchen team monitors kitchen operations to ensure no faults happen during production. When the order is ready for delivery, a drone picks it up and flies it to the customer. A dedicated team of engineers called the delivery team monitors this process to ensure the operational excellence of the delivery process.

This completes our analysis of the organizational structure of CoffeeMesh. We're now ready to design a microservices architecture based on this analysis.

3.3.2 Decomposing microservices by business capabilities

To decompose services by business capability, we map each business team to a microservice. Based on the analysis in section 3.3.1, we can map the following business teams to microservices:

- *Products team maps to the products service*—This service owns CoffeeMesh product catalogue data. The products team uses this service to maintain CoffeeMesh's catalogue by adding new products or updating existing products through the service's interface.
- *Ingredients team maps to the ingredients service*—This service owns data about CoffeeMesh stock of ingredients. The ingredients team uses this service to keep the ingredients database in sync with CoffeeMesh warehouses.
- *Sales team maps to the sales service*—This service guides customers through their journey to place orders and keep track of them. The sales team owns data about customer orders, and it manages the life cycle of each order. It collects data from this service to analyze and improve the customer journey.
- *Finance team maps to the finance service*—This service implements payment processors, and it owns data about user payment details and payment history. The finance team uses this service to keep the company accounts up to date and to ensure payments work correctly.
- *Kitchen team maps to the kitchen service*—This service sends orders to the automated kitchen system and keeps track of its progress. It owns data about the orders produced in the kitchen. The kitchen team collects data from this service to monitor the performance of the automated kitchen system.
- *Delivery team maps to the delivery service*—This service arranges the delivery of the order to the customer once it has been produced by the kitchen. This service

knows how to translate the user location into coordinates and how to calculate the best route to that destination. It owns data about every delivery made by CoffeeMesh. The delivery team collects data from this service to monitor the performance of the automated delivery system.

In this microservices architecture, we named every service after the business structure it represents. We did this for convenience in this example, but it does not have to be that way. For example, the finance service could be renamed to payments service, since all user interactions with this service will be related to their payments.

Decomposition by business capability gives us an architecture in which every service maps to a business team. Is this result in agreement with the principles of microservices design we learned in section 3.2? Let's look at this question.

From the previous analysis, it's clear that every service owns its own data: the products service owns product data, the ingredients service owns ingredients data, and so on. The SRP also applies, as every service is restricted to one business area: the finance service only processes payments, the delivery service only manages deliveries, and so on.

However, as you can see in figure 3.4, this solution doesn't satisfy the loose coupling principle. To serve the CoffeeMesh catalogue, the products service needs to determine the availability of each product, which depends on the available stock of ingredients. Since the stock of ingredients data is owned by the ingredients service, the products service needs to make an API call per product to the ingredients service.

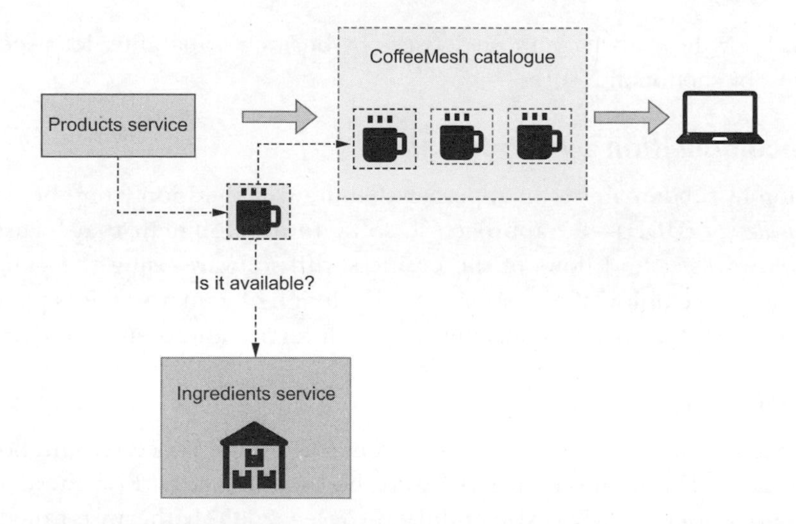

Figure 3.4 To determine whether a product is available, the products service checks the stock of ingredients with the ingredients service.

There's a high degree of coupling between the products and ingredients services, and therefore both business capabilities should be implemented within the same service.

Figure 3.5 shows the final layout of the CoffeeMesh microservices architecture using the decomposition by business capability strategy.

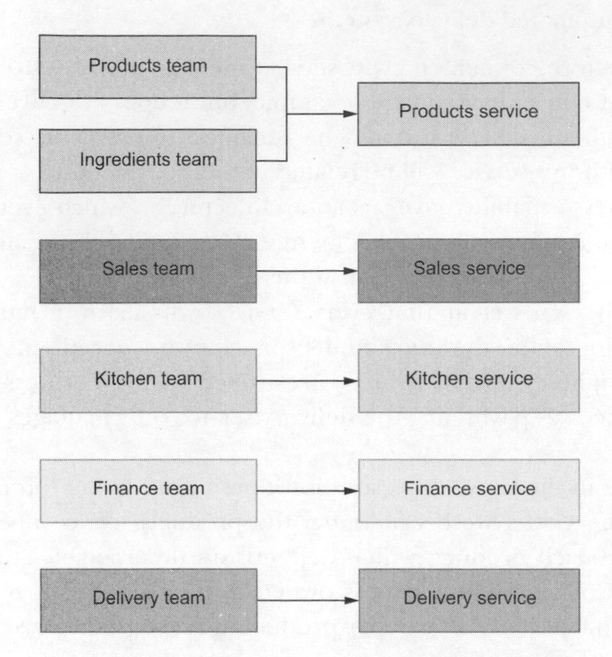

Figure 3.5 When we decompose services by business capability, we map every team to a service.

Now that we know how to decompose services by business capability, let's see how decomposition by subdomain works.

3.4 Service decomposition by subdomains

Decomposition by subdomains is an approach that draws inspiration from the field of *domain-driven design* (DDD)—an approach to software development that focuses on modeling the processes and flows of the business with software using the same language business users employ. When applied to the design of a microservices platform, DDD helps us define the core responsibilities of each service and their boundaries.

3.4.1 What is domain-driven design?

DDD is an approach to software that focuses on modeling the processes and flows of the business users. The methods of DDD were best described by Eric Evans in his influential book *Domain-Driven Design* (Addison-Wesley, 2003), otherwise called "the big blue book." DDD offers an approach to software development that tries to reflect as accurately as possible the ideas and the language that businesses, or end users of the software, use to refer to their processes and flows. To achieve this alignment, DDD encourages developers to create a rigorous, model-based language that software developers can share with the end users. Such language must not have ambiguous meanings and is called *ubiquitous language*.

To create an ubiquitous language, we must identify the core domain of a business, which corresponds with the main activity an organization performs to generate value. For a logistics company, it may be the shipment of products around the world. For an e-commerce company, it may be the sale of products. For a social media platform, it may be feeding a user with relevant content. For a dating app, it may be matching users. For CoffeeMesh, the core domain is to deliver high-quality coffee to customers as quickly as possible regardless of their location.

The core domain is often not sufficient to cover all areas of activity in a business, so DDD also distinguishes supportive subdomains and generic subdomains. A *supportive subdomain* represents an area of the business that is not directly related to value generation, but it is fundamental to support it. For a logistics company, it may be providing customer support to the users shipping their products, leasing equipment, managing partnerships with other businesses, and so on. For an e-commerce company, it may be marketing, customer support, warehousing, and so on.

The core domain gives you a definition of the *problem space*: the problem you are trying to solve with software. The solution consists of a model, understood here as a system of abstractions that describes the domain and solves the problem. Ideally, there is only one generic model that provides a *solution space* for the problem, with a clearly defined ubiquitous language. However, in practice, most problems are complex enough that they require the collaboration of different models, with their own ubiquitous languages. We call the process of defining such models *strategic design*.

3.4.2 Applying strategic analysis to CoffeeMesh

How does DDD work in practice? How do we apply it to decompose CoffeeMesh into subdomains? To break down a system into subdomains, it helps to think about the operations the system has to perform to accomplish its goal. With CoffeeMesh, we want to model the process of taking an order and delivering it to the customer. As you can see in figure 3.6, we break down this process into eight steps:

1. When the customer lands on the website, we show them the product catalogue. Each product is marked as available or unavailable. The customer can filter the list by availability and sort it by price (from lowest to highest and highest to lowest).
2. The customer selects products.
3. The customer pays for their order.
4. Once the customer has paid, we pass on the details of the order to the kitchen.
5. The kitchen picks up the order and produces it.
6. The customer monitors progress on their order.
7. Once the order is ready, we arrange its delivery.
8. The customer tracks the drone's itinerary until their order is delivered.

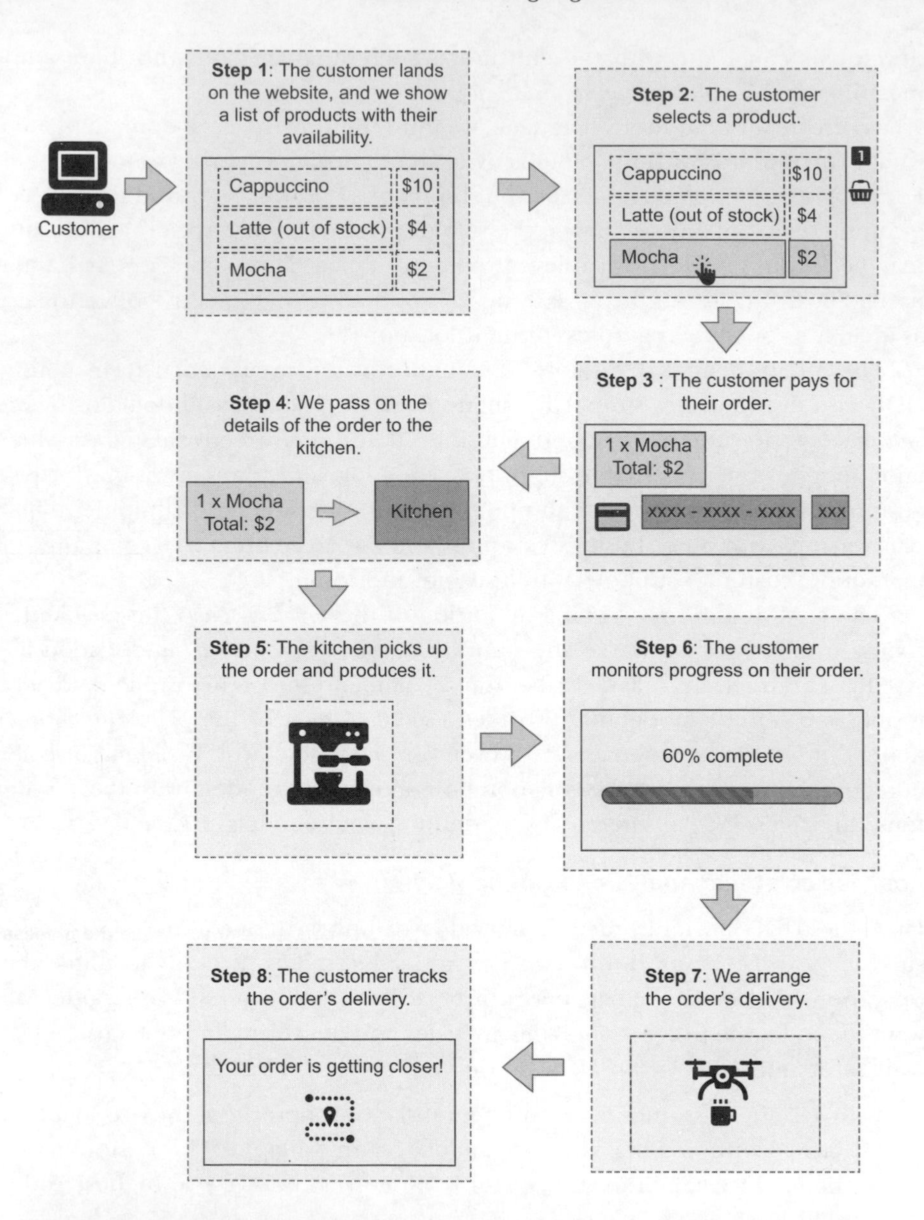

Figure 3.6 To place an order, the customer lands on the CoffeeMesh website, selects items from the product catalogue, and pays for the order. After payment, we pass the order's details to the kitchen, which produces it while the customer monitors its progress. Finally, we arrange the order's delivery.

Let's map each step to its corresponding subdomain (see figure 3.7 for a representation of this analysis). The first step represents a subdomain that serves the CoffeeMesh product catalogue. We can call it the *products subdomain*. This subdomain tells us which

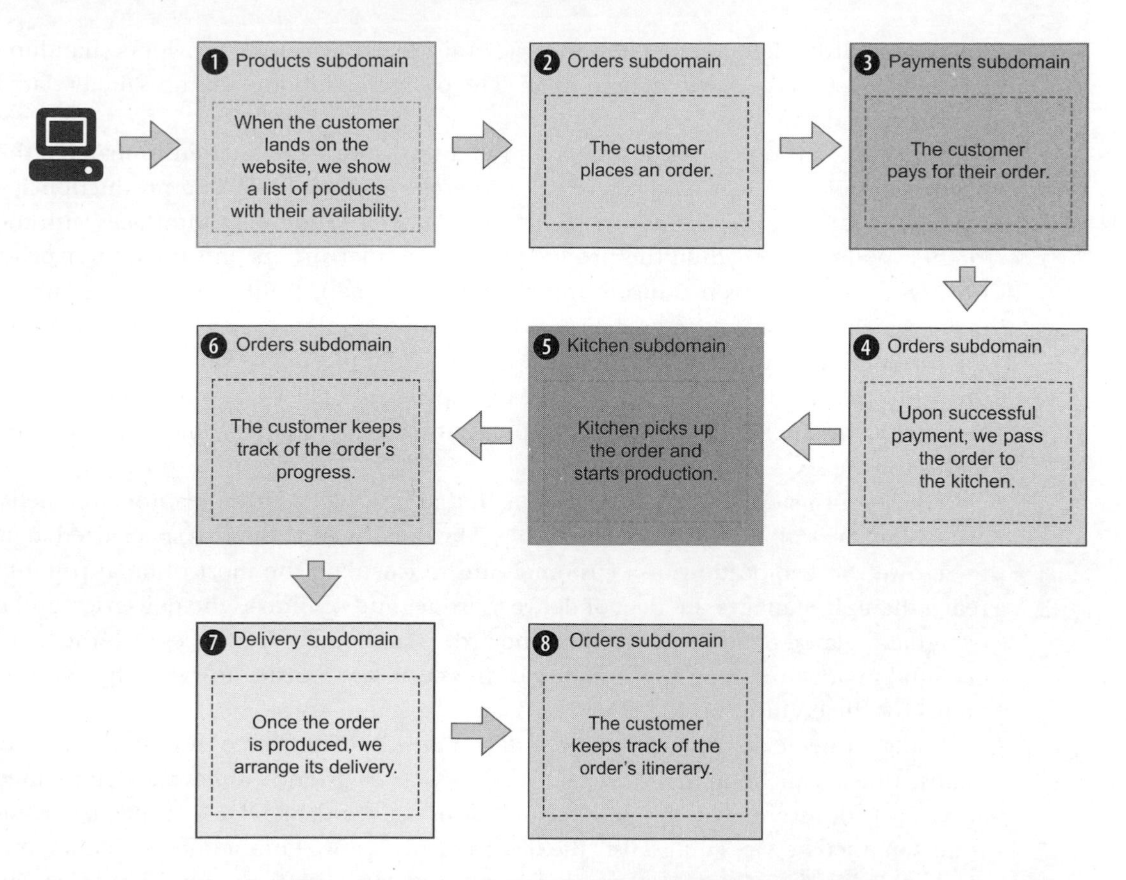

Figure 3.7 We map to a subdomain every step in the process of placing and delivering an order. For example, the process of serving the product catalogue is satisfied by the products subdomain, while the process of taking an order is satisfied by the orders subdomain.

products are available and which are not. To do so, the products subdomain tracks the amount of each product and ingredient in stock.

The second step represents a subdomain that allows users to select products. This subdomain manages the life cycle of each order, and we call it the *orders subdomain.* This subdomain owns data about users' orders, and it exposes an interface that allows us to manage orders and check their status. It hides the complexity of the platform so that the user doesn't have to know about different endpoints and know what to do with them. The orders subdomain also takes care of the second part of the fourth step: passing the details of the order to the kitchen once the payment has been successfully processed. It also meets the requirements for step 6: allow the user to check the state of their order. As an orders manager, the orders subdomain also works with the delivery subdomain to arrange the delivery.

The third step represents a subdomain that can handle user payments. We will call it the *payments subdomain.* This domain contains specialized logic for payment processing, including card validation, integration with third-party payment providers, handling different methods of payment, and so on. The payments subdomain owns data related to user payments.

The fifth step represents a subdomain that works with the kitchen to manage the production of customer orders. We call it the *kitchen subdomain*. The production system in the kitchen is fully automated, and the kitchen subdomain interfaces with the kitchen system to schedule the production of customer orders and track their progress. Once an order is produced, the kitchen subdomain notifies the orders subdomain, which then arranges its delivery. The kitchen subdomain owns data related to the production of customer orders, and it exposes an interface that allows us to send orders to the kitchen and keep track of their progress. The orders subdomain interfaces with the kitchen subdomain to update the order's status to meet the requirements for the sixth step.

The seventh step represents a subdomain that interfaces with the automated delivery system. We call it the *delivery subdomain*. This subdomain contains specialized logic to resolve the geolocation of a customer and to calculate the most optimal route to reach them. It manages the fleet of delivery drones and optimizes the deliveries, and it owns data related to all the deliveries. The orders subdomain interfaces with the delivery subdomain to update the itinerary of the customer's order to meet the requirements for the eighth step.

Using strategic analysis, we obtain a decomposition for CoffeeMesh in five subdomains, which can be mapped to microservices, as each encapsulates a well-defined and clearly differentiated area of logic that owns its own data. DDD's strategic analysis results in microservices that satisfy the design principles we enumerated in section 3.2: all these subdomains can perform their core tasks without relying on other microservices, and therefore we say they're loosely coupled; each service owns its own data, hence complying with the database-per-service principle; finally, each service performs tasks within a narrowly defined subdomain, which complies with the SRP.

As you can see in figure 3.8, strategic analysis gives us the following microservices architecture:

- *Products subdomain maps to the products service*—Manages CoffeeMesh's product catalogue
- *Orders subdomain maps to the orders service*—Manages customer orders
- *Payments subdomain maps to the payments service*—Manages customer payments
- *Kitchen subdomain maps to the kitchen service*—Manages the production of orders in the kitchen
- *Delivery subdomain maps to the delivery service*—Manages customer deliveries

In the next section, we compare the results of DDD's strategic analysis with the outcome of service decomposition by business capability, and we evaluate the benefits and challenges of each approach.

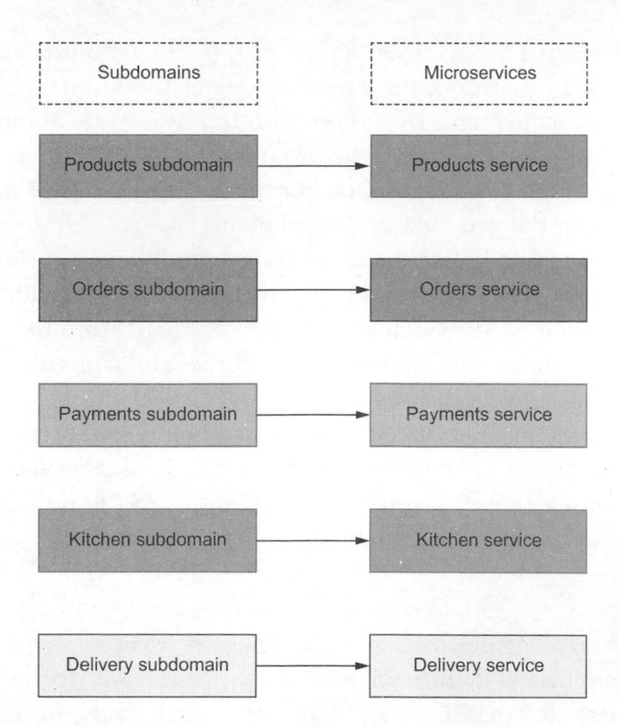

Figure 3.8 Applying DDD's strategic analysis breaks down the CoffeeMesh platform into five subdomains that can be mapped directly to microservices.

3.5 Decomposition by business capability vs. decomposition by subdomain

Which service decomposition strategy should we use to design our microservices: decomposition by business capability or decomposition by subdomains? While decomposition by business capability focuses on business structure and organization, decomposition by subdomain analyzes business processes and flows. Therefore, both approaches give us different perspectives on the business, and if you can spare the time, the best strategy is to apply both approaches to service decomposition.

Sometimes we can combine the results of both approaches. For example, the CoffeeMesh platform could allow customers to write reviews for each product, and CoffeeMesh could leverage this information to recommend new products to other customers. The company could have an entire team dedicated to this aspect of the business. From a technical point of view, reviews could be just another table in the Products database. However, to facilitate collaboration with the business, it could make sense to build a reviews service. The reviews service would be able to feed new reviews into the recommendation system, and the orders service would use the reviews service's interface to serve recommendations to new users.

The advantage of decomposition by business capability is that the architecture of the platform aligns with the existing organizational structure of the business. This alignment might facilitate the collaboration between business and technical teams. The downside of this approach is that the existing organizational structure of the business is not necessarily the most efficient one. As a matter of fact, it can be outdated and reflect old business processes. In that case, the inefficiencies of the business will be mirrored in the microservices architecture. Decomposition by business capability also risks falling out of alignment with the business if the organization is restructured.

When we applied decomposition by business capability in section 3.3.2, we obtained an undesirable division between the products and ingredients services. After further analysis of the dependencies between both services, we concluded that both capabilities should go into the same service. However, in real-life situations, this additional analysis is often missing, and the resulting architecture isn't optimal. From the analysis in sections 3.3 and 3.4, we can say that decomposition by subdomain gives you a better architectural fit to model the business processes and flows, and if you must choose only one approach, decomposition by subdomain is the better strategy.

Now that we know how to design our microservices, it's time to design and build their interfaces. In the upcoming chapters, you'll learn to build REST and GraphQL interfaces for microservices.

Summary

- We call the process of breaking down a system into microservices service decomposition. Service decomposition defines the boundaries between services, and we must get this process right to avoid the risk of building a distributed monolith.
- Decomposition by business capability analyzes the structure of the business and designs microservices for each team in the organization. This approach aligns the business with our system architecture, but it also reproduces the inefficiencies of the business into the platform.
- Decomposition by subdomains applies DDD to model the processes and flows of the business through subdomains. By using this approach, we design a microservice for each subdomain, which results in a more robust technical design.
- To assess the quality of our microservices architecture, we apply three design principles:
  - *Database-per-service principle*—Each microservice owns its own data, and access to that data happens through the service's API.
  - *Loose coupling principle*—You must be able to update a service without impacting other services, and each service should be able to work without constantly calling other services.
  - *Single Responsibility Principle*—We must design each service around a specific business capability or subdomain.

Part 2

Designing and building REST APIs

In part 1, you learned what microservice APIs are and how to decompose a system into microservices. The natural questions now are, "How do you build a microservice?" and "How do you make your services talk to each other?"

We make services talk to each other using APIs, and in part 2 you learn to design and build REST APIs. Representational State Transfer (REST) is the most popular technology for building APIs, and in chapter 4 you learn all the fundamental principles of REST API design. We'll keep the approach practical: in chapter 1, we introduced CoffeeMesh, an on-demand coffee delivery application, and in chapter 6, you learn to build CoffeeMesh's orders and kitchen APIs using Python's popular FastAPI and Flask frameworks.

In chapter 1 we introduced documentation-driven development and highlighted the importance of API documentation, which tells your API clients how the API works; therefore, good documentation is essential to deliver successful integrations. We document REST APIs using the OpenAPI standard, and in chapter 5 you learn step by step how to document a REST API.

Finally, in chapter 7 you learn everything you need to build microservices. You learn to implement your data layer using SQLAlchemy and to manage migrations using Alembic. You learn to structure your application using hexagonal architecture, as well as many other useful patterns and principles to encapsulate your code and maintain loose coupling between layers.

By the end of part 2 you'll be able to design great REST APIs, produce excellent API documentation, and write highly readable and maintainable service implementations. I can't wait to get started!

4 Principles of REST API design

This chapter covers

- The design principles of REST APIs
- How the Richardson maturity model helps us understand the advantages of REST best design principles
- The concept of resource and the design of endpoints for REST APIs
- Using HTTP verbs and HTTP status codes to create highly expressive REST APIs
- Designing high-quality payloads and URL query parameters for REST APIs

Representational state transfer (REST) describes an architectural style for applications that communicate over a network. Originally, the concept of REST included a list of constraints for the design of distributed and scalable web applications. Over time, detailed protocols and specifications have emerged that give us well-defined guidelines for designing REST APIs. Today, REST is by far the most popular choice for building web APIs.[1] In this chapter, we study the design principles of REST and

[1] The 2022 "State of the API Report" by Postman found that the majority of participants in the survey (89%) use REST (https://www.postman.com/state-of-api/api-technologies/#api-technologies).

learn to apply them by designing the orders API of the CoffeeMesh platform, the on-demand coffee delivery application we introduced in chapter 1.

We explain the concept of a resource, and what it means for the design of REST APIs. You'll also learn to leverage features of the HTTP protocol, such as HTTP verbs and status codes, to create highly expressive APIs. The final part of this chapter covers best practices for designing API payloads and URL query parameters.

4.1 What is REST?

REST, a term coined by Roy Fielding in his doctoral dissertation "Architectural Styles and the Design of Network-based Software Architectures" (PhD diss., University of California, Irvine, 2000, p. 109), describes an architectural style for loosely coupled and highly scalable applications that communicate over a network. It refers to the ability to transfer the representation of a resource's state. The concept of resource is fundamental in REST applications.

DEFINITION REST is an architectural style for building loosely coupled and highly scalable APIs. REST APIs are structured around resources, entities that can be manipulated through the API.

A *resource* is an entity that can be referenced by a unique hypertext reference (i.e., URL). There are two types of resources: collections and singletons. A *singleton* represents a single entity, while *collections* represent lists of entities.[2] What does this mean in practice? It means that we use different URL paths for each type of resource. For example, CoffeeMesh's orders service manages orders, and through its API we can access a specific order through the `/orders/{order_id}` URL path, while a collection of orders is available under the `/orders` URL path. Therefore, `/orders/{order_id}` is a singleton endpoint, while `/orders` is a collections endpoint.

Some resources can be nested within another resource, such as a payload for an order with several items listed in a nested array.

Listing 4.1 Example of payload with nested resources

```
{
    "id": "924721eb-a1a1-4f13-b384-37e89c0e0875",
    "status": "progress",
    "created": "2023-09-01",
    "order": [
        {
            "product": "cappuccino",
            "size": "small",
            "quantity": 1
        },
```

[2] See Prakash Subramaniam's excellent article "REST API Design—Resource Modeling" for an in-depth discussion of resources and resource modeling in REST APIs (https://www.thoughtworks.com/en-gb/insights/blog/rest-api-design-resource-modeling).

```
            {
                "product": "croissant",
                "size": "medium",
                "quantity": 2
            }
        ]
    }
```

We can create nested endpoints to represent nested resources. Nested endpoints allow us to access specific details of a resource. For example, we can expose a GET `/orders/{order_id}/status` endpoint that allows us to get an order's status without all the other details about the order. Using nested endpoints is a common optimization strategy when resources are represented by large payloads since they help us avoid costly data transfers when we are only interested in one property.

The resource-oriented nature of REST APIs may sometimes appear limiting. A common concern is how to model actions through endpoints while keeping our APIs RESTful. For example, how do we represent the action of cancelling an order? A common heuristic is to represent actions as nested resources. For example, we can have a POST `/orders/{order_id}/cancel` endpoint to cancel orders. In this case, we model the order's cancellation as creating a cancellation event.

Designing clean endpoints is the first step toward building REST APIs that are easy to maintain and to consume. The patterns you've learned in this section go a long way to achieving clean endpoints, and in the rest of this chapter, you'll learn additional patterns and principles for clean API design. In the next section, you'll learn about the six architectural constraints of REST API applications.

4.2 Architectural constraints of REST applications

In this section, we study the architectural constraints of REST applications. These constraints were enumerated by Fielding, and they specify how a server should process and respond to a client request. Before we delve into the details, let's first provide a brief overview of each constraint:

- *Client-server architecture*—The user interface (UI) must be decoupled from the backend.
- *Statelessness*—The server must not manage states between requests.
- *Cacheability*—Requests that always return the same response must be cacheable.
- *Layered system*—The API may be architected in layers, but such complexity must be hidden from the user.
- *Code on demand*—The server can inject code into the user interface on demand.
- *Uniform interface*—The API must provide a consistent interface for accessing and manipulating resources.

Let's discuss each of these constraints in more detail.

4.2.1 Separation of concerns: The client-server architecture principle

REST relies on the principle of separation of concerns, and consequently it requires that user interfaces are decoupled from data storage and server logic. This allows server-side components to evolve independently from UI elements. As you can see in figure 4.1, a common implementation of the client-server architectural pattern is building the UI as a standalone application, for example, as a single-page application (SPA).

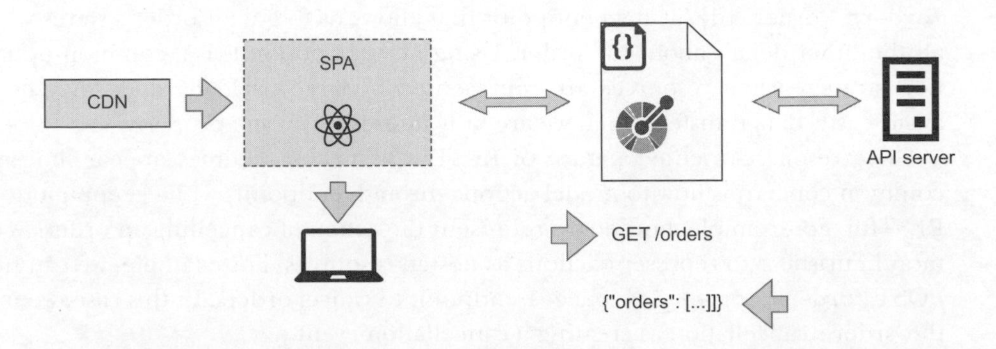

Figure 4.1 REST's client-server architecture principle states that the server implementation must be decoupled from the client.

4.2.2 Make it scalable: The statelessness principle

In REST, every request to the server must contain all the information necessary to process it. In particular, the server must not keep state from one request to the next. As you can see in figure 4.2, removing state management from server components makes

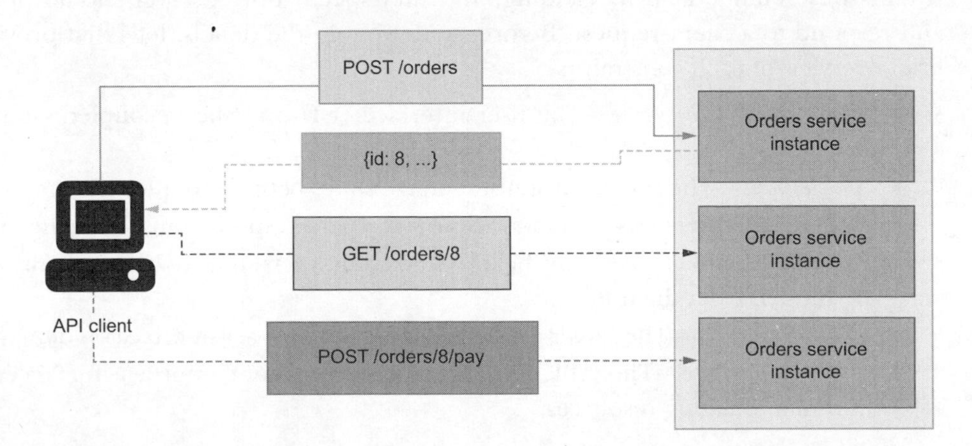

Figure 4.2 REST's statelessness principle states that the server must not manage the state of the client. This allows us to deploy multiple instances of the API server and respond to the API client with any of them.

it easier to scale the backend horizontally. This allows us to deploy multiple instances of the server, and because none of those instances manages the API client's state, the client can communicate with any of them.

4.2.3 Optimize for performance: The cacheability principle

When applicable, server responses must be cached. Caching improves the performance of APIs because it means we don't have to perform all the calculations required to serve a response again and again. GET requests are suitable for caching, since they return data already saved in the server. As you can see in figure 4.3, by caching a GET request, we avoid having to fetch data from the source every time a user requests the same information. The longer it takes to assemble the response for a GET request, the greater the benefits of caching it.

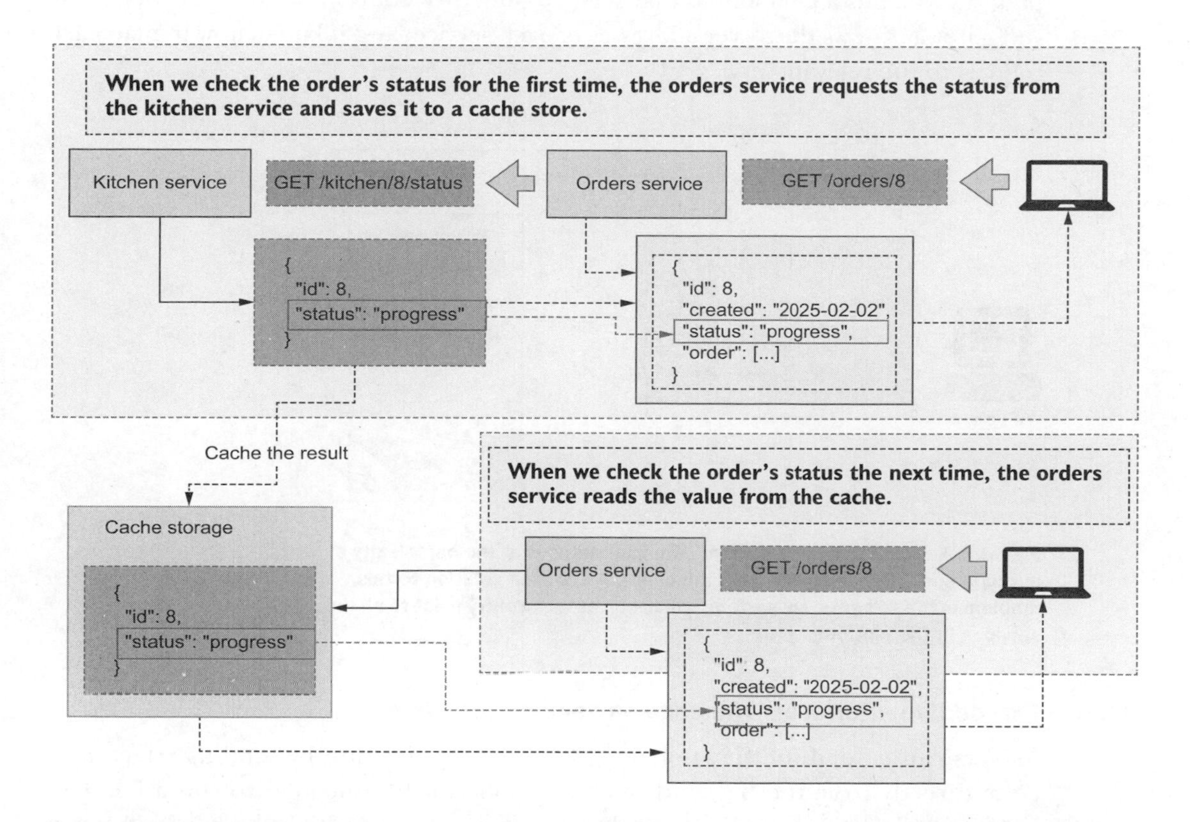

Figure 4.3 REST's cacheability principle states that cacheable responses must be cached, which helps to boost the API server performance. In this example, we cache the order's status for a short period of time to avoid multiple requests to the kitchen service.

Figure 4.3 illustrates the benefits of caching. As we learned in chapter 3, customers can track the progress on their orders once they've been submitted to the kitchen.

The orders service interfaces with the kitchen service to obtain information on the order's progress. To save time the next time the customer checks the order's status, we cache its value for a short period of time.

4.2.4 Make it simple for the client: The layered system principle

In a REST architecture, clients must have a unique point of entry to your API and must not be able to tell whether they are connected directly to the end server or to an intermediary layer such as a load balancer. You can deploy different components of a server-side application in different servers, or you can deploy the same component across different servers for redundancy and scalability. This complexity should be hidden from the user by exposing a single endpoint that encapsulates access to your services.

As you can see in figure 4.4, a common solution to this problem is the API gateway pattern, which is a component that serves as an entry point for all microservices. The API gateway knows the server addresses of each service, and it knows how to map each request to the relevant service.[3]

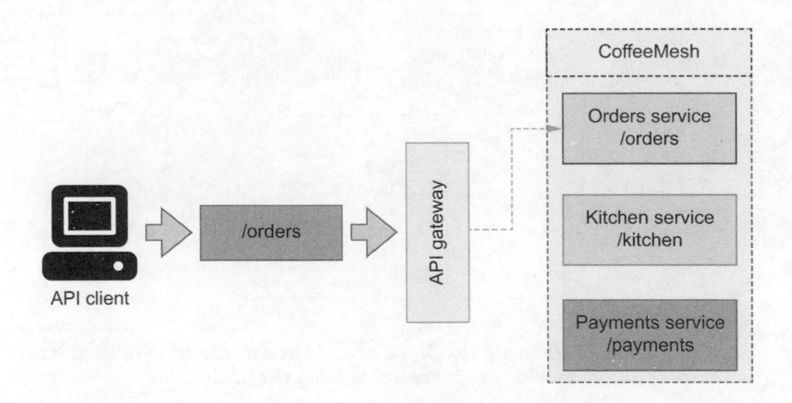

Figure 4.4 REST's layered system principle states that the complexity of our backend must be hidden from the client. A common solution to this problem is the API gateway pattern, which serves as an entry point to all the services in the platform.

4.2.5 Extendable interfaces: The code-on-demand principle

Servers can extend the functionality of a client application by sending executable code directly from the backend, such as JavaScript files needed to run a UI. This constraint is optional and only applies to applications in which the backend serves the client interface.

[3] For more information on this pattern, see Chris Richardson, *Microservices Patterns* (Manning, 2019, pp. 259–291; https://livebook.manning.com/book/microservices-patterns/chapter-8/point-8620-53-297-0).

4.2.6 Keep it consistent: The uniform interface principle

REST applications must expose a uniform and consistent interface to their consumers. The interface must be documented, and the API specification must be followed strictly by the server and the client. Individual resources are identified by a Uniform Resource Identifier (URI),[4] and each URI must be unique and always return the same resource. For example, the URI `/orders/8` represents an order with ID 8, and a GET request on this URI always returns the state of the order with ID 8. If the order is deleted from the system, the ID must not be reused to represent a different order.

Resources must be represented using a serialization method of choice, and that approach should be used consistently across the API. Nowadays, REST APIs typically use JSON as the serialization format, although other formats are also possible, such as XML.

The architectural constraints of REST give us solid ground for designing robust and scalable APIs. But as we'll see in the following sections of this chapter, there are more factors we need to consider when designing an API. In the next section, you'll learn to make your APIs discoverable by enriching a resource's description with related hypermedia links.

4.3 Hypermedia as the engine of application state

Now that we understand the most important design constraints of REST APIs, let's look at another important concept in REST: hypermedia as the engine of application state (HATEOAS). HATEOAS is a paradigm in the design of REST APIs that emphasizes the concept of discoverability. HATEOAS makes APIs easier to use by enriching responses with all the information users need to interact with a resource. In this section, we explain how HATEOAS works, and we discuss the benefits and disadvantages of this approach.

What exactly is HATEOAS? In an article written in 2008 with the title "REST APIs Must Be Hypertext-Driven" (http://mng.bz/p6y5), Fielding suggested that REST APIs must include related links in their responses to allow clients to navigate the API by following those links.

> **DEFINITION** *Hypermedia as the engine of application state* (HATEOAS) is a design paradigm of REST that emphasizes the idea of discoverability. Whenever a client requests a resource from the server, the response must contain a list of related links to the resource. For example, if a client requests the details of an order, the response must include the links to cancel and pay for the order.

For example, as you can see in figure 4.5, when a client requests the details of an order, the API includes a collection of links related to the order. With those links, we can cancel the order, or we can pay for it.

---

[4] For the latest specification on URIs, see "RFC 7320: URI Design and Ownership" by M. Nottingham (July 2004, https://tools.ietf.org/html/rfc7320).

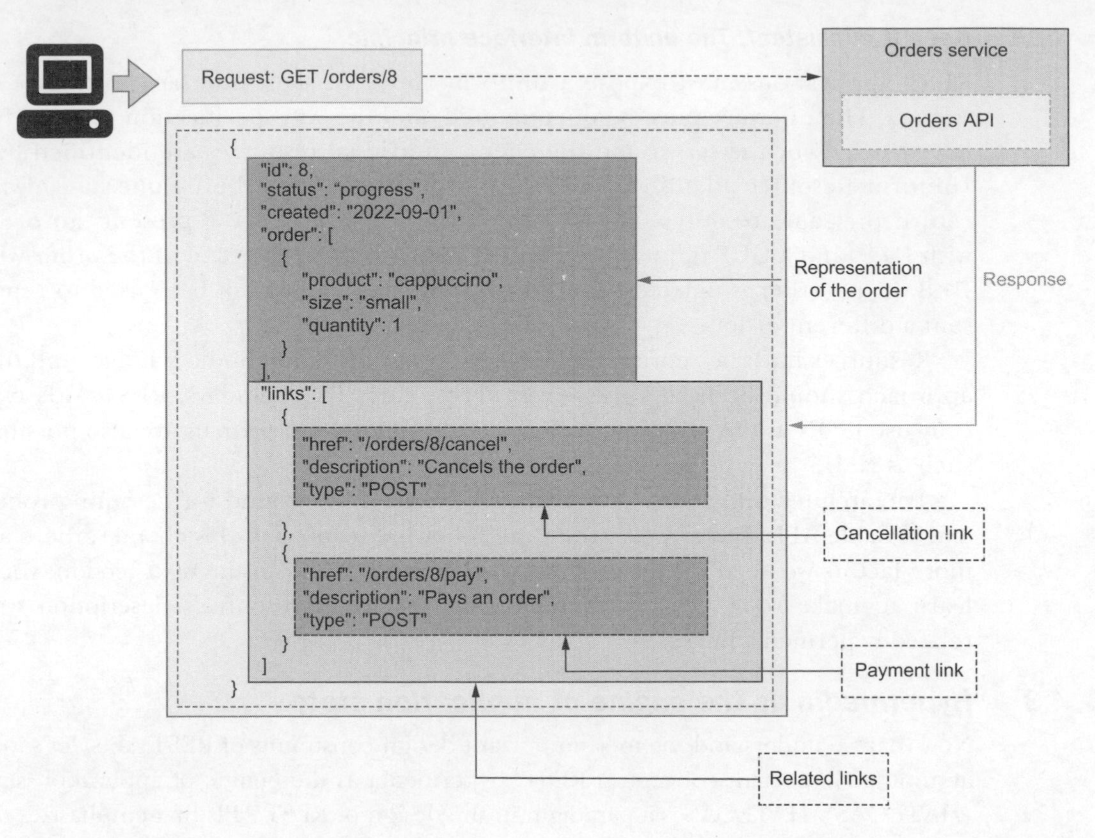

Figure 4.5 In the HATEOAS paradigm, the API sends a representation of the requested resource with other links related to the resource.

Listing 4.2 Representation of an order including hypermedia links

```
{
    "id": 8,
    "status": "progress",
    "created": "2023-09-01",
    "order": [
        {
            "product": "cappuccino",
            "size": "small",
            "quantity": 1
        },
        {
            "product": "croissant",
            "size": "medium",
            "quantity": 2
        }
    ],
    "links": [
        {
            "href": "/orders/8/cancel",
```

```
                "description": "Cancels the order",
                "type": "POST"
            },
            {
                "href": "/orders/8/pay",
                "description": "Pays for the order",
                "type": "POST"
            }
        ]
}
```

Providing relational links makes APIs navigational and easier to use, since every resource comes with all the URLs we need to work with it. However, in practice, many APIs are not implemented that way for several reasons:

- The information supplied by hyperlinks is already available in the API documentation. In fact, the information contained in an OpenAPI specification is far richer and more structured than what you can provide in a list of related links for specific resources.
- It's not always clear exactly what links should be returned. Different users have different levels of permissions and roles, which allow them to perform different actions and access different resources. For example, external users can use the POST `/orders` endpoint in the CoffeeMesh API to place an order, and they are also able to use the GET `/orders/{order_id}` endpoint to retrieve the details of an order. However, they cannot use the DELETE `/orders/{order_id}` endpoint to delete an order, since this endpoint is restricted to internal users of the CoffeeMesh platform. If the point of HATEOAS is to make the API navigational from a single point of entry, it wouldn't make sense to return the DELETE `/orders/{order_id}` endpoint to external users since they are not able to use it. Therefore, it's necessary to return different lists of related links to different users according to their permissions. However, this level of flexibility introduces additional complexity in our API designs and implementations and couples the authorization layer with the API layer.
- Depending on the state of the resource, certain actions and resources may not be available. For example, you can call the POST `/orders/1234/cancel` endpoint on an active order but not on a cancelled order. This level of ambiguity makes it hard to define and implement robust interfaces that follow the HATEOAS principles.
- Finally, in some APIs, the list of related links may be large and therefore make the response payload too big, hence compromising the performance of the API and the reliability of the connection for small devices with low network connectivity.

When working on your own APIs, you can decide whether to follow the HATEOAS principles. There's a certain level of benefit in providing lists of related resources in some cases. For example, in a wiki application, the linked resources section of a payload can be used to list content related to a specific article, links to the same article in other languages, and links to actions that can be performed on the article. Overall, you may want to strike a balance between what your API documentation already provides to the client in a more clear and detailed way, and what you can offer in your responses to facilitate the interaction between the client and the API. If you're building a public-facing API, your clients will benefit from relational links. However, if it's a small internal API, it's probably unnecessary to include relational links.

Now that we know how we make our APIs discoverable and when it's worth doing so, let's study the Richardson maturity model, which will help you understand to what extent your APIs comply with the design principles of REST.

4.4 Analyzing the maturity of an API with the Richardson maturity model

This section discusses the Richardson maturity model, a mental model developed by Leonard Richardson to help us think about the degree to which an API complies with the principles of REST.[5] The Richardson maturity model distinguishes four levels (from level 0 to level 3) of "maturity" in an API. Each level introduces additional elements of good REST API design (figure 4.6). Let's discuss each level in detail.

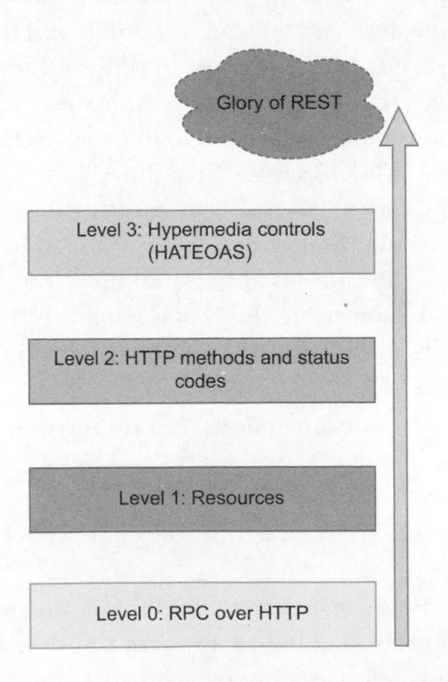

Figure 4.6 The Richardson maturity model distinguishes four levels of API maturity, where the highest level represents an API design that abides by the best practices and standards of REST, while the lowest level represents a type of API that doesn't apply any of the principles of REST.

[5] Leonard Richardson presented his maturity model in his talk "Justice Will Take Us Millions of Intricate Moves" at QCon San Francisco in 2008 (https://www.crummy.com/writing/speaking/2008-QCon/).

4.4.1 Level 0: Web APIs à la RPC

At level 0, HTTP is essentially used as a transport system to carry interactions with the server. The notion of API in this case is closer to the idea of a *remote procedure call* (RPC; see appendix A). All the requests to the server are made on the same endpoint and with the same HTTP method, usually GET or POST. The details of the client's request are carried in an HTTP payload. For example, to place an order through the CoffeeMesh website, the client might send a POST request on a generic `/api` endpoint with the following payload:

```
{
    "action": "placeOrder",
    "order": [
        {
            "product": "mocha",
            "size": "medium",
            "quantity": 2
        }
    ]
}
```

The server invariably responds with 200 status codes and an accompanying payload letting us know the outcome of processing the request. Similarly, to get the details of an order, a client might make the following POST request on the generic `/api` endpoint (assuming the ID of the order is 8):

```
{
    "action": "getOrder",
    "order": [
        {
            "id": 8
        }
    ]
}
```

4.4.2 Level 1: Introducing the concept of resource

Level 1 introduces the concept of resource URLs. Instead of a generic `/api` endpoint, the server exposes URLs that represent resources. For example, the `/orders` URL represents a collection of orders, while the `/orders/{order_id}` URL represents a single order. To place an order, the client sends a POST request on the `/orders` endpoint with a similar payload as in level 0:

```
{
    "action": "placeOrder",
    "order": [
        {
            "product": "mocha",
            "size": "medium",
            "quantity": 2
```

```
        }
    ]
}
```

This time when requesting the details of the last order, the client will make a POST request on the URI representing that order: `/orders/8`. At this level, the API doesn't distinguish between HTTP methods to represent different actions.

4.4.3 Level 2: Using HTTP methods and status codes

Level 2 introduces the concept of HTTP verbs and status codes. At this level, HTTP verbs are used to represent specific actions. For example, to place an order, a client sends a POST request on the `/orders` endpoint with the following payload:

```
{
    "order": [
        {
            "product": "mocha",
            "size": "medium",
            "quantity": 2
        }
    ]
}
```

In this case, the HTTP method POST indicates the operation we want to perform, and the payload only includes the details of the order we want to place. Similarly, to get the details of an order, we send a GET request on the order's URI: `/orders/{order_id}`. In this case, we use the HTTP verb GET to tell the server that we want to retrieve details of the resource specified in the URI.

While previous levels include the same status code (usually 200) in all responses, level 2 introduces the semantic use of HTTP status codes to report the outcome of processing the client's request. For example, when we create a resource using a POST request, we get a 201 response status code, and a request for a nonexistent resource gets a 404 response status code. For more information on HTTP status codes and best practices using them, see section 4.6.

4.4.4 Level 3: API discoverability

Level 3 introduces the concept of discoverability by applying the principles of HATEOAS and by enriching responses with links that represent the actions we can perform on a resource. For example, a GET request on the `/orders/{order_id}` endpoint returns a representation of an order, and it includes a list of related links.

Listing 4.3 Representation of an order, including hypermedia links

```
{
    "id": 8
    "status": "progress",
    "created": "2023-09-01",
```

```
    "order": [
        {
            "product": "cappuccino",
            "size": "small",
            "quantity": 1
        },
        {
            "product": "croissant",
            "size": "medium",
            "quantity": 2
        }
    ],
    "links": [
        {
            "href": "/orders/8/cancel",
            "description": "Cancels the order",
            "type": "POST"

        },
        {
            "href": "/orders/8/pay",
            "description": "Pays for the order",
            "type": "GET"
        }
    ]
}
```

In the Richardson maturity model, level 3 represents the last step toward what he calls the "Glory of REST."

What does the Richardson maturity model mean for the design of our APIs? The model gives us a framework to think about where our API designs stand within the overall principles of REST. This model isn't meant to measure the degree to which an API "complies" with the principles of REST, or to otherwise assess the quality of an API design; instead, it gives us a framework to think about how well we leverage the HTTP protocol to create expressive APIs that are easy to understand and to consume.

Now that we understand the main design principles of REST APIs, it's time to start designing the orders API! In the next section, we'll begin by designing the API endpoints by learning to use HTTP methods.

4.5 Structured resource URLs with HTTP methods

As we learned in section 4.4, using HTTP methods and status codes is associated with a mature API design in the Richardson maturity model. In this section, we learn to use HTTP methods correctly by applying them to the design of the CoffeeMesh application's orders API.

HTTP methods are special keywords used in HTTP requests to indicate the type of action we want to perform in the server. Proper use of HTTP methods makes our APIs more structured and elegant, and since they're part of the HTTP protocol, they also make the API more understandable and easier to use.

DEFINITION *HTTP request methods* are keywords used in HTTP requests to indicate the type of action we wish to perform. For example, the GET method retrieves the details of a resource, while the POST method creates a new resource. The most important HTTP methods for REST APIs are GET, POST, PUT, PATCH, and DELETE. HTTP methods are also known as verbs.

In my experience, there's often confusion around the proper use of HTTP methods. Let's clear up that confusion by learning the semantics of each method. The most relevant HTTP methods in REST APIs are GET, POST, PUT, PATCH, and DELETE:

- *GET*—Returns information about the requested resource
- *POST*—Creates a new resource
- *PUT*—Performs a full update by replacing a resource
- *PATCH*—Updates specific properties of a resource
- *DELETE*—Deletes a resource

Semantics of the PUT method

According to the HTTP specification, PUT can be idempotent, and therefore we can use it to create a resource if it doesn't exist. However, the specification also highlights "[a] service that selects a proper URI on behalf of the client, after receiving a state-changing request, SHOULD be implemented using the POST method rather than PUT." This means that, when the server is in charge of generating the URI of a new resource, we should create resources using the POST method, and PUT can only be used for updates.

See R. Fielding, "Hypertext Transfer Protocol (HTTP/1.1): Semantics and Content" (RFC 7231, June 2014, https://tools.ietf.org/html/rfc7231#section-4.3.4).

HTTP methods allow us to model the basic operations we can perform on a resource: create (POST), read (GET), update (PUT and PATCH), and delete (DELETE). We refer to these operations with the acronym CRUD, which comes from the field of databases,[6] but is very popular in the world of APIs. You'll often hear about CRUD APIs, which are APIs designed to perform these operations on resources.

PUT vs. PATCH: What's the difference, and when do you use them?

We can use both PUT and PATCH to perform updates. So, what's the difference between the two? While PUT requires the API client to send a whole new representation of the resource (hence the replacement semantics), PATCH allows you to send only those properties that changed.

[6] The CRUD acronym was reportedly introduced by James Martin in his influential book *Managing the Data-Base Environment* (Prentice-Hall, 1983, p. 381).

For example, imagine that an order has the following representation:

```
{
    "id": "96247264-7d42-4a95-b073-44cedf5fc07d",
    "status": "progress",
    "created": "2023-09-01",
    "order": [
        {
            "product": "cappuccino",
            "size": "small",
            "quantity": 1
        },
        {
            "product": "croissant",
            "size": "medium",
            "quantity": 2
        }
    ]
}
```

Now suppose that the user wants to make a small amendment in this order and update the size of the croissants from `"medium"` to `"small"`. Although the user wants to change one specific field, with PUT they must send the whole payload back to the server. However, with PATCH they only need to send the fields that must be updated in the server. PATCH requests are more optimal, since the payloads sent to the server are smaller. However, as you can see in the following example, PATCH requests also have a more complex structure, and sometimes they're more difficult to process in the backend:

```
{
    "op": "replace",
    "path": "order/1/size",
    "value": "medium"
}
```

This follows the guidelines of the JSON Patch specification:[a] a JSON Patch request must specify the type of operation we want to perform, plus the target attribute and its desired value. We use JSON Patch to declare the target attribute.

While implementing PATCH endpoints is good practice for public-facing APIs, internal APIs often only implement PUT endpoints for updates since they're easier to handle. In the orders API, we'll implement updates as PUT requests.

[a] P. Bryan and M. Nottingham, "JavaScript Object Notation (JSON) Patch" (https://www.rfc-editor.org/rfc/rfc6902).

How do we use HTTP methods to define the endpoints of CoffeeMesh's orders API? We use HTTP methods in combination with URLs, so let's first define the resource URLs. In section 4.1, we learned to distinguish between two types of resource URLs in

REST: singletons, which represent a single resource, and collections, which represent a list of resources. In the orders API, we have these two resource URLs:

- /orders—Represents a list of orders.
- /orders/{orders_id}—Represents a single order. The curly braces around {order_id} indicates that this is a URL path parameter and must be replaced by the ID of an order.

As you can see in figure 4.7, we use the singleton URL /orders/{order_id} to perform actions on an order, such as updating it, and the collections URL /orders to place and to list past orders. HTTP methods help us model these operations:

- POST /orders to place orders since we use POST to create new resources.
- GET /orders to retrieve a list of orders since we use GET to obtain information.
- GET /orders/{order_id} to retrieve the details of a particular order.
- PUT /orders/{order_id} to update an order since we use PUT to update a resource.
- DELETE /orders/{order_id} to delete an order since we use DELETE for deletes.
- POST /orders/{order_id}/cancel to cancel an order. We use POST to create a cancellation.
- POST /orders/{order_id}/pay to pay for an order. We use POST to create a payment.

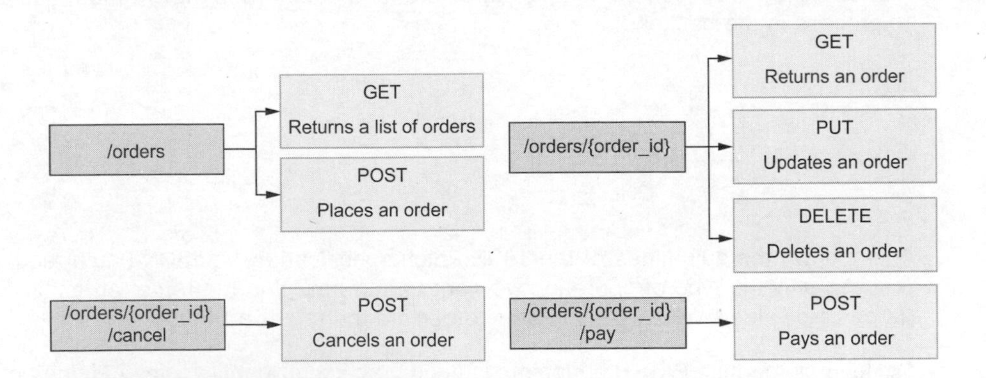

Figure 4.7 We combine HTTP methods with URL paths to design our API endpoints. We leverage the semantics of HTTP methods to convey the intention of each endpoint. For example, we use the POST method to create new resources, so we use it in the POST /orders endpoint to place orders.

Now that we know how to design API endpoints by combining URL paths with HTTP methods, let's see how to leverage the semantics of HTTP status codes to return expressive responses.

4.6 Using HTTP status codes to create expressive HTTP responses

This section explains how we use HTTP status codes in the responses of a REST API. We begin by clarifying what HTTP status codes are and how we classify them into groups, and then we explain how to use them to model our API responses.

4.6.1 What are HTTP status codes?

We use status codes to signal the result of processing a request in the server. When properly used, HTTP status codes help us deliver expressive responses to our APIs' consumers. Status codes fall into the following five groups:

- *1xx group*—Signals that an operation is in progress
- *2xx group*—Signals that a request was successfully processed
- *3xx group*—Signals that a resource has been moved to a new location
- *4xx group*—Signals that something was wrong with the request
- *5xx group*—Signals that there was an error while processing the request

NOTE HTTP response status codes are used to indicate the outcome of processing an HTTP request. For example, the 200 status code indicates that the request was successfully processed, while the 500 status code indicates that an internal server error was raised while processing the request. HTTP status codes are associated with a reasoned phrase that explains the intent of the code. For example, the reasoned phrase for the 404 status code is "Not Found." You can check out the full list of status codes and learn more about them at http://mng.bz/z5lw.

The full list of HTTP status codes is long, and enumerating them one by one wouldn't do much to help us understand how we use them. Instead, let's look at the most commonly used codes and see how we apply them in our API designs.

When thinking about HTTP status codes, it's useful to distinguish between successful and unsuccessful responses. A successful response means the request was successfully processed, while an unsuccessful response means that something went wrong while processing the request. For each of the endpoints that we defined in section 4.5, we use the following successful HTTP status codes:

- POST `/orders`: 201 (Created)—Signals that a resource has been created.
- GET `/orders`: 200 (OK)—Signals that the request was successfully processed.
- GET `/orders/{order_id}`: 200 (OK)—Signals that the request was successfully processed.
- PUT `/orders/{order_id}`: 200 (OK)—Signals that the resource was successfully updated.
- DELETE `/orders/{order_id}`: 204 (No Content)—Signals that the request was successfully processed but no content is delivered in the response. Contrary to all other methods, a DELETE request doesn't require a response with payload, since, after all, we are instructing the server to delete the resource. Therefore, a 204 (No Content) code is a good choice for this type of HTTP request.

- POST `/orders/{order_id}/cancel`: 200 (OK)—Although this is a POST endpoint, we use the 200 (OK) status code since we're not really creating a resource, and all the client wants to know is that the cancellation was successfully processed.
- POST `/orders/{order_id}/pay`: 200 (OK)—Although this is a POST endpoint, we use the 200 (OK) status code since we're not really creating a resource, and all the client wants to know is that the payment was successfully processed.

That's all good for successful responses, but what about error responses? What kinds of errors can we encounter in the server while processing requests, and what kinds of HTTP status codes are appropriate for them? We distinguish two groups of errors:

- Errors made by the user when sending the request, for example, due to a malformed payload, or due to the request being sent to a nonexistent endpoint. We address this type of error with an HTTP status code in the 4xx group.
- Errors unexpectedly raised in the server while processing the request, typically due to a bug in our code. We address this type of error with an HTTP status code in the 5xx group.

Let's talk about each of these error types in more detail.

4.6.2 Using HTTP status codes to report client errors in the request

An API client can make different types of errors when sending a request to an API. The most common type of error in this category is sending a malformed payload to the server. We distinguish two types of malformed payloads: payloads with invalid syntax and unprocessable entities.

Payloads with *invalid syntax* are payloads that the server can neither parse nor understand. A typical example of a payload with invalid syntax is malformed JSON. As you can see in figure 4.8, we address this type of error with a 400 (Bad Request) status code.

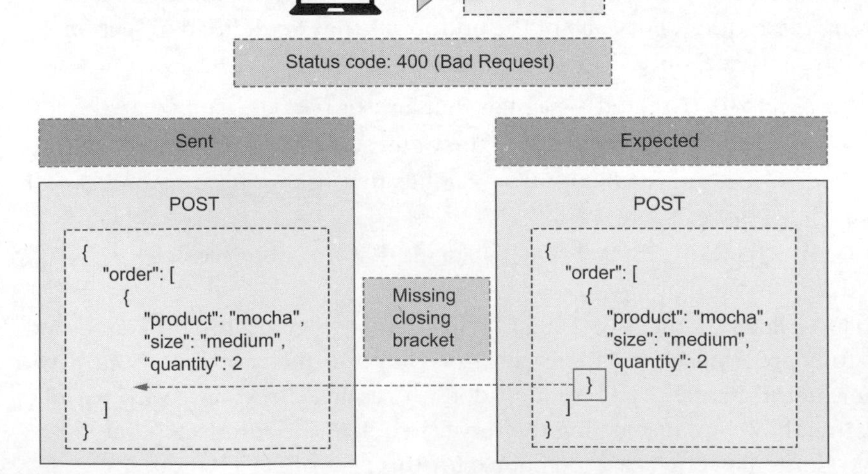

Figure 4.8 When a client sends a malformed payload, we respond with a 400 (Bad Request) status code.

Unprocessable entities are syntactically valid payloads that miss a required parameter, contain invalid parameters, or assign the wrong value or type to a parameter. For example, let's say that, to place an order, our API expects a POST request on the /orders URL path with a payload like this:

```
{
    "order": [
        {
            "product": "mocha",
            "size": "medium",
            "quantity": 2
        }
    ]
}
```

That is, we expect the user to send us a list of elements, where each element represents an item of the order. Each item is described by the following properties:

- product—Identifies the product the user is ordering
- size—Identifies the size that applies to the ordered product
- quantity—Tells us how many items of the same product and size the user wishes to order

As you can see in figure 4.9, an API client can send a payload missing one of the required properties, such as product. We address this type of error with the 422 (Unprocessable Entity) status code, which signals that something was wrong with the request and it couldn't be processed.

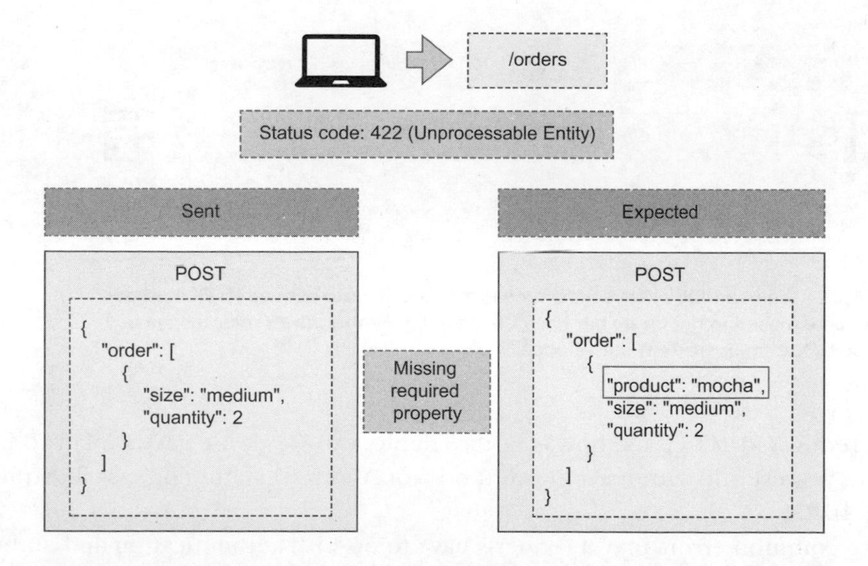

Figure 4.9 When an API client sends a malformed payload, the server responds back with a 400 (Bad Request) status code.

Another common error happens when an API client requests a resource that doesn't exist. For example, we know that the GET `/orders/{order_id}` endpoint serves the details of an order. If a client uses that endpoint with a nonexistent order ID, we should respond with an HTTP status code signaling that the order doesn't exist. As you can see in figure 4.10, we address this error with the 404 (Not Found) status code, which signals that the requested resource is not available or couldn't be found.

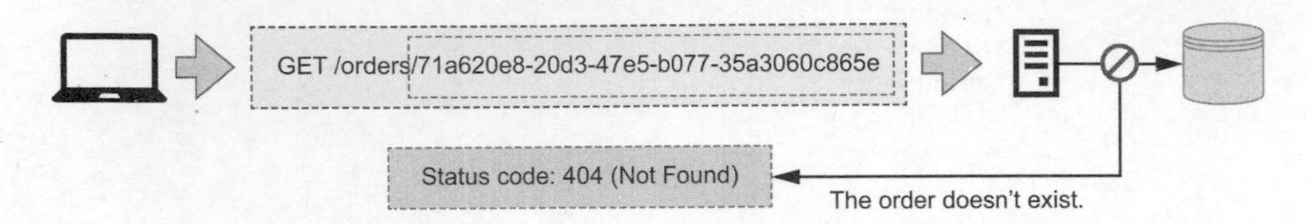

Figure 4.10 When an API client requests a resource that doesn't exist, the server responds with status code 404 (Not Found).

Another common error happens when API clients send a request using an HTTP method that is not supported. For example, if a user sent a PUT request on the `/orders` endpoint, we must tell them that the PUT method is not supported on that URL path. There are two HTTP status codes we can use to address this situation. As you can see in figure 4.11, we can return a 501 (Not Implemented) if the method hasn't been implemented but will be available in the future (i.e., we have a plan to implement it).

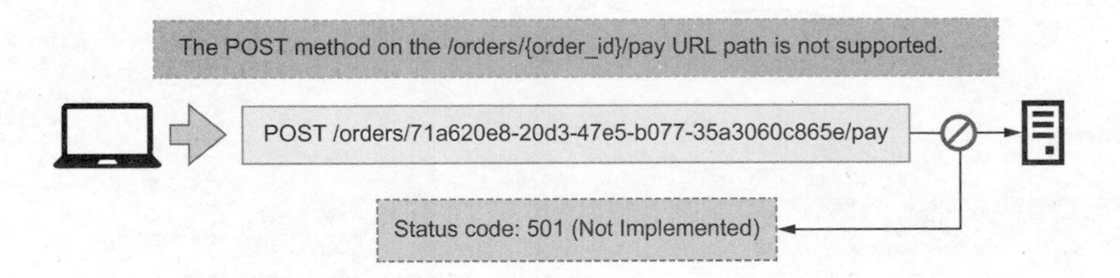

Figure 4.11 When an API client sends a request to a URL path with an HTTP method that will be exposed in the future but hasn't been implemented, the server responds with a 501 (Not Implemented) status code.

If the requested HTTP method is not available and we don't have a plan to implement it, we respond with the 405 (Method Not Allowed) status code, as illustrated in figure 4.12.

Two common errors in API requests have to do with authentication and authorization. The first happens when a client sends an unauthenticated request to a protected endpoint. In that case, we must tell them that they should first authenticate. As you

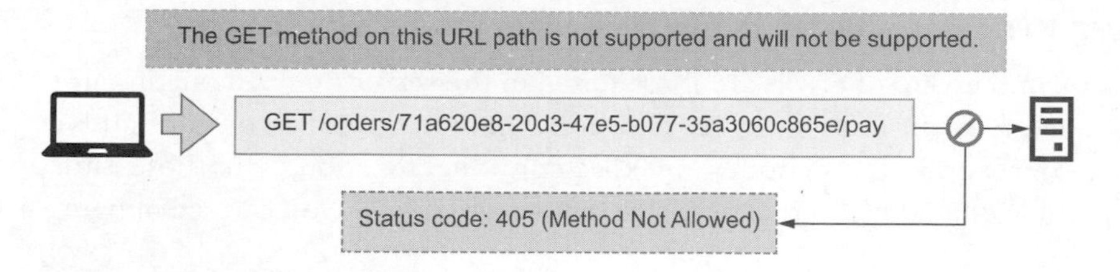

Figure 4.12 When an API client makes a request on a URL path with an HTTP method that is not supported and will not be supported, the server responds with a 405 (Method Not Allowed) status code.

can see in figure 4.13, we address this situation with the 401 (Unauthorized) status code, which signals that the user hasn't been authenticated.

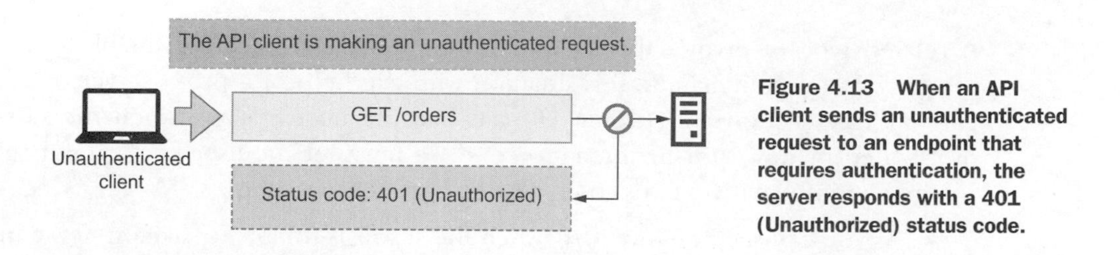

Figure 4.13 When an API client sends an unauthenticated request to an endpoint that requires authentication, the server responds with a 401 (Unauthorized) status code.

The second error happens when a user is correctly authenticated and tries to use an endpoint or a resource they are not authorized to access. An example is a user trying to access the details of an order that doesn't belong to them. As you can see in figure 4.14, we address this scenario with the 403 (Forbidden) status code, which signals that the user doesn't have permissions to access the requested resource or to perform the requested operation.

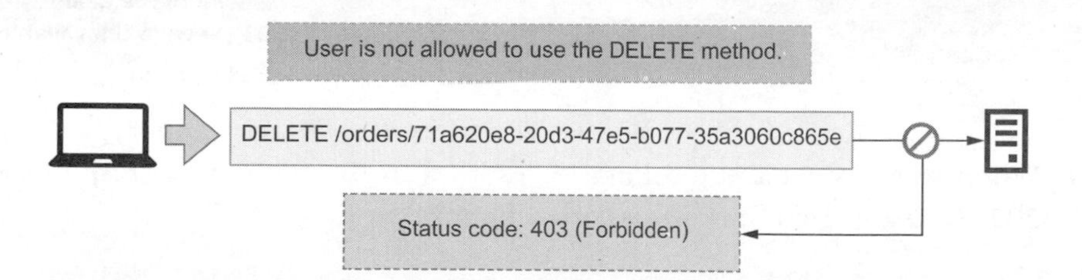

Figure 4.14 When an authenticated user makes a request using an HTTP method they're not allowed to use, the server responds with a 403 (Forbidden) status code.

Now that we know how to use HTTP status codes to report user errors, let's turn our attention to status codes for server errors.

4.6.3 Using HTTP status codes to report errors in the server

The second group of errors are those raised in the server due to a bug in our code or to a limitation in our infrastructure. The most common type of error within this category is when our application crashes unexpectedly due to a bug. In those situations, we respond with a 500 (Internal Server Error) status code, as you can see in figure 4.15.

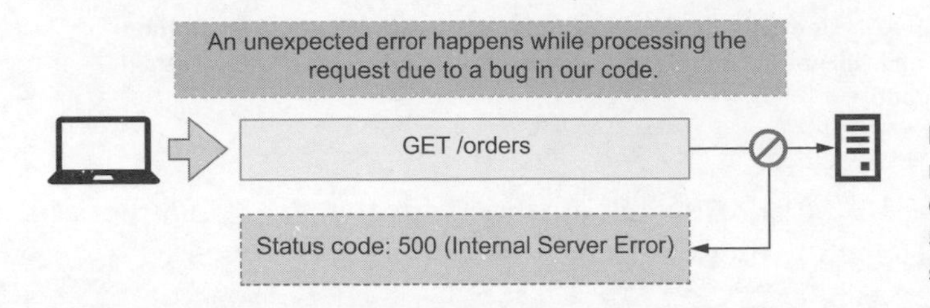

Figure 4.15 When the server raises an error due to a bug in our code, we respond with a 500 (Internal Server Error) status code.

A related type of error happens when our application becomes unable to service requests. We usually handle this situation with the help of a proxy server or an API gateway (see section 4.2.4). Our API can become unresponsive when the server is overloaded or down for maintenance, and we must let the user know about this by sending an informative status code. We distinguish two scenarios:

- As you can see in figure 4.16, when the server is unable to take on new connections, we must respond with a 503 (Service Unavailable) status code, which signals that the server is overloaded or down for maintenance and therefore cannot service additional requests.

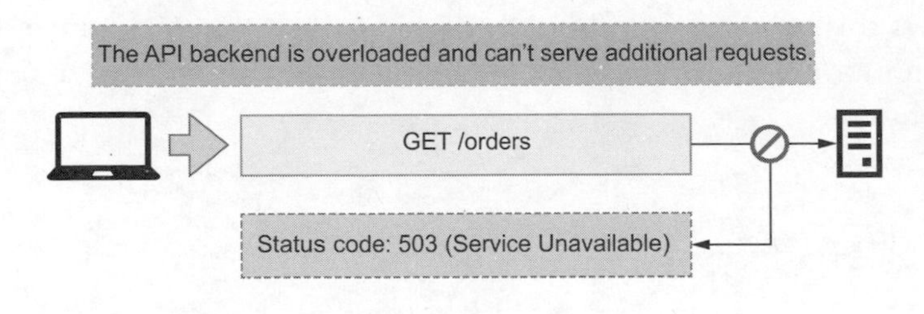

Figure 4.16 When the API server is overloaded and can't serve additional requests, we respond to the client with a 503 (Service Unavailable) status code.

- When the server takes too long to respond to the request, we respond with a 504 (Gateway Timeout) status code, as shown in figure 4.17.

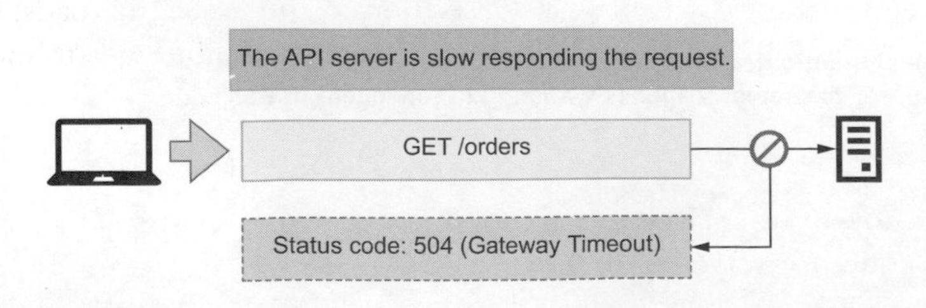

Figure 4.17 When the API server is very slow responding to the request, a proxy server responds to the client with a 504 (Gateway Timeout) status code.

This completes our overview of the HTTP status codes most commonly used in the design of web APIs. The correct use of status codes goes a long way toward delivering a good developer experience for your API clients, but there's one more thing we need to design well: API payloads. In the next section, we turn our attention to this important topic.

4.7 Designing API payloads

This section explains best practices for designing user-friendly HTTP request and response payloads. *Payloads* represent the data exchanged between a client and a server through an HTTP request. We send payloads to the server when we want to create or update a resource, and the server sends us payloads when we request data. The usability of an API is very much dependent on good payload design. Poorly designed payloads make APIs difficult to use and result in bad user experiences. It's therefore important to spend some effort designing high-quality payloads, and in this section you'll learn some patterns and best practices to help you in that task.[7]

4.7.1 What are HTTP payloads, and when do we use them?

An HTTP request is a message an application client sends to a web server, and an HTTP response is the server's reply to the request. An HTTP *request* includes a URL, an HTTP method, a set of headers, and, optionally, a body or payload. HTTP headers include metadata about the request's contents, such as the encoding format. Similarly, an HTTP *response* includes a status code, a set of headers, and, optionally, a payload. We can represent payloads with different data serialization methods, such as XML and JSON. In REST APIs, data is typically represented as a JSON document.

DEFINITION An *HTTP message body* or *payload* is a message that contains the data exchanged in an HTTP request. Both HTTP requests and responses can contain a message body. The message body is encoded in one of the media types supported by HTTP, such as XML or JSON. The Content-Type header of the HTTP request tells us the encoding type of the message. In REST APIs, the message body is typically encoded as JSON.

HTTP requests include a payload when we need to send data to the server. For example, a POST request typically sends data to create a resource. The HTTP specification allows us to include payloads in all HTTP methods, but it discourages their use in GET (http://mng.bz/O69K) and DELETE (http://mng.bz/YKeo) requests.

The wording of the HTTP specification is intentionally vague on whether DELETE and GET requests can include a payload. It doesn't forbid the use of payloads, but it states that they don't have any defined semantics. This allows some APIs to include

---

[7] In addition to learning best practices, you'll find it useful to read about anti-patterns. My article, "How Bad Models Ruin an API (or Why Design-First is the Way to Go)," contains an overview of common anti-patterns you should avoid (https://www.microapis.io/blog/how-bad-models-ruin-an-api).

payloads in GET requests. A famous example is Elasticsearch, which allows clients to send query documents in the body of a GET request (http://mng.bz/G14M).

What about HTTP responses? Responses may contain a payload depending on the status code. According to the HTTP specification, responses with a 1xx status code, as well as the 204 (No Content) and 304 (Not Modified) status codes, must not include a payload. All other responses do. In the context of REST APIs, the most important payloads are those in the 4xx and 5xx error responses, as well as 2xx success responses with the exception of the 204 status code. In the next section, you'll learn to design high-quality payloads for all those responses.

4.7.2 HTTP payload design patterns

Now that we know when we use payloads, let's learn best practices for designing them. We'll focus on the design of response payloads, since they present more variety. As we learned in section 4.6.1, we distinguish between error and success responses. Error responses' payloads should include an `"error"` keyword detailing why the client is getting an error. For example, a 404 response, which is generated when the requested resource cannot be found in the server, can include the following error message:

```
{
    "error": "Resource not found"
}
```

`"error"` is a commonly used keyword for error messages, but you can also use other keywords such as `"detail"` and `"message"`. Most web development frameworks handle HTTP errors and have default templates for error responses. For example, FastAPI uses `"detail"`, so we'll use that keyword in the orders API specification.

Among success responses, we distinguish three scenarios: when we create a resource, when we update a resource, and when we get the details of a resource. Let's see how we design responses for each of these scenarios.

RESPONSE PAYLOADS FOR POST REQUESTS

We use POST requests to create resources. In CoffeeMesh's orders API, we place orders through the POST `/orders` endpoint. To place an order, we send the list of items we want to buy to the server, which takes responsibility for assigning a unique ID to the order, and therefore the order's ID must be returned in the response payload. The server also sets the time when the order was taken and its initial status. We call the properties set by the server *server-side* or *read-only properties*, and we must include them in the response payload. As you can see in figure 4.18, it's good practice to return a full representation of the resource in the response to a POST request. This payload serves to validate that the resource was correctly created.

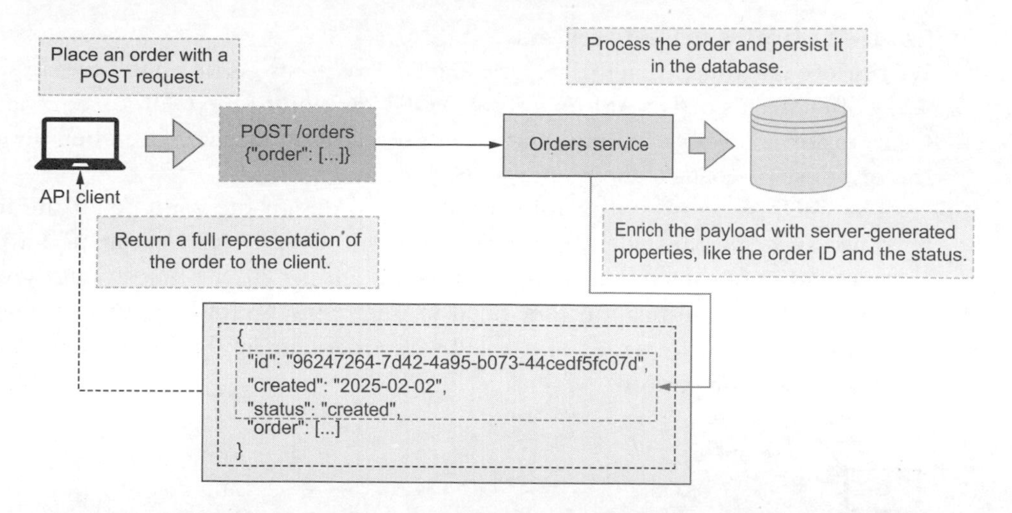

Figure 4.18 When an API client sends a POST request to create a new resource, the server responds with a full representation of the resource just created with its ID and any other properties set by the server.

Response payloads for PUT and PATCH requests

To update a resource, we use a PUT or a PATCH request. As we saw in section 4.5, we make PUT/PATCH requests on a singleton resource URI, such as the PUT `/orders/{order_id}` endpoint of CoffeeMesh's orders API. As you can see in figure 4.19, in this case it's also good practice to return a full representation of the resource, which the client can use to validate that the update was correctly processed.

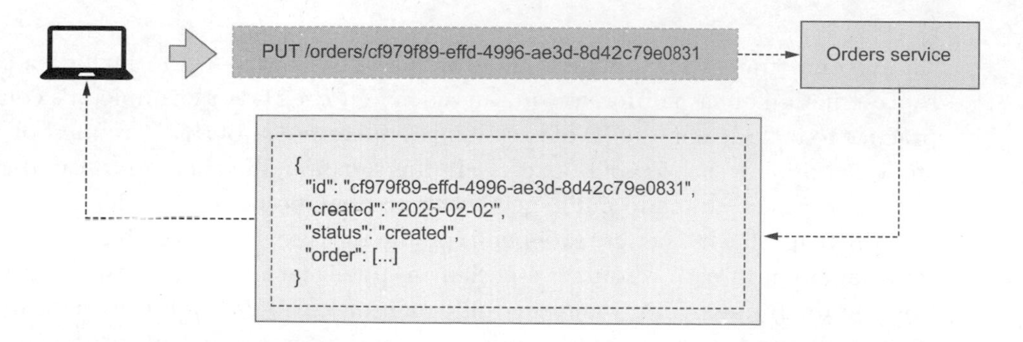

Figure 4.19 When an API client sends a PUT request to update a resource, the server responds with a full representation of the resource.

RESPONSE PAYLOADS FOR GET REQUESTS

We retrieve resources from the server using GET requests. As we established in section 4.5, CoffeeMesh's orders API exposes two GET endpoints: the GET `/orders` and the GET `/orders/{orders_id}` endpoints. Let's see what options we have when designing the response payloads of these endpoints.

The GET `/orders` returns a list of orders. To design the contents of the list, we have two strategies: include a full representation of each order or include a partial representation of each order. As you can see in figure 4.20, the first strategy gives the API client all the information they need in one request. However, this strategy may compromise the performance of the API when the items in the list are big, resulting in a large response payload.

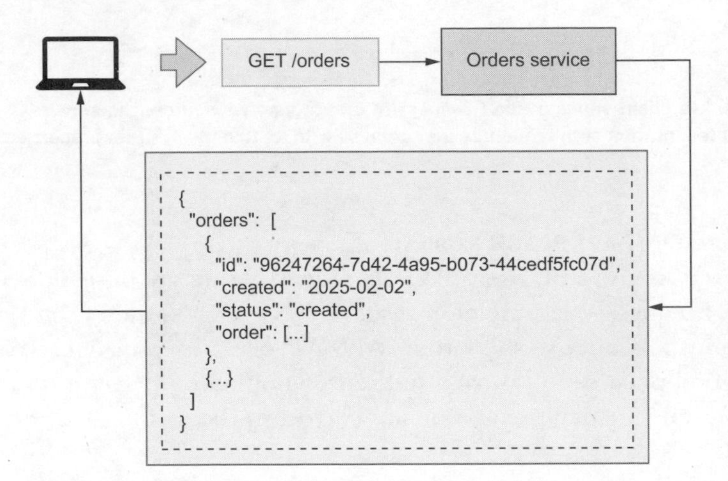

Figure 4.20 When an API client sends a request to the GET `/orders` endpoint, the server responds with a list of orders, where each order object contains full details about the order.

The second strategy for the GET `/orders` endpoint's payload is to include a partial representation of each order, as you can see in figure 4.21. For example, it's common practice to include only the ID of each item in the response of a GET request on a collection endpoint, such as GET `/orders`. In this situation, the client must call the GET `/orders/{order_id}` endpoint to get a full representation of each order.

Which approach is better? It depends on the use case. It's preferable to send a full representation of each resource, especially in public-facing APIs. However, if you're working on an internal API and the full details of each item aren't needed, you can shorten the payload by including only the properties the client needs. Smaller payloads are faster to process, which results in a better user experience. Finally, singleton endpoints, such as the GET `/orders/{order_id}`, must always return a full representation of the resource.

Now that we know how to design API payloads, let's turn our attention to URL query parameters.

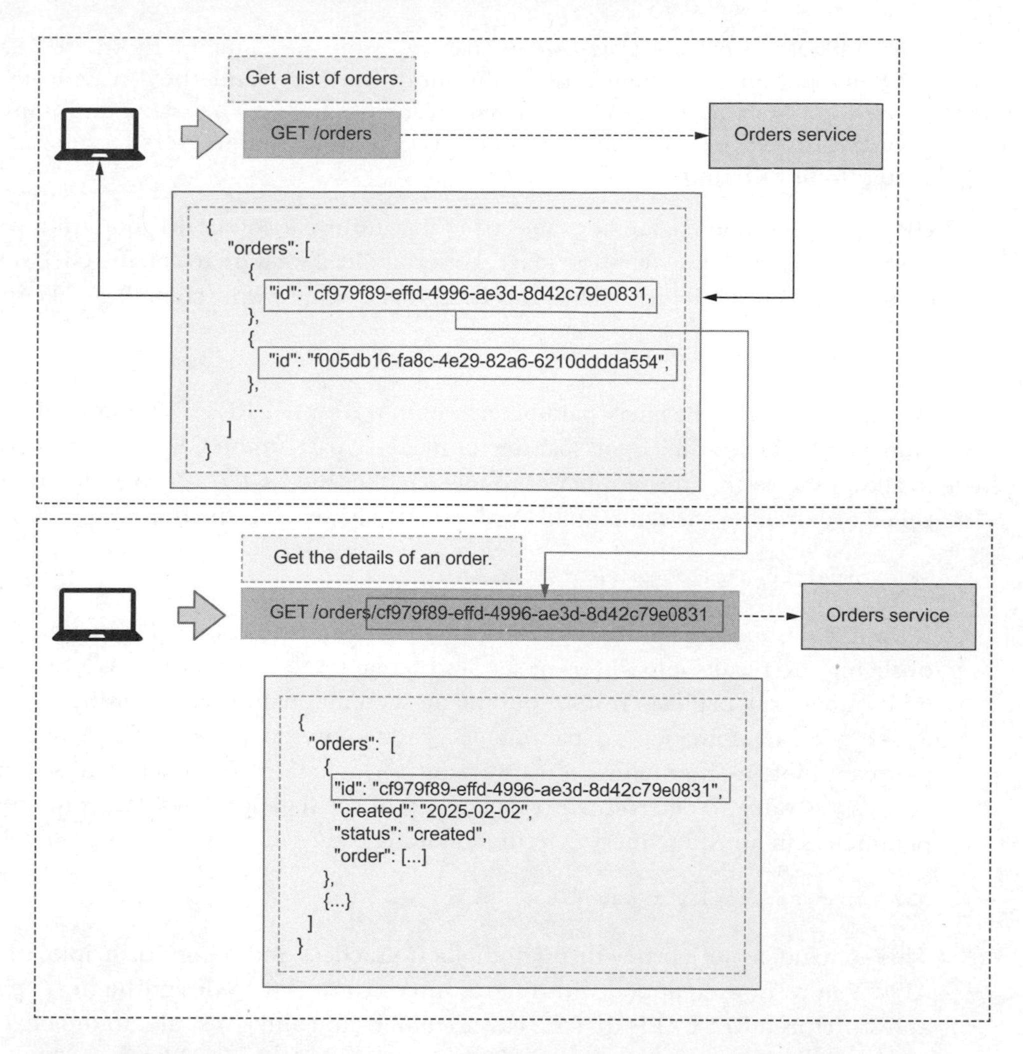

Figure 4.21 When the API client makes a GET request on the `/orders` URL path, the server responds with a list of order IDs. The client uses those IDs to request the details of each order on the GET `/orders/{order_id}` endpoint.

4.8 Designing URL query parameters

Now let's talk about URL query parameters and how, why, and when you should use them. Some endpoints, such as the GET `/orders` endpoint of the orders API, return a list of resources. When an endpoint returns a list of resources, it's best practice to allow users to filter and paginate the results. For example, when using the GET `/orders` endpoint, we may want to limit the results to only the five most recent orders or to list only cancelled orders. URL query parameters allow us to accomplish those goals and should always be optional, and, when appropriate, the server may assign default values for them.

DEFINITION *URL query parameters* are key-value parameters in the URL. Query parameters come after a question mark (?), and they're typically used to filter the results of an endpoint, such as the GET `/orders` endpoint of the orders API. We can combine multiple query parameters by separating them with ampersands (&).

URL query parameters are key-value pairs that form part of a URL but are separated from the URL path by a question mark. For example, if we want to call the GET `/orders` endpoint and filter the results by cancelled orders, we may write something like this:

```
GET /orders?cancelled=true
```

We can chain multiple query parameters within the same URL by separating them with ampersands. Let's add a query parameter named `limit` to the GET `/orders` endpoint to allow us to restrict the number of results. To filter the GET `/orders` endpoint by cancelled orders and restrict the number of results to 5, we make the following API request:

```
GET /orders?cancelled=true&Limit=5
```

It's also common practice to allow API clients to paginate results. Pagination consists of slicing the results into different sets and serving one set at a time. We can use several strategies to paginate results, but the most common approach is using a `page` and a `per_page` combination of parameters. `page` represents a set of the data, while `per_page` tells us how many items we want to include in each set. The server uses `per_page`'s value to determine how many sets of the data we'll get. We combine both parameters in an API request as in the following example:

```
GET /orders?page=1&per_page=10
```

This concludes our journey through the best practices and design principles of REST APIs. You're now equipped with the resources you need to design highly expressive and structured REST APIs that are easy to understand and consume. In the next chapter, you'll learn to document your API designs using the OpenAPI standard.

Summary

- Representational state transfer (REST) defines the design principles of well-architected REST APIs:
  - *Client-server architecture*—Client and server code must be decoupled.
  - *Statelessness*—The server must not keep state between requests.
  - *Cacheability*—Cacheable requests must be cached.
  - *Layered system*—The architectural complexity of the backend must not be exposed to end users.
  - *Code on demand (optional)*—Client applications may be able to download executable code from the server.
  - *Uniform interface*—The API must provide a uniform and consistent interface.

- Hypermedia as the engine of application state (HATEOAS) is a paradigm that states that REST APIs must include referential links in their responses. HATEOAS makes APIs navigational and easier to use.
- Good REST API design leverages features of the HTTP protocol, such as HTTP methods and status codes, to create well-structured and highly expressive APIs that are easy to consume.
- The most important HTTP methods for REST APIs are
  - GET for retrieving resources from the server
  - POST for creating new resources
  - PUT and PATCH for updating resources
  - DELETE for deleting resources
- We exchange data with an API server using payloads. A payload goes in the body of an HTTP request or response. Clients send request payloads using the POST, PUT, and PATCH HTTP methods. Server responses always include a payload, except when the status code is 204, 304, or one from the 1xx group.
- URL query parameters are key-value pairs in the URL, and we use them for filtering, paginating, and sorting the results of a GET endpoint.

Documenting REST APIs with OpenAPI

5

This chapter covers

- Using JSON Schema to create validation models for JSON documents
- Describing REST APIs with the OpenAPI documentation standard
- Modeling the payloads for API requests and responses
- Creating reusable schemas in OpenAPI specifications

In this chapter, you'll learn to document APIs using OpenAPI: the most popular standard for describing RESTful APIs, with a rich ecosystem of tools for testing, validating, and visualizing APIs. Most programming languages have libraries that support OpenAPI specifications, and in chapter 6 you'll learn to use OpenAPI-compatible libraries from the Python ecosystem.

OpenAPI uses JSON Schema to describe an API's structure and models, so we start by providing an overview of how JSON Schema works. JSON Schema is a specification for defining the structure of a JSON document, including the types and formats of the values within the document.

After learning about JSON Schema, we study how an OpenAPI document is structured, what its properties are, and how we use it to provide informative API specifications for our API consumers. API endpoints constitute the core of the specification, so we pay particular attention to them. We break down the process of defining the endpoints and schemas for the payloads of the API's requests and responses, step by step. For the examples in this chapter, we work with the API of CoffeeMesh's orders service. As we mentioned in chapter 1, CoffeeMesh is a fictional on-demand coffee-delivery platform, and the orders service is the component that allows customers to place and manage their orders. The full specification for the orders API is available under ch05/oas.yaml in the GitHub repository for this book.

5.1 Using JSON Schema to model data

This section introduces the specification standard for JSON Schema and explains how we leverage it to produce API specifications. OpenAPI uses an extended subset of the JSON Schema specification for defining the structure of JSON documents and the types and formats of its properties. It's useful for documenting interfaces that use JSON to represent data and to validate that the data being exchanged is correct. The JSON Schema specification is under active development, with the latest version being 2020-12.[1]

DEFINITION *JSON Schema* is a specification standard for defining the structure of a JSON document and the types and formats of its properties. OpenAPI uses JSON Schema to describe the properties of an API.

A JSON Schema specification usually defines an object with certain attributes or properties. A JSON Schema `object` is represented by an associative array of key-value pairs. A JSON Schema specification usually looks like this:

```
{
    "status": {                  <- Each property in a JSON Schema specification
                                    comes as a key whose values are the
                                    descriptors of the property.
        "type": "string"         <- The minimum descriptor necessary for a
                                    property is the type. In this case, we
                                    specify that the status property is a string.
    }
}
```

In this example, we define the schema of an object with one attribute named `status`, whose type is `string`.

JSON Schema allows us to be very explicit with respect to the data types and formats that both the server and the client should expect from a payload. This is fundamental

[1] A. Wright, H. Andrews, B. Hutton, "JSON Schema: A Media Type for Describing JSON Documents" (December 8, 2020); https://datatracker.ietf.org/doc/html/draft-bhutton-json-schema-00. You can follow the development of JSON Schema and contribute to its improvement by participating in its repository in GitHub: https://github.com/json-schema-org/json-schema-spec. Also see the website for the project: https://json-schema.org/.

for the integration between the API provider and the API consumer, since it lets us know how to parse the payloads and how to cast them into the right data types in our runtime.

JSON Schema supports the following basic data types:

- `string` for character values
- `number` for integer and decimal values
- `object` for associative arrays (i.e., dictionaries in Python)
- `array` for collections of other data types (i.e., lists in Python)
- `boolean` for `true` or `false` values
- `null` for uninitialized data

To define an object using JSON Schema, we declare its type as `object`, and we list its properties and their types. The following shows how we define an object named `order`, which is one of the core models of the orders API.

Listing 5.1 Defining the schema of an object with JSON Schema

```
{
    "order": {
        "type": "object",          <- We can declare the schema as an object.
        "properties": {            <- We describe the object's properties under the properties keyword.
            "product": {
                "type": "string"
            },
            "size": {
                "type": "string"
            },
            "quantity": {
                "type": "integer"
            }
        }
    }
}
```

Since `order` is an object, the `order` attribute also has properties, defined under the `properties` attribute. Each property has its own type. A JSON document that complies with the specification in listing 5.1 is the following:

```
{
    "order": {
        "product": "coffee",
        "size": "big",
        "quantity": 1
    }
}
```

As you can see, each of the properties described in the specification is used in this document, and each of them has the expected type.

A property can also represent an array of items. In the following code, the `order` object represents an array of objects. As you can see, we use the `items` keyword to define the elements within the array.

Listing 5.2 Defining an array of objects with JSON Schema

```
{
    "order": {
        "type": "array",
        "items": {                  <-- We define the elements
            "type": "object",           within the array using
            "properties": {             the items keyword.
                "product": {
                    "type": "string"
                },
                "size": {
                    "type": "string"
                },
                "quantity": {
                    "type": "integer"
                }
            }
        }
    }
}
```

In this case, the `order` property is an array. Array types require an additional property in their schema, which is the `items` property that defines the type of each of the elements contained in the array. In this case, each of the elements in the array is an object that represents an item in the order.

An object can have any number of nested objects. However, when too many objects are nested, indentation grows large and makes the specification difficult to read. To avoid this problem, JSON Schema allows us to define each object separately and to use JSON pointers to reference them. A *JSON pointer* is a special syntax that allows us to point to another object definition within the same specification.

As you can see in the following code, we can extract the definition of each item within the `order` array as a model called `OrderItemSchema` and use a JSON pointer to reference `OrderItemSchema` using the special `$ref` keyword.

Listing 5.3 Using JSON pointers to reference other schemas

```
{
    "OrderItemSchema": {
        "type": "object",
        "properties": {
            "product": {
                "type": "string"
            },
            "size": {
                "type": "string"
            },
```

```
            "quantity": {
                "type": "integer"
            }
        }
    },
    "Order": {
        "status": {
            "type": "string"
        },
        "order": {
            "type": "array",
            "items": {
                "$ref": '#/OrderItemSchema'     <-- We can specify the type of the array's items using a JSON pointer.
            }
        }
    }
}
```

JSON pointers use the special keyword `$ref` and JSONPath syntax to point to another definition within the schema. In JSONPath syntax, the root of the document is represented by the hashtag symbol (#), and the relationship of nested properties is represented by forward slashes (/). For example, if we wanted to create a pointer to the `size` property of the `OrderItemSchema` model, we would use the following syntax: `'#/OrderItemSchema/size'`.

DEFINITION A *JSON pointer* is a special syntax in JSON Schema that allows us to point to another definition within the same specification. We use the special keyword `$ref` to declare a JSON pointer. To build the path to another schema, we use JSONPath syntax. For example, to point to a schema called `OrderItemSchema`, defined at the top level of the document, we use the following syntax: `{"$ref": "#/OrderItemSchema"}`.

We can refactor our specification using JSON pointers by extracting common schema objects into reusable models, and we can reference them using JSON pointers. This helps us avoid duplication and keep the specification clean and succinct.

In addition to being able to specify the type of a property, JSON Schema also allows us to specify the format of the property. We can develop our own custom formats or use JSON Schema's built-in formats. For example, for a property representing a date, we can use the `date` format—a built-in format supported by JSON Schema that represents an ISO date (e.g., 2025-05-21). Here's an example:

```
{
    "created": {
        "type": "string",
        "format": "date"
    }
}
```

In this section, we've worked with examples in JSON format. However, JSON Schema documents don't need to be written in JSON. In fact, it's more common to write them in YAML format, as it's more readable and easier to understand. OpenAPI specifications are also commonly served in YAML format, and for the remainder of this chapter, we'll use YAML to develop the specification of the orders API.

5.2 Anatomy of an OpenAPI specification

In this section, we introduce the OpenAPI standard, and we learn to structure an API specification. OpenAPI's latest version is 3.1; however, this version still has little support in the current ecosystem, so we'll document the API using OpenAPI 3.0. There's not much difference between the two versions, and nearly everything you learn about OpenAPI 3.0 applies to 3.1.[2]

OpenAPI is a standard specification format for documenting RESTful APIs (figure 5.1). OpenAPI allows us to describe in detail every element of an API, including its endpoints, the format of its request and response payloads, its security schemes, and so on. OpenAPI was created in 2010 under the name of Swagger as an open source specification format for describing RESTful web APIs. Over time, this framework grew in popularity, and in 2015 the Linux Foundation and a consortium of major companies sponsored the creation of the OpenAPI initiative, a project aimed at improving the protocols and standards for building RESTful APIs. Today, OpenAPI is by far the most popular specification format used to document RESTful APIs,[3] and it benefits from a rich ecosystem of tools for API visualization, testing, and validation.

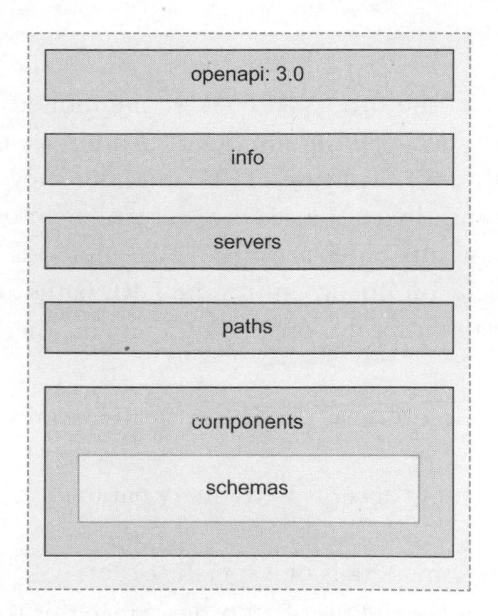

Figure 5.1 An OpenAPI specification contains five sections. For example, the `paths` section describes the API endpoints, while the `components` section contains reusable schemas referenced across the document.

[2] For a detailed analysis of the differences between OpenAPI 3.0 and 3.1, check out OpenAPI's migration from 3.0 to 3.1 guide: https://www.openapis.org/blog/2021/02/16/migrating-from-openapi-3-0-to-3-1-0.

[3] According to the 2022 "State of the API" report by Postman (https://www.postman.com/state-of-api/api-technologies/#api-technologies).

An OpenAPI specification contains everything that the consumer of the API needs to know to be able to interact with the API. As you can see in figure 5.1, an OpenAPI is structured around five sections:

- `openapi`—Indicates the version of OpenAPI that we used to produce the specification.
- `info`—Contains general information, such as the title and version of the API.
- `servers`—Contains a list of URLs where the API is available. You can list more than one URL for different environments, such as the production and staging environments.
- `paths`—Describes the endpoints exposed by the API, including the expected payloads, the allowed parameters, and the format of the responses. This is the most important part of the specification, as it represents the API interface, and it's the section that consumers will be looking for to learn how to integrate with the API.
- `components`—Defines reusable elements that are referenced across the specification, such as schemas, parameters, security schemes, request bodies, and responses.[4] A *schema* is a definition of the expected attributes and types in your request and response objects. OpenAPI schemas are defined using JSON Schema syntax.

Now that we know how to structure an OpenAPI specification, let's move on to documenting the endpoints of the orders API.

5.3 Documenting the API endpoints

In this section, we declare the endpoints of the orders API. As we mentioned in section 5.2, the `paths` section of an OpenAPI specification describes the interface of your API. It lists the URL paths exposed by the API, with the HTTP methods they implement, the types of requests they expect, and the responses they return, including the status codes. Each path is an object whose attributes are the HTTP methods it supports. In this section, we'll focus specifically on documenting the URL paths and the HTTP methods. In chapter 4, we established that the orders API contains the following endpoints:

- POST `/orders`—Places an order. It requires a payload with the details of the order.
- GET `/orders`—Returns a list of orders. It accepts URL query parameters, which allow us to filter the results.
- GET `/orders/{order_id}`—Returns the details of a specific order.
- PUT `/orders/{order_id}`—Updates the details of an order. Since this is a PUT endpoint, it requires a full representation of the order.
- DELETE `/orders/{order_id}`—Deletes an order.

---

[4] See https://swagger.io/docs/specification/components/ for a full list of reusable elements that can be defined in the `components` section of the API specification.

- POST /orders/{order_id}/pay—Pays for an order.
- POST /orders/{order_id}/cancel—Cancels the order.

The following shows the high-level definitions of the orders API endpoints. We declare the URLs and the HTTP implemented by each URL, and we add an operation ID to each endpoint so that we can reference them in other sections of the document.

Listing 5.4 High-level definition of the orders API endpoints

```
paths:
  /orders:              <-- We declare a URL path.
    get:                <-- An HTTP method supported by the /orders URL path
      operationId: getOrders
    post:  # creates a new order
      operationId: createOrder

  /orders/{order_id}:
    get:
      operationId: getOrder
    put:
      operationId: updateOrder
    delete:
      operationId: deleteOrder

  /orders/{order_id}/pay:
    post:
      operationId: payOrder

  /orders/{order_id}/cancel:
    post:
      operationId: cancelOrder
```

Now that we have the endpoints, we need to fill in the details. For the GET /orders endpoint, we need to describe the parameters that the endpoint accepts, and for the POST and PUT endpoints, we need to describe the request payloads. We also need to describe the responses for each endpoint. In the following sections, we'll learn to build specifications for different elements of the API, starting with the URL qucry parameters.

5.4 Documenting URL query parameters

As we learned in chapter 4, URL query parameters allow us to filter and sort the results of a GET endpoint. In this section, we learn to define URL query parameters using OpenAPI. The GET /orders endpoint allows us to filter orders using the following parameters:

- cancelled—Whether the order was cancelled. This value will be a Boolean.
- limit—Specifies the maximum number of orders that should be returned to the user. The value for this parameter will be a number.

Both `cancelled` and `limit` can be combined within the same request to filter the results:

```
GET /orders?cancelled=true&limit=5
```

This request asks the server for a list of five orders that have been cancelled. Listing 5.5 shows the specification for the GET `/orders` endpoint's query parameters. The definition of a parameter requires a `name`, which is the value we use to refer to it in the actual URL. We also specify what `type` of parameter it is. OpenAPI 3.1 distinguishes four types of parameters: path parameters, query parameters, header parameters, and cookie parameters. Header parameters are parameters that go in an HTTP header field, while cookie parameters go into a cookie payload. Path parameters are part of the URL path and are typically used to identify a resource. For example, in `/orders/{order_id}`, `order_id` is a path parameter that identifies a specific order. Query parameters are optional parameters that allow us to filter and sort the results of an endpoint. We define the parameter's type using the `schema` keyword (Boolean in the case of `cancelled`, and a number in the case of `limit`), and, when relevant, we specify the `format` of the parameter as well.[5]

Listing 5.5 Specification for the GET `/orders` endpoint's query parameters

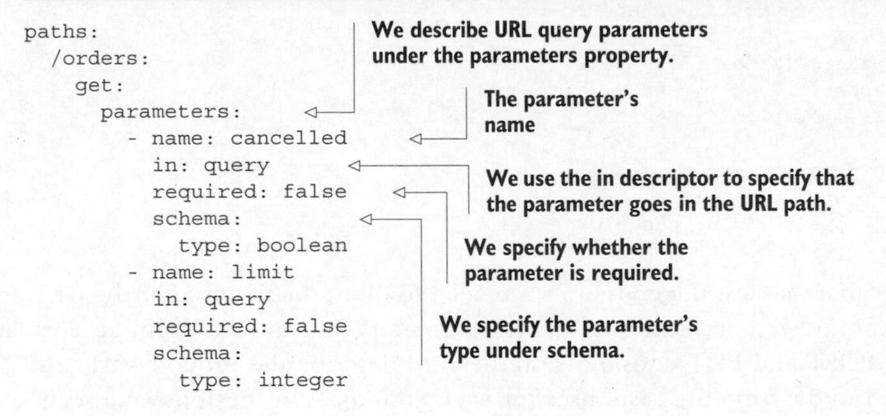

Now that we know how to describe URL query parameters, in the next section we'll tackle something more complex: documenting request payloads.

5.5 Documenting request payloads

In chapter 4, we learned that a request represents the data sent by a client to the server through a POST or a PUT request. In this section, we learn to document the request payloads of the orders API endpoints. Let's start with the POST `/orders` method. In section 5.1, we established that the payload for the POST `/orders` endpoint looks like this:

---

[5] To learn more about the date types and formats available in OpenAPI 3.1 see http://spec.openapis.org/oas/v3.1.0#data-types.

```
{
    "order": [
        {
            "product": "cappuccino",
            "size": "big",
            "quantity": 1
        }
    ]
}
```

This payload contains an attribute `order`, which represents an array of items. Each item is defined by the following three attributes and constraints:

- `product`—The type of product the user is ordering.
- `size`—The size of the product. It can be one of the three following choices: `small`, `medium`, and `big`.
- `quantity`—The amount of the product. It can be any integer number equal to or greater than 1.

Listing 5.6 shows how we define the schema for this payload. We define request payloads under the `content` property of the method's `requestBody` property. We can specify payloads in different formats. In this case, we allow data only in JSON format, which has a media type definition of `application/json`. The schema for our payload is an object with one property: `order`, whose type is `array`. The items in the array are objects with three properties: the `product` property, with type `string`; the `size` property, with type `string`; and the `quantity` property, with type `integer`. In addition, we define an enumeration for the `size` property, which constrains the accepted values to `small`, `medium`, and `big`. Finally, we also provide a default value of `1` for the `quantity` property, since it's the only nonrequired field in the payload. Whenever a user sends a request containing an item without the `quantity` property, we assume that they want to order only one unit of that item.

Listing 5.6 Specification for the POST `/orders` endpoint

```
paths:
  /orders:
    post:
      operationId: createOrder
      requestBody:                  ◁ We describe request payloads under requestBody.
        required: true              ◁ We specify whether the payload is required.
        content:                    ◁ We specify the payload's content type.
          application/json:
            schema:                 ◁ We define the payload's schema.
              type: object
              properties:
                order:
                  type: array
                  items:
                    type: object
                    properties:
```

```
              product:
                type: string
              size:
                type: string
                enum:              <- We can constrain the property's values using an enumeration.
                  - small
                  - medium
                  - big
              quantity:
                type: integer
                required: false
                default: 1         <- We specify a default value.
            required:
              - product
              - size
```

Embedding payload schemas within the endpoints' definitions, as in listing 5.6, can make our specification more difficult to read and understand. In the next section, we learn to refactor payload schemas for reusability and for readability.

5.6 Refactoring schema definitions to avoid repetition

In this section, we learn strategies for refactoring schemas to keep the API specification clean and readable. The definition of the POST `/orders` endpoint in listing 5.6 is long and contains several layers of indentation. As a result, it's difficult to read, and that means in the future it'll become difficult to extend and to maintain. We can do better by moving the payload's schema to a different section of the API specification: the `components` section. As we explained in section 5.2, the `components` section is used to declare schemas that are referenced across the specification. Every schema is an object where the key is the name of the schema, and the values are the properties that describe it.

Listing 5.7 Specification for the POST `/orders` endpoint using a JSON pointer

```
paths:
  /orders:
    post:
      operationId: createOrder
      requestBody:
        required: true
        content:
          application/json:
            schema:
              $ref: '#/components/schemas/CreateOrderSchema'   <- We use a JSON pointer to reference a schema defined somewhere else in the document.

components:                  <- Schema definitions go under components.
  schemas:
    CreateOrderSchema:       <- Every schema is an object, where the key is the name and the values are the properties that describe it.
      type: object
      properties:
        order:
          type: array
          items:
```

```
            type: object
            properties:
              product:
                type: string
              size:
                type: string
                enum:
                  - small
                  - medium
                  - big
              quantity:
                type: integer
                required: false
                default: 1
            required:
              - product
              - size
```

Moving the schema for the POST `/orders` request payload under the `components` section of the API makes the document more readable. It allows us to keep the `paths` section of the document clean and focused on the higher-level details of the endpoint. We simply need to refer to the `CreateOrderSchema` schema using a JSON pointer:

```
#/components/schemas/CreateOrderSchema
```

The specification is looking good, but it can get better. `CreateOrderSchema` is a tad long, and it contains several layers of nested definitions. If `CreateOrderSchema` grows in complexity, over time it'll become difficult to read and maintain. We can make it more readable by refactoring the definition of the `order` item in the array in the following code. This strategy allows us to reuse the schema for the order's item in other parts of the API.

Listing 5.8 Schema definitions for `OrderItemSchema` and `Order`

```
components:
  schemas:
      OrderItemSchema:          <- We introduce the OrderItemSchema.
        type: object
        properties:
          product:
            type: string
          size:
            type: string
            enum:
              - small
              - medium
              - big
          quantity:
            type: integer
            default: 1
      CreateOrderSchema:
        type: object
```

```
      properties:
        order:
          type: array
          items:
            $ref: '#/OrderItemSchema'
```

We use a JSON pointer to point to OrderItemSchema.

Our schemas are looking good! The `CreateOrderSchema` schema can be used to create an order or to update it, so we can reuse it in the PUT `/orders/{order_id}` endpoint, as you can see in listing 5.9. As we learned in chapter 4, the `/orders/{order_id}` URL path represents a singleton resource, and therefore the URL contains a path parameter, which is the order's ID. In OpenAPI, path parameters are represented between curly braces. We specify that the `order_id` parameter is a string with a UUID format (a long, random string often used as an ID).[6] We define the URL path parameter directly under the URL path to make sure it applies to all HTTP methods.

Listing 5.9 Specification for the PUT `/orders/{order_id}` endpoint

```
paths:
  /orders:
    get:
      ...

  /orders/{order_id}:
    parameters:
      - in: path
        name: order_id
        required: true
        schema:
          type: string
          format: uuid
    put:
      operationId: updateOrder
      requestBody:
        required: true
        content:
          application/json:
            schema:
          $ref: '#/components/schemas/CreateOrderSchema'
```

- We declare the order's resource URL.
- We define the URL path parameter.
- The order_id parameter is part of the URL path.
- The name of the parameter
- The order_id parameter is required.
- We specify the parameter's format (UUID).
- We define the HTTP method PUT for the current URL path.
- We document the request body of the PUT endpoint.

Now that we understand how to define the schemas for our request payloads, let's turn our attention to the responses.

5.7 Documenting API responses

In this section, we learn to document API responses. We start by defining the payload for the GET `/orders/{order_id}` endpoint. The response of the GET `/orders/{order_id}` endpoint looks like this:

---

[6] P. Leach, M. Mealling, and R. Salz, "A Universally Unique Identifier (UUID) URN Namespace," RFC 4112 (https://datatracker.ietf.org/doc/html/rfc4122).

```
{
    "id": "924721eb-a1a1-4f13-b384-37e89c0e0875",
    "status": "progress",
    "created": "2022-05-01",
    "order": [
        {
            "product": "cappuccino",
            "size": "small",
            "quantity": 1
        },
        {
            "product": "croissant",
            "size": "medium",
            "quantity": 2
        }
    ]
}
```


This payload shows the products ordered by the user, when the order was placed, and the status of the order. This payload is similar to the request payload we defined in section 5.6 for the POST and PUT endpoints, so we can reuse our previous schemas.

Listing 5.10 Definition of the `GetOrderSchema` schema

```
components:
  schemas:
    OrderItemSchema:
      ...

  GetOrderSchema:                  <-- We define the GetOrderSchema schema.
    type: object
    properties:
      status:
        type: string
        enum:                      <-- We constrain the values of the status property with an enumeration.
          - created
          - paid
          - progress
          - cancelled
          - dispatched
          - delivered
      created:
        type: string
        format: date-time          <-- A string with date-time format
      order:
        type: array
        items:
          $ref: '#/components/schemas/OrderItemSchema'   <-- We reference the OrderItemSchema schema using a JSON pointer.
```

In listing 5.10, we use a JSON pointer to point to `GetOrderSchema`. An alternative way to reuse the existing schemas is to use inheritance. In OpenAPI, we can inherit and extend a schema using a strategy called *model composition*, which allows us to combine the properties of different schemas in a single object definition. The special keyword `allOf` is used in these cases to indicate that the object requires all the properties in the listed schemas.

DEFINITION *Model composition* is a strategy in JSON Schema that allows us to combine the properties of different schemas into a single object. It is useful when a schema contains properties that have already been defined elsewhere, and therefore allows us to avoid repetition.

The following code shows an alternative definition of `GetOrderSchema` using the `allOf` keyword. In this case, `GetOrderSchema` is the composition of two other schemas: `CreateOrderSchema` and an anonymous schema with two keys—`status` and `created`.

Listing 5.11 Alternative implementation of `GetOrderSchema` using the `allOf` keyword

```
components:
  schemas:
    OrderItemSchema:
      ...

    GetOrderSchema:
      allOf:
        - $ref: '#/components/schemas/CreateOrderSchema'
        - type: object
          properties:
            status:
              type: string
              enum:
                - created
                - paid
                - progress
                - cancelled
                - dispatched
                - delivered
            created:
              type: string
              format: date-time
```

- We use the allOf keyword to inherit properties from other schemas. (annotates `allOf:`)
- We use a JSON pointer to reference another schema. (annotates `$ref`)
- We define a new object to include properties that are specific to GetOrderSchema. (annotates `- type: object`)

Model composition results in a cleaner and more succinct specification, but it only works if the schemas are strictly compatible. If we decide to extend `CreateOrderSchema` with new properties, then this schema may no longer be transferable to the `GetOrder-Schema` model. In that sense, it's sometimes better to look for common elements among different schemas and refactor their definitions into standalone schemas.

Now that we have the schema for the GET `/orders/{order_id}` endpoint's response payload, we can complete the endpoint's specification. We define the endpoint's responses as objects in which the key is the response's status code, such as 200. We also describe the response's content type and its schema, `GetOrderSchema`.

Listing 5.12 Specification for the GET `/orders/{order_id}` endpoint

```
paths:
  /orders:
```

```
    get:
      ...

  /orders/{order_id}:
    parameters:
      - in: path
        name: order_id
        required: true
        schema:
          type: string
          format: uuid

    put:
      ...

    get:
      summary: Returns the details of a specific order
      operationId: getOrder
      responses:
        '200':
          description: OK
          content:
            application/json:
              schema:
                $ref: '#/components/schemas/GetOrderSchema'
```

We define the GET endpoint of the /orders/{order_id} URL path.

We provide a summary description of this endpoint.

We define this endpoint's responses.

Each response is an object where the key is the status code.

A brief description of the response

We describe the content types of the response.

We use a JSON pointer to reference GetOrderSchema.

As you can see, we define response schemas within the `responses` section of the endpoint. In this case, we only provide the specification for the 200 (OK) successful response, but we can also document other status codes, such as error responses. The next section explains how we create generic responses we can reuse across our endpoints.

5.8 Creating generic responses

In this section, we learn to add error responses to our API endpoints. As we mentioned in chapter 4, error responses are more generic, so we can use the `components` section of the API specification to provide generic definitions of those responses, and then reuse them in our endpoints.

We define generic responses within the `responses` header of the API's `components` section. The following shows a generic definition for a 404 response named `NotFound`. As with any other response, we also document the content's payload, which in this case is defined by the `Error` schema.

Listing 5.13 Generic `404` status code response definition

```
components:
  responses:
    NotFound:
      description: The specified resource was not found.
```

We name the response.

Generic responses go under responses in the components section.

We describe the response.

```
      content:                                         # We define the response's content.
        application/json:
          schema:
            $ref: '#/components/schemas/Error'         # We reference the Error schema.

  schemas:
    OrderItemSchema:
      ...

    Error:                                             # We define the schema for the Error payload.
      type: object
      properties:
        detail:
          type: string
      required:
        - detail
```

This specification for the 404 response can be reused in the specification of all our endpoints under the /orders/{order_id} URL path, since all of those endpoints are specifically designed to target a specific resource.

NOTE You may be wondering, if certain responses are common to all the endpoints of a URL path, why can't we define the responses directly under the URL path and avoid repetition? The answer is this isn't possible as of now. The responses keyword is not allowed directly under a URL path, so we must document all the responses for every endpoint individually. There's a request in the OpenAPI GitHub repository to allow including common responses directly under the URL path, but it hasn't been implemented (http://mng.bz/097p).

We can use the generic 404 response from listing 5.13 under the GET /orders/{order_id} endpoint.

Listing 5.14 Using the 404 response schema under GET /orders/{order_id}

```
paths:
  ...

  /orders/{order_id}:
    parameters:
      - in: path
        name: order_id
        required: true
        schema:
          type: string
          "format": uuid
    get:
      summary: Returns the details of a specific order
      operationId: getOrder
      responses:
        '200':
          description: OK
          content:
            application/json:
```

```
            schema:
                $ref: '#/components/schemas/GetOrderSchema'
        '404':
            $ref: '#/components/responses/NotFound'
```

We define a 404 response.

We reference the NotFound response using a JSON pointer.

The orders API specification in the GitHub repository for this book also contains a generic definition for 422 responses and an expanded definition of the `Error` component that accounts for the different error payloads we get from FastAPI.

We're nearly done. The only remaining endpoint is GET `/orders`, which returns a list of orders. The endpoint's payload reuses `GetOrderSchema` to define the items in the `orders` array.

Listing 5.15 Specification for the GET `/orders` endpoint

```
paths:
  /orders:
    get:
      operationId: getOrders
      responses:
        '200':
          description: A JSON array of orders
          content:
            application/json:
              schema:
                type: object
                properties:
                  orders:
                    type: array
                    items:
                      $ref: '#/components/schemas/GetOrderSchema'
                required:
                  - order

    post:
      ...

  /orders/{order_id}:
    parameters:
      ...
```

We define the new GET method of the /orders URL path.

orders is an array.

Each item in the array is defined by GetOrderSchema.

Our API's endpoints are now fully documented! You can use many more elements within the definitions of your endpoints, such as `tags` and `externalDocs`. These attributes are not strictly necessary, but they can help to provide more structure to your API or make it easier to group the endpoints. For example, you can use `tags` to create groups of endpoints that logically belong together or share common features.

Before we finish this chapter, there's one more topic we need to address: documenting the authentication scheme of our API. That's the topic of the next section!

5.9 Defining the authentication scheme of the API

If our API is protected, the API specification must describe how users need to authenticate and authorize their requests. This section explains how we document our API's security schemes. The security definitions of the API go within the `components` section of the specification, under the `securitySchemes` header.

With OpenAPI, we can describe different security schemes, such as HTTP-based authentication, key-based authentication, Open Authorization 2 (OAuth2), and OpenID Connect.[7] In chapter 11, we'll implement authentication and authorization using the OpenID Connect and OAuth2 protocols, so let's go ahead and add definitions for these schemes. Listing 5.16 shows the changes we need to make to our API specification to document the security schemes.

We describe three security schemes: one for OpenID Connect, another one for OAuth2, and another for bearer authorization. We'll use OpenID Connect to authorize user access through a frontend application, and for direct API integrations, we'll offer OAuth's client credentials flow. We'll explain how each protocol and each authorization flow works in detail in chapter 11. For OpenID Connect, we must provide a configuration URL that describes how our backend authentication works under the `openIdConnectUrl` property. For OAuth2, we must describe the authorization flows available, together with a URL that clients must use to obtain their authorization tokens and the available scopes. The bearer authorization tells users that they must include a JSON Web Token (JWT) in the Authorization header to authorize their requests.

Listing 5.16 Documenting an API's security scheme

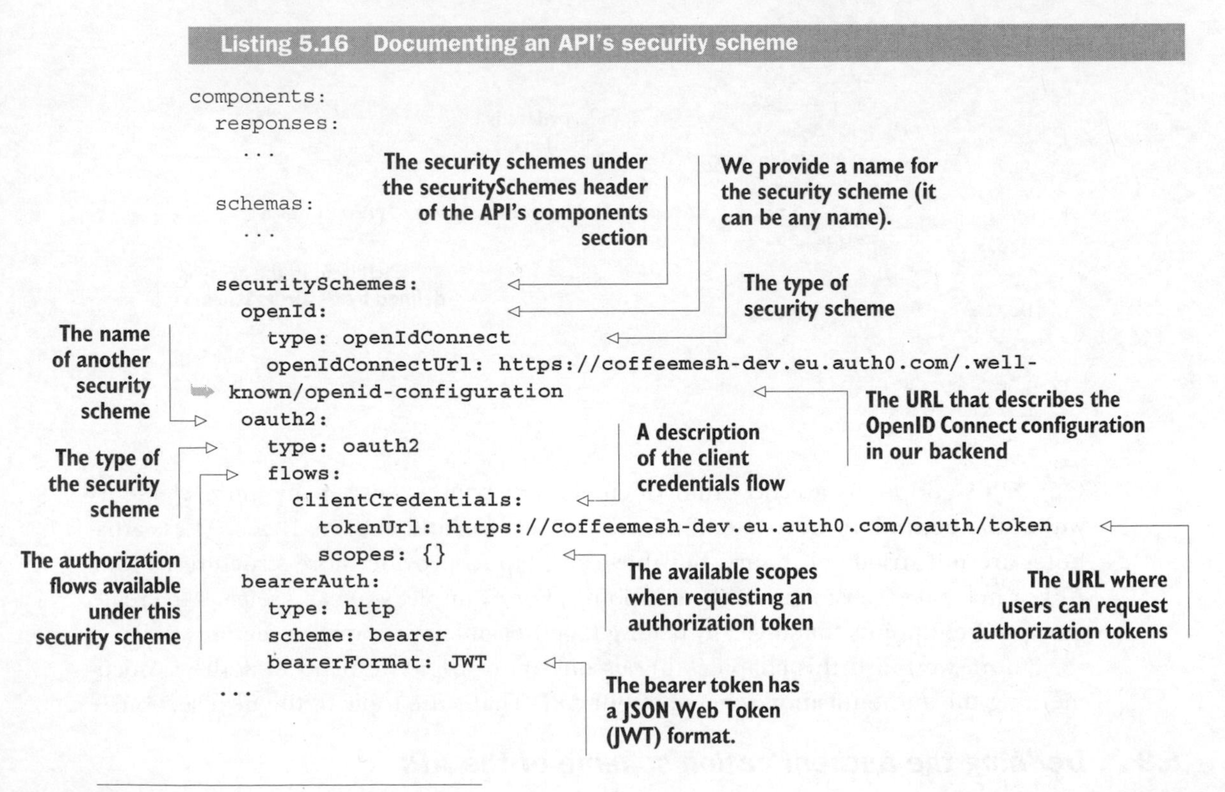

```
components:
  responses:
    ...

  schemas:
    ...

  securitySchemes:
    openId:
      type: openIdConnect
      openIdConnectUrl: https://coffeemesh-dev.eu.auth0.com/.well-
➥ known/openid-configuration
    oauth2:
      type: oauth2
      flows:
        clientCredentials:
          tokenUrl: https://coffeemesh-dev.eu.auth0.com/oauth/token
          scopes: {}
    bearerAuth:
      type: http
      scheme: bearer
      bearerFormat: JWT
    ...
```


[7] For a complete reference of all the security schemas available in OpenAPI, see https://swagger.io/docs/specification/authentication/.

```
security:
  - oauth2:
      - getOrders
      - createOrder
      - getOrder
      - updateOrder
      - deleteOrder
      - payOrder
      - cancelOrder
  - bearerAuth:
      - getOrders
      - createOrder
      - getOrder
      - updateOrder
      - deleteOrder
      - payOrder
      - cancelOrder
```

This concludes our journey through documenting REST APIs with OpenAPI. And what a ride! You've learned how to use JSON Schema; how OpenAPI works; how to structure an API specification; how to break down the process of documenting your API into small, progressive steps; and how to produce a full API specification. The next time you work on an API, you'll be well positioned to document its design using these standard technologies.

Summary

- JSON Schema is a specification for defining the types and formats of the properties of a JSON document. JSON Schema is useful for defining data validation models in a language-agnostic manner.
- OpenAPI is a standard documentation format for describing REST APIs and uses JSON Schema to describe the properties of the API. By using OpenAPI, you're able to leverage the whole ecosystem of tools and frameworks built around the standard, which makes it easier to build API integrations.
- A JSON pointer allows you to reference a schema using the `$ref` keyword. Using JSON pointers, we can create reusable schema definitions that can be used in different parts of an API specification, keeping the API specification clean and easy to understand.
- An OpenAPI specification contains the following sections:
  - `openapi`—Specifies the version of OpenAPI used to document the API
  - `info`—Contains information about the API, such as its title and version
  - `servers`—Documents the URLs under which the API is available
  - `paths`—Describes the endpoints exposed by the API, including the schemas for the API requests and responses and any relevant URL path or query parameters
  - `components`—Describes reusable components of the API, such as payload schemas, generic responses, and authentication schemes

6 Building REST APIs with Python

This chapter covers

- Adding URL query parameters to an endpoint using FastAPI
- Disallowing the presence of unknown properties in a payload using pydantic and marshmallow
- Implementing a REST API using flask-smorest
- Defining validation schemas and URL query parameters using marshmallow

In previous chapters, you learned to design and document REST APIs. In this chapter, you'll learn to implement REST APIs by working on two examples from the CoffeeMesh platform, the on-demand coffee delivery application that we introduced in chapter 1. We'll build the APIs for the orders service and for the kitchen service. The orders service is the main gateway to CoffeeMesh for customers of the platform. Through it they can place orders, pay for those orders, update them, and keep track of them. The kitchen service takes care of scheduling orders for production in the CoffeeMesh factories and keeps track of their progress. We'll learn best practices for implementing REST APIs as we work through these examples.

In chapter 2, we implemented part of the orders API. In the first sections of this chapter, we pick up the orders API where we left it in chapter 2 and implement its remaining features using FastAPI, a highly performant API framework for Python and a popular choice for building REST APIs. We'll learn how to add URL query parameters to our endpoints using FastAPI. As we saw in chapter 2, FastAPI uses pydantic for data validation, and in this chapter we'll use pydantic to forbid unknown fields in a payload. We'll learn about the tolerant reader pattern and balance its benefits against the risk of API integration failures due to errors such as typos.

After completing the implementation of the orders API, we'll implement the API for the kitchen service. The kitchen service schedules orders for production in the factory and keeps track of their progress. We'll implement the kitchen API using flask-smorest, a popular API framework built on top of Flask and marshmallow. We'll learn to implement our APIs following Flask application patterns, and we'll define validation schemas using marshmallow.

By the end of this chapter, you'll know how to implement REST APIs using FastAPI and Flask, two of the most popular libraries in the Python ecosystem. You'll see how the principles for implementing REST APIs transcend the implementation details of each framework and can be applied regardless of the technology that you use. The code for this chapter is available under folder ch06 in the repository provided with this book. Folder ch06 contains two subfolders: one for the orders API (ch06/orders) and one for the kitchen API (ch06/kitchen). With that said, and without further ado, let's get cracking!

6.1 Overview of the orders API

In this section, we recap the minimal implementation of the orders API that we undertook in chapter 2. You can find the full specification of the orders API under ch06/orders/oas.yaml in the GitHub repository for this book. Before we jump directly into the implementation, let's briefly analyze the specification and see what's left to implement.

In chapter 2, we implemented the API endpoints of the orders API, and we created pydantic schemas to validate request and response payloads. We intentionally skipped implementing the business layer of the application, as that's a complex task that we'll tackle in chapter 7.

As a reminder, the endpoints exposed by the orders API are the following:

- `/orders`—Allows us to retrieve lists (GET) of orders and to place orders (POST)
- `/orders/{order_id}`—Allows us to retrieve the details of a specific order (GET), to update an order (PUT), and to delete an order (DELETE)
- `/orders/{order_id}/cancel`—Allows us to cancel an order (POST)
- `/orders/{order_id}/pay`—Allows us to pay for an order (POST)

POST `/orders` and PUT `/orders/{order_id}` require request payloads that define the properties of an order, and in chapter 2 we implemented schemas for those payloads. What's missing from the implementation is the URL query parameters for the GET `/orders` endpoint. Also, the pydantic schemas we implemented in chapter 2 don't invalidate payloads with illegal properties in the payloads. As we'll see in section 6.3, this is fine in some situations, but it may lead to integration issues in other cases, and you'll learn to configure the schemas to invalidate payloads with illegal properties.

If you want to follow along with the examples in this chapter, create a folder called ch06 and copy into it the code from ch02 as ch06/orders. Remember to install the dependencies and activate the virtual environment:

```
$ mkdir ch06
$ cp -r ch02 ch06/orders
$ cd ch06/orders
$ pipenv install --dev && pipenv shell
```

You can start the web server by running the following command:

```
$ uvicorn orders.app:app --reload
```

FASTAPI + UVICORN REFRESHER We implement the orders API using the FastAPI framework, a popular Python framework for building REST APIs. FastAPI is built on top of Starlette, an asynchronous web server implementation. To execute our FastAPI application, we use Uvicorn, another asynchronous server implementation that efficiently handles incoming requests.

The `--reload` flag makes Uvicorn watch for changes on your files so that any time you make an update, the application is reloaded. This saves you the time of having to restart the server every time you make changes to the code. With this covered, let's complete the implementation of the orders API!

6.2 URL query parameters for the orders API

In this section, we enhance the GET `/orders` endpoint of the orders API by adding URL query parameters. We also implement validation schemas for the parameters. In chapter 4, we learned that URL query parameters allow us to filter the results of a GET endpoint. In chapter 5, we established that the GET `/orders` endpoint accepts URL query parameters to filter orders by cancellation and also to limit the list of orders returned by the endpoint.

Listing 6.1 Specification for the GET `/orders` URL query parameters

```
# file: orders/oas.yaml

paths:
  /orders:
    get:
      parameters:
        - name: cancelled
          in: query
          required: false
          schema:
            type: boolean
        - name: limit
          in: query
          required: false
```

```
        schema:
          type: integer
```

We need to implement two URL query parameters: `cancelled` (Boolean) and `limit` (integer). Neither are required, so users must be able to call the GET `/orders` endpoint without specifying them. Let's see how we do that.

Implementing URL query parameters for an endpoint is easy with FastAPI. All we need to do is include them in the endpoint's function signature and use type hints to add validation rules for them. Since the query parameters are optional, we'll mark them as such using the `Optional` type, and we'll set their default values to `None`.

Listing 6.2 Implementation of URL query parameters for GET `/orders`

```
# file: orders/orders/api/api.py

import uuid
from datetime import datetime
from typing import Optional
from uuid import UUID

...

@app.get('/orders', response_model=GetOrdersSchema)
def get_orders(cancelled: Optional[bool] = None, limit: Optional[int] = None):
    ...
```

We include URL query parameters in the function signature.

Now that we have query parameters available in the GET `/orders` endpoint, how should we handle them within the function? Since the query parameters are optional, we'll first check whether they've been set. We can do that by checking whether their values are something other than `None`. Listing 6.3 shows how we can handle URL query parameters within the function body of the GET `/orders` endpoint. Study figure 6.1 to understand the decision flow for filtering the list of orders based on the query parameters.

Listing 6.3 Implementation of URL query parameters for GET `/orders`

```
# file: orders/orders/api/api.py

@app.get('/orders', response_model=GetOrdersSchema)
def get_orders(cancelled: Optional[bool] = None, limit: Optional[int] = None):
    if cancelled is None and limit is None:
        return {'orders': orders}

    query_set = [order for order in orders]

    if cancelled is not None:
        if cancelled:
            query_set = [
                order
                for order in query_set
                if order['status'] == 'cancelled'
            ]
```

If the parameters haven't been set, we return immediately.

If any of the parameters has been set, we filter list into a query_set.

We check whether cancelled is set.

```
        else:
            query_set = [
                order
                for order in query_set
                if order['status'] != 'cancelled'
            ]

    if limit is not None and len(query_set) > limit:
        return {'orders': query_set[:limit]}

    return {'orders': query_set}
```

If limit is set and its value is lower than the length of query_set, we return a subset of query_set.

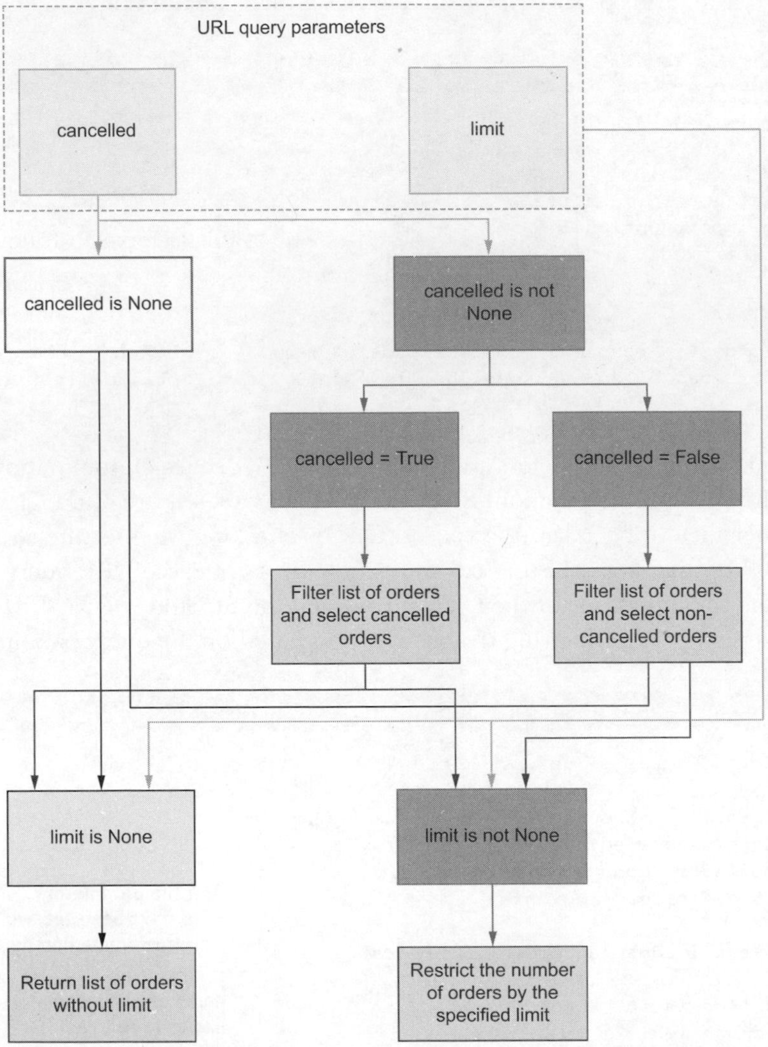

Figure 6.1 Decision flow for filtering orders based on query parameters. If the `cancelled` parameter is set to `True` or `False`, we use it to filter the list of orders. After this step, we check whether the `limit` parameter is set. If `limit` is set, we only return the corresponding number of orders from the list.

Now that we know how to add URL query parameters to our endpoints, let's see how we enhance our validation schemas.

6.3 Validating payloads with unknown fields

Until now, our pydantic models have been tolerant with the request payloads. If an API client sends a payload with fields that haven't been declared in our schemas, the payload will be accepted. As you'll see in this section, this may be convenient in some cases but misleading or dangerous in other contexts. To avoid integration errors, in this section, we learn how to configure pydantic to forbid the presence of unknown fields. Unknown fields are fields that haven't been defined in a schema.

> **PYDANTIC REFRESHER** As we saw in chapter 2, FastAPI uses pydantic to define validation models for our APIs. Pydantic is a popular data validation library for Python with a modern interface that allows you to define data validation rules using type hints.

In chapter 2, we implemented the schema definitions of the orders API following the tolerant reader pattern (https://martinfowler.com/bliki/TolerantReader.html), which follows Postel's law that recommends to be conservative in what you do and be liberal in what you accept from others.[1]

In the field of web APIs, this means that we must strictly validate the payloads we send to the client, while allowing for unknown fields in the payloads we receive from API clients. JSON Schema follows this pattern by default, and unless explicitly declared, a JSON Schema object accepts any kind of property. To disallow undeclared properties using JSON Schema, we set `additionalProperties` to `false`. If we use model composition, a better strategy is setting `unevaluatedProperties` to `false`, since `additionalProperties` causes conflicts between different models.[2] OpenAPI 3.1 allows us to use both `additionalProperties` and `unevaluatedProperties`, but OpenAPI 3.0 only accepts `additionalProperties`. Since we're documenting our APIs using OpenAPI 3.0.3, we'll ban undeclared properties using `additionalProperties`:

```
# file: orders/oas.yaml

    GetOrderSchema:
      additionalProperties: false
      type: object
      required:
        - order
        - id
        - created
        - status
```

[1] Jon Postel, Ed., "Transmission Control Protocol," RFC 761, p. 13, https:// tools.ietf.org/html/rfc761.

[2] To understand why `additionalProperties` doesn't work when using model composition, see the excellent discussion about this topic in JSON Schema's GitHub repository: https://github.com/json-schema-org/json-schema-spec/issues/556.

```
properties:
  id:
    type: string
    format: uuid
...
```

Check out the orders API specification under ch06/orders/oas.yaml in the GitHub repository for this book to see additional examples of `additionalProperties`.

The tolerant reader pattern is useful when an API is not fully consolidated or is likely to change frequently and when we want to be able to make changes to it without breaking integrations with existing clients. However, in other cases, like we saw in chapter 2 (section 2.5), the tolerant reader pattern can introduce new bugs or lead to unexpected integration issues.

For example, `OrderItemSchema` has three properties: `product`, `size`, and `quantity`. `product` and `size` are required properties, but `quantity` is optional, and if missing, the server assigns to it the default value of `1`. In some scenarios, this can lead to confusing situations. Imagine a client sends a payload with a typo in the representation of the `quantity` property, for example with the following payload:

```
{
  "order": [
    {
      "product": "capuccino",
      "size": "small",
      "quantit": 5
    }
  ]
}
```

Using the tolerant reader implementation, we ignore the field `quantit` from the payload, and we assume that the `quantity` property is missing and set its value to the default of `1`. This situation can be confusing for the client, who intended to set a different value for `quantity`.

> **THE API CLIENT SHOULD'VE TESTED THEIR CODE!** You can argue that the client should've tested their code and verified that it works properly before calling the server. And you're right. But in real life, code often goes untested, or is not properly tested, and a little bit of extra validation in the server will help in those situations. If we check the payload for the presence of illegal properties, this error will be caught and reported to the client.

How can we accomplish this using pydantic? To disallow unknown attributes, we need to define a `Config` class within our models and set the `extra` property to `forbid`.

Listing 6.4 Disallowing additional properties in models

```
# file: orders/orders/api/schemas.py

from datetime import datetime
from enum import Enum
```

```
from typing import List, Optional
from uuid import UUID

from pydantic import BaseModel, Extra, conint, conlist, validator

...

class OrderItemSchema(BaseModel):
    product: str
    size: Size
    quantity: int = Optional[conint(ge=1, strict=True)] = 1

    class Config:                 ◁── We use Config to ban
        extra = Extra.forbid          properties that haven't been
                                      defined in the schema.

class CreateOrderSchema(BaseModel):
    order: List[OrderItemSchema]

    class Config:
        extra = Extra.forbid


class GetOrderSchema(CreateOrderSchema):
    id: UUID
    created: datetime
    status: StatusEnum
```

Let's test this new functionality. Run the following command to start the server:

```
$ uvicorn orders.app:app --reload
```

As we saw in chapter 2, FastAPI generates a Swagger UI from the code, which we can use to test the endpoints. We'll use this UI to test our new validation rules with the following payload:

```
{
  "order": [
    {
      "product": "string",
      "size": "small",
      "quantit": 5
    }
  ]
}
```

DEFINITION A *Swagger UI* is a popular style for representing interactive visualizations of REST APIs. They provide a user-friendly interface that helps us understand the API implementation. Another popular UI for REST interfaces is Redoc (https://github.com/Redocly/redoc).

To get to the Swagger UI, visit http://127.0.0.1:8000/docs and follow the steps in figure 6.2 to learn how to execute a test against the POST `/orders` endpoint.

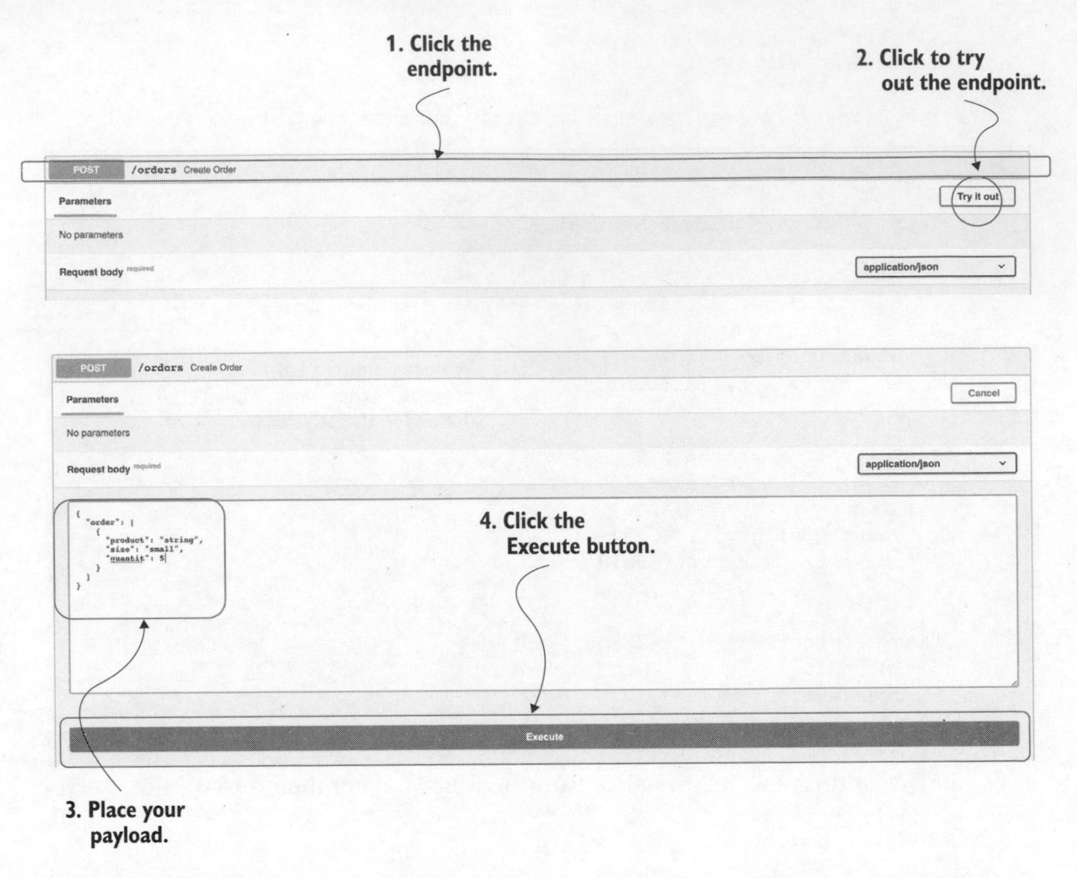

Figure 6.2 Testing the API with the Swagger UI: to test an endpoint, click the endpoint itself, then click the Try it Out button, then click the Execute button.

After running this test, you'll see that now FastAPI invalidates this payload and returns a helpful 422 response with the following message: "extra fields not permitted."

6.4 Overriding FastAPI's dynamically generated specification

So far, we've relied on FastAPI's dynamically generated API specification to test, visualize, and document the orders API. The dynamically generated specification is great to understand how we've implemented the API. However, our code can contain implementation errors, and those errors can translate to inaccurate documentation. Additionally, API development frameworks have limitations when it comes to generating API documentation, and they typically lack support for certain features of OpenAPI. For example, a common missing feature is documenting OpenAPI links, which we'll add to our API specification in chapter 12.

To understand how the API is supposed to work, we need to look at our API design document, which lives under orders/oas.yaml, and therefore is the specification we want to show when we deploy the API. In this section, you'll learn to override FastAPI's dynamically generated API specification with our API design document.

To load the API specification document, we need PyYAML, which you can install with the following command:

```
$ pipenv install pyyaml
```

In the orders/app.py file, we load the API specification, and we overwrite our application's object openapi property.

Listing 6.5 Overriding FastAPI's dynamically generated API specification

```
# file: orders/orders/app.py

from pathlib import Path

import yaml
from fastapi import FastAPI

app = FastAPI(debug=True)

oas_doc = yaml.safe_load(
    (Path(__file__).parent / '../oas.yaml').read_text()
)

app.openapi = lambda: oas_doc

from orders.api import api
```

We load the API specification using PyYAML.

We override FastAPI's openapi property so that it returns our API specification.

To be able to test the API using the Swagger UI, we need to add the localhost URL to the API specification. Open the orders/oas.yaml file and add the localhost address to the servers section of the specification:

```
# file: orders/oas.yaml

servers:
  - url: http://localhost:8000
    description: URL for local development and testing
  - url: https://coffeemesh.com
    description: main production server
  - url: https://coffeemesh-staging.com
    description: staging server for testing purposes only
```

By default, FastAPI serves the Swagger UI under the /docs URL, and the OpenAPI specification under /openapi.json. That's great when we only have one API, but CoffeeMesh has multiple microservice APIs; therefore, we need multiple paths to access each API's documentation. We'll serve the orders API's Swagger UI under /docs/orders, and its OpenAPI specification under /openapi/orders.json. We can override those paths directly in FastAPI's application object initializer:

```
# file: orders/app.py

app = FastAPI(
    debug=True, openapi_url='/openapi/orders.json', docs_url='/docs/orders'
)
```

This concludes our journey through building the orders API with FastAPI. It's now time to move on to building the API for the kitchen service, for which we'll use a new stack: Flask + marshmallow. Let's get on with it!

6.5 Overview of the kitchen API

In this section, we analyze the implementation requirements for the kitchen API. As you can see in figure 6.3, the kitchen service manages the production of customer orders. Customers interface with the kitchen service through the orders service when they place an order or check its status. CoffeeMesh staff can also use the kitchen service to check how many orders are scheduled and to manage them.

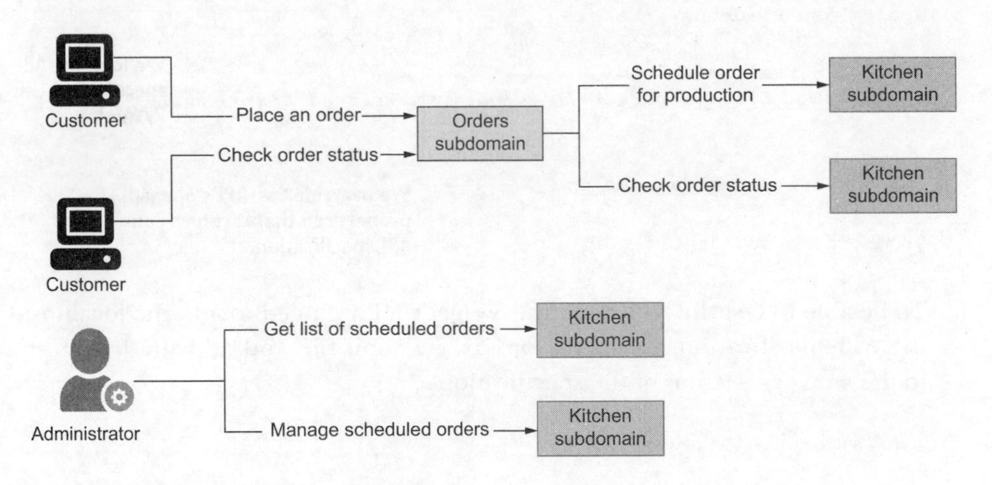

Figure 6.3 The kitchen service schedules orders for production, and it tracks their progress. CoffeeMesh staff members use the kitchen service to manage scheduled orders.

The specification for the kitchen API is provided under ch06/kitchen/oas.yaml in the repository provided with this book. The kitchen API contains four URL paths (see figure 6.4 for additional clarification):

- /kitchen/schedules—Allows us to schedule an order for production in the kitchen (POST) and to retrieve a list of orders scheduled for production (GET)
- /kitchen/schedules/{schedule_id}—Allows us to retrieve the details of a scheduled order (GET), to update its details (PUT), and to delete it from our records (DELETE)

- `/kitchen/schedules/{schedule_id}/status`—Allows us to read the status of an order scheduled for production
- `/kitchen/schedules/{schedule_id}/cancel`—Allows us to cancel a scheduled order

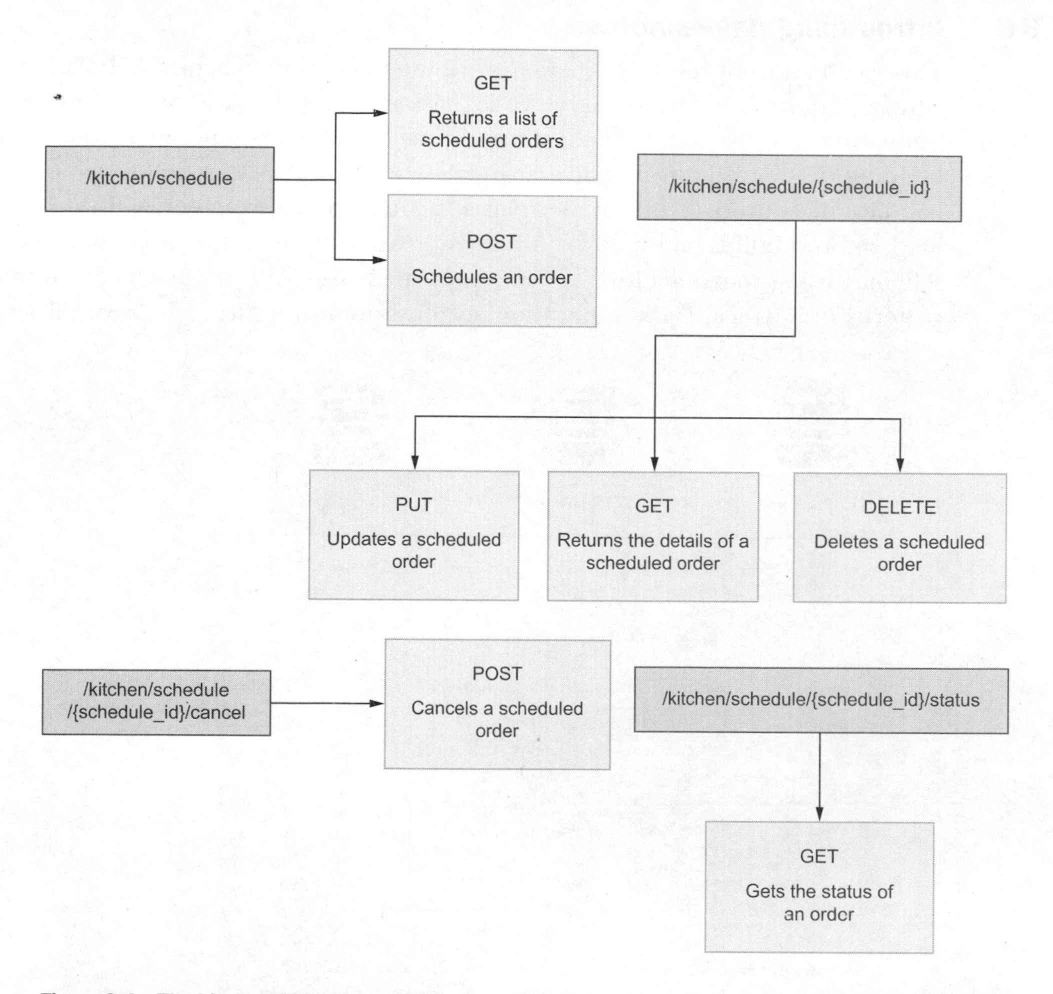

Figure 6.4 The kitchen API has four URL paths: `/kitchen/schedules` exposes a GET and a POST endpoint; `/kitchen/schedules/{schedule_id}` exposes PUT, GET, and DELETE endpoints; `/kitchen/schedules/{schedule_id}/cancel` exposes a POST endpoint; and `/kitchen/schedules/{schedule_id}/status` exposes a GET endpoint.

The kitchen API contains three schemas: `OrderItemSchema`, `ScheduleOrderSchema`, and `GetScheduledOrderSchema`. The `ScheduleOrderSchema` represents the payload required to schedule an order for production, while the `GetScheduledOrderSchema` represents the details of an order that has been scheduled. Just like in the orders API, `OrderItemSchema` represents the details of each item in an order.

Just as we did in chapter 2, we'll keep the implementation simple and focus only on the API layer. We'll mock the business layer with an in-memory representation of the schedules managed by the service. In chapter 7, we'll learn service implementation patterns that will help us implement the business layer.

6.6 Introducing flask-smorest

This section introduces the framework we'll use to build the kitchen API: flask-smorest (https://github.com/marshmallow-code/flask-smorest). Flask-smorest is a REST API framework built on top of Flask and marshmallow. Flask is a popular framework for building web applications, while marshmallow is a popular data validation library that handles the conversion of complex data structures to and from native Python objects. Flask-smorest builds on top of both frameworks, which means we implement our API schemas using marshmallow, and we implement our API endpoints following the patterns of a typical Flask application, as illustrated in figure 6.5. As you'll see, the

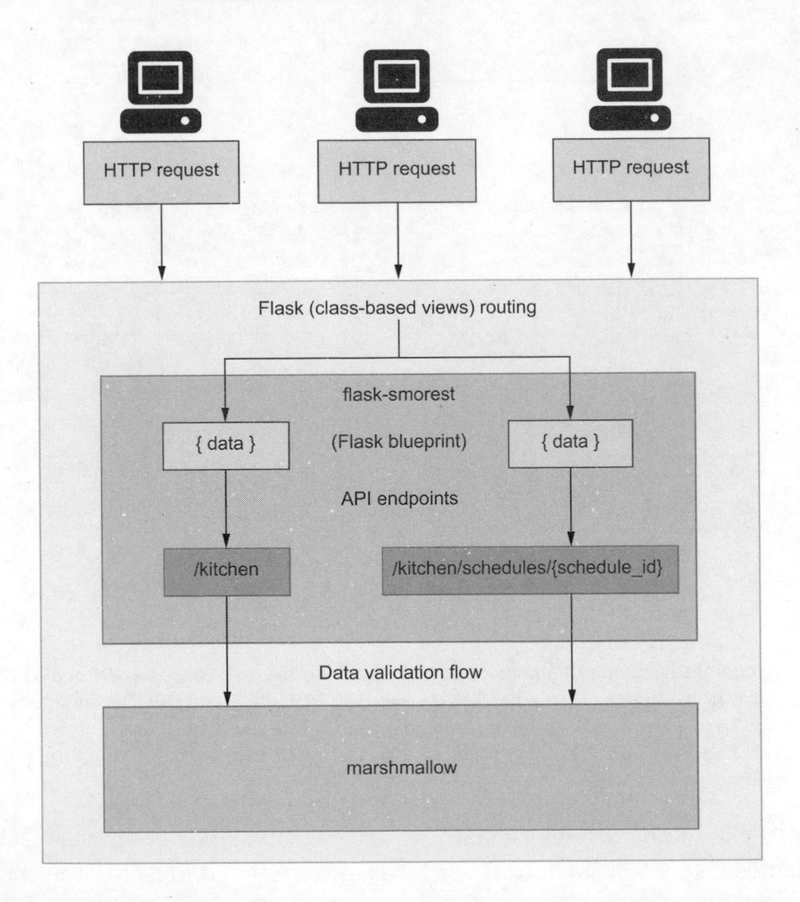

Figure 6.5 Architecture of an application built with flask-smorest. Flask-smorest implements a typical Flask blueprint, which allows us to build and configure our API endpoints just as we would in a standard Flask application.

principles and patterns we used when we built the orders API with FastAPI can be applied regardless of the framework, and we'll use the same approach to build the kitchen API with flask-smorest.

Building APIs with flask-smorest offers an experience similar to building them with FastAPI, with only two major differences:

- *FastAPI uses pydantic for data validation, while flask-smorest uses marshmallow.* This means that with FastAPI we use native Python-type hints to create data validation rules, while in marshmallow we use field classes.
- *Flask allows us to implement API endpoints with class-based views.* This means that we can use a class to represent a URL path and implement its HTTP methods as methods of the class. Class-based views help you write more structured code and encapsulate the specific behavior of each URL path within the class. In contrast, FastAPI allows you only to define endpoints using functions. Notice that Starlette allows you to implement class-based routes, so this limitation of FastAPI may go away in the future.

With this covered, let's kick off the implementation of the kitchen API!

6.7 Initializing the web application for the API

In this section, we set up the environment to start working on the kitchen API. We'll also create the entry point for the application and add basic configuration for the web server. In doing so, you'll learn how to set up a project with flask-smorest and how to inject configuration objects into your Flask applications.

Flask-smorest is built on top of the Flask framework, so we'll lay out our web application following the patterns of a typical Flask application. Create a folder called ch06/kitchen for the kitchen API implementation. Within that folder, copy the kitchen API specification, which is available under ch06/kitchen/oas.yaml in this book's GitHub repository. oas.yaml contains the API specification for the kitchen API. Use the `cd` command to navigate into the ch06/kitchen folder, and run the following commands to install the dependencies that we'll need to proceed with the implementation:

```
$ pipenv install flask-smorest
```

NOTE If you want to ensure that you're installing the same version of the dependencies that I used when writing this chapter, copy the ch06/kitchen/Pipfile and the ch06/kitchen/Pipfile.lock files from the GitHub repository onto your local machine, and run `pipenv install`.

Also, run the following command to activate the environment:

```
$ pipenv shell
```

Now that we have the libraries we need, let's create a file called kitchen/app.py. This file will contain an instance of the `Flask` application object, which represents our web server. We'll also create an instance of flask-smorest's `Api` object, which will represent our API.

Listing 6.6 Initialization of the `Flask` application object and the `Api` object

```
# file: kitchen/app.py

from flask import Flask
from flask_smorest import Api

app = Flask(__name__)

kitchen_api = Api(app)
```

- `app = Flask(__name__)`: We create an instance of the Flask application object.
- `kitchen_api = Api(app)`: We create an instance of flask-smorest's Api object.

Flask-smorest requires some configuration parameters to work. For example, we need to specify the version of OpenAPI we are using, the title of our API, and the version of our API. We pass this configuration through the `Flask` application object. Flask offers different strategies for injecting configuration, but the most convenient method is loading configuration from a class. Let's create a file called kitchen/config.py for our configuration parameters. Within this file we create a `BaseConfig` class, which contains generic configuration for the API.

Listing 6.7 Configuration for the orders API

```
# file: kitchen/config.py

class BaseConfig:
    API_TITLE = 'Kitchen API'
    API_VERSION = 'v1'
    OPENAPI_VERSION = '3.0.3'
    OPENAPI_JSON_PATH = 'openapi/kitchen.json'
    OPENAPI_URL_PREFIX = '/'
    OPENAPI_REDOC_PATH = '/redoc'
    OPENAPI_REDOC_URL =
     'https://cdn.jsdelivr.net/npm/redoc@next/bundles/redoc.standalone.js'
    OPENAPI_SWAGGER_UI_PATH = '/docs/kitchen'
    OPENAPI_SWAGGER_UI_URL = 'https://cdn.jsdelivr.net/npm/swagger-ui-
➥ dist/'
```

- `API_TITLE`: The title of our API
- `API_VERSION`: The version of our API
- `OPENAPI_VERSION`: The version of OpenAPI we are using
- `OPENAPI_JSON_PATH`: Path to the dynamically generated specification in JSON
- `OPENAPI_URL_PREFIX`: URL path prefix for the OpenAPI specification file
- `OPENAPI_REDOC_PATH`: Path to the Redoc UI of our API
- `OPENAPI_REDOC_URL`: Path to a script to be used to render the Redoc UI
- `OPENAPI_SWAGGER_UI_PATH`: Path to the Swagger UI of our API
- `OPENAPI_SWAGGER_UI_URL`: Path to a script to be used to render the Swagger UI

Now that the configuration is ready, we can pass it to the `Flask` application object.

Listing 6.8 Loading configuration

```
# file: kitchen/app.py

from flask import Flask
from flask_smorest import Api

from config import BaseConfig
```

- `from config import BaseConfig`: We import the BaseConfig class we defined earlier.

```
app = Flask(__name__)
app.config.from_object(BaseConfig)

kitchen_api = Api(app)
```

We use the from_object method to load configuration from a class.

With the entry point for our application ready and configured, let's move on to implementing the endpoints for the kitchen API!

6.8 Implementing the API endpoints

This section explains how we implement the endpoints of the kitchen API using flask-smorest. Since flask-smorest is built on top of Flask, we build the endpoints for our API exactly as we'd do any other Flask application. In Flask, we register our endpoints using Flask's `route` decorator:

```
@app.route('/orders')
def process_order():
    pass
```

Using the `route` decorator works for simple cases, but for more complex application patterns, we use Flask blueprints. Flask blueprints allow you to provide specific configuration for a group of URLs. To implement the kitchen API endpoints, we'll use the flask-smorest's `Blueprint` class. Flask-smorest's `Blueprint` is a subclass of Flask's `Blueprint`, so it provides the functionality that comes with Flask blueprints, enhances it with additional functionality and configuration that generates API documentation, and supplies payload validation models, among other things.

We can use `Blueprint`'s `route` decorators to create an endpoint or URL path. As you can see from figure 6.6, functions are convenient for URL paths that only expose one HTTP method. When a URL exposes multiple HTTP methods, it's more convenient to use class-based routes, which we implement using Flask's `MethodView` class.

As you can see in figure 6.7, using `MethodView`, we represent a URL path as a class, and we implement the HTTP methods it exposes as methods of the class.

For example, if we have a URL path `/kitchen` that exposes GET and POST endpoints, we can implement the following class-based view:

```
class Kitchen(MethodView):

    def get(self):
        pass

    def post(self):
        pass
```

Listing 6.9 illustrates how we implement the endpoints for the kitchen API using class-based views and function-based views. The content in listing 6.9 goes into the kitchen/api/api.py file. First, we create an instance of flask-smorest's `Blueprint`. The `Blueprint` object allows us to register our endpoints and add data validation to them.

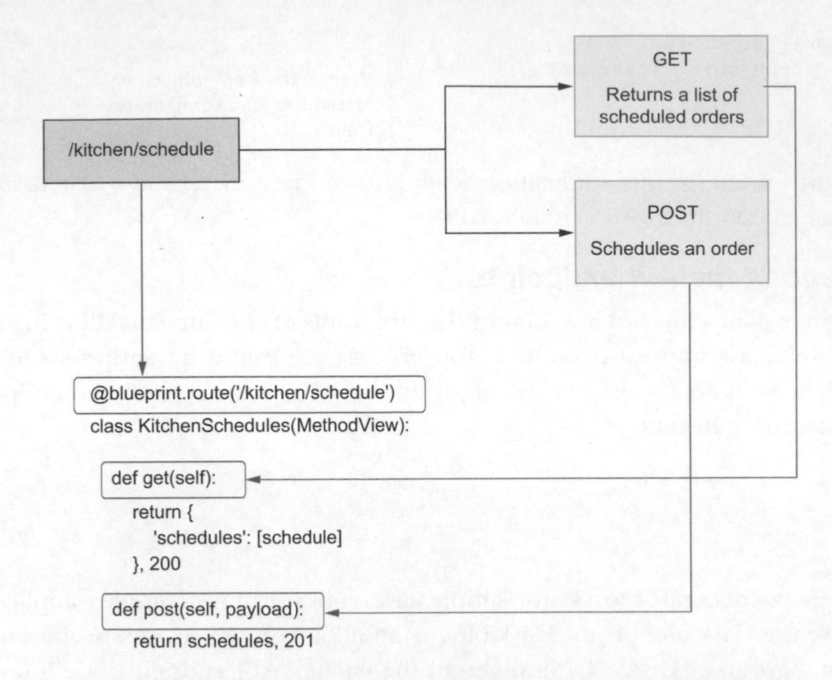

Figure 6.6 When a URL path exposes more than one HTTP method, it's more convenient to implement it as a class-based view, where the class methods implement each of the HTTP methods exposed.

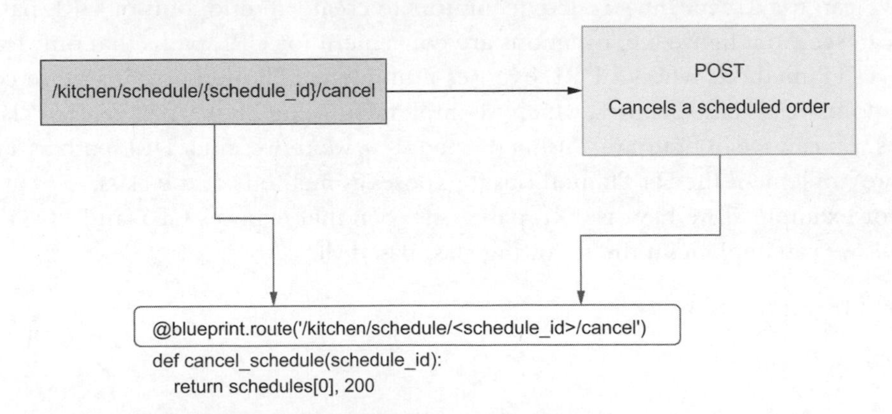

Figure 6.7 When a URL path exposes only one HTTP method, it's more convenient to implement it as a function-based view.

To instantiate `Blueprint`, we must pass two required positional arguments: the name of the `Blueprint` itself and the name of the module where the `Blueprint`'s routes are implemented. In this case, we pass the module's name using the `__name__` attribute, which resolves to the name of the file.

Once the Blueprint is instantiated, we register our URL paths with it using the route() decorator. We use class-based routes for the /kitchen/schedules and the /kitchen/schedules/{schedule_id} paths since they expose more than one HTTP method, and we use function-based routes for the /kitchen/schedules/{schedule_id}/cancel and /kitchen/schedules/{schedule_id}/status paths because they only expose one HTTP method. We return a mock schedule object in each endpoint for illustration purposes, and we'll change that into a dynamic in-memory collection of schedules in section 6.12. The return value of each function is a tuple, where the first element is the payload and the second is the status code of the response.

Listing 6.9 Implementation of the endpoints of the orders API

```
# file: kitchen/api/api.py

import uuid
from datetime import datetime

from flask.views import MethodView
from flask_smorest import Blueprint


blueprint = Blueprint('kitchen', __name__, description='Kitchen API')


schedules = [{
    'id': str(uuid.uuid4()),
    'scheduled': datetime.now(),
    'status': 'pending',
    'order': [
        {
            'product': 'capuccino',
            'quantity': 1,
            'size': 'big'
        }
    ]
}]


@blueprint.route('/kitchen/schedules')
class KitchenSchedules(MethodView):

    def get(self):
        return {
            'schedules': schedules
        }, 200

    def post(self, payload):
        return schedules[0], 201


@blueprint.route('/kitchen/schedules/<schedule_id>')
class KitchenSchedule(MethodView):
```

We create an instance of flask-smorest's Blueprint class.

We declare a hardcoded list of schedules.

We use the Blueprint's route() decorator to register a class or a function as a URL path.

We implement the /kitchen/schedules URL path as a class-based view.

Every method view in a class-based view is named after the HTTP method it implements.

We return both the payload and the status code.

We define URL parameters within angle brackets.

```
    def get(self, schedule_id):          <-- We include the URL path parameter in the function signature.
        return schedules[0], 200

    def put(self, payload, schedule_id):
        return schedules[0], 200

    def delete(self, schedule_id):
        return '', 204

@blueprint.route(
    '/kitchen/schedules/<schedule_id>/cancel', methods=['POST']
)                                        <-- We implement the /kitchen/schedules/<schedule_id>/cancel URL path as a function-based view.
def cancel_schedule(schedule_id):
    return schedules[0], 200

@blueprint.route('/kitchen/schedules/<schedule_id>/status, methods=[GET])
def get_schedule_status(schedule_id):
    return schedules[0], 200
```

Now that we have created the blueprint, we can register it with our API object in the kitchen/app.py file.

Listing 6.10 Registering the blueprint with the API object

```
# file: kitchen/app.py

from flask import Flask
from flask_smorest import Api

from api.api import blueprint          <-- We import the blueprint we defined earlier.
from config import BaseConfig


app = Flask(__name__)
app.config.from_object(BaseConfig)

kitchen_api = Api(app)

kitchen_api.register_blueprint(blueprint)          <-- We register the blueprint with the kitchen API object.
```

Using the cd command, navigate to the ch06/kitchen directory and run the application with the following command:

```
$ flask run --reload
```

Just like in Uvicorn, the `--reload` flag runs the server with a watcher over your files so that the server restarts when you make changes to the code.

If you visit the http://127.0.0.1:5000/docs URL, you'll see an interactive Swagger UI dynamically generated from the endpoints we implemented earlier. You can also see the OpenAPI specification dynamically generated by flask-smorest under http://127.0.0.1:5000/openapi.json. At this stage in our implementation, it's not possible to interact with the endpoints through the Swagger UI. Since we don't yet have marshmallow models, flask-smorest doesn't know how to serialize data and therefore doesn't return payloads. However, it's still possible to call the API using cURL and inspect the responses. If you run `curl http://127.0.0.1:5000/kitchen/schedules`, you'll get the mock object we defined in the kitchen/api/api.py module.

Things are looking good, and it's time to spice up the implementation by adding marshmallow models. Move on to the next section to learn how to do that!

6.9 Implementing payload validation models with marshmallow

Flask-smorest uses marshmallow models to validate request and response payloads. In this section, we learn to work marshmallow models by implementing the schemas of the kitchen API. The marshmallow models will help flask-smorest validate our payloads and serialize our data.

As you can see in the kitchen API specification under ch06/kitchen/oas.yaml in this book's GitHub repository, the kitchen API contains three schemas: `ScheduleOrderSchema` schema, which contains the details needed to schedule an order; `GetScheduledOrderSchema`, which represents the details of a scheduled order; and `OrderItemSchema`, which represents a collection of items in an order. Listing 6.11 shows how to implement these schemas as marshmallow models under kitchen/api/schemas.py.

To create marshmallow models, we create subclasses of marshmallow's `Schema` class. We define the models' properties with the help of marshmallow's field classes, such as `String` and `Integer`. Marshmallow uses these property definitions to validate a payload against a model. To customize the behavior of marshmallow's models, we use the `Meta` class to set the unknown attribute to `EXCLUDE`, which instructs marshmallow to invalidate the payload with unknown properties.

Listing 6.11 Schema definitions for the orders API

```
# file: kitchen/api/schemas.py

from marshmallow import Schema, fields, validate, EXCLUDE


class OrderItemSchema(Schema):
    class Meta:                         <-- We use the Meta class to ban unknown properties.
        unknown = EXCLUDE

    product = fields.String(required=True)
    size = fields.String(
        required=True, validate=validate.OneOf(['small', 'medium', 'big'])
    )
    quantity = fields.Integer(
        validate=validate.Range(1, min_inclusive=True), required=True
    )
```

```
class ScheduleOrderSchema(Schema):
    class Meta:
        unknown = EXCLUDE

    order = fields.List(fields.Nested(OrderItemSchema), required=True)


class GetScheduledOrderSchema(ScheduleOrderSchema):    <-- We use class inheritance to reuse the definitions of an existing schema.
    id = fields.UUID(required=True)
    scheduled = fields.DateTime(required=True)
    status = fields.String(
        required=True,
        validate=validate.OneOf(
            ["pending", "progress", "cancelled", "finished"]
        ),
    )


class GetScheduledOrdersSchema(Schema):
    class Meta:
        unknown = EXCLUDE

    schedules = fields.List(
        fields.Nested(GetScheduledOrderSchema), required=True
    )


class ScheduleStatusSchema(Schema):
    class Meta:
        unknown = EXCLUDE

    status = fields.String(
        required=True,
        validate=validate.OneOf(
            ["pending", "progress", "cancelled", "finished"]
        ),
    )
```

Now that our validation models are ready, we can link them with our views. Listing 6.12 shows how we use the models to add validation for request and response payloads on our endpoints. To add request payload validation to a view, we use the blueprint's `arguments()` decorator in combination with a marshmallow model. For response payloads, we use the blueprint's `response()` decorator in combination with a marshmallow model.

By decorating our methods and functions with the blueprint's `response()` decorator, we no longer need to return a tuple of payload plus a status code. Flask-smorest takes care of adding the status code for us. By default, flask-smorest adds a 200 status code to our responses. If we want to customize that, we simply need to specify the desired status code using the `status_code` parameter in the decorator.

While the blueprint's `arguments()` decorator validates and deserializes a request payload, the blueprint's `response()` decorator doesn't perform validation and only serializes the payload. We'll discuss this feature in more detail in section 6.11, and we'll see how we can ensure that data is validated before being serialized.

Listing 6.12 Adding validation to the API endpoints

```
# file: kitchen/api/api.py

import uuid
from datetime import datetime

from flask.views import MethodView
from flask_smorest import Blueprint

from api.schemas import (
    GetScheduledOrderSchema,
    ScheduleOrderSchema,
    GetScheduledOrdersSchema,
    ScheduleStatusSchema,
)

blueprint = Blueprint('kitchen', __name__, description='Kitchen API')

...

@blueprint.route('/kitchen/schedulles')
class KitchenSchedules(MethodView):

    @blueprint.response(status_code=200, schema=GetScheduledOrdersSchema)
    def get(self):
        return {'schedules': schedules}

    @blueprint.arguments(ScheduleOrderSchema)
    @blueprint.response(status_code=201, schema=GetScheduledOrderSchema)
    def post(self, payload):
        return schedules[0]

@blueprint.route('/kitchen/schedules/<schedule_id>')
class KitchenSchedule(MethodView):

    @blueprint.response(status_code=200, schema=GetScheduledOrderSchema)
    def get(self, schedule_id):
        return schedules[0]

    @blueprint.arguments(ScheduleOrderSchema)
    @blueprint.response(status_code=200, schema=GetScheduledOrderSchema)
    def put(self, payload, schedule_id):
        return schedules[0]

    @blueprint.response(status_code=204)
    def delete(self, schedule_id):
        return
```

We import our marshmallow models.

We use the blueprint's response() decorator to register a marshmallow model for the response payload.

We use the blueprint's arguments() decorator to register a marshmallow model for the request payload.

We set the status_code parameter to the desired status code.

```
@blueprint.response(status_code=200, schema=GetScheduledOrderSchema)
@blueprint.route(
    '/kitchen/schedules/<schedule_id>/cancel', methods=['POST']
)
def cancel_schedule(schedule_id):
    return schedules[0]

@blueprint.response(status_code=200, schema=ScheduleStatusSchema)
@blueprint.route(
    '/kitchen/schedules/<schedule_id>/status', methods=['GET']
)
def get_schedule_status(schedule_id):
    return schedules[0]
```

To see the effects of the new changes in the implementation, visit http://127.0.0.1:5000/docs URL again. If you're running the server with the `--reload` flag, the changes will be automatically reloaded. Otherwise, stop the server and run it again. As you can see in figure 6.8, flask-smorest now recognizes the validation schemas that need to be used in the API, and therefore they're represented in the Swagger UI. If you play around with the UI now, for example by hitting the GET `/kitchen/schedules` endpoint, you'll be able to see the response payloads.

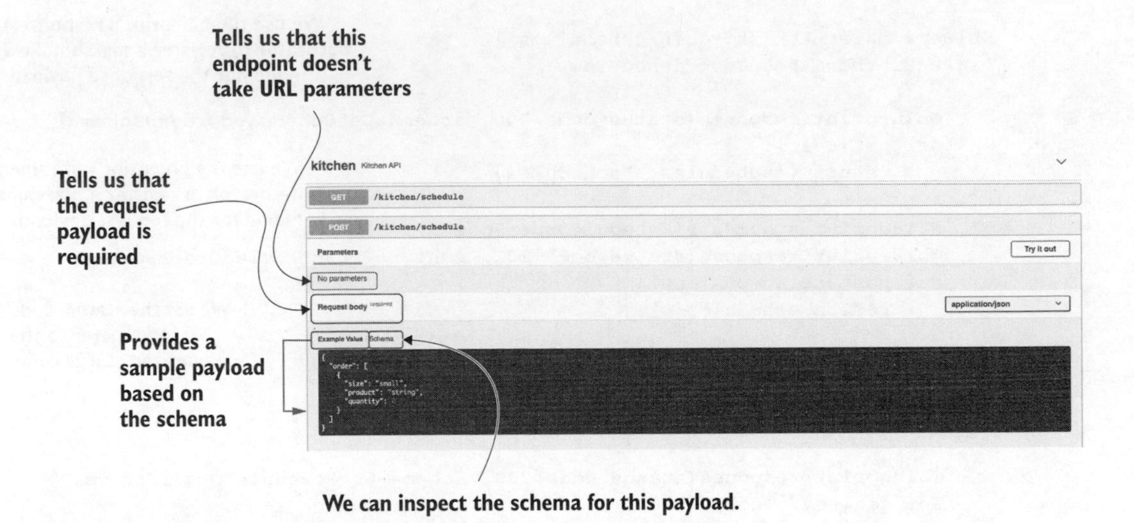

Figure 6.8 The Swagger UI shows the schema for the request for the POST `/kitchen/schedules` endpoint's payload and provides an example of it.

The API is looking good, and we are nearly finished with the implementation. The next step is adding URL query parameters to the GET `/kitchen/schedules` endpoint. Move on to the next section to learn how to do that!

6.10 Validating URL query parameters

In this section, we learn how to add URL query parameters to the GET `/kitchen/schedules` endpoint. As shown in listing 6.13, the GET `/kitchen/schedules` endpoint accepts three URL query parameters:

- `progress` *(Boolean)*—Indicates whether an order is in progress.
- `limit` *(integer)*—Limits the number of results returned by the endpoint.
- `since` *(date-time)*—Filters results by the time when the orders were scheduled. A date in date-time format is an ISO date with the following structure: `YYYY-MM-DDTHH:mm:ssZ`. An example of this date format is 2021-08-31T01:01:01Z. For more information on this format, see https://tools.ietf.org/html/rfc3339#section-5.6.

Listing 6.13 Specification for the GET `/kitchen/schedules` URL query parameters

```
# file: kitchen/oas.yaml

paths:
  /kitchen/schedules:
    get:
      summary: Returns a list of orders scheduled for production
      parameters:
        - name: progress
          in: query
          description: >-
            Whether the order is in progress or not.
            In progress means it's in production in the kitchen.
          required: false
          schema:
            type: boolean
        - name: limit
          in: query
          required: false
          schema:
            type: integer
        - name: since
          in: query
          required: false
          schema:
            type: string
            format: 'date-time'
```

How do we implement URL query parameters in flask-smorest? To begin, we need to create a new marshmallow model to represent them. We define the URL query parameters for the kitchen API using marshmallow. You can add the model for the URL query parameters to kitchen/api/schemas.py with the other marshmallow models.

Listing 6.14 URL query parameters in marshmallow

```
# file: kitchen/api/schemas.py

from marshmallow import Schema, fields, validate, EXCLUDE

...

class GetKitchenScheduleParameters(Schema):
    class Meta:
        unknown = EXCLUDE

    progress = fields.Boolean()        <-- We define the fields
    limit = fields.Integer()               of the URL query
    since = fields.DateTime()              parameters.
```

We register the schema for URL query parameters using the blueprint's `arguments()` decorator. We specify that the properties defined in the schema are expected in the URL, so we set the `location` parameter to query.

Listing 6.15 Adding URL query parameters to GET `/kitchen/schedules`

```
# file: kitchen/api/api.py

import uuid
from datetime import datetime

from flask.views import MethodView
from flask_smorest import Blueprint

from api.schemas import (
    GetScheduledOrderSchema, ScheduleOrderSchema, GetScheduledOrdersSchema,
    ScheduleStatusSchema, GetKitchenScheduleParameters   <-- We import the marshmallow model
)                                                            for URL query parameters.

blueprint = Blueprint('kitchen', __name__, description='Kitchen API')

...

@blueprint.route('/kitchen/schedules')
class KitchenSchedules(MethodView):

    @blueprint.arguments(GetKitchenScheduleParameters, location='query')   <-- We register the model using the arguments() decorator and set the location parameter to query.
    @blueprint.response(status_code=200, schema=GetScheduledOrdersSchema)
    def get(self, parameters):     <-- We capture URL query
        return schedules               parameter in the function
                                       signature.
...
```

If you reload the Swagger UI, you'll see that the GET `/kitchen/schedules` endpoint now accepts three optional URL query parameters (shown in figure 6.9). We should

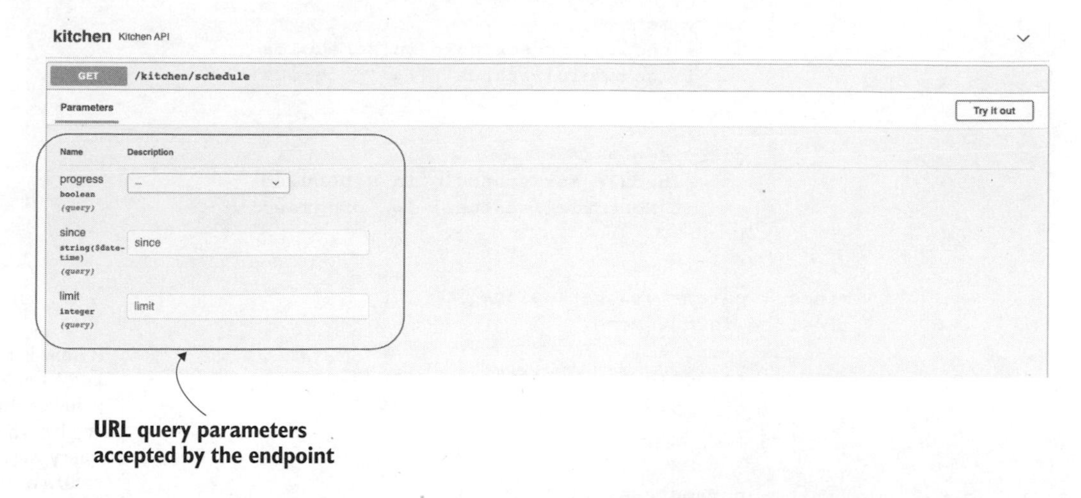

Figure 6.9 The Swagger UI shows the URL query parameters of the GET `/kitchen/schedules` endpoint, and it offers form fields that we can fill in to experiment with different values.

pass these parameters to our business layer, which will use them to filter the list of results. URL query parameters come in the form of a dictionary. If the user didn't set any query parameters, the dictionary will be empty and therefore and evaluate to `False`. Since URL query parameters are optional, we check for their presence by using the dictionary's `get()` method. Since `get()` returns `None` when a parameter isn't set, we know that a parameter is set when its value isn't `None`. We won't be implementing the business layer until chapter 7, but we can use query parameters to filter our in-memory list of schedules.

Listing 6.16 Use filters in GET `/kitchen/schedules`

```
# file: kitchen/api/api.py

...

@blueprint.route('/kitchen/schedules')
class KitchenSchedules(MethodView):

    @blueprint.arguments(GetKitchenScheduleParameters, location='query')
    @blueprint.response(status_code=200, schema=GetScheduledOrdersSchema)
    def get(self, parameters):
        if not parameters:
            return {'schedules': schedules}

        query_set = [schedule for schedule in schedules]

        in_progress = parameters.get(progress)
        if in_progress is not None:
            if in_progress:
```

If no parameter is set, we return the full list of schedules.

If the user set any URL query parameters, we use them to filter the list of schedules.

We check for the presence of each URL query parameter by using the dictionary's get() method.

```
            query_set = [
                schedule for schedule in schedules
                if schedule['status'] == 'progress'
            ]
        else:
            query_set = [
                schedule for schedule in schedules
                if schedule['status'] != 'progress'
            ]

    since = parameters.get('since')
    if since is not None:
        query_set = [
            schedule for schedule in schedules
            if schedule['scheduled'] >= since
        ]

    limit = parameters.get('limit')
    if limit is not None and len(query_set) > limit:
        query_set = query_set[:limit]

    return {'schedules': query_set}
...
```

If limit is set and its value is lower than the length of query_set, we return a subset of query_set.

We return the filtered list of schedules.

Now that we know how to handle URL query parameters with flask-smorest, there's one more topic we need to cover, and that is data validation before serialization. Move on to the next section to learn more about this!

6.11 Validating data before serializing the response

Now that we have schemas to validate our request payloads and we have hooked them up with our routes, we have to ensure that our response payloads are also validated. In this section, we learn how to use marshmallow models to validate data. We'll use this functionality to validate our response payloads, but you could use the same approach to validate any kind of data, such as configuration objects.

When we send a payload in a response, flask-smorest serializes the payload using marshmallow. However, as shown in figure 6.10, it doesn't validate if it's correctly formed.[3] As you can see in figure 6.11, in contrast to marshmallow, FastAPI does validate our data before it's serialized for a response.

The fact that marshmallow doesn't perform validation before serialization is not necessarily undesirable. In fact, it can be argued that it's a desirable behavior, as it decouples the task of serializing from the task of validating the payload. There are two

[3] Before version 3.0.0, marshmallow used to perform validation before serialization (see the change log: https://github.com/marshmallow-code/marshmallow/blob/dev/CHANGELOG.rst#300-2019-08-18).

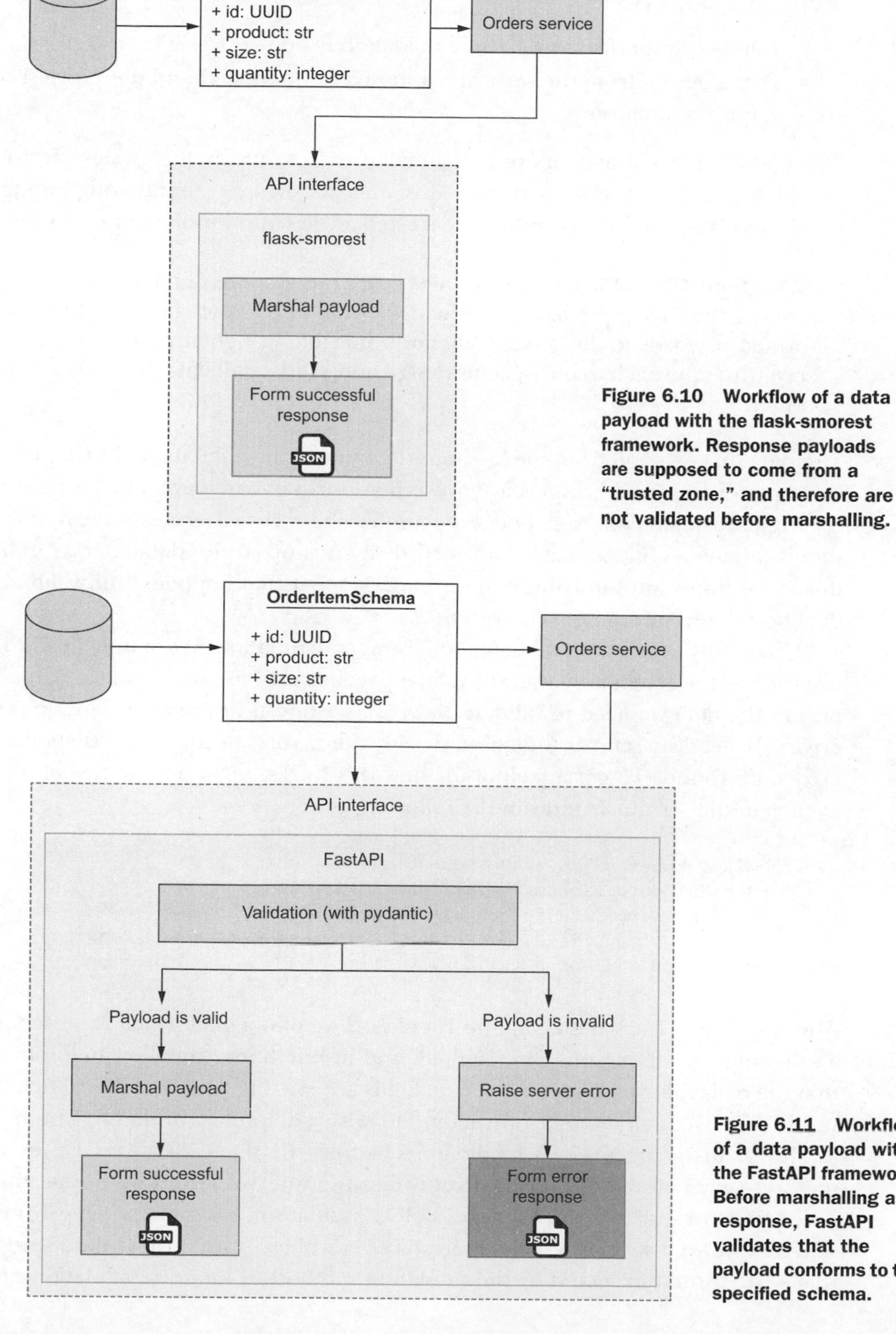

Figure 6.10 Workflow of a data payload with the flask-smorest framework. Response payloads are supposed to come from a "trusted zone," and therefore are not validated before marshalling.

Figure 6.11 Workflow of a data payload with the FastAPI framework. Before marshalling a response, FastAPI validates that the payload conforms to the specified schema.

rationales to justify why marshmallow doesn't perform validation before serialization (http://mng.bz/9Vwx):

- It improves performance, since validation is slow.
- Data coming from the server is supposed to be trusted and therefore shouldn't require validation.

The reasons the maintainers of marshmallow use to justify this design decision are fair. However, if you've worked with APIs, and websites in general, long enough, you know there's generally very little to be trusted, even from within your own system.

> **ZERO-TRUST APPROACH FOR ROBUST APIS** API integrations fail due to the server sending the wrong payload as much as they fail due to the client sending malformed payloads to the server. Whenever possible, it's good practice to take a zero-trust approach to our systems design and validate all data, regardless of its origin.

The data that we send from the kitchen API comes from a database. In chapter 7, we'll learn patterns and techniques to ensure that our database contains the right data in the right format. However, and even under the strictest access security measures, there's always a chance that malformed data ends up in the database. As unlikely as this is, we don't want to ruin the user experience if that happens, and validating our data before serializing helps us with that.

Thankfully, it's easy to validate data using marshmallow. We simply need to get an instance of the schema we want to validate against and use its `validate()` method to pass in the data we need to validate. `validate()` doesn't raise an exception if it finds errors. Instead, it returns a dictionary with the errors, or an empty dictionary if no errors are found. To get a feeling for how this works, open a Python shell by typing `python` in the terminal, and run the following code:

```
>>> from api.schemas import GetScheduledOrderSchema
>>> GetScheduledOrderSchema().validate({'id': 'asdf'})
{'order': ['Missing data for required field.'], 'scheduled': ['Missing
➥ data for required field.'], 'status': ['Missing data for required
➥ field.'], 'id': ['Not a valid UUID.']}
```

After importing the schema on line 1, in line 2 we pass a malformed representation of a schedule containing only the `id` field, and in line 3 marshmallow helpfully reports that the `order`, `scheduled`, and `status` fields are missing, and that the `id` field is not a valid UUID. We can use this information to raise a helpful error message in the server, as shown in listing 6.17. We validate schedules in the GET `/kitchen/schedules` method view before building and returning the query set, and we iterate the list of schedules to validate one at a time. Before validation, we make a deep copy of the schedule so that we can transform its `datetime` object into an ISO date string, since that's the format expected by the validation method. If we get a validation error, we raise marshmallow's `ValidationError` exception, which automatically formats the error message into an appropriate HTTP response.

Listing 6.17 Validating data before serialization

```
# file: kitchen/api/api.py

import copy
import uuid
from datetime import datetime

from flask.views import MethodView
from flask_smorest import Blueprint
from marshmallow import ValidationError     <- We import the ValidationError class from marshmallow.

...

@blueprint.route('/kitchen/schedules')
class KitchenSchedules(MethodView):

    @blueprint.arguments(GetKitchenScheduleParameters, location='query')
    @blueprint.response(status_code=200, schema=GetScheduledOrdersSchema)
    def get(self, parameters):
        for schedule in schedules:
            schedule = copy.deepcopy(schedule)
            schedule['scheduled'] = schedule['scheduled'].isoformat()
            errors = GetScheduledOrderSchema().validate(schedule)   <- We capture validation errors in the errors variable.
            if errors:
                raise ValidationError(errors)   <- If validate() finds errors, we raise a ValidationError exception.
        ...
        return {'schedules': query_set}
...
```

Please be aware that there are known issues with validation in marshmallow, especially when your models contain complex configurations for determining which fields should be serialized and which fields shouldn't (see https://github.com/marshmallow-code/marshmallow/issues/682 for additional information). Also, take into account that validation is known to be a slow process, so if you are handling large payloads, you may want to use a different tool to validate your data, validate only a subset of your data, or skip validation altogether. However, whenever possible, you're better off performing validation on your data.

This concludes the implementation of the functionality of the kitchen API. However, the API is still returning the same mock schedule across all endpoints. Before concluding this chapter, let's add a minimal implementation of an in-memory list of schedules so that we can make our API dynamic. This will allow us to verify that all endpoints are functioning as intended.

6.12 Implementing an in-memory list of schedules

In this section, we implement a simple in-memory representation of schedules so that we can obtain dynamic results from the API. By the end of this section, we'll be able to schedule orders, update them, and cancel them through the API. Because the schedules are managed as an in-memory list, any time the server is restarted, we'll lose information from our previous session. In the next chapter, we'll address this problem by adding a persistence layer to our service.

Our in-memory collection of schedules will be represented by a Python list, and we'll simply add and remove elements from it in the API layer. Listing 6.18 shows the changes that we need to make to kitchen/api/api.py to make this possible. We initialize an empty list and assign it to a variable named `schedules`. We also refactor our data validation code into an independent function named `validate_schedule()` so that we can reuse it in other view methods or functions. When a schedule payload arrives in the `KitchenSchedules`' `post()` method, we set the server-side attributes, such as the ID, the scheduled time, and the status. In the singleton endpoints, we look for the requested schedule by iterating the list of schedules and checking their IDs. If the requested schedule isn't found, we return a 404 response.

Listing 6.18 In-memory implementation of schedules

```
# file: kitchen/api/api.py

import copy
import uuid
from datetime import datetime

from flask import abort
...

schedules = []                          <- We initialize schedules as an empty list.


def validate_schedule(schedule):        <- We refactor our data validation code into a function.
    schedule = copy.deepcopy(schedule)
    schedule['scheduled'] = schedule['scheduled'].isoformat()
    errors = GetScheduledOrderSchema().validate(schedule)
    if errors:
        raise ValidationError(errors)


@blueprint.route('/kitchen/schedules')
class KitchenSchedules(MethodView):

    @blueprint.arguments(GetKitchenScheduleParameters, location='query')
    @blueprint.response(GetScheduledOrdersSchema)
    def get(self, parameters):
        ...

    @blueprint.arguments(ScheduleOrderSchema)
    @blueprint.response(status_code=201, schema=GetScheduledOrderSchema,)
```

```
    def post(self, payload):
        payload['id'] = str(uuid.uuid4())                    <-- We set the server-side
        payload['scheduled'] = datetime.utcnow()                 attributes of a schedule,
        payload['status'] = 'pending'                            such as the ID.
        schedules.append(payload)
        validate_schedule(payload)
        return payload


@blueprint.route('/kitchen/schedules/<schedule_id>')
class KitchenSchedule(MethodView):

    @blueprint.response(status_code=200, schema=GetScheduledOrderSchema)
    def get(self, schedule_id):
        for schedule in schedules:
            if schedule['id'] == schedule_id:
                validate_schedule(schedule)
                return schedule
        abort(404, description=f'Resource with ID {schedule_id} not found')
                                    # If a schedule isn't found, we return a 404 response.

    @blueprint.arguments(ScheduleOrderSchema)
    @blueprint.response(status_code=200, schema=GetScheduledOrderSchema)
    def put(self, payload, schedule_id):
        for schedule in schedules:
            if schedule['id'] == schedule_id:
                schedule.update(payload)      <-- When a user updates a schedule, we update the
                validate_schedule(schedule)       schedule's properties with the contents of the payload.
                return schedule
        abort(404, description=f'Resource with ID {schedule_id} not found')

    @blueprint.response(status_code=204)
    def delete(self, schedule_id):
        for index, schedule in enumerate(schedules):
            if schedule['id'] == schedule_id:
                schedules.pop(index)          <-- We remove the schedule from the list and return
                return                            an empty response.
        abort(404, description=f'Resource with ID {schedule_id} not found')


@blueprint.response(status_code=200, schema=GetScheduledOrderSchema)
@blueprint.route(
    '/kitchen/schedules/<schedule_id>/cancel', methods=['POST']
)
def cancel_schedule(schedule_id):
    for schedule in schedules:
        if schedule['id'] == schedule_id:
            schedule['status'] = 'cancelled'      <-- We set the status of the schedule to
            validate_schedule(schedule)               cancelled.
            return schedule
    abort(404, description=f'Resource with ID {schedule_id} not found')


@blueprint.response(status_code=200, schema=ScheduleStatusSchema)
@blueprint.route(
    '/kitchen/schedules/<schedule_id>/status', methods=['GET']
)
```

```
def get_schedule_status(schedule_id):
    for schedule in schedules:
        if schedule['id'] == schedule_id:
            validate_schedule(schedule)
            return {'status': schedule['status']}
    abort(404, description=f'Resource with ID {schedule_id} not found')
```

If you reload the Swagger UI and test the endpoints, you'll see you're now able to add schedules, update them, cancel them, list and filter them, get their details, and delete them. In the next section, you'll learn to override flask-smorest's dynamically generated API specification to make sure we serve our API design instead of our implementation.

6.13 Overriding flask-smorest's dynamically generated API specification

As we learned in section 6.4, API specifications dynamically generated from code are good for testing and visualizing our implementation, but to publish our API, we want to make sure we serve our API design document. To do that, we'll override flask-smorest's dynamically generated API documentation. First, we need to install PyYAML, which we'll use to load the API design document:

```
$ pipenv install pyyaml
```

We override the API object's `spec` property with a custom `APISpec` object. We also override `APISpec`'s `to_dict()` method so that it returns our API design document.

Listing 6.19 Overriding flask-smorest's dynamically generated API specification

```
# file: kitchen/app.py

from pathlib import Path

import yaml
from apispec import APISpec
from flask import Flask
from flask_smorest import Api

from api.api import blueprint
from config import BaseConfig


app = Flask(__name__)

app.config.from_object(BaseConfig)

kitchen_api = Api(app)

kitchen_api.register_blueprint(blueprint)

api_spec = yaml.safe_load((Path(__file__).parent / "oas.yaml").read_text())
spec = APISpec(
    title=api_spec["info"]["title"],
```

```
    version=api_spec["info"]["version"],
    openapi_version=api_spec["openapi"],
)
spec.to_dict = lambda: api_spec
kitchen_api.spec = spec
```

This concludes our journey through implementing REST APIs using Python. In the next chapter, we'll learn patterns to implement the rest of the service following best practices and useful design patterns. Things are spicing up!

Summary

- You can build REST APIs in Python using frameworks like FastAPI and flask-smorest, which have great ecosystems of tools and libraries that make it easier to build APIs.
- FastAPI is a modern API framework that makes it easier to build highly performant and robust REST APIs. FastAPI is built on top of Starlette and pydantic. Starlette is a highly performant asynchronous server framework, and pydantic is a data validation library that uses type hints to create validation rules.
- Flask-smorest is built on top of Flask and works as a Flask blueprint. Flask is one of Python's most popular frameworks, and by using flask-smorest you can leverage its rich ecosystem of libraries to make it easier to build APIs.
- FastAPI uses pydantic for data validation. Pydantic is a modern framework that uses type hints to define validation rules, which results in cleaner and easy-to-read code. By default, FastAPI validates both request and response payloads.
- Flask-smorest uses marshmallow for data validation. Marshmallow is a battle-tested framework that uses class fields to define validation rules. By default, flask-smorest doesn't validate response payloads, but you can validate responses by using marshmallow models' `validate()` method.
- With flask-smorest, you can use Flask's `MethodView` to create class-based views that represent URL paths. In a class-based view, you implement HTTP methods as methods of the class, such as `get()` and `post()`.
- The tolerant reader pattern follows Postel's law, which recommends being tolerant with errors in HTTP requests and validating response payloads. When designing your APIs, you must balance the benefits of the tolerant reader pattern with risk of integration failure due to bugs like typos.

7 Service implementation patterns for microservices

This chapter covers

- How hexagonal architecture helps us design loosely coupled services
- Implementing the business layer for a microservice and implementing database models using SQLAlchemy
- Using the repository pattern to decouple the data layer from the business layer
- Using the unit of work pattern to ensure the atomicity of all transactions and using the dependency inversion principle to build software that is resilient to changes
- Using the inversion of control principle and the dependency injection pattern to decouple components that are dependent on each other

In this chapter, we'll learn how to implement the business layer of a microservice. In previous chapters, we learned how to design and implement REST APIs. In those implementations, we used an in-memory representation of the resources managed by the service. We took that approach to keep the implementation simple and allow ourselves to focus on the API layer of the service.

In this chapter, we'll complete our implementation of the orders service by adding a business layer and a data layer. The business layer will implement the capabilities of the orders service, such as taking orders, processing their payments, or scheduling them for production. For some of these tasks, the orders service requires the collaboration of other services, and we'll learn useful patterns to handle those integrations.

The data layer will implement the data management capabilities of the service. The orders service owns and manages data about orders, so we'll implement a persistent storage solution and an interface to it. However, as a gateway to users regarding the life cycle of an order, the orders service also needs to fetch data from other services—for example, to keep track of the order during production and delivery. We'll also learn useful patterns to handle access to those services.

To articulate the implementation patterns of the service, we'll also cover elements of the architectural layout required to keep all pieces of our microservices loosely coupled. Loose coupling will help us ensure that we can change the implementation of a specific component without having to make changes to other components that rely on it. It'll also make our codebase generally more readable, maintainable, and testable. The code for this chapter is available in the ch07 directory in the repository provided with this book.

7.1 Hexagonal architectures for microservices

This chapter introduces the concept of hexagonal architecture and how we'll apply it to the design of the orders service. In chapter 2, we introduced the three-tier architecture pattern to help us organize the components of our application in a modular and loosely coupled way. In this section, we'll take this idea further by applying the concept of hexagonal architecture to our design.

In 2005, Alistair Cockburn introduced the concept of *hexagonal architecture,* also called the architecture of *ports and adapters,* as a way to help software developers structure their code into loosely coupled components.[1] As you can see in figure 7.1, the idea behind the hexagonal or ports-and-adapters architecture is that, in any application, there's a core piece of logic that implements the capabilities of a service, and around that core we "attach" *adapters* that help the core communicate with external components. For example, a web API is an adapter that helps the core communicate with web clients over the internet. The same goes for a database, which is simply an external component that helps a service persist data. We should be able to swap the

[1] Alistair Cockburn, "Hexagonal Architecture," https://alistair.cockburn.us/hexagonal-architecture/. You may be wondering why hexagonal and not pentagonal or heptagonal. As Alistair points out, it "is not a hexagon because the number six is important," but because it helps to visually highlight the idea of a core application communicating with external components through ports (the sides of the hexagon), and it allows us to represent the two main sides of an application: the public-facing side (web components, APIs, etc.) and the internal side (databases, third-party integrations, etc.).

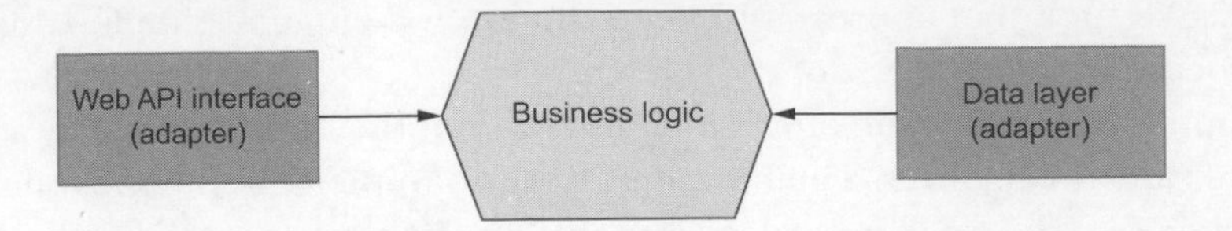

Figure 7.1 In hexagonal architecture, we distinguish a core layer in our application, the business layer, which implements the service's capabilities. Other components, such as a web API interface or a database, are considered adapters that depend on the business layer.

database if we want, and the service would still be the same. Therefore, the database is also an adapter.

How does this help us build loosely coupled services? Hexagonal architecture requires that we keep the core logic of the service and the logic for the adapters strictly separated. In other words, the logic that implements our web API layer shouldn't interfere with the implementation of the core business logic. And the same goes for the database: regardless of the technology we choose, and its design and idiosyncrasies, it shouldn't interfere with the core business logic. How do we achieve that? By building ports between the core business layer and the adapters. *Ports* are technology-agnostic interfaces that connect the business layer with the adapters. Later in this chapter, we'll learn some design patterns that will help us design those ports or interfaces.

When working out the relationship between the core business logic and the adapters, we apply the dependency inversion principle, which states that (see figure 7.2 for clarification)

- High-level modules shouldn't depend on low-level details. Instead, both should depend on abstractions, such as interfaces. For example, when saving data, we want to do it through an interface that doesn't require understanding of the specific implementation details of the database. Whether it's an SQL or a NoSQL database or a cache store, the interface should be the same.
- Abstractions shouldn't depend on details. Instead, details should depend on abstractions.[2] For example, when designing the interface between the business layer and the data layer, we want to make sure that the interface doesn't change based on the implementation details of the database. Instead, we make changes to the data layer to make it work with the interface. In other words, the data layer depends on the interface, not the other way around.

DEFINITION The *dependency inversion principle* encourages us to design our software against interfaces and to make sure we don't create dependencies between the low-level details of our components.

[2] Robert C. Martin, *Agile Software Development, Principles, Patterns, and Practices* (Prentice Hall, 2003), pp. 127–131.

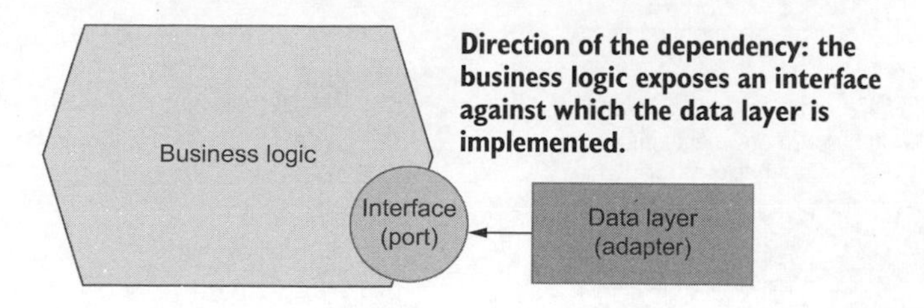
Direction of the dependency: the business logic exposes an interface against which the data layer is implemented.
Business logic
Interface (port)
Data layer (adapter)

Figure 7.2 We apply the dependency inversion principle to determine which components drive the changes. In hexagonal architecture, this means that our adapters will depend on the interface exposed by the core business layer.

The concept of dependency inversion often appears with the concepts of inversion of control and dependency injection. These are related but different concepts. As we'll see in section 7.5, the inversion of control principle consists of supplying code dependencies through the execution context (also called the inversion of control container). To supply such dependencies, we can use the dependency injection pattern, which we'll describe in section 7.5.

What does this mean in practice? It means we should make the adapters depend on the interface exposed by the core business logic. That is, it's okay for our API layer to know about the core business logic's interface, but it's not okay for our business logic to know specific details of our API layer or low-level details of the HTTP protocol. The same goes for the database: our data layer should know how the application works and how to accommodate the application's needs to our choice of storage technology, but the core business layer should know nothing specific about the database. Our business layer will expose an interface, and all other components will be implemented against it.

What exactly are we inverting with the dependency inversion principle? This principle inverts the way we think about software. Instead of the more conventional approach of building the low-level details of our software first, and then building interfaces on top of them, the dependency inversion principle encourages us to think of the interfaces first and then build the low-level details against them.[3]

As you can see in figure 7.3, when it comes to the orders service, we'll have a core package that implements the capabilities of the service. This includes the ability to process an order and its payment, to schedule its production, or to keep track of its progress. The core service package will expose interfaces for other components of the application. Another package implements the web API layer, and our API modules will use functions and classes from the business layer interface to serve the requests of our users. Another package implements the data layer, which knows how to interact with the database and return business objects for the core business layer.

[3] For an excellent introduction to the dependency inversion principle, see Eric Freeman, Elizabeth Robson, Kathy Sierra, and Bert Bates, *Head First Design Patterns* (O'Reilly, 2014), pp. 141–143.

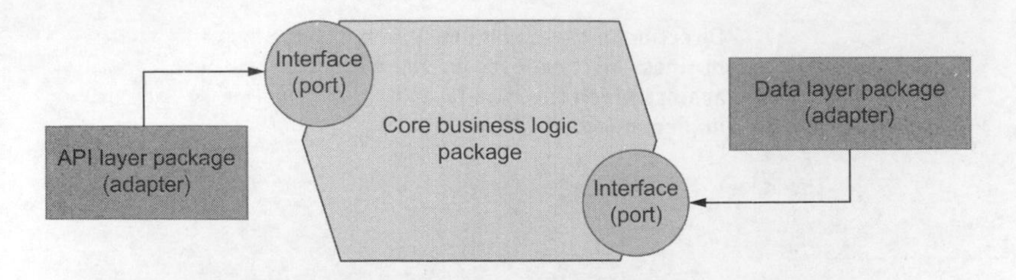

Figure 7.3 The orders service consist of three packages: the core business logic, which implements the capabilities of the service; an API layer, which allows clients to interact with the service over HTTP; and a data layer, which allows the service to interact with the database. The core business logic exposes interfaces against which the API layer and the data layer are implemented.

Now that we know how we are going to structure the application, it's time to start implementing it! In the next section, we'll set up the environment to start working on the service.

7.2 Setting up the environment and the project structure

In this section, we set up the environment to work on the orders service and lay out the high-level structure of the project. As in previous chapters, we'll use Pipenv to manage our dependencies. Run the following commands to set up a Pipenv environment and activate it:

```
$ pipenv --three
$ pipenv shell
```

We'll install our dependencies as we need in the following sections. Or if you prefer, copy the Pipfile and Pipfile.lock files from the GitHub repository under the ch07 folder and run `pipenv install`.

Our service implementation will live under a folder named orders, so go ahead and create it. To reinforce the separation of concerns between the core business layer and the API and database adapters, we'll implement each of them in different directories, as shown in figure 7.4. The business layer will live under orders/orders_service.

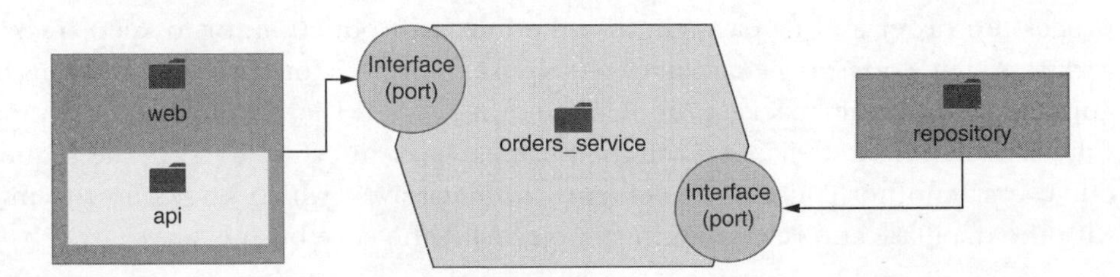

Figure 7.4 To reinforce the separation of concerns, we implement each layer of the application in different directories: orders_service for the core business layer; repository for the data layer; and web/api for the API layer.

Since the API layer is a web component, it will live under orders/web, which contains web adapters for the orders service. In this case, we are only including one type of web adapter, namely, a REST API, but nothing prevents you from adding a web adapter that returns dynamically rendered content from the server, as you would in a more traditional Django application.

The data layer will live under orders/repository. "Repository" might look like an unlikely name for our data layer, but we're choosing this name because we'll implement the repository pattern to interface with our data. This concept will become clearer in section 7.4. In chapters 2 and 6 we covered the implementation of the API layer, so go ahead and copy over the files from the GitHub repository under ch07/order/web into your local directory. Notice that the API implementation has been adapted for this chapter.

Listing 7.1 High-level structure of the orders service

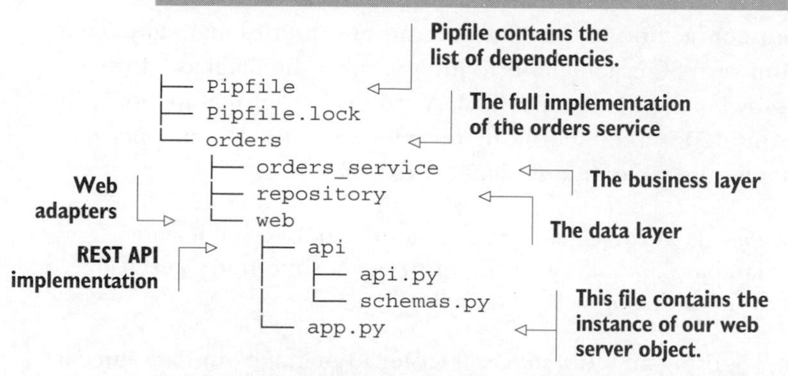

Since the folder structure has changed, the path to our FastAPI application object has also changed location, and therefore the command to run the API server is now

```
$ uvicorn orders.web.app:app --reload
```

Due to the new folder structure, a few import paths and file locations have also changed. For the full list of changes, please refer to the ch07 folder under the GitHub repository for this book.

Now that our project is set up and ready to go, it's time to get on with the implementation. Move on to the next section to learn how to add database models to the service!

7.3 Implementing the database models

In the previous section, we learned how we'll structure our project into three different layers: the core business layer, the API layer, and the data layer. This structure reinforces the separation of concerns among each layer, as recommended by the hexagonal architecture pattern that we learned in section 7.1. Now that we know how we'll structure our code, it's time to focus on the implementation. In this section, we'll define the database models for the orders service; that is, we'll design the database tables and their fields. We start our implementation from the database since it will facilitate the rest of the discussion in this chapter. In a real-world context, you might start with the business layer, mocking the data layer and iterating back and forth between each layer until you're done with the implementation. Just bear in mind that the linear approach we take in this chapter is not meant to reflect the actual development process, but is instead intended to illustrate concepts that we want to explain.

To keep things simple in this chapter, we'll use SQLite as our database engine. SQLite is a file-based relational database system. To use it, we don't need to set up and run a server, as we would with PostgreSQL or MySQL, and there's no configuration needed to start using it. Python's core library has built-in support for interfacing with SQLite, which makes it a suitable choice for quick prototyping and experimentation before we are ready to move on to a production-ready database system.

We won't manage our connection to the database and our queries manually. That is, we won't be writing our own SQL statements to interact with the database. Instead, we'll use SQLAlchemy—by far the most popular ORM (object relational mapper) in the Python ecosystem. An ORM is a framework that implements the data mapper pattern, which allows us to map the tables in our database to objects.

DEFINITION A *data mapper* is an object wrapper around database tables and rows. It encapsulates database operations in the form of class methods, and it allows us to access data fields through class attributes.[4]

As you can see in figure 7.5, using an ORM makes it easier to manage our data since it gives us a class interface to the tables in the database. This allows us to leverage the benefits of object-oriented programming, including the ability to add custom methods and properties to our database models that enhance their functionality and encapsulate their behavior.

Over time, our database models will change, and we need to be able to keep track of those changes. Changing the schema of our database is called a *migration*. As our database evolves, we'll accumulate more and more migrations. We need to keep track of our migrations, since they allow us to reliably replicate the database schema in different environments and to roll out database changes to production with confidence. To manage this complex task, we'll use Alembic. Alembic is a schema migration library that integrates seamlessly with SQLAlchemy.

Let's start by installing both libraries by running the following command:

```
$ pipenv install sqlalchemy alembic
```

Before we start working on our database models, let's set up Alembic. (For additional help, please check out my video tutorial about setting up Alembic with SQLAlchemy

[4] Martin Fowler, *Patterns of Enterprise Architecture* (Addison-Wesley, 2003), pp. 165–181.

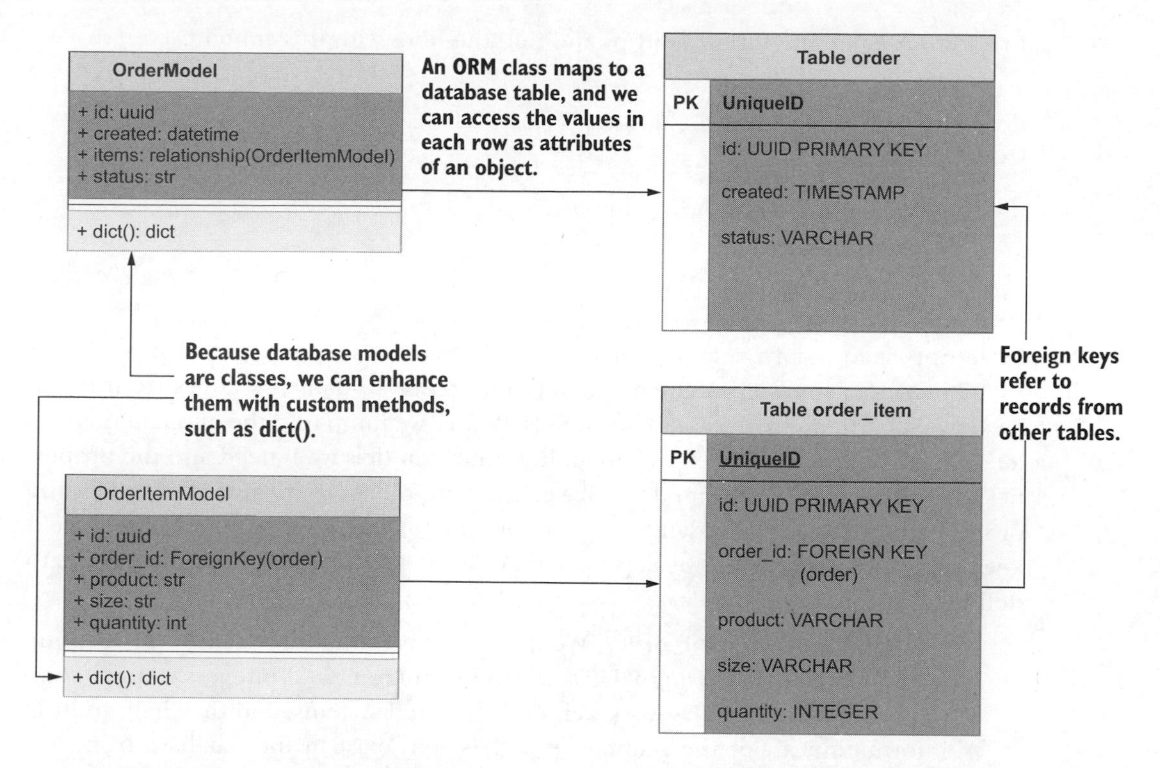

Figure 7.5 Using an ORM, we can implement our data models as classes that map to database tables. Since the models are classes, we can enhance them with custom methods to add new functionality.

at https://youtu.be/nt5sSr1A_qw.) Run the following command to create a migrations folder, which will contain the history of all migrations in our database:

```
$ alembic init migrations
```

This creates a folder called migrations, which comes with a configuration file called env.py and a versions/ directory. The versions/ directory will contain the migration files. The setup command also creates a configuration file called alembic.ini. To make Alembic work with an SQLite database, open alembic.ini, find a line that contains a declaration for the `sqlalchemy.url` variable, and replace it with the following content:

```
sqlalchemy.url = sqlite:///orders.db
```

COMMIT THE FILES GENERATED BY ALEMBIC The migrations folder contains all the information required to manage our database schema changes, so you should commit this folder, as well as alembic.ini. This will allow you to replicate the database setup in new environments.

In addition, open migrations/env.py and find the lines with this content:[5]

```
# from myapp import mymodel
# target_metadata = mymodel.Base.metadata
target_metadata = None
```

Replace them with the following content:

```
from orders.repository.models import Base
target_metadata = Base.metadata
```

By setting `target_metadata` to our `Base` model's `metadata`, we make it possible for Alembic to load our SQLAlchemy models and generate database tables from them. Next, we'll implement our database models. Before we jump into the implementation, let's pause for a moment to think about how many models we'll need and the properties we should expect each model to have. The core object of the orders service is the order. Users place, pay, update, or cancel orders. Orders have a life cycle, and we'll keep track of it through a `status` property. We'll use the following list of properties to define our order model:

- *ID*—Unique ID for the order. We'll give it the format of a Universally Unique Identifier (UUID). Using UUIDs instead of incremental integers is quite common these days. UUIDs work well in distributed systems, and they help to hide information about the number of orders that exist in the database from our users.
- *Creation date*—When the order was placed.
- *Items*—The list of items included in the order and the amount of each product. Since an order can have any number of items linked to it, we'll use a different model for items, and we'll create a one-to-many relationship between the order and the items.
- *Status*—The status of the order throughout the system. An order can have the following statuses:
  - *Created*—The order has been placed.
  - *Paid*—The order has been successfully paid.
  - *Progress*—The order is being produced in the kitchen.
  - *Cancelled*—The order has been cancelled.
  - *Dispatched*—The order is being delivered to the user.
  - *Delivered*—The order has been delivered to the user.
- *Schedule ID*—The ID of the order in the kitchen service. This ID is created by the kitchen service after scheduling the order for production, and we'll use it to keep track of its progress in the kitchen.

[5] The shape and format of this file may change over time, but for reference, at the time of this writing, those lines are 18–20.

- *Delivery ID*—The ID of the order in the delivery service. This ID is created by the delivery service after scheduling it for dispatch, and we'll use it to keep track of its progress during delivery.

When users place an order, they add any number of items to the order. Each item contains information about the product selected by the user, the size of the product, and the amount of it that the user wishes to purchase. There's a one-to-many relationship between orders and items, and therefore we'll implement a model for items and link them with a foreign key relationship. The item model will have the following list of attributes:

- *ID*—A unique identifier for the item in UUID format.
- *Order ID*—A foreign key representing the ID of the order the item belongs to. This is what allows us to connect items and orders that belong together.
- *Product*—The product selected by the user.
- *Size*—The size of the product.
- *Quantity*—The amount of the product that the user wishes to purchase.

Our SQLAlchemy models will live under the orders/repository folder, which we created to encapsulate our data layer, in a file called orders/repository/models.py. We'll use these classes to interface with the database and rely on SQLAlchemy to translate these models into their corresponding database tables behind the scenes. Listing 7.2 shows the definition of the database models for the orders service. First, we create a declarative base model by using SQLALchemy's `declarative_base()` function. The declarative base model is a class that can map ORM classes to database tables and columns, and therefore all our database models must inherit from it. We map class attributes to specific database columns by setting them to instances of SQLAlchemy's `Column` class.

To map an attribute to another model, we use SQLAlchemy's `relationship()` function. In listing 7.2, we use `relationship()` to create a one-to-many relationship between `OrderModel`'s `items` attribute and the `OrderItemModel` model. This means that we can access the list of items in an order through `OrderModel`'s `items` attribute. Each item also maps to the order it belongs to through the `order_id` property, which is defined as a foreign key column. Furthermore, `relationship()`'s `backref` argument allows us to access the full order object from an item directly through a property called `order`.

Since we want our IDs to be in UUID format, we create a function that SQLAlchemy can use to generate the value. If we later switch to a database engine with built-in support for generating UUID values, we'll leave it to the database to generate the IDs. Each database model is enhanced with a `dict()` method, which allows us to output the properties of a record in dictionary format. Since we'll use this method to translate database models to business objects, the `dict()` method only returns the properties relevant to the business layer.

Listing 7.2 SQLAlchemy models for the orders service

```
# file: orders/repository/models.py

import uuid
from datetime import datetime

from sqlalchemy import Column, Integer, String, ForeignKey, DateTime
from sqlalchemy.ext.declarative import declarative_base
from sqlalchemy.orm import relationship

Base = declarative_base()    # We create our declarative base model.


def generate_uuid():    # Custom function to create random UUIDs for our models
    return str(uuid.uuid4())


class OrderModel(Base):    # All our models must inherit from Base.
    __tablename__ = 'order'    # Name of the table that maps to this model

    id = Column(String, primary_key=True, default=generate_uuid)    # Every class property maps to a database column by using the Column class.
    items = relationship('OrderItemModel', backref='order')    # We use relationship() to create a one-to-many relationship with the OrderItemModel model.
    status = Column(String, nullable=False, default='created')
    created = Column(DateTime, default=datetime.utcnow)
    schedule_id = Column(String)
    delivery_id = Column(String)

    def dict(self):    # Custom method to render our objects as Python dictionaries
        return {
            'id': self.id,
            'items': [item.dict() for item in self.items],    # We call dict() on each item to get its dictionary representation.
            'status': self.status,
            'created': self.created,
            'schedule_id': self.schedule_id,
            'delivery_id': self.delivery_id,
        }


class OrderItemModel(Base):
    __tablename__ = 'order_item'

    id = Column(String, primary_key=True, default=generate_uuid)
    order_id = Column(Integer, ForeignKey('order.id'))
    product = Column(String, nullable=False)
    size = Column(String, nullable=False)
    quantity = Column(Integer, nullable=False)

    def dict(self):
        return {
            'id': self.id,
            'product': self.product,
            'size': self.size,
            'quantity': self.quantity
        }
```

To apply the models to the database, run the following command from the ch07 directory:

```
$ PYTHONPATH=`pwd` alembic revision --autogenerate -m "Initial migration"
```

This will create a migration file under migrations/versions. We set the `PYTHONPATH` environment variable to the current directory using the `pwd` command so that Python looks for our models relative to this directory. You should commit your migration files and keep them in your version control system (e.g., a Git repository) since they'll allow you to re-create your database for different environments. You can look in those files to understand the database operations that SQLAlchemy will perform to apply the migrations. To apply the migrations and create the schemas for these models in the database, run the following command:

```
$ PYTHONPATH=`pwd` alembic upgrade heads
```

This will create the desired schemas in our database. Now that our database models are implemented and our database contains the desired schemas, it's time to move on to the next step. Go to the next section to learn about the repository pattern!

7.4 Implementing the repository pattern for data access

In the previous section, we learned to design the database models for the orders service and to manage changes to the database schema through migrations. With our database models ready, we can interact with the database to create orders and manage them. Now we have to decide how we make the data accessible to the business layer. In this section, we'll first discuss different strategies to connect the business layer with the data layer, and we'll learn what the repository pattern is and how we can use it to create an interface between the business layer and the database. Then we'll move on to implementing it.

7.4.1 The case for the repository pattern: What is it, and why is it useful?

In this section, we discuss different strategies for interfacing with the database from the business layer, and we introduce the repository pattern as a strategy that helps us decouple the business layer from the implementation details of the database.

As shown in figure 7.6, a common strategy to enable interactions between the business layer and the database is to use the database models directly within the business layer. Our database models already contain data about the orders, so we could enhance them with methods that implement business capabilities. This is called the *active record pattern*, which represents objects that carry both data and domain logic.[6] This pattern

[6] Fowler, *Patterns of Enterprise Architecture*, pp. 160–164.

is useful when we have one-to-one mapping between service capabilities and database operations, or when we don't need the collaboration of multiple domains.

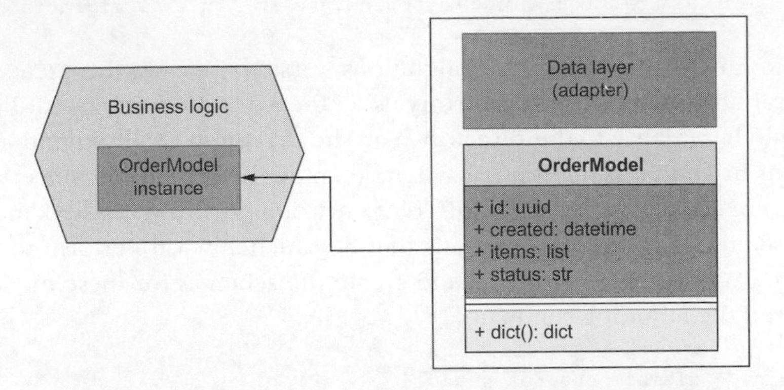

Figure 7.6 A common approach to enable interactions between the data layer and the business layer is by using the database models directly in the business layer.

This approach works for simple cases; however, it couples the implementation of the business layer to the database and to the ORM framework of choice. What happens if we want to change the ORM framework later on, or if we want to switch to a different data storage technology that doesn't involve SQL? In those cases, we'd have to make changes to our business layer. This breaks the principles we introduced in section 7.1. Remember, the database is an adapter that the orders service uses to persist data, and the implementation details of the database should not leak into the business logic. Instead, data access will be encapsulated by our data access layer.

To decouple the business layer from the data layer, we'll use the repository pattern. This pattern gives us an in-memory list interface of our data. This means that we can get, add, or delete orders from the list, and the repository will take care of translating these operations into database-specific commands. Using the repository pattern means the data layer exposes a consistent interface to the business layer to interact with the database, regardless of the database technology we use to store our data. Whether we use an SQL database such as PostgreSQL, a NoSQL database like MongoDB, or an in-memory cache such as Redis, the repository pattern's interface will remain the same and will encapsulate whichever specific operations are required to interact with the database. Figure 7.7 illustrates how the repository pattern helps us invert the dependency between the data layer and the business layer.

DEFINITION The *repository pattern* is a software development pattern that provides an in-memory list interface to our data store. This helps us decouple our components from the low-level implementation details of the database. The repository takes care of managing interactions with the database and provides

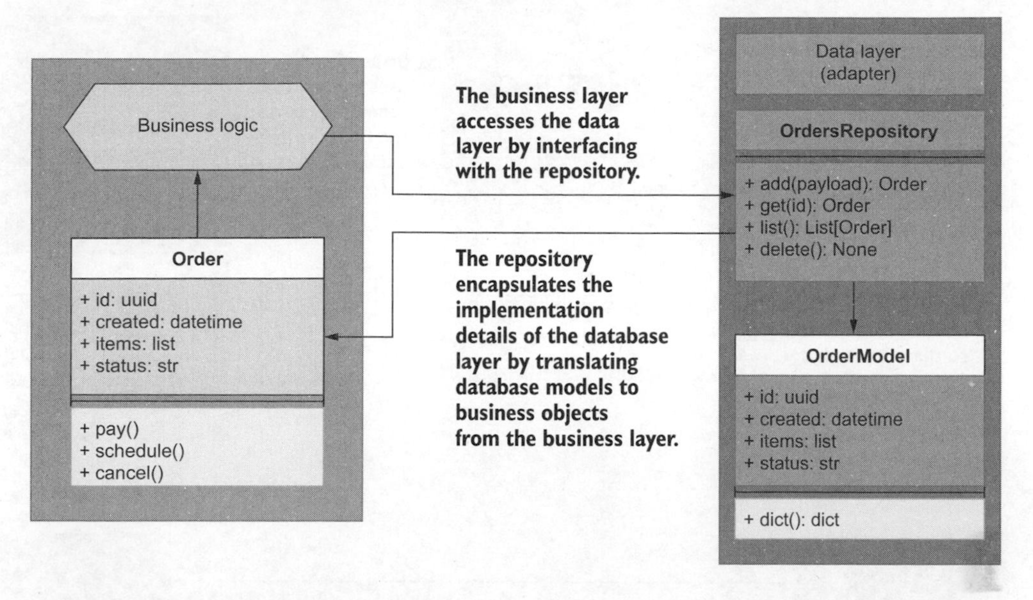

Figure 7.7 The repository pattern encapsulates the implementation details of the data layer by exposing an in-memory list interface to the business layer, and it translates database models to business objects.

a consistent interface to our components, regardless of the database technology used. This allows us to change the database system without having to change our core business logic.

Now that we know how we can use the repository pattern to allow the business layer to interface with the database while decoupling its implementation from low-level details of the database, we'll learn to implement the repository pattern.

7.4.2 Implementing the repository pattern

How do we implement the repository pattern? We can use different approaches to this as long as we meet the following constraint: none of the operations carried out by the repository can be committed by the repository. What does this mean? It means that when we add an order object to the repository, the repository will add the order to a database session, but it will not commit the changes. Instead, it will be the responsibility of the consumer of `OrdersService` (i.e., the API layer) to commit the changes. Figure 7.8 illustrates this process.

Why can't we commit database changes within the repository? First, because the repository acts just like an in-memory list representation of our data, and as such it doesn't have a concept of database sessions and transactions; second, because the repository is not the right place to execute a database transaction. Instead, the context in which the repository is invoked provides the right context for executing database

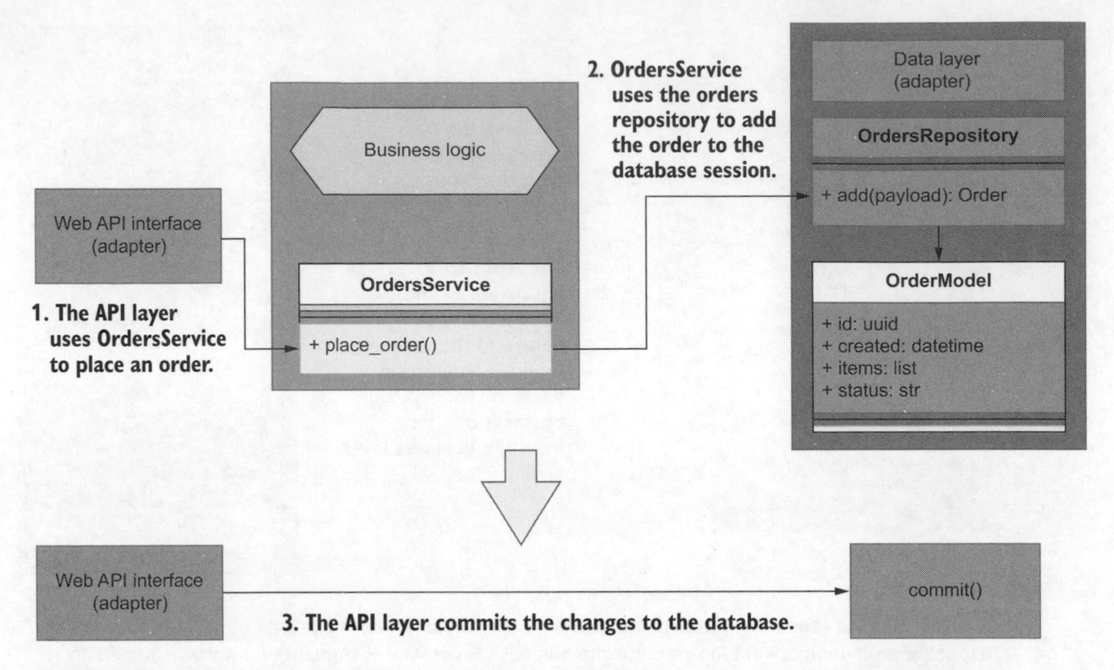

Figure 7.8 **Using the repository pattern, the API layer uses the `place_order()` capability of `OrdersService` to place an order. To place the order, `OrdersService` interfaces with the orders repository to add the order to the database. Finally, the API layer must commit the changes to persist them in the database.**

transactions. In many cases, our applications will execute multiple operations that involve one or more repositories and also call to other services. For example, figure 7.9 shows the number of operations involved in processing a payment:

1. The API layer receives the request from the user and uses the `OrdersService`'s `pay_order()` method to process the request.
2. `OrdersService` talks to the payments service to process the payment.
3. If the payment is successful, `OrdersService` schedules the order with the kitchen service.
4. `OrdersService` updates the state of the order in the database using the orders repository.
5. If all the previous operations were successful, the API layer commits the transaction in the database; otherwise, it rolls back the changes.

These steps can be taken synchronously, one after the other, or asynchronously, in no specific order, but regardless of the approach, all steps must succeed or fail all together. As the unit of execution context, it's the responsibility of the API layer to ensure that all changes are committed or rolled back as required. In section 7.6, we'll learn how exactly the API layer controls the database session and commits the transactions.

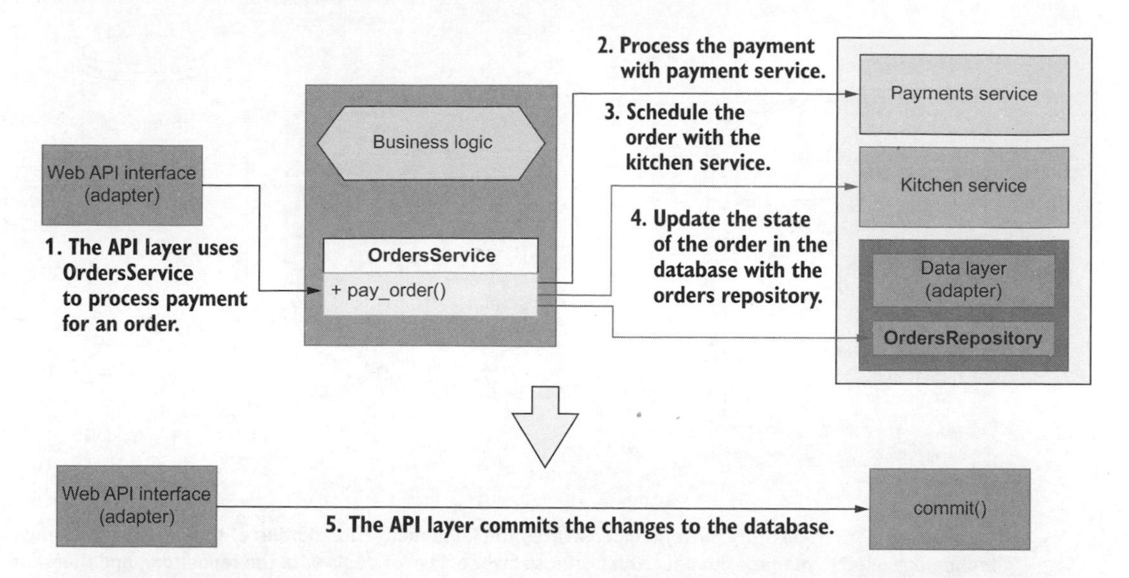

Figure 7.9 In some situations, `OrdersService` has to interface with multiple repositories or services to perform an operation. In this example, `OrdersService` interfaces with the payments service to process a payment, then with the kitchen service to schedule the order for production, and finally updates the status of the order through the orders repository. All these operations must succeed or fail together, and it's the responsibility of the API layer to commit or rollback accordingly.

At a minimum, a repository pattern implementation consists of a class that exposes a `get()` and an `add()` method, respectively, to be able to retrieve and add objects to the repository. For our purposes, we'll also implement the following methods: `update()`, `delete()`, and `list()`. This will simplify the CRUD interface of the repository.

The following question bears some consideration in this context: when we fetch data through the repository, what kind of object should the repository return? In many implementations, you'll see repositories returning instances of the database models (i.e., the classes defined in orders/repository/models.py). We won't do that in this chapter. Instead, we'll return objects that represent orders from the business layer domain. Why is it a bad idea to return instances of the database models through the repository? Because it defeats the purpose of the repository, which is to decouple the business layer from the data layer. Remember, we may want to change our persistence storage technology or our ORM framework. If that happens, the database classes we implemented in section 7.2 will no longer exist, and there's no guarantee that a new framework would allow us to return objects with the same interfaces. For this reason, we don't want to couple our business layer with them. Figure 7.10 illustrates the relationship between the business layer and the orders repository.

Our orders repository implementation will live under orders/repository/orders_repository.py. Listing 7.3 shows the implementation of the orders repository. It takes one required argument that represents the database session. Objects are added and deleted from the database session. The `add()` and `update()` methods take payloads

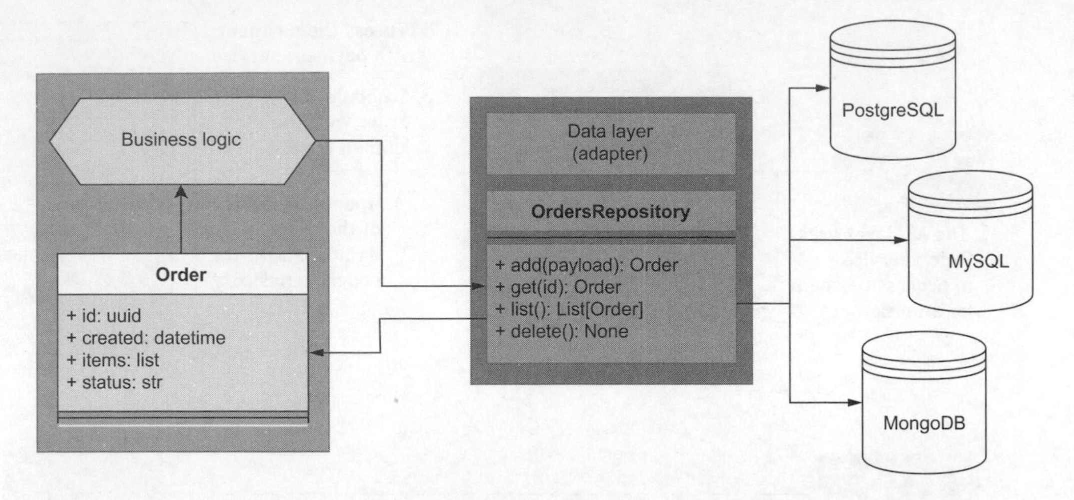

Figure 7.10 The repository pattern encapsulates the implementation details of the persistent storage technology used to manage our data. Our business layer only ever deals with the repository, and therefore we are free to change our persistent storage solution to a different technology without affecting our core application implementation.

that represent orders in the form of a Python dictionary. Our payloads are fairly simple, so a dictionary is sufficient here, but if we have more complex payloads, we should consider using objects instead.

With the exception of the `delete()` method, all methods of the repository return `Order` objects from the business layer (see section 7.5 for `Order`'s implementation details). To create instances of `Order`, we pass dictionary representations of the SQLAlchemy models using our custom `dict()` method from listing 7.2. In the `add()` method, we also include a pointer to the actual SQLAlchemy model through `Order`'s `order_` parameter. As we'll see in section 7.5, this pointer will help us access the order's ID after committing the database transaction.

`OrdersRepository`'s `get()`, `update()`, and `delete()` methods use the same logic to pull a record before returning, updating, or deleting it, so we define a common `_get()` method that knows how to obtain a record given an ID and optional filters. We fetch the record using the `first()` method of SQLAlchemy's query object. `first()` returns an instance of the record if it exists, and otherwise it returns `None`. Alternatively, it's also possible to use the `one()` method, which raises an error if the record doesn't exist. `_get()` returns a database record, so it's not meant to be used by the service layer, and we signal that by prefixing the method's name with an underscore.

The `list()` method accepts a `limit` parameter and optional filters. We build our query dynamically using SQLAlchemy's `query` object. We also leverage SQLAlchemy's `filter_by()` method to include additional filters in the query as keyword arguments, and we limit the query results by adding the `limit` parameter. Finally, we transform the database records into `Order` objects for consumption by the business layer by using the `dict()` method we implemented in listing 7.2.

The repository implementation is tightly coupled to the methods of SQLAlchemy's `Session` object, but it also encapsulates these details, and to the business layer the repository appears as an interface to which we submit IDs and payloads, and we get `Order` objects in return. This is the point of the repository: to encapsulate and hide the implementation details of the data layer from the business layer. This means that if we switch to a different ORM framework, or to a different database system, we only need to make changes to the repository.

Listing 7.3 Orders repository

```
# file: orders/repository/orders_repository.py

from orders.orders_service.orders import Order
from orders.repository.models import OrderModel, OrderItemModel


class OrdersRepository:
    def __init__(self, session):
        self.session = session

    def add(self, items):
        record = OrderModel(
            items=[OrderItemModel(**item) for item in items]
        )
        self.session.add(record)
        return Order(**record.dict(), order_=record)

    def _get(self, id_):
        return (
            self.session.query(OrderModel)
            .filter(OrderModel.id == str(id_))
            .filter_by(**filters)
            .first()
        )

    def get(self, id_):
        order = self._get(id_)
        if order is not None:
            return Order(**order.dict())

    def list(self, limit=None, **filters):
        query = self.session.query(OrderModel)
        if 'cancelled' in filters:
            cancelled = filters.pop('cancelled')
            if cancelled:
                query = query.filter(OrderModel.status == 'cancelled')
            else:
                query = query.filter(OrderModel.status != 'cancelled')
        records = query.filter_by(**filters).limit(limit).all()
        return [Order(**record.dict()) for record in records]
```

Annotations:
- The repository's initializer method requires a session object.
- When creating a record for an order, we also create a record for each item in the order.
- We add the record to the session object.
- We return an instance of the Order class.
- Generic method to retrieve a record by ID
- We fetch the record using SQLAlchemy's first() method.
- We retrieve a record using _get().
- If the order exists, we return an Order object.
- list() accepts a limit parameter and other optional filters.
- We build our query dynamically.
- We filter by whether an order is cancelled using the SQLAlchemy's filter() method.
- We return a list of Order objects.

```
    def update(self, id_, **payload):
        record = self._get(id_)
        if 'items' in payload:                          <-- To update an order, we first delete the
            for item in record.items:                       items linked to the order and then create
                self.session.delete(item)                   new items from the supplied payload.
            record.items = [
                OrderItemModel(**item) for item in payload.pop('items')
            ]
        for key, value in payload.items():              <-- We dynamically update the
            setattr(record, key, value)                     database object using the
        return Order(**record.dict())                       setattr() function.

    def delete(self, id_):
        self.session.delete(self._get(id_))             <-- To delete a record,
                                                            we call SQLAlchemy's
                                                            delete() method.
```

This completes the implementation of our data layer. We have implemented a persistent storage solution with the help of SQLAlchemy, and we have encapsulated the details of this solution with the help of the repository pattern. It's now time to work on the business layer and see how it will interact with the repository!

7.5 Implementing the business layer

We've done a lot of work designing the database models for the orders service and using the repository pattern to build the interface to the data. It's now time to focus on the business layer! In this section, we'll implement the business layer of the orders service. That's the core of the hexagon we introduced in section 7.1 and illustrated in figure 7.1, which is reproduced here as figure 7.11 for your convenience. The business layer implements the service's capabilities. What are the business capabilities of the orders service? From the analysis in chapter 3 (section 3.4.2), we know that the orders service allows users of the platform to place their orders and manage them.

Figure 7.11 In hexagonal architecture, we distinguish a core layer in our application, the business layer, which implements the service's capabilities. Other components, such as a web API interface or a database, are considered adapters that depend on the business layer.

As illustrated in figure 7.12, the orders service manages the life cycle of an order through integrations with other services. The following list describes the capabilities of the orders service and highlights integrations with other services (refer to figure 7.9 for further clarification):

- *Place orders*—Creates a record of an order in the system. The order won't be scheduled in the kitchen until the user pays for it.
- *Process payments*—Processes payment for an order with the help of the payments service. If the payments service confirms the payment is successful, the orders service schedules the order for production with the kitchen service.
- *Update orders*—Users can update their order any time to add or remove items from it. To confirm a change, a new payment must be made and processed with the help of the payments service.
- *Cancel orders*—Users can cancel their orders anytime. Depending on the status of the order, the orders service will communicate with the kitchen or the delivery service to cancel the order.
- *Schedule order for production in the kitchen*—After payment, the orders service schedules the order for production in the kitchen with the help of the kitchen service.
- *Keep track of orders' progress*—Users can keep track of their orders' status through the orders service. Depending on the status of the order, the orders service checks with the kitchen or the delivery service to get updated information about the state of the order.

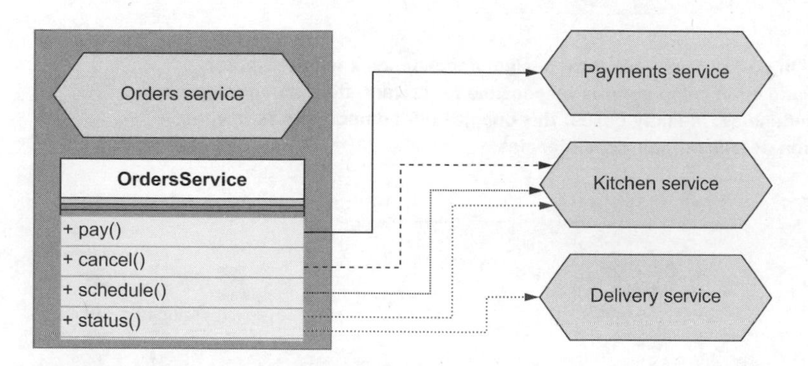

Figure 7.12 In order to perform some of its functions, the orders service needs to interact with orders services. For example, to process payments, it must interact with the payments service, and to schedule an order for production, it must interact with the kitchen service.

What's the best way to model these actions in our business layer? We can use different approaches, but to make it easy for other components to interact with the business layer, we'll expose a single unified interface through a class called `OrdersService`. We'll define this class under orders/orders_service/orders_service.py. To fulfill its duties, `OrdersService` uses the orders repository to interface with the database. We could let `OrdersService` import and initialize the orders repository as in the following code:

```
from repository.orders_repository import OrdersRepository

class OrdersService:
    def __init__(self):
        self.repository = OrdersRepository()
```

However, doing this would place too much responsibility on the orders service since it would need to know how to configure the orders repository. It would also tightly couple the implementation of the orders repository and the orders service, and we wouldn't be able to use different repositories if we needed to. As you can see in figures 7.13 and 7.14, a better approach is to use dependency injection in combination with the inversion of control principle.

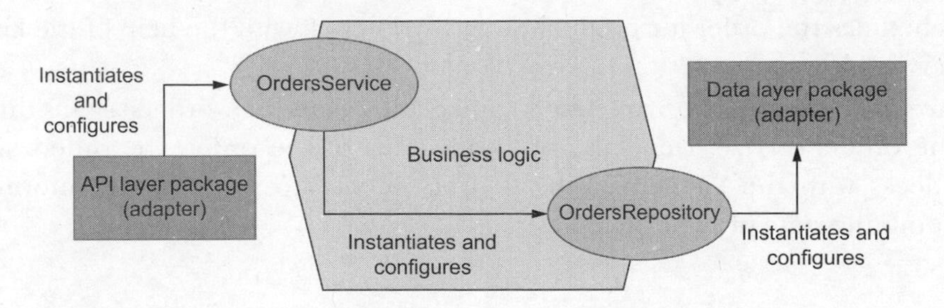

Figure 7.13 In conventional software design, dependencies follow a linear relationship, and each component is responsible for instantiating and configuring its own dependencies. In many cases, this couples our components to low-level implementation details in their dependencies.

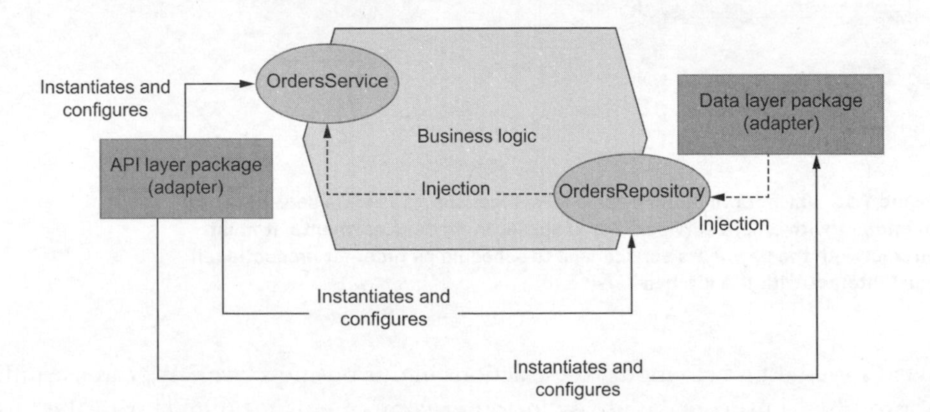

Figure 7.14 With inversion of control, we decouple components from their dependencies by supplying them at runtime using methods such as dependency injection. In this approach, it's the responsibility of the context to provide correctly configured instances of the dependencies. The solid lines show relationships of dependency, while the dotted lines show how dependencies are injected.

DEFINITION *Inversion of control* is a software development principle that encourages us to decouple our components from their dependencies by supplying them at runtime. This allows us to control how the dependencies are supplied. One popular pattern to accomplish this is dependency injection. The context in which the dependencies are instantiated and supplied is called an *inversion of control container*. In the orders service, a suitable inversion of control container is the request object since most operations are specific to the context of a request.

The inversion of control principle states that we should decouple the dependencies in our code by letting the execution context supply those dependencies at runtime. This means that, instead of letting the orders service import and instantiate the orders repository, we should supply the repository at runtime. How do we do that? We can use different patterns to supply dependencies to our code, but one of the most popular, due to its simplicity and effectiveness, is dependency injection.

DEFINITION *Dependency injection* is a software development pattern whereby we supply code dependencies at runtime. This helps us decouple our components from the specific implementation details of the code they depend on, since they don't need to know how to configure and instantiate their dependencies.

To make the orders repository injectable into the orders service, we parameterize it:

```
class OrdersService:
    def __init__(self, orders_repository):
        self.orders_repository = orders_repository
```

It's now the responsibility of the caller to instantiate and configure the orders repository correctly. As you can see in figure 7.11, this has a very desirable outcome: depending on the context, we can supply different implementations of the repository or add different configurations. This makes the orders service easier to use in different contexts.[7]

Listing 7.4 shows the interface exposed by `OrdersService`. The class initializer takes an instance of the orders repository as a parameter to make it injectable. As per the inversion of control principle, when we integrate `OrdersService` with the API layer, it will be the responsibility of the API to get a valid instance of the orders repository and pass it to `OrdersService`. This approach is convenient, since it allows us to swap repositories at will when necessary, and it'll make it very easy to write our tests in the next chapter.

[7] For more details on the inversion of control principle and the dependency injection pattern, see Martin Fowler, "Inversion of Control Containers and the Dependency Injection pattern," https://martinfowler.com/articles/injection.html.

Listing 7.4 Interface of the `OrdersService` class

```
# file: orders/orders_service/orders_service.py

class OrdersService:
    def __init__(self, orders_repository):
        self.orders_repository = orders_repository

    def place_order(self, items):
        pass

    def get_order(self, order_id):
        pass

    def update_order(self, order_id, items):
        pass

    def list_orders(self, **filters):
        pass

    def pay_order(self, order_id):
        pass

    def cancel_order(self, order_id):
        pass
```

Some of the actions listed under `OrdersService`, such as payment or scheduling, take place at the level of individual orders. Since orders contain data, it will be useful to have a class that represents orders and has methods to perform tasks related to an order. Within the context of the orders service, an order is a core object of the orders domain. In domain-driven design (DDD), we call these objects *domain objects*. These are the objects returned by the orders repository. We'll implement our `Order` class under orders/orders_service/orders.py. Listing 7.5 shows a preliminary implementation of the `Order` class.

In addition to the `Order` class, listing 7.5 also provides an `OrderItem` class that represents each of the items in an order. We'll use the `Order` class to represent orders before and after saving them to the database. Some of the properties of an order, such as the creation time or its ID, are set by the data layer and can be known only after the changes to the database have been committed. As we explained in section 7.4, committing changes is out of the scope of a repository, which means that when we add an order to the repository, the returned object won't have those properties. The order's ID and its creation time become available through the order's database record after committing the transaction. For this reason, `Order`'s initializer binds the order's ID, creation time, and status as private properties with a leading underscore (like in `self._id`), and we use the `order_` parameter in the `Order` class to hold a pointer to the order's database record. If we retrieve the details of an order already saved to the database, `_id`, `_created`, and `_status` will have their corresponding values in the initializer; otherwise, they'll be `None` and we'll pull their values from `order_`. That's why we define `Order`'s `id`, `created`, and `status` properties using the `property()` decorator, since it allows us to resolve their value depending on the state of the object. This is the only degree of coupling we'll allow between the business layer and the data layer. And to make sure this dependency can be easily removed if we ever have to, we're setting `order_` to `None` by default.

Listing 7.5 Implementation of the `Order` business object class

```
# file: orders/orders_service/orders.py

class OrderItem:
    def __init__(self, id, product, quantity, size):
        self.id = id
        self.product = product
        self.quantity = quantity
        self.size = size


class Order:
    def __init__(self, id, created, items, status, schedule_id=None,
                 delivery_id=None, order_=None):
        self._id = id
        self._created = created
        self.items = [OrderItem(**item) for item in items]
        self._status = status
        self.schedule_id = schedule_id
        self.delivery_id = delivery_id

    @property
    def id(self):
        return self._id or self._order.id

    @property
    def created(self):
        return self._created or self._order.created

    @property
    def status(self):
        return self._status or self._order.status
```

Since we resolve the ID dynamically, we store the provided ID as a private property.

Business object that represents an order item

We declare the parameters of OrderItem's initializer method.

The order_ parameter represents a database model instance.

We build an OrderItem object for each order item.

We resolve the ID dynamically using the property() decorator.

In addition to holding data about an order, the `Order` class also needs to handle tasks such as cancelling, paying, and scheduling an order. To fulfill those tasks, we must interface with external dependencies, such as the kitchen and payments services. As we explained in section 7.1, the goal of hexagonal architecture is to encapsulate access to external dependencies through adapters. However, to keep things simple in this chapter, we'll implement the external API calls within the `Order` class. A good adapter pattern for encapsulating external API calls is the *facade pattern*.[8]

[8] Erich Gamma, Richard Helm, Ralph Johnsohn, and John Vlissides, *Design Patterns* (Addison-Wesley, 1995), pp. 185–193.

Before we proceed with the implementation, we should know what those API calls look like.

To build the integration between the orders service and the kitchen and payments services, we'd want to run the kitchen and payments services and see how they work. However, we don't need to run the actual services. The folder for this chapter in the GitHub repository for this book contains three OpenAPI files: one for the orders API (ch07/oas.yaml), one for the kitchen API (ch07/kitchen.yaml), and one for the payments API (ch07/payments.yaml). kitchen.yaml and payments.yaml tell us how the kitchen and payments APIs work, and that's all the information we need to build our integration. Make sure to pull the kitchen.yaml and payments.yaml files from GitHub to be able to work with the following examples.

As it turns out, we can also use the kitchen and payments API specifications to simulate their behavior using mock servers. API mock servers replicate the server behind the APIs, validating our requests and returning valid responses. We'll use Prism CLI (https://github.com/stoplightio/prism), a library built and maintained by Stoplight, to mock the API server for the kitchen and payments services. Prism is a Node.js library, but don't worry, it's just a CLI tool; you don't need to know any JavaScript to use it. To install the library, run the following command:

```
$ yarn add @stoplight/prism-cli
```

DEALING WITH ERRORS RUNNING PRISM You may run into errors when running Prism. A common error is not having a compatible version of Node.js. I recommend you install nvm to manage your Node versions and use the latest stable version of Node to run Prism. Also, make sure the port you select to run Prism is available.

This command will create a node_modules/ folder within your application folder, where Prism and all its dependencies will be installed. You don't want to commit this folder, so make sure you add it to your .gitignore file. You'll also see a new file called package.json, and another one called yarn.lock within your application directory. These are the files you want to commit since they'll allow you to re-create the same node_modules/ directory in any other environment.

To see Prism in action with the kitchen API, run the following command:

```
$ ./node_modules/.bin/prism mock kitchen.yaml --port 3000
```

This will start a server on port 3000 that runs a mock service for the kitchen API. To get a taste of what we can do with it, run the following command to hit the GET `/kitchen/schedules` endpoint, which returns a list of schedules:

```
$ curl http://localhost:3000/kitchen/schedules
```

DISPLAY JSON IN THE TERMINAL LIKE A PRO WITH JQ When outputting JSON to the terminal, either using cURL to interact with an API or catting a JSON file, I recommend you use JQ—a command-line utility that parses the JSON and produces a beautiful display. You can use JQ like this: `curl http://localhost:3000/kitchen/schedules | jq`.

You'll see that the mock server started by Prism is able to return a perfectly valid payload representing a list of schedules. Impressive, to say the least! Now that we know how to run mock servers for the kitchen and payments APIs, let's analyze the requirements of the API integrations with them:

- *Kitchen service (kitchen.yaml)*—To schedule an order with the kitchen service, we must call the POST `/kitchen/schedules` endpoint with a payload containing the list of items in the order. In the response to this call, we'll find the `schedule_id`, which we can use to keep track of the state of the order.
- *Payments service (payments.yaml)*—To process the payment for an order, we must call the POST `/payments` endpoint with a payload containing the ID of the order. This is a mock endpoint for integration testing purposes.

Before we can cancel an order, we need to check its status. If the order is scheduled for production, we must hit the POST `/kitchen/schedules/{schedule_id}/cancel` endpoint to cancel the schedule. If the order is out for delivery, we won't allow users to cancel the order, and therefore we raise an exception.

To implement the API integrations, we'll use the popular Python `requests` library. Run the following command to install the library with `pipenv`:

```
$ pipenv install requests
```

Listing 7.6 extends the implementation of the `Order` class by adding methods that implement API calls to the kitchen and payment services. For testing purposes, we're expecting the kitchen API to run on port 3001 and the payments service to run on port 3000. You can accomplish this by running the following commands:

```
$ ./node_modules/.bin/prism mock kitchen.yaml --port 3000
$ ./node_modules/.bin/prism mock payments.yaml --port 3001
```

In each API call, we check that the response contains the expected status code, and if it doesn't, we raise a custom `APIIntegrationError` exception. Also, if a user tries to perform an invalid action, such as cancelling an order when it's already out for delivery, we raise an `InvalidActionError` exception.

Listing 7.6 Encapsulating per-order capabilities within the `Order` class

```
# file: orders/orders_service/orders.py

import requests
```

```
from orders.orders_service.exceptions import (
    APIIntegrationError, InvalidActionError
)

...
class Order:
    ...

    def cancel(self):
        if self.status == 'progress':
            kitchen_base_url = "http://localhost:3000/kitchen"
            response = requests.post(
                f"{kitchen_base_url}/schedules/{self.schedule_id}/cancel",
                json={"order": [item.dict() for item in self.items]},
            )
            if response.status_code == 200:
                return
            raise APIIntegrationError(
                f'Could not cancel order with id {self.id}'
            )
        if self.status == 'delivery':
            raise InvalidActionError(
                f'Cannot cancel order with id {self.id}'
            )

    def pay(self):
        response = requests.post(
            'http://localhost:3001/payments', json={'order_id': self.id}
        )
        if response.status_code == 201:
            return
        raise APIIntegrationError(
            f'Could not process payment for order with id {self.id}'
        )

    def schedule(self):
        response = requests.post(
            'http://localhost:3000/kitchen/schedules',
            json={'order': [item.dict() for item in self.items]}
        )
        if response.status_code == 201:
            return response.json()['id']
        raise APIIntegrationError(
            f'Could not schedule order with id {self.id}'
        )
```

If an order is in progress, we cancel its schedule by calling the kitchen API.

If the response from the kitchen service is successful, we return.

Otherwise, we raise an APIIntegrationError.

We don't allow orders that are being delivered to be cancelled.

We process a payment by calling the payments API.

We schedule an order for production by calling the kitchen API.

If the response from the kitchen service is successful, we return the schedule ID.

Listing 7.7 contains the implementation of the custom exceptions we use in the order service to signal that something has gone wrong. We'll use `OrderNotFoundError` in the `OrdersService` class when a user tries to fetch the details of an order that doesn't exist.

Listing 7.7 Orders service custom exceptions

```
# file: orders/orders_service/exceptions.py

class OrderNotFoundError(Exception):      # Exception to signal that an order doesn't exist
    pass


class APIIntegrationError(Exception):     # Exception to signal that an API integration error has taken place
    pass


class InvalidActionError(Exception):      # Exception to signal that the action being performed is invalid
    pass
```

As we mentioned earlier, the API module won't use the `Order` class directly. Instead, it will use a unified interface to all our adapters through the `OrdersService` class, whose interface we showed in listing 7.4. `OrdersService` encapsulates the capabilities of the orders domain, and it takes care of using the orders repository to get orders objects and perform actions on them. Listing 7.8 shows the implementation of the `OrdersService` class.

To instantiate the `OrdersService` class, we require an orders repository object that we can use to add or delete orders from our records. To place an order, we create a database record using the orders repository, and to retrieve the details of an order, we fetch the corresponding record from the database. If the requested order isn't found, we raise an `OrderNotFoundError` exception. The `list_orders()` method accepts filters in the form of a dictionary. To get a list of orders, the orders repository forces us to pass a specific value for the `limit` argument, and therefore we extract its value from the `filters` dictionary by using the `pop()` method, which allows us to set a default value and also removes the key from the dictionary. In the `pay_order()` method, we process the payment using the payments API, and if the payment is successful, we schedule the order by calling the kitchen API. After scheduling the order, we update the order record by setting its `schedule_id` attribute to the schedule ID returned by the kitchen API.

Listing 7.8 Implementation of the `OrdersService`

```
# file: orders/orders_service/orders_service.py

from orders.orders_service.exceptions import OrderNotFoundError


class OrdersService:
    def __init__(self, orders_repository):      # To instantiate the OrdersService class, we require an instance of the orders repository.
        self.orders_repository = orders_repository

    def place_order(self, items):
        return self.orders_repository.add(items)     # We place an order by creating a database record.
```

```
    def get_order(self, order_id):
        order = self.orders_repository.get(order_id)
        if order is not None:
            return order
        raise OrderNotFoundError(f'Order with id {order_id} not found')

    def update_order(self, order_id, items):
        order = self.orders_repository.get(order_id)
        if order is None:
            raise OrderNotFoundError(f'Order with id {order_id} not found')
        return self.orders_repository.update(order_id, {'items': items})

    def list_orders(self, **filters):
        limit = filters.pop('limit', None)
        return self.orders_repository.list(limit, **filters)

    def pay_order(self, order_id):
        order = self.orders_repository.get(order_id)
        if order is None:
            raise OrderNotFoundError(f'Order with id {order_id} not found')
        order.pay()
        schedule_id = order.schedule()
        return self.orders_repository.update(
            order_id, {'status': 'scheduled', 'schedule_id': schedule_id}
        )

    def cancel_order(self, order_id):
        order = self.orders_repository.get(order_id)
        if order is None:
            raise OrderNotFoundError(f'Order with id {order_id} not found')
        order.cancel()
        return self.orders_repository.update(order_id, status="cancelled")
```

We get the details of an order using the orders repository and passing in the requested ID.

If the order doesn't exist, we raise an OrderNotFoundError exception.

We capture filters as a dictionary by using keyword arguments.

After scheduling the order, we update its schedule_id attribute.

The orders service is ready to be used in our API module. However, before we continue with this integration, there's one more piece in this puzzle that we need to solve. As we mentioned in section 7.4, the orders repository doesn't commit any actions to the database. It's the responsibility of the API, as the consumer of the `OrdersService`, to ensure that everything is committed at the end of an operation. How exactly does that work? Move on to section 7.6 to learn how!

7.6 Implementing the unit of work pattern

In this section, we'll learn to handle database commits and rollbacks when interacting with the `OrdersService`. As you can see in figure 7.15, when we use the `OrdersService` class to access any of its capabilities, we must inject an instance of the `OrdersRepository` class. We must also open an SQLAlchemy session before we perform any actions, and we must commit any changes to our data to persist them in the database.

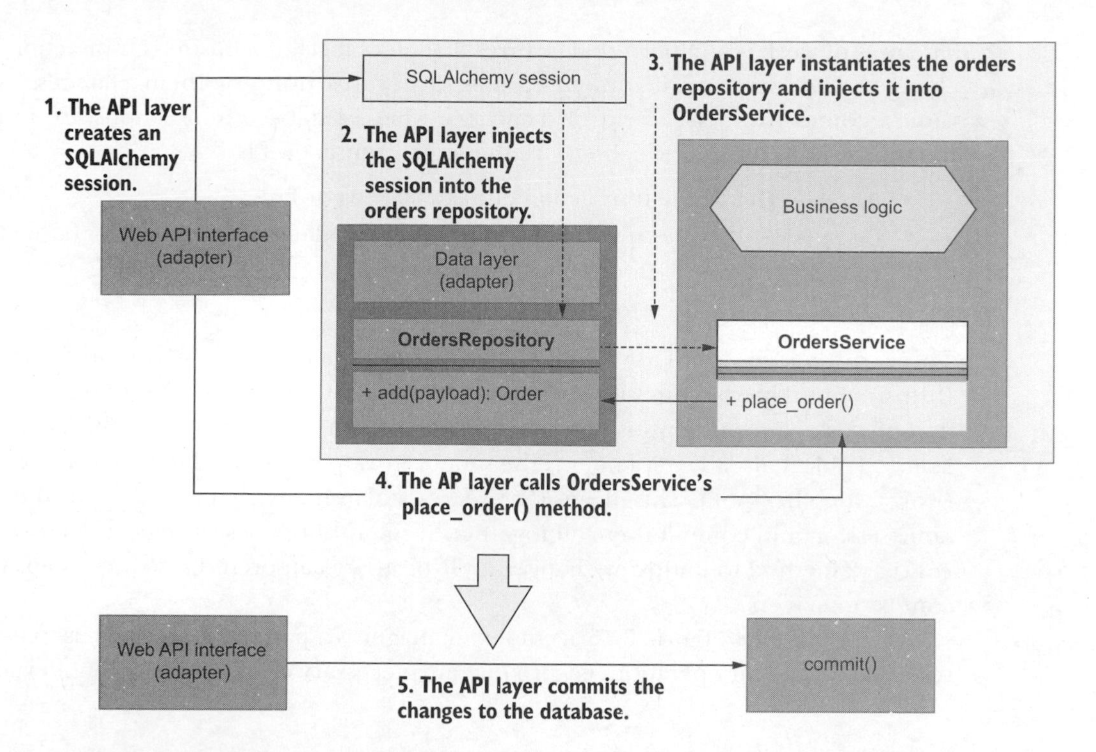

Figure 7.15 To persist our changes to the database, we could simply make the API layer use the SQLAlchemy session object to commit the transaction. In this figure, the solid lines represent calls, while the dashed lines represent injections of dependencies.

What's the best way to orchestrate these operations? We can use different approaches for this implementation. We could simply use SQLAlchemy session objects to wrap our calls to `OrdersService`, and once our operations succeed, use the session to commit, or roll back otherwise. This would work if `OrdersService` only ever had to deal with a single SQL database. However, what if we had to interact with a different type of database at the same time? We'd need to open a new session for it as well. What if we also had to handle integrations with other microservices within the same operation, and ensure we make the right API calls at the end of the transaction in case we had to roll back? Again, we could just add special clauses and guards to our code. The same code would have to be repeated in every API function that interacts with the `OrdersService`, so wouldn't it be nice if there was pattern that can help us put it all together in a single place? Enter the unit of work pattern.

DEFINITION The *unit of work* is a design pattern that guarantees the atomicity of our business transactions, ensuring that all transactions are committed at once, or rolled back if any of them fails.

The unit of work is a pattern that ensures that all objects of a business transaction are changed together, and if something fails, it ensures none of them changes.[9] The notion comes from the world of databases, where database transactions are implemented as units of work which ensure that every transaction is

- *Atomic*—The whole transaction either succeeds or fails.
- *Consistent*—It conforms to the constrains of the database.
- *Isolated*—It doesn't interfere with other transactions.
- *Durable*—It's written to persistent storage.

These properties are known as the *ACID principles* in the world of databases (https://en.wikipedia.org/wiki/Database_transaction). When it comes to services, the unit of work pattern helps us apply these principles in our operations. SQLAlchemy's `Session` object already implements the unit of work pattern for database transactions (http://mng.bz/jA5z). This means that we can add as many changes as we need to the same session and commit them all together. If something goes wrong, we can call the `rollback` method to undo any changes. In Python, we can orchestrate these steps with context managers.

As you can see in figure 7.16, a context manager is a pattern that allows us to lock a resource during an operation, ensure that any necessary cleanup jobs are undertaken

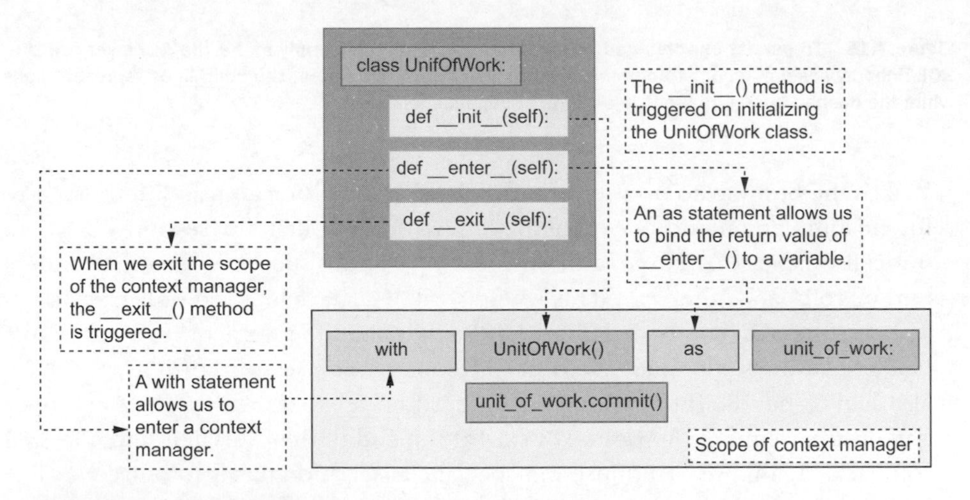

Figure 7.16 A class-based context manager has an `__init__()`, an `__enter__()`, and an `__exit__()` method. `__init__()` is triggered when we initialize the context manager. The `__enter__` method allows us to enter the context, and it's called when we use the `with` statement. Using an `as` statement within the same line allows us to bind the return value of the `__enter__()` method to a variable (`unit_of_work` in this case). Finally, when we exit the context manager, the `__exit__()` method is triggered.

[9] Fowler, *Patterns of Enterprise Architecture* (pp. 184–194).

in case anything goes wrong, and finally release the lock once the operation is finished. The key syntactical feature of a context manager is the use of the `with` statement, as illustrated in figure 7.16. As you can see in the illustration, context managers can return objects, which we can capture by using Python's `as` clause. This is useful if the context manager is creating access to a resource, such as a file, on which we want to operate.

In Python, we can implement context managers in multiple ways, including as a class or using the `contextmanager()` decorator from the `contextlib` module.[10] In this section, we'll implement our unit of work context manager as a class. A context manager class must implement at least the two following special methods:

- `__enter__()`—Defines the operations that must be undertaken upon entering the context, such as creating a session or opening a file. If we need to perform actions on any of the objects created within the `__enter__()` method, we can return the object and capture its value through an `as` clause, as illustrated in figure 7.16.
- `__exit__()`—Defines the operations that must be undertaken upon exiting the context, for example, closing a file or a session. The `__exit__()` method captures any exceptions raised during the execution of the context through three parameters in its method signature:
  - `exc_type`—Captures the type of exception raised
  - `exc_value`—Captures the value bound to the exception, typically the error message
  - `traceback`—A traceback object that can be used to pinpoint the exact place where the exception took place

If no exceptions are raised, the value of these three parameters will be `None`.

Listing 7.9 shows the implementation of the unit of work pattern as a context manager for the orders service. In the initializer method, we obtain a session factory object using SQLAlchemy's `sessionmaker()` function, which requires a connection object that we produce with the help of SQLAlchemy's `create_engine()` function. To keep the example simple, we're hardcoding the database connection string to point to our local SQLite database. In chapter 13, you'll learn to parameterize this value and pull it from the environment.

When we enter the context, we create a new database session, and we bind it to the `UnitOfWork` instance so that we can access it in other methods. We also return the context manager object itself so that the caller can access any of its attributes, such as the `session` object or the `commit()` method. On exiting the context, we check whether any exceptions were raised while adding or removing objects to the session, and if that's the case, we roll back the changes to avoid leaving the database in an inconsistent state.

[10] Ramalho, *Fluent Python* (O'Reilly, 2015), pp. 463–478.

We have access to the exception's type (exc_type) and value (exc_val), and the traceback (traceback) context, which we can use to log the details of the error. If no exception took place, all three parameters will be set to None. Finally, we close the database session to release database resources and to end the scope of the transaction. We also add wrappers around SQLAlchemy's commit() and rollback() methods to avoid exposing database internals to the business layer.

Listing 7.9 Unit of work pattern as a context manager

```
# file: orders/repository/unit_of_work.py

from sqlalchemy import create_engine
from sqlalchemy.orm import sessionmaker


class UnitOfWork:

    def __init__(self):
        self.session_maker = sessionmaker(
            bind=create_engine('sqlite:///orders.db')
        )

    def __enter__(self):
        self.session = self.session_maker()
        return self

    def __exit__(self, exc_type, exc_val, traceback):
        if exc_type is not None:
            self.rollback()
            self.session.close()
        self.session.close()

    def commit(self):
        self.session.commit()

    def rollback(self):
        self.session.rollback()
```

We obtain a session factory object.

We return an instance of the unit of work object.

We open a new database session.

We check whether an exception took place.

On existing the context, we have access to any exceptions raised during the context's execution.

If an exception took place, roll back the transaction.

We close the database session.

Wrapper around SQLAlchemy's commit() method

Wrapper around SQLAlchemy's rollback() method

This is all very good, but how exactly are we supposed to use the UnitOfWork in combination with the orders repository and the OrdersService? In the next section, we'll delve more into the details of this, but before we do that, listing 7.10 gives you a template for how to use all these components together. We enter the unit of work context with Python's syntax for context managers using a with statement. We also use an as statement to bind the return value of UnitOfWork's __enter__() method to the unit_of_work variable. Then we get an instance of the orders repository passing in the UnitOfWork's database session object, and an instance of the OrdersService class passing in the orders repository object. Then we use the orders service object to place an order, and we commit the transaction using UnitOfWork's commit() method.

Listing 7.10 Template pattern for using the unit of work and the repository

```
with UnitOfWork() as unit_of_work:
    repo = OrdersRepository(unit_of_work.session)
    orders_service = OrdersService(repo)
    orders_service.place_order(order_details)
    unit_of_work.commit()
```

We enter the unit of work context.

We get an instance of the orders repository passing in the UnitOfWork's session.

We get an instance of the OrdersService class passing in the orders repository object.

We place an order.

We commit the transaction.

Now that we have a unit of work that we can use to commit our transactions, let's see how we put this all together by integrating the API layer with the service layer! Move on to section 7.7 to learn how we do that.

7.7 Integrating the API layer and the service layer

In this section, we put everything we have learned in this chapter together to integrate the service layer with the API layer. We'll make use of the template pattern we showed in listing 7.10 to use the `UnitOfWork` class in combination with `OrdersRepository` and `OrdersService`. When a user tries to perform an action on an order, we make sure we have checks in place to verify that the order exists in the first place; otherwise, we return a 404 (Not Found) error response.

Listing 7.11 shows the new version of the orders/web/api/api.py module. The first thing we do in every function is enter the context of `UnitOfWork`, making sure we bind the context object to a variable, `unit_of_work`. Then we create an instance of `OrdersRepository` using the session object from the `UnitOfWork` context object. Once we have an instance of the repository, we inject it into `OrdersService` as we create an instance of the service. Then we use the service to perform the operations required in each endpoint. In endpoints that perform actions on a specific order, we guard against the possibility of an `OrderNotFoundError` being raised by `OrdersService` if the requested order doesn't exist.

In the `create_order()` function, we retrieve the dictionary representation of the order using `order.dict()` before we exit the `UnitOfWork` context so that we can access properties generated by the database during the commit process, such as the order's ID. Remember that the order ID doesn't exist until the changes are committed to the database, and therefore it's only accessible within the scope of the database session. In our implementation, that means that we must access the ID before we exit the `UnitOfWork` context, since the database session closes right before exiting the context. Figure 7.17 illustrates this process.

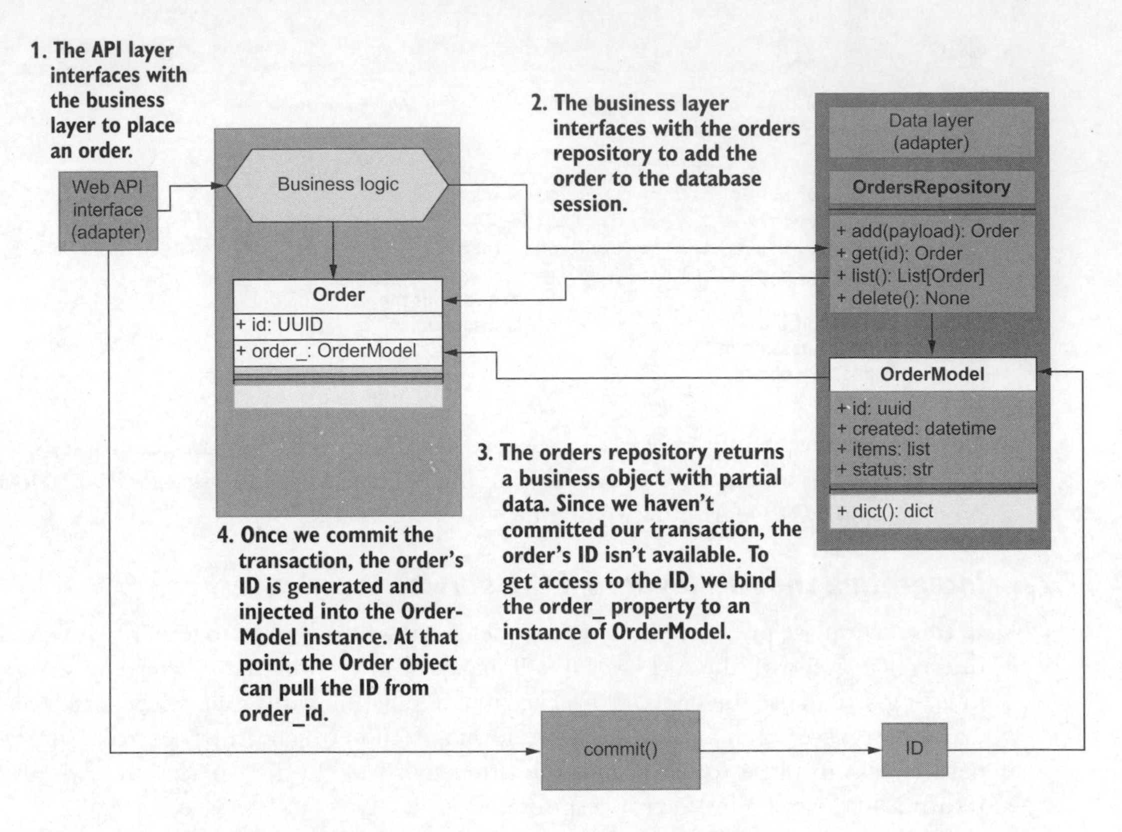
1. The API layer interfaces with the business layer to place an order.
Web API interface (adapter)
Business logic
Order
+ id: UUID
+ order_: OrderModel
2. The business layer interfaces with the orders repository to add the order to the database session.
Data layer (adapter)
OrdersRepository
+ add(payload): Order
+ get(id): Order
+ list(): List[Order]
+ delete(): None
OrderModel
+ id: uuid
+ created: datetime
+ items: list
+ status: str
+ dict(): dict
3. The orders repository returns a business object with partial data. Since we haven't committed our transaction, the order's ID isn't available. To get access to the ID, we bind the order_ property to an instance of OrderModel.
4. Once we commit the transaction, the order's ID is generated and injected into the Order-Model instance. At that point, the Order object can pull the ID from order_id.
commit()
ID

Figure 7.17 When we place an order, the object returned by the orders repository doesn't contain an ID. The ID will be available once we commit the database transaction through the `OrderModel` instance. Therefore, we bind an instance of the model to the `Order` object so that it can pull the ID from the model after the commit.

Listing 7.11 Integration between API layer and service layer

```
# file: orders/web/api/api.py

from http import HTTPStatus
from typing import List, Optional
from uuid import UUID

from fastapi import HTTPException
from starlette import status
from starlette.responses import Response

from orders.orders_service.exceptions import OrderNotFoundError
from orders.orders_service.orders_service import OrdersService
from orders.repository.orders_repository import OrdersRepository
from orders.repository.unit_of_work import UnitOfWork
from orders.web.app import app
from orders.web.api.schemas import (
    GetOrderSchema,
```

```
    CreateOrderSchema,
    GetOrdersSchema,
)


@app.get('/orders', response_model=GetOrdersSchema)
def get_orders(
    cancelled: Optional[bool] = None,
    limit: Optional[int] = None,
):
    with UnitOfWork() as unit_of_work:          <- We enter the unit of work context.
        repo = OrdersRepository(unit_of_work.session)
        orders_service = OrdersService(repo)
        results = orders_service.list_orders(
            limit=limit, cancelled=cancelled
        )
    return {'orders': [result.dict() for result in results]}


@app.post(
    '/orders',
    status_code=status.HTTP_201_CREATED,
    response_model=GetOrderSchema,
)
def create_order(payload: CreateOrderSchema):
    with UnitOfWork() as unit_of_work:
        repo = OrdersRepository(unit_of_work.session)
        orders_service = OrdersService(repo)
        order = orders_service.place_order(payload.dict()['order'])
        order = payload.dict()['order']
        for item in order:
            item['size'] = item['size'].value
        order = orders_service.place_order(order)          <- We place an order.

        unit_of_work.commit()
        return_payload = order.dict()          <- We access the order's dictionary representation before exiting the unit of work context.
    return return_payload

@app.get('/orders/{order_id}', response_model=GetOrderSchema)
def get_order(order_id: UUID):
    try:          <- We use a try/except block to catch the OrderNotFoundError exception.
        with UnitOfWork() as unit_of_work:
            repo = OrdersRepository(unit_of_work.session)
            orders_service = OrdersService(repo)
            order = orders_service.get_order(order_id=order_id)
        return order.dict()
    except OrderNotFoundError:
        raise HTTPException(
            status_code=404, detail=f'Order with ID {order_id} not found'
        )


@app.put('/orders/{order_id}', response_model=GetOrderSchema)
def update_order(order_id: UUID, order_details: CreateOrderSchema):
```

```
    try:
        with UnitOfWork() as unit_of_work:
            repo = OrdersRepository(unit_of_work.session)
            orders_service = OrdersService(repo)
            order = order_details.dict()['order']
            for item in order:
                item['size'] = item['size'].value
            order = orders_service.update_order(
                order_id=order_id, items=order
            )
            unit_of_work.commit()
        return order.dict()
    except OrderNotFoundError:
        raise HTTPException(
            status_code=404, detail=f'Order with ID {order_id} not found'
        )


@app.delete(
    "/orders/{order_id}",
    status_code=status.HTTP_204_NO_CONTENT,
    response_class=Response,
)
def delete_order(order_id: UUID):
    try:
        with UnitOfWork() as unit_of_work:
            repo = OrdersRepository(unit_of_work.session)
            orders_service = OrdersService(repo)
            orders_service.delete_order(order_id=order_id)
            unit_of_work.commit()
        return
    except OrderNotFoundError:
        raise HTTPException(
            status_code=404, detail=f'Order with ID {order_id} not found'
        )


@app.post('/orders/{order_id}/cancel', response_model=GetOrderSchema)
def cancel_order(order_id: UUID):
    try:
        with UnitOfWork() as unit_of_work:
            repo = OrdersRepository(unit_of_work.session)
            orders_service = OrdersService(repo)
            order = orders_service.cancel_order(order_id=order_id)
            unit_of_work.commit()
        return order.dict()
    except OrderNotFoundError:
        raise HTTPException(
            status_code=404, detail=f'Order with ID {order_id} not found'
        )


@app.post('/orders/{order_id}/pay', response_model=GetOrderSchema)
def pay_order(order_id: UUID):
```

```
try:
    with UnitOfWork() as unit_of_work:
        repo = OrdersRepository(unit_of_work.session)
        orders_service = OrdersService(repo)
        order = orders_service.pay_order(order_id=order_id)
        unit_of_work.commit()
    return order.dict()
except OrderNotFoundError:
    raise HTTPException(
        status_code=404, detail=f'Order with ID {order_id} not found'
    )
```

This concludes our journey through the implementation of the service layer for the orders service. The patterns we learned in this chapter are not only applicable to the world of APIs and microservices, but to all application models generally. In particular, the repository pattern will always help you ensure that you keep your data access layer fully decoupled from the business layer, and the unit of work pattern will help you ensure that all transactions of a business operation are handled atomically and consistently.

Summary

- Hexagonal architecture, or architecture of ports and adapters, is a software architectural pattern that encourages us to decouple the business layer from the implementation details of the database and the application interface.
- The dependency inversion principle teaches us that the implementation details of our application components should depend on interfaces. This helps us decouple our components from the implementation details of their dependencies.
- To interface with the database, you can use an ORM library such as SQLAlchemy, which can translate database tables and rows into classes and objects. This provides the possibility of enhancing our database models with useful functionality for our application needs.
- Repository is a software development pattern that helps to decouple the data layer from the business layer by adding an abstraction layer, which exposes an in-memory list interface of the data. Regardless of the database engine we use, the business layer will always receive the same objects from the repository.
- The unit of work pattern helps ensure that all the business transactions that are part of an application operation succeed or fail together. If one of the transactions fails, the unit of work pattern ensures that all changes are rolled back. This mechanism ensures that data is never left in an inconsistent state.

Part 3

Designing and building GraphQL APIs

In part 2, you learned that REST is an API technology that allows us to alter or retrieve the state of a resource from the server. When a resource is represented by a large payload, fetching it from the server translates to a large amount of data transfer. With the emergence of API clients running in mobile devices with restricted network access and limited storage and memory capacity, exchanging large payloads often results in unreliable communication. In 2012, Facebook was acutely aware of these problems, and it developed a new technology to allow API clients to run granular data queries on the server. This technology was released in 2015 under the name of GraphQL.

GraphQL is a query language for APIs. Instead of fetching full representations of resources, GraphQL allows you to fetch one or more properties of a resource, such as the price of a product or the status of an order. With GraphQL, we can also model the relationship between different objects, which allows us to retrieve, in a single request, the properties of various resources from the server, such as a product's ingredients and its stock availability.

Despite its benefits, many developers aren't familiar with GraphQL or don't know how it works, and therefore it isn't usually the first choice of technology for building an API. In part 3, you learn everything you need to know to design and build high-quality GraphQL APIs and how to consume them. After reading part 3, you'll know what GraphQL is, how it works, and when to use it so that you can make better decisions in your API strategy.

8 Designing GraphQL APIs

This chapter covers

- Understanding how GraphQL works
- Producing an API specification using the Schema Definition Language (SDL)
- Learning GraphQL's built-in scalar types and data structures and building custom object types
- Creating meaningful connections between GraphQL types
- Designing GraphQL queries and mutations

GraphQL is one of the most popular protocols for building web APIs. It's a suitable choice for driving integrations between microservices and for building integrations with frontend applications. GraphQL gives API consumers full control over the data they want to fetch from the server and how they want to fetch it.

In this chapter, you'll learn to design a GraphQL API. You'll do it by working on a practical example: you'll design a GraphQL API for the products service of the CoffeeMesh platform. The products service owns data about CoffeeMesh's products as well as their ingredients. Each product and ingredient contains a rich list of properties that describe their features. However, when a client requests a list of products, they are most likely interested in fetching only a few details about each product. Also, clients may be interested in being able to traverse the relationships between products, ingredients, and other objects owned by the products service. For these reasons, GraphQL is an excellent choice for building the products API.

As we build the specification for the products API, you'll learn about GraphQL's scalar types, designing custom object types, as well as queries and mutations. By the end of this chapter, you'll understand how GraphQL compares with other types of APIs and when it makes the most sense to use it. We've got a lot to cover, so without further ado, let's start our journey!

To follow along with the specification we develop in this chapter, you can use the GitHub repository provided with this book. The code for this chapter is available under the folder named ch08.

8.1 Introducing GraphQL

This section covers what GraphQL is, what its advantages are, and when it makes sense to use it. The official website of the GraphQL specification defines GraphQL as a "query language for APIs and a runtime for fulfilling those queries with your existing data."[1] What does this really mean? It means that GraphQL is a specification that allows us to run queries in an API server. In the same way SQL provides a query language for databases, GraphQL provides a query language for APIs.[2] GraphQL also provides a specification for how those queries are resolved in a server so that anyone can implement a GraphQL runtime in any programming language.[3]

Just as we can use SQL to define schemas for our database tables, we can use GraphQL to write specifications that describe the type of data that can be queried from our servers. A GraphQL API specification is called a schema, and it's written in a standard called Schema Definition Language (SDL). In this chapter, we will learn how to use the SDL to produce a specification for the products API.

GraphQL was first released in 2015, and since then it's gained traction as one of the most popular choices for building web APIs. I should say there's nothing in the GraphQL specification saying that GraphQL should be used over HTTP, but in practice, this is the most common type of protocol used in GraphQL APIs.

What's great about GraphQL? It shines in giving users full control over which data they want to obtain from the server. For example, as we'll see in the next section, in the products API we store many details about each product, such as its name, price, availability, and ingredients, among others. As you can see in figure 8.1, if a user wishes to get a list of just product names and prices, with GraphQL they can do that. In contrast, with other types of APIs, such as REST, you get a full list of details for each product. Therefore, whenever it's important to give the client full control over how they fetch data from the server, GraphQL is a great choice.

---

[1] This definition appears in the home page of the GraphQL specification: https://graphql.org/.

[2] I owe the comparison between GraphQL and SQL to Eve Porcello and Alex Banks, *Learning GraphQL, Declarative Data Fetching for Modern Web Apps* (O'Reilly, 2018), pp. 31–32.

[3] The GraphQL website maintains a list of runtimes available for building GraphQL servers in different languages: https://graphql.org/code/.

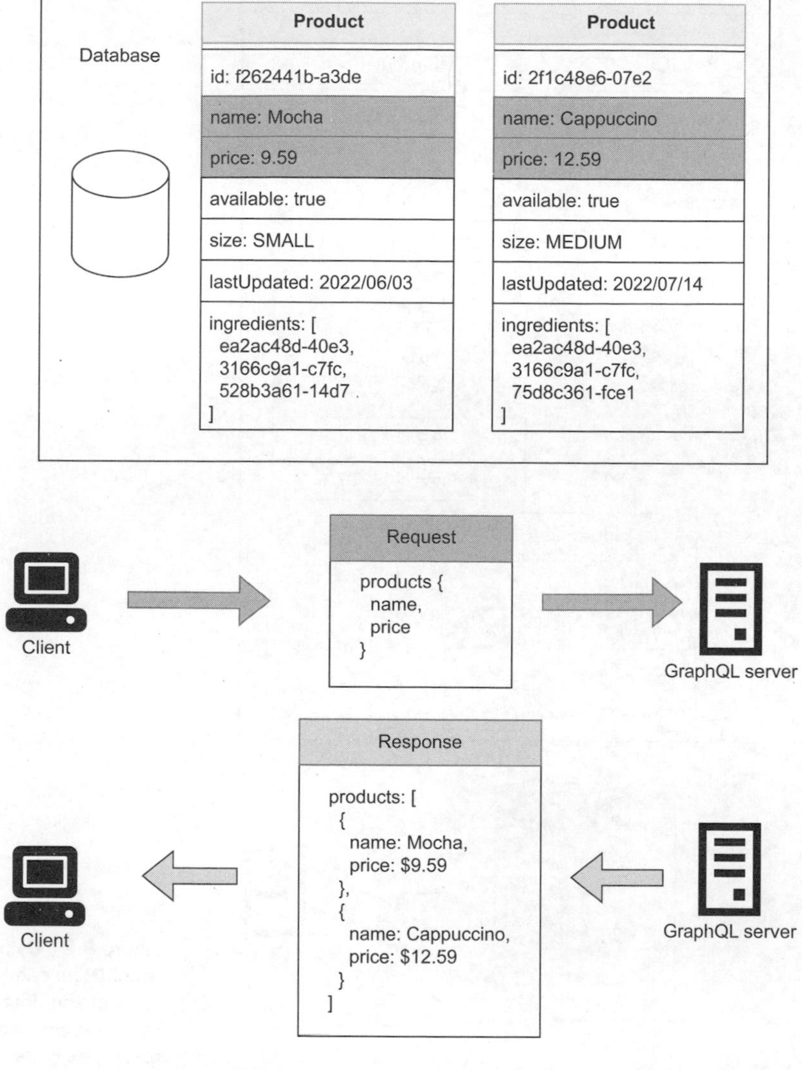

Figure 8.1 Using a GraphQL API, a client can request a list of items with specific details. In this example, a client is requesting the name and price of each product in the products API.

Another great advantage of GraphQL is the ability to create connections between different types of resources, and to expose those connections to our clients for use in their queries. For example, in the products API, products and ingredients are different but related types of resources. As you can see in figure 8.2, if a user wants to get a list of products, including their names, prices, and their ingredients, with GraphQL they can do that by leveraging the connections between these resources. Therefore, in services where we have highly interconnected resources, and where it's useful for our clients to explore and query those connections, GraphQL makes an excellent choice.

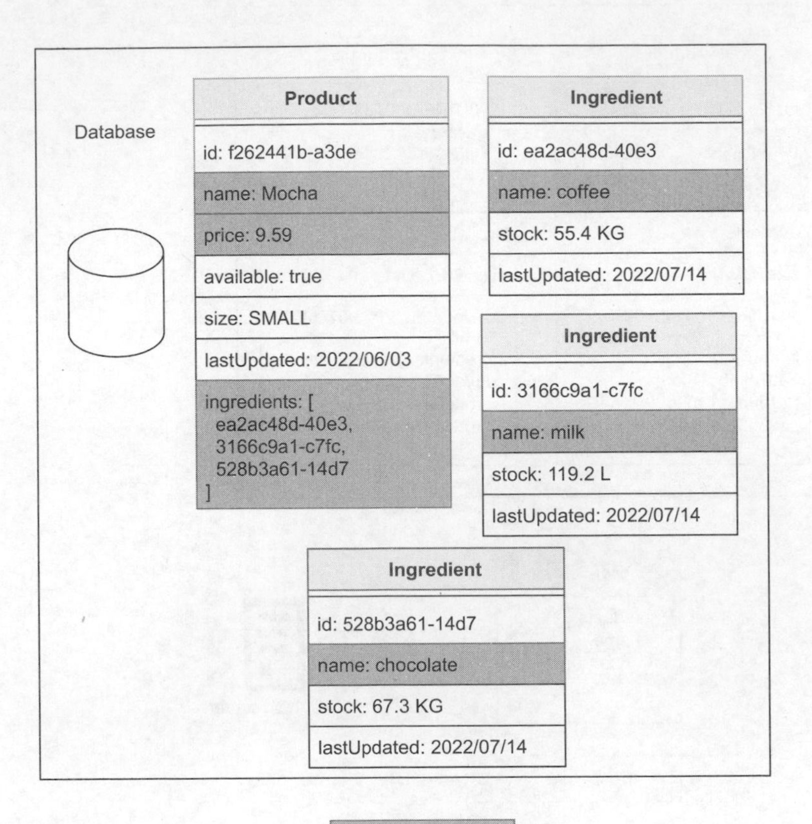

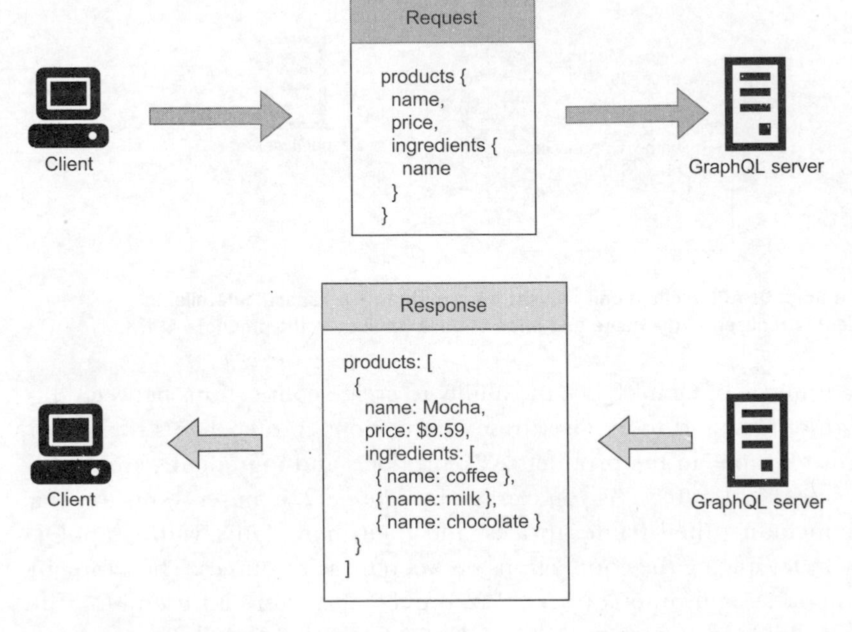

Figure 8.2 Using GraphQL, a client can request the details of a resource and other resources linked to it. In this example, the products API has two types of resources: products and ingredients, both of which are connected through product's `ingredients` field. Using this connection, a client can request the name and price of each product, as well as the name of each product's ingredient.

In the sections that follow, we'll learn how to produce a GraphQL specification for the products service. We'll learn how to define the types of our data, how to create meaningful connections between resources, and how to define operations for querying the data and changing the state of the server. But before we do that, we ought to understand the requirements for the products API, and that's what we do in the next section!

8.2 Introducing the products API

This section discusses the requirements of the products API. Before working on an API specification, it's important to gather information about the API requirements. As you can see in figure 8.3, the products API is the interface to the products service. To determine the requirements of the products API, we need to know what users of the products service can do with it.

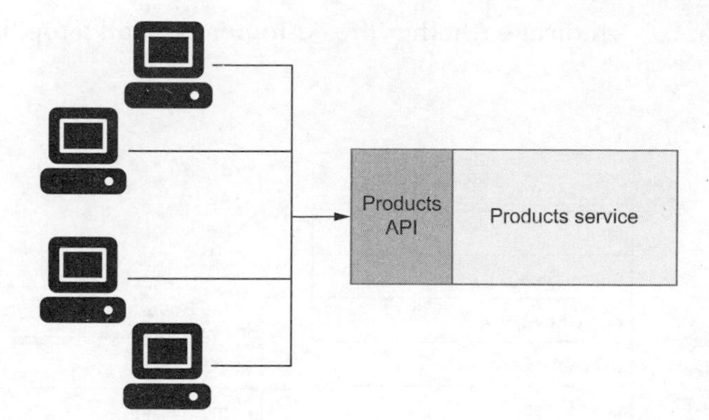

Figure 8.3 To interact with the products service, clients use the products API.

The products service owns data about the products offered by the CoffeeMesh platform. As you can see in figure 8.4, the CoffeeMesh staff must be able to use the products service to manage the available stock of each product, as well as to keep the products' ingredients up to date. In particular, they must be able to query the stock of a product

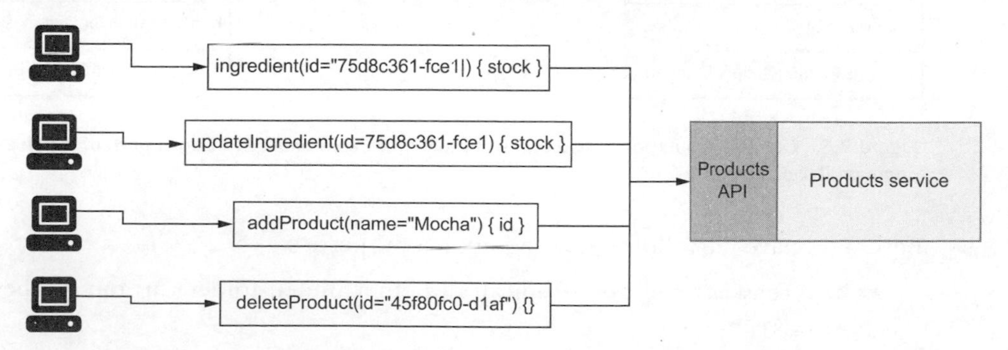

Figure 8.4 The CoffeeMesh staff uses the products service to manage products and ingredients.

or ingredient, and to update them when new stock arrives to the warehouse. They must also be able to add new products or ingredients to the system and delete old ones. This information already gives us a complex list of requirements, so let's break it down into specific technical requirements.

Let's start with by modeling the resources managed by the products API. We want to know which type of resources we should expose through the API and the products' properties. From the description in the previous paragraph, we know that the products service manages two types of resources: products and ingredients. Let's analyze products first.

The CoffeeMesh platform offers two types of products: cakes and beverages. As you can see in figure 8.5, both cakes and beverages have a common set of properties, including the product's name, price, size, list of ingredients, and its availability. Cakes have two additional properties:

- `hasFilling`—Indicates whether the cake has a filling
- `hasNutsToppingOption`—Indicates whether the customer can add a topping of nuts to the cake

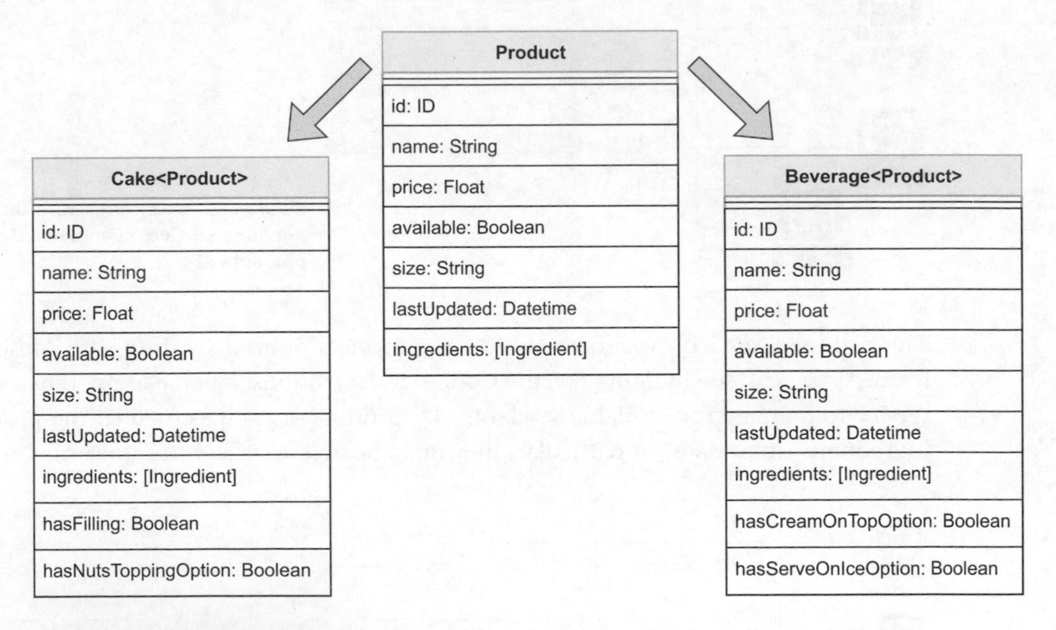

Figure 8.5 CoffeeMesh exposes two types of products: `Cake` and `Beverage`, both of which share a common list of properties.

Beverages have the following two additional properties:

- `hasCreamOnTopOption`—Indicates whether the customer can top the beverage with cream
- `hasServeOnIceOption`—Indicates whether the customer can choose to get the beverage served on ice

What about ingredients? As you can see in figure 8.6, we can represent all ingredients through one entity with the following attributes:

- `name`—The ingredient's name.
- `stock`—The ingredient's available stock. Since different ingredients are measured with different units, such as kilograms or liters, we express the available stock in terms of amounts of per unit of measure.
- `description`—A collection of notes that CoffeeMesh employees can use to describe and qualify the product.
- `supplier`—Information about the company that supplies the ingredient to CoffeeMesh, including their name, address, contact number, and email.

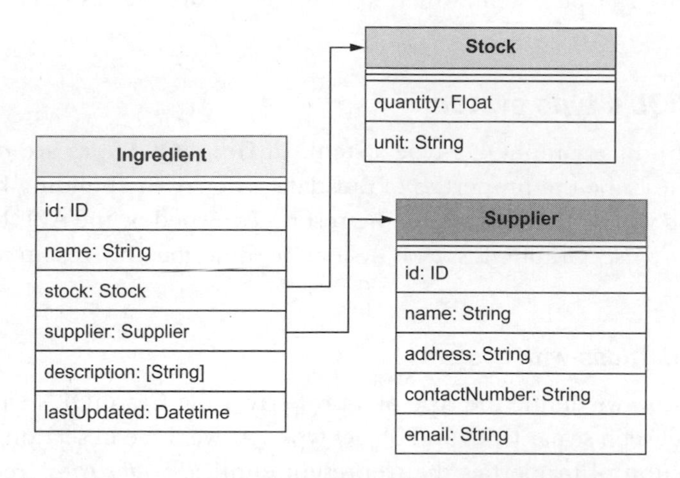

Figure 8.6 List of properties that describe an ingredient. The ingredient's supplier is described by a resource called `Supplier`, while the ingredient's stock is described through a `Stock` object.

Now that we've modeled the main resources managed by the products service, let's turn our attention to the operations we must expose through the API. We'll distinguish read operations from write/delete operations. This distinction will make sense when we look more closely at these operations in sections 8.8 and 8.9.

Based on the previous discussion, we'll expose the following read operations:

- `allProducts()`—Returns the full list of products available in the CoffeeMesh catalogue
- `allIngredients()`—Returns the full list of ingredients used by CoffeeMesh to make their products
- `products()`—Allows users to filter the full list of products by certain criteria such as availability, maximum price, and others
- `product()`—Allows users to obtain information about a single product
- `ingredient()`—Allows users to obtain information about a single ingredient

In terms of write/delete operations, from the previous discussion it's clear that we should expose the following capabilities:

- `addIngredient()`—To add new ingredients
- `updateStock()`—To update an ingredient's stock
- `addProduct()`—To add new products
- `updateProduct()`—To update existing products
- `deleteProduct()`—To delete products from the catalogue

Now that we understand the requirements of the products API, it's time to move on to creating the API specification! In the following sections, we'll learn to create a GraphQL specification for the products API, and along the way we'll learn how GraphQL works. Our first stop is GraphQL's type system, which we'll use to model the resources managed by the APIs.

8.3 Introducing GraphQL's type system

In this section, we introduce GraphQL's type system. In GraphQL, types are definitions that allow us to describe the properties of our data. They're the building blocks of a GraphQL API, and we use them to model the resources owned by the API. In this section, you'll learn to use GraphQL's type system to describe the resources we defined in section 8.2.

8.3.1 Creating property definitions with scalars

This section explains how we define the type of a property using GraphQL's type system. We distinguish between scalar types and object types. As we'll see in section 8.3.2, object types are collection of properties that represent entities. *Scalar types* are types such as Booleans or integers. The syntax for defining a property's type is very similar to how we use type hints in Python: we include the name of the property followed by a colon, and the property's type to the right of the colon. For example, in section 8.2 we discussed that cakes have two distinct properties: `hasFilling` and `hasNutsToppingOption`, both of which are Booleans. Using GraphQL's type system, we describe these properties like this:

```
hasFilling: Boolean
hasNutsToppingOption: Boolean
```

GraphQL supports the following types of scalars:

- *Strings* (`String`)—For text-based object properties.
- *Integers* (`Int`)—For numerical object properties.
- *Floats* (`Float`)—For numerical object properties with decimal precision.
- *Booleans* (`Boolean`)—For binary properties of an object.
- *Unique identifiers* (`ID`)—For describing an object ID. Technically, IDs are strings, but GraphQL checks and ensures that the ID of each object is unique.

In addition to defining the type of a property, we can also indicate whether the property is non-nullable. Nullable properties are properties that can be set to `null` when we don't know their value. We mark a property as non-nullable by placing an exclamation point at the end of the property definition:

```
name: String!
```

This line defines a property `name` of type `String`, and it marks it as non-nullable by using an exclamation point. This means that, whenever we serve this property from the API, it will always be a string.

Now that we've learned about properties and scalars, let's see how we use this knowledge to model resources!

8.3.2 Modeling resources with object types

This section explains how we use GraphQL's type system to model resources. Resources are the entities managed by the API, such as the ingredients, cakes, and beverages that we discussed in section 8.2. In GraphQL, each of these resources is modeled as an object type. *Object types* are collections of properties, and as the name indicates, we use them to define objects. To define an object type, we use the `type` keyword followed by the object name, and the list of object properties wrapped between curly braces. A property is defined by declaring the property name followed by a colon, and its type on the right side of the colon. In GraphQL, `ID` is a type with a unique value. An exclamation point at the end of a property indicates that the property is non-nullable. The following illustrates how we describe the cake resource as an object type. The listing contains the basic properties of the cake type, such as the ID, the name, and its price.

Listing 8.1 Definition of the `Cake` object type

```
type Cake {
  id: ID!
  name: String!
  price: Float
  available: Boolean!
  hasFilling: Boolean!
  hasNutsToppingOption: Boolean!
}
```

We define an object type.

We define a non-nullble ID property.

TYPES AND OBJECT TYPES For convenience, throughout the book, we use the concepts of type and object type interchangeably unless otherwise stated.

Some of the property definitions in listing 8.1 end with an exclamation point. In GraphQL, an exclamation point means that a property is non-nullable, which means that every cake object returned by our API will contain an ID, a name, its availability, as well as the `hasFilling` and `hasNutsToppingOption` properties. It also guarantees that none of these properties will be set to `null`. For API client developers, this information is very valuable because they know they can count on these properties to always be present and build their applications with that assumption. The following code shows the definitions for the `Beverage` and `Ingredient` types. It also shows the definition for the `Supplier` type, which contains information about the business that supplies a certain ingredient, and in section 8.5.1 we'll see how we connect it with the `Ingredient` type.

Listing 8.2 Definitions of the `Beverage` and `Ingredient` object types

```
type Beverage {
  id: ID!
  name: String!
  price: Float
  available: Boolean!
  hasCreamOnTopOption: Boolean!
  hasServeOnIceOption: Boolean!
}

type Ingredient {
  id: ID!
  name: String!
}

type Supplier {
  id: ID!
  name: String!
  address: String!
  contactNumber: String!
  email: String!
}
```

Now that we know how to define object types, let's complete our exploration of GraphQL's type system by learning how to create our own custom types!

8.3.3 Creating custom scalars

This section explains how we create custom scalar definitions. In section 8.3.1, we introduced GraphQL's built-in scalars: `String`, `Int`, `Float`, `Boolean`, and `ID`. In many cases, this list of scalar types is sufficient to model our API resources. In some cases, however, GraphQL's built-in scalar types might prove limited. In such cases, we can define our own custom scalar types. For example, we may want to be able to represent a date type, a URL type, or an email address type.

Since the products API is used to manage products and ingredients and make changes to them, it is useful to add a `lastUpdated` property that tells us the last time a record changed. `lastUpdated` should be a `Datetime` scalar. GraphQL doesn't have a built-in scalar of that type, so we have to create our own. To declare a custom date-time scalar, we use the following statement:

```
scalar Datetime
```

We also need to define how this scalar type is validated and serialized. We define the rules for validation and serialization of a custom scalar in the server implementation, which will be the topic of chapter 10.

Listing 8.3 Using a custom `Datetime` scalar type

```
scalar Datetime                          <-- We declare a custom
                                             Datetime scalar.
type Cake {
  id: ID!
  name: String!
  price: Float
  available: Boolean!
  hasFilling: Boolean!
  hasNutsToppingOption: Boolean!
  lastUpdated: Datetime!             <-- We declare a non-nullable property
}                                        with type Datetime.
```

This concludes our exploration of GraphQL scalars and object types. You're now in a position to define basic object types in GraphQL and create your own custom scalars. In the following sections, we'll learn to create connections between different object types, and we'll learn how to use lists, interfaces, enumerations, and more!

8.4 Representing collections of items with lists

This section introduces GraphQL lists. Lists are arrays of types, and they're defined by surrounding a type with square brackets. Lists are useful when we need to define properties that represent collections of items. As discussed in section 8.2, the `Ingredient` type contains a property called `description`, which contains collections of notes about the ingredient, as shown in the following code.

Listing 8.4 Representing a list of strings

```
type Ingredient {
  id: ID!
  name: String!
  description: [String!]          <-- We define a list of
}                                     non-nullable items.
```

Look closely at the use of exclamation points in the `description` property: we're defining it as a nullable property with non-nullable items. What does this mean? When we return an ingredient from the API, it may or may not contain a `description` field, and if that field is present, it will contain a list of strings.

When it comes to lists, you must pay careful attention to the use of exclamation points. In list properties, we can use two exclamation points: one for the list itself and another for the item within the list. To make both the list and its contents non-nullable, we use exclamation points for both. The use of exclamation points for list types is one of the most common sources of confusion among GraphQL users. Table 8.1 summarizes the possible return values for each combination of exclamation points in a list property definition.

> **USE EXCLAMATION POINTS AND LISTS CAREFULLY!** In GraphQL, an exclamation point indicates that a property is non-nullable, which means that the property needs to be present in an object and its value cannot be `null`. When it comes to lists, we can use two exclamation points: one for the list itself and another for the item within the list. Different combinations of the exclamation points will yield different representations of the property. Table 8.1 shows which representations are valid for each combination.

Table 8.1 Valid return values for list properties

	`[Word]`	`[Word!]`	`[Word]!`	`[Word!]!`
`null`	Valid	Valid	Invalid	Invalid
`[]`	Valid	Valid	Valid	Valid
`["word"]`	Valid	Valid	Valid	Valid
`[null]`	Valid	Invalid	Valid	Invalid
`["word", null]`	Valid	Invalid	Valid	Invalid

Now that we've learned about GraphQL's type system and list properties, we're ready to explore one of the most powerful and exciting features of GraphQL: connections between types.

8.5 Think graphs: Building meaningful connections between object types

This section explains how we create connections between objects in GraphQL. One of the great benefits of GraphQL is being able to connect objects. By connecting objects, we make it clear how our entities are related. As we'll see in the next chapter, this makes our GraphQL API more easily consumed.

8.5.1 Connecting types through edge properties

This section explains how we connect types by using *edge properties*: properties that point to another type. Types can be connected by creating a property that points to another type. As you can see in figure 8.7, a property that connects with another object is called an *edge*. The following code shows how we connect the `Ingredient` type with the `Supplier` type by adding a property called `supplier` to `Ingredient` that points to `Supplier`.

Listing 8.5 Edge for one-to-one connection

```
type Ingredient {
  id: ID!
  name: String!
```

```
  supplier: Supplier!
  description: [String!]
}
```
We use an edge property to connect the Ingredient and the Supplier types.

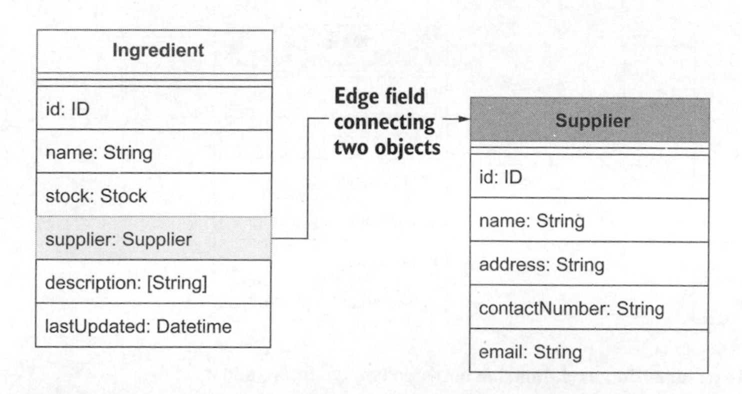

Figure 8.7 To connect the `Ingredient` type with the `Supplier` type, we add a property to `Ingredient` called `supplier`, which points to the `Supplier` type. Since the `Ingredient`'s `supplier` property is creating a connection between two types, we call it an edge.

This is an example of *one-to-one connection*: a property in an object that points to exactly one object. The property in this case is called an edge because it connects the `Ingredient` type with the `Supplier` type. It's also an example of a *directed connection*: as you can see in figure 8.7, we can reach the `Supplier` type from the `Ingredient` type, but not the other way around, so the connection only works in one direction.

To make the connection between `Supplier` and the `Ingredient` bidirectional,[4] we need to add a property to the `Supplier` type that points to the `Ingredient` type. Since a supplier can provide more than one ingredient, the `ingredients` property points to a list of `Ingredient` types. This is an example of a *one-to-many connection*. Figure 8.8 shows what the new relationship between the `Ingredient` and the `Supplier` types looks like.

Listing 8.6 Bidirectional relationship between `Supplier` and `Ingredient`

```
type Supplier {
  id: ID!
  name: String!
  address: String!
  contactNumber: String!
  email: String!
```

[4] In the literature about GraphQL, you'll often find a digression about how GraphQL is inspired by graph theory, and how we can use some of the concepts from graph theory to illustrate the relationships between types. Following that tradition, the bidirectional relationship we refer to here is an example of an undirected graph, since the `Supplier` type can be reached from the `Ingredient` type, and vice versa. For a good discussion of graph theory in the context of GraphQL, see Eve Porcello and Alex Banks, *Learning GraphQL, Declarative Data Fetching for Modern Web Apps* (O'Reilly, 2018), pp. 15–30.

```
    ingredients: [Ingredient!]!
}
```

We create a bidirectional relationship between the Ingredient and the Supplier types.

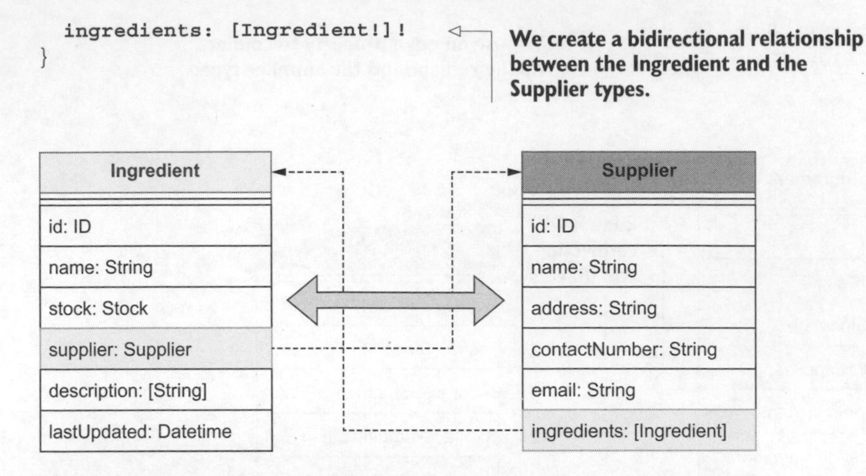

Figure 8.8 To create a bidirectional relationship between two types, we add properties to each of them that point to each other. In this example, the `Ingredient`'s `supplier` property points to the `Supplier` type, while the `Supplier`'s `ingredients` property points to a list of ingredients.

Now that we know how to create simple connections through edge properties, let's see how we create more complex connections using dedicated types.

8.5.2 Creating connections with through types

This section discusses *through types*: types that tell us how other object types are connected. They add additional information about the connection itself. We'll use through types to connect our products, cakes, and beverages, with their ingredients. We could connect them by adding a simple list of ingredients to `Cake` and `Beverage`, as shown in figure 8.9, but this wouldn't tell us how much of each ingredient goes into a product's recipe.

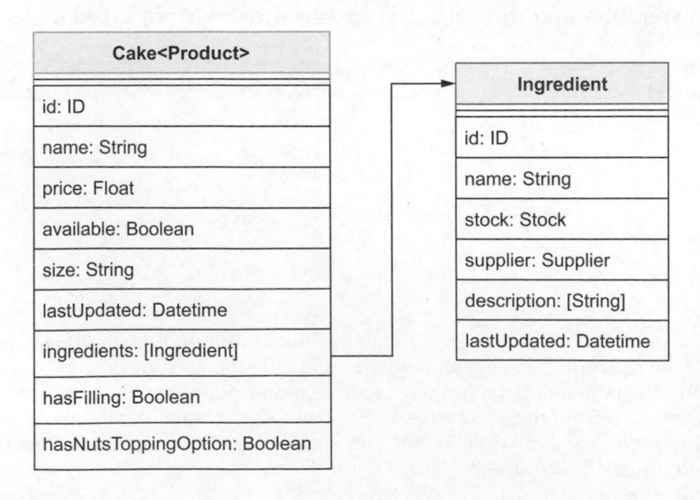

Figure 8.9 We can express `Cake`'s `ingredients` field as a list of `Ingredient` types, but that wouldn't tell us how much of each ingredient goes into a cake recipe.

To connect cakes and beverages with their ingredients, we'll use a through type called `IngredientRecipe`. As you can see in figure 8.10, `IngredientRecipe` has three properties: the ingredient itself, its amount, and the unit in which the amount is measured. This gives us more meaningful information about how our products relate to their ingredients.

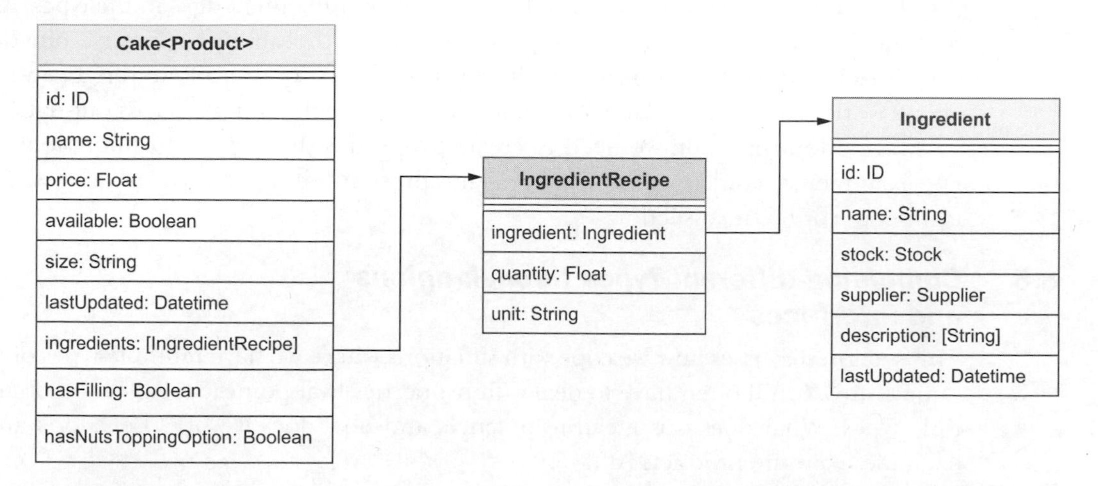

Figure 8.10 To express how an `Ingredient` is connected with a `Cake`, we use the `IngredientRecipe` through type, which allows us to detail how much of each ingredient goes into a cake recipe.

Listing 8.7 Through types that represent a relationship between two types

```
type IngredientRecipe {          <-- We declare the IngredientRecipe through type.
  ingredient: Ingredient!
  quantity: Float!
  unit: String!
}

type Cake {
  id: ID!
  name: String!
  price: Float
  available: Boolean!
  hasFilling: Boolean!
  hasNutsToppingOption: Boolean!
  lastUpdated: Datetime!
  ingredients: [IngredientRecipe!]!     <-- We declare ingredients as a list of IngredientRecipe through types.
}

type Beverage {
  id: ID!
  name: String!
  price: Float
  available: Boolean!
```

```
  hasCreamOnTopOption: Boolean!
  hasServeOnIceOption: Boolean!
  lastUpdated: Datetime!
  ingredients: [IngredientRecipe!]!
}
```

By creating connections between different object types, we give our API consumers the ability to explore our data by just following the connecting edges in the types. And by creating bidirectional relationships, we give users the ability to traverse our data graph back and forth. This is one of the most powerful features of GraphQL, and it's always worth spending the time to design meaningful connections across our data.

More often than not, we need to create properties that represent multiple types. For example, we could have a property that represents either cakes or beverages. This is the topic of the next section.

8.6 Combining different types through unions and interfaces

This section discusses how we cope with situations where we have multiple types of the same entity. You'll often have to deal with properties that point to a collection of multiple types. What does this mean in practice, and how does it work? Let's look at an example from the products API!

In the products API, `Cake` and `Beverage` are two types of products. In section 8.4.2, we saw how we connect `Cake` and `Beverage` with the `Ingredient` type. But how do we connect `Ingredient` to `Cake` and `Beverage`? We could simply add a property called `products` to the `Ingredient` type, which points to a list of `Cakes` and `Beverages`, like this:

```
products: [Cake, Beverage]
```

This works, but it doesn't allow us to represent `Cakes` and `Beverages` as a single product entity. Why would we want to do that? Because of the following reasons:

- `Cake` and `Beverage` are the same thing: a product, and as such, it makes sense to treat them as the same entity.
- As we'll see in sections 8.8 and 8.9, we'll have to refer to our products in other parts of the code, and it will be very helpful to be able to use one single type for that.
- If we add new types of products to the system in the future, we don't want to have to change all parts of the specification that refer to products. Instead, we want to have a single type that represents them all and update only that type.

GraphQL offers two ways to bring various types together under a single type: unions and interfaces. Let's look at each in detail.

Interfaces are useful when we have types that share properties in common. This is the case for the `Cake` and the `Beverage` types, which share most of their properties. GraphQL interfaces are similar to class interfaces in programming languages, such as

Python: they define a collection of properties that must be implemented by other types. Listing 8.8 shows how we use an interface to represent the collection of properties shared by `Cake` and `Beverage`. As you can see, we declare interface types using the `interface` keyword. The `Cake` and `Beverage` types implement `ProductInterface`, and therefore they must define all the properties defined in the `ProductInterface` type. By looking at the `ProductInterface` type, any user of our API can quickly get an idea of which properties are accessible on both the `Beverage` and `Cake` types.

Listing 8.8 Representing common properties through interfaces

```
interface ProductInterface {          <-- We declare the ProductInterface interface type.
  id: ID!
  name: String!
  price: Float
  ingredients: [IngredientRecipe!]
  available: Boolean!
  lastUpdated: Datetime!
}

type Cake implements ProductInterface {          <-- The Cake type implements the ProductInterface interface.
  id: ID!
  name: String!
  price: Float
  available: Boolean!
  hasFilling: Boolean!          <-- We define properties specific to Cake.
  hasNutsToppingOption: Boolean!
  lastUpdated: Datetime!
  ingredients: [IngredientRecipe!]!
}

type Beverage implements ProductInterface {          <-- Beverage implements the ProductInterface interface.
  id: ID!
  name: String!
  price: Float
  available: Boolean!
  hasCreamOnTopOption: Boolean!
  hasServeOnIceOption: Boolean!
  lastUpdated: Datetime!
  ingredients: [IngredientRecipe!]!
}
```

By creating interfaces, we make it easier for our API consumers to understand the common properties shared by our product types. As we'll see in the next chapter, interfaces also make the API easier to consume.

While interfaces help us define the common properties of various types, unions help us bring various types under the same type. This is very helpful when we want to treat various types as a single entity. In the products API, we want to be able to treat the `Cake` and `Beverage` types as a single `Product` type, and unions allow us to do that. A union type is the combination of different types using the pipe (`|`) operator.

Listing 8.9 A union of different types

```
type Cake implements ProductInterface {
  id: ID!
  name: String!
  price: Float
  available: Boolean!
  hasFilling: Boolean!
  hasNutsToppingOption: Boolean!
  lastUpdated: Datetime!
  ingredients: [IngredientRecipe!]!
}

type Beverage implements ProductInterface {
  id: ID!
  name: String!
  price: Float
  available: Boolean!
  hasCreamOnTopOption: Boolean!
  hasServeOnIceOption: Boolean!
  lastUpdated: Datetime!
  ingredients: [IngredientRecipe!]!
}

union Product = Beverage | Cake     <- We create a union of the Beverage and the Cake types.
```

Using unions and interfaces makes our API easier to maintain and to consume. If we ever add a new type of product to the API, we can make sure it offers a similar interface to `Cake` and `Beverage` by making it implement the `ProductInterface` type. And by adding the new product to the `Product` union, we make sure it's available on all operations that use the `Product` union type.

Now that we know how to combine multiple object types, it's time to learn how we constrain the values of object type properties through enumerations.

8.7 Constraining property values with enumerations

This section covers GraphQL's enumeration type. Technically, an *enumeration* is a specific type of scalar that can only take on a predefined number of values. Enumerations are useful in properties that can accept a value only from a constrained list of choices. In GraphQL, we declare enumerations using the `enum` keyword followed by the enumeration's name, and we list its allowed values within curly braces.

In the products API, we need enumerations for expressing the amounts of the ingredients. For example, in section 8.5.2, we defined a through type called `IngredientRecipe`, which indicates the amount of each ingredient that goes into a product. `IngredientRecipe` expresses amounts in terms of quantity per unit of measure. We can measure ingredients in different ways. For example, we can measure milk in pints, liters, ounces, gallons, and so on. For the sake of consistency, we want to ensure that everyone uses the same units to describe the amounts of our ingredients, so we'll create an enumeration type called `MeasureUnit` that can be used to constrain the values for the unit property.

Listing 8.10 Using the `MeasureUnit` enumeration type

```
enum MeasureUnit {        <-- We declare an enumeration.
  LITERS                  <-- We list the allowed values within this enumeration.
  KILOGRAMS
  UNITS
}

type IngredientRecipe {
    ingredient: Ingredient!
    quantity: Float!
    unit: MeasureUnit!    <-- unit is a non-nullable property of type MeasureUnit.
}
```

We also want to use the `MeasureUnit` enumeration to describe the available stock of an ingredient. To do so, we define a `Stock` type, and we use it to define the `stock` property of the `Ingredient` type.

Listing 8.11 Using the `Stock` enumeration type

```
type Stock {              <-- We declare the Stock type to help us express information about the available stock of an ingredient.
  quantity: Float!
  unit: MeasureUnit!      <-- Stock's unit property is an enumeration.
}

type Ingredient {
  id: ID!
  name: String!
  stock: Stock            <-- We connect the Ingredient type with the Stock type through Ingredient's stock property.
  products: [Product!]!
  supplier: Supplier!
  description: [String!]
}
```

Enumerations are useful to ensure that certain values remain consistent through the interface. This helps avoid errors that happen when you let users choose and write those values by themselves.

This concludes our journey through GraphQL's type system. Types are the building blocks of an API specification, but without a mechanism to query or interact with them, our API is very limited. To perform actions on the server, we need to learn about GraphQL queries and mutations. Those will be the topic of the rest of the chapter!

8.8 Defining queries to serve data from the API

This section introduces GraphQL *queries*: operations that allow us to fetch or read data from the server. Serving data is one of the most important functions of any web API, and GraphQL offers great flexibility to create a powerful query interface. Queries correspond to the group of read operations that we discussed in section 8.2. As a reminder, these are the query operations that the products API needs to support:

- `allProducts()`
- `allIngredients()`

- `products()`
- `product()`
- `ingredient()`

We'll work on the `allProducts()` query first since it's the simplest, and then move on to the `products()` query. As we work on `products()`, we'll see how we add arguments to our query definitions, we'll learn about pagination, and, finally, we'll learn how to refactor our query parameters into their own type to improve readability and maintenance.

The specification of a GraphQL query looks similar to the signature definition of a Python function: we define the query name, optionally define a list of parameters for the query between parentheses, and specify the return type after a colon. The following code shows the simplest query in the products API: the `allProducts()` query, which returns a list of all products. `allProducts()` doesn't take any parameters and simply returns a list of all products that exist in the server.

Listing 8.12 Simple GraphQL query to return a list of products

```
type Query {                          <- All queries are defined under the Query object type.
  allProducts: [Products!]!           <- We define the allProducts() query. After the colon, we indicate what the return type of the query is.
}
```

`allProducts()` returns a list of all products that exist in the CoffeeMesh database. Such a query is useful if we want to run an exhaustive analysis of all products, but in real life our API consumers want to be able to filter the results. They can do that by using the `products()` query, which, according to the requirements we gathered in section 8.2, returns a filtered list of products.

Query arguments are defined within parentheses, similar to how we define the parameters of a Python function. Listing 8.13 shows how we define the `products()` query. It includes arguments that allows our API consumers to filter products by availability, or by maximum and minimum price. All the arguments are optional. API consumers are free to use any or all of the query arguments, or none. If they don't specify any of the arguments when using the `products()` query, they'll get a list of all the products.

Listing 8.13 Simple GraphQL query to return a list of products

```
type Query {
  products(available: Boolean, maxPrice: Float, minPrice: Float):
    [Product!]                        <- Query parameters are defined within parentheses.
}
```

In addition to filtering the list of products, API consumers will likely want to be able to sort the list and paginate the results. Pagination is the ability to deliver the result of a query in different sets of a specified size, and it's commonly used in APIs to ensure that API clients receive a sensible amount of data in each request. As illustrated in figure 8.11, if the result of a query yields 10 or more records, we can divide the query result into groups of five items each and serve one set at a time. Each set is called a *page*.

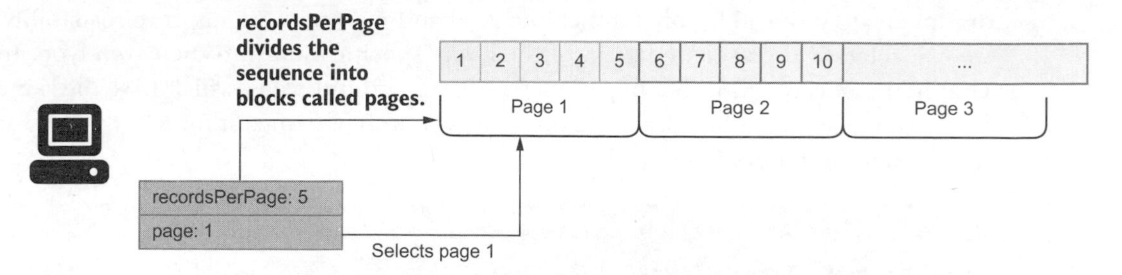

Figure 8.11 A more common approach to pagination is to let users decide how many results per page they want to see and let them select the specific page they want to get.

We enable pagination by adding a `resultsPerPage` argument to the query, as well as a `page` argument. To sort the result set, we expose a `sort` argument. The following snippet shows in bold the changes to the `products()` query after we add these arguments:

```
type Query {
  products(available: Boolean, maxPrice: Float, minPrice: Float, sort: String,
      resultsPerPage: Int, page: Int): [Product!]!
}
```

Offering numerous query arguments gives a lot of flexibility to our API consumers, but it can be cumbersome to set values for all of them. We can make our API easier to use by setting default values for some of the arguments. We'll set a default sorting order, as well as a default value for the `resultsPerPage` argument and a default value for the `page` argument. The following code shows how we assign default values to some of the arguments in the `products()` query and includes a `SortingOrder` enumeration that constrains the values of the `sort` argument to either `ASCENDING` or `DESCENDING`.

Listing 8.14 Setting default values for query arguments

```
enum SortingOrder {          <-- We declare the SortingOrder
  ASCENDING                      enumeration.
  DESCENDING
}

type Query {
  products(
    maxPrice: Float
    minPrice: Float                          We assign default
    available: Boolean = true           <--  values for some of
    sort: SortingOrder = DESCENDING          the parameters.
    resultsPerPage: Int = 10            <-- We constrain sort's values
    page: Int = 1                           by setting its type to the
                                            SortingOrder enumeration.
```

```
  ): [Product!]!
}
```

The signature of the products() query is becoming a bit cluttered. If we keep adding arguments to it, it will become difficult to read and maintain. To improve readability, we can refactor the arguments out of the query specification into their own type. In GraphQL, we can define lists of parameters by using input types, which have the same look and feel as any other GraphQL object type, but they're meant for use as input for queries and mutations.

Listing 8.15 Refactoring query arguments into input types

```
input ProductsFilter {                  <- We declare the ProductsFilter input type.
  maxPrice: Float                       <- We define ProductsFilter's parameters.
  minPrice: Float
  available: Boolean = true,            <- We assign default values to some parameters.
  sort: SortingOrder = DESCENDING
  resultsPerPage: Int = 10
  page: Int = 1
}

type Query {
  products(input: ProductsFilter): [Product!]!     <- We set the input parameter's type to ProductsFilter.
}
```

The remaining API queries, namely, allIngredients(), product(), and ingredient(), are shown in listing 8.16 in bold. allIngredients() returns a full list of ingredients and therefore takes no arguments, as in the case of the allProducts() query. Finally, product() and ingredient() return a single product or ingredient by ID, and therefore have a required id argument of type ID. If a product or ingredient is found for the provided ID, the queries will return the details of the requested item; otherwise, they'll return null.

Listing 8.16 Specification for all the queries in the products API

```
type Query {
  allProducts: [Product!]!
  allIngredients: [Ingredient!]!
  products(input: ProductsFilter!): [Product!]!
  product(id: ID!): Product              <- product() returns a nullable result of type Product.
  ingredient(id: ID!): Ingredient
}
```

Now that we know how to define queries, it's time to learn about mutations, which are the topic of the next section.

8.9 Altering the state of the server with mutations

This section introduces GraphQL *mutations*: operations that allow us to trigger actions that change the state of the server. While the purpose of a query is to let us fetch data from the server, mutations allow us to create new resources, to delete them, or to alter their state. Mutations have a return value, which can be a scalar, such as a Boolean, or an object. This allows our API consumers to verify that the operation completed successfully and to fetch any values generated by the server, such as IDs.

In section 8.2, we discussed that the products API needs to support the following operations for adding, deleting, and updating resources in the server:

- `addIngredient()`
- `updateStock()`
- `addProduct()`
- `updateProduct()`
- `deleteProduct()`

In this section, we'll document the `addProduct()`, `updateProduct()`, and `deleteProduct()` mutations. The specification for the other mutations is similar to these, and you can check them out in the GitHub repository provided with this book.

A GraphQL mutation looks similar to the signature of a function in Python: we define the name of the mutation, describe its parameters between parentheses, and provide its return type after a colon. Listing 8.17 shows the specification for the `addProduct()` mutation. `addProduct()` accepts a long list of arguments, and it returns a `Product` type. All the arguments are optional except `name` and `type`. We use `type` to indicate what kind of product we're creating, a cake or a beverage. We also include a `ProductType` enumeration to constrain the values of the `type` argument to either `cake` or `beverage`. Since this mutation is used to create cakes and beverages, we allow users to specify properties of each type, namely `hasFilling` and `hasNutsToppingOption` for cakes, as well as `hasCreamOnTopOption` and `hasServeOnIceOption` for beverages, but we set them by default to `false` to make the mutation easier to use.

Listing 8.17 Defining a GraphQL mutation

```
enum ProductType {          <-- We declare a ProductType enumeration.
  cake
  beverage
}

input IngredientRecipeInput {
  ingredient: ID!
  quantity: Float!
  unit: MeasureUnit!
}

enum Sizes {
  SMALL
  MEDIUM
  BIG
}

type Mutation {          <-- We declare mutations under the Mutation object type.
  addProduct(
```

```
    name: String!
    type: ProductType!
    price: String
    size: Sizes
    ingredients: [IngredientRecipeInput!]!
    hasFilling: Boolean = false
    hasNutsToppingOption: Boolean = false
    hasCreamOnTopOption: Boolean = false
    hasServeOnIceOption: Boolean = false
  ): Product!          <-- We specify the return type of addProduct().
}
```

You'd agree that the signature definition of the addProduct() mutation looks a bit cluttered. We can improve readability and maintainability by refactoring the list of parameters into their own type. Listing 8.18 shows how we refactor the addProduct() mutation by moving the list of parameters into an input type. AddProductInput contains all the optional parameters that can be set when we create a new product. We set aside the name parameter, which is the only required parameter when we create a new product. As we'll see shortly, this allows us to reuse the AddProductInput input type in other mutations that don't require the name parameter.

Listing 8.18 Refactoring parameters with input types

```
input AddProductInput {          <-- We declare the AddProductInput input type.
  price: String                  <-- We list AddProductInput's parameters.
  size: Sizes
  ingredients: [IngredientRecipeInput!]!
  hasFilling: Boolean = false                <-- We assign default values
  hasNutsToppingOption: Boolean = false          to some parameters.
  hasCreamOnTopOption: Boolean = false
  hasServeOnIceOption: Boolean = false
}

type Mutation {
  addProduct(
    name: String!
    type: ProductType!
    input: AddProductInput!
  ): Product!          <-- addProduct()'s input parameter has the AddProduct input type.
}
```

Input types not only help us make our specification more readable and maintainable, but they also allow us to create reusable types. We can reuse the AddProductInput input type in the signature of the updateProduct() mutation. When we update the configuration for a product, we may want to change only some of its parameters, such as the name, the price, or its ingredients. The following snippet shows how we reuse the AddProductInput parameters in updateProduct(). In addition to AddProductInput, we also include a mandatory product `id` parameter, which is necessary to identify the product we want to update. We also include the `name` parameter, which in this case is optional:

```
type Mutation {
  updateProduct(id: ID!, input: AddProductInput!): Product!
}
```

Let's now look at the `deleteProduct()` mutation, which removes a product from the catalogue. To do that, the user must provide the ID for the product they want to delete. If the operation is successful, the mutation returns `true`; otherwise, it returns `false`. The next snippet shows the specification for the `deleteProduct()` mutation:

```
deleteProduct(id: ID!): Boolean!
```

This concludes our journey through GraphQL's SDL! You're now equipped with everything you need to define your own API schemas. In chapter 9, we'll learn how to launch a mock server using the products API specification and how to consume and interact with the GraphQL API.

Summary

- GraphQL is a popular protocol for building web APIs. It shines in scenarios where it's important to give API clients full control over the data they want to fetch and in situations where we have highly interconnected data.
- A GraphQL API specification is called a schema, and it's written using the Schema Definition Language (SDL).
- We use GraphQL's scalar types to define the properties of an object type: Booleans, strings, floats, integers, and IDs. In addition, we can also create our own custom scalar types.
- GraphQL's object types are collections of properties, and they typically represent the resource or entities managed by the API server.
- We can connect objects by using edge properties, namely, properties that point to another object, and by using through types. Through types are object types that add additional information about how two objects are connected.
- To constrain the values of a property, we use enumeration types.
- GraphQL queries are operations that allow API clients to fetch data from the server.
- GraphQL mutations are operations that allow API clients to trigger actions that change the state of the server.
- When queries and mutations have long lists of parameters, we can refactor them into input types to increase readability and maintainability. Input types can also be reused in more than one query or mutation.

9 Consuming GraphQL APIs

This chapter covers

- Running a GraphQL mock server to test our API design
- Using the GraphiQL client to explore and consume a GraphQL API
- Running queries and mutations against a GraphQL API
- Consuming a GraphQL API programmatically using cURL and Python

This chapter teaches you how to consume GraphQL APIs. As we learned in chapter 8, GraphQL offers a query language for web APIs, and in this chapter you'll learn how to use this language to run queries on the server. In particular, you'll learn how to make queries against a GraphQL API. You'll learn to explore a GraphQL API to discover its available types, queries, and mutations. Understanding how GraphQL APIs work from the client side is an important step toward mastering GraphQL.

Learning to interact with GraphQL APIs will help you learn to consume the APIs exposed by other vendors, it'll let you run tests against your own APIs, and it'll help you design better APIs. You'll learn to use the GraphiQL client to explore and visualize a GraphQL API. As you'll see, GraphiQL offers an interactive query panel that makes it easier to run queries on the server.

To illustrate the concepts and ideas behind GraphQL's query language, we'll run practical examples using the products API we designed in chapter 8. Since we haven't implemented the API specification for the products API, we'll learn to run a mock server—an important part of the API development process, as it makes testing and validating an API design so much easier. Finally, you'll also learn to run queries against a GraphQL API programmatically using tools such as cURL and Python.

9.1 Running a GraphQL mock server

In this section, we explain how we can run a GraphQL mock server to explore and test our API. A mock server is a fake server that emulates the behavior of the real server, offering the same endpoints and capabilities, but using fake data. For example, a mock server for the products API is a server that mimics the implementation of the products API and offers the same interface that we developed in chapter 8.

> **DEFINITION** *Mock servers* are fake servers that mimic the behavior of a real server. They are commonly used for developing API clients while the backend is being implemented. You can launch a mock server using the specification for an API. Mock servers return fake data and typically don't persist data.

Mock servers are instrumental in the development of web APIs since they allow our API consumers to start working on the client-side code while we work on the backend implementation. In this section, we'll run a mock server on the products API. The only thing we need to run a mock server is the API specification, which we developed in chapter 8. You'll find the API specification under ch08/schema.graphql in the GitHub repository for this book.

You can choose from among many different libraries to run a GraphQL mock server. In this chapter, we'll use GraphQL Faker (https://github.com/APIs-guru/graphql-faker), which is one of the most popular GraphQL mocking tools. To install GraphQL Faker, run the following command:

```
$ npm install graphql-faker
```

This will create a package-lock.json file under your current directory, as well as a node_modules folder. package-lock.json contains information about the dependencies installed together with graphql-faker, while node_modules is the directory where those dependencies are installed. To run the mock server, execute the following command:

```
$ ./node_modules/.bin/graphql-faker schema.graphql
```

GraphQL Faker normally runs on port 9002, and it exposes three endpoints:

- `/editor`—An interactive editor where you can develop your GraphQL API.
- `/graphql`—A GraphiQL interface to your GraphQL API. This is the interface we'll use to explore the API and run our queries.
- `/voyager`—An interactive display of your API, which helps you understand the relationships and dependencies between your types (see figure 9.1).

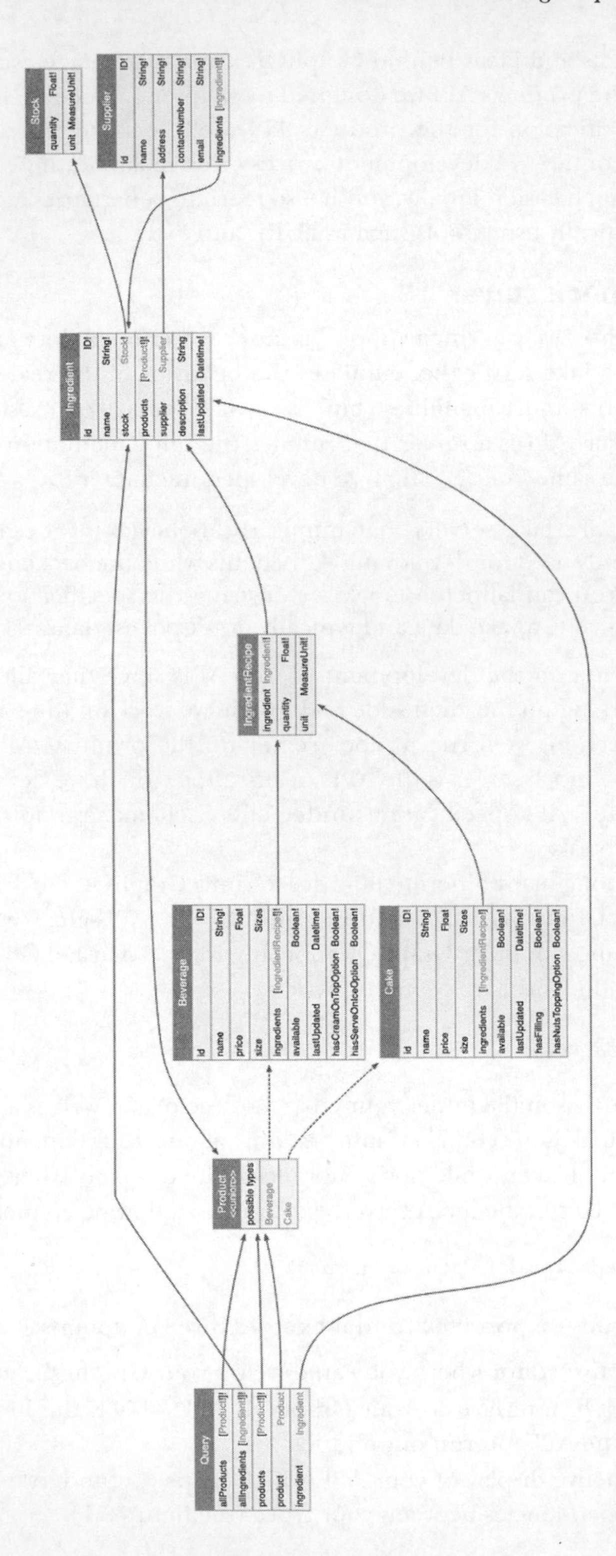

Figure 9.1 Voyager UI for the products API. This UI shows the relationships between object types captured by the queries available in the API. By following the connecting arrows, you can see which objects we can reach from each query.

To start exploring and testing the products API, visit the following address in your browser: http://localhost:9002/graphql (if you're running GraphQL Faker in a different port, your URL will look different). This endpoint loads a GraphiQL interface for our products API. Figure 9.2 illustrates what this interface looks like and highlights the most important elements in it.

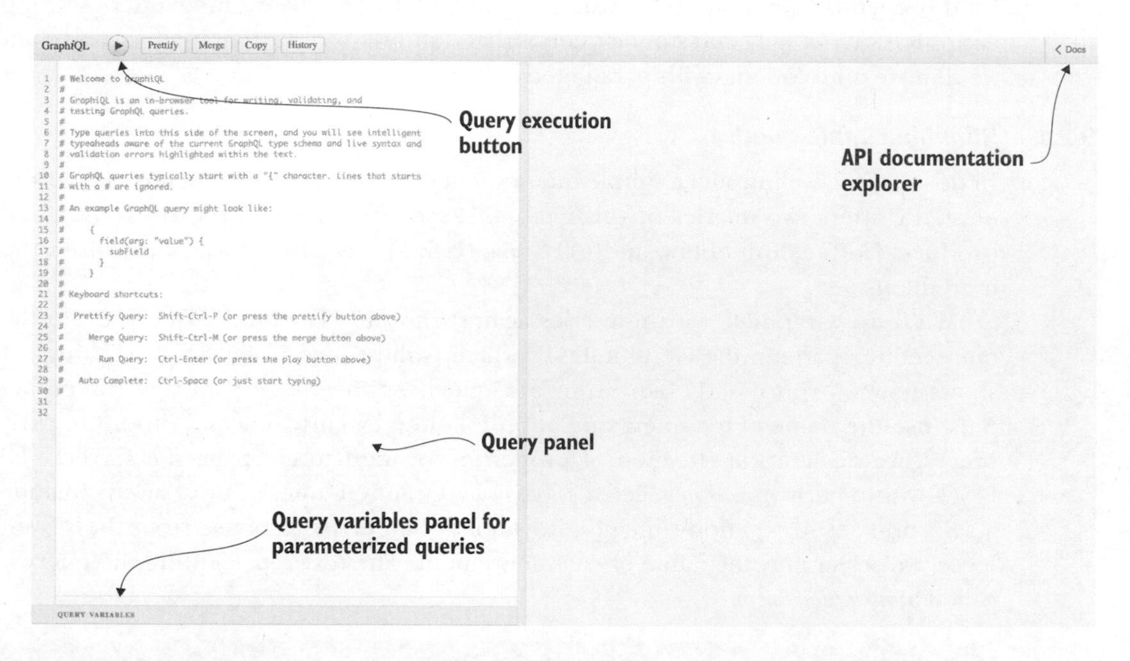

Figure 9.2 API documentation explorer and query panel interface in GraphiQL

To discover the queries and mutations exposed by the API, click the Docs button on the top-right corner of the UI. Upon clicking the Docs button, a side navigation bar will pop up offering two choices: queries or mutations (see figure 9.3 for an illustration). If you

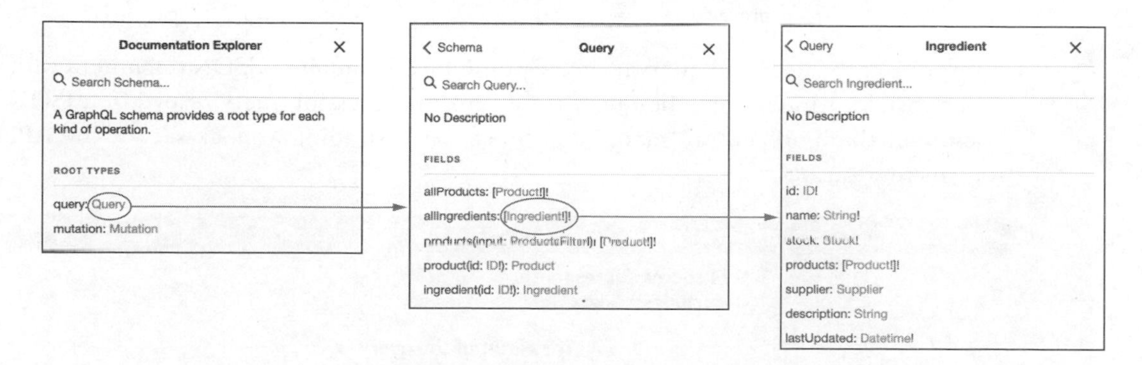

Figure 9.3 By clicking through the Documentation Explorer in GraphiQL, you can inspect all the queries and mutations available in the API, as well as the types they return and their properties.

select queries, you'll see the list of queries exposed by the server with their return types. You can click the return types to explore their properties, as you can see in figure 9.3. In the next section, we'll start testing the GraphQL API!

9.2 Introducing GraphQL queries

In this section, we learn to consume a GraphQL API by running queries using GraphiQL. We'll start with simple queries that don't require any parameters, and then we'll move on to queries with parameters.

9.2.1 Running simple queries

In this section, we introduce simple queries that don't take any parameters. The products API offers two queries of this type: `allProducts()`, which returns a list of all products CoffeeMesh offers, and `allIngredients()`, which returns a list of all the ingredients.

We'll use GraphiQL to run queries against the API. To run the query, go to the query editor pane in the GraphiQL UI, which is illustrated in figure 9.2. Listing 9.1 shows how we run the `allIngredients()` query. As you can see, to run a query we must use the name of the query operation followed by curly braces. Within the curly braces, we declare the selection of properties we want to get from the server. The block within curly braces is called a *selection set*. GraphQL queries must always include a selection set. If you don't include it, you'll get an error response from the server. Here, we select only the name of each ingredient. The text representing the query is called a *query document*.

Listing 9.1 Query document running the `allIngredients()` query

```
{                       <- We wrap queries within curly braces.
  allIngredients {      <- We run the allIngredients() query.
    name                <- We query the name property.
  }
}
```

A response to a successful query from a GraphQL API contains a JSON document with a "data" field, which wraps the query result. An unsuccessful query results in a JSON document that contains an "error" key. Since we're running a mock server, the API returns random values.

Listing 9.2 Example of successful response for the `allIngredients()` query

```
{
  "data": {                 <- A successful response includes a "data" key.
    "allIngredients": [     <- The result of the query is indexed under a key named after the query itself.
      {
        "name": "string"
      },
```

```
        {
          "name": "string"
        }
      ]
    }
  }
```

Now that we know the basics of GraphQL queries, let's spice up our queries by adding parameters!

9.2.2 Running queries with parameters

This section explains how we use parameters in GraphQL queries. `allIngredients()` is a simple query that doesn't take any parameters. Now let's see how we can run a query that requires a parameter. One example of such a query is the `ingredient()` query, which requires an `id` parameter. The following code shows how we can call the `ingredient()` query with a random ID. As you can see, we include the query parameters as key-value pairs separated by a colon within parentheses.

Listing 9.3 Running a query with a required parameter

```
{
  ingredient(id: "asdf") {      <-- We call ingredient()
    name                            with the ID parameter
  }                                 set to "asdf".
}
```

Now that we know how to run queries with parameters, let's look at the kinds of problems we can run into when running queries and how to deal with them.

9.2.3 Understanding query errors

This section explains some of the most common errors you'll find when running GraphQL queries, and it teaches you how to read and interpret them.

If you omit the required parameter when running the `ingredient()` query, you'll get an error from the API. Error responses include an error key pointing to a list of all the errors found by the server. Each error is an object with the following keys:

- `message`—Includes a human-readable description of the error
- `locations`—Specifies where in the query the error was found, including the line and column

Listing 9.4 shows what happens when you run the query with empty parentheses. As you can see, we get a syntax error with a somewhat cryptic message: `Expected Name, found )`. This is a common error that occurs whenever you make a syntax error in GraphQL. In this case, it means that GraphQL was expecting a parameter after the opening parenthesis, but instead it found a closing parenthesis.

Listing 9.4 Missing query parameter errors

```
# Query:
{
  ingredient() {        <-- We run the ingredient() query without the required parameter id.
    name
  }
}

# Error:
{
  "errors": [          <-- An unsuccessful response includes an "errors" key.
    {
      "message": "Syntax Error: Expected Name, found )",      <-- We get a generic syntax error.
      "locations": [    <-- The precise location of the error in our query
        {
          "line": 2,    <-- The error was found in the second line of our query document.
          "column": 14  <-- The error was found at the 14th character in the second line.
        }
      ]
    }
  ]
}
```

On the other hand, if you run the `ingredient()` query without any parentheses at all, as shown in listing 9.5, you'll get an error specifying that you missed the required parameter id.

> **USE OF PARENTHESES IN GRAPHQL QUERIES AND MUTATIONS** In GraphQL, the parameters of a query are defined within parentheses. If you run a query with required parameters, such as `ingredient`, you must include the parameters within parentheses (see listing 9.3). Failing to do so will throw an error (see listings 9.4 and 9.5). If you run a query without parameters, you must omit the parentheses. For example, when we run the `allIngredients()` query, we omit parentheses (see listing 9.1), since `allIngredients()` doesn't require any parentheses.

Listing 9.5 Missing query parameter errors

```
# Query:
{
  ingredient {          <-- We run the ingredient() query without the parentheses.
    name
  }
}

# Error:
{
  "errors": [
    {
      "message": "Field \"ingredient\" argument \"id\" of type \"ID!\" is
➥ required, but it was not provided.",      <-- The error message says that the id parameter is missing in the query.
```

```
        "locations": [
          {
            "line": 2,                    <-- The error was found in the second
                                              line of our query document.
            "column": 3                   <-- The error was found at
          }                                   the third character of
        ]                                     the second line.
      }
    ]
}
```

Now that we know how to read and interpret error messages when we make mistakes in our queries, let's explore queries that return multiple types.

9.3 Using fragments in queries

This section explains how we run queries that return multiple types. The queries that we've seen so far in this chapter are simple since they only return one type, which is `Ingredient`. However, our product-related queries, such as `allProducts()` and `product()`, return the `Product` union type, which is the combination of the `Cake` and `Beverage` types. How do we run our queries in this case?

When a GraphQL query returns multiple types, we must create selection sets for each type. For example, if you run the `allProducts()` query with a single selector, you get the error message saying that the server doesn't know how to resolve the properties in the selection set.

Listing 9.6 Calling `allProducts()` with a single selector set

```
# Query
{
  allProducts {          <-- We run the allProducts()
                             query without parameters.
    name                 <-- We include the
  }                          name property in
}                            the selection set.

# Error message
{
  "errors": [            <-- We get an error
                             response.
    {
      "message": "Cannot query field \"name\" on type \"Product\". Did you
➥ mean to use an inline fragment on \"ProductInterface\", \"Beverage\",
➥ or \"Cake\"?",                <-- The server doesn't know how
                                     to resolve the properties in
                                     the selection set.
      "locations": [
        {
          "line": 3,             <-- The error was found in the
                                     third line of the query
                                     document.
          "column": 5            <-- The error was found at the
                                     fifth position of the third line.
        }
      ]
    }
  ]
}
```

The error message in listing 9.6 asks you whether you meant to use an inline fragment on either ProductInterface, Beverage, or Cake. What is an inline fragment? An *inline fragment* is an anonymous selection set on a specific type. The syntax for inline fragments includes three dots (the spread operator in JavaScript) followed by the on keyword and the type on which the selection set applies, as well as a selection of properties between curly braces:

```
...on ProductInterface {
    name
  }
```

Listing 9.7 fixes the allProducts() query by adding inline fragments that select properties on the ProductInterface, Cake, and Beverage types. allProducts()'s return type is Product, which is the union of Cake and Beverage, so we can select properties from both types. From the specification, we also know that Cake and Beverage implement the ProductInterface interface type, so we can conveniently select properties common to both Cake and Beverage directly on the interface.

Listing 9.7 Adding inline fragments for each return type

```
{
  allProducts {
    ...on ProductInterface {      <-- Inline fragment with a selection set on the ProductInterface type
      name
    }
    ...on Cake {                  <-- Inline fragment with a selection set on the Cake type
      hasFilling
    }
    ...on Beverage {              <-- Inline fragment with a selection set on the Beverage type
      hasCreamOnTopOption
    }
  }
}
```

Listing 9.7 uses inline fragments, but the real benefit of fragments is we can define them as standalone variables. This makes fragments reusable, and it also makes our queries more readable. Listing 9.8 shows how we can refactor listing 9.7 to use standalone fragments. The queries are so much cleaner! In real-life situations, you're likely to work with large selection sets, so organizing your fragments into standalone, reusable pieces of code will make your queries easier to read.

Listing 9.8 Using standalone fragments

```
{
  allProducts {
    ...commonProperties
    ...cakeProperties
    ...beverageProperties
  }
}
```

```
fragment commonProperties on ProductInterface {
  name
}

fragment cakeProperties on Cake {
  hasFilling
}

fragment beverageProperties on Beverage {
  hasCreamOnTopOption
}
```

Now that we know how to deal with queries that return multiple object types, let's take our querying skills to the next level. In the next section, we'll learn to run queries with a specific type of parameter called an input parameter.

9.4 Running queries with input parameters

This section explains how we run queries with input type parameters. In section 8.8, we learned that input types are similar to object types, but they're meant for use as parameters for a GraphQL query or mutation. One example of an input type in the products API is `ProductsFilter`, which allows us to filter products by factors such as availability, minimum or maximum price, and others. `ProductsFilter` is the parameter of the `products()` query. How do we call the `products()` query?

When a query takes parameters in the form of an input type, the query's input type parameter must be passed in the form of an input object. This may sound complicated, but it's actually very simple. We call the `products()` query using `ProductsFilter`'s `maxPrice` parameter. To use any of the parameters in the input type, we simply wrap them with curly braces.

Listing 9.9 Calling a query with a required parameter

```
{
  products(input: {maxPrice: 10}) {      <- We specify ProductFilter's maxPrice parameter.
    ...on ProductInterface {             <- Inline fragment on the ProductInterface type
      name
    }
  }
}
```

Now that we know how to call queries with input parameters, let's take a deeper look at the relationships between the objects defined in the API specification and see how we can build queries that allow us to traverse our data graph.

9.5 Navigating the API graph

This section explains how we select properties from multiple types by leveraging their connections. In section 8.5, we learned to create connections between object types by using edge properties and through types. These connections allow API clients to traverse the graph of relationships between the resources managed by the API. For example, in the products API, the `Cake` and `Beverage` types are connected with the `Ingredient` type by means of a through type called `IngredientRecipe`. By leveraging this connection, we can run queries that fetch information about the ingredients related to each product. In this section, we'll learn to build such queries.

In our queries, whenever we add a selector for a property that points to another object type, we must include a nested selection set for said object type. For example, if we add a selector for the `ingredient` property on the `ProductInterface` type, we have to include a selection set with any of the properties in `IngredientRecipe` nested within the `ingredients` property. We include a nested selection set for the `ingredients` property of `ProductInterface` in the `allProducts()` query. The query selects the name of each product as well as the name of each ingredient in the product's recipe.

Listing 9.10 Querying nested object types

```
{
  allProducts {
    ...on ProductInterface {        <-- Inline fragment on the ProductInterface type
      name,
      ingredients {                 <-- Selector for ProductInterface's ingredients property
        ingredient {                <-- Selector for IngredientRecipe's ingredient property
          name
        }
      }
    }
  }
}
```

Listing 9.10 leverages the connection between the `ProductInterface` and `Ingredient` types to fetch information from both types in a single query, but we can take this further. The `Ingredient` type contains a `supplier` property, which points to the `Supplier` type. Say we want to get a list of products, including their names and ingredients, together with the supplier's name of each ingredient. (I encourage you to head over to the Voyager UI generated by `graphql-faker` to visualize the relationships captured by this query; figure 9.1 is an illustration of the Voyager UI.)

Listing 9.11 Traversing the products API graph through connections between types

```
{
  allProducts {
    ...on ProductInterface {        <-- Inline fragment on the ProudctInterface type
      name
      ingredients {                 <-- Selector for ProductInterface's ingredients property
        ingredient {                <-- Selector for IngredientRecipe's ingredient property
          name
          supplier {                <-- Selector for Ingredient's supplier property
            name
          }
        }
```

```
        }
      }
    }
}
```

Listing 9.11 is traversing our graph of types. Starting from the `ProductInterface` type, we are able to fetch details about other objects, such as `Ingredient` and `Supplier`, by leveraging their connections.

Here lies one the most powerful features of GraphQL, and one of its main advantages in comparison with other types of APIs, such as REST. Using REST, we'd need to make multiple requests to obtain all the information we were able to fetch in one request in listing 9.11. GraphQL gives you the power to obtain all the information you need, and just the information you need, in a single request.

Now that we know how to traverse the graph of types in a GraphQL API, let's take our querying skills to the next level by learning how to run multiple queries within a single request!

9.6 Running multiple queries and query aliasing

This section explains how to run multiple queries per request and how to create aliases for the responses returned by the server. Aliasing our queries means changing the key under which the dataset returned by the server is indexed. As we'll see, aliases can improve the readability of the results returned by the server, especially when we make multiple queries per request.

9.6.1 Running multiple queries in the same request

In previous sections, we ran only one query per request. However, GraphQL also allows us to send several queries in one request. This is yet another powerful feature of GraphQL that can help us save unnecessary network round-trips to the server, improving the overall performance of our applications and therefore user experience.

Let's say we wanted to obtain a list of all the products and ingredients available in the CoffeeMesh platform, as shown in figure 9.4. To do that, we can run `allIngredients()` with the `allProducts()` queries. Listing 9.12 shows how we include both operations within the same query document. By including multiple queries within the same query document, we make sure all of them are sent to the server in the same request, and therefore we save round-trips to the server. The code also includes a named fragment that selects properties on the `ProductInterface` type. Named fragments are useful to keep our queries clean and focused.

Listing 9.12 Multiple queries per request

```
{
  allProducts {                  <-- We run the allProducts() query without parameters.
    ...commonProperties          <-- We select properties using a named fragment.
  }
```

```
  allIngredients {      <-- We run the
    name                    allIngredients() query.
  }
}
                                                          Named fragment with
                                                          selection set on the
fragment commonProperties on ProductInterface {      <--  ProductInterface type
  name
}
```

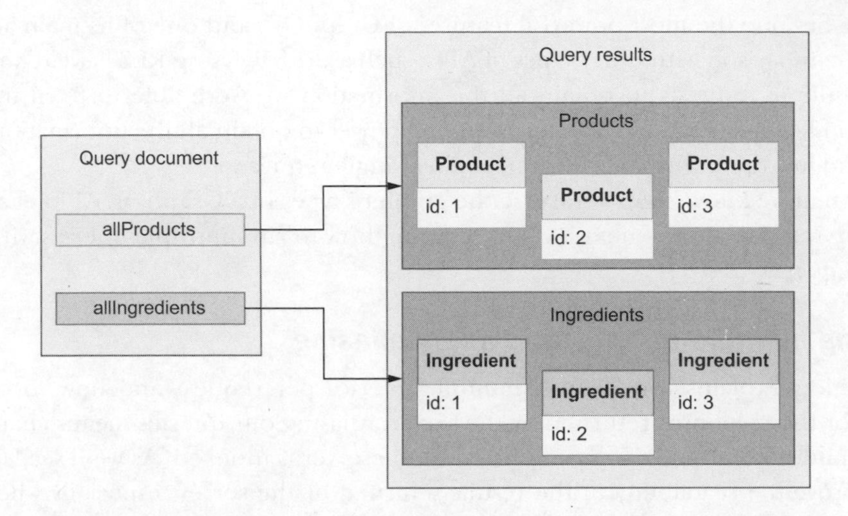

Figure 9.4 In GraphQL, we can run multiple queries within the same request, and the response will contain one dataset for each query.

9.6.2 *Aliasing our queries*

All the queries we've run in previous sections are anonymous queries. When we make an anonymous query, the data returned by the server appears under a key named after the name of the query we're calling.

Listing 9.13 Result of an anonymous query

```
# Query:
{
  allIngredients {      <-- We run the
    name                    allIngredients()
  }                         query.
}

# Result:                   Successful
{                           response from
  "data": {             <-- the query
    "allIngredients": [     <-- Query
      {                         result
        "name": "string"
      },
```

```
            {
                "name": "string"
            }
        ]
    }
}
```

Running anonymous queries can sometimes be confusing. `allIngredients()` returns a list of ingredients, so it is helpful to index the list of ingredients under an `ingredients` key, instead of `allIngredients()`. Changing the name of this key is called *query aliasing*. We can make our queries more readable by using aliasing. The benefits of aliasing become clearer when we include multiple queries in the same request. For example, the query for all products and ingredients shown in listing 9.12 becomes more readable if we use aliases. The following code shows how we use aliases to rename the results of each query: the result of `allProducts()` appears under the `product` alias, and the result of the `allIngredients()` query appears under the `ingredients` alias.

Listing 9.14 Using query aliasing for more readable queries

```
{
  products: allProducts {           ← Alias for the allProducts() query
    ...commonProperties             ← We select properties using a named fragment.
  }
  ingredients: allIngredients {     ← Alias for the allIngredients() query
    name
  }
}

fragment commonProperties on ProductInterface {   ← Named fragment with selection set on the ProductInterface
  name
}
```

In some cases, using query aliases is necessary to make our requests work. For example, in listing 9.15, we run the `products()` query twice to select two datasets: one for available products and another for unavailable products. Both datasets are produced by the same query: `products`. As you can see, without query aliasing, this request results in conflict error, because both datasets return under the same key: `products`.

Listing 9.15 Error due to calling the same query multiple times without aliases

```
{
  products(input: {available: true}) {    ← We run the products() query filtering for available products.
    ...commonProperties                   ← We select properties using the commonProperties fragment.
  }
  products(input: {available: false}) {   ← We run the products() query filtering for unavailable products.
    ...commonProperties
  }
}
```

```
fragment commonProperties on ProductInterface {    <-- Named fragment with selection set on the ProductInterface type.
  name
}

# Error
{
  "errors": [    <-- The query returns an unsuccessful response, so the payload includes an error key.
    {
      "message": "Fields \"products\" conflict because they have differing
➥ arguments. Use different aliases on the fields to fetch both if this
➥ was intentional.",    <-- The error message says that the query document contains a conflict.
      "locations": [
        {
          "line": 2,    <-- The server found errors in lines 2 and 5 from the query document.
          "column": 3
        },
        {
          "line": 5,
          "column": 3
        }
      ]
    }
  ]
}
```

To resolve the conflict created by the queries in listing 9.15, we must use aliases. Listing 9.16 fixes the query by adding an alias to each operation: `availableProducts` for the query that filters for available products and `unavailableProducts` for the query that filters for unavailable products.

Listing 9.16 Calling the same query multiple times with aliases

```
{
  availableProducts: products(input: {available: true}) {    <-- Alias for the available products() query
    ...commonProperties
  }
  unavailableProducts: products(input: {available: false}) {    <-- unavailableProducts alias for the unavailable products() query
    ...commonProperties
  }
}

fragment commonProperties on ProductInterface {
  name
}

# Result (datasets omitted for brevity)
{
  "data": {    <-- Successful response from the server
    "availableProducts": [...],    <-- Result of the available products() query
    "unavailableProducts": [...]    <-- Result of the unavailable products() query
  }
}
```

This concludes our overview of GraphQL queries. You've learned to run queries with parameters, with input types, with inline and named fragments, and with aliases, and you've learned to include multiple queries within the same request. We've come a long way! But no overview of the GraphQL query language would be complete without learning how to run mutations.

9.7 Running GraphQL mutations

This section explains how we run GraphQL mutations. Mutations are GraphQL functions that allow us to create resources or change the state of the server. Running a mutation is similar to running a query. The only difference between the two is in their intent: queries are meant to read data from the server, while mutations are meant to create or change data in the server.

Let's illustrate how we run a mutation with an example. Listing 9.17 shows how we run the `deleteProduct()` mutation. When we use mutations, we must start our query document by qualifying our operation as a mutation. The `deleteProduct()` mutation has one required argument, a product ID, and its return value is a simple Boolean, so in this case, we don't have to include a selection set.

Listing 9.17 Calling a mutation

```
mutation {                          <-- We qualify the operation we're going to run as a mutation.
  deleteProduct(id: "asdf")         <-- We call the deleteProduct() mutation, passing in the required id parameter.
}
```

Let's now look at a more complex mutation, like `addProduct()`, which is used to add new products to the CoffeeMesh catalogue. `addProduct()` has three required parameters:

- `name`—The product name.
- `type`—The product type. The values for this parameter are constrained by the `ProductType` enumeration, which offers two choices: cake and beverage.
- `input`—Additional product properties, such as its price, size, list of ingredients, and others. The full list of properties is given by the `AddProductInput` type.

`addProduct()` returns a value of type `Product`, which means, in this case, we must include a selection set. Remember that `Product` is the union of the `Cake` and `Beverage` types, so our selection set must use fragments to indicate which type's properties we want to include in our return payload. In the following example, we select the `name` property on the `ProductInterface` type.

Listing 9.18 Calling a mutation with input parameters and complex return type

```
mutation {     <-- We qualify the operation we're going to run as a mutation.
  addProduct(name: "Mocha", type: beverage, input: {price: 10, size: BIG,
     ingredients: [{ingredient: 1, quantity: 1, unit: LITERS}]}) {     <-- We call the addProduct() mutation.
```

```
    ...commonProperties
  }
}

fragment commonProperties on ProductInterface {
  name
}
```

We select properties using a named fragment.

Now that we know how to run mutations, it's time to learn how we write more structured and readable query documents by parameterizing the arguments.

9.8 Running parameterized queries and mutations

This section introduces parameterized queries and explains how we can use them to build more structured and readable query documents. In previous sections, when using queries and mutations that require parameters, we defined the values for each parameter in the same line we called the function. In queries with lots of arguments, this approach can lead to query documents, which are cluttered and difficult to read and maintain. GraphQL offers a solution for this, which is to use parameterized queries.

Parameterized queries allow us to decouple our query/mutation calls from the data. Figure 9.5 illustrates how we parameterize the call to the `addProduct()` mutation using GraphiQL (the code for the query is also shown in listing 9.19 so that you can inspect it and copy it more easily). There're two things we need to do when we parameterize a query or mutation: create a function wrapper around the query/mutation, and

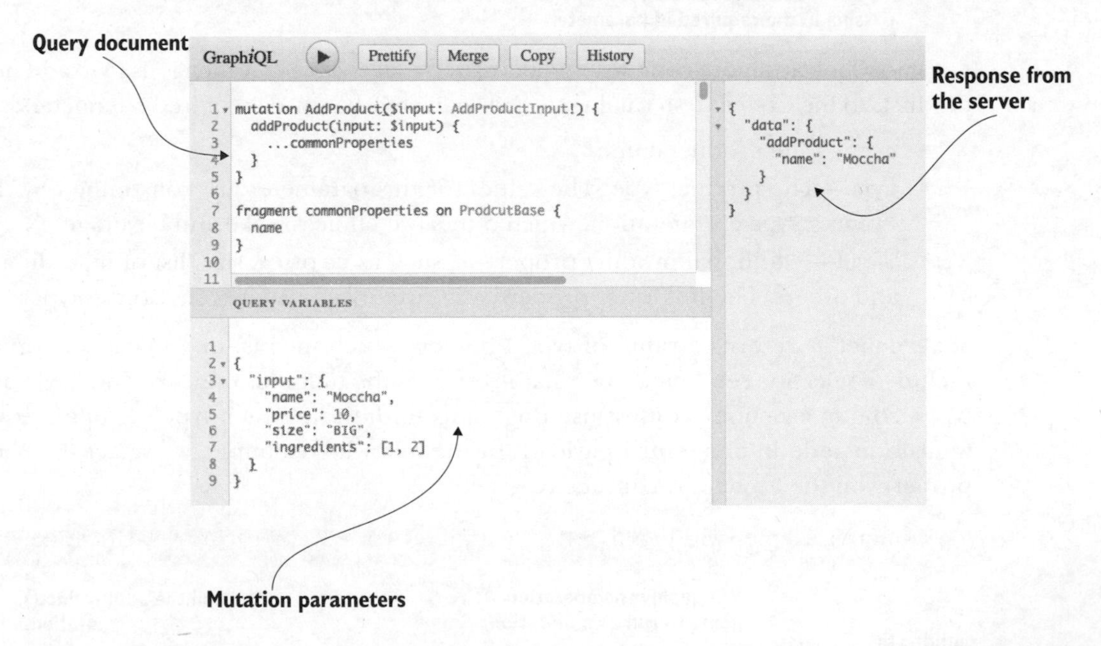

Figure 9.5 GraphiQL offers a Query Variables panel where we can include the input values for our parameterized queries.

assign values for the query/mutation parameters in a query variables object. Figure 9.6 illustrates how all these pieces fit together to bind the parameterized values to the `addProduct()` mutation call.

Listing 9.19 Using parameterized syntax

```
# Query document
mutation CreateProduct(                                  <- We create a wrapper named CreateProduct().
  $name: String!
  $type: ProductType!
  $input: AddProductInput!
) {
  addProduct(name: $name, type: $type, input: $input) {  <- We call the addProduct() mutation.
    ...commonProperties                                  <- We select properties using a named fragment.
  }
}

fragment commonProperties on ProductInterface {
  name
}

# Query variables
{
  "name": "Mocha",                                       <- We assign a value to the name parameter.
  "type": "beverage",                                    <- We assign a value to the type parameter.
  "input": {                                             <- We assign a value to the input parameter.
    "price": 10,
    "size": "BIG",
    "ingredients": [{"ingredient": 1, "quantity": 1, "unit": "LITERS"}]
  }
}
```

Let's look at each of these steps in detail.

1. *Creating a query/mutation wrapper.* To parameterize our queries, we create a function wrapper around the query or mutation. In figure 9.5, we call the wrapper `CreateProduct()`. The syntax for the wrapper looks very similar to the syntax we use to define a query. Parameterized arguments must be included in the wrapper's function signature. In figure 9.5, we parameterize the `name`, `type`, and `input` parameters of the `addProduct()` mutation. The parameterized argument is marked with a dollar sign (`$`). In the wrapper's signature (i.e., in `CreateProduct()`), we specify the expected type of the parameterized arguments.
2. *Parameterizing through a query variables object.* Separately, we define our query variables as a JSON document. As you can see in figure 9.5, in GraphiQL we define query variables within the Query Variables panel. For further clarification on how parameterized queries work, look at figure 9.6.

In figure 9.5, we used parameterized syntax to wrap only one mutation, but nothing prevents us from wrapping more mutations within the same query document. When we wrap multiple queries or mutations, all the parameterized arguments must be defined

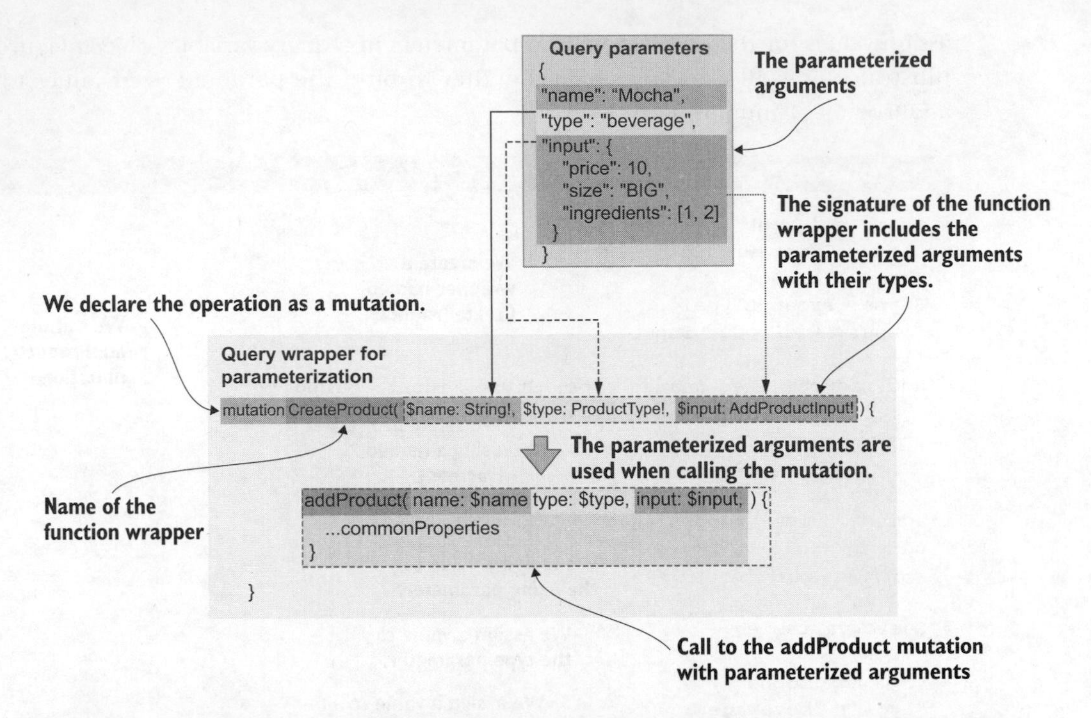

Figure 9.6 To parameterize queries and mutations, we create a function wrapper around the query or mutation. In the wrapper's signature we include the parameterized arguments. Parameterized variables carry a leading dollar (`$`) sign.

within the wrapper's function signature. The following code shows how we extend the query from listing 9.19 to include a call to the `deleteProduct()` mutation. Here, we call the wrapper `CreateAndDeleteProduct()` to better represent the actions in this request.

Listing 9.20 Using parameterized syntax

```
# Query document
mutation CreateAndDeleteProduct(     ◁ We created a wrapper named CreateAndDeleteProduct().
  $name: String!
  $type: ProductType!
  $input: AddProductInput!
  $id: ID!
) {
  addProduct(name: $name, type: $type, input: $input) {     ◁ We call the addProduct() mutation.
    ...commonProperties     ◁ We select properties using a named fragment.
  }
  deleteProduct(id: $id)     ◁ We call the deleteProduct() mutation.
}

fragment commonProperties on ProductInterface {
  name
}
```

```
# Query variables
{
  "name": "Mocha",             <-- We assign values
  "type": "beverage",              to addProduct()'s
  "input": {                       parameters.
    "price": 10,
    "size": "BIG",
    "ingredients": [{"ingredient": 1, "quantity": 1, "unit": "LITERS"}]
  },
  "id": "asdf"              <-- We set the value for
}                               deleteProduct()'s id
                                parameter.
```

This completes our journey through learning how to consume GraphQL APIs. You can now inspect any GraphQL API, explore its types, and play around with its queries and mutations. Before we close this chapter, I'd like to show you how a GraphQL API request works under the hood.

9.9 Demystifying GraphQL queries

This section explains how GraphQL queries work under the hood in the context of HTTP requests. In previous sections, we used the GraphiQL client to explore our GraphQL API and to interact with it. GraphiQL translates our query documents into HTTP requests that the GraphQL server understands. GraphQL clients such as GraphiQL are interfaces that make it easier to interact with a GraphQL API. But nothing prevents you from sending an HTTP request directly to the API, say, from your terminal, using something like cURL. Contrary to a popular misconception, you don't really need any special tools to work with GraphQL APIs.[1]

To send a request to a GraphQL API, you can use either of the GET or POST methods. If you use GET, you send your query document using URL query parameters, and if you use POST, you include the query in the request payload. GraphQL Faker's mock server only accepts GET requests, so I'll illustrate how you send a query using GET.

Let's run the `allIngredients()` query, selecting only the `name` property of each ingredient. Since this is a GET request, our query document must be included in the URL as a query parameter. However, the query document contains special characters, such as curly braces, which are considered unsafe and therefore cannot be included in a URL. To deal with special characters in URLs, we URL encode them. *URL encoding* is the process of translating special characters, such as braces, punctuation marks, and others, into a suitable format for URLs. URL-encoded characters start with a

[1] Unless you want to use subscriptions (connections with the GraphQL server that allow you to receive notifications when something happens in the server, e.g., when the state of a resource changes). Subscriptions require a two-way connection with the server, so you need something more sophisticated than cURL. To learn more about GraphQL subscriptions, see Eve Porcello and Alex Banks, *Learning GraphQL, Declarative Data Fetching for Modern Web Apps* (O'Reilly, 2018), pp. 50–53 and 150–160.

percent sign, so this type of encoding is also known as *percent encoding*.[2] cURL takes care of URL encoding our data when we use the `--data-urlencode` option. By using `--data-urlencode`, cURL translates our command into a GET request with the following URL: http://localhost:9002/graphql?query=%7BallIngredients%7Bname%7D%7D. The following snippet shows the cURL command you need to run to make this call:

```
$ curl http://localhost:9002/graphql --data-urlencode \
'query={allIngredients{name}}'
```

Now that you understand how GraphQL API requests work under the hood, let's see how we can leverage this knowledge to write code in Python that consumes a GraphQL API.

9.10 Calling a GraphQL API with Python code

This section illustrates how we can interact with a GraphQL API using Python. GraphQL clients like GraphiQL are useful to explore and get familiar with a GraphQL API, but in practice, you'll spend most of your time writing applications that consume those APIs programmatically. In this section, we learn to consume the products API using a GraphQL client written in Python.

To work with GraphQL APIs, the Python ecosystem offers libraries such as `gql` (https://github.com/graphql-python/gql) and `sgqlc` (https://github.com/profusion/sgqlc). These libraries are useful when we want to use advanced features of GraphQL, such as subscriptions. You'll rarely need those features in the context of microservices, so for the purposes of this section, we'll take a simpler approach and use the popular `requests` library (https://github.com/psf/requests). Remember that GraphQL queries are simply GET or POST requests with a query document.

Listing 9.21 shows how we call the `allIngredients()` query, adding a selector for `Ingredient`'s `name` property. The listing is also available under ch09/client.py in this book's GitHub repository. Since our GraphQL mock server only accepts GET requests, we send the query document in the form of URL-encoded data. With requests, we accomplish this by passing the query document through the `get` method's `params` argument. As you can see, the query document looks the same as what we wrote in the GraphiQL query panel, and the result from the API also looks the same. This is great news, because it means that, when working out your queries, you can start working with GraphiQL, leveraging its great support for syntax highlighting and query validation, and when you're ready, you can move your queries directly to your Python code.

[2] Tim Berners-Lee, R. Fielding, and L. Masinter, "Uniform Resource Identifer (URI): Generic Syntax," RFC 3986, section 2.1, https://datatracker.ietf.org/doc/html/rfc3986#section-2.1.

Listing 9.21 Calling a GraphQL query using Python

```
# file: ch09/client.py

import requests                                    ◁ We import the requests library.

URL = 'http://localhost:9002/graphql'              ◁ The base URL of our GraphQL server

query_document = '''                               ◁ The query document
{
  allIngredients {
    name
  }
}
'''

result = requests.get(URL, params={'query': query_document})   ◁ We send a GET request to the server with the query document as a URL query parameter.

print(result.json())                               ◁ We parse and print the JSON payload returned by the server.

# Result
{'data': {'allIngredients': [{'name': 'string'}, {'name': 'string'},
➥ {'name': 'string'}]}}
```

This concludes our journey through GraphQL. You went from learning about the basic scalar types supported by GraphQL in chapter 8 to making complex queries using tools as varied as GraphiQL, cURL, and Python in this chapter. Along the way, we built the specification for the products API, and we interacted with it using a GraphQL mock server. That's no small feat. If you've read this far, you've learned a great deal of things about APIs, and you should be proud of it!

GraphQL is one of the most popular protocols in the world of web APIs, and its adoption grows every year. GraphQL is a great choice for building microservices APIs and for integration with frontend applications. In the next chapter, we'll undertake the actual implementation of the products API and its service. Stay tuned!

Summary

- When we call a query or mutation that returns an object type, our query must include a selection set. A selection set is a list of the properties we want to fetch from the object returned by the query.
- When a query or mutation returns a list of multiple types, our selection set must include fragments. Fragments are selections of properties on a specific type, and they're prefixed by the spread operator (three dots).
- When calling a query or mutation that includes arguments, we can parameterize those arguments by building a wrapper around the query or queries. This allows us to write more readable and maintainable query documents.
- When designing a GraphQL API, it's a good idea to put it to work with a mock server, which allows us to build API clients while the server is implemented.

- You can run a GraphQL mock server using `graphql-faker`, which also creates a GraphiQL interface to the API. This is useful to test that our design conforms to our expectations.
- Behind the scenes, a GraphQL query is a simple HTTP request that uses either of the GET or POST methods. When using GET, we must ensure our query document is URL encoded, and when using POST, we include it in the request payload.

10 Building GraphQL APIs with Python

This chapter covers

- Creating GraphQL APIs using the Ariadne web server framework
- Validating request and response payloads
- Creating resolvers for queries and mutations
- Creating resolvers for complex object types, such as union types
- Creating resolvers for custom scalar types and object properties

In chapter 8, we designed a GraphQL API for the products service, and we produced a specification detailing the requirements for the products API. In this chapter, we implement the API according to the specification. To build the API, we'll use the Ariadne framework, which is one of the most popular GraphQL libraries in the Python ecosystem. Ariadne allows us to leverage the benefits of documentation-driven development by automatically loading data validation models from the specification. We'll learn to create resolvers, which are Python functions that implement the logic of a query or mutation. We'll also learn to handle queries that return multiple types. After reading this chapter, you'll have all the tools you need to start developing your own GraphQL APIs!

The code for this chapter is available in the GitHub repository provided with this book, under the folder ch10. Unless otherwise specified, all the file references within this chapter are relative to the ch10 folder. For example, server.py refers to the ch10/server.py file, and web/schema.py refers to the ch10/web/schema.py file. Also, to ensure all the commands used in this chapter work as expected, use the `cd` command to move the ch10 folder in your terminal.

10.1 Analyzing the API requirements

In this section, we analyze the requirements of the API specification. Before jumping into implementing an API, it's worth spending some time analyzing the API specification and what it requires. Let's do this analysis for the products API!

The products API specification is available under ch10/web/products.graphql in the GitHub repository for this book. The specification defines a collection of object types that represent the data we can retrieve from the API and a set of queries and mutations that expose the capabilities of the products service. We must create validation models that faithfully represent the schemas defined in the specification, as well as functions that correctly implement the functionality of the queries and mutations. We'll work with a framework that can handle schema validation automatically from the specification, so we don't need to worry about implementing validation models.

Our implementation will focus mainly on the queries and mutations. Most of the queries and mutations defined in the schema return either an array or a single instance of the `Ingredient` and `Product` types. `Ingredient` is simpler since it's an object type, so we'll look at queries and mutations that use this type first. `Product` is the union of the `Beverage` and `Cake` types, both of which implement the `ProductInterface` type. As we'll see, implementing queries and mutations that return union types is slightly more complex. A query that returns a list of `Product` objects contains instances of both the `Beverage` and `Cake` types, so we need to implement additional functionality that makes it possible for the server to determine which type each element in the list belongs to.

With that said, let's analyze the tech stack that we'll use for this chapter, and then move straight into the implementation!

10.2 Introducing the tech stack

In this section, we discuss the tech stack that we'll use to implement the products API. We discuss which libraries are available for implementing GraphQL APIs in Python, and we choose one of them. We also discuss the server framework that we'll use to run the application.

Since we're going to implement a GraphQL API, the first thing we want to look for is a good GraphQL server library. GraphQL's website (https://graphql.org/code/) is an excellent resource for finding tools and frameworks for the GraphQL ecosystem. As the ecosystem is constantly evolving, I recommend you check out that website every once in a while for any new additions. The website lists four Python libraries that support GraphQL:

- *Graphene* (https://github.com/graphql-python/graphene) is one of the first GraphQL libraries built for Python. It's battle tested and one of the most widely used libraries.
- *Ariadne* (https://github.com/mirumee/ariadne) is a library built for schema-first (or documentation-driven) development. It's a highly popular framework, and it handles schema validation and serialization automatically.
- *Strawberry* (https://github.com/strawberry-graphql/strawberry) is a more recent library that makes it easy to implement GraphQL schema models by offering a clean interface inspired by Python data classes.
- *Tartiflette* (https://github.com/tartiflette/tartiflette) is another recent addition to the Python ecosystem that allows you to implement a GraphQL server using a schema-first approach, and it's built on top of asyncio, which is Python's core library for asynchronous programming.

For this chapter, we'll use Ariadne, since it supports a schema-first or documentation-driven development approach, and it's a mature project. The API specification is already available, so we don't want to spend time implementing each schema model in Python. Instead, we want to use a library that can handle schema validation and serialization directly from the API specification, and Ariadne can do that.

We'll run the Ariadne server with the help of Uvicorn, which we encountered in chapters 2 and 6 when we worked with FastAPI. To install the dependencies for this chapter, you can use the Pipfile and Pipfile.lock files available under the ch10 folder in the repository provided with this book. Copy the Pipfile and Pipfile.lock files into your ch10 folder, `cd` into it, and run the following command:

```
pipenv install
```

If you prefer to install the latest versions of Ariadne and Uvicorn, simply run

```
pipenv install ariadne uvicorn
```

Now that we have the dependencies installed, let's activate the environment:

```
pipenv shell
```

With all the dependencies installed, now we are ready to start coding, so let's do it!

10.3 Introducing Ariadne

In this section, we introduce the Ariadne framework, and we learn how it works by using a simple example. We'll learn how to run a GraphQL server with Ariadne, how to load a GraphQL specification, and how to implement a simple GraphQL resolver. As we saw in chapter 9, users interact with GraphQL APIs by running queries and mutations. A GraphQL resolver is a function that knows how to execute one of those queries or mutations. In our implementation, we'll have as many resolvers as queries and mutations there are in the API specification. As you can see from figure 10.1, resolvers are the pillars of a GraphQL server since it's through resolvers that we can return actual data to the API users.

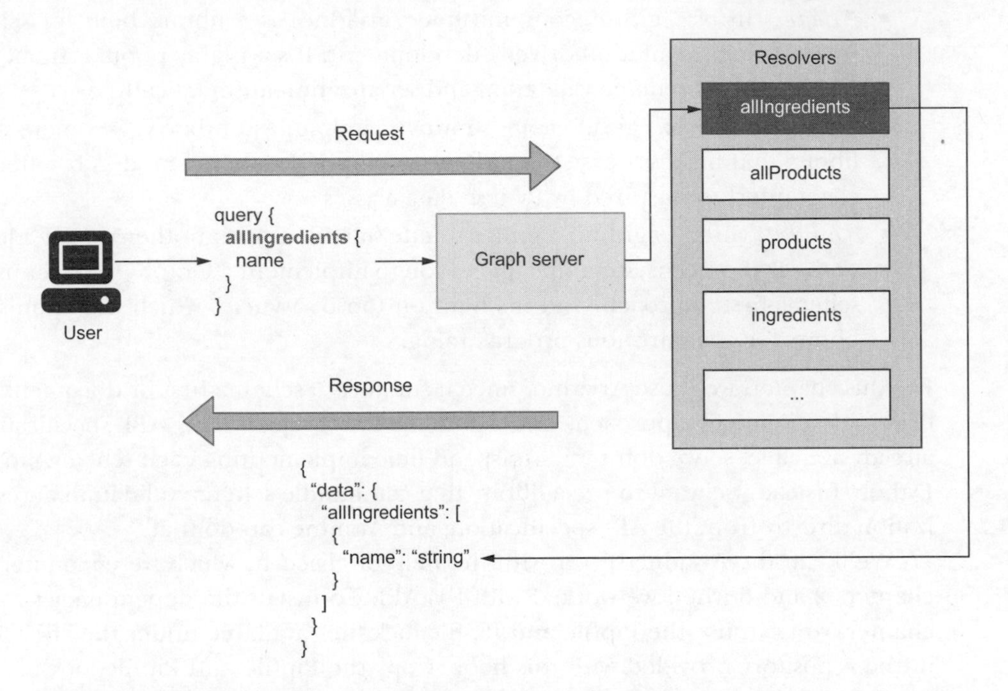

Figure 10.1 To serve data to a user, a GraphQL server uses resolvers, which are functions that know how to build the payload for a given query.

Let's start by writing a very simple GraphQL schema. Open the server.py file and copy the following content into it:

```
# file: server.py

schema = '''
  type Query {
    hello: String
  }
'''
```

We define a variable called `schema`, and we point it to a simple GraphQL schema. This schema defines only one query, named `hello()`, which returns a string. The return value of the `hello()` query is optional, which means `null` is also a valid return value. To expose this query through our GraphQL server, we need to implement a resolver using Ariadne.

Ariadne can run a GraphQL server from this simple schema definition. How do we do that? First, we need to load the schema using Ariadne's `make_executable_schema()` function. `make_executable_schema()` parses the document, validates our definitions, and builds an internal representation of the schema. As you can see in figure 10.2, Ariadne uses the output of this function to validate our data. For example, when we return the payload for a query, Ariadne validates the payload against the schema.

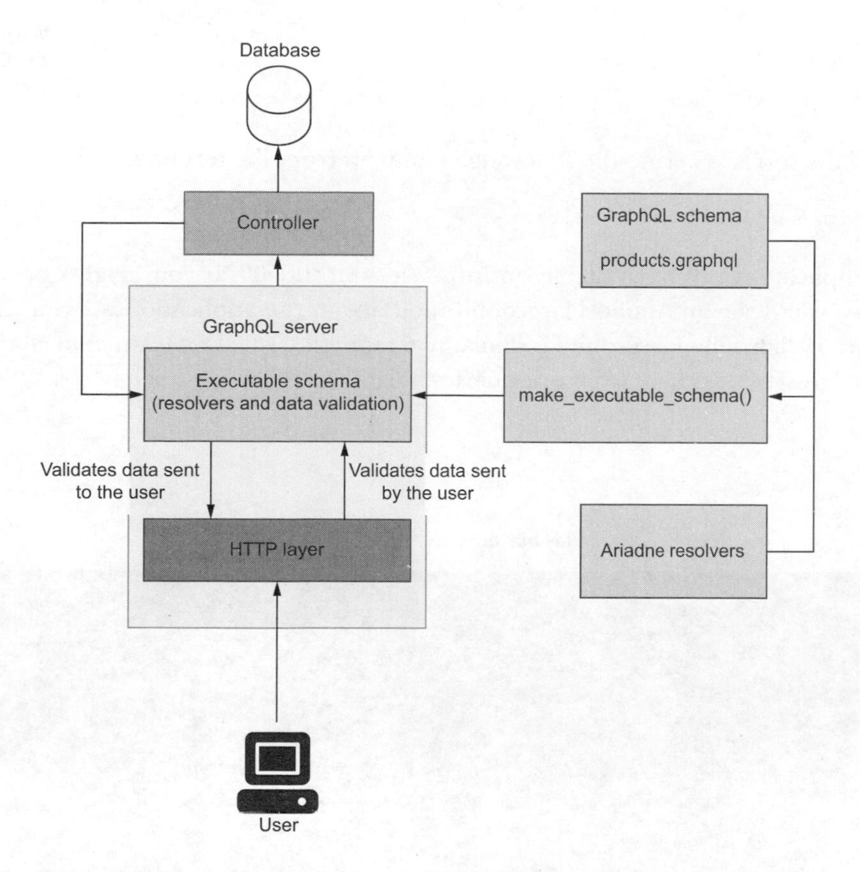

Figure 10.2 To run the GraphQL server with Ariadne, we produce an executable schema by loading the GraphQL schema for the API and a collection of resolvers for the queries and mutations. Ariadne uses the executable schema to validate data the user sent to the server, as well as data sent from the server to the user.

Once we've loaded the schema, we can initialize our server using Ariadne's `GraphQL` class (listing 10.1). Ariadne provides two implementations of the server: a synchronous implementation, which is available under the `ariande.wsgi` module, and an asynchronous implementation, which is available under the `ariande.asgi` module. In this chapter, we'll use the asynchronous implementation.

Listing 10.1 Initializing a GraphQL server using Ariadne

```
# file: server.py

from ariadne import make_executable_schema
from ariadne.asgi import GraphQL

schema = '''
  type Query {
    hello: String
  }
'''

server = GraphQL(make_executable_schema(schema), debug=True)
```

We declare a simple schema.

We instantiate the GraphQL server.

To run the server, execute the following command from the terminal:

```
$ uvicorn server:server --reload
```

Your application will be available on http://localhost:8000. If you head over to that address, you'll see an Apollo Playground interface to the application. As you can see in figure 10.3, Apollo Playground is similar to GraphiQL, which we learned in chapter 8. On the left-side panel, we write our queries. Write the following query:

```
{
  hello
}
```

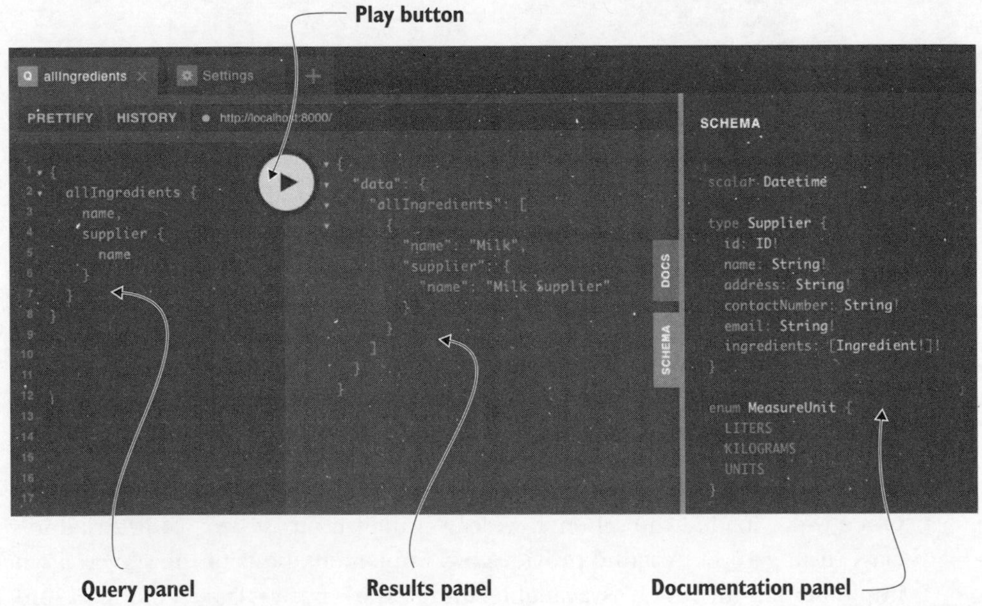

Figure 10.3 The Apollo Playground interface contains a query panel where we execute queries and mutations; a results panel where the queries and mutations are evaluated; and a documentation panel where we can inspect the API schemas.

This query executes the query function that we defined in listing 10.1. If you press the execute button, you'll get the results of this query on the right-side panel:

```
{
  "data": {
    "hello": null
  }
}
```

The query returns `null`. This shouldn't come as a surprise, since the return value of the `hello()` query is a nullable string. How can we make the `hello()` query return a string? Enter resolvers. *Resolvers* are functions that let the server know how to produce a value for a type or an attribute. To make the `hello()` query return an actual string, we need to implement a resolver. Let's create a resolver that returns a string of 10 random characters.

In Ariadne, a resolver is a Python callable (e.g., a function) that takes two positional parameters: `obj` and `info`.

Resolver parameters in Ariadne

Ariadne's resolvers always have two positional-only parameters, which are commonly called `obj` and `info`. The signature of a basic Ariadne resolver is

```
def simple_resolver(obj: Any, info: GraphQLResolveInfo):
    pass
```

As you can see in the figure, `obj` will normally be set to `None`, unless the resolver has a parent resolver, in which case `obj` will be set to the value returned by the parent resolver. We encounter the latter case when a resolver doesn't return an explicit type. For example, the resolver for the `allProducts()` query, which we'll implement in section 10.4.4, doesn't return an explicit type. It returns an object of type `Product`, which is the union of the `Cake` and `Beverage` types. To determine the type of each object, Ariadne needs to call a resolver for the `Product` type.

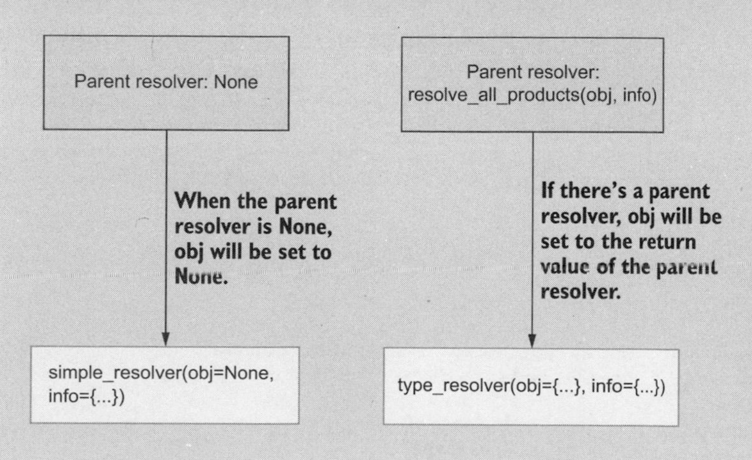

(continued)

The `info` parameter is an instance of `GraphQLResolveInfo`, which contains information required to execute a query. Ariadne uses this information to process and serve each request. For the application developer, the most interesting attribute exposed by the `info` object is `info.context`, which contains details about the context in which the resolver is called, such as the HTTP context. To learn more about the `obj` and `info` objects, check out Ariadne's documentation: https://ariadnegraphql.org/docs/resolvers.html.

A resolver needs to be bound to its corresponding object type. Ariadne provides bindable classes for each GraphQL type:

- `ObjectType` for object types.
- `QueryType` for query types. In GraphQL, the query type represents the collection of all queries available in a schema. As we saw in chapter 8 (section 8.8), a query is a function that reads data from a GraphQL server.
- `MutationType` for mutation types. As we saw in chapter 8 (section 8.9), a mutation is a function that alters the state of the GraphQL server.
- `UnionType` for union types.
- `InterfaceType` for interface types.
- `EnumType` for enumeration types.

Since `hello()` is a query, we need to bind its resolver to an instance of Ariadne's `QueryType`. Listing 10.2 shows how we do that. We first create an instance of the `QueryType` class and assign it to a variable called `query`. We then use `QueryType`'s `field()` decorator method to bind our resolver, which is available on most of Ariadne's bindable classes and allows us to bind a resolver to a specific field. By convention, we prefix our resolvers' names with `resolve_`. Ariadne's resolvers always get two positional-only parameters by default: `obj` and `info`. We don't need to make use of those parameters in this case, so we use a wildcard followed by an underscore (`*_`), which is a convention in Python to ignore a list of positional parameters. To make Ariadne aware of our resolvers, we need to pass our bindable objects as an array to the `make_executable_schema()` function. The changes go under server.py.

Listing 10.2 Implementing a GraphQL resolver with Ariadne

```
# file: server.py

import random
import string

from ariadne import QueryType, make_executable_schema
from ariadne.asgi import GraphQL

query = QueryType()        <-- Instance of QueryType
```

We bind a resolver for the hello() query using QueryType's field() decorator.

We skip positional-only parameters.

We return a list of randomly generated ASCII characters.

```
@query.field('hello')
def resolve_hello(*_):
    return ''.join(
        random.choice(string.ascii_letters) for _ in range(10)
    )
```

We declare our GraphQL schema.

Instance of the GraphQL server

```
schema = '''
type Query {
    hello: String
}
'''

server = GraphQL(make_executable_schema(schema, [query]), debug=True)
```

Since we're running the server with the hot reloading flag (`--reload`), the server automatically reloads once you save the changes to the file. Go back to the Apollo Playground interface in http://127.0.0.1:8000 and run the `hello()` query again. This time, you should get a random string of 10 characters as a result.

This completes our introduction to Ariadne. You've learned how to load a GraphQL schema with Ariadne, how to run the GraphQL server, and how to implement a resolver for a query function. In the rest of the chapter, we'll apply this knowledge as we build the GraphQL API for the products service.

10.4 Implementing the products API

In this section, we'll use everything we learned in the previous section to build the GraphQL API for the products service. Specifically, you'll learn to build resolvers for the queries and mutations of the products API, to handle query parameters, and to structure your project. Along the way, we'll learn additional features of the Ariadne framework and various strategies for testing and implementing GraphQL resolvers. By the end of this section, you'll be able to build GraphQL APIs for your own microservices. Let the journey begin!

10.4.1 Laying out the project structure

In this section, we structure our project for the products API implementation. So far, we've included all our code under the server.py file. To implement a whole API, we need to split our code into different files and add structure to the project; otherwise, the codebase would become difficult to read and to maintain. To keep the implementation simple, we'll use an in-memory representation of our data.

If you followed along with the code in the previous section, delete the code we wrote earlier under server.py, which represents the entry point to our application and therefore will contain an instance of the GraphQL server. We'll encapsulate the web server implementation within a folder called web/. Create this folder, and within it, create the following files:

- data.py will contain the in-memory representation of our data.
- mutations.py will contain resolvers for the mutations in the products API.
- queries.py will contain resolvers for queries.
- schema.py will contain all the code necessary to load an executable schema.
- types.py will contain resolvers for object types, custom scalar types, and object properties.

The products.graphql specification file also goes under the web folder, since it's handled by the code under the web/schema.py file. You can copy the API specification from the ch10/web/products.graphql file in the GitHub repository for this book. The directory structure for the products API looks like this:

```
.
├── Pipfile
├── Pipfile.lock
├── server.py
└── web
    ├── data.py
    ├── mutations.py
    ├── products.graphql
    ├── queries.py
    ├── schema.py
    └── types.py
```

The GitHub repository for this book contains an additional module called `exceptions.py`, which you can check for examples of how to handle exceptions in your GraphQL APIs. Now that we have structured our project, it's time to start coding!

10.4.2 Creating an entry point for the GraphQL server

Now that we have structured our project, it's time to work on the implementation. In this section, we'll create the entry point for the GraphQL server. We need to create an instance of Ariadne's `GraphQL` class and load an executable schema from the products specification.

As we mentioned in section 10.4.1, the entry point for the products API server lives under server.py. Include the following content in this file:

```
# file: server.py

from ariadne.asgi import GraphQL

from web.schema import schema

server = GraphQL(schema, debug=True)
```

Next, let's create the executable schema under web/schema.py:

```
# file: web/schema.py

from pathlib import Path

from ariadne import make_executable_schema

schema = make_executable_schema(
    (Path(__file__).parent / 'products.graphql').read_text()
)
```

The API specification for the products API is available under the web/products.graphql file. We read the schema file contents and pass them on to Ariadne's `make_executable_schema()` function. We then pass the resulting schema object to Ariadne's `GraphQL` class to instantiate the server. If you haven't started the server, you can do it now by executing the following command:

```
$ uvicorn server:server --reload
```

Like before, the API is available on http://localhost:8000. If you visit this address again, you'll see the familiar Apollo Playground UI. At this point, we could try running any of the queries defined in the products API specification; however, most of them will fail since we haven't implemented any resolvers. For example, if you run the following query

```
{
  allIngredients {
    name
  }
}
```

you'll get the following error message: "Cannot return null for non-nullable field Query.allProducts." The server doesn't know how to produce a value for the `Ingredient` type since we don't have a resolver for it, so let's build it!

10.4.3 Implementing query resolvers

In this section, we learn to implement query resolvers. As you can see from figure 10.4, a query resolver is a Python function that knows how to return a valid payload for a given query. We'll build a resolver for the `allIngredients()` query, which is one of the simplest queries in the products API specification (listing 10.3).

To implement a resolver for the `allIngredients()` query, we simply need to create a function that returns a data structure with the shape of the `Ingredient` type, which has four non-nullable properties: `id`, `name`, `stock`, and `products`. The `stock` property is, in turn, an instance of the `Stock` object type, which, as per the specification, must contain the `quantity` and `unit` properties. Finally, the `products` property must be an array of `Product` objects. The contents of the array are non-nullable, but an empty array is a valid return value.

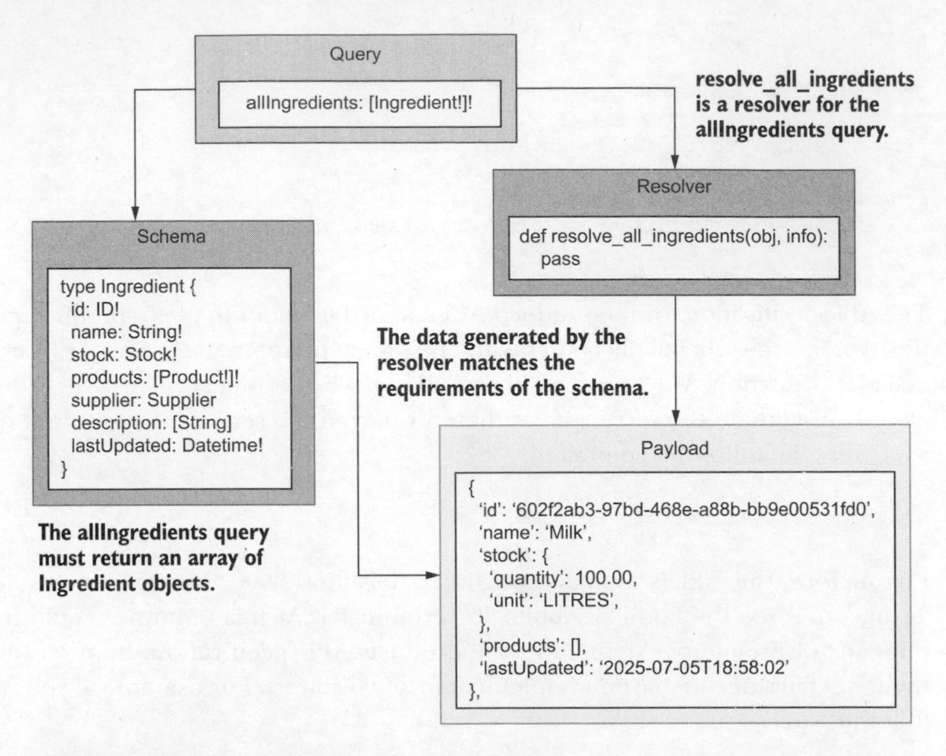

Figure 10.4 GraphQL uses resolvers to serve the query requests sent by the user to the server. A resolver is a Python function that knows how to return a valid payload for a given query.

Listing 10.3 Specification for the `Ingredient` type

```
# file: web/products.graphql

type Stock {                        ← We declare the Stock type.
    quantity: Float!                ← quantity is a non-nullable float.
    unit: MeasureUnit!
}

type Ingredient {
    id: ID!
    name: String!
    stock: Stock!
    products: [Product!]!           ← products is a non-nullable list of products.
    supplier: Supplier              ← supplier is a nullable through type that points to the Supplier type.
    description: [String!]
    lastUpdated: Datetime!
}
```

Let's add a list of ingredients to the in-memory list representation of our data under the web/data.py file:

```
# file: web/data.py

from datetime import datetime


ingredients = [
    {
        'id': '602f2ab3-97bd-468e-a88b-bb9e00531fd0',
        'name': 'Milk',
        'stock': {
            'quantity': 100.00,
            'unit': 'LITRES',
        },
        'supplier': '92f2daae-a4f8-4aae-8d74-51dd74e5de6d',
        'products': [],
        'lastUpdated': datetime.utcnow(),
    },
]
```

Now that we have some data, we can use it in the `allIngredients()`' resolver. Listing 10.4 shows what `allIngredients()`' resolver looks like. As we did in section 10.3, we first create an instance of the `QueryType` class, and we bind the resolver with this class. Since this is a resolver for a query type, the implementation goes under the web/queries.py file.

Listing 10.4 A resolver for the `allIngredients()` query

```
# file: web/queries.py

from ariadne import QueryType

from web.data import ingredients

query = QueryType()


@query.field('allIngredients')            <-- We bind allIngredients()' resolver using the decorator.
def resolve_all_ingredients(*_):
    return ingredients                   <-- We return a hardcoded response.
```

To enable the query resolver, we have to pass the query object to the `make_executable_schema()` function under web/schema.py:

```
# file: web/schema.py

from pathlib import Path

from ariadne import make_executable_schema

from web.queries import query

schema = make_executable_schema(
    (Path(__file__).parent / 'products.graphql').read_text(), [query]
)
```

If we go back to the Apollo Playground UI and we run the query

```
{
  allIngredients {
    name
  }
}
```

we get a valid payload. The query selects only the ingredient's name, which in itself is not very interesting, and it doesn't really tell us whether our current resolver works as expected for other fields. Let's write a more complex query to test our resolver more thoroughly. The following query selects the `id`, `name`, and `description` of an ingredient, as well as the `name` of each product it's related to:

```
{
  allIngredients {
    id,
    name,
    products {
      ...on ProductInterface {
        name
      }
    },
    description
  }
}
```

The response payload to this query is also valid:

```
{
  "data": {
    "allIngredients": [
      {
        "id": " "602f2ab3-97bd-468e-a88b-bb9e00531fd0",
        "name": "Milk",
        "products": [],
        "description": null
      }
    ]
  }
}
```

The products list is empty because we haven't associated any products with the ingredient, and `description` is `null` because this is a nullable field. Now that we know how to implement resolvers for simple queries, in the next section, we'll learn to implement resolvers that handle more complex situations.

10.4.4 Implementing type resolvers

In this section, we'll learn to implement resolvers for queries that return multiple types. The `allIngredients()` query is fairly simple since it only returns one type of object: the `Ingredient` type. Let's now consider the `allProducts()` query. As you can see from figure 10.5, `allProducts()` is more complex since it returns the `Product` type, which is a union of the `Beverage` and `Cake` types, both of which implement the `ProductInterface` type.

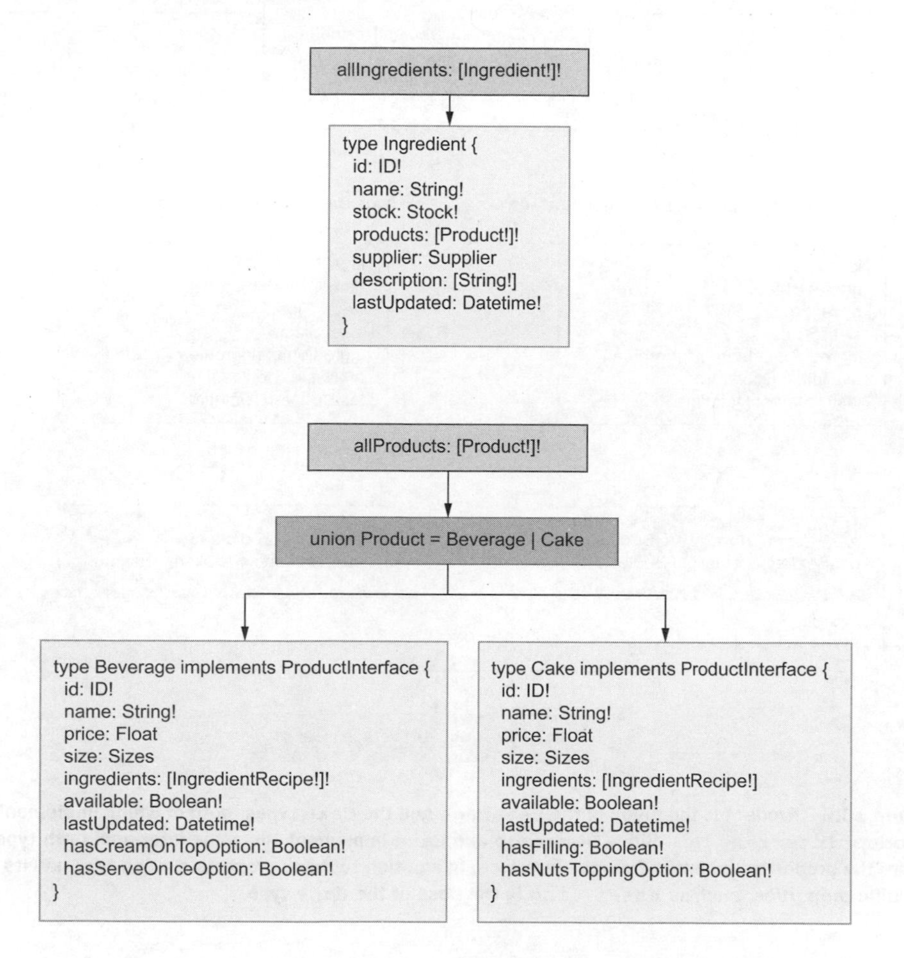

Figure 10.5 The `allIngredients()` query returns an array of `Ingredient` objects, while the `allProducts()` query returns an array of `Product` objects, where `Product` is the union of two types: `Beverage` and `Cake`.

Let's begin by adding a list of products to our in-memory list of data under the web/data.py file. We'll add two products: one `Beverage` and one `Cake`. What fields should we include in the products? As you can see in figure 10.6, since `Beverage` and `Cake` implement the `ProductInterface` type, we know they both require an `id`, a `name`, a list of `ingredients`, and a field called `available`, which signals if the product is available. On top of these common fields inherited from `ProductInterface`, `Beverage` requires two additional fields: `hasCreamOnTopOption` and `hasServeOnIceOption`,

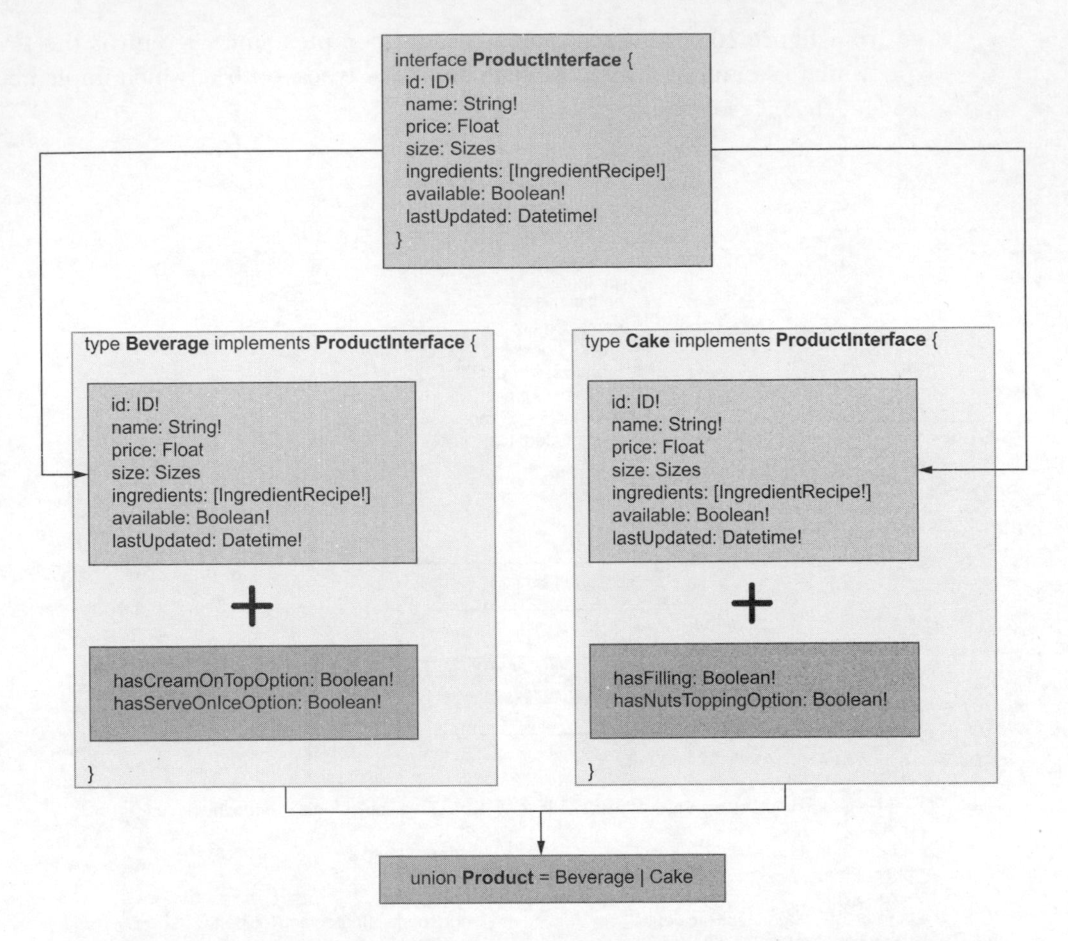

Figure 10.6 Product is the union of the `Beverage` and the `Cake` types, both of which implement the `ProductInterface` type. Since `Beverage` and `Cake` implement the same interface, both types share the properties inherited from the interface. In addition to those properties, each type has its own specific properties, such as `hasFilling` in the case of the `Cake` type.

both of which are Booleans. In turn, `Cake` requires the properties `hasFilling` and `hasNutsToppingOption`, which are also Booleans.

Listing 10.5 Resolver for the `allProducts()` query

```
# file: web/data.py

...

products = [
    {
        'id': '6961ca64-78f3-41d4-bc3b-a63550754bd8',
        'name': 'Walnut Bomb',
        'price': 37.00,
        'size': 'MEDIUM',
```

```
        'available': False,
        'ingredients': [
            {
                'ingredient': '602f2ab3-97bd-468e-a88b-bb9e00531fd0',
                'quantity': 100.00,
                'unit': 'LITRES',
            }
        ],
        'hasFilling': False,
        'hasNutsToppingOption': True,
        'lastUpdated': datetime.utcnow(),
    },
    {
        'id': 'e4e33d0b-1355-4735-9505-749e3fdf8a16',
        'name': 'Cappuccino Star',
        'price': 12.50,
        'size': 'SMALL',
        'available': True,
        'ingredients': [
            {
                'ingredient': '602f2ab3-97bd-468e-a88b-bb9e00531fd0',
                'quantity': 100.00,
                'unit': 'LITRES',
            }
        ],
        'hasCreamOnTopOption': True,
        'hasServeOnIceOption': True,
        'lastUpdated': datetime.utcnow(),
    },
]
```

This ID references the ID of the milk ingredient we added earlier to web/data.py.

Now that we have a list of products, let's use it in the `allProducts()`' resolver.

Listing 10.6 Adding the `allProducts()` resolver

```
# file: web/queries.py

from ariadne import QueryType

from web.data import ingredients, products

query = QueryType()

...

@query.field('allProducts')
def resolve_all_products(*_):
    return products
```

We bind allProducts()' resolver using the field() decorator.

We return a hardcoded response.

Let's run a simple query to test the resolver:

```
{
  allProducts {
```

```
    ...on ProductInterface {
      name
    }
  }
}
```

If you run this query, you'll get an error saying that the server can't determine what types each of the elements in our list are. In these situations, we need a type resolver. As you can see in figure 10.7, a *type resolver* is a Python function that determines what type an object is, and it returns the name of the type.

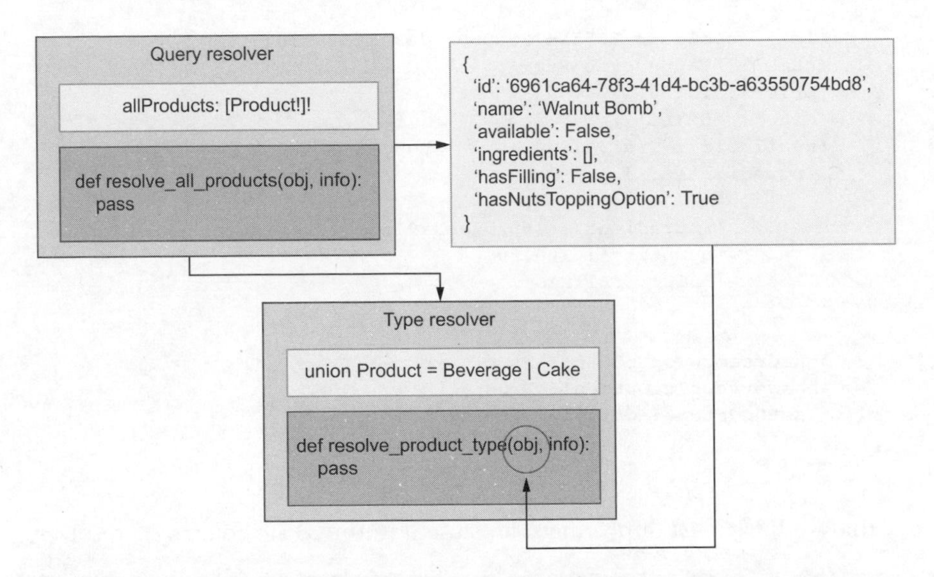

Figure 10.7 A type resolver is a function that determines the type of an object. This example shows how the `resolve_product_type()` resolver determines the type of an object returned by the `resolve_all_products()` resolver.

We need type resolvers in queries and mutations that return more than one object type. In the products API, this affects all queries and mutations that return the `Product` type, such as `allProducts()`, `addProduct()`, and `product()`.

> **RETURNING MULTIPLE TYPES** Whenever a query or mutation returns multiple types, you'll need to implement a type resolver. This applies to queries and mutations that return union types and object types that implement interfaces.

Listing 10.7 shows how we implement a type resolver for the `Product` type in Ariadne. The type resolver function takes two positional parameters, the first of which is an object. We need to determine the type of this object. As you can see in figure 10.8, since we know that `Cake` and `Beverage` have different required fields, we can use this information to determine their types: if the object has a `hasFilling` property, we know it's a `Cake`; otherwise, it's a `Beverage`.

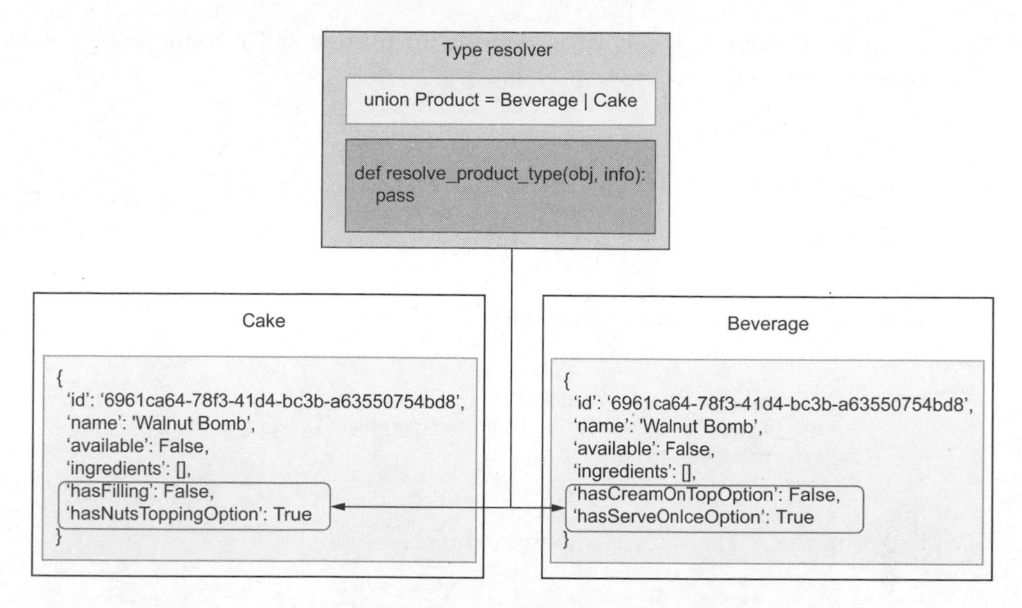

Figure 10.8 A type resolver inspects the properties of a payload to determine its type. In this example, `resolve_product_type()` looks for distinguishing properties that differentiate a `Cake` from a `Beverage` type.

The type resolver must be bound to the `Product` type. Since `Product` is a union type, we create a bindable object of it using the `UnionType` class. Ariadne guarantees that the first argument in a resolver is an object, and we inspect this object to resolve its type. We don't need any other parameters, so we ignore them with Python's `*_` syntax, which is standard for ignoring positional parameters. To resolve the type of the object, we check if it has a `hasFilling` attribute. If it does, we know it's a `Cake` object; otherwise, it's a `Beverage`. Finally, we pass the product bindable to the `make_executable_schema()` function. Since this is a type resolver, this code goes into the web/types.py.

Listing 10.7 Implementing a type resolver for the `Product` union type

```
# file: web/types.py

from ariadne import UnionType

product_type = UnionType('Product')


@product_type.type_resolver
def resolve_product_type(obj, *_):
    if 'hasFilling' in obj:
        return 'Cake'
    return 'Beverage'
```

- We create a bindable object for the Product type using the UnionType class.
- We bind Product's resolver using the resolver() decorator.
- We capture the resolver's first positional argument as obj.

To enable the type resolver, we need to add the product object to the `make_executable_schema()` function under web/schema.py:

```
# file: web/schema.py

from pathlib import Path

from ariadne import make_executable_schema

from web.queries import query
from web.types import product_type


schema = make_executable_schema(
    (Path(__file__).parent / 'products.graphql').read_text(),
    [query, product_type]
)
```

Let's run the `allProducts()` query again:

```
{
  allProducts {
    ...on ProductInterface {
      name
    }
  }
}
```

You'll now get a successful response. You have just learned to implement type resolvers and to handle queries that return multiple types! In the next section, we continue exploring queries by learning how to handle query parameters.

10.4.5 Handling query parameters

In this section, we learn to handle query parameters in the resolvers. Most of the queries in the products API accept filtering parameters, and all the mutations require at least one parameter. Let's see how we access parameters by studying one example from the products API: the `products()` query, which accepts an `input` filter object whose type is `ProductsFilter`. How do we access this filter object in a resolver?

As you can see in figure 10.9, when a query or mutation takes parameters, Ariadne passes those parameters to our resolvers as keyword arguments. Listing 10.8 shows how we access the `input` parameter for the `products()` query resolver. Since the `input` parameter is optional and therefore nullable, we set it by default to `None`. The `input` parameter is an instance of the `ProductsFilter` input type, so when it's present in the query, it comes in the form of a dictionary. From the API specification, we know that `ProductsFilter` guarantees the presence of the following fields:

- `available`—Boolean field that filters products by whether they're available
- `sortBy`—An enumeration type that allows us to sort products by price or name

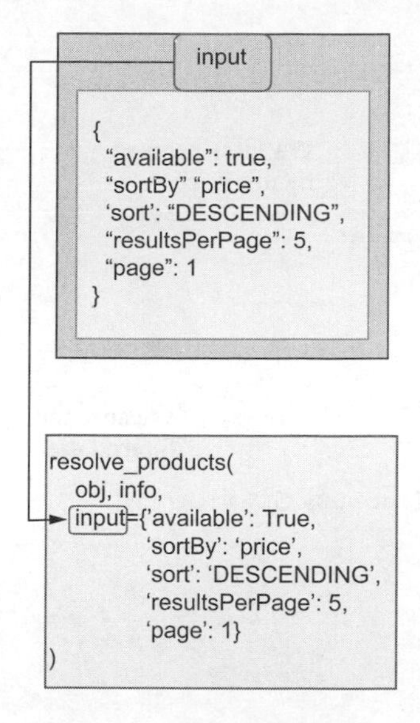

Figure 10.9 Query parameters are passed to our resolvers as keyword arguments. This example illustrates how the `resolve_products()` resolver is called, with the `input` parameter passed as a keyword argument. The parameter `input` is an object of type `ProductsFilter`, and therefore it comes in the form of a dictionary.

- `sort`—Enumeration type that allows us to sort the results in ascending or descending order
- `resultsPerPage`—Indicates how many results should be shown per page
- `page`—Indicates which page of the results we should return

In addition to these parameters, `ProductsFilter` may also include two optional parameters: `maxPrice`, which filters results by maximum price, and `minPrice`, which filters results by minimum price. Since `maxPrice` and `minPrice` are not required fields, we check for their presence using the Python dictionary's `get()` method, which returns `None` if they're not found. Let's implement the filtering and sorting functionality first, and deal with pagination afterwards. The following code goes under web/queries.py.

Listing 10.8 Accessing `input` parameters in a resolver

```
# file: web/queries.py

...

Query = QueryType()

...


@query.field('products')
def resolve_products(*_, input=None):
    filtered = [product for product in products]
    if input is None:
        return filtered
    filtered = [
```

We bind products()' resolver using the field() decorator.

We ignore the default positional arguments and instead capture the input parameter.

We copy the list of products.

If input is None, we return the whole dataset.

We filter products by availability.

```
            product for product in filtered
            if product['available'] is input['available']
        ]
    if input.get('minPrice') is not None:     <-- We filter products by minPrice.
        filtered = [
            product for product in filtered
            if product['price'] >= input['minPrice']
        ]
    if input.get('maxPrice') is not None:
        filtered = [
            product for product in filtered
            if product['price'] <= input['maxPrice']
        ]
    filtered.sort(                             <-- We sort the filtered dataset.
        key=lambda product: product.get(input['sortBy'], 0],
        reverse=input['sort'] == 'DESCENDING'
    )
    return filtered                            <-- We return the filtered dataset.
```

Let's run a query to test this resolver:

```
{
  products(input: {available: true}) {
    ...on ProductInterface {
      name
    }
  }
}
```

You should get a valid response from the server. Now that we have filtered the results, we need to paginate them. Listing 10.9 adds a generic pagination function called `get_page()` to web/queries.py. Just a word of warning: in normal circumstances, you'll be storing your data in a database and delegating filtering and pagination to the database. The examples here are to illustrate how you use the query parameters in the resolver. We paginate the results using the `islice()` function from the `itertools` module.

As you can see in figure 10.10, `islice()` allows us to extract a slice of an iterable object. `islice()` requires us to provide the start and stop indices of the portion that

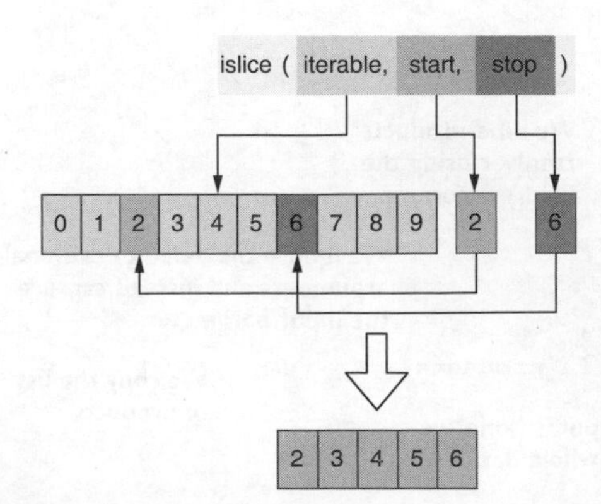

Figure 10.10 The `islice()` function from the `itertools` module allows you to get a slice of an iterable object by selecting the `start` and `stop` indices of the subset that you want to slice.

we want to slice. For example, a list of 10 items comprising the numbers 0 to 9, providing a start index of 2 and a stop index of 6, would give us a slice with the following items: `[2, 3, 4, 5]`. The API paginates results starting at 1, while `islice()` uses zero-based indexing, so `get_page()` subtracts one unit from the page parameter to account for that difference.

Listing 10.9 Paginating results

```
# file: web/queries.py

From itertools import islice          ◁—— We import islice().

from ariadne import QueryType

from web.data import ingredients, products

...

def get_page(items, items_per_page, page):
    page = page - 1
    start = items_per_page * page if page > 0 else page      ◁—— We resolve the start index.
    stop = start + items_per_page     ◁—— We calculate the stop index.
    return list(islice(items, start, stop))     ◁—— We return a slice of the list.

@query.field('products')
def resolve_products(*_, input=None):
    ...
    return get_page(filtered, input['resultsPerPage'], input['page'])     ◁—— We paginate the results.
```

Our hardcoded dataset only contains two products, so let's test the pagination with `resutlsPerPage` set to 1, which will split the list into two pages:

```
{
  products(input: {resultsPerPage: 1, page: 1}) {
    ...on ProductInterface {
      name
    }
  }
}
```

You should get exactly one result. Once we implement the `addProduct()` mutation in the next section, we'll be able to add more products through the API and make more use of the pagination parameters.

You just learned how to handle query parameters! We're now in a good position to learn how to implement mutations. Mutation resolvers are similar to query resolvers, but they always have parameters. But that's enough of a spoiler; move on to the next section to learn more about mutations.

10.4.6 Implementing mutation resolvers

In this section, we learn to implement mutation resolvers. Implementing a mutation resolver follows the same guidelines we saw for queries. The only difference is the class we use to bind the mutation resolvers. While queries are bound to an instance of the `QueryType` class, mutations are bound to an instance of the `MutationType` class.

Let's have a look at implementing the resolver for the `addProduct()` mutation. From the specification, we know that the `addProduct()` mutation has three required parameters: `name`, `type`, and `input`. The shape of the `input` parameter is given by the `AddProductInput` object type. `AddProductInput` defines additional properties that can be set when creating a new product, all of which are optional and therefore nullable. Finally, the `addProduct()` mutation must return a product type.

Listing 10.10 shows how we implement the resolver for the `addProduct()` mutation (see figure 10.11 for an illustration). We first import the `MutationType` bindable class and instantiate it. We then declare our resolver and bind it to `MutationType` using its `field()` decorator. We don't need to use Ariadne's default positional parameters `obj` and `info`, so we skip them using a wildcard followed by an underscore (`*_`). We don't set default values for `addProduct()`'s parameters, since the specification states they're all required. `addProduct()` must return a valid `Product` object, so we

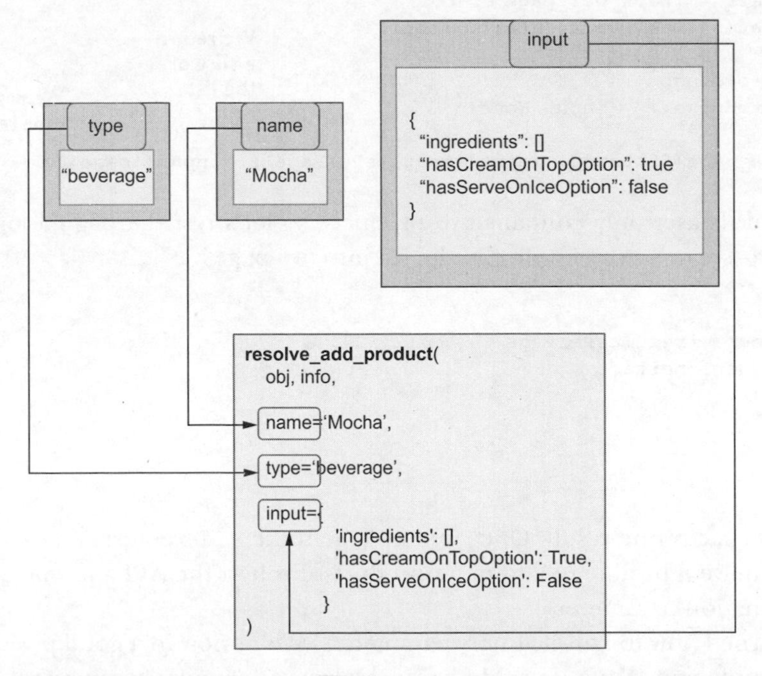

Figure 10.11 Mutation parameters are passed to our resolvers as keyword arguments. This example illustrates how the `resolve_add_product()` resolver is called, with the `name`, `type`, and `input` parameters passed as keyword arguments.

build the object with its expected attributes in the body of the resolver. Since `Product` is the union of the `Cake` and `Beverage` types, and each type requires different sets of properties, we check the `type` parameter to determine which fields we should add to our object. The following code goes into the web/mutations.py file.

Listing 10.10 Resolver for the `addProduct()` mutation

```
# file: web/mutations.py

import uuid
from datetime import datetime

from ariadne import MutationType

from web.data import products


mutation = MutationType()    <-- Bindable object for mutations

@mutation.field('addProduct')    <-- We bind addProduct()'s resolver using the field() decorator.
def resolve_add_product(*_, name, type, input):    <-- We capture addProduct()'s parameters.
    product = {    <-- We declare the new product as a dictionary.
        'id': uuid.uuid4(),    <-- We set server-side properties such as the ID.
        'name': name,
        'available': input.get('available', False),    <-- We parse optional parameters and set their default values.
        'ingredients': input.get('ingredients', []),
        'lastUpdated': datetime.utcnow(),
    }
    if type == 'cake':    <-- We check whether the product is a Beverage or a Cake.
        product.update({
            'hasFilling': input['hasFilling'],
            'hasNutsToppingOption': input['hasNutsToppingOption'],
        })
    else:
        product.update({
            'hasCreamOnTopOption': input['hasCreamOnTopOption'],
            'hasServeOnIceOption': input['hasServeOnIceOption'],
        })
    products.append(product)    <-- We return the newly created product.
    return product
```

To enable the resolver implemented in listing 10.10, we need to add the `mutation` object to the `make_executable_schema()` function in web/schema.py:

```
# file: web/schema.py

from pathlib import Path

from ariadne import make_executable_schema

from web.mutations import mutation
from web.queries import query
from web.types import product_type
```

```
schema = make_executable_schema(
    (Path(__file__).parent / 'products.graphql').read_text(),
    [query, mutation, product_type]
)
```

Let's put the new mutation to work by running a simple test. Go to the Apollo Playground running on http://127.0.0.1:8000, and run the following mutation:

```
mutation {
  addProduct(name: "Mocha", type: beverage, input:{ingredients: []}) {
    ...on ProductInterface {
      name,
      id
    }
  }
}
```

You'll get a valid response, and a new product will be added to our list. To verify things are working correctly, run the following query and check that the response contains the new item just created:

```
{
  allProducts {
    ...on ProductInterface {
      name
    }
  }
}
```

Remember that we are running the service with an in-memory list representation of our data, so if you stop or reload the server, the list will be reset and you'll lose any newly created data.

You just learned how to build mutations! This is a powerful feature: with mutations, you can create and update data in a GraphQL server. We've now covered nearly all the major aspects of the implementation of a GraphQL server. In the next section, we'll take this further by learning how to implement resolvers for custom scalar types.

10.4.7 Building resolvers for custom scalar types

In this section, we learn how to implement resolvers for custom scalar types. As we saw in chapter 8, GraphQL provides a decent amount of scalar types, such as Boolean, integer, and string. And in many cases, GraphQL's default scalar types are sufficient to develop an API. Sometimes, however, we need to define our own custom scalars. The products API contains a custom scalar called `Datetime`. The `lastUpdated` field in both the `Ingredient` and `Product` types have a `Datetime` scalar type. Since `Datetime` is a custom scalar, Ariadne doesn't know how to handle it, so we need to implement a resolver for it. How do we do that?

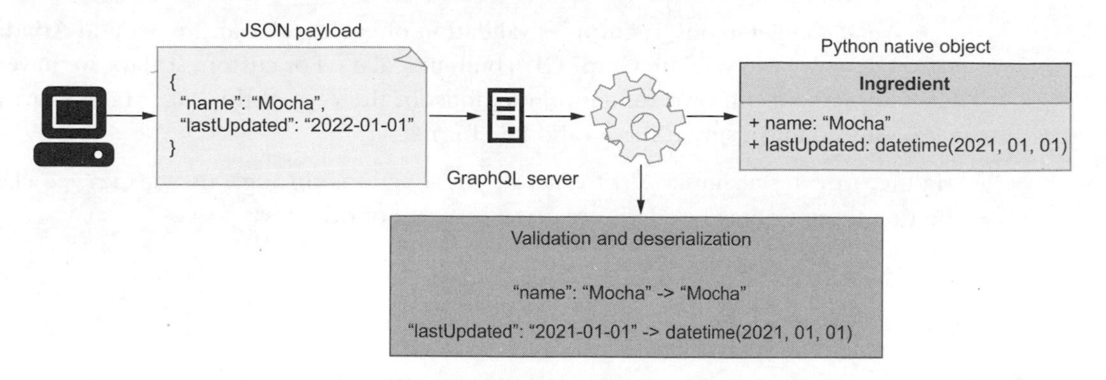

Figure 10.12 When a GraphQL server receives data from the user, it validates and deserializes the data into native Python objects. In this example, the server deserializes the name `"Mocha"` into a Python string, and the date `"2021-01-01"` into a Python datetime.

As you can see in figures 10.12 and 10.13, when we encounter a custom scalar type in a GraphQL API, we need to make sure we can perform the following three actions on the custom scalar:

- *Serialization*—When a user requests data from the server, Ariadne has to be able to serialize the data. Ariadne knows how to serialize GraphQL's built-in scalars, but for custom scalars, we need to implement a custom serializer. In the case of the `Datetime` scalar in the products API, we have to implement a method to serialize a `datetime` object.
- *Deserialization*—When a user sends data to our server, Ariadne deserializes the data and makes it available to us as a Python native data structure, such as a dictionary. If the data includes a custom scalar, we need to implement a method that lets Ariadne know how to parse and load the scalar into a native Python data structure. For the `Datetime` scalar, we want to be able to load it as a `datetime` object.

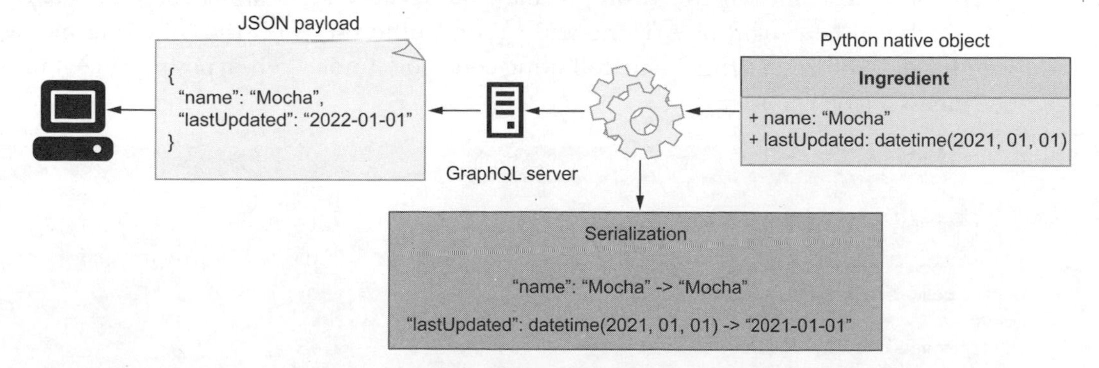

Figure 10.13 When the GraphQL server sends data to the user, it transforms native Python objects into serializable data. In this example, the server serializes the both the name and the date as strings.

- *Validation*—GraphQL enforces validation of each scalar and type, and Ariadne knows how to validate GraphQL's built-in scalars. For custom scalars, we have to implement our own validation methods. In the case of the `Datetime` scalar, we want to make sure it has a valid ISO format.

Ariadne provides a simple API to handle these actions through its `ScalarType` class. The first thing we need to do is create an instance of this class:

```
from ariadne import ScalarType

datetime_scalar = ScalarType('Datetime')
```

`ScalarType` exposes decorator methods that allow us to implement serialization, deserialization, and validation. For serialization, we use `ScalarType`'s `serializer()` decorator. We want to serialize `datetime` objects into ISO standard date format, and Python's `datetime` library provides a convenient method for ISO formatting, the `isoformat()` method:

```
@datetime_scalar.serializer
def serialize_datetime(value):
  return value.isoformat()
```

For validation and deserialization, `ScalarType` provides the `value_parser()` decorator. When a user sends data to the server containing a `Datetime` scalar, we expect the date to be in ISO format and therefore parsable by Python's `datetime.fromisoformat()` method:

```
from datetime import datetime


@datetime_scalar.value_parser
def parse_datetime_value(value):
  return datetime.fromisoformat(value)
```

If the date comes in the wrong format, `fromisoformat()` will raise a `ValueError`, which will be caught by Ariadne and shown to the user with the following message: "Invalid isoformat string." The following code goes under web/types.py since it implements a type resolver.

Listing 10.11 Serializing and parsing a custom scalar

```
# file: web/types.py

import uuid
from datetime import datetime

from ariadne import UnionType, ScalarType

...
```

```
datetime_scalar = ScalarType('Datetime')


@datetime_scalar.serializer
def serialize_datetime_scalar(date):
    return date.isoformat()


@datetime_scalar.value_parser
def parse_datetime_scalar(date):
    return datetime.fromisoformat(date)
```

We create a bindable object for the Datetime scalar using the ScalarType class.

We serialize the date object.

We bind Datetime's serializer using the serializer() decorator.

We capture the serializer's argument as date.

We capture the parser's argument.

We bind Datetime's parser using the value_parser() decorator.

We parse a date.

To enable the `Datetime` resolvers, we add `datetime_scalar` to the array of bindable objects for the `make_executable_schema()` function under web/schema.py:

```
from pathlib import Path

from ariadne import make_executable_schema

from web.mutations import mutation
from web.queries import query
from web.types import product_type, datetime_scalar

schema = make_executable_schema(
    (Path(__file__).parent / 'products.graphql').read_text(),
    [query, mutation, product_type, datetime_scalar]
)
```

Let's put the new resolvers to the test! Go back to the Apollo Playground running on http://127.0.0.1:8000 and execute the following query:

```
# Query document
{
  allProducts {
    ...on ProductInterface {
      name,
      lastUpdated
    }
  }
}

# result:
{
  "data": {
    "allProducts": [
      {
        "name": "Walnut Bomb",
        "lastUpdated": "2022-06-19T18:27:53.171870"
      },
      {
        "name": "Cappuccino Star",
```

```
        "lastUpdated": "2022-06-19T18:27:53.171871"
      }
    ]
  }
}
```

You should get a list of all products with their names, and with an ISO-formatted date in the `lastUpdated` field. You now have the power to implement your own custom scalar types in GraphQL. Use it wisely! Before we close the chapter, there's one more topic we need to explore: implementing resolvers for the fields of an object type.

10.4.8 Implementing field resolvers

In this section, we learn to implement resolvers for the fields of an object type. We've implemented nearly all the resolvers that we need to serve all sorts of queries on the products API, but there's still one type of query that our server can't resolve: queries involving fields that map to other GraphQL types. For example, the `Products` type has a field called `ingredients`, which maps to an array of `IngredientRecipe` objects. According to the specification, the shape of the `IngredientRecipe` type looks like this:

```
# file: web/products.graphql

type IngredientRecipe {
    ingredient: Ingredient!
    quantity: Float!
    unit: String!
}
```

Each `IngredientRecipe` object has an `ingredient` field, which maps to an `Ingredient` object type. This means that, when we query the `ingredients` field of a product, we should be able to pull information about each ingredient, such as its name, description, or supplier information. In other words, we should be able to run the following query against the server:

```
{
  allProducts {
    ...on ProductInterface {
      name,
      ingredients {
        quantity,
        unit,
        ingredient{
          name
        }
      }
    }
  }
}
```

If you run this query in Apollo Playground at this juncture, you'll get an error with the following message: "Cannot return null for non-nullable field Ingredient.name."

Why is this happening? If you look at the list of products in listing 10.5, you'll notice that the `ingredients` field maps to an array of objects with three fields: `ingredient`, `quantity`, and `unit`. For example, the Walnut Bomb has the following ingredients:

```
# file: web/data.py

ingredients = [
  {
    'ingredient': '602f2ab3-97bd-468e-a88b-bb9e00531fd0',
    'quantity': 100.00,
    'unit': 'LITRES',
  }
]
```

The `ingredient` field maps to an ingredient ID, not a full ingredient object. This is our internal representation of the product's ingredients. It's how we store product data in our database (in-memory list in this implementation). And it's a useful representation since it allows us to identify each ingredient by ID. However, the API specification tells us that the `ingredients` field should map to an array of `IngredientRecipe` objects and that each `ingredient` should represent an `Ingredient` object, not just an ID.

How do we solve this problem? We can use different approaches. For example, we could make sure that each ingredient payload is correctly built in the resolvers for each query that returns a `Product` type. For example, listing 10.12 shows how we can modify the `allProducts()` resolver to accomplish this. The snippet modifies every product's `ingredients` property to make sure it contains a full ingredient payload. Since every product is represented by a dictionary, we make a deep copy of each product to make sure the changes we apply in this function don't affect our in-memory list of products.

Listing 10.12 Updating products to contain full ingredient payloads, not just IDs

```
# file: web/queries.py

...

@query.field('allProducts')
def resolve_all_products(*_):
    products_with_ingredients = [deepcopy(product) for product in products]
    for product in products_with_ingredients:
        for ingredient_recipe in product['ingredients']:
            for ingredient in ingredients:
                if ingredient['id'] == ingredient_recipe['ingredient']:
                    ingredient_recipe['ingredient'] = ingredient
    return products_with_ingredients
```

- We make a deep copy of each object in the products list. (products_with_ingredients = ...)
- We update the ingredient property with a full representation of the ingredient. (ingredient_recipe['ingredient'] = ingredient)
- We return the list of products with ingredients. (return products_with_ingredients)

The approach in listing 10.12 is perfectly fine, but as you can see, it makes the code grow in complexity. If we had to do this for a few more properties, the function would quickly become difficult to understand and to maintain.

As you can see in figure 10.14, GraphQL offers an alternative way of resolving object properties. Instead of modifying the product payload within the `allProducts()` resolver, we can create a specific resolver for the product's `ingredients` property and make any necessary changes within that resolver. Listing 10.13 shows what the resolver for the product's `ingredients` property looks like and goes under web/types.py since it implements a resolver for object properties.

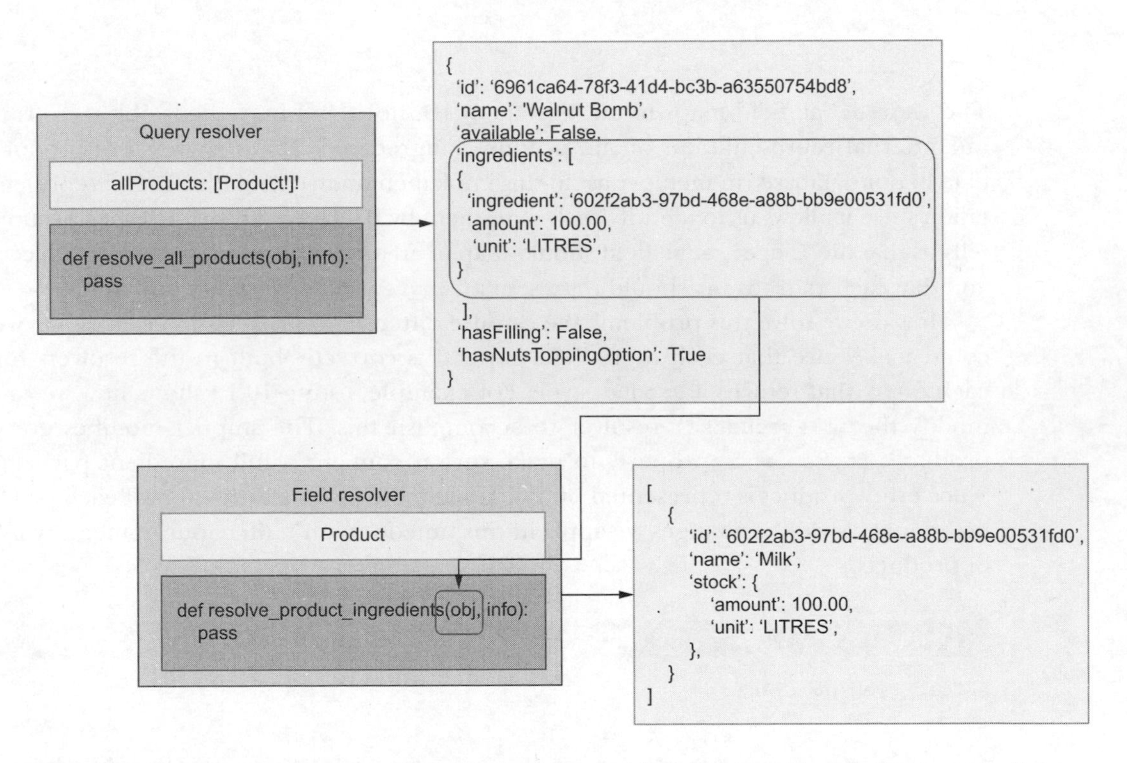

Figure 10.14 GraphQL allows us to create resolvers for specific fields of an object. In this example, the `resolve_product_ingredients()` resolver takes care of returning a valid payload for the `ingredients` property of a product.

Listing 10.13 Implementing a field resolver

```
# file: web/types.py

...

@product_interface.field('ingredients')
def resolve_product_ingredients(product, _):
    recipe = [
```

We create a deep copy of each ingredient.

```
        copy.copy(ingredient)
        for ingredient in product.get("ingredients", [])
    ]

    for ingredient_recipe in recipe:
        for ingredient in ingredients:
            if ingredient['id'] == ingredient_recipe['ingredient']:
                ingredient_recipe['ingredient'] = ingredient
    return recipe
```

Object property resolvers help us keep our code more modular because every resolver does only one thing. They also help us avoid repetition. By having a single resolver that takes care of updating the `ingredients` property in product payloads, we avoid having to perform this operation in every resolver that returns a product type. On the downside, property resolvers may be more difficult to trace and debug. If something is wrong with the `ingredients` payload, you won't find the bug within the `allProducts()` resolver. You have to know that there's a resolver for products' ingredients and look into that resolver. Application logs will help to point you in the right direction when debugging this kind of issues, but bear in mind that this design will not be entirely obvious to other developers who are not familiar with GraphQL. As with everything else in software design, make sure that code reusability doesn't impair the readability and ease of maintenance of your code.

Summary

- The Python ecosystem offers various frameworks for implementing GraphQL APIs. See GraphQL's official website for the latest news on available frameworks: https://graphql.org/code/.
- You can use the Ariadne framework to implement GraphQL APIs following a schema-first approach, which means we first design the API, and then we implement the server against the specification. This approach is beneficial since it allows the server and client development teams to work in parallel.
- Ariadne can validate request and response payloads automatically using the specification, which means we don't have to spend time implementing custom validation models.
- For each query and mutation in the API specification, we need to implement a resolver. A resolver is a function that knows how to process the request for a given query or mutation. Resolvers are the code that allow us to expose the capabilities of a GraphQL API and therefore represent the backbone of the implementation.
- To register a resolver, we use one of Ariadne's bindable classes, such as `QueryType` or `MutationType`. These classes expose decorators that allow us to bind a resolver function.
- GraphQL specifications can contain complex types, such as union types, which combine two or more object types. If our API specification contains a union

type, we must implement a resolver that knows how to determine the type of an object; otherwise, the GraphQL server doesn't know how to resolve it.

- With GraphQL, we can define custom scalars. If the specification contains a custom scalar, we must implement resolvers that know how to serialize, parse, and validate the custom scalar type; otherwise, the GraphQL server doesn't know how to handle them.

Part 4

Securing, testing, and deploying microservice APIs

As we learned in chapter 1, APIs are programmatic interfaces to our applications, and making our APIs public allows other organizations to build integrations with our own APIs. The growing offering of APIs as a means of delivering software products has given rise to the API economy. APIs open new opportunities for business growth, but they also represent a security risk. Lack of proper testing or wrongly implemented security protocols render our APIs vulnerable. Part 4 of this book will get you up and running on the major topics of API testing, security, and operations.

The modern standard for API authentication is OpenID Connect, and for API authorization it's Open Authorization (OAuth) 2.1. Chapter 11 kicks off part 4 by introducing these standards. In my experience, this is one of the most misunderstood areas of API development, which leads to security vulnerabilities and breaches. Chapter 11 teaches you everything you need to know to implement a robust API authentication and authorization strategy for your APIs.

When you drive integrations using APIs, you need a reliable API testing and validation method. You must ensure that your API backend serves the interface defined in your API specification. How do we do that? As you'll learn in chapter 12, a powerful approach to API testing is using contract-testing tools, such as

Dredd and Schemathesis, and applying property-based testing. With these strategies, you can test and validate your code with confidence before releasing it to production.

Finally, what about deployments and operations? The final chapters of this book teach you how to Dockerize and deploy your microservice APIs using Kubernetes. You'll learn to deploy and operate a Kubernetes cluster using AWS EKS, one of the most popular solutions for running Kubernetes in the cloud. After reading part 4, you'll be ready to test, protect, and operate your microservice APIs at scale.

11 API authorization and authentication

This chapter covers

- Using Open Authorization to allow access to our APIs
- Using OpenID Connect to verify the identity of our API users
- What kinds of authorization flows exist, and which flow is more suitable for each authorization scenario
- Understanding JSON Web Tokens (JWT) and using Python's PyJWT library to produce and validate them
- Adding authentication and authorization middleware to our APIs

In 2018, a weakness in the API authentication system of the US postal system (https://usps.com) allowed hackers to obtain data from 60 million users, including their email addresses, phone numbers, and other personal details.[1] API security

[1] The issue was reported first by Brian Krebs, "USPS Site Exposed Data on 60 Million Users," KrebsOnSecurity, November 21, 2018, https://krebsonsecurity.com/2018/11/usps-site-exposed-data-on-60-million-users/.

attacks like this have become more and more common, with an estimated growth of over 300% in the number of attacks in 2021.[2] API vulnerabilities don't only risk exposing sensitive data from your users; they can also put you out of business![3] The good news is there are steps you can take to reduce the risk of an API breach. The first line of defense is a robust authentication and authorization system. In this chapter, you'll learn to prevent unauthorized access to your APIs by using standard authentication and authorization protocols.

In my experience, API authentication and authorization are two of the most confusing topics for developers, and they're also areas where implementation mistakes happen often. Before you implement the security layer of your API, I highly recommend you read this chapter to make sure you know what you're doing and know how to do it correctly. I've done my best to provide a comprehensive summary of how API authentication and authorization work, and by the end of this chapter you should be able to add a robust authorization flow to your own APIs.

Authentication is the process of verifying the identity of a user, while authorization is the process of determining whether a user has access to certain resources or operations. The concepts and standards about authentication and authorization that you'll learn in this chapter are applicable to all types of web APIs.

You'll learn different authentication and authorization protocols and flows and how to validate authorization tokens. You'll also learn to use Python's PyJWT library to produce signed tokens and to validate them. We'll walk through a practical example of adding authentication and authorization to the orders API. We've got a lot to cover, so let's get started!

11.1 Setting up the environment for this chapter

Let's set up the environment for this chapter. The code for this chapter is available under the directory called ch11 in the GitHub repository for this book. In chapter 7, we implemented a fully functional orders service, complete with a business layer, database, and API. This chapter picks up the orders service from where we left it in chapter 7. If you want to follow along with the changes in this chapter, copy over the code from chapter 7 into a new folder called ch11:

```
$ cp -r ch07 ch11
```

`cd` into ch11 and install the dependencies by running `pipenv install`. For this chapter, we need a few additional dependencies, so run the following command to install them:

```
$ pipenv install cryptography pyjwt
```

[2] Bill Doerfeld, "API Attack Traffic Grew 300+% In the Last Six Months," *Security Boulevard*, July 30, 2021, https://securityboulevard.com/2021/07/api-attack-traffic-grew-300-in-the-last-six-months/.

[3] Joe Galvin, "60 Percent of Small Businesses Fold Within 6 Months of a Cyber Attack," *Inc.*, May 7, 2018, https://www.inc.com/joe-galvin/60-percent-of-small-businesses-fold-within-6-months-of-a-cyber-attack-heres-how-to-protect-yourself.html.

PyJWT is a Python library that allows us to work with JSON Web Tokens, while `cryptography` will allow us to verify the tokens' signatures. (For a list of alternative JWT libraries in the Python ecosystem, check out https://jwt.io/libraries?language=Python.)

Our environment is now ready, so let's begin our quest through the wondrous world of user authentication and authorization. It's a journey full of pitfalls, but a necessary one. Hold tight, and watch carefully as we go along!

11.2 Understanding authentication and authorization protocols

When it comes to API authentication, the two most important protocols you need to know are OAuth (Open Authorization) and OpenID Connect (OIDC). This section explains how each protocol works and how they fit within the authentication and authorization flows for our APIs.

11.2.1 Understanding Open Authorization

OAuth is a standard protocol for access delegation.[4] As you can see in figure 11.1, OAuth allows a user to grant a third-party application access to protected resources they own in another website without having to share their credentials.

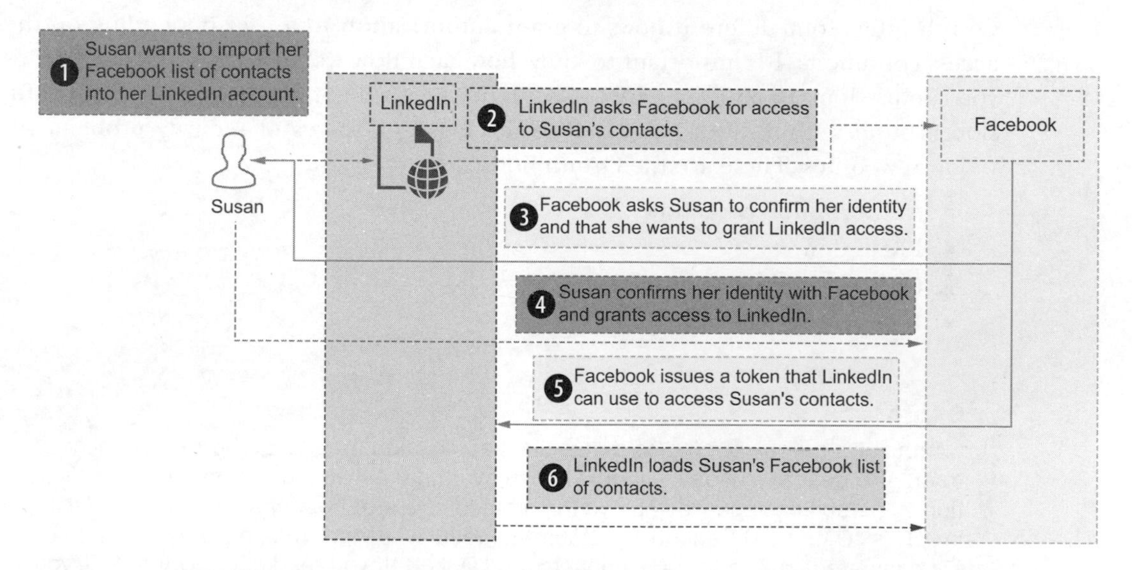

Figure 11.1 With OAuth, a user can grant a third-party application access to their information on another website.

DEFINITION *OAuth* is an open standard that allows users to grant access to third-party applications to their information on other websites. Typically, access is granted by issuing a token, which the third-party application uses to access the user's information.

[4] https://oauth.net/ is a pretty good website with tons of resources to learn more about the OAuth specification.

For example, let's say Susan has a list of contacts in her Facebook account. One day, Susan signs into LinkedIn, and she wants to import her list of contacts from Facebook. To allow LinkedIn to import her Facebook contacts, Susan has to grant LinkedIn access to that resource. How can she grant LinkedIn access to her list of contacts? She could give LinkedIn her Facebook credentials to access her account. But that would be a major security risk. Instead, OAuth defines a protocol that allows Susan to tell Facebook that LinkedIn can access her list of contacts. With OAuth, Facebook issues a temporary token LinkedIn can use to import Susan's contacts.

OAuth distinguishes various roles in the process of granting access to a resource:

- *Resource owner*—The user who's granting access to the resource. In the previous example, Susan is the resource owner.
- *Resource server*—The server hosting the user's protected resources. In the previous example, Facebook is the resource server.
- *Client*—The application or server requesting access to the user's resources. In the previous example, LinkedIn is the client.
- *Authorization server*—The server that grants the client access to the resources. In the previous example, Facebook is the authorization server.

OAuth offers four different flows to grant authorization to a user depending on the access conditions. It's important to know how each flow works and in which scenarios you can use it in. In my experience, OAuth flows are one of the biggest areas of confusion around authorization, and one of the biggest sources of security problems in modern websites. These are the OAuth flows:

- Authorization code flow
- PKCE flow
- Client credentials flow
- Refresh token flow

OAuth

OAuth flows are the strategies that a client application uses to authorize their access to an API. Best practices in OAuth change over time as we learn more about application vulnerabilities and we improve the protocol. Current best practices are described in IETF's "OAuth 2.0 Security Best Current Practice" (http://mng.bz/o58v), written by T. Lodderstedt, J. Bradley, A. Labunets, and D. Fett. If you read about OAuth 2.0, you may encounter references to two flows that we don't describe in this chapter: the resource owner password flow and the implicit flow. Both are now deprecated since they expose serious vulnerabilities, and therefore you shouldn't use them.

Another popular extension that we don't discuss in this chapter is the device authorization grant (http://mng.bz/5mZD), which allows input-constrained devices such as smart TVs to obtain access tokens. The latest version of OAuth is 2.1, which is described in the IETF's "The OAuth 2.1 Authorization Framework" (http://mng.bz/69m6).

Let's delve into each flow to understand how they work and when we use them!

AUTHORIZATION CODE FLOW

In the authorization code flow, the client server exchanges a secret with the authorization server to produce a signing URL. As you can see in figure 11.2, after the user signs in using this URL, the client server obtains a one-time code it can exchange for an access token. This flow uses a client secret, and therefore is only appropriate for applications in which the code is not publicly exposed, such as traditional web applications where the user interface is rendered in the backend. OAuth 2.1 recommends using the authorization code flow in combination with PKCE, which is described in the next section.

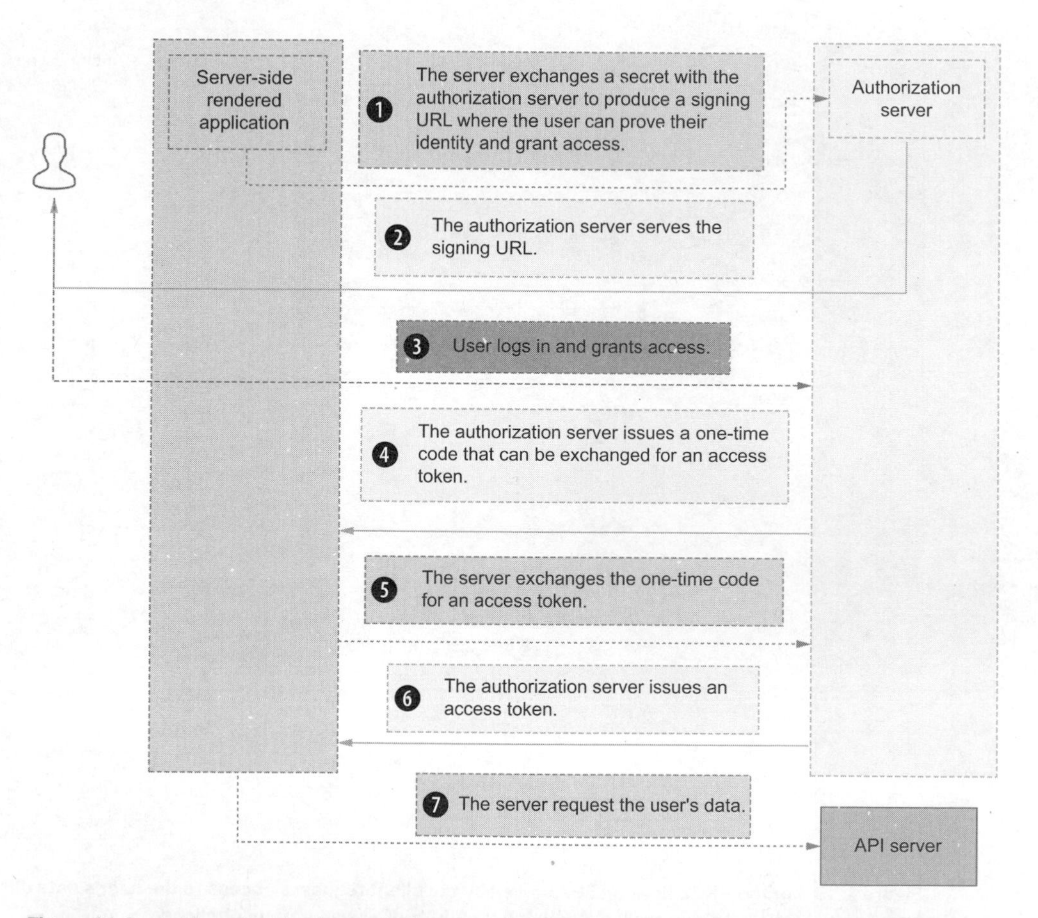

Figure 11.2 In the authorization code flow, the authorization server produces a signing URL, which the user can use to prove their identity and grant access to the third-party application.

PROOF OF KEY FOR CODE EXCHANGE FLOW

The *Proof of Key for Code Exchange* (PKCE, pronounced "pixie") is an extension of the authorization code flow designed to protect applications whose source code is publicly exposed, such as mobile applications and single-page applications (SPAs).[5] Since the source is publicly exposed, the client cannot use a secret because it would also be publicly exposed.

As you can see in figure 11.3, in the PKCE flow, the client generates a secret called the *code verifier*, and it encodes it. The encoded code is called the *code challenge*. When sending an authorization request to the server, the client includes both the code verifier and the code challenge in the request. In return, the server produces an *authorization code*, which the client can exchange for an access token. To get the access token, the client must send both the authorization code and the code challenge.

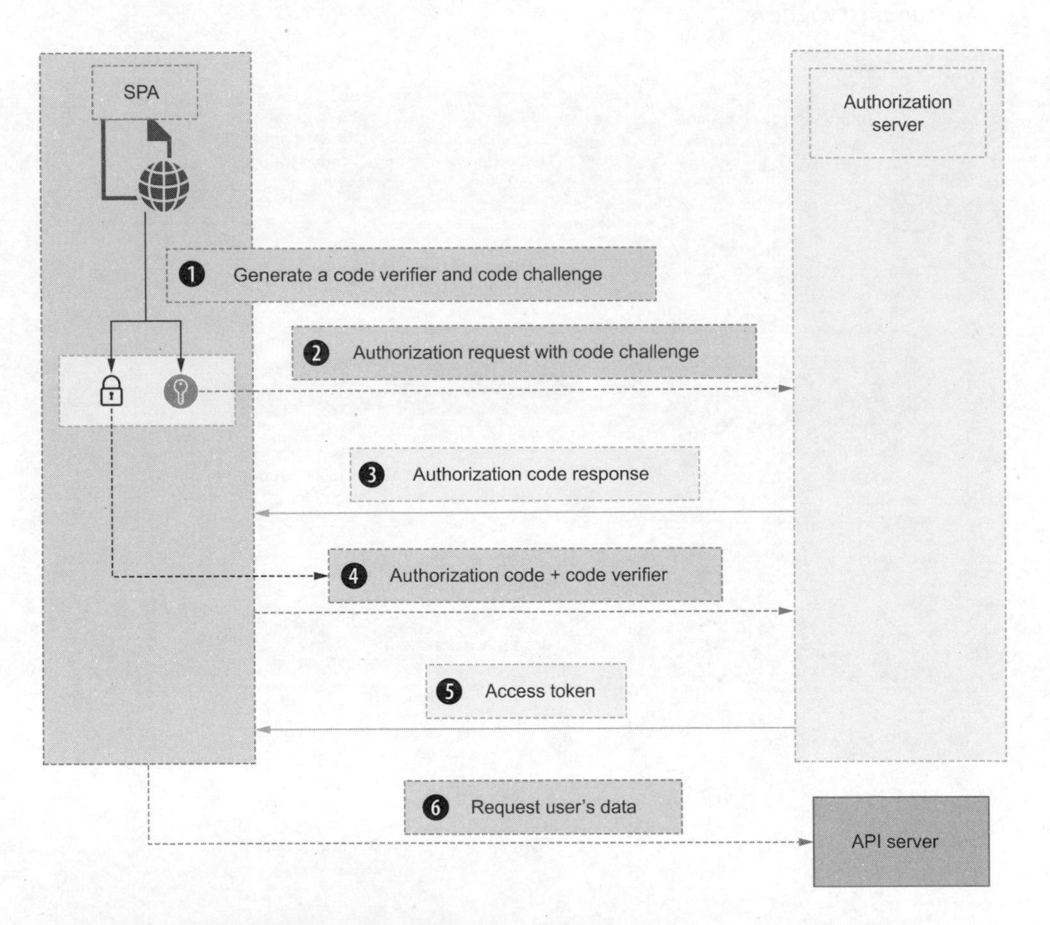

Figure 11.3 In the PKCE flow, an SPA served by the client requests access to the user's data directly from the authorization server by exchanging a code verifier and a code challenge.

[5] N. Sakimura, J. Bradley, and N. Agarwal, "Proof Key for Code Exchange by OAuth Public Clients," IETF RFC 7636, September 2015, https://datatracker.ietf.org/doc/html/rfc7636.

Thanks to the code challenge, the PKCE flow also prevents authorization code injection attacks, in which a malicious user intercepts the authorization code and uses it to get hold of an access token. Due to the security benefits of this flow, PKCE is also recommended for server-side applications. We'll see an example of this flow using an SPA in appendix C.

CLIENT CREDENTIALS FLOW

The client credentials flow is aimed for server-to-server communication, and as you can see in figure 11.4, it involves the exchange of a secret to obtain an access token. This flow is suitable for enabling communication between microservices over a secure network. We'll see an example of this flow in appendix C.

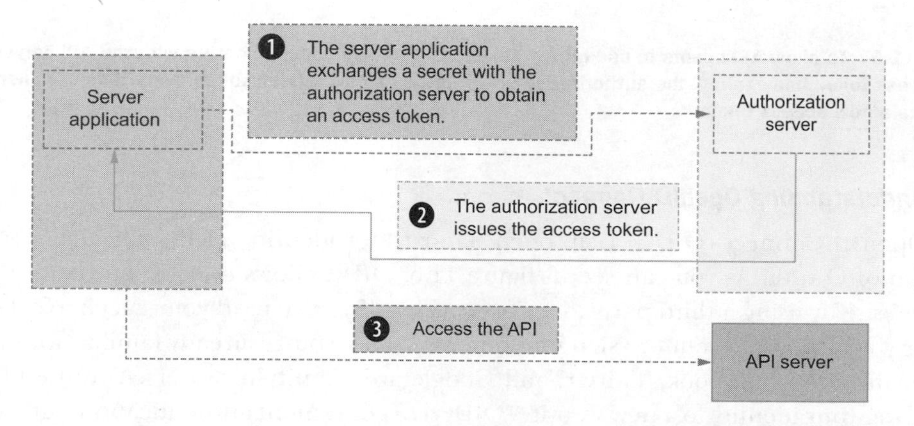

Figure 11.4 In the client credentials flow, a server application exchanges a secret with the authorization server to obtain an access token.

REFRESH TOKEN FLOW

The refresh token flow allows clients to exchange a refresh token for a new access token. For security reasons, access tokens are valid for a limited period of time. However, API clients often need to be able to communicate with the API server after an access token has expired, and to obtain the new token they use the refresh token flow.

As you can see in figure 11.5, API clients typically receive both an access token and a refresh token when they successfully gain access to the API. Refresh tokens are usually valid for a limited period of time, and they're valid for one-time use. Every time you refresh your access token, you'll get a new refresh token.

Now that we understand how OAuth works, let's turn our attention to OpenID Connect!

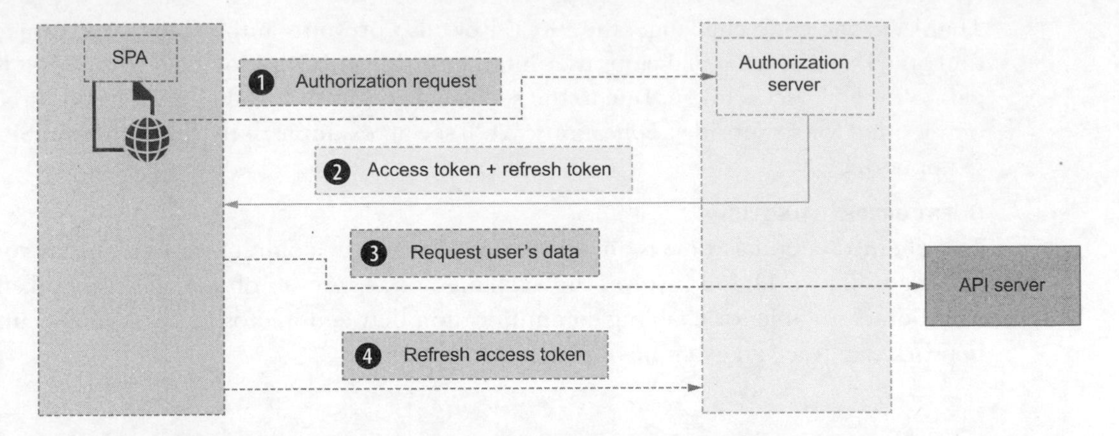

Figure 11.5 To allow API clients to use refresh tokens to continue communicating with the API server after the access token has expired, the authorization server issues a new refresh token every time the client requests a new access token.

11.2.2 Understanding OpenID Connect

OpenID Connect (OIDC) is an open standard for identity verification that's built on top of OAuth. As you can see in figure 11.6, OIDC allows users to authenticate to a website by using a third-party identity provider. If you've used your Facebook, Twitter, or your Google account to sign into other websites, you're already familiar with OIDC. In this case, Facebook, Twitter, and Google are identity providers. You use them to bring your identity to a new website. OIDC is a convenient authentication system since it allows users to use the same identity across different websites without having to create and manage new usernames and passwords.

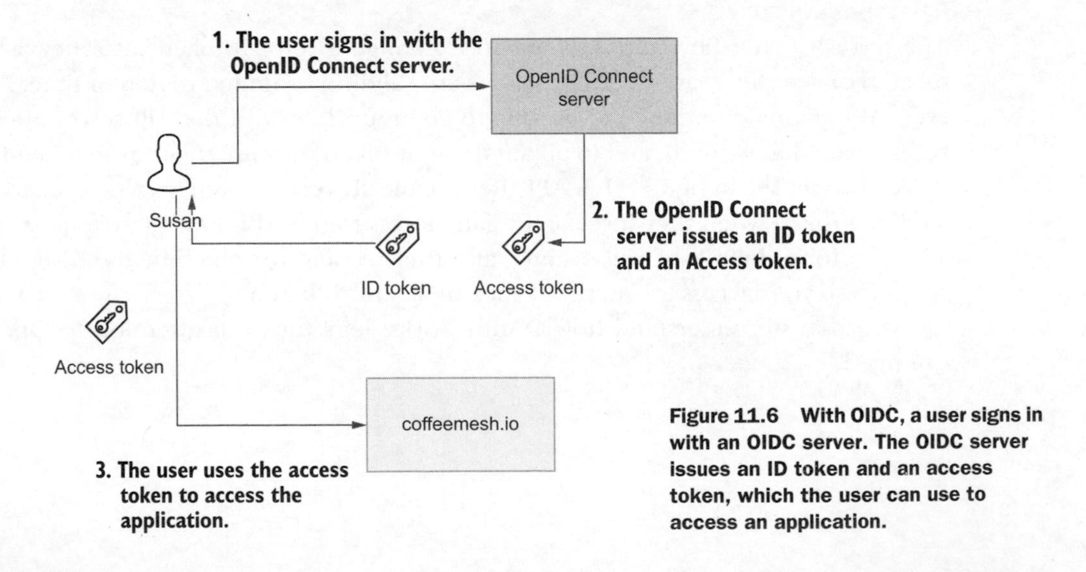

Figure 11.6 With OIDC, a user signs in with an OIDC server. The OIDC server issues an ID token and an access token, which the user can use to access an application.

DEFINITION *OpenID Connect* (OIDC) is an identity verification protocol that allows users to bring their identity from one website (the identity provider) to another. OIDC is built on top of OAuth, and we can use the same flows defined by OAuth to authenticate users.

Since OIDC is built on top of OAuth, we can use any of the authorization flows described in the previous section to authenticate and authorize users. As you can see in figure 11.6, when we authenticate using the OIDC protocol, we distinguish two types of tokens: ID tokens and access tokens. Both tokens come in the form of JSON Web Tokens, but they serve different purposes: *ID tokens* identify the user, and they contain information such as the user's name, their email, and other personal details. You use ID tokens only to verify the user identity, and never to determine whether a user has access to an API. API access is validated with access tokens. *Access tokens* typically don't contain user information but a set of claims about the access rights of the user.

ID TOKENS VS. ACCESS TOKENS A common security problem is the misuse of ID tokens and access tokens. ID tokens are tokens that carry the identity of the user. They must be used exclusively for verifying the user's identity and not for validating access to an API. API access is validated through access tokens. Access tokens rarely contain a user's identity details, and instead contain claims about the user's right to access the API. A fundamental difference between ID tokens and access tokens is the audience: the ID token's audience is the authorization server, while the access token's audience is our API server.

Identity providers that offer OIDC integrations expose a `/.well-known/openid-configuration` endpoint (with a leading period!), also known as the *discovery endpoint*, which tells the API consumer how to authenticate and obtain their access tokens. For example, the OIDC's well-known endpoint for Google Accounts is https://accounts.google.com/.well-known/openid-configuration. If you call this endpoint, you'll obtain the following payload (the example is truncated with an ellipsis):


```
{
  "issuer": "https://accounts.google.com",
  "authorization_endpoint": "https://accounts.google.com/o/oauth2/v2/auth",
  "device_authorization_endpoint":
➥ "https://oauth2.googleapis.com/device/code",
  "token_endpoint": "https://oauth2.googleapis.com/token",
  "userinfo_endpoint": "https://openidconnect.googleapis.com/v1/userinfo",
  "revocation_endpoint": "https://oauth2.googleapis.com/revoke",
  "jwks_uri": "https://www.googleapis.com/oauth2/v3/certs",
  "response_types_supported": [
    "code",
    "token",
    "id_token",
    "code token",
    "code id_token",
    "token id_token",
```

```
      "code token id_token",
      "none"
    ],
    ...
  }
```

As you can see, the well-known endpoint tells us which URL we must use to obtain the authorization access token, which URL returns user information, or which URL we use to revoke an access token. There are other bits of information in this payload, such as available claims or the JSON Web Keys URI (JWKS). Typically, you use a library to handle these endpoints on your behalf, or you use an identity-as-a-service provider to take care of these integrations. If you want to learn more about OpenID Connect, I recommend Prabath Siriwardena's *OpenID Connect in Action* (Manning, 2022).

Now that we know how OAuth and OpenID Connect work, it's time get into the details of how authentication and authorization work. We'll start by studying what JSON Web Tokens are in the next section.

11.3 Working with JSON Web Tokens

In OAuth and OpenID Connect, user access is verified by means of a token known as *JSON Web Token*, or JWT. This section explains what JSON Web Tokens are, how they're structured, what kinds of claims they contain, and how to produce and validate them.

A JWT is a token that represents a JSON document. The JSON document contains claims, such as who issued the token, the audience of the token, or when the token expires. The JSON document is typically encoded as a Base64 string. JWTs are normally signed with a private secret or a cryptographic key.[6] A typical JSON Web Token looks like this:


```
eyJ0eXAiOiJKV1QiLCJhbGciOiJSUzI1NiJ9.eyJpc3MiOiJodHRwczovL2F1dGguY29mZmVlbW
➥ VzaC5pby8iLCJzdWIiOiJlYzdiYmNjZi1jYTg5LTRhZjMtODJhYy1iNDFlNDgzMWE5NjIiL
➥ CJhdWQiOiJodHRwOi8vMTI3LjAuMC4xOjgwMDAvb3JkZXJzIiwiaWF0IjoxNjM4MjI4NDg2
➥ LjE1Otg4MSwiZXhwIjoxNjM4MzE0Odg2LjE1Otg4Mswic2NvcGUiOiJvcGVuaWQifQ.oblJ
➥ 5wV9GqrhIDzNSzcClrpEQTMK8hZGzn1S707tDtQE__OCDsP9J2Wa70aBua6X81-
➥ zrvWBfzrcX--nSyT-
➥ A9uQxL5j3RHHycToqSVi87I9H6jgP4FEKH6ClwZfabVwzNIy52Zs7zRdcSI4WRz1OpHoCM-
➥ 2hNtZ67dMJQgBVIlrXcwKAeKQWP8SxSDgFbwnyRTZJt6zijRnCJQqV4KrK_M4pv2UQYqf9t
➥ Qpj2uflTsVcZq6XsrFLAgqvAg-YsIarYw9d63rs4H_I2aB3_T_1dGPY6ic2R8WDT1_Axzi-
➥ crjoWq9A51SN-kMaTLhE_v2MSBB3A0zrjbdC4ZvuszAqQ
```


If you look closely at the example, you'll see the string contains two periods. The periods act as delimiters that separate each component of the JSON Web Token. As you can see in figure 11.7, a JSON Web Token document has three sections:

---

[6] The full specification for how JSON Web Tokens should be produced and validated is available under J. Jones, J. Bradley, and N. Sakimura, "JSON Web Token (JWT)," RFC-7519, May 2015, https://datatracker.ietf.org/doc/html/rfc7519.

- *Header*—Identifies the type of token as well as the algorithm and the key that were used sign the token. We use this information to apply the right algorithm to verify the token's signature.
- *Payload*—Contains the document's set of claims. The JWT specification includes a list of reserved claims that identify the issuer of the token (the authorization server), the token's audience or intended recipient (our API server), and its expiry date, among other details. In addition to JWT's standard claims, a payload can also include custom claims. We use this information to determine whether the user has access to the API.
- *Signature*—A string representing the token's signature.

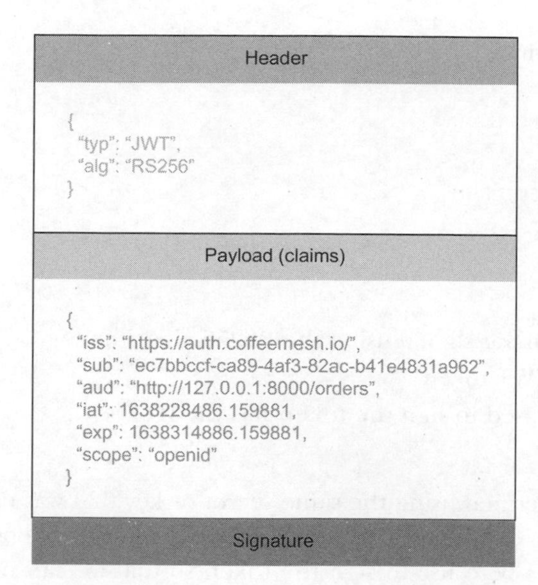

Figure 11.7 A JWT is composed of three parts: a header that contains information about the token itself, a payload with claims about the user's access to the website, and a signature that proves the authenticity of the token.

Now that we understand what a JWT is and what its structure looks like, let's delve deeper into its properties. The next sections explain the main types of claims and properties we can find in JWT payloads and headers and how we use them.

11.3.1 Understanding the JWT header

JWTs contain a header that describes the type of token, as well as the algorithm and the key used to sign the token. JWTs are commonly signed using the HS256 and the RS256 algorithms. HS256 uses a secret to encrypt the token, while RS256 uses a private/public key pair to sign the token. We use this information to apply the right algorithm to verify the token's signature.

> **Signing algorithms for JWTs**
>
> The two most common algorithms used for signing JWTs are HS256 and RS256. HS256 stands for HMAC-SHA256, and it's a form of encryption that uses a key to produce a hash.
>
> RS256 stands for RSA-SHA256. RSA (Rivest-Shamir-Adleman) is a form of encryption that uses a private key to encrypt the payload. In this case, we can verify that the token's signature is correct by using a public key.
>
> You can learn more about HMAC and RSA in David Wong's *Real-World Cryptography* (Manning, 2021).

A typical JWT header is the following:

```
{
  "alg": "RS256",
  "typ": "JWT",
  "kid": "ZweIFRR4l1dJlVPHOoZqf"
}
```

Let's analyze this header:

- `alg`—Tells us that the token was signed using the RS256 algorithm
- `typ`—Tells us that this is a JWT token
- `kid`—Tells us that the key used to sign the token has the ID `ZweIFRR4l1dJlVPHOoZqf`

A token's signature can only be verified using the same secret or key that was used to sign it. For security, we often use a collection of secrets or keys to sign the tokens. The `kid` field tells us which secret or key to use to sign the token so that we can use the right value when verifying the token's signature.

Some tokens also contain a `nonce` field in the header. If you see one of those tokens, chances are the token isn't for your API server unless you're the creator of the token and you know what the value for `nonce` is. The `nonce` field typically contains an encrypted secret that adds an additional layer of security to the JWT. For example, the tokens issued by the Azure Active Directory to access its Graph API contain a `nonce` token, which means you shouldn't use those tokens to authorize access to your custom APIs. Now that we understand the properties of a token's header, the next section explains how to read the token's claims.

11.3.2 Understanding JWT claims

The payload of a JWT contains a set of claims. Since a JWT payload is a JSON document, the claims come in the form of key-value pairs.

There are two types of claims: *reserved claims*, which are part of the JWT specification, and *custom claims*, which are claims we can add to enrich the tokens with additional information.[7] The JWT specification defines seven reserved claims:

- `iss` *(issuer)*—Identifies the issuer of the JWT. If you use an identity-as-a-service provider, the issuer identifies that service. It typically comes in the form of an ID or a URL.
- `sub` *(subject)*—Identifies the subject of the JWT (i.e., the user sending the request to the server). It typically comes in the form of an opaque ID (i.e., an ID that doesn't disclose the user's personal details).
- `aud` *(audience)*—Indicates the recipient for which the JWT is intended. This is our API server. It typically comes in the form of an ID or a URL. It's crucial to check this field to validate that the token is intended for our APIs. If we don't recognize the value in this field, it means the token isn't for us, and we must disregard the request.
- `exp` *(expiration time)*—A UTC timestamp that indicates when the JWT expires. Requests with expired tokens must be rejected.
- `nbf` *(not before time)*—A UTC timestamp that indicates the time before which the JWT must not be accepted.
- `iat` *(issued at time)*—A UTC timestamp that indicates when the JWT was issued. It can be used to determine the age of the JWT.
- `jti` *(JWT ID)*—A unique identifier for the JWT.

The reserved claims are not required in the JWT payload, but it's recommended to include them to ensure interoperability with third-party integrations.

Listing 11.1 Example of JWT payload claims

```
{
  "iss": "https://auth.coffeemesh.io/",
  "sub": "ec7bbccf-ca89-4af3-82ac-b41e4831a962",
  "aud": "http://127.0.0.1:8000/orders",
  "iat": 1667155816,
  "exp": 1667238616,
  "azp": "7c2773a4-3943-4711-8997-70570d9b099c",
  "scope": "openid"
}
```

Let's dissect the claims in listing 11.1:

- `iss` tells us that the token has been issued by the https://auth.coffeemesh.io server identity service.
- `sub` tell us that the user has the identifier `ec7bbccf-ca89-4af3-82ac-b41e4831a962`. The value of this identifier is owned by the identity service. Our APIs can use this value to control access to the resources owned by this user in

[7] You can see a full list of the most commonly used JWT claims under https://www.iana.org/assignments/jwt/jwt.xhtml.

an opaque way. We say this ID is opaque because it doesn't disclose any personal information about the user.

- `aud` tells us that this token has been issued to grant access to the orders API. If the value of this field is a different URL, the orders API will reject the request.
- `iat` tells us that the token was issued on the 30th of October of 2022 at 6:50 p.m. UTC.
- `exp` tells us that the token expires on the 31st of October of 2022 at 5:50 p.m. UTC.
- `azp` tells us that the token has been requested by an application with identifier `7c2773a4-3943-4711-8997-70570d9b099c`. This is typically a frontend application. This claim is common in tokens that have been issued using the OpenID Connect protocol.
- The `scope` field tells us that this token was issued using the OpenID Connect protocol.

Now that we know how to work with token claims, let's see how we produce and validate tokens!

11.3.3 Producing JWTs

To form the final JWT, we encode the header, the payload, and the signature using base64url encoding. As documented in RFC 4648 (http://mng.bz/aPRj), base64url encoding is similar to Base64, but it uses non-alphanumeric characters and omits padding. The header, payload, and signature are then concatenated using periods as separators. Libraries like PyJWT take care of the heavy lifting of producing a JWT. Let's say we want to produce a token for the payload we saw in listing 11.1:

```
payload = {
  "iss": "https://auth.coffeemesh.io/",
  "sub": "ec7bbccf-ca89-4af3-82ac-b41e4831a962",
  "aud": "http://127.0.0.1:8000/orders",
  "iat": 1667155816,
  "exp": 1667238616,
  "azp": "7c2773a4-3943-4711-8997-70570d9b099c",
  "scope": "openid"
}
```

To produce a signed token with this payload, we use PyJWT's `encode()` function, passing in the token, the key to sign the token, and the algorithm we want to use to sign the token:

```
>>> import jwt
>>> jwt.encode(payload=payload, key='secret', algorithm='HS256')
➥ 'eyJ0eXAiOiJKV1QiLCJhbGciOiJIUzI1NiJ9.eyJpc3MiOiJodHRwczovL2F1dGguY29mZ
➥ mVlbWVzaC5pby8iLCJzdWIiOiJlYzdiYmNjZi1jYTg5LTRhZjMtODJhYy1iNDFlNDgzMWE5
➥ NjIiLCJhdWQiOiJodHRwOi8vMTI3LjAuMC4xOjgwMDAvb3JkZXJzIiwiaWF0IjoxNjY3MTU
➥ 1ODE2LCJleHAiOjE2NjcyMzg2MTYsImF6cCI6IjdjMjc3M2E0LTM5NDMtNDcxMS04Otk3Lt
➥ cwNTcwZDliMDk5YyIsInNjb3BlIjoib3BlbmlkIn0.sZEXZVitCv0iVrbxGN54GJr8QecZf
➥ HA_pdvfEMzT1dI'
```

In this case, we're signing the token with a secret keyword using the HS256 algorithm. For a more secure encryption, we use a private/public key pair to sign the token with the RS256 algorithm. To sign JWTs, we typically use certificates that follow the X.509 standard, which allows us to bind an identity to a public key. To generate a private/public key pair, run the following command from your terminal:

```
$ openssl req -x509 -nodes -newkey rsa:2048 -keyout private_key.pem \
-out public_key.pem -subj "/CN=coffeemesh"
```

The minimum input for an X.509 certificate is the subject's common name (CN), which in this case we set to `coffeemesh`. If you omit the `-subj` flag, you'll be prompted with a series of questions about the identity you want to bind the certificate to. This command produces a private key under a file named private_key.pem, and the corresponding public certificate under a file named public_key.pem. If you're unable to run these commands, you can find a sample key pair in the GitHub repository provided with this book, under ch11/private_key.pem and ch11/public_key.pem.

Now that we have a private/public key pair, we can use them to sign our tokens and to validate them. Create a file named jwt_generator.py and paste into it the contents of listing 11.2, which shows how to generate JWT tokens signed with a private key. The listing defines a function, `generate_jwt()`, which generates a JWT for the payload defined within the function. In the payload, we set the `iat` and the `exp` properties dynamically: `iat` is set to the current UTC time; `exp` is set to 24 hours from now. We load the private key using `cryptography`'s `serialization()` function, passing in as parameters the content of our private key file encoded in bytes, as well as the passphrase encoded in bytes. Finally, we encode the payload using PyJWT's `encode()` function, passing in the payload, the loaded private key, and the algorithm we want to use to sign the token (RS256).

Listing 11.2 Generating JWTs signed with a private key

```
# file: jwt_generator.py

from datetime import datetime, timedelta
from pathlib import Path

import jwt
from cryptography.hazmat.primitives import serialization


def generate_jwt():
    now = datetime.utcnow()
    payload = {
        "iss": "https://auth.coffeemesh.io/",
        "sub": "ec7bbccf-ca89-4af3-82ac-b41e4831a962",
        "aud": "http://127.0.0.1:8000/orders",
        "iat": now.timestamp(),
        "exp": (now + timedelta(hours=24)).timestamp(),
        "scope": "openid",
    }
```

```
    private_key_text = Path("private_key.pem").read_text()
    private_key = serialization.load_pem_private_key(
        private_key_text.encode(),
        password=None,
    )
    return jwt.encode(payload=payload, key=private_key, algorithm="RS256")


print(generate_jwt())
```

To see this code at work, activate your virtual environment by running `pipenv shell`, and execute the following command:

```
$ python jwt_generator.py
➥ eyJ0eXAiOiJKV1QiLCJhbGciOiJSUzI1NiJ9.eyJpc3MiOiJodHRwczovL2F1dGguY29mZm
➥ VlbWVzaC5pby8iLCJzdWIiOiJlYzdiYmNjZi1jYTg5LTRhZjMtODJhYy1iNDFlNDgzMWE5N
➥ jIiLCJhdWQiOiJodHRwOi8vMTI3LjAuMC4xOjgwMDAvb3JkZXJzIiwiaWF0IjoxNjM4MDMx
➥ LjgzOTY5ODczOTEsImV4cCI6MTYzODExOC4yMzk2Otg5OTMsInNjb3BlIjoib3BlbmlkIn0
➥ .GipMvEvZG8ErmMA99geYUq5IkeWpRrnHoViLb1CkRufqC5vgM9555re4IsLLa7yVxNAXIp
➥ FVFBqaoWrloJl6dSQ5r00dvUBSM1EM78KMZ7f0gQqUDFWNoKWCeyQu1QCBzuHTouS4l_mzz
➥ Ii75Sal3DJLTaj4zr6c_bQdUuDU1GyrIOJiPSCHSlnKPgg9tjrX8eOcB_ESGSo9ipnCbPAl
➥ uWp0cDjPRPBNRuiU53sbli-
➥ dTy7WoCD1mXAbqhztwO39kG3DZBkysB4vTnKU4Eul2yNNYK2hHVZQEvAqq8TJjETUS7iekf
➥ 0NSt1qQArJ7cxg6Jh5D7y5pbKmYYsBlFohPg
```

Now you know how to generate JWTs! The JWT generator from listing 11.2 is handy for running tests, and we'll use it in the upcoming sections to test our code. Now that we understand how JWTs are generated, let's see how to inspect their payloads and how to validate them.

11.3.4 Inspecting JWTs

Often when working with JWTs you'll run into validation issues. To understand why a token validation is failing, it's useful to inspect the payload and verify whether its claims are correct. In this section, you'll learn to inspect JWTs using three different tools: jwt.io (https://jwt.io), the terminal's `base64` command, and with Python. To try out these tools, run the jwt_generator.py script we created in section 11.3.3 to issue a new token.

jwt.io is an excellent tool that offers an easy way to inspect a JWT. As you can see in figure 11.8, all you need to do is paste the JWT in the input panel on the left. The display panel on the right will show you the contents of the token's header and payload. You can also verify the token's signature by providing your public key. To extract the public key from our public certificate, you can use the following command:

```
$ openssl x509 -pubkey -noout < public_key.pem > pubkey.pem
```

This command outputs the public key to a file named pubkey.pem. You need to copy the contents of that file into the public key input panel in jwt.io to verify the token's signature.

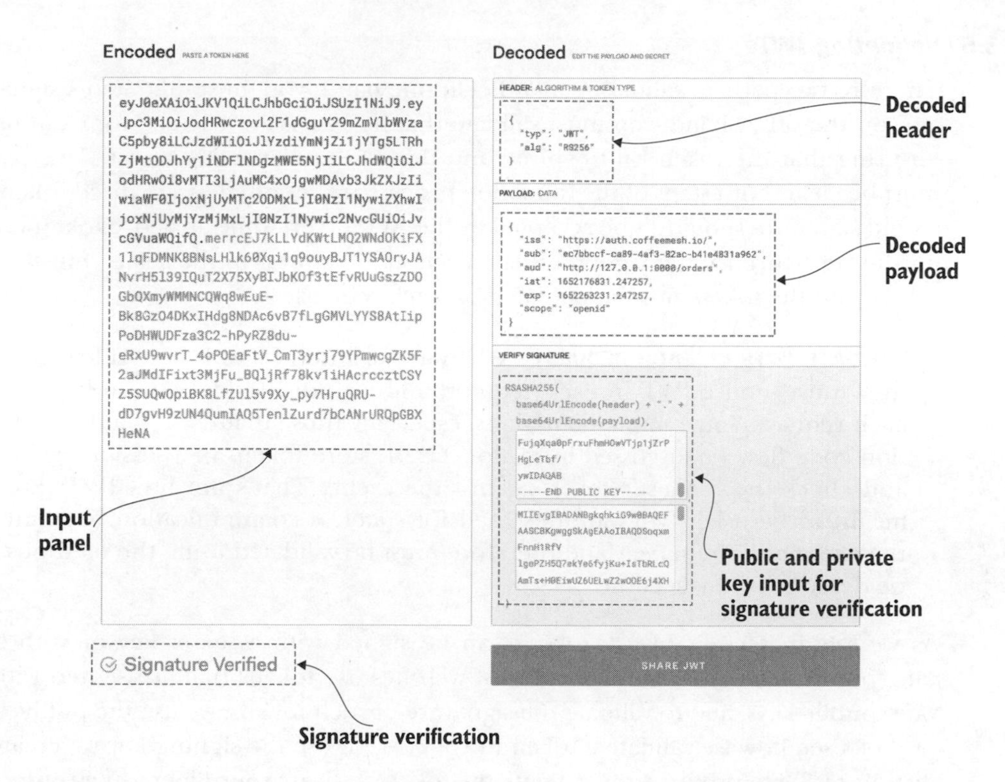

Figure 11.8 jwt.io is a tool that helps you to easily inspect and visualize JWTs. Simply paste the token on the left-side panel. You can also verify the token's signature by pasting the public key in the VERIFY SIGNATURE box on the right.

You can also inspect the contents of the JWT by decoding the header and payload in the terminal using the `base64` command. For example, to decode the token's header in the terminal, run the following command:

```
$ echo eyJ0eXAiOiJKV1QiLCJhbGciOiJSUzI1NiJ9 | base64 --decode
{"alg":"RS256","typ":"JWT"}
```

We can also inspect the contents of a JWT using Python's `base64` library. To decode a JWT header with Python, open a Python shell and run the following code:

```
>>> import base64
>>> base64.decodebytes('eyJ0eXAiOiJKV1QiLCJhbGciOiJSUzI1NiJ9'.encode())
b'{"alg":"RS256","typ":"JWT",}'
```

Since the JWT payload is also base64url encoded, we use the same methods for decoding it. Now that we know how to inspect JWT payloads, let's see how we validate them!

11.3.5 Validating JWTs

There're two parts to validating a JWT. On one hand, you must validate its signature, and on the other hand, you must validate that its claims are correct, for example, by ensuring that the token isn't expired and that the audience is correct. This process must be clear; both steps of the validation process are required. An expired token with a valid signature shouldn't be accepted by the API server, while an active token with an invalid signature isn't any good either. Every user request to the server must carry a token, and the token must be validated on each request.

> **VALIDATE JWTS ON EACH REQUEST** When a user interacts with our API server, they must send a JWT in each request, and we must validate the token on each request. Some implementations, especially those that use the authorization code flow we discussed in section 11.2.1, store tokens in a session cache and check the request's token against the cache. That's not how JWTs are meant to be used. JWTs are designed for stateless communication between the client and the server, and therefore must be validated using the methods we describe in this section.

As we saw in section 11.3.3, tokens can be signed with a secret key or with a private/public key pair. For security, most websites use tokens that are signed with private/public keys, and to validate the signature of such tokens, we use the public key.

Let's see how we validate a token in code. We'll use the signing key we created in section 11.3.3 to produce and validate the token. Activate your Pipenv environment by running `pipenv shell`, and execute the jwt_generator.py script to issue a new token.

To validate the token, we must first load the public key using the following code:

```
>>> from cryptography.x509 import load_pem_x509_certificate
>>> from pathlib import Path
>>> public_key_text = Path('public_key.pem').read_text()
>>> public_key = load_pem_x509_certificate(public_key_text.encode('utf-
➥ 8')).public_key()
```

Now that we have the public key available, we can use it to validate a token with the following code:

```
>>> import jwt
>>> access_token = "eyJ0eXAiOiJKV1QiLCJhbGciOiJSUzI1NiJ..."
>>> jwt.decode(access_token, key=public_key, algorithms=['RS256'],
➥ audience=["http://127.0.0.1:8000/orders"])
{'iss': 'https://auth.coffeemesh.io/', 'sub': 'ec7bbccf-ca89-4af3-82ac-
➥ b41e4831a962', 'aud': 'http://127.0.0.1:8000/orders', 'iat':
➥ 1638114196.49375, 'exp': 1638200596.49375, 'scope': 'openid'}
```

As you can see, if the token is valid, we'll get back the JWT payload. If the token is invalid, this code will raise an exception. Now that we know how to work with and validate JWTs, let's see how we authorize requests in an API server.

11.4 Adding authorization to the API server

Now that we know how to validate access tokens, let's put all this code together in our API server. In this section, we add authorization to the orders API. Some endpoints of the orders API are protected, while others must be accessible to everyone. Our goal is to ensure that our server checks for valid access tokens under the protected endpoints.

We'll allow public access to the /docs/orders and the /openapi/orders.json endpoints since they serve the API documentation that must be available for all consumers. All other endpoints require valid tokens. If the token is invalid or is missing in the request, we must reject the request with a 401 (Unauthorized) status code, which indicates that credentials are missing.

How do we add authorization to our APIs? There're two major strategies: handling validation in an API gateway or handling validation in each service. An *API gateway* is a network layer that sits in front of our APIs.[8] The main role of an API gateway is to facilitate service discovery, but it can also be used to authorize user access, validate access tokens, and enrich the request with custom headers that add information about the user.

The second method is to handle authorization within each API. You'll handle authorization at the service level when your API gateway can't handle authorization or when an API gateway doesn't fit in your architecture. In this section, we'll learn to handle authorization within the service since we don't have an API gateway.

A question that often comes up is, where exactly in our code do we handle authorization? Since authorization is needed to validate user access to the service through the API, we implement it in the API middleware. As you can see in figure 11.9, *middleware* is a layer of code that provides common functionality to process all our requests. Most web servers have a concept of middleware or request preprocessors, and that's where our authorization code goes. Middleware components are usually executed in order, and typically we can choose the order in which they're executed. Since authorization controls access to our server, the authorization middleware must be executed early.

11.4.1 Creating an authorization module

Let's first create a module to encapsulate our authorization code. Create a file named orders/web/api/auth.py and copy the code in listing 11.3 into it. We start by loading the public key we created in section 11.3.3. To validate the token, we first retrieve the headers and load the public key. We use PyJWT's `decode()` function to validate the token, passing in as parameters the token itself, the public key required to validate the token, the expected list of audiences, and the algorithms used to sign the key.

[8] See Chris Richardson, "Pattern: API Gateway/Backends for Frontends," https://microservices.io/patterns/apigateway.html.

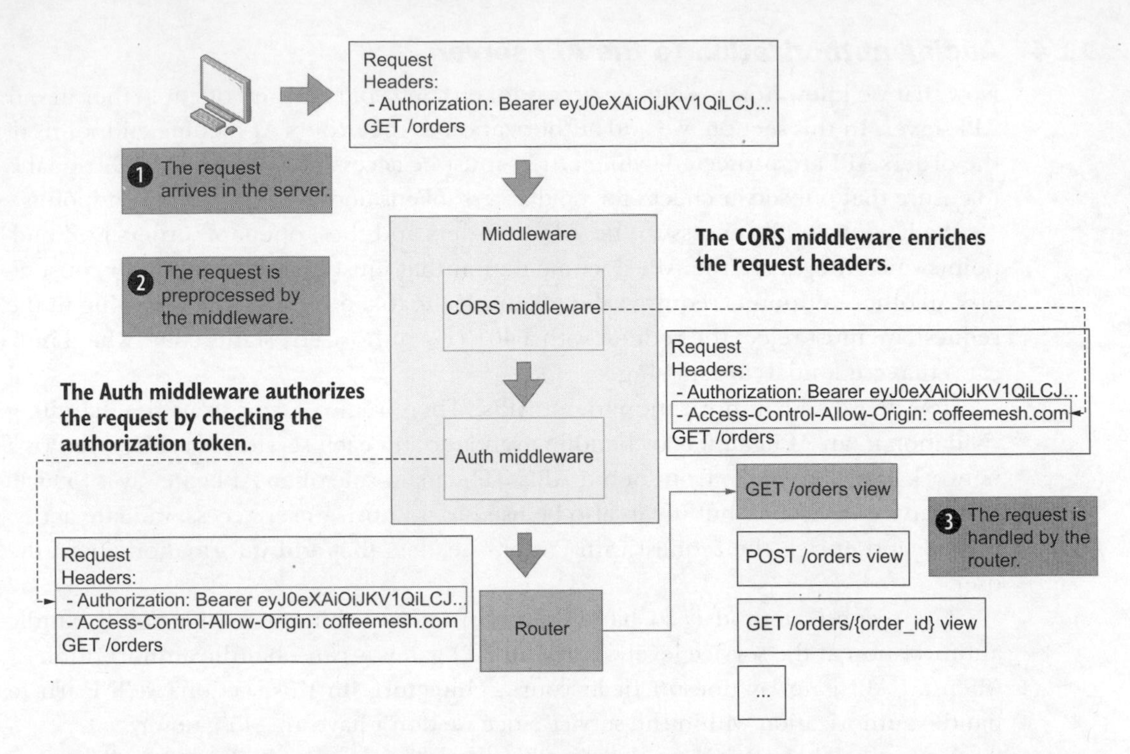

Figure 11.9 A request is first processed by the server middleware, such as the CORS and auth middleware, before making it to the router, which maps the request to the corresponding view function.

Listing 11.3 Adding an authorization module to the API

```
# file: orders/web/api/auth.py

from pathlib import Path

import jwt
from cryptography.x509 import load_pem_x509_certificate


public_key_text = (
    Path(__file__).parent / "../../../public_key.pem"
).read_text()
public_key = load_pem_x509_certificate(
    public_key_text.encode()
).public_key()


def decode_and_validate_token(access_token):
    """
    Validates an access token. If the token is valid, it returns the token payload.
    """
    return jwt.decode(
        access_token,
```

```
        key=public_key,
        algorithms=["RS256"],
        audience=["http:/ /127.0.0.1:8000/orders"],
    )
```

Now that we created a module that encapsulates the functionality necessary to validate a JWT, let's incorporate it into the API by adding a middleware that uses it to validate access to the API.

11.4.2 Creating an authorization middleware

To add authorization to our API, we create an authorization middleware. Listing 11.4 shows how to implement the authorization middleware. The code in listing 11.4 goes into the orders/web/app.py file, with the newly added code in bold. We implement the middleware as a simple class called `AuthorizeRequestMiddleware`, which inherits from Starlette's `BaseHTTPMiddleware` class. The entry point for the middleware must be implemented in a function called `dispatch()`.

We use a flag to determine whether we should enable authorization. The flag is an environment variable called `AUTH_ON`, and we set it to `False` by default. Often when working on a new feature or when debugging an issue in our API, it's convenient to run the server locally without authorization. Using a flag allows us to switch authentication on and off according to our needs. If authorization is off, we add the default ID `test` for the request user.

Next, we check whether the user is requesting the API documentation. In that case, we don't block the request since we want to make the API documentation visible to all users; otherwise, they wouldn't know how to form their requests correctly.

We also check the request's method. If it's an OPTIONS request, we won't attempt to authorize the request. OPTIONS requests are preflight requests, also known as cross-origin resource sharing (CORS) requests. The purpose of a preflight request is to check which origins, methods, and request headers are accepted by the API server, and according to W3's specification, CORS requests must not require credentials (https://www.w3.org/TR/2020/SPSD-cors-20200602/). CORS requests are typically handled by the web server framework.

> **DEFINITION** *CORS requests*, also known as preflight requests, are requests sent by the web browser to understand which methods, origins, and headers are accepted by the API server. If we don't process CORS requests correctly, the web browser will abort communication with the API. Fortunately, most web frameworks contain plug-ins or extensions that handle CORS requests correctly. CORS requests aren't authenticated, so when we add authorization to our server, we must ensure that preflight requests don't require credentials.

If it's not a CORS request, we attempt to capture the token from the request headers. We expect the token under the Authorization header. If the Authorization header isn't found, we reject the request with a 401 (Unauthorized) status code response.

The format of the Authorization header's value is `Bearer <ACCESS_TOKEN>`, so if the Authorization header is found, we capture the token by splitting the header value around the space, and we attempt to validate it. If the token is invalid, PyJWT will raise an exception. In our middleware, we capture PyJWT's invalidation exceptions to make sure we can return a 401 status code response. If no exception is raised, it means the token is valid, and therefore we can process the request, so we return a call to the next callback. We also store the user ID from the token payload in the request's `state` object so that we can access it later in the API views. Finally, to register the middleware, we use FastAPI's `add_middleware()` method.

WHERE DO JSON WEB TOKENS GO? JWTs go in the request headers, typically under the Authorization header. An Authorization header with a JWT usually has the following format: `Authorization: Bearer <JWT>`.

Listing 11.4 Adding an authorization middleware to the orders API

```
# file: orders/web/app.py

import os

from fastapi import FastAPI
from jwt import (
    ExpiredSignatureError,
    ImmatureSignatureError,
    InvalidAlgorithmError,
    InvalidAudienceError,
    InvalidKeyError,
    InvalidSignatureError,
    InvalidTokenError,
    MissingRequiredClaimError,
)
from starlette import status
from starlette.middleware.base import (
    RequestResponseEndpoint,
    BaseHTTPMiddleware,
)
from starlette.requests import Request
from starlette.responses import Response, JSONResponse

from orders.api.auth import decode_and_validate_token

app = FastAPI(debug=True)

class AuthorizeRequestMiddleware(BaseHTTPMiddleware):
    async def dispatch(
        self, request: Request, call_next: RequestResponseEndpoint
    ) -> Response:
```

We create a middleware class by inheriting from Starlette's BaseHTTPMiddleware base class.

We implement the middleware's entry point.

```
        if os.getenv("AUTH_ON", "False") != "True":
            request.state.user_id = "test"
            return await call_next(request)

        if request.url.path in ["/docs/orders", "/openapi/orders.json"]:
            return await call_next(request)
        if request.method == "OPTIONS":
            return await call_next(request)

        bearer_token = request.headers.get("Authorization")
        if not bearer_token:
            return JSONResponse(
                status_code=status.HTTP_401_UNAUTHORIZED,
                content={
                    "detail": "Missing access token",
                    "body": "Missing access token",
                },
            )
        try:
            auth_token = bearer_token.split(" ")[1].strip()
            token_payload = decode_and_validate_token(auth_token)
        except (
            ExpiredSignatureError,
            ImmatureSignatureError,
            InvalidAlgorithmError,
            InvalidAudienceError,
            InvalidKeyError,
            InvalidSignatureError,
            InvalidTokenError,
            MissingRequiredClaimError,
        ) as error:
            return JSONResponse(
                status_code=status.HTTP_401_UNAUTHORIZED,
                content={"detail": str(error), "body": str(error)},
            )
        else:
            request.state.user_id = token_payload["sub"]
        return await call_next(request)


app.add_middleware(AuthorizeRequestMiddleware)

from orders.api import api
```

We authorize the request if AUTH_ON is set to True.

If authorization is off, we bind a default user named test to the request.

We return by calling the next callback.

The documentation endpoints are publicly available, so we don't authorize them.

We attempt to fetch the Authorization header.

If the Authorization header isn't set, we return a 401 response.

We validate and retrieve the token's payload.

We capture the token from the Authorization header.

If the token is invalid, we return a 401 response.

We capture the user ID from the token's sub field.

We register the middleware using FastAPI's add_middleware() method.

Our server is ready to start validating requests with JWTs! Let's run a test to see our authorization code at work. Activate the virtual environment by running `pipenv shell`, and start the server with the following command:

```
$ AUTH_ON=True uvicorn orders.web.app:app --reload
```

From a different terminal, make an unauthenticated request using cURL (some of the output is truncated) with the `-i` flag, which displays additional information, such as the response status code:

```
$ curl -i http://localhost:8000/orders
HTTP/1.1 401 Unauthorized
[...]

{"detail":"Missing access token","body":"Missing access token"}
```

As you can see, a request with a missing token is rejected with a 401 error and a message telling us that the access token is missing. Now generate a token using the jwt_generator.py script we implemented in section 11.3.3, and use the token to make a new request:

```
curl http://localhost:8000/orders -H 'Authorization: Bearer
➥ eyJ0eXAiOiJKV1QiLCJhbGciOiJSUzI1NiIsImtpZCI6ImI3NTQwM2QxLWUzZDktNDgzYy0
➥ 5MjZhLTM4NDRhM2Q4OWY1YyJ9.eyJpc3MiOiJodHRwczovL2F1dGguY29mZmVlbWVzaC5pb
➥ y8iLCJzdWIiOiJlYzdiYmNjZi1jYTg5LTRhZjMtODJhYy1iNDFlNDgzMWE5NjIiLCJhdWQi
➥ OiJodHRwOi8vMTI3LjAuMC4xOjgwMDAvb3JkZXJzIiwiaWF0IjoxNjM4MTE3MjEyLjc5OTE
➥ 3OSwiZXhwIjoxNjM4MjAzNjEyLjc5OTE3OSwic2NvcGUiOiJvcGVuaWQifQ.F1bmgYm1acf
➥ i1NMm5JGkbYQYWFNvG1-7BAXEnIqNdF0th_DYcnEm_p3YZ5hQ93v4QWxDx9muit6InKs-
➥ MHqhChP2k6DakpSocaqbgJ_IHpqNhTaEzByqZjoNfZFyQLZMo3yEaQB8S_x0LcKOOqeoPYl
➥ GSWM1eAUy7VFBXmvMUZrUj-yoK721U9vevgM-wdVyYFVtpTRuyjCoWMjJEVadNn-
➥ Zrxr0ghlRQnwEx-YdTbbEMkk_vVLWoWeEgj7mkBE167fr-
➥ fyGUKBqa2F71Zwh8DaDQz79Ph_STOY6BTlCnAVL8XwnlIOhJWpSHuc90Kynn_RX49_yJrQH
➥ KF-xLoflWg'
{"orders":[]}
```

If the token is valid, this time you'll get a successful response with a list of orders. Our authorization code is working! The next step is to ensure that users can access only their own resources in the server. Before we do that, though, let's add one more piece of middleware to handle CORS requests.

11.4.3 Adding CORS middleware

Since we're going to allow interactions with a frontend application, we also need to enable the CORS middleware. As we saw in section 11.4.2, CORS requests are sent by the browser to know which headers, methods, and origins are allowed by the server. FastAPI's CORS middleware takes care of populating our responses with the right information. Listing 11.5 shows how to modify the orders/web/app.py file to register the CORS middleware, with the newly added code in bold and omitting some of the code in listing 11.5 with an ellipsis.

As we did previously, we use FastAPI's `add_middleware()` method to register the CORS middleware, and we pass along the necessary configuration. For testing purposes, we're using wildcards to allow all origins, methods, and headers, but in your production environment you must be more specific. In particular, you must restrict the allowed origins to your website's domain and other trusted origins.

The order in which we register our middleware matters. Middleware is executed in reverse order of registration, so the latest registered middleware is executed first. Since the CORS middleware is required for all interactions between the frontend client and the API server, we register it last, which ensures it's always executed.

Listing 11.5 Adding CORS middleware

```
# file: orders/web/app.py

import os

from fastapi import FastAPI
from jwt import (
    ExpiredSignatureError,
    ImmatureSignatureError,
    InvalidAlgorithmError,
    InvalidAudienceError,
    InvalidKeyError,
    InvalidSignatureError,
    InvalidTokenError,
    MissingRequiredClaimError,
)
from starlette import status
from starlette.middleware.base import RequestResponseEndpoint,
    BaseHTTPMiddleware
from starlette.middleware.cors import CORSMiddleware      # We import Starlette's CORSMiddleware class.
from starlette.requests import Request
from starlette.responses import Response, JSONResponse

from orders.api.auth import decode_and_validate_token

app = FastAPI(debug=True)

...

app.add_middleware(AuthorizeRequestMiddleware)


app.add_middleware(
    CORSMiddleware,                  # We register CORSMiddleware using FastAPI's add_middleware() method.
    allow_origins=["*"],             # We allow all origins.
    allow_credentials=True,          # We support cookies for cross-origin requests.
    allow_methods=["*"],             # We allow all HTTP methods.
    allow_headers=["*"],             # We allow all headers.
)


from orders.api import api
```

We're almost ready! Our server can now authorize users and handle CORS requests. The next step is to ensure each user can only access their data.

11.5 Authorizing resource access

We've protected our API by making sure only authenticated users can access it. Now we must ensure that the details of each order are only accessible to the user who placed it; we don't want to allow users to access each other's data. We call this type of validation *authorization*, and in this section, you'll learn to add it to your APIs.

11.5.1 Updating the database to link users and orders

We'll start by removing the orders currently present in the database. Those orders are not associated with a user and therefore won't work once we enforce an association between each order and a user. cd into the ch11 directory, activate the virtual environment by running pipenv shell, and open a Python shell by running the python command. Within the Python shell, run the following code:

```
>>> from orders.repository.orders_repository import OrdersRepository
>>> from orders.repository.unit_of_work import UnitOfWork
>>> with UnitOfWork() as unit_of_work:
...     orders_repository = OrdersRepository(unit_of_work.session)
...     orders = orders_repository.list()
...     for order in orders: order.delete(order.id)
...     unit_of_work.commit()
```

Our database is now clean, so we're ready to get rolling. How do we associate each order with a user? A typical strategy is to create a user table and link our orders to user records via foreign keys. But does it really make sense to create a user table for the orders service? Do we want to have a user table per service?

No, we don't want to have a user table per service since it would involve lots of duplication. As you can see in figure 11.10, we want to have just one user table, and that table must be owned by the user service. Our user service is our identity-as-a-service provider, and therefore our user table already exists. Each user has already an ID, and as we saw in section 11.3.1, the ID is present in the JWT payload under the sub field. All we need to do is add a new column to the orders table to store the ID of the user who created the order.

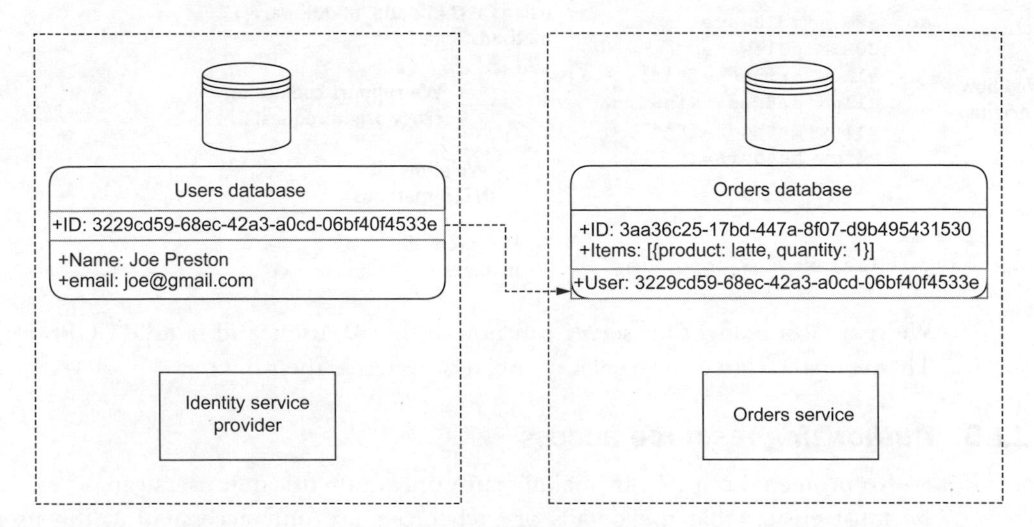

Figure 11.10 To avoid duplication, we keep only one user table under the identity service provider. And to avoid tight coupling between services, we avoid foreign keys between the tables owned by different services.

LINKING USERS TO THEIR RESOURCES Two common anti-patterns in microservices architecture is to create one user table per service and to have a shared user table that is directly accessed by multiple services to create foreign keys between users and other resources. Having a user table per service is unnecessary and involves duplicates, while a shared user table across multiple services creates tight coupling between the services and risks breaking them the next time you change the user table's schema. Since JWTs already contain opaque user IDs under the `sub` field, it's good practice to rely on that identifier to link users to their resources.

Listing 11.6 shows how we add a `user_id` field to the `OrderModel` class. The following code goes in the orders/repository/models.py file, and the newly added code is highlighted in bold.

Listing 11.6 Adding a user ID foreign key to the order table

```
# file: orders/repository/models.py

class OrderModel(Base):
    __tablename__ = 'order'

    id = Column(String, primary_key=True, default=generate_uuid)
    user_id = Column(String, nullable=False)    # We add a new column called user_id.
    items = relationship('OrderItemModel', backref='order')
    status = Column(String, nullable=False, default='created')
    created = Column(DateTime, default=datetime.utcnow)
    schedule_id = Column(String)
    delivery_id = Column(String)
```

Now that we've updated the models, we need to update the database by running a migration. As we saw in chapter 7, running a migration is the process of updating the database schema. As we did in chapter 7, we use Alembic to manage our migrations, which is Python's best database migration management library. Alembic checks the difference between the `OrderModel` model and the `order` table's current schema, and it performs the necessary updates to add the `user_id` column.

ALTERING TABLES IN SQLITE SQLite has limited support for `ALTER` statements. For example, SQLite doesn't support adding a new column to a table through an `ALTER` statement. As you can see in figure 11.11, to work around this problem, we need to copy the table's data to a temporary table and drop the original table. Then we re-create the table with the new fields, copy the data from the temporary table, and drop the temporary table. Alembic handles these operations with its batch operations strategy.

Before we can run the migration, we need to update the Alembic configuration. The change in listing 11.6 adds a new column to the order table, which translates into an `ALTER TABLE` SQL statement. For local development, we're working with SQLite, which has limited support for `ALTER` statements. To ensure that Alembic generates the

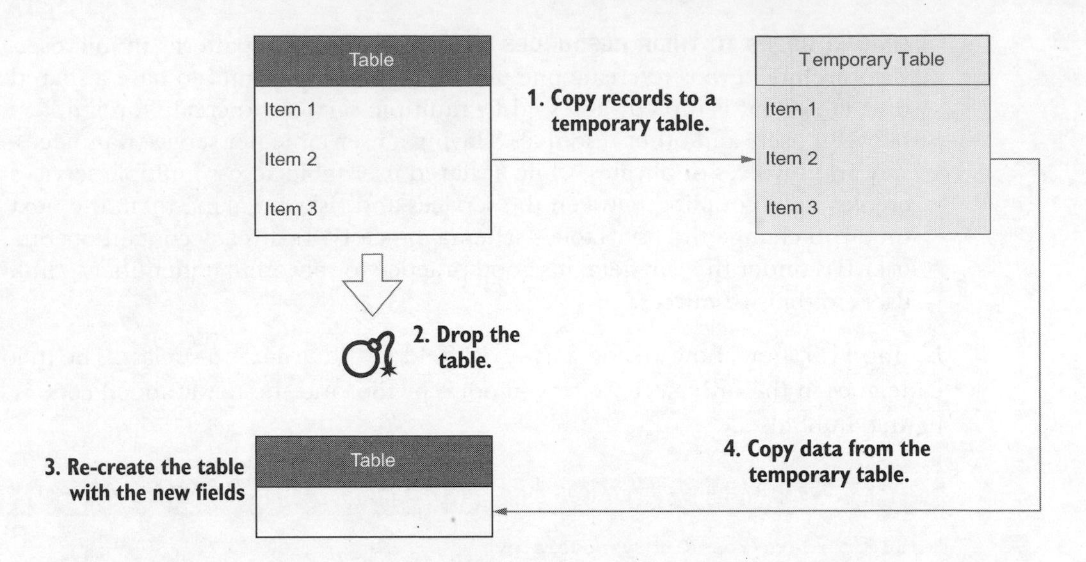

Figure 11.11 When working with SQLite, we use batch operations to make changes to our tables. In a batch operation, we copy data from the original table to a temporary table; then, we drop the original table and re-create it with the new fields; and, finally, we copy back data from the temporary table.

right migrations for SQLite, we need to update its configuration to run batch operations. *You only need to do this if you work with SQLite.*

To update the Alembic configuration so that we can run the migration, open the migrations/env.py file and search for a function called `run_migrations_online()`. This is the function that runs the migrations against our database. Within that function, search for the following block:

```
# file: migrations/env.py

with connectable.connect() as connection:
    context.configure(
        connection=connection,
        target_metadata=target_metadata

    )
```

And add the following line (highlighted in bold) within the call to the `configure()` method:

```
# file: migrations/env.py

with connectable.connect() as connection:
    context.configure(
        connection=connection,
        target_metadata=target_metadata,
        render_as_batch=True
    )
```

Now we can generate the Alembic migration and update the database. Run the following command to create the new migration:

```
$ PYTHONPATH=`pwd` alembic revision --autogenerate -m "Add user id to order table"
```

Next, we run the migration with the following command:

```
$ PYTHONPATH=`pwd` alembic upgrade heads
```

Our database is now ready to start linking orders and users. The next section explains how we fetch the user ID from the `request` object and feed it to our data repositories.

11.5.2 Restricting user access to their own resources

Now that our database is ready, we need to update our API views to capture the user ID when creating or updating an order, or when retrieving the list of orders. Since the changes that we need to make to our view functions are all quite similar, we'll illustrate how to apply the changes to some of the views. You can refer to the GitHub repository for this book for the full list of changes.

Listing 11.7 shows how to update the `create_order()` view function to capture the user ID when placing the order. The newly added code is highlighted in bold. As we saw in section 11.4.2, we store the user ID under the request's `state` property, so the first change we make is changing the signature of the `create_order()` function to include the `request` object. The second change is passing the user ID to the `OrderService`'s `place_order()` method.

Listing 11.7 Capturing the user ID when placing an order

```
# file: orders/web/api/api.py

@app.post(
    "/orders", status_code=status.HTTP_201_CREATED,
     response_model=GetOrderSchema
)
def create_order(request: Request, payload: CreateOrderSchema):    # We capture the request object in the function signature.
    with UnitOfWork() as unit_of_work:
        repo = OrdersRepository(unit_of_work.session)
        orders_service = OrdersService(repo)
        order = payload.dict()["order"]
        for item in order:
            item["size"] = item["size"].value
        order = orders_service.place_order(order, request.state.user_id)    # We capture the user ID from the request's state object.
        unit_of_work.commit()
        return_payload = order.dict()
    return return_payload
```

We also need to change the `OrdersService` and the `OrdersRepository` to ensure they too capture the user ID. The following code shows how to update the `OrdersService` to capture the user ID:

```
# file: orders/orders_service/orders_service.py

class OrdersService:
    def __init__(self, orders_repository: OrdersRepository):
        self.orders_repository = orders_repository

    def place_order(self, items, user_id):
        return self.orders_repository.add(items, user_id)
```

And the following code shows how to update the `OrdersRepository` to capture the user ID:

```
# file: orders/repository/orders_repository.py

class OrdersRepository:
    def __init__(self, session):
        self.session = session

    def add(self, items, user_id):
        record = OrderModel(
            items=[OrderItemModel(**item) for item in items],
            user_id=user_id
        )
        self.session.add(record)
        return Order(**record.dict(), order_=record)
```

Now that we know how to save an order with the user ID, let's see how we make sure a user gets only a list of their own orders when they call the GET `/orders` endpoint. Listing 11.8 shows the changes required to the `get_orders()` function, which implements the GET `/orders` endpoint. The newly added code is shown in bold. As you can see, in this case we also need to change the function's signature to capture the request object. Then we simply pass on the user ID as one of the query filters. No additional changes are required anywhere else in the code since both `OrdersService` and `OrdersRepository` are designed to accept arbitrary dictionaries of filters.

Listing 11.8 Ensuring a user only gets a list of their own orders

```
# file: orders/web/api/api.py

@app.get("/orders", response_model=GetOrdersSchema)
def get_orders(
    request: Request,
    cancelled: Optional[bool] = None,
    limit: Optional[int] = None
):
    with UnitOfWork() as unit_of_work:
        repo = OrdersRepository(unit_of_work.session)
        orders_service = OrdersService(repo)
        results = orders_service.list_orders(
            limit=limit, cancelled=cancelled, user_id=request.state.user_id
        )
    return {"orders": [result.dict() for result in results]}
```

Let's now turn our attention to the GET /orders/{order_id} endpoint. What happens if a user tries to retrieve the details of an order that doesn't belong to them? We can respond with two strategies: return a 404 (Not Found) response indicating that the requested order doesn't exist, or respond with a 403 (Forbidden) response, indicating that the user doesn't have access to the requested resource.

Technically, a 403 response is more correct than a 404 when a user is trying to access a resource that doesn't belong to them. But it also exposes unnecessary information. A malicious user who has valid credentials could leverage our 403 responses to build a map of the existing resources in the server. To avoid that problem, we opt for disclosing less information and return a 404 response. The user ID will become an additional filter when we attempt to retrieve an order from the database.

The following code shows the changes required to the `get_order()` function to include the user ID in our queries, with the newly added code in bold. Again, we include the request object in the function signature, and we pass on the user ID to the `OrderService`'s `get_order()` method.

Listing 11.9 Filtering orders with order ID and user ID

```
# file: orders/web/api/api.py

@app.get("/orders/{order_id}", response_model=GetOrderSchema)
def get_order(request: Request, order_id: UUID):
    try:
        with UnitOfWork() as unit_of_work:
            repo = OrdersRepository(unit_of_work.session)
            orders_service = OrdersService(repo)
            order = orders_service.get_order(
                order_id=order_id, user_id=request.state.user_id
            )
        return order.dict()
    except OrderNotFoundError:
        raise HTTPException(
            status_code=404, detail=f"Order with ID {order_id} not found"
        )
```

To be able to query orders by user ID as well, we also need to update the `OrdersService` and the `OrdersRepository` classes. We'll change their methods to accept an optional dictionary of arbitrary filters. The `OrdersService`'s `get_order()` method changes like this:

```
# file: orders/orders_service/orders_service.py

def get_order(self, order_id, **filters):
    order = self.orders_repository.get(order_id, **filters)
    if order is not None:
        return order
    raise OrderNotFoundError(f"Order with id {order_id} not found")
```

And the OrdersRepository's get() and _get() methods require the following changes:

```
# file: orders/repository/orders_repository.py

def _get(self, id_, **filters):
    return (
        self.session.query(OrderModel)
        .filter(OrderModel.id == str(id_)).filter_by(**filters)
        .first()
    )

def get(self, id_, **filters):
    order = self._get(id_, **filters)
    if order is not None:
        return Order(**order.dict())
```

The rest of the view functions in the orders/web/api/api.py file require changes similar to the ones we've seen in this section, and the same goes for the remaining methods of the OrdersService and the OrdersRepository classes. As an exercise, I recommend you try to complete the changes necessary to add authorization to the remaining API endpoints. The GitHub repository for this book contains the full list of changes, so feel free to check it out for guidance.

This concludes our journey through API authentication and authorization, and what a journey! You've learned what OAuth and OpenID Connect are and how they work. You've learned about OAuth flows and when to use each flow. You've learned what JWTs are, how to inspect their payloads, and how to produce and validate them. Finally, you've learned how to authorize API requests and how to authorize user access to specific resources. You've got all you need to start adding robust authentication and authorization to your own APIs!

Appendix C teaches you how to integrate with an identity provider such as Auth0. You'll also see practical examples of how to use the PKCE and client credentials flows, and you'll learn to authorize your requests using a Swagger UI.

Summary

- We authorize access to our APIs using the standard protocols OAuth and OpenID Connect.
- OAuth is an access delegation protocol that allows a user to grant an application access to resources they own in a different website. It distinguishes four authorization flows:
  - *Authorization code*—The API server exchanges a code with the authorization server to request the user's access token.
  - *PKCE*—The client application, typically an SPA, uses a code verifier and a code challenge to obtain an access token from the authorization server.

  - *Client credentials*—The client, typically another microservice, exchanges a private secret in return for an access token.
  - *Refresh token*—A client obtains a new access token in exchange for a refresh token.

- OpenID Connect is an identity verification protocol that builds on top of OAuth. It helps users easily authenticate to new websites by bringing their identity from other websites, such as Google or Facebook.
- JWTs are JSON documents that contain claims about the user's access permissions. JWTs are encoded using base64url encoding and are typically signed using a private/public key.
- To authenticate a request, users send their access tokens in the request's Authorization header. The expected format of this header is `Authorization: Bearer <ACCESS_TOKEN>`.
- We use PyJWT to validate access tokens. PyJWT checks that the token isn't expired, that the audience is correct, and that the signature can be verified with one of the available public keys. If the token is invalid, we reject the request with a 401 (Unauthorized) response.
- To link users to their resources, we use the user ID as represented in the `sub` claim of the JWT.
- If a user tries to access a resource that doesn't belong to them, we respond with a 403 (Forbidden) response.
- OPTIONS requests are known as CORS requests or preflight requests. CORS requests must not be protected by credentials.

12 Testing and validating APIs

This chapter covers

- Generating automatic tests for REST APIs using Dredd and Schemathesis
- Writing Dredd hooks to customize the behavior of your Dredd test suite
- Using property-based testing to test APIs
- Leveraging OpenAPI links to enhance your Schemathesis test suite
- Testing GraphQL APIs with Schemathesis

This chapter teaches you how to test and validate API implementations. Thus far, we've learned to design and build APIs to drive integrations between microservices. Along the way, we did some manual tests to ensure our implementations exhibited the correct behavior. However, those tests were minimal, and most importantly, they were purely manual and therefore not repeatable in an automated fashion.

In this chapter, we learn how to run an exhaustive test suite against our API implementations using tools such as Dredd and Schemathesis, tools for API testing that are part of every API developer's tool kit. Both Dredd and Schemathesis work by looking at the API specification and automatically generating tests against our

API server. For an API developer, this is very handy because it means you can focus your efforts on building your APIs instead of testing them.

By using tools such as Dredd and Schemathesis, you can save time and energy while resting assured that the implementation you're delivering is correct. You can run Dredd and Schemathesis in combination, or you can choose one of them. As you'll see, Dredd runs a more basic test suite that is very useful in the early stages of your API development cycle, while Schemathesis runs a robust test suite that is useful before you release your APIs to production.

To illustrate how we test REST APIs, we'll use the orders API, which we implemented in chapters 2 and 6. To illustrate how we test GraphQL APIs, we'll use the products API, which we implemented in chapter 10. As a recap, both APIs are part of CoffeeMesh, the fictional on-demand coffee delivery platform that we're building in this book. The orders API is the interface to the orders service, which manages customers' orders, while the products API is the interface to the products service, which manages the catalogue of products CoffeeMesh offers.

The code for this chapter is available in GitHub, under the folder named ch12. In section 12.1, we set up the folder structure and the environments to work on this chapter's examples, so make sure you go through that section if you want to follow along with the examples in this chapter.

12.1 Setting up the environment for API testing

In this section, we set up the environment to follow along with the examples in this chapter. Let's start by setting up the folder structure. Create a new folder called ch12 and `cd` into it. Within this folder, we'll copy the orders API and the products API. To keep things simple in this chapter, we use the implementation of the orders API as we left it in chapter 6. Chapter 6 contains a full implementation of the orders API, but it lacks a real database and integration with other services (those features were added in chapter 7). Since the goal of this chapter is to learn how to test APIs, the implementation in chapter 6 is sufficient and will help us stay focused, as we won't have to set up the database and run additional services. In real life, you'd want to test the API layer in isolation and run integration tests, including on the database. See the README.md file under the ch12/orders folder in the GitHub repository for this chapter for instructions on running the tests against the state of the application after chapters 7 and 11.

Within the ch12 folder, copy the implementation of the orders API from ch06/orders by running the following command:

```
$ cp -r ../ch06/orders orders
```

`cd` into ch12/orders and run the following command to install the dependencies:

```
$ pipenv install --dev
```

Don't forget to include the `--dev` flag when you run `pipenv install`, which tells `pipenv` to install both production and development dependencies. In this chapter, we'll use development packages to test the orders API. To run the tests, we'll need pytest, dredd_hooks, and schemathesis, which you can install with the following command:

```
$ pipenv install --dev dredd_hooks pytest schemathesis
```

To run the tests, we'll use a slightly modified version of the orders API specification without the bearerAuth security scheme, which you can find under the ch12/orders/oas.yaml file in the GitHub repository for this book. In this chapter, we'll focus on testing that the API implementation complies with the API specification, namely, ensuring the API uses the right schemas, the right status codes, and so on. API security testing is a whole different topic, and for that I recommend chapter 11 of Mark Winteringham's *Testing Web APIs* (Manning, 2022) and Corey J. Ball's *Hacking APIs* (No Starch Press, 2022).

Let's now copy the implementation of the products API from chapter 10. Go back to the top level of the ch12 directory by running cd .. and then execute the following command:

```
$ cp -r ../ch10 products
```

cd into ch12/products and run pipenv install --dev to install the dependencies. We'll use pytest and schemathesis to test the products API, which you can install by running the following command:

```
$ pipenv install pytest schemathesis
```

We're now all set up to start testing the APIs. We'll start our journey by learning about the Dredd API testing framework.

12.2 Testing REST APIs with Dredd

This section explains what Dredd is and how we use it to test REST APIs. Dredd is an API testing framework that automatically generates tests to validate the behavior of our API server. It generates tests by parsing the API specification and learning from it how the API is expected to work. Using Dredd is very helpful during development because it means we can focus our efforts on building the API while Dredd ensures that our work is going in the right direction. Dredd was released by Apiary in 2017 as the first tool of its kind (http://mng.bz/5maq), and ever since it's been part of every API developer's essential tool kit.

In this section, we'll learn how Dredd works by using it to validate the implementation of the orders API. We'll start by first running a basic test suite against the API, and then we'll explore more advanced features of the framework.

12.2.1 What is Dredd?

Before we start working with Dredd, let's take a moment to understand what Dredd is and how it works. Dredd is an API testing framework. As shown in figure 12.1, Dredd works by parsing the API specification and discovering the available URL paths and the HTTP methods they accept.

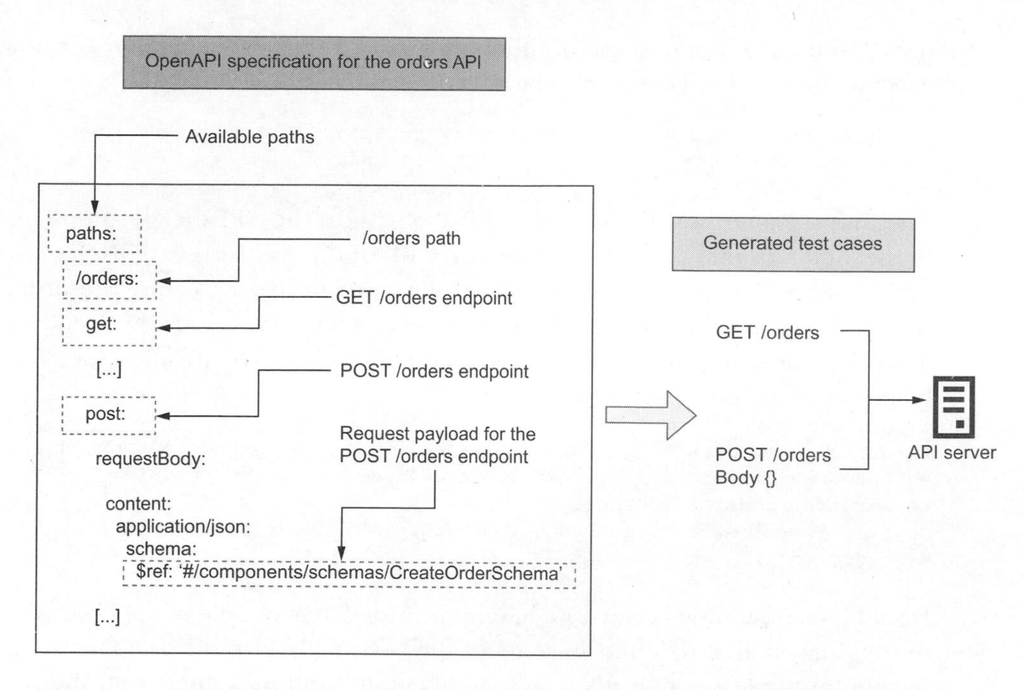

Figure 12.1 Dredd works by parsing the API specification, discovering the available endpoints, and launching tests for each endpoint.

To test the API, Dredd sends requests to each of the endpoints defined in the API specification with the expected payloads, if any, as well as any query parameters accepted by the endpoint. Finally, it checks whether the responses the API receives conform to the schemas declared in the API specification and whether they carry the expected status codes.

Now that we understand how Dredd works, let's start using it! The next section explains how to install Dredd.

12.2.2 Installing and running Dredd's default test suite

In this section, we install Dredd and run its default test suite against the orders API. `cd` into ch12/orders and run `pipenv shell` to activate the environment. Dredd is an npm package, which means you need to have a Node.js runtime available in your machine, as well as a package management tool for JavaScript, such as npm or Yarn. To install Dredd with npm, run the following command from your ch12/orders directory:

```
$ npm install dredd
```

This will install Dredd under a folder called node_modules/. Once the installation is complete, we can start using Dredd to test the API. Dredd comes with a CLI that is available under the following directory: node_modules/.bin/dredd. The Dredd CLI exposes optional arguments that give us great flexibility in how we want to run our tests. We'll make use of some of those arguments later in this section. For now, let's execute the simplest Dredd command to run a test:

```
$ ./node_modules/.bin/dredd oas.yaml http://127.0.0.1:8000 --server \
 "uvicorn orders.app:app"
```

The first argument for the Dredd CLI is the path to the API specification file, while the second argument represents the base URL of the API server. With the `--server` option, we tell Dredd which command needs to be used to start the orders API server. If you run this command now, you'll get a few warnings from Dredd with the following message (the ellipsis omits the path to the API specification file, which will be different in your machine):

```
warn: [...] (Orders API > /orders/{order_id}/cancel > Cancels an order >
➥ 200 > application/json): Ambiguous URI parameter in template:
➥ /orders/{order_id}/cancel
No example value for required parameter in API description document:
➥ order_id
```

Dredd is complaining because we haven't provided an example of the URL parameter `order_id`, which is required in some of the URL paths. Dredd complains about the missing example because it's unable to generate random values from the specification. To address Dredd's complaint, we add an example of the `order_id` parameter in each URL where it's used. For example, for the `/orders/{order_id}` URL path, we make the modification shown in listing 12.1 (the ellipses represent omitted code). The `/orders/{order_id}/pay` and the `/orders/{order_id}/cancel` URLs also contain descriptions of the `order_id` parameter, so add examples to them as well. Dredd will use the exact value provided in the examples to test the API.

Listing 12.1 Adding examples for the `order_id` URL path parameter

```
# file: orders/oas.yaml

[...]
  /orders/{order_id}:
    parameters:
      - in: path
        name: order_id
        required: true
        schema:
          type: string
        example: d222e7a3-6afb-463a-9709-38eb70cc670d    <- We add an example for the order_id URL parameter.
    get:
      [...]
```

Once we've added examples for the `order_id` parameter, we can run the Dredd CLI again. This time, the tests suite runs without problems, and you'll get a result like this:

```
complete: 7 passing, 5 failing, 0 errors, 0 skipped, 12 total
complete: Tests took 90ms
```

```
INFO:     Shutting down
INFO:     Finished server process [23593]
```

This summary tells us that Dredd ran 18 tests, of which 7 passed and 11 failed. The full outcome of the test is too long to reproduce here, but if you scroll up in the terminal, you'll see that the failing tests are on endpoints that target specific resources:

- GET, PUT, and DELETE `/orders/{order_id}`
- POST `/orders/{order_id}/pay`
- POST `/orders/{order_id}/cancel`

Dredd runs three tests for each of those endpoints, and it expects to obtain one successful response per endpoint. However, in the previous execution, Dredd only obtained 404 responses, which means the server couldn't find the resources Dredd requested. Dredd is using the ID we provided as an example in listing 12.1 when testing those endpoints. To address this problem, we could add a hardcoded order with that ID to our in-memory list of orders (we'd add it to the database if we were using one for the tests). As we'll see in the next section, however, a better approach is to use Dredd hooks.

There's also a failing test for the POST `/orders` endpoint in which Dredd expects a 422 response. The failed tests for 422 responses happen because Dredd doesn't know how to create tests that generate those responses, and Dredd hooks will also help us address this problem.

12.2.3 Customizing Dredd's test suite with hooks

Dredd's default behavior can be limited. As we've seen in section 12.2.1, Dredd doesn't know how to handle endpoints with URL path parameters, such as `order_id` in the `/orders/{order_id}` URL. Dredd doesn't know how to produce a random resource ID, and if we provide an example, it expects the sample ID to be present in the system during the execution of the test suite. This expectation is unhelpful, since it means our API is only testable when it's in a certain state—when certain resources or fixtures have been loaded into the database.

> **DEFINITION** In software testing, *fixtures* are the preconditions required to run a test. Typically, fixtures are data that we load into a database for testing, but they can also include configuration, directories and files, or infrastructure resources.

Instead of using fixtures, we can take a better approach by using Dredd hooks. This section explains what Dredd hooks are and how we use them. Dredd hooks are scripts that allow us to customize Dredd's behavior during the execution of the test suite. Using Dredd hooks, we can create resources for use during the test, save their IDs, and clean them up after finishing the test.

Dredd hooks allow us to trigger actions before and after the whole test suite, and before and after each endpoint-specific test. They are useful for stateful tests that involve creating resources and performing operations on them. For example, we can use hooks to place an order using the POST `/orders` endpoint, save the ID of the order, and reuse the ID to perform operations on the order, such as payments and cancellations, with other endpoints. Using this approach, we can test that the POST `/orders` endpoint fulfills its job of creating a resource, and we can test other endpoints with a real resource. As illustrated in figures 12.2, 12.3, and 12.4, we'll create the following hooks with these steps:

1. After the POST `/orders` test, we use a hook to save the ID returned by the server for the newly created order.
2. Before the GET, PUT, and DELETE `/orders/{order_id}` tests, we use hooks to tell Dredd to use the ID from the order created at point (1). These endpoints are used to retrieve the details of the order (GET), to update the order (PUT), and to remove the order from the server (DELETE). Therefore, after running the DELETE `/orders/{order_id}` test, the order will no longer exist in the server.
3. Before the POST `/orders/{order_id}/pay` and the POST `/orders/ {order_id}/cancel` endpoints, we use hooks to create new orders for use in these tests. We won't be able to reuse the ID from point (1), since the DELETE `/orders/{order_id}` test from point (2) deletes the order from the server.
4. For the 422 responses, we need a strategy that generates a 422 response from the server. We'll use two approaches: for the POST `/orders` endpoint, we'll send an invalid payload, while for the remaining endpoints, we'll modify the order's URI and include an invalid identifier.

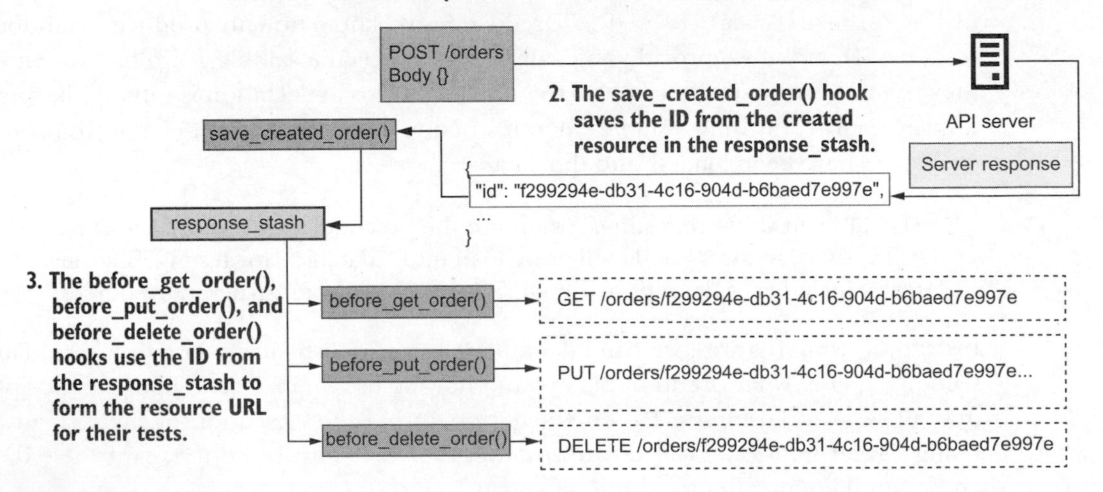

Figure 12.2 After the POST `/orders` endpoint test, the `save_created_order()` hook saves the ID from the server response body in the `response_stash`. The `before_get_order()`, `before_put_order()`, and `before_delete_order()` hooks use the ID from `response_stash` to form their resource URLs.

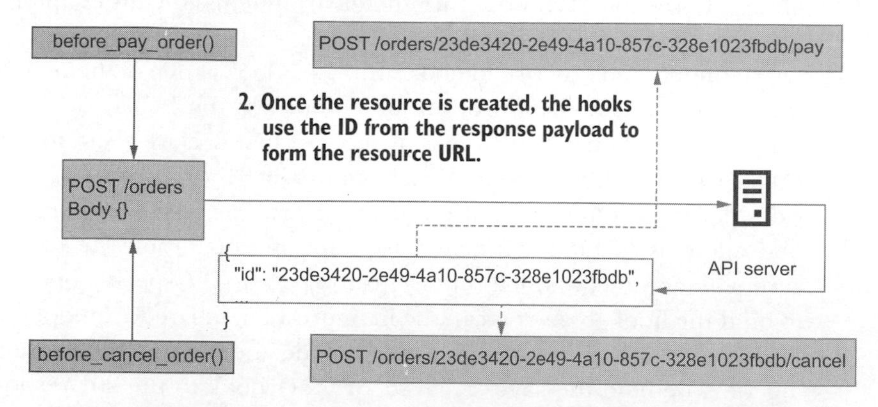

Figure 12.3 Before executing the test, the `before_pay_order()` and the `before_cancel_order()` hooks use the POST `/orders` endpoint to place a new order and use the ID from the response payload form their resource URLs.

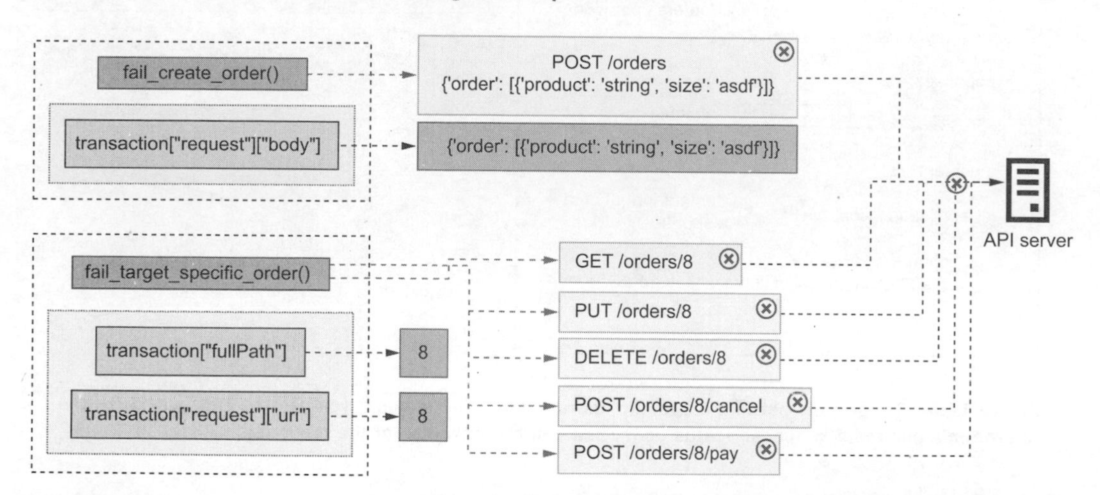

Figure 12.4 The `fail_create_order()` and the `fail_target_specific_order()` hooks inject invalid payloads and invalid order identifiers to trigger a 422 response from the server.

Using Dredd hooks to save the ID of a created resource

Now that we know what we want to do, let's write our hooks! First, if you haven't done it yet, `cd` into ch12/orders and activate the virtual environment by running `pipenv` shell. Create a file called orders/hooks.py, where we'll write our hooks. Although Dredd is an npm package, we can write our hooks in Python by using the dredd-hooks library. In section 12.1, we set up the environments for this chapter, so dredd-hooks has already been installed.

To understand how Dredd hooks work, let's look at one of them in detail. Listing 12.2 shows the implementation of an after hook for the POST /orders endpoint. This code goes into the orders/hooks.py file. We first declare a variable called response_stash, which we'll use to store data from the POST /orders request. dredd-hooks provides decorator functions, such as dredd_hooks.before() and dredd_hooks.after(), that allow us to bind a function to a specific operation. dredd-hooks' decorators accept an argument, which represents the path to the specific operation that we want to bind the hook to. As you can see in figure 12.5, in Dredd, an operation is defined as a URL endpoint with its response status code and its content-encoding format. In listing 12.2, we bind the save_created_order() hook to the 201 response of the POST /orders endpoint.

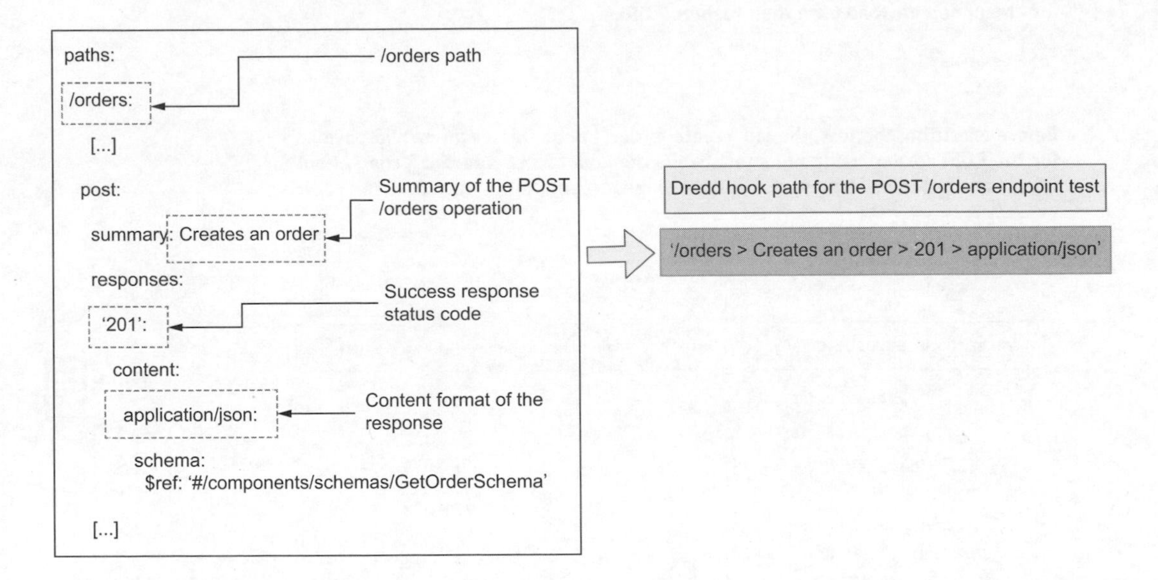

Figure 12.5 To form the path for a specific operation in a Dredd hook, you use the URL path with the operation's summary, response status code, and content encoding of the response.

DEFINING OPERATION PATHS IN DREDD HOOKS When defining the path for an operation using dredd-hooks, you can't use HTTP methods as part of the operation path; that is, the following syntax won't work: /orders > post > 201 > application/json. Instead, we use other properties of the POST endpoint, such as summary or operationId, as in the following example: /orders > Creates an order > 201 > application/json.

Dredd hooks take an argument that represents the transaction Dredd performed during the test. The argument comes in the form of a dictionary. In listing 12.2, we name the hook's argument `transaction`. Since our goal in the `save_created_order()` hook is to fetch the ID of the created order, we inspect the payload returned by the POST `/orders` endpoint, which can be found under `transaction['real']['body']`. Since our API returns JSON payloads, we load its contents using Python's `json` library. Once we get hold of the order's ID, we save it for later use in our global state dictionary, which we named `response_stash`.

Listing 12.2 Implementation of an after hook for the POST `/orders` endpoint

```
# file: orders/hooks.py

import json
import dredd_hooks

response_stash = {}

@dredd_hooks.after('/orders > Creates an order > 201 > application/json')
def save_created_order(transaction):
    response_payload = transaction['real']['body']
    order_id = json.loads(response_payload)['id']
    response_stash['created_order_id'] = order_id
```

- We import the dredd_hooks library. (`import dredd_hooks`)
- We create a global object to store and manage the state of the test suite. (`response_stash = {}`)
- We create a hook to be triggered after the POST /orders endpoint test. (`@dredd_hooks.after(...)`)
- We access the response payload from the POST /orders endpoint. (`response_payload = ...`)
- We load the response using Python's json library and retrieve the order's ID. (`order_id = ...`)
- We store the order ID in our global response_stash object. (`response_stash['created_order_id'] = ...`)

USING HOOKS TO MAKE DREDD USE CUSTOM URLS

Now that we know how to save the ID of the order created in a POST request, let's see how we use the ID to form the order's resource URL. Listing 12.3 shows how we build hooks for the order resource endpoints. The code shown in listing 12.3 goes into the orders/hooks.py file. The code from listing 12.2 is omitted using ellipses, while the new additions are shown in bold.

To specify which URL Dredd should use when testing the `/orders/{order_id}` path, we need to modify the transaction payload. In particular, we need to modify the transaction's `fullPath` and its `request`'s `uri` properties and make sure they point to the right URL. To form the URL, we access the order's ID from the `response_stash` dictionary.

Listing 12.3 Using before hooks to tell Dredd which URL to use

```
# file: orders/hooks.py

import json
import dredd_hooks

response_stash = {}

[...]
```

```
@dredd_hooks.before(
    '/orders/{order_id} > Returns the details of a specific order > 200 > '
    'application/json'
)
def before_get_order(transaction):
    transaction["fullPath"] = (
        "/orders/" + response_stash["created_order_id"]
    )
    transaction['request']['uri'] = (
        '/orders/' + response_stash['created_order_id']
    )
```

We create a hook to be triggered before the GET /orders/{order_id} endpoint test.

We change the GET /orders/{order_id} endpoint test's URL to include the ID of the order we created earlier.

```
@dredd_hooks.before(
    '/orders/{order_id} > Replaces an existing order > 200 > '
    'application/json'
)
def before_put_order(transaction):
    transaction['fullPath'] = (
        '/orders/' + response_stash['created_order_id']
    )
    transaction['request']['uri'] = (
        '/orders/' + response_stash['created_order_id']
    )

@dredd_hooks.before('/orders/{order_id} > Deletes an existing order > 204')
def before_delete_order(transaction):
    transaction['fullPath'] = (
        '/orders/' + response_stash['created_order_id']
    )
    transaction['request']['uri'] = (
        '/orders/' + response_stash['created_order_id']
    )
```

USING DREDD HOOKS TO CREATE RESOURCES BEFORE A TEST

The DELETE `/orders/{order_id}` endpoint deletes the order from the database, so we can't use the same order ID to test the `/orders/{order_id}/pay` and `/orders/{order_id}/cancel` endpoints. Instead, we'll use hooks to create new orders before testing those endpoints. Listing 12.4 shows how we accomplish that. The code in listing 12.4 goes into the orders/hooks.py file. The new code is shown in bold, while the code from previous listings is omitted with ellipses.

To create new orders, we'll call the POST `/orders` endpoint using the `requests` library, which makes it easy to make HTTP requests. To launch a POST request, we use `requests`' `post()` function, passing in the target URL for the request and the JSON payload required to create an order. In this case, we hardcode the server base URL to http://127.0.0.1:8000, but you may want to make this value configurable if you want to be able to run the test suite in different environments. Once we've created the order, we fetch its ID from the response payload and use the ID to modify the `transaction`'s `fullPath` and its `request`'s `uri` properties.

Listing 12.4 Using before hooks to create resources before a test

```
# file: orders/hooks.py

import json
import dredd_hooks
import requests                  <-- We import the requests library.

response_stash = {}

[...]

@dredd_hooks.before(
    '/orders/{order_id}/pay > Processes payment for an order > 200 > '
    'application/json'
)
def before_pay_order(transaction):
    response = requests.post(           <-- We place a new order.
        "http://127.0.0.1:8000/orders",
        json={
            "order": [{"product": "string", "size": "small", "quantity":1}]
        },
    )
    id_ = response.json()['id']         <-- We fetch the newly created order's ID.
    transaction['fullPath'] = '/orders/' + id_ + '/pay'
    transaction['request']['uri'] = '/orders/' + id_ + '/pay'


@dredd_hooks.before(
    '/orders/{order_id}/cancel > Cancels an order > 200 > application/json'
)
def before_cancel_order(transaction):
    response = requests.post(
        "http://127.0.0.1:8000/orders",
        json={
            "order": [{"product": "string", "size": "small", "quantity":1}]
        },
    )
    id_ = response.json()['id']
    transaction['fullPath'] = '/orders/' + id_ + '/cancel'
    transaction['request']['uri'] = '/orders/' + id_ + '/cancel'
```

We change the POST /orders/{order_id}/pay endpoint test's URL by to include the ID of the order we created earlier.

USING HOOKS TO GENERATE 422 RESPONSES

Some of the endpoints in the orders API accept request payloads or URL path parameters. If an API client sends an invalid payload or uses an invalid URL path parameter, the API responds with a 422 response. As we saw earlier, Dredd doesn't know how to generate 422 responses from the server, so we'll create hooks for that.

As you can see in listing 12.5, we only need two functions:

- `fail_create_order()` intercepts the request for the POST `/orders` endpoint before it reaches the server, and it modifies its payload with an invalid value for the `size` property.
- `fail_target_specific_order()` modifies the order's URI with an invalid identifier. Since we know that Dredd fires this test using the example ID we provided in the API specification, we simply need to replace that ID with an invalid value. The type of the `order_id` path parameter is a UUID, so by replacing it with an integer, the server will respond with a 422 status code.

These hooks are a good opportunity to test how the server behaves with different types of payloads and parameters, and if you need to, you can create specific tests for each endpoint for more comprehensive test coverage.

Listing 12.5 Generating 422 responses with Dredd hooks

```
# file: orders/hooks.py

@dredd_hooks.before('/orders > Creates an order > 422 > application/json')
def fail_create_order(transaction):
    transaction["request"]["body"] = json.dumps(
        {"order": [{"product": "string", "size": "asdf"}]}
    )


@dredd_hooks.before(
    "/orders/{order_id} > Returns the details of a specific order > 422 > "
    "application/json"
)
@dredd_hooks.before(
    "/orders/{order_id}/cancel > Cancels an order > 422 > application/json"
)
@dredd_hooks.before(
    "/orders/{order_id}/pay > Processes payment for an order > 422 > "
    "application/json"
)
@dredd_hooks.before(
    "/orders/{order_id} > Replaces an existing order > 422 > "
    "application/json"
)
@dredd_hooks.before(
    "/orders/{order_id} > Deletes an existing order > 422 > "
    "application/json"
)
def fail_target_specific_order(transaction):
    transaction["fullPath"] = transaction["fullPath"].replace(
        "d222e7a3-6afb-463a-9709-38eb70cc670d", "8"
    )
    transaction["request"]["uri"] = transaction["request"]["uri"].replace(
        "d222e7a3-6afb-463a-9709-38eb70cc670d", "8"
    )
```

Running Dredd with custom hooks

Now that we have Dredd hooks to make sure that each URL is correctly formed, we can run the Dredd test suite again. The following command shows how to run Dredd using a hooks file:

```
$ ./node_modules/.bin/dredd oas.yaml http://127.0.0.1:8000 --server \
 "uvicorn orders.app:app" --hookfiles=./hooks.py --language=python
```

As you can see, we simply need to pass the path to our hooks file using the `--hookfiles` flag. We also need to specify the language in which the hooks are written by using the `--language` flag. If you run the command now, you'll see now that all tests pass.

12.2.4 Using Dredd in your API testing strategy

Dredd is a fantastic tool for testing API implementations, but its test suite is limited. Dredd only tests the happy path of each endpoint. For example, to test the POST `/orders` endpoint, Dredd sends only a valid payload to the endpoint and expects it to be processed correctly. It doesn't send malformed payloads, so by using Dredd alone, we don't know how the server reacts in those situations. This is fine when we're in the early stage development of our service and we don't want to be carried away by the API layer.

However, before we release our code, we must ensure it works as expected in all situations, and to run tests that go beyond the happy path, we need to use a different library: `schemathesis`. We'll learn about Schemathesis in section 12.4, but before we do that, we need to understand the core approach to testing that Schemathesis uses: property-based testing. That's the topic of our next section, so move on to learn more about it!

12.3 Introduction to property-based testing

This section explains what property-based testing is, how it works, and how it helps us write more exhaustive tests for our APIs. Along the way, you'll also lean about Python's excellent property-based testing library, `hypothesis`. As you'll see, property-based testing helps us create robust test suites for APIs, allowing us to easily generate hundreds of test cases with multiple combinations of properties and types. This section paves the way for the upcoming sections of this chapter, where we'll learn about Schemathesis, an API testing framework that uses property-based testing.

12.3.1 What is property-based testing?

As you can see in figure 12.6, property-based testing is a testing strategy in which we feed test data to our code and design our tests to make claims about the properties of the result of running our code.[1] Typically, a property-based framework generates test cases for us given a set of conditions that we define.

[1] See the excellent article by David R. MacIver for a more detailed explanation of what property-based testing is: "What is Property Based Testing?," https://hypothesis.works/articles/what-is-property-based-testing/.

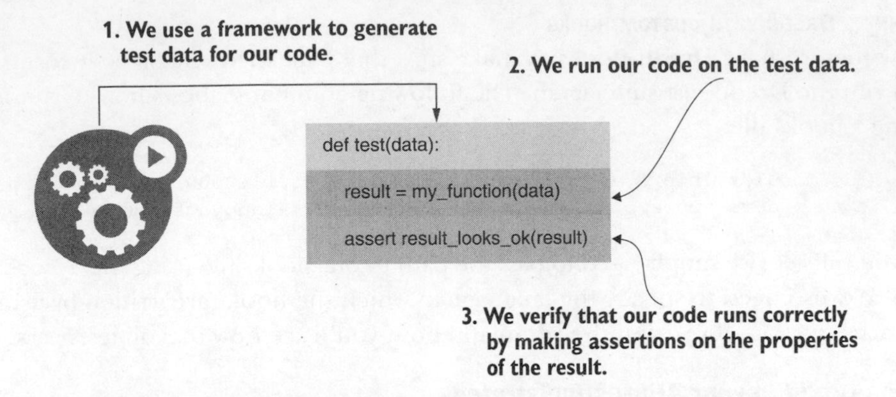
1. We use a framework to generate test data for our code.
2. We run our code on the test data.
def test(data):
result = my_function(data)
assert result_looks_ok(result)
3. We verify that our code runs correctly by making assertions on the properties of the result.

Figure 12.6 In property-based testing, we use a framework to generate test cases for our functions, and we make assertions on the result of running our code on such cases.

DEFINITION Property-based testing is an approach to testing in which we make claims about the properties of the return value of our functions or methods. Instead of manually writing lots of different tests with various inputs, we let a framework generate the inputs for us, and we define how we expect our code to handle them. In Python, an excellent library for property-based testing is Hypothesis (https://github.com/HypothesisWorks/hypothesis).

12.3.2 The traditional approach to API testing

Let's say we want to test our POST `/orders` endpoint to ensure it only accepts valid payloads. As you can see from the OpenAPI specification for the orders API under the ch012/orders/oas.yaml file, a valid payload for the POST `/orders` endpoint contains a key named `order`, which represents an array of ordered items. Each item has two required keys: `product` and `size`.

Listing 12.6 Schema for the POST `/orders` endpoint's request payload

```
# file: orders/oas.yaml

components:
  schemas:
    OrderItemSchema:
      type: object
      additionalProperties: false
      required:
        - product
        - size
      properties:
        product:
          type: string
        size:
          type: string
          enum:
            - small
            - medium
```

```
          - big
        quantity:
          type: integer
          format: int64
          default: 1
          minimum: 1

    CreateOrderSchema:
      type: object
      additionalProperties: false
      required:
        - order
      properties:
        order:
          type: array
          minItems: 1
          items:
            $ref: '#/components/schemas/OrderItemSchema'
```

In a traditional approach, we'd write various payloads manually, then submit them to the POST `/orders` endpoint and write the expected result for each payload. Listing 12.7 illustrates how we test the POST `/orders` endpoint with two different payloads. If you want to try out the code in listing 12.7, create a file called orders/test.py and run the tests with the following command: `pytest test.py`.

In listing 12.7, we define two test cases: one with an invalid payload missing the required `size` property of an order item and another with a valid payload. In both cases, we use FastAPI's test client to send the payloads to our API server, and we test the server's behavior by checking the status code from the response. We expect the response for an invalid payload to carry the 422 status code (Unprocessable Entity), and the response for the valid payload to carry the 201 status code (Created). FastAPI uses pydantic to validate our payloads, and it automatically generates a 422 response for malformed payloads. Therefore, this test serves to validate that our pydantic models are correctly implemented.

Listing 12.7 Testing the POST `/orders` endpoint with different payloads

```
# file: orders/test.py

from fastapi.testclient import TestClient        # We import FastAPI's TestClient class.

from orders.app import app

test_client = TestClient(app=app)        # We instantiate the test client.


def test_create_order_fails():        # We create a test.
    bad_payload = {
        'order': [{'product': 'coffee'}]        # We define a bad payload for the POST /orders endpoint.
    }
```

```
    response = test_client.post('/orders', json=bad_payload)    <-- We test the payload.
    assert response.status_code == 422

def test_create_order_succeeds():
    good_payload = {
        'order': [{'product': 'coffee', 'size': 'big'}]    <-- We define a valid payload for the POST /orders endpoint.
    }
    response = test_client.post('/orders', json=good_payload)
    assert response.status_code == 201    <-- We confirm that the response status code is 201.
```

We confirm that the response status code is 422.

12.3.3 Property-based testing with Hypothesis

The testing strategy in listing 12.7, where we write all the test cases manually, is a common approach to API testing. The problem with this approach is that it's quite limited unless we're willing to spend many hours writing exhaustive test suites. The test suite in listing 12.7 is far from complete: it's not testing what happens if the `size` property contains an invalid value, or if the `quantity` property is present with a negative value, or if the list of order items is empty.

For a more comprehensive approach to API testing, we want to be able to use a framework that can generate all possible types of payloads and test them against our API server. This is exactly what property-based testing allows us to do. In Python, we can run property-based tests with the help of the excellent `hypothesis` library.

Hypothesis uses the concept of strategy to generate test data. For example, if we want to generate random integers, we use Hypothesis's `integers()` strategy, and if we want to generate text data, we use Hypothesis's `text()` strategy. Hypothesis's strategies expose a method called `example()` that you can use to get an idea of the values they produce. You can get a feeling of how Hypothesis's strategies work by playing with them in a Python shell (since Hypothesis produces random values, you'll see different results in your shell):

```
>>> from hypothesis import strategies as st
>>> st.integers().example()
0
>>> st.text().example()
'r'
```

As you can see in figure 12.7, Hypothesis also allows us to combine various strategies using the `pipe` operator (`|`). For example, we can define a strategy that produces either integers or text:

```
>>> strategy = st.integers() | st.text()
>>> strategy.example()
-2781
```

To test the POST `/orders` endpoint with Hypothesis, we want to define a strategy that produces dictionaries with random values. To work with dictionaries, we can use

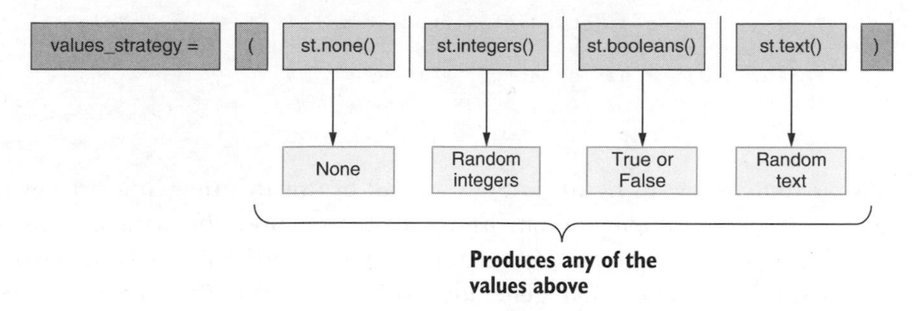

Figure 12.7 We can combine various Hypothesis strategies into one. The resulting strategy will produce a value from any of the combined strategies at random.

either Hypothesis's `dictionaries()` or `fixed_dictionaries()` strategies. For example, if we want to generate a dictionary with two keys, such as `product` and `size`, where each key can be either an integer or a text, we'd use the following declaration:

```
>>> strategy = st.fixed_dictionaries(
    {
        "product": st.integers() | st.text(),
        "size": st.integers() | st.text(),
    }
)

>>> strategy.example()
{'product': -7958791642907854994, 'size': 16875}
```

12.3.4 Using Hypothesis to test a REST API endpoint

Let's put all of this together to create an actual test for the POST `/orders` endpoint. First, let's define a strategy for all the values that a property in our payload can take. We'll keep it simple for illustration purposes and assume properties can only be null, Booleans, text, or integers:

```
>>> values_strategy = (
        st.none() |
        st.booleans() |
        st.text() |
        st.integers()
)
```

Now, let's define a strategy for the schema that represents an order item. To keep it simple, we use a fixed dictionary with valid keys, that is, `product`, `size`, and `quantity`. Since the `size` property can only take on values from an enumeration whose choices are `small`, `medium`, or `big`, we define a strategy that allows Hypothesis to choose a value either from that enumeration or from the `values_strategy` strategy that we defined earlier:

```
>>> order_item_strategy = st.fixed_dictionaries(
    {
        "product": values_strategy,
```

```
        "size": st.one_of(st.sampled_from(("small", "medium", "big")))
        | values_strategy,
        "quantity": values_strategy,
    }
)
```

Finally, as you can see in figure 12.8, we put all of this together in a strategy for the `CreateOrderSchema` schema. From listing 12.4, we know that `CreateOrderSchema` requires a property called `order`, whose value is a list of order items. Using Hypothesis, we can define a strategy that generates payloads to test the `CreateOrderSchema` schema like this:

```
>>> strategy = st.fixed_dictionaries({
    'order': st.lists(order_item_strategy)
})
>>> strategy.example()
{'order': [{'product': None, 'size': 'small', 'quantity': None}]}
```

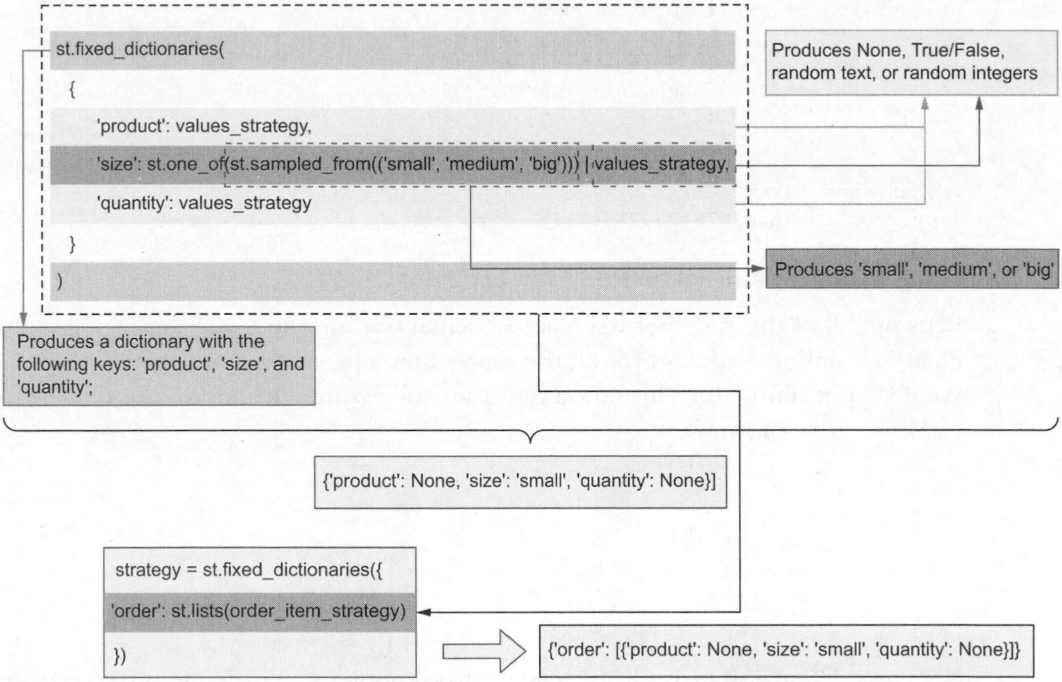

Figure 12.8 By combining Hypothesis's `fixed_dictionaries()` strategy with the `lists()` strategy and the `values_strategy`, we can produce payloads that resemble the `CreateOrderSchema` schema.

We're now ready to rewrite our test suite from listing 12.6 into a more generic and comprehensive test for the POST `/orders` endpoint. Listing 12.7 shows how we inject Hypothesis strategies into a test function. The code in listing 12.7 goes into the orders/test.py file. I've omitted the definitions of some variables in listing 12.7, such as `values_strategy` and `order_item_strategy`, since we already came across them in the previous examples.

The testing strategy in listing 12.8 uses the `jsonschema` library to validate the payloads generated by Hypothesis. To validate payloads with the `jsonschema` library, we first load the OpenAPI specification for the orders API, which lives under ch012/orders/oas.yaml. We read the file contents using pathlib's `Path().read_text()` method, and we parse them using Python's `yaml` library. To check whether a payload is valid, we create a utility function called `is_valid_payload()`, which returns `True` if the payload is valid and, otherwise, returns `False`.

We validate the payload using `jsonschema`'s `validate()` function, which requires two arguments: the payload that we want to validate and the schema that we want to validate against. Since `CreateOrderSchema` contains a reference to another schema within the API specification, namely, the `OrderItemSchema` schema, we also provide a resolver, which `jsonschema` can use to resolve references to other schemas within the document. `jsonschema`'s `validate()` function raises a `ValidationError` if the payload is invalid, so we call it within a try/except block, and we return `True` or `False` depending on the result.

To inject data into our test functions, Hypothesis provides the `given()` decorator, which takes a Hypothesis strategy as an argument and uses it to feed test cases to our test function. If the payloads are valid, we expect our API to return a response with the 201 status code, while for bad payloads we expect a 422 status code.

Listing 12.8 Using `hypothesis` to run property-based tests against an API

```
# file: orders/test.py
from pathlib import Path

import hypothesis.strategies as st
import jsonschema
import yaml
from fastapi.testclient import TestClient
from hypothesis import given, Verbosity, settings
from jsonschema import ValidationError, RefResolver

from orders.app import app


orders_api_spec = yaml.full_load(
    (Path(__file__).parent / 'oas.yaml').read_text()     <-- We load the API specification.
)
create_order_schema = (
    orders_api_spec['components']['schemas']['CreateOrderSchema']     <-- Pointer to the CreateOrderSchema schema
)


def is_valid_payload(payload, schema):     <-- Helper function to determine whether a payload is valid
    try:
        jsonschema.validate(
```

```
            payload, schema=schema,
            resolver=RefResolver('', orders_api_spec)    <-- We validate a payload
        )                                                    with jsonschema's
    except ValidationError:                                  validate() function.
        return False
    else:
        return True


test_client = TestClient(app=app)    <-- We instantiate
                                         the test client.
values_strategy = [...]

order_item_strategy = [...]

strategy = [...]                  We feed the hypothesis
                                  strategies into our test function.

@given(strategy)    <--     We capture each test case
def test(payload):  <--     through the payload argument.
    response = test_client.post('/orders', json=payload)    <-- We send the payload to the POST /orders endpoint.
    if is_valid_payload(payload, create_order_schema):    <-- We assert the expected
        assert response.status_code == 201                    status code depending on
    else:                                                     whether the payload is valid.
        assert response.status_code == 422
```

As it turns out, Hypothesis is very suitable for generating datasets based on JSON Schema schemas, and there's already a library that translates schemas into Hypothesis strategies, so you don't have to do it yourself: `hypothesis-jsonschema` (https://github.com/Zac-HD/hypothesis-jsonschema). I strongly encourage you to look at this library before trying to generate your own Hypothesis strategies for testing web APIs. Now that we understand what property-based testing is and how Hypothesis works, we're ready to learn about Schemathesis, which is the topic of our next section!

12.4 Testing REST APIs with Schemathesis

This section introduces Schemathesis and explains how it works and how we use it to test REST APIs. Schemathesis is an API testing framework that uses property-based testing to validate our APIs. It uses the `hypothesis` library under the hood, and thanks to its approach, it's capable of running a more exhaustive test suite than Dredd. Once you're getting ready to release your APIs to production, I recommend you test them with Schemathesis to make sure you cover all edge cases.

12.4.1 Running Schemathesis's default test suite

In this section, we'll get familiar with Schemathesis by running its default test suite. Since we already installed our dependencies in section 12.1, all we need to do is `cd` into the orders folder and activate our environment by running `pipenv shell`. In contrast with Dredd, Schemathesis requires you to have your API server running before you run your test suite. You can start the server by opening a new terminal window and running the server there or by starting the server and pushing it to the background with the following command:

```
$ uvicorn orders.app:app &
```

The & symbol pushes the process to the background. Then you can run Schemathesis with the following command:

```
$ schemathesis run oas.yaml --base-url=http://localhost:8000 \
--hypothesis-database=none
```

Hypothesis, the library that Schemathesis uses to generate test cases, creates a folder called .hypothesis/ where it caches some of its tests. In my experience, Hypothesis's cache sometimes causes misleading results in subsequent test executions, so until this is fixed, my recommendation is to avoid caching the tests. We set the `--hypothesis-database` flag to `none` so that Schemathesis doesn't cache test cases.

After executing the command, you'll see that Schemathesis runs around 700 tests against the API, testing all possible combinations of parameters, types, and formats. All tests should pass correctly. Once Schemathesis has finished, you can bring the Uvicorn process to the foreground by running the `fg` command, and stop it if you wish. (I'm sure know you know, but remember that to stop a process you use the Ctrl-C key combination).

12.4.2 Using links to enhance Schemathesis' test suite

The test suite we just ran with Schemathesis has one major limitation: it doesn't test whether the POST `/orders` endpoint is creating orders correctly nor if we can perform the expected operations, such as payments and cancellations, on an order. It's simply launching independent and unrelated requests to each of the endpoints in the orders API. To check whether we are creating resources correctly, we need to enhance our API specification with links. As you can see in figure 12.9, in the OpenAPI standard, links are declarations that allow us to describe the relationships between different endpoints.[2]

For example, using links, we can specify that the POST `/orders` endpoint returns a payload with an ID, and that we can use that ID to form the resource URL of the order just created under the GET `/orders/{order_id}` endpoint. We use operation IDs to describe the relationships between our endpoints. As we learned in chapter 5 (section 5.3), operation IDs are unique identifiers for each endpoint in the API. Listing 12.9 shows how we enhance the orders API with a link that describes the relationship between the POST `/orders` endpoint and the GET `/orders/{order_id}` endpoint. For the full list of links, please see the ch12/orders/oas_with_links.yaml file in the GitHub repository for this book. Ellipses are used to hide parts of the code that are not relevant to the example, and newly added code is in bold.

[2] For a good explanation of how links work and how you leverage them in your API documentation, see https://swagger.io/docs/specification/links/.

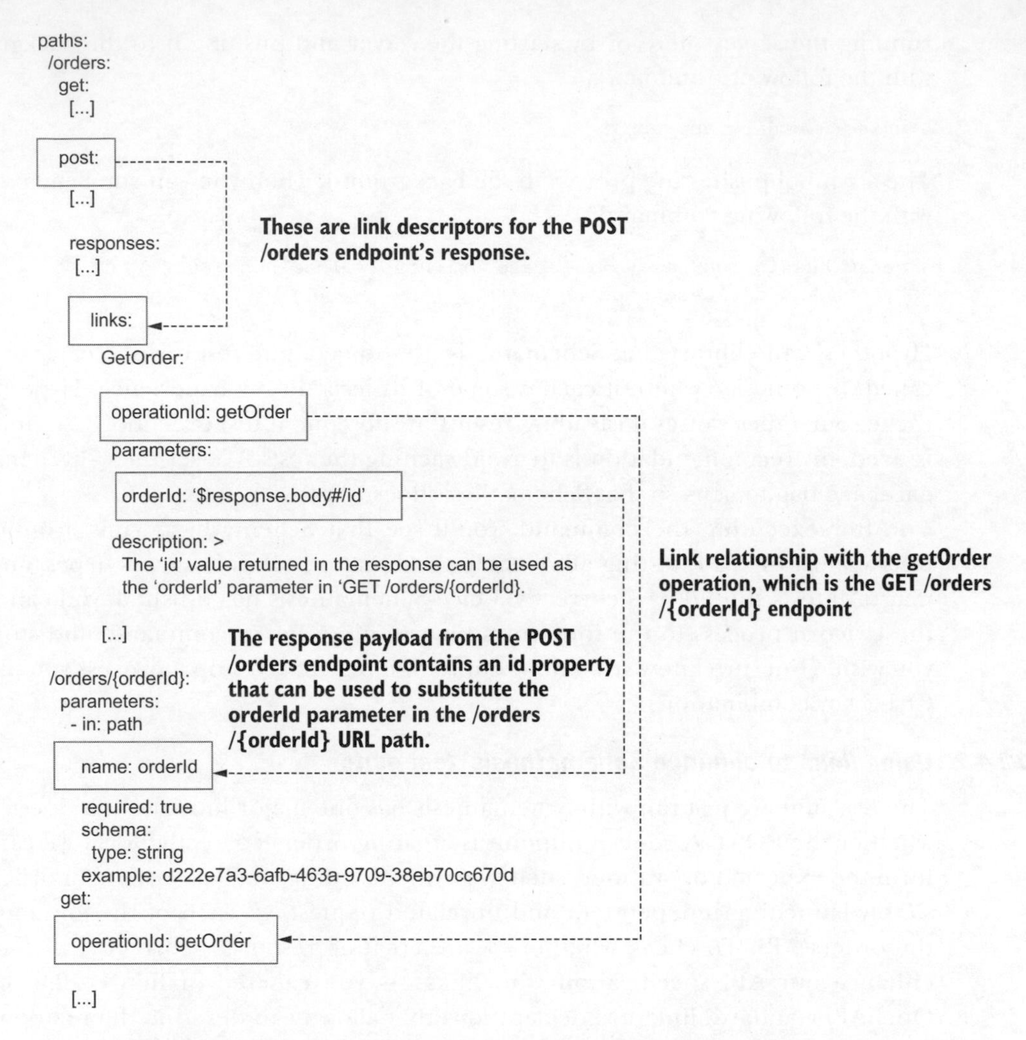

Figure 12.9 In OpenAPI, we can use links to describe the relationships between endpoints. For example, the POST `/orders` response contains an `id` property that we can use to replace the `order_id` parameter in the `/orders/{order_id}` URL.

In listing 12.9, we name the link between the POST `/orders` and the GET `/order/{order_id}` endpoints `GetOrder`. `GetOrder`'s `operationId` property identifies the endpoint this link refers to (`getOrder`). The GET `/order/{order_id}` endpoint has an URL parameter named `order_id`, and `GetOrder`'s `parameters` property tells us that the response body from the POST `/orders` endpoint contains an `id` property, which we can use to replace `order_id` in the GET `/order/{order_id}` endpoint.

Listing 12.9 Adding links to create relationships between endpoints in OpenAPI

```
# file: orders/oas.yaml

paths:
  /orders:
    get:
      [...]

    post:
      operationId: createOrder
      summary: Creates an order
      requestBody:
        required: true
        content:
          application/json:
            schema:
              $ref: '#/components/schemas/CreateOrderSchema'
      responses:
        '201':
          description: A JSON representation of the created order
          content:
            application/json:
              schema:
                $ref: '#/components/schemas/GetOrderSchema'
          links:
            GetOrder:
              operationId: getOrder
              parameters:
                order_id: '$response.body#/id'
              description: >
                The `id` value returned in the response can be used as
                the `order_id` parameter in `GET /orders/{order_id}`
          [...]

  /orders/{order_id}:
    [...]
    get:
      operationId: getOrder
      [...]
```

We add links to the POST /orders endpoint.

We define a link with the GET /orders/{order_id} endpoint.

The order_id URL parameter in the getOrder endpoint can be replaced with the response payload's id property.

We explain how this link works.

We can now run Schemathesis and take advantage of our links by running the following command:

```
$ schemathesis run oas_with_link.yaml --base-url=http://localhost:8000 \
--stateful=links
```

The `--stateful=links` flag instructs Schemathesis to look for links in our documentation and use them to run tests on the resources created through the POST `/orders` endpoint. If you run Schemathesis now, you'll see that it runs well over a thousand tests against the API. Since Schemathesis generates random tests, the exact number of tests cases may differ from time to time. Listing 12.10 shows the output of the Schemathesis test suite after running it with the `--stateful` parameter set to `links`. The listing omits the first few lines of the test suite as they contain only system-specific metadata. Notice that some of the tests appear nested within the POST `/orders` endpoint (the lines starting with the `->` symbol). Nested tests are tests that leverage links from our API documentation. If the tests on the POST `/orders` endpoint's links pass, we can rest assured that our resources are being created correctly.

Listing 12.10 Output of a Schemathesis test suite

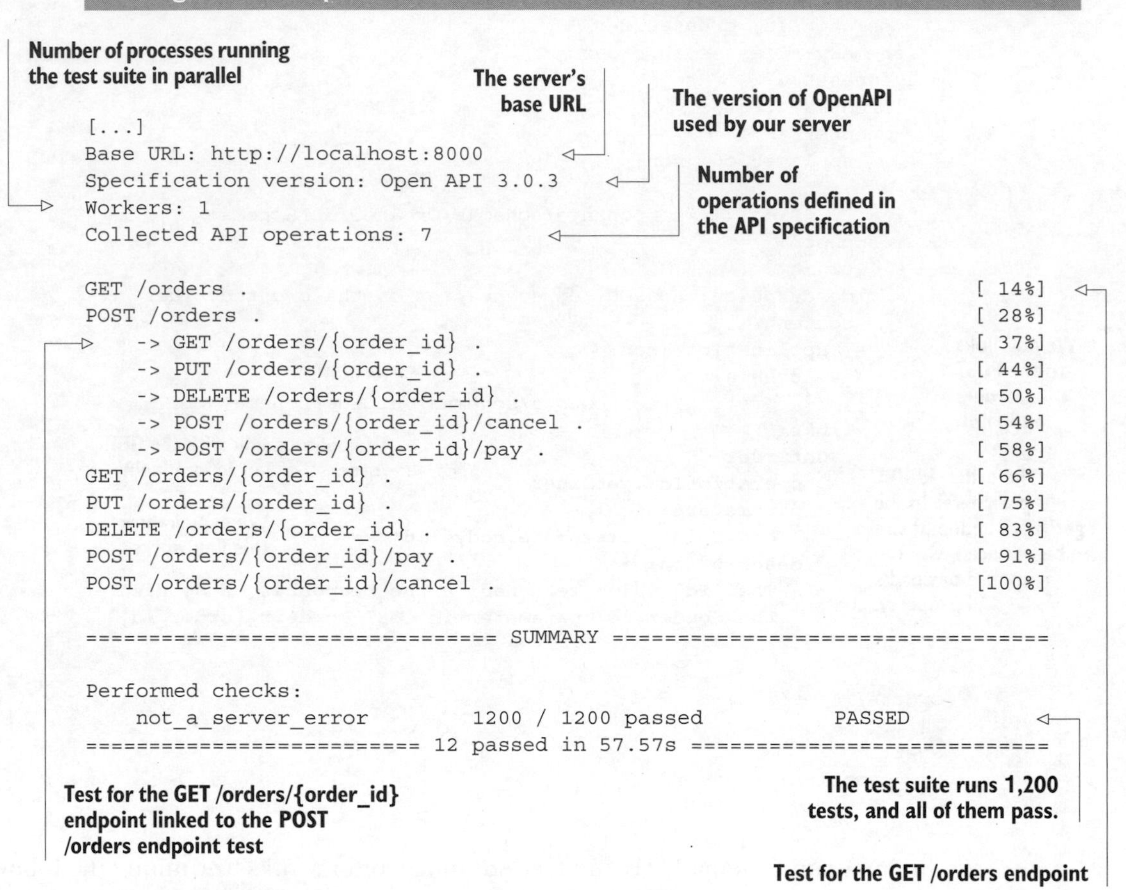

```
[...]
Base URL: http://localhost:8000
Specification version: Open API 3.0.3
Workers: 1
Collected API operations: 7

GET /orders .                                                    [ 14%]
POST /orders .                                                   [ 28%]
    -> GET /orders/{order_id} .                                  [ 37%]
    -> PUT /orders/{order_id} .                                  [ 44%]
    -> DELETE /orders/{order_id} .                               [ 50%]
    -> POST /orders/{order_id}/cancel .                          [ 54%]
    -> POST /orders/{order_id}/pay .                             [ 58%]
GET /orders/{order_id} .                                         [ 66%]
PUT /orders/{order_id} .                                         [ 75%]
DELETE /orders/{order_id} .                                      [ 83%]
POST /orders/{order_id}/pay .                                    [ 91%]
POST /orders/{order_id}/cancel .                                 [100%]

================================= SUMMARY =================================

Performed checks:
    not_a_server_error          1200 / 1200 passed          PASSED
========================== 12 passed in 57.57s ============================
```


The output from the previous test says that our API passed all checks in the `not_a_server_error` category. By default, Schemathesis only checks that the API doesn't raise server errors, but it can be configured to also verify that our API uses the right status codes, content types, headers, and schemas as documented in the API specification. To apply all these checks, we use the `--checks` flag and we set it to `all`:

```
$ schemathesis run oas_with_link.yaml --base-url=http://localhost:8000 \
--hypothesis-database=none --stateful=links --checks=all
```

As you can see, this time Schemathesis runs over a thousand test cases per check:

```
================================= SUMMARY ==================================

Performed checks:
    not_a_server_error                 1200 / 1200 passed          PASSED
    status_code_conformance            1200 / 1200 passed          PASSED
    content_type_conformance           1200 / 1200 passed          PASSED
    response_headers_conformance       1200 / 1200 passed          PASSED
    response_schema_conformance        1200 / 1200 passed          PASSED

========================== 12 passed in 70.54s ============================
```

In some cases, Schemathesis may complain that it takes too long to generate test cases. You can suppress that warning by using the `--hypothesis-suppress-health-check=too_slow` flag. By running the whole set of Schemathesis checks against your API, you can be certain that it works as expected and complies with the API specification. If you'd like to extend the tests with additional custom payloads or scenarios, you can do that as well. Since `schemathesis` is a Python library, it's very easy to add additional custom tests. Check the documentation for examples on how to do that (http://mng.bz/69Q5).

This concludes our journey through testing REST APIs. It's now time to move on to the world of GraphQL API testing, which is the topic of the next section!

12.5 Testing GraphQL APIs

This section explains how we test and validate GraphQL APIs so that we can ensure they work as expected before we release them to production. We'll use the products API, which we implemented in chapter 10, as a guiding example. To work through the examples in this section, `cd` into ch12/products and activate the environment by running `pipenv shell`.

In sections 12.2 and 12.4, we learned about Dredd and Schemathesis, which automatically generate tests for REST APIs based on the API specification. For GraphQL, there's less support for automatic test generation. In particular, Dredd doesn't support GraphQL APIs, while Schemathesis only provides partial support. However, this is an active area of development, so expect to see increasing support for automatic GraphQL testing in the future.

12.5.1 Testing GraphQL APIs with Schemathesis

This section explains how we use Schemathesis to test and validate a GraphQL API. As we explained in section 12.4, Schemathesis is an API testing framework that uses an approach known as property-based testing to validate our APIs. Schemathesis can be used to test both REST and GraphQL APIs. In both cases, as you can see in figure 12.10, Schemathesis looks at the API specification to learn about its endpoints and schemas, and to decide which tests to run.

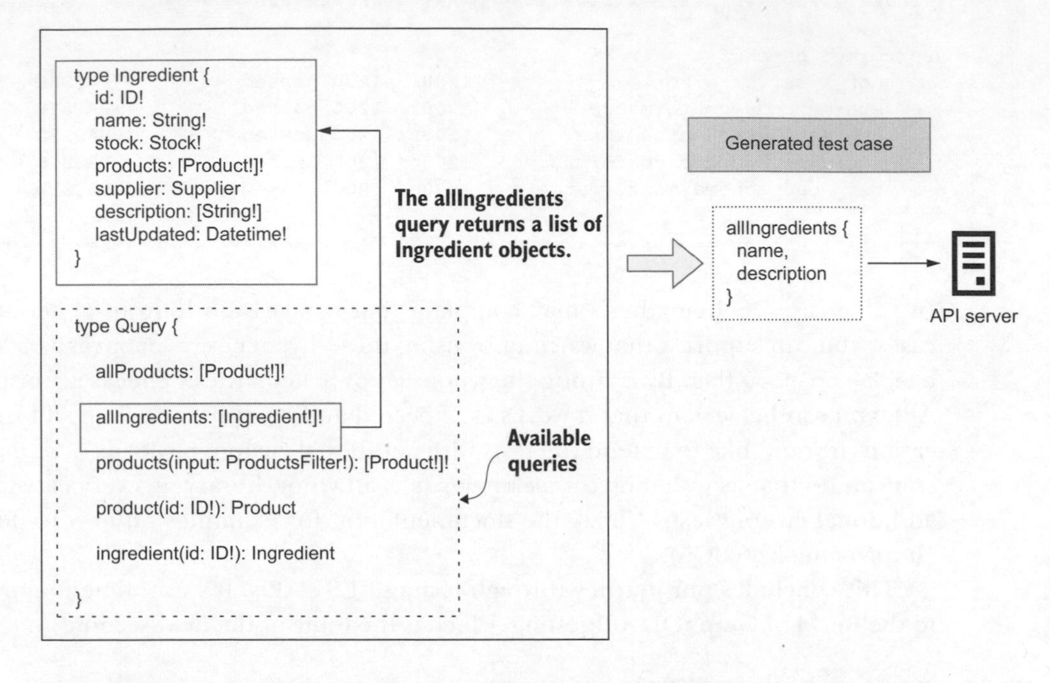

Figure 12.10 Schemathesis parses a GraphQL API specification in search of available operations and generates query documents with both valid and invalid parameters and selection sets to test the server's response.

To generate tests for a GraphQL API, Schemathesis uses `hypothesis-graphql` (http://mng.bz/o5Pj), a library that generates Hypothesis strategies from a GraphQL schema. Before we run our test, we need to start the GraphQL API server. You can do that in a different terminal window, or you can run the process in the background with the following command:

```
$ uvicorn server:server &
```

The `&` symbol pushes the Uvicorn process to the background. To test a GraphQL API with Schemathesis, we simply need to give it the URL where our API specification is hosted. In our case, the GraphQL API is hosted under the following URL: http://127.0.0.1:8000/graphql. Armed with this information, we can now run our tests:

```
$ schemathesis run --hypothesis-deadline=None http://127.0.0.1:8000/graphql
```

The `--hypothesis-deadline=None` flag instructs Schemathesis to avoid timing the requests. This is useful in cases where our queries may be slow, which sometimes happens with GraphQL APIs. The following shows the output of the test suite, omitting the first few lines that contain platform-specific metadata. As you can see, Schemathesis tests all of the queries and mutations exposed by the products API, generating a very solid battery of tests: 1,100 test cases!

Listing 12.11 Output of a Schemathesis test suite for a GraphQL API

```
[...]
Schema location: http://127.0.0.1:8000/graphql
Base URL: http://127.0.0.1:8000/graphql
Specification version: GraphQL
Workers: 1
Collected API operations: 11
Query.allProducts .                                                    [  9%]
Query.allIngredients .                                                 [ 18%]
Query.products .                                                       [ 27%]
Query.product .                                                        [ 36%]
Query.ingredient .                                                     [ 45%]
Mutation.addSupplier .                                                 [ 54%]
Mutation.addIngredient .                                               [ 63%]
Mutation.addProduct .                                                  [ 72%]
Mutation.updateProduct .                                               [ 81%]
Mutation.deleteProduct .                                               [ 90%]
Mutation.updateStock .                                                 [100%]

================================= SUMMARY ==================================

Performed checks:
    not_a_server_error.            1100 / 1100 passed          PASSED

========================== 11 passed in 36.82s ============================
```

After running the Schemathesis test suite against the products API, we can be certain that our queries and mutations work as expected. You can further customize your tests to make sure the application works correctly under certain conditions. To learn how to add custom tests cases, check out Schemathesis' excellent documentation (https://schemathesis.readthedocs.io/en/stable/).

12.6 Designing your API testing strategy

You've learned a lot in this chapter. You've learned to use frameworks such as Dredd and Schemathesis, which run automated test suites against your APIs based on the API documentation. You've also learned about property-based testing and how to use Hypothesis to automatically generate test cases to test your REST and GraphQL APIs.

As we saw in section 12.2, Dredd runs a simple test suite against your APIs. Dredd only tests the happy path: it makes sure your API accepts the expected payloads and responds with the expected payloads. It doesn't test what happens when the wrong payloads are sent to your server.

Dredd's testing strategy is useful in the early development stage of your API, when you want to be able to focus on the overall functionality of your application rather than get bogged down with specific corner cases of your API integration. However, before you release your APIs to production, you want to make sure your APIs are tested with Schemathesis. Schemathesis runs a more comprehensive test suite, which ensures that your API works exactly as expected.

I recommend you run Dredd and Schemathesis locally during development, and also in your continuous integration (CI) server before releasing your code. For an example of how you can incorporate Dredd and Schemathesis into your CI server, check out my talk, "API Development Workflows for Successful Integrations," at Manning's API Conference (August 3 2021, https://youtu.be/SUKqmEX_uwg).

Some of the technologies and skills that you've learned in this chapter are still very new and experimental, so you've got an edge in your team and in the job market. Use your new powers wisely!

Summary

- Dredd and Schemathesis are API testing tools that automatically generate validation tests for APIs from the documentation. This helps you to avoid the effort of writing tests manually and to focus on building your APIs and services.
- Dredd is a REST API testing framework. It runs a basic test suite against your API without covering edge cases, and therefore it's convenient in the early stages of your API cycle.
- You can customize Dredd's behavior by adding Dredd hooks to your tests. Although Dredd is an npm package, you can write your hooks in Python. Dredd hooks are useful for saving information from one test for reuse in another test, and for creating or deleting resources before and after each test.
- Schemathesis is a more generic API test framework that runs an exhaustive test suite against your APIs. Before releasing your APIs to production, you want to make sure you've tested them with Schemathesis. You can use Schemathesis to test both REST and GraphQL APIs.
- To test that your POST endpoints are creating resources correctly, you can enrich your OpenAPI specification with links and instruct Schemathesis to use them in its test suite. Links are properties that describe the relationship between different operations in an OpenAPI specification.
- Property-based testing is an approach in which you let a framework generate random test cases, and you validate the behavior of your code by making assertions about the properties of the test result. This approach saves you the time of having to write test cases manually. In Python, you can run property-based tests with the excellent `hypothesis` library.

13 Dockerizing microservice APIs

This chapter covers

- How to Dockerize an application
- How to run Docker containers
- How to run an application with Docker Compose
- Publishing a Docker image to AWS Elastic Container Registry

Docker is a virtualization technology that allows us to run our applications anywhere by simply having a Docker execution runtime. Docker takes away the pain and effort required to tune and configure an environment to run code. It also makes deployments more predictable since it produces replicable artifacts (container images) that we can run locally as well as in the cloud.

In this chapter, you'll learn to Dockerize a Python application. Dockerizing is the process of packaging an application as a Docker image. You can think of a Docker image as a build or artifact that is ready to be deployed and executed. To execute an image, Docker creates running instances of the image, known as *containers*. To deploy Docker images, we typically use a container orchestrator, such as Kubernetes, which takes care of managing the life cycle of a container. In the next chapter, you'll learn to deploy Docker builds with Kubernetes. We'll illustrate how to Dockerize an application using the orders service of the CoffeeMesh platform. You'll also learn to publish your Docker builds to a container registry by uploading images to AWS's Elastic Container Registry (ECR).

All the code examples are available under folder ch13 in the GitHub repository for this book. We'll begin by setting up the environment to work on this chapter in section 13.1.

13.1 Setting up the environment for this chapter

In this section, we set up the environment so that you can follow along with the examples in the rest of the chapter. We continue the implementation of the orders service where we left it in chapter 11, where we added the authentication and authorization layers. First, copy over the code from chapter 11 into a new folder called ch13:

```
$ cp -r ch11 ch13
```

`cd` into ch13, and install the dependencies and activate the virtual environment by running the following commands:

```
$ cd ch13 && pipenv install --dev && pipenv shell
```

When we deploy the application, we use a PostgreSQL engine, which is one of the most popular SQL engines for running applications in production. To communicate with the database, we use `psycopg2`, which is one of Python's most popular PostgreSQL drivers:

```
$ pipenv install psycopg2
```

> **INSTALLING PSYCOPG2** If you run into issues installing and compiling `psycopg2`, try installing the compiled package by running `pipenv install psycopg2-binary`, or pull ch13/Pipfile and ch13/Pipfile.lock from this book's GitHub repository and run `pipenv install --dev`. Two other powerful PostgreSQL drivers are `asyncpg` (https://github.com/MagicStack/asyncpg) and `pscycopg3` (https://github.com/psycopg/psycopg), both of which support asynchronous operations. I encourage you to check them out!

To build and run Docker containers, you'll need a Docker runtime on your machine. Installation instructions are platform specific, so please see the official documentation to learn how to install Docker on your system (https://docs.docker.com/get-docker/).

Since we're going to publish our Docker images to AWS's ECR, we need to install the AWS CLI:

```
$ pipenv install --dev awscli
```

Next, go to https://aws.amazon.com/. Create an AWS account and obtain an access key to be able to access AWS services programmatically. The user profile you use to create the AWS account is the account's root user. For security, it is recommended that you don't use the root user to generate your access key. Instead, create an IAM user and generate an access key for that user. IAM is AWS's Identity Access Management service, which allows you to create users, roles, and granular policies for granting access to other services in your account. Follow the AWS documentation to learn how to create an IAM user (http://mng.bz/neP8) and to learn how to generate your access keys and configure the AWS CLI (http://mng.bz/vXxq).

Now that our environment is ready, it's time to Dockerize our applications!

13.2 Dockerizing a microservice

What does Dockerizing an application mean? *Dockerizing* is the process of packaging an application as a Docker image. You can think of a Docker image as a build or artifact that can be deployed and executed in a Docker runtime. All the system dependencies are already installed in the Docker image, and to run the image, we only need a Docker runtime. To execute the image, the Docker runtime creates a container, which is a running instance of the image. As you can see in figure 13.1, working with Docker is very convenient since it allows us to run our applications in isolated processes. There are different options for installing a Docker runtime depending on your platform, so please see the official documentation to determine which option works best for you (https://docs.docker.com/get-docker/).

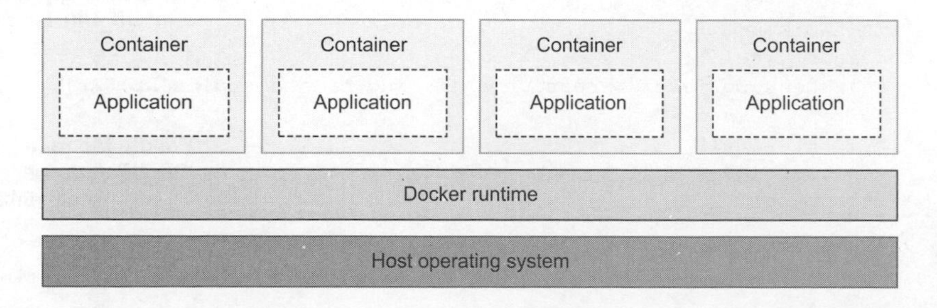

Figure 13.1 Docker containers run in isolated processes on top of the host operating system.

In this section, we create an optimized Docker image of the orders service. Along the way, you'll learn how to write a Dockerfile, which is a document that contains all the instructions required to build a Docker image. You'll also learn how to run Docker containers and to map ports from the container to the host operating system so that you can interact with the application running inside the container. Finally, you'll also learn how to manage containers with the Docker CLI.

DOCKER FUNDAMENTALS If you want to know more about how Docker works and how it interacts with the host operating system, check out Prabath Siriwardena and Nuwan Dias's excellent "Docker Fundamentals" from their book *Microservices Security in Action* (Manning, 2020, http://mng.bz/49Ag).

Before we build the image, we need to make two small changes to our application code to get it ready for deployment. So far, the orders service has been using a hard-coded database URL, but to operate the service in different environments, we need to make this setting configurable. The following code shows the changes needed to the orders/repository/unit_of_work.py file to pull the database URL from the environment, with the newly added code in bold characters. We use an assert statement to exit the application immediately if no database URL is provided.

Listing 13.1 Pulling the database URL from the environment

```
# file: orders/repository/unit_of_work.py

import os

from sqlalchemy import create_engine
from sqlalchemy.orm import sessionmaker

DB_URL = os.getenv('DB_URL')    # We pull the database URL from the DB_URL environment variable.

assert DB_URL is not None, 'DB_URL environment variable needed.'    # We exit the application if DB_URL isn't set.


class UnitOfWork:
    def __init__(self):
        self.session_maker = sessionmaker(bind=create_engine(DB_URL))    # We use the value from DB_URL to connect to the database.

    def __enter__(self):
        self.session = self.session_maker()
        return self

    ...
```

We also need to update our Alembic files to pull the database URL from the environment. The following code shows the changes required to migrations/env.py to accomplish that, with the newly added code in bold. We omitted nonrelevant parts of the code with ellipses to make it easier to observe the changes.

Listing 13.2 Pulling the database URL from the environment for alembic

```
# file: migrations/env.py

import os
from logging.config import fileConfig

from sqlalchemy import create_engine
from sqlalchemy import pool

from alembic import context

...
```

```
def run_migrations_online():
    """...
    """

    url = os.getenv('DB_URL')

    assert url is not None, 'DB_URL environment variable needed.'

    connectable = create_engine(url)

    context.configure(
        url=url,
        target_metadata=target_metadata,
        literal_binds=True,
        dialect_opts={"paramstyle": "named"},
    )

    ...
```

We pull the database URL from the DB_URL environment variable.

We exit the application if DB_URL isn't set.

Now that our code is ready, it's time to Dockerize it! To build a Docker image, we need to write a Dockerfile. Create a file named Dockerfile. Listing 13.3 shows this file's contents. We use the slim version of the official Python 3.9 Docker image as our base image. Slim images contain just the dependencies that we need to run our applications, which results in lighter images. To use a base image, we use Docker's `FROM` directive. Then we create the folder for the application code called /orders/orders. To run bash commands, such as `mkdir` in this case, we use Docker's `RUN` directive. We also set /orders/orders as the working directory using Docker's `WORKDIR` directive. The working directory is the directory from which the application runs.

Next, we install `pipenv`, copy our Pipenv files, and install the dependencies. We use Docker's `COPY` directive to copy files from our filesystem into the Docker image. Since we're running in Docker, we don't need a virtual environment, so we install the dependencies using `pipenv`'s `--system` flag. We also use `pipenv`'s `--deploy` flag, which checks that our Pipenv files are up to date. Finally, we copy over our source code and specify the command that needs to be executed to get the orders service up and running. The command that Docker must use to execute our application is specified using Docker's `CMD` directive. We also use Docker's `EXPOSE` directive to make sure the running container listens on port 8000, the port on which our API runs. If we don't expose the port, we can't interact with the API.

The order of our statements in the Dockerfile matters because Docker caches each step of the build. Docker will only execute a step again if the previous step changed, for example, if we installed a new dependency, or if one of our files changed. Since our application code is likely to change more often than our dependencies, we copy the code at the end of the build. That way, Docker will only install the dependencies once and cache the step until they change.

Listing 13.3 Dockerfile for the orders service

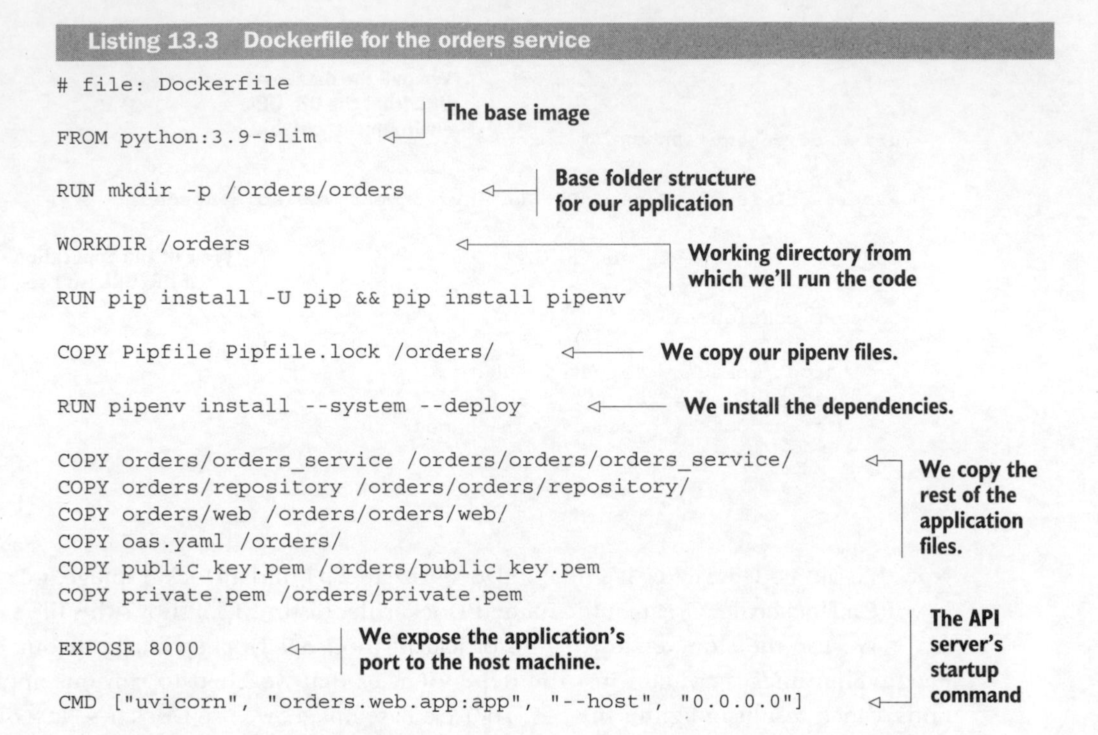

```
# file: Dockerfile

FROM python:3.9-slim

RUN mkdir -p /orders/orders

WORKDIR /orders

RUN pip install -U pip && pip install pipenv

COPY Pipfile Pipfile.lock /orders/

RUN pipenv install --system --deploy

COPY orders/orders_service /orders/orders/orders_service/
COPY orders/repository /orders/orders/repository/
COPY orders/web /orders/orders/web/
COPY oas.yaml /orders/
COPY public_key.pem /orders/public_key.pem
COPY private.pem /orders/private.pem

EXPOSE 8000

CMD ["uvicorn", "orders.web.app:app", "--host", "0.0.0.0"]
```

The base image
Base folder structure for our application
Working directory from which we'll run the code
We copy our pipenv files.
We install the dependencies.
We copy the rest of the application files.
We expose the application's port to the host machine.
The API server's startup command

To build the Docker image from listing 13.3, you need to run the following command from the ch13 directory:

```
$ docker build -t orders:1.0 .
```

The `-t` flag stands for *tag*. A Docker tag has two parts: the image name on the left of the colon and the tag name on the right of the colon. The tag name is typically the version of the build. In this case, we're naming the image orders and tagging it with `1.0`. Make sure you don't miss the period at the end of the build statement: it represents the path to the source code for the build (the *context* in Docker parlance). A period means the current directory.

Once the image has built, you can execute it with the following command:

```
$ docker run --env DB_URL=sqlite:///orders.db \
-v $(pwd)/orders.db:/orders/orders.db -p 8000:8000 -it orders:1.0
```

As you can see in figure 13.2, the `--env` flag allows us to set environment variables in the container, and we use it to set the URL of the database. To make the application accessible to the host machine, we use the `-p` flag, which allows us to bind the port on which the application is running inside the container to a port in the host machine. We also use the `-v` flag to mount a volume on the SQLite database file. Docker volumes allow containers to access files from the host machine's file system.

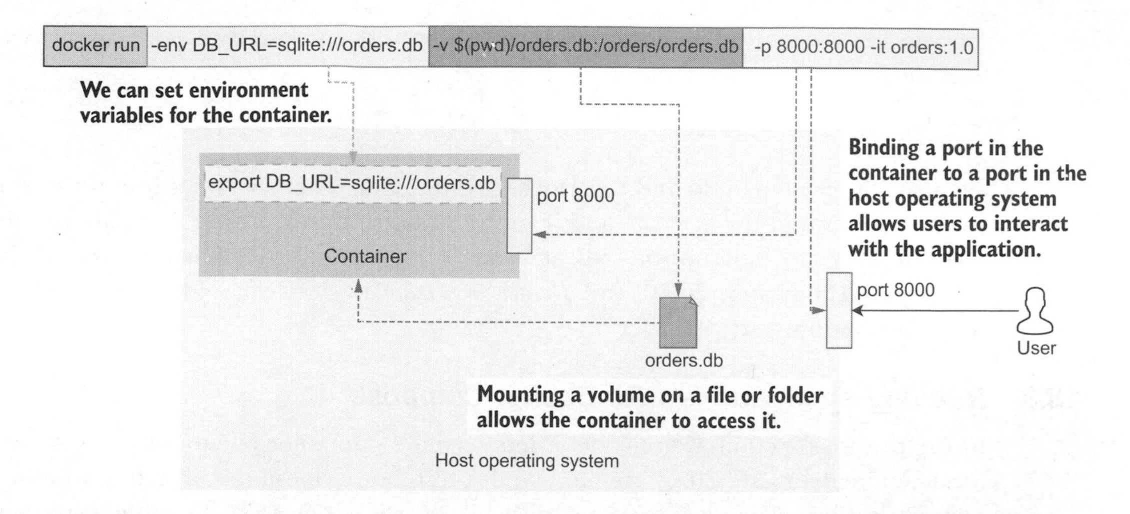

Figure 13.2 When we run a container, we can include various configurations to set environment variables within the container or to allow it to access files in the host operating system.

You can now access the application on the following URL: http://127.0.0.1:8000/docs/orders. The previous command executes the container attached to your current terminal session, which allows you to see the logs unfold as you interact with the application. In this case, you can stop the container just like any other process by pressing the Ctrl-C key combination.

You can also run containers in detached mode, which means the process isn't linked to your terminal session, so when you close your terminal, the process will continue running. This is convenient if you just want to run a container to interact with it, and you don't need to watch the logs. We typically run containerized databases in detached mode. To run the container in detached mode, you use the `-d` flag:

```
$ docker run -d --env DB_URL=sqlite:///orders.db \
 v $(pwd)/orders.db:/orders/orders.db -p 8000:8000 orders:1.0
```

In this case, you'll need to stop the container with the `docker stop` command. First, you need to figure out the ID of the running container with the following command:

```
$ docker ps
```

This command will list all currently running containers in your machine. The output looks like this (output truncated with ellipses):

```
CONTAINER ID   IMAGE        COMMAND        CREATED          STATUS...
83e6189a02ee   orders:1.0   "uvicorn..."   7 seconds ago    Up 6 seconds
```

Pick up the container ID (in this case 83e6189a02ee) and use it to stop the process with the following command:

```
$ docker stop 83e6189a02ee
```

That's all it takes to build and run Docker containers! There's a lot more to Docker than we've seen in this section, and if you're interested in learning more about this technology, I recommend you look at *Docker in Practice* by Ian Miell and Aidan Hobson Sayers (Manning, 2019) and *Docker in Action* by Jeff Nickoloff and Stephen Kuenzli (Manning, 2019).

13.3 Running applications with Docker Compose

In the previous section, we ran the orders service's container by mounting it on our local SQLite database. This is fine for a quick test, but it doesn't really tell us whether our application will work as expected with a PostgreSQL database. A common strategy to connect our containerized applications to a database is using Docker Compose, which allows us to run multiple containers within a shared network, so they can talk to each other. In this section, you'll learn how to run the orders service with a PostgreSQL database using docker-compose.

To use Docker Compose, first we need to install it. It is a Python package, so we install it with pip:

```
$ pip install docker-compose
```

Next, let's write our Docker Compose file—a declaration of the resources we need to run our application. Listing 13.4 shows the docker-compose file for the orders service. We use Docker Compose's latest specification format, version 3.9, and we declare two services: database and api. database runs PostgreSQL's official Docker image, while api runs the orders service. We use the build keyword to point to the Docker build context, and we give it a period value (.). By using a period, we instruct Docker Compose to look for a Dockerfile and build the image relative to the current directory. Through the environment keyword, we configure the environment variables required to run our applications. We expose database's 5432 port so that we can connect to the database from our host machine, as well as api's 8000 port so that we can access the API. Finally, we use a volume called database-data, which docker-compose will use to persist our data. This means that if you restart docker-compose, you won't lose your data.

Listing 13.4 docker-compose file for the orders service

```
# file: docker-compose.yaml

version: "3.9"          <-- The version of docker-compose's format for this file.

services:               <-- We declare our services.
```

```
  database:
    image: postgres:14.2
    ports:
      - 5432:5432
    environment:
      POSTGRES_PASSWORD: postgres
      POSTGRES_USER: postgres
      POSTGRES_DB: postgres
    volumes:
      - database-data:/var/lib/postgresql/data

  api:
    build: .
    ports:
      - 8000:8000
    depends_on:
      - database
    environment:
      DB_URL: postgresql://postgres:postgres@database:5432/postgres

volumes:
  database-data:
```

The database service

The database service's Docker image

We expose the database ports to the host machine.

Database environment configuration

We mount our database's data folder on a local volume.

The API service

The API's build context

We expose the API's port to the host machine.

The API depends on the database.

The API's environment configuration

The database's volume

Execute the following command to run our Docker Compose file:

```
$ docker-compose up --build
```

The `--build` flag instructs Docker Compose to rebuild your images if your files changed. Once the web API is up and running, you can access it on http://localhost:8000/docs/orders. If you try any of the endpoints, your tables don't exist. That's because we haven't run the migrations against our fresh PostgreSQL database! To run the migrations, open a new terminal window, `cd` into the ch13 folder, activate your `pipenv` environment, and run the following command:

```
$ PYTHONPATH=`pwd` \
DB_URL=postgresql://postgres:postgres@localhost:5432/postgres alembic \
upgrade heads
```

Once the migrations have been applied, you can hit the API endpoints again, and everything should work. To stop `docker-compose`, run the following command from another terminal window and inside the ch13 folder:

```
$ docker-compose down
```

This is all it takes to run Docker Compose! You've just learned to use one of the most powerful automation tools. Docker Compose is often used to run integration tests and to have an easy way to run the backend for developers who work on client applications, such as SPAs.

With our Docker stack ready and our images tested, it's time to learn how to push images to a container registry. Move on to the next section to learn how!

13.4 Publishing Docker builds to a container registry

To deploy our Docker builds, we need to publish them first to a Docker container registry. A container registry is a repository of Docker images. In the next chapter, we will deploy our applications to AWS's Elastic Kubernetes Service, so we publish our builds to AWS's ECR. Keeping our Docker images within AWS will make it easier to deploy them to EKS.

First, let's create an ECR repository for our images with the following command:

```
$ aws ecr create-repository --repository-name coffeemesh-orders
{
    "repository": {
        "repositoryArn":
➥ "arn:aws:ecr:<aws_region>:<aws_account_id>:repository/coffeemesh-orders",
        "registryId": "876701361933",
        "repositoryName": "coffeemesh-orders",
        "repositoryUri":
➥ "<aws_account_id>.dkr.ecr.<aws_region>.amazonaws.com/coffeemesh-orders",
        "createdAt": "2021-11-16T10:08:42+00:00",
        "imageTagMutability": "MUTABLE",
        "imageScanningConfiguration": {
            "scanOnPush": false
        },
        "encryptionConfiguration": {
            "encryptionType": "AES256"
        }
    }
}
```

In this command, we create a ECR repository named `coffeemesh-orders`. The output from the command is a payload describing the repository we just created. When you run the command, the placeholder for `<aws_account_id>` in the output payload will contain your AWS account ID, and `<aws_region>` will contain your default AWS region. To publish our Docker build to ECR, we need to tag our build with the name of the ECR repository. Get hold of the `repository.repositoryArn` property of the previous command's output (in bold), and use it to tag the Docker build we created in section 13.2 with the following command:

```
$ docker tag orders:1.0 \
<aws_account_id>.dkr.ecr.<aws_region>.amazonaws.com/coffeemesh-orders:1.0
```

To publish our images to ECR, we need to obtain login credentials with the following command:

```
$ aws ecr get-login-password --region <aws_region> | docker login \
--username AWS --password-stdin \
<aws_account_id>.dkr.ecr.<region>.amazonaws.com
```

Make sure you replace `<aws_region>` in this command for the AWS region where you created the Docker repository, such as eu-west-1 for Europe (Ireland) or us-east-2 for US East (Ohio). Also replace `<aws_account_id>` with your AWS account ID. Check out the AWS documentation to learn how to find your AWS account ID (http://mng.bz/Qnye).

> **AWS REGIONS** When you deploy services to AWS, you deploy them to specific regions. Each region has an identifier, such as eu-west-1 for Ireland and eu-east-2 for Ohio. For an up-to-date list of the regions available in AWS, see http://mng.bz/XaPM.

The `aws ecr get-login-password` command produces an instruction that Docker knows how to use to log in to ECR. We're now ready to publish our build! Run the following command to push the image to ECR:

```
$ docker push \
<aws_account_id>.dkr.ecr.<aws_region>.amazonaws.com/coffeemesh-orders:1.0
```

Voila! Our Docker build is now in ECR. In the next chapter, you'll learn how to deploy this build to a Kubernetes cluster in AWS.

Summary

- Docker is a virtualization technology that allows us to run our applications anywhere by simply having a Docker execution runtime. A Docker build is called an image, which is executed in processes called Docker containers.
- Docker Compose is a container orchestration framework that allows you to run multiple containers simultaneously, such as databases and APIs. Using Docker Compose is an easy and effective way to run your whole backend without having to install and configure additional dependencies.
- To deploy Docker images, we publish them to a container registry, such as AWS's ECR—a robust and secure container registry that makes it easy to deploy our containers to AWS services.

14 Deploying microservice APIs with Kubernetes

This chapter covers

- Creating a cluster with AWS's Elastic Kubernetes Service (EKS)
- Exposing services using the AWS Load Balancer Controller
- Deploying services to a Kubernetes cluster
- Managing secrets securely in Kubernetes
- Deploying an Aurora Serverless database

Kubernetes is an open source container orchestration framework, and it's fast becoming a standard way for deploying and managing applications across platforms. You can deploy Kubernetes yourself to your own servers, or you can use a managed Kubernetes service. In either case, you'll get a consistent interface to your services, which means moving across cloud providers becomes less disruptive for your operations. You can also deploy a Kubernetes cluster in your machine and run your tests locally in much the same way you'd do in the cloud.

RUN KUBERNETES LOCALLY WITH MINIKUBE You can run a Kubernetes cluster locally using minikube. Although we won't cover it in this chapter, minikube is a great tool to get more familiar with Kubernetes. Check out the official documentation for minikube (https://minikube.sigs.k8s.io/docs/start/).

Deploying Kubernetes yourself is a good exercise to get more familiar with the technology, but in practice most companies use a managed service. In this chapter, we'll use a Kubernetes managed service to deploy our cluster. Plenty of vendors offer Kubernetes managed services. The major players are Google Cloud's Google Kubernetes Engine (GKE), Azure's Kubernetes Service (AKS), and AWS's Elastic Kubernetes Service (EKS). All three services are very robust and offer similar features.[1] In this chapter, we'll use EKS, which is currently the most popular managed Kubernetes service.[2]

To illustrate how to deploy applications to a Kubernetes cluster, we'll use the example of the orders service. We'll also create an Aurora Serverless database, and we'll see how to securely feed the database connection credentials to the service using Kubernetes secrets.

The chapter doesn't assume previous knowledge of AWS or Kubernetes. I've made an effort to explain every Kubernetes and AWS concept in detail so that you can follow along with the examples, even if you have no previous experience with either technology. Entire books have been written on these topics, so this chapter is just an overview, and I provide references to other resources you can use to dive deeper into these matters.

Before proceeding, please bear in mind that EKS and other AWS services used in this chapter are for-fee services, so this is the only chapter in the book that will cost you some money if you follow along with the examples. The base cost of a Kubernetes cluster in AWS EKS is $0.10 per hour, which amounts to $2.40 per day and roughly $72 per month. If budget is an issue, my recommendation is to read the chapter first to get an understanding of what we're doing and then try out the EKS examples afterward. If this is your first time working with EKS and Kubernetes, it may take you one or two days to work through the examples, so try to schedule this time to work on the examples. Section 14.9 describes how to delete the EKS cluster, and all the other resources created in this chapter, to make sure you don't incur additional costs.

Without further ado, let's get started! We'll begin by setting up the environment.

14.1 Setting up the environment for this chapter

In this section, we set up the environment so that you can follow along with the examples in the rest of the chapter. Even if you're not planning to try out the examples, I recommend you take at least a quick look at this section to learn about the tools we're going to use. This chapter is heavy in tooling, so here we install the most important dependencies, and in the coming sections you'll find additional instructions for other tools.

---

[1] For a quick comparison between GKE, AKS, and EKS, see Alexander Postasnick, "AWS vs EKS vs GKE: Managed Kubernetes Services Compared," June 9, 2021, https://acloudguru.com/blog/engineering/aks-vs-eks-vs-gke-managed-kubernetes-services-compared.

[2] Flexera, "2022 State of the Cloud Report" (pp. 52–53), https://info.flexera.com/CM-REPORT-State-of-the-Cloud.

First, copy over the code from chapter 13 into a new folder called ch14 by running the following command:

```
$ cp -r ch13 ch14
```

`cd` into ch14, install the dependencies, and activate the virtual environment by running the following commands:

```
$ cd ch14 && pipenv install --dev && pipenv shell
```

Since we'll deploy to AWS, we need to be able to access AWS services programmatically. In chapter 13, we installed and configured the AWS CLI. If you haven't done so, please go back to section 13.1 and follow the steps to install and configure the AWS CLI.

You're going to learn how to deploy services to Kubernetes, so you also need to install the Kubernetes CLI, known as kubectl. There're different ways to install kubectl depending on the platform that you're using, so please refer to the official documentation to see which option works best for you (https://kubernetes.io/docs/tasks/tools/).

Finally, in this chapter we will make heavy use of `jq`—a CLI tool that helps us parse and query JSON documents. `jq` is not strictly necessary to follow along with the examples in this chapter, but it does make everything easier, and if you haven't used the tool before, I highly encourage you to learn about it. We'll use `jq` mostly for filtering JSON payloads and retrieving specific properties from them. As with Kubernetes, there are different installation options depending on your platform, so please refer to the official documentation to find out which strategy is best for you (https://stedolan.github.io/jq/download/).

Now that our environment is ready, it's deployment time! Before we create the cluster, the next section explains some of the main concepts related to Kubernetes to make sure you can follow the upcoming sections. If you have previous experience with Kubernetes, you can skip section 14.2.

14.2 How Kubernetes works: The "CliffsNotes" version

So, what is Kubernetes? If you don't have previous experience with Kubernetes or are still confused about how it works, this section offers a hyper-compressed introduction to its main components.

Kubernetes is an open source container orchestration tool. *Container orchestration* is the process of running containerized applications. In addition to container orchestration, Kubernetes also helps us automate deployments, and it handles graceful rollouts and rollbacks, scaling applications, and more.

Figure 14.1 offers a high-level overview of the main components of a Kubernetes cluster. The core of a Kubernetes cluster is the control plane, a process that runs the Kubernetes API for our cluster, controls its state, and manages the available resources,

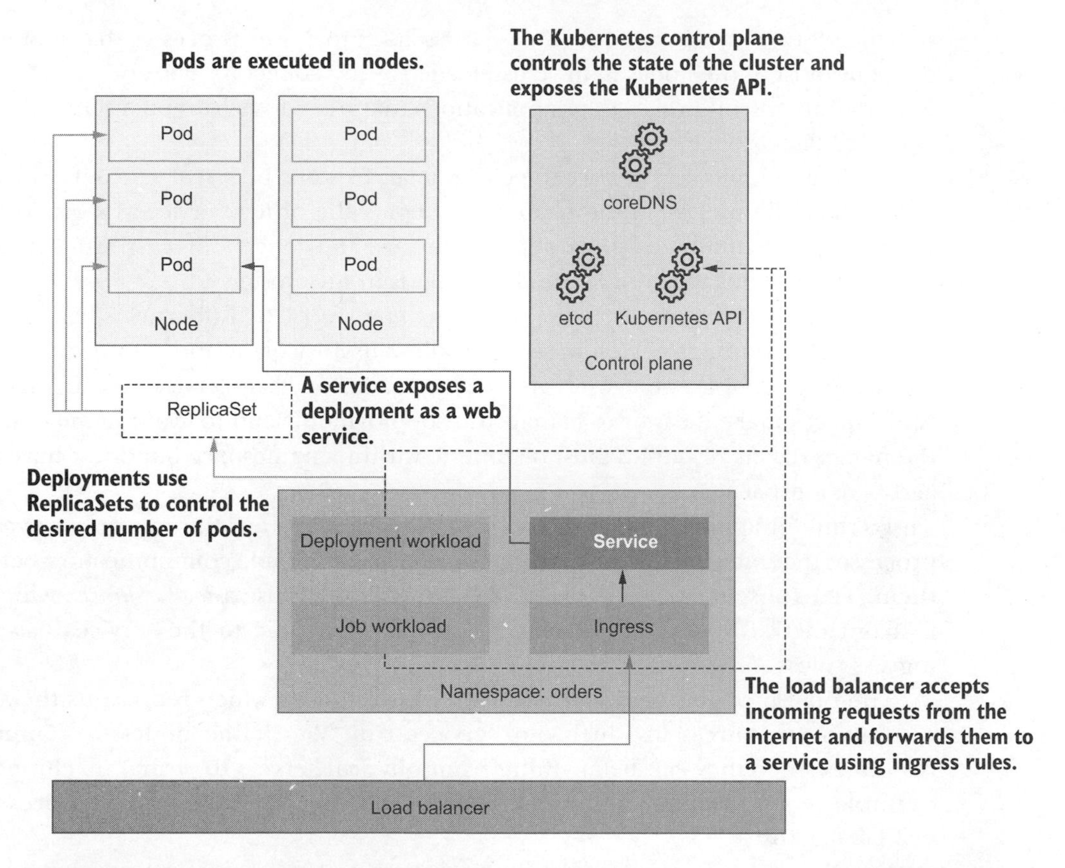

Figure 14.1 High-level architecture of a Kubernetes cluster showing how all components of a cluster come together.

among many other tasks. It's also possible to install add-ons on the control plane, including specific DNS servers such as CoreDNS.

> **DEFINITION** The *Kubernetes control plane* is a process that runs the Kubernetes API and controls the state of the cluster and manages the available resources, scheduling, and many other tasks. For more information about the control plane, see chapters 11 (http://mng.bz/yayE) and 12 (http://mng.bz/M0dm) from *Core Kubernetes* by Jay Vyas and Chris Love (Manning, 2022).

The smallest unit of computing in Kubernetes is the *pod*: a wrapper around containers that can include one or more containers. The most common practice is to run one container per pod, and in this chapter, we deploy the orders service as a single container per pod.

To deploy pods into the cluster, we use *workloads*. Kubernetes has four types of workloads: `Deployment`, `StatefulSet`, `DaemonSet`, and `Job/CronJob`. `Deployment` is the most common type of Kubernetes workload and is useful for running stateless distributed applications. `StatefulSet` is used for running distributed applications whose state needs to be synchronized. You use DaemonSet to define processes that should run on all or most of the nodes in the cluster, such as log collectors. Job and CronJob help us to define one-off processes or applications that need to be run on a schedule, such as once a day or once a week.

To deploy a microservice, we use either a Deployment or a StatefulSet. Since our services are all stateless, in this chapter we deploy the orders service as a Deployment. To manage the number of pods, deployments use the concept of a ReplicaSet, a process that maintains the desired number of pods in the cluster.

Workloads are normally scoped within *namespaces*. In Kubernetes, namespaces are logical groupings of resources that allow us to isolate and scope our deployments. For example, we can create a namespace for each service in our platform. Namespaces make it easier to manage our deployments and to avoid name conflicts: the names of our resources must be unique within a namespace but don't have to be across namespaces.

To run our applications as web services, Kubernetes offers the concept of *services*—processes that manage the interfaces of our pods and enable communication between them. To expose our services through the internet, we use a *load balancer*, which sits in front of the Kubernetes cluster, and forwards traffic to the services based on ingress rules.

The final piece of the Kubernetes system is the *node*, which represents the actual computing resources in which our services run. We define nodes as computing resources since they can be anything from physical servers to virtual machines. For example, when running a Kubernetes cluster in AWS, our nodes will be represented by EC2 machines.

Now that we understand what the main parts of Kubernetes are, let's create a cluster!

14.3 Creating a Kubernetes cluster with EKS

In this section, you'll learn how to create a Kubernetes cluster using the AWS EKS. We launch the Kubernetes cluster using eksctl, which is the recommended tool for managing Kubernetes in AWS.

eksctl is an open source tool created and maintained by Weaveworks. It uses CloudFormation behind the scenes to create and manage changes to our Kubernetes clusters. This is excellent news, because it means we can reuse the CloudFormation templates to replicate the same infrastructure across different environments. It also makes all our changes to the cluster visible through CloudFormation.

DEFINITION *CloudFormation* is AWS's infrastructure-as-code service. With CloudFormation, we can declare our resources in YAML or JSON files called *templates*. When we submit the templates to CloudFormation, AWS creates a CloudFormation *stack*, the collection of resources defined in the templates. CloudFormation templates shouldn't contain sensitive information and can be committed in our code repositories, which makes changes to our infrastructure very visible and replicable across different environments.

There are various ways to install eksctl depending on the platform you're using, so please refer to the official documentation to find out which strategy works best for you (https://github.com/weaveworks/eksctl).

To run the containers in the Kubernetes cluster, we use AWS Fargate. As you can see in figure 14.2, Fargate is AWS's serverless container service that allows us to run containers in the cloud without having to provision servers. With AWS Fargate, you don't need to worry about scaling your servers up or down, since Fargate takes care of that.

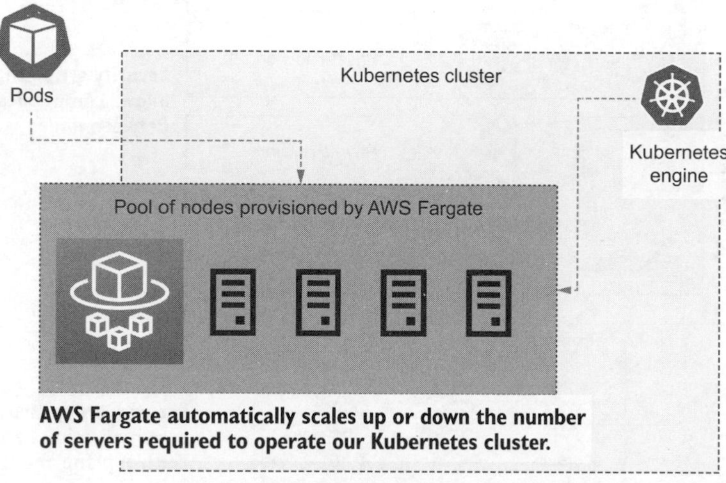

Figure 14.2 AWS Fargate automatically provisions the servers required to operate our Kubernetes cluster.

To create a Kubernetes cluster using eksctl, run the following command:

```
$ eksctl create cluster --name coffeemesh --region <aws_region> --fargate \
--alb-ingress-access
```

The creation process takes approximately 30 minutes to complete. Let's look at each flag in this command:

- `--name`—The name of the cluster. We're calling the cluster `coffeemesh`.
- `--region`—The AWS region where you want to deploy the cluster. This region should be the same you used to create the ECR repository in section 13.4.
- `--fargate`—Creates a Fargate profile to schedule pods in the `default` and the `kube-system` namespaces. Fargate profiles are policies that determine which pods must be launched by Fargate.
- `--alb-ingress-access`—Enables access to the cluster through an Application Load Balancer.

Figure 14.3 illustrates the architecture of the stack created by eksctl when launching the Kubernetes cluster. By default, eksctl creates a dedicated Virtual Private Cloud (VPC) for the cluster.

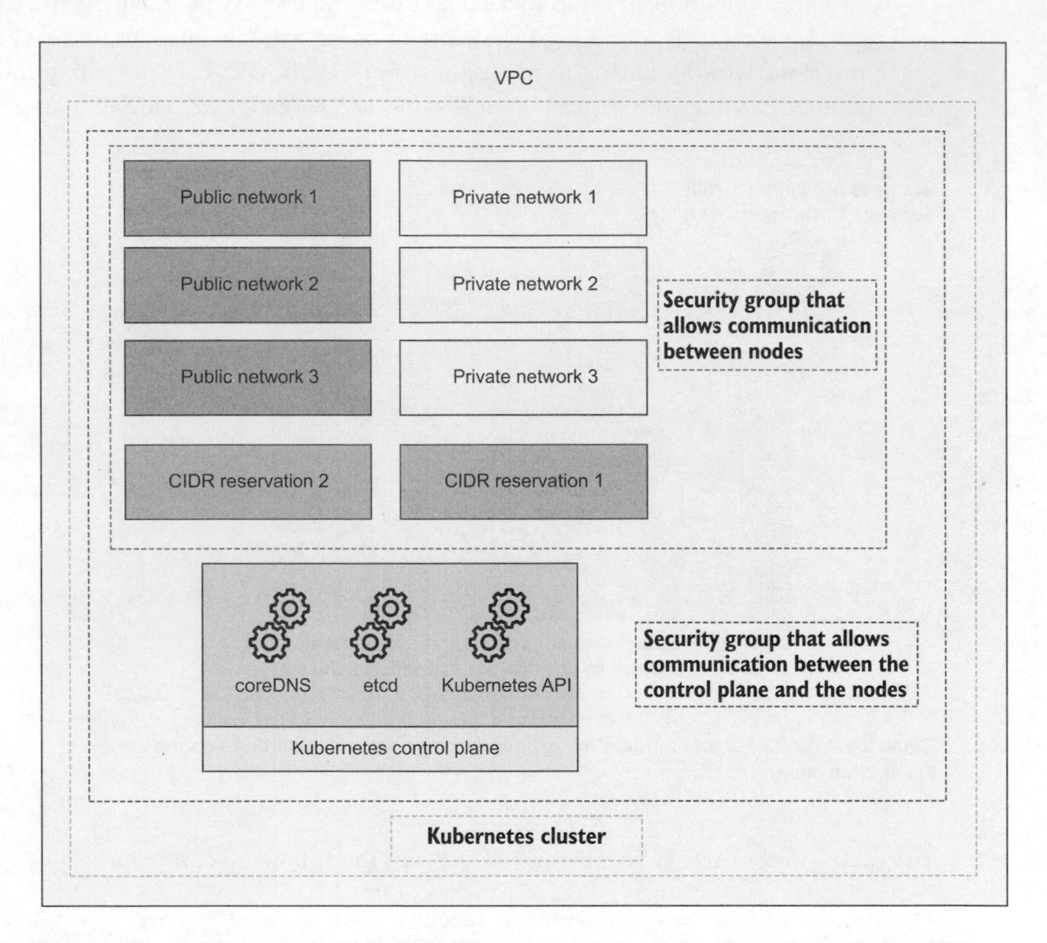

Figure 14.3 eksctl creates a VPC with three public networks, three private networks, two CIDR reservations, and two VPC security groups. It also deploys the Kubernetes cluster within the VPC.

> **KUBERNETES NETWORKING** To make advanced use of Kubernetes, you need to understand how networking works in Kubernetes. To learn more about Kubernetes networking, check out *Networking and Kubernetes: A Layered Approach* by James Strong and Vallery Lancey (O'Reilly, 2021).

It's also possible to launch the cluster within an existing VPC by specifying the subnets in which you want to run the deployment. If launching within an existing VPC, you must make sure the VPC and the provided subnets are correctly configured for operating the Kubernetes cluster. See the eksctl documentation to learn about the networking requirements of a Kubernetes cluster (https://eksctl.io/usage/vpc-networking/) and the official AWS documentation on the VPC networking requirements for a Kubernetes cluster (http://mng.bz/aPRY).

As you can see in figure 14.3, eksctl creates six subnets by default: three public and three private, with their corresponding NAT gateways and routing tables. A *subnet* is a subset of the IP addresses available in a VPC. Public subnets are accessible through the internet, while private subnets are not. eksctl also creates two subnet CIDR reservations for internal use by Kubernetes, as well as two security groups; one of them allows communication between all nodes in the cluster, and the other allows communication between the control plane and the nodes.

> **DEFINITION** *CIDR* stands for Classless Inter-Domain Routing, and it's a notation used for representing ranges of IP addresses. CIDR notation includes an IP address followed by a slash and a decimal number, where the decimal number represents the range of addresses. For example, 255.255.255.255/32 represents a range for one address. To learn more about CIDR notation, see Wikipedia's article: https://en.wikipedia.org/wiki/Classless_Inter-Domain_Routing.

Once we've created the cluster, we can configure kubectl to point to it, which will allow us to manage the cluster with the command line. Use the following command to point kubectl to the cluster:

```
$ aws eks update-kubeconfig --name coffeemesh --region <aws_region>
```

Now that we're connected to the cluster, we can inspect its properties. For example, we can get a list of running nodes with the following command:

```
$ kubectl get nodes
# output truncated:
NAME                                        STATUS  ROLES   AGE    VERSION
fargate-ip-192-168-157-75.<aws_region>...   Ready   <none>  4d16h  v1.20.7...
fargate-ip-192-168-170-234.<aws_region>...  Ready   <none>  4d16h  v1.20.7...
fargate-ip-192-168-173-63.<aws_region>...   Ready   <none>  4d16h  v1.20.7...
```

To get the list of pods running in the cluster, run the following command:

```
$ kubectl get pods -A
NAMESPACE    NAME                      READY  STATUS   RESTARTS  AGE
kube-system  coredns-647df9f975-2ns5m  1/1    Running  0         2d15h
kube-system  coredns-647df9f975-hcgjq  1/1    Running  0         2d15h
```

There are many more useful commands you can run to learn more about your cluster. Check out the official documentation about the Kubernetes CLI for additional commands and options (https://kubernetes.io/docs/reference/kubectl/). A good starting point is the kubectl cheat sheet (https://kubernetes.io/docs/reference/kubectl/cheatsheet/). Now that our cluster is up and running, in the next section, we'll create an IAM role for our Kubernetes service accounts.

14.4 Using IAM roles for Kubernetes service accounts

Every process that runs in your Kubernetes cluster has an identity, and that identity is given by a *service account*. Service accounts determine the access privileges of a process within the cluster. Sometimes, our services need to interact with AWS resources using the AWS API. To give access to the AWS API, we need to create *IAM roles*—entities that give applications access to the AWS API—for our services. As you can see in figure 14.4, to link a Kubernetes service account to an IAM role, we use OpenID Connect (OIDC). By using OIDC, our pods can obtain temporary credentials to access the AWS API.

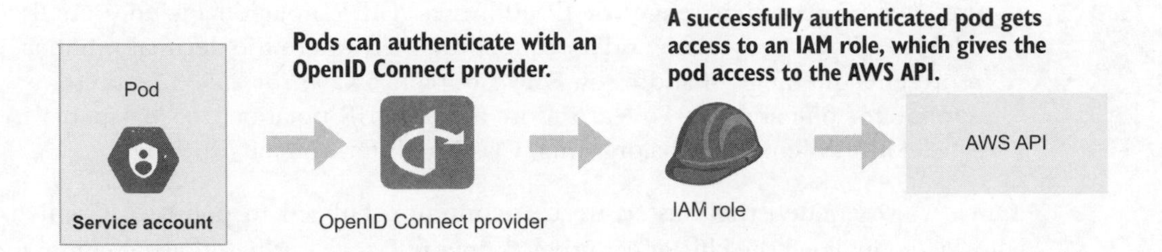

Figure 14.4 Pods can authenticate with an OIDC provider to assume an IAM role, which gives them access to the AWS API, and therefore gives them access to AWS services.

To check if your cluster has an OIDC provider, run the following command, replacing `<cluster_name>` with the name of your cluster:

```
$ aws eks describe-cluster --name coffeemesh \
--query "cluster.identity.oidc.issuer" --output text
```

You'll get an output like the following:

```
https://oidc.eks.<aws_region>.amazonaws.com/id/BE4E5EE7DCDF9FB198D06FC9883F
➥ F1BE
```

In this case, the ID of the cluster's OIDC provider is `BE4E5EE7DCDF9FB198D06FC9883FF1BE`. Grab the OIDC provider's ID and run the following command:

```
$ aws iam list-open-id-connect-providers | \
grep BE4E5EE7DCDF9FB198D06FC9883FF1BE
```

This command lists all the OIDC providers in your AWS account, and it uses `grep` to filter by the ID of your cluster's OIDC provider. If you get a result, it means you already have an OIDC provider for your cluster. If you don't get any output, it means you don't have an OIDC provider, so let's create one! To create an OIDC provider for your cluster, run the following command, replacing `<cluster_name>` with the name of your cluster:

```
$ eksctl utils associate-iam-oidc-provider --cluster <cluster_name> \
--approve
```

That's all it takes. Now we can link IAM roles to our service accounts! In the next section, we deploy a Kubernetes load balancer to enable external traffic to the cluster.

14.5 Deploying a Kubernetes load balancer

Right now, our cluster is not accessible from outside of the VPC. If we deploy our applications, they'll only get internal IPs and therefore won't be accessible to the external world. To enable external access to the cluster, we need an *ingress controller*. As you can see in figure 14.5, an ingress controller accepts traffic from outside of the Kubernetes cluster and load balances it among our pods. To redirect traffic to specific pods, we create *ingress resources* for each service. The ingress controller takes care of managing ingress resources.

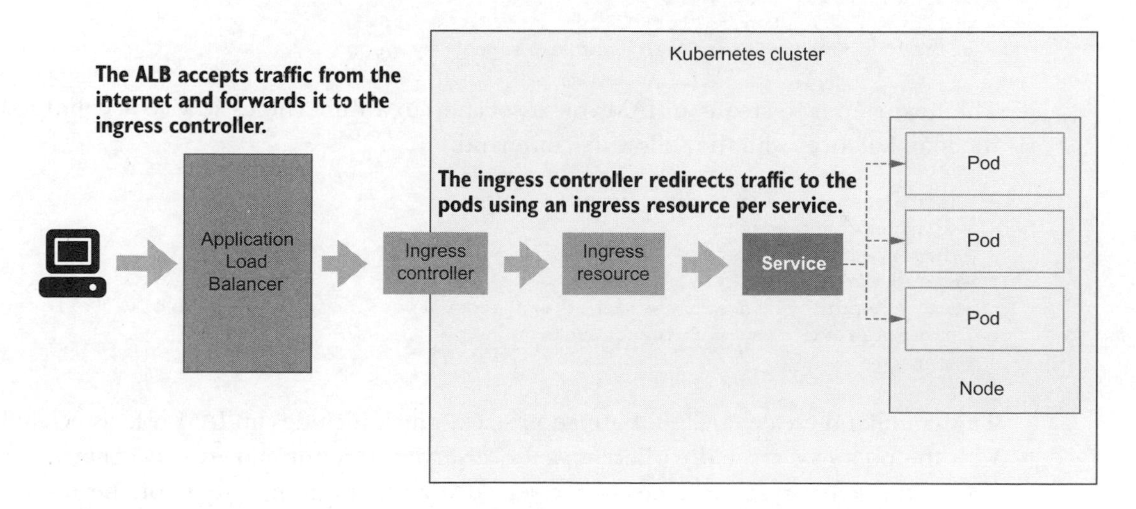

Figure 14.5 An ingress controller accepts traffic from outside of the Kubernetes cluster and forwards it to the pods according to rules defined by ingress resources.

In this section, we'll deploy a Kubernetes ingress controller as an AWS Load Balancer Controller.[3] As you can see in figure 14.5, the AWS Load Balancer Controller deploys an AWS Application Load Balancer (ALB), which sits in front of our cluster, captures incoming traffic, and forwards it to our services. To forward traffic to our services, the

[3] The AWS Load Balancer Controller is an open source project hosted on GitHub (https://github.com/kubernetes-sigs/aws-load-balancer-controller/). The project was originally created by Ticketmaster and CoreOS.

ALB uses the concept of *target groups*—a rule for how traffic should be forwarded from the ALB to a specific resource. For example, we can have target groups based on IPs, services IDs, and other factors. The load balancer monitors the health of its registered targets and makes sure traffic is only redirected to healthy targets.

To install the AWS Load Balancer Controller, we need to have an OIDC provider in the cluster, so make sure you've gone through section 14.4 before proceeding. The first step to deploying an AWS Load Balancer Controller is to create an IAM policy that gives the controller access to the relevant AWS APIs. The open source community that maintains the AWS Load Balancer Controller project provides a sample of the policy that we need, so we simply need to fetch it:

```
$ curl -o alb_controller_policy.json \
https://raw.githubusercontent.com/kubernetes-sigs/aws-load-balancer-
➥ controller/main/docs/install/iam_policy.json
```

After running this command, you'll see a file called alb_controller_policy.json in your directory. Now we can create the IAM policy using this file:

```
$ aws iam create-policy \
--policy-name ALBControllerPolicy \
--policy-document file://alb_controller_policy.json
```

The next step is to create an IAM role associated to a Kubernetes service account for the load balancer with the following command:

```
$ eksctl create iamserviceaccount \
  --cluster=coffeemesh \
  --namespace=kube-system \
  --name=alb-controller \
  --attach-policy-arn=arn:aws:iam::<aws_account_id>:policy/ALBControllerPolicy \
  --override-existing-serviceaccounts \
  --approve
```

This command creates a CloudFormation stack, which includes an IAM role associated with the policy we created earlier, as well as a service account named `alb-controller` within the `kube-system` namespace reserved for system components of the Kubernetes cluster.

Now we can install the Load Balancer Controller. We'll use Helm to install the controller, a package manager for Kubernetes. If you don't have Helm available in your machine, you need to install it. There are different strategies for installing Helm depending on your platform, so make sure you check out the documentation to see which option works best for you (https://helm.sh/docs/intro/install/).

Once Helm is available on your machine, you need to update it by adding the EKS charts repository to your local `helm` (in Helm, packages are called *charts*). To add the EKS charts, run the following command:

```
$ helm repo add eks https://aws.github.io/eks-charts
```

Now let's update helm to make sure we pick up the most recent updates to the charts:

```
$ helm repo update
```

Now that helm is up to date, we can install the AWS Load Balancer Controller. To install the controller, we need to get hold of the ID of the VPC eksctl created when we launched the cluster. To find the VPC ID, run the following command:

```
$ eksctl get cluster --name coffeemesh -o json | \
jq '.[0].ResourcesVpcConfig.VpcId'
# output: "vpc-07d35ccc982a082c9"
```

To run the previous command successfully, you need to have jq installed. Please refer to section 14.1 to learn how to install it. Now we can install the controller by running the following command:

```
$ helm install aws-load-balancer-controller eks/aws-load-balancer-
➥ controller \
  -n kube-system \
  --set clusterName=coffeemesh \
  --set serviceAccount.create=false \
  --set serviceAccount.name=alb-controller \
  --set vpcId=<vpc_id>
```

Since the controller is an internal Kubernetes component, we install it within the kube-system namespace. We make sure that the controller is installed for the coffeemesh cluster. We also instruct Helm not to create a new service account for the controller, and instead use the alb-controller service account we created earlier.

It'll take a few minutes until all the resources are created. To verify that the deployment went well, run the following command:

```
$ kubectl get deployment -n kube-system aws-load-balancer-controller
NAME              READY    UP-TO-DATE    AVAILABLE    AGE
alb-controller    2/2      2             2            84s
```

You'll know that the controller is up and running when the READY column shows 2/2, which means the desired number of resources are up. Our cluster is now ready, so it's time to deploy the orders service!

14.6 Deploying microservices to the Kubernetes cluster

Now that our Kubernetes cluster is ready, it's time to start deploying our services! In this section, we walk through the steps required to deploy the orders service. You can follow the same steps to deploy other services of the CoffeeMesh platform.

As you can see in figure 14.6, we deploy the orders service to a new namespace called orders-service. This allows us to logically group and isolate all the resources required to operate the orders service. To create a new namespace, we run the following command:

```
$ kubectl create namespace orders-service
```

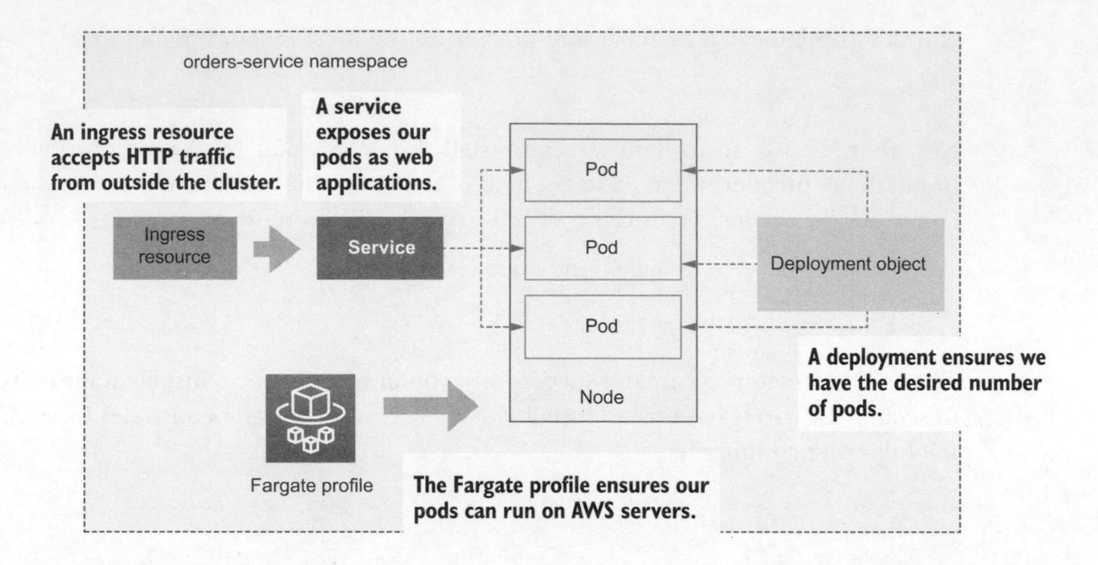

Figure 14.6 To deploy a microservice, we create a new namespace, and within this namespace we deploy all the components needed to operate the microservice, such as a `Deployment` object and a `Service` object.

Since we'll run the orders service in the new namespace, we also need to create a new Fargate profile configured to schedule jobs within the `orders-service` namespace. To create the new Fargate profile, run the following command:

```
$ eksctl create fargateprofile --namespace orders-service --cluster \
coffeemesh --region <aws_region>
```

With the `orders-service` namespace and the Fargate profile ready, we can deploy the orders service. To make the deployment, we take the following steps:

1. Create a deployment object for the orders service.
2. Create a service object.
3. Create an ingress resource to expose the service.

The following sections explain in detail how to proceed in each step.

14.6.1 Creating a deployment object

Let's begin by creating a deployment for the orders service using a service manifest file. As you can see in figure 14.7, deployments are Kubernetes objects that operate our pods and provision them with everything they need to run, including a Docker image and port configuration. Create a file named orders-service-deployment.yaml and copy the contents of listing 14.1 into it.

We use Kubernetes' API version apps/v1 and declare this object a `Deployment`. In metadata, we name the deployment `orders-service`, we specify its namespace, and

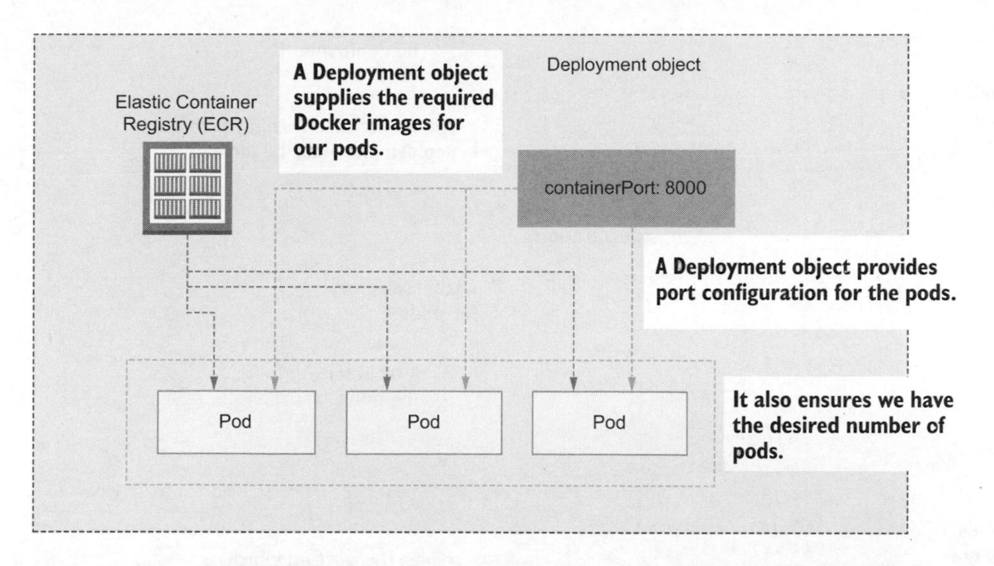

Figure 14.7 A `Deployment` object provides necessary configuration for the pods, such as their Docker image and port configuration, and ensures we have the desired number of pods running.

we add the label `app: orders-service`. *Labels* are custom identifiers for Kubernetes objects, and they can be used for monitoring, tracing, or scheduling tasks, among other uses.[4]

In the `spec` section, we define a selector rule that matches pods with the label `app: orders-service`, which means this deployment will only operate pods with this label. We also declare that we'd like to run only one replica of the pod.

Within the `spec.template` section, we define the pod operated by this deployment. We label the pod with the `app: orders-service` key-value pair in agreement with the deployment's selector rule. Within the pod's `spec` section, we declare the containers that belong in the pod. In this case, we want to run just one container, which is the orders service application. Within the definition of the orders service container, we specify the image that must be used to run the application with the port on which the application runs.

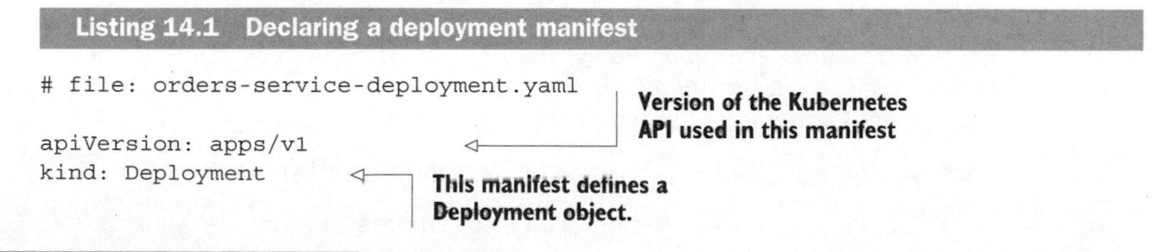

Listing 14.1 Declaring a deployment manifest

```
# file: orders-service-deployment.yaml

apiVersion: apps/v1
kind: Deployment
```


[4] To learn more about labels and how to use them, see the official documentation, https://kubernetes.io/docs/concepts/overview/working-with-objects/labels/, and Zane Hitchcox's "matchLabels, Labels, and Selectors Explained in Detail, for Beginners," *Medium* (July 15, 2018), https://medium.com/@zwhitchcox/matchlabels-labels-and-selectors-explained-in-detail-for-beginners-d421bdd05362.

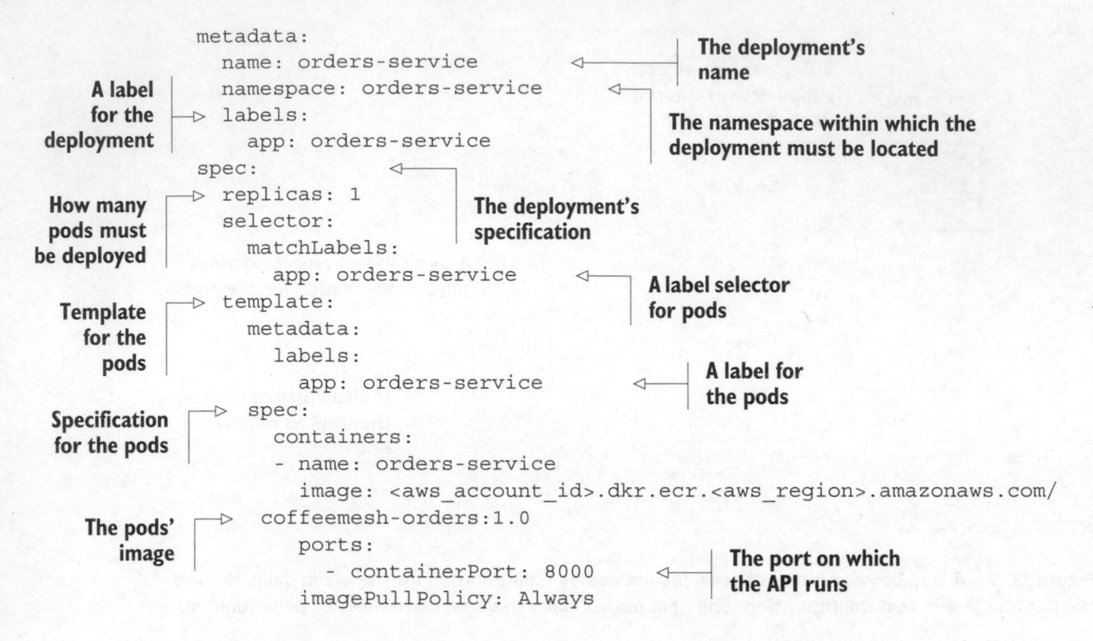

metadata:
  name: orders-service
  namespace: orders-service
  labels:
    app: orders-service
spec:
  replicas: 1
  selector:
    matchLabels:
      app: orders-service
  template:
    metadata:
      labels:
        app: orders-service
    spec:
      containers:
      - name: orders-service
        image: <aws_account_id>.dkr.ecr.<aws_region>.amazonaws.com/
     coffeemesh-orders:1.0
        ports:
          - containerPort: 8000
        imagePullPolicy: Always
The deployment's name
The namespace within which the deployment must be located
A label for the deployment
The deployment's specification
How many pods must be deployed
A label selector for pods
Template for the pods
A label for the pods
Specification for the pods
The pods' image
The port on which the API runs

To create the deployment, we run the following command:

```
$ kubectl apply -f orders-service-deployment.yaml
```

This command creates the deployment and launches the pods we defined in the manifest file. It'll take a few seconds for the pods to become available. You can check their state with the following command:

```
$ kubectl get pods -n orders-service
```

The initial state of the pods will be `Pending`, and once they're up and running their state will change to `Running`.

What is a Kubernetes manifest file?

In Kubernetes, we can create objects using manifest files. Objects are resources such as namespaces, deployments, services, and so on. A manifest file is a YAML file that describes the properties of the object and its desired state. Using manifest files is convenient because they can be tracked in source control, which helps us trace changes to our infrastructure.

Each manifest file contains, at a minimum, the following properties:

- `apiVersion`—The version of the Kubernetes API that we want to use. Each Kubernetes object has its own stable version. You can check the latest stable version of each object for your Kubernetes cluster by running the following command: `kubectl api-resources`.

- `kind`—The kind of object that we're creating. Possible values include `Service`, `Ingress`, and `Deployment`, among others.
- `metadata`—A collection of properties that provide identifying information about the object, such as its name, its namespace, and additional labels.
- `spec`—The specification for the object. For example, if we're creating a service, we use this section to specify the type of service we're creating (e.g., `NodePort`) and selector rules.

To create an object from a manifest file, we use the `kubectl apply` command. For example, if we have a manifest file called deployment.yaml, we apply it using the following command:

```
$ kubectl apply -f deployment.yaml
```

14.6.2 Creating a service object

Now that our deployment is ready, we will create a service object for the orders service. As we learned in section 14.2, services are Kubernetes objects that allow us to expose our pods as networking services. As you can see in figure 14.8, a service object exposes our applications as web services and redirects traffic from the cluster to our pods on the specified ports. Create a file named orders-service.yaml, and copy into it the contents of listing 14.2, which shows how to configure a simple service manifest.

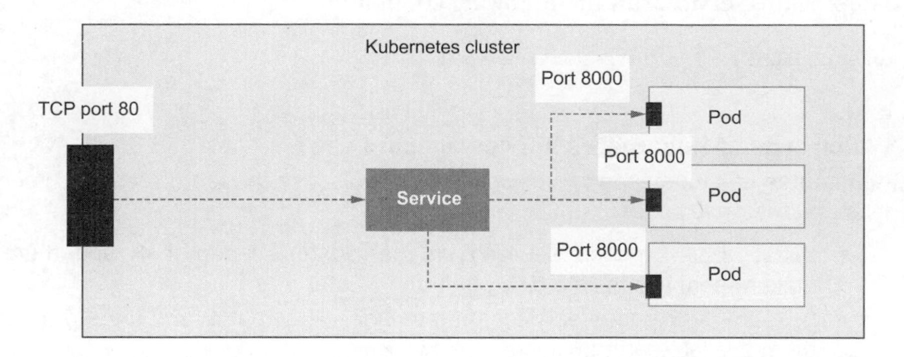

Figure 14.8 A service object redirects traffic from the cluster to the pods on the specified ports. In this example, incoming traffic to the cluster on port 80 is redirected to port 8000 in the pods.

We use version v1 of the Kubernetes API to declare our service. In metadata, we specify that the service's name is `orders-service` and that it's to be launched within the `orders-service` namespace. We also add a label: `app: orders-service`. In the service's `spec` section, we configure a `ClusterIP` type, which means the pod will only be accessible from within the cluster. There are other types of services in Kubernetes, such as NodePort and LoadBalancer. (To learn more about the types of services and when to use each type, see the sidebar, "Which type of Kubernetes service should I use?")

We also create a forwarding rule to redirect traffic from port 80 to port 8000, which is the port on which our containers run. Finally, we specify a selector for the app: orders-service label, which means this service will only operate pods with that label.

Listing 14.2 Declaring a service manifest

```
# file: orders-service.yaml

apiVersion: v1
kind: Service                      <- This manifest defines a Service object.
metadata:
  name: orders-service
  namespace: orders-service
  labels:
    app: orders-service
spec:
  selector:
    app: orders-service
  type: ClusterIP                  <- This is a ClusterIP type of Service.
  ports:
    - protocol: http               <- The service communicates over HTTP.
      port: 80                     <- The service must be mapped to port 80.
      targetPort: 8000             <- The service runs internally on port 8000.
```

To deploy this service, run the following command:

```
$ kubectl apply -f orders-service.yaml
```

> **Which type of Kubernetes service should I use?**
>
> Kubernetes has four types of services. Here we discuss the features of each service type and their use cases:
>
> - ClusterIP—Exposes services on the cluster's internal IP and therefore makes them accessible only within the cluster
> - NodePort—Exposes services on the node's external IP and therefore makes them available on the cluster's network
> - LoadBalancer—Exposes the service directly through a dedicated cloud load balancer
> - ExternalName—Exposes the service through an internal DNS record within the cluster
>
> Which of these types should you use? It depends on your needs. NodePort is useful if you want to be able to access your services externally on the IP of the node in which they're running. The downside is the service uses the static port of the node, so you can only run one service per node. ClusterIP is useful if you'd rather access the service on the cluster's IP. ClusterIP services are not directly reachable from outside the cluster, but you can expose them by creating ingress rules that forward traffic to them.

`LoadBalancer` is useful if you'd like to use one cloud load balancer per service. Using a load balancer per service makes configuration somewhat simpler, as you won't have to configure multiple ingress rules. However, load balancers are usually the most expensive components of your cluster, so if budget is a factor, you may not want to use this option. Finally, `ExternalName` is useful if you want to be able to access your services from within the cluster using custom domains.

14.6.3 Exposing services with ingress objects

The final step is to expose the service through the internet. To expose the service, we need to create an ingress resource that routes traffic to the service. As you can see in figure 14.9, an ingress resource is a service that redirects HTTP traffic to the pods running in our Kubernetes cluster on the specified ports and URL paths. Create a file named orders-service-ingress.yaml and copy the content of listing 14.3 to it.

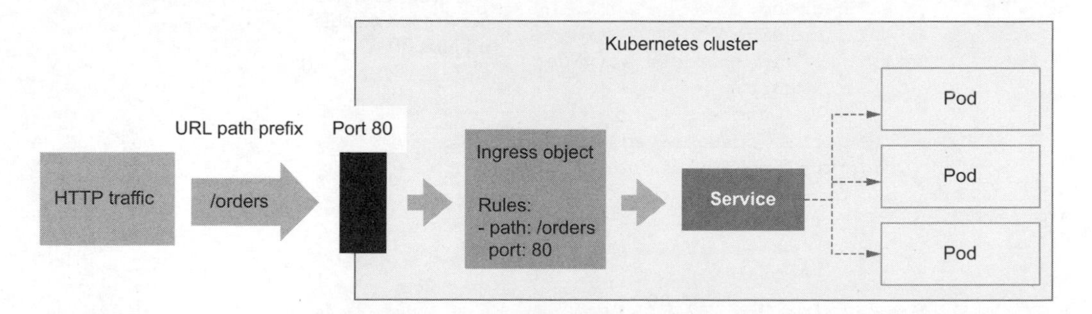

Figure 14.9 An ingress object allows us to redirect HTTP traffic on a specific port and URL path to a service object.

In the ingress manifest, we use version networking.k8s.io/v1 of the Kubernetes API, and we declare the object as an `Ingress` type. In `metadata`, we name the ingress object `orders-service-ingress`, and we specify that it should be deployed within the `orders-service` namespace. We use annotations to bind the ingress object to the AWS Load Balancer we deployed in section 14.5. Within the `spec` section, we define the forwarding rules of the ingress resource. We declare an HTTP rule that forwards all traffic under the `/orders` path to the orders service and additional rules to access the service's API documentation.

Listing 14.3 Declaring an ingress manifest

```
# file: orders-service-ingress.yaml

apiVersion: networking.k8s.io/v1
kind: Ingress
```

The manifest defines an Ingress object.

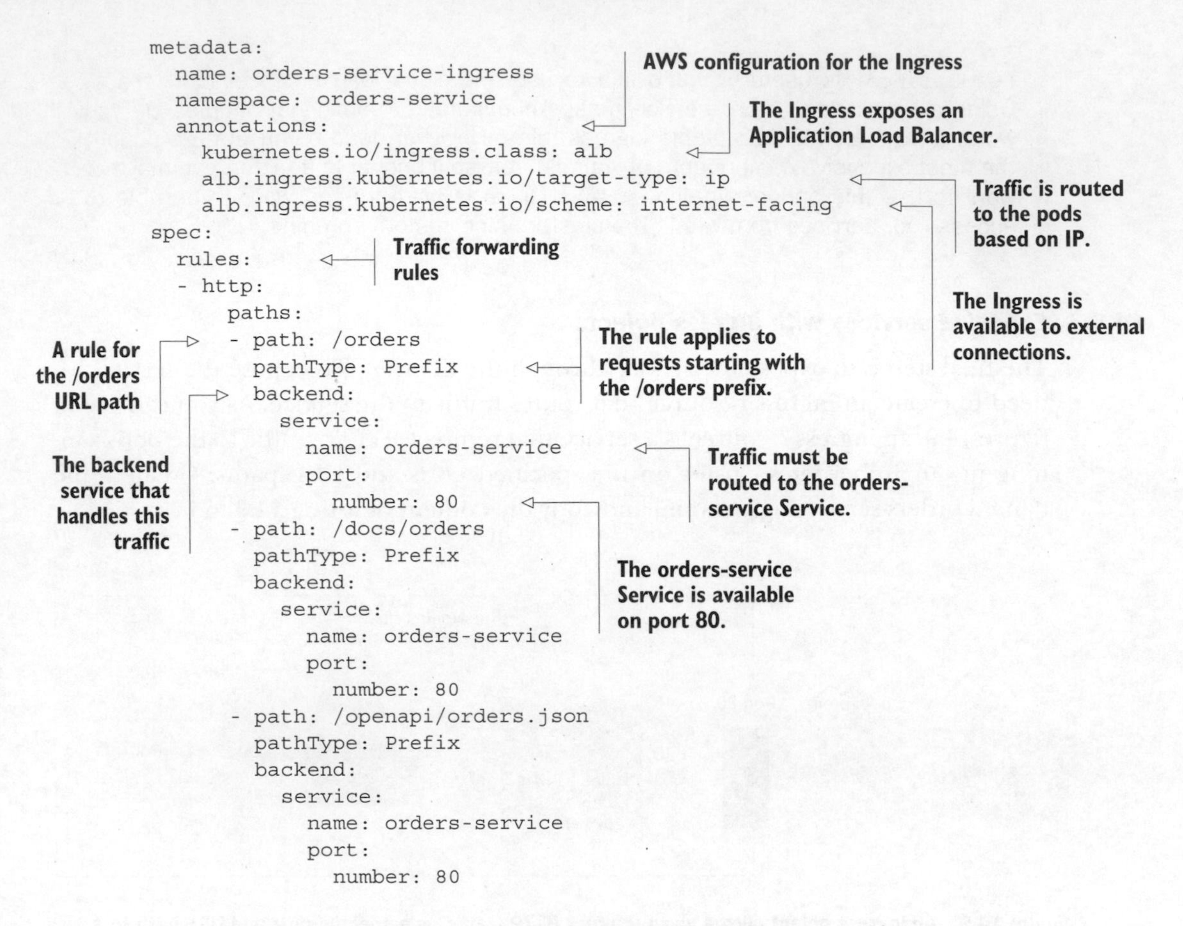
AWS configuration for the Ingress
The Ingress exposes an Application Load Balancer.
Traffic is routed to the pods based on IP.
The Ingress is available to external connections.
Traffic forwarding rules
A rule for the /orders URL path
The rule applies to requests starting with the /orders prefix.
The backend service that handles this traffic
Traffic must be routed to the orders-service Service.
The orders-service Service is available on port 80.

```
metadata:
  name: orders-service-ingress
  namespace: orders-service
  annotations:
    kubernetes.io/ingress.class: alb
    alb.ingress.kubernetes.io/target-type: ip
    alb.ingress.kubernetes.io/scheme: internet-facing
spec:
  rules:
  - http:
      paths:
      - path: /orders
        pathType: Prefix
        backend:
          service:
            name: orders-service
            port:
              number: 80
      - path: /docs/orders
        pathType: Prefix
        backend:
          service:
            name: orders-service
            port:
              number: 80
      - path: /openapi/orders.json
        pathType: Prefix
        backend:
          service:
            name: orders-service
            port:
              number: 80
```

To create this ingress resource, we run the following command:

```
$ kubectl apply -f orders-service-ingress.yaml
```

The orders API is now accessible. To call the API, we first need to find out the endpoint for the ingress rule we just created. Run the following command to get the details of the ingress resource:

```
$ kubectl get ingress/orders-service-ingress -n orders-service
# output truncated:
NAME                     CLASS    HOSTS   ADDRESS...
orders-service-ingress   <none>   *       k8s-ordersse-ordersse-3c391193...
```

The value under the `ADDRESS` field is the URL of the load balancer. You can also get hold of this value by running the following command:

```
$ kubectl get ingress/orders-service-ingress -n orders-service -o json | \
jq '.status.loadBalancer.ingress[0].hostname'
"k8s-ordersse-ordersse-3c39119336-236890178.<aws_region>.elb.amazonaws.com"
```

We can use this URL to call the orders service API. Since the database isn't yet ready, the API itself won't work, but we can access the API documentation:

```
$ curl http://k8s-ordersse-ordersse-3c39119336-
➥ 236890178.<aws_region>.elb.amazonaws.com/openapi/orders.json
```

It may take some time for the load balancer to become available, and in the meantime `curl` won't be able to resolve the host. If that happens, wait a few minutes and try again. To be able to interact with the API, we must set up a database, which will be the goal of our next section!

14.7 Setting up a serverless database with AWS Aurora

The orders service is almost ready: the application is up and running, and we can access it through the internet. Only one component is missing: the database. We have multiple choices for setting up the database. We can set up the database as a deployment within our Kubernetes cluster with a mounted volume, or we can choose one of the many managed database services that cloud providers offer.

To keep it simple and cost-effective, in this section, we'll set up an Aurora Serverless database in AWS—a powerful database engine that is cost-effective since you only pay for what you use and is very convenient since you don't have to worry about managing or scaling the database.

14.7.1 Creating an Aurora Serverless database

We'll launch our Aurora database within the Kubernetes cluster's VPC. To be able to launch a database within an existing VPC, we need to create a *database subnet group*: a collection of subnets within the VPC. As we learned in section 14.3, eksctl divides the Kubernetes cluster's VPC into six subnets: three public and three private. The six subnets are distributed across three *availability zones* (data centers within an AWS region), with one public and one private subnet per availability zone.

When choosing the subnets for our database subnet group, we need to consider the following constraints:

- Aurora Serverless only supports one subnet per availability zone.
- When creating a database subnet group, the subnets must all be either private or public.[5]

For security, it's best practice to use private subnets in database subnet groups as it ensures that the database server is not accessible from outside of the VPC, which means external and unauthorized users are unable to connect to it directly. To find

[5] For more information on this point, see the official AWS documentation: https://docs.aws.amazon.com/AmazonRDS/latest/UserGuide/USER_VPC.WorkingWithRDSInstanceinaVPC.html.

the list of private subnets in the VPC, we first need to obtain the ID of the Kubernetes cluster's VPC with the following command:

```
$ eksctl get cluster --name coffeemesh -o json | \
jq '.[0].ResourcesVpcConfig.VpcId'
```

Then use the following command to get the IDs of the private subnets in the VPC:

```
$ aws ec2 describe-subnets --filters Name=vpc-id,Values=<vpc_id> \
--output json | jq '.Subnets[] | select(.MapPublicIpOnLaunch == false) | \
.SubnetId'
```

The previous command lists all the subnets in the Kubernetes cluster's VPC, and it uses `jq` to filter the public subnets. Armed with all this information, we can now create the database subnet group using the following command:

```
$ aws rds create-db-subnet-group --db-subnet-group-name \
coffeemesh-db-subnet-group --db-subnet-group-description "Private subnets" \
--subnet-ids "<subnet_id>" "<subnet_id>" "<subnet_id>"
```

As you can see in figure 14.10, this command creates a database subnet group named `coffeemesh-db-subnet-group`. When running the command, make sure you replace the `<subnet_id>` placeholders with the IDs of your private subnets. We'll deploy our Aurora database within this database subnet group.

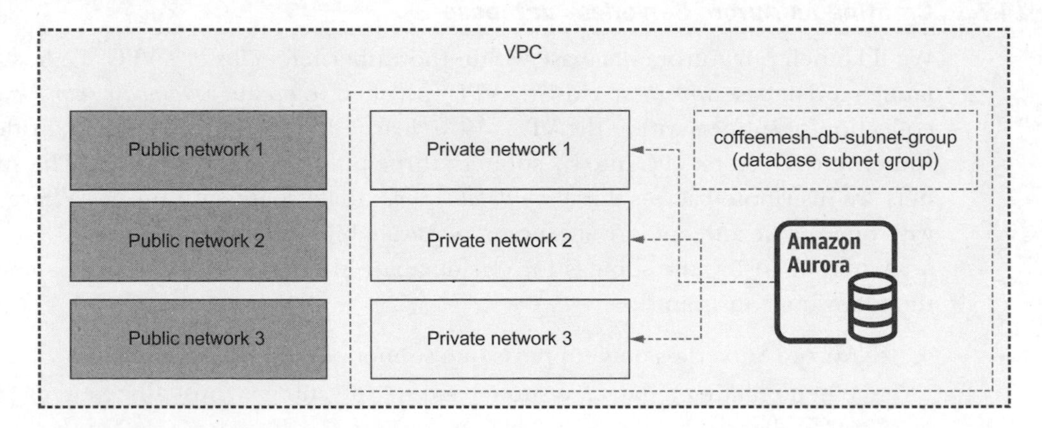

Figure 14.10 We deploy an Aurora database within a database subnet group named `coffeemesh-db-subnet-group`. The database subnet group is created on top of the three private subnets of our VPC to prevent unauthorized access.

Next, we need to create a *VPC security group*—a set of rules that define what incoming and outgoing traffic is allowed from the VPC—that allows traffic to the database so that our applications can connect to it. The following command creates a security group called `db-access`:

```
$ aws ec2 create-security-group --group-name db-access --vpc-id <vpc-id> \
--description "Security group for db access"
# output:
{
   "GroupId": "sg-00b47703a4299924d"
}
```

In the previous command, replace `<vpc-id>` with the ID of your Kubernetes cluster's VPC. The output from the previous command is the ID of the security group we just created. We'll allow traffic from all IP addresses on PostgreSQL's default port, which is 5432. Since we're going to deploy the database into private subnets, it's okay to listen on all IPs, but for additional security, you may want to restrict the range of addresses to those of your pods. We use the following command to create an inbound traffic rule for our database access security group:

```
$ aws ec2 authorize-security-group-ingress --group-id \
<db-security-group-id> --ip-permissions \
'FromPort=5432,IpProtocol=TCP,IpRanges=0.0.0.0/0'
```

In this command, replace `<db-security-group-id>` with the ID of your database access security group.

Now that we have a database subnet group and a security group that allows our pods to connect to it, we can use the subnet group to launch an Aurora Serverless cluster within our VPC! Run the following command to launch an Aurora Serverless cluster:

```
$ aws rds create-db-cluster --db-cluster-identifier coffeemesh-orders-db \
--engine aurora-postgresql --engine-version 10.14 \
--engine-mode serverless \
--scaling-configuration MinCapacity=8,MaxCapacity=64,
➥ SecondsUntilAutoPause=1000,AutoPause=true \
--master-username <username> \
--master-user-password <password> \
--vpc-security-group-ids <security_group_id> \
--db-subnet-group <db_subnet_group_name>
```

Let's take a close look at the command's parameters:

- `--db-cluster-identifier`—The name of the database cluster. We're naming the cluster `coffeemesh-orders-db`.
- `--engine`—The database engine you want to use. We're using a PostgreSQL-compatible engine, but you can also choose a MySQL-compatible engine if you prefer.
- `--engine-version`—The version of the Aurora engine you want to use. We're choosing version 10.14, which is the only version available for Aurora PostgreSQL serverless right now. See the AWS documentation to keep up to date with new versions (http://mng.bz/gRyn).

- `--engine-mode`—The database engine mode. We're choosing serverless to keep the example simple and cost-effective.
- `--scaling-configuration`—The autoscaling configuration for the Aurora cluster. We configure the cluster with minimum Aurora capacity units (ACU) of 8 and a maximum of 64. Each ACU provides approximately 2 GB of memory. We also configure the cluster to scale down to 0 ACUs automatically after 1,000 seconds without activity.[6]
- `--master-username`—The username of the database master user.
- `--master-user-password`—The password of the database master user.
- `--vpc-security-group-ids`—The ID of the database access security group we created in the previous step.
- `--db-subnet-group`—The name of the database security group we created earlier.

After running this command, you'll get a large JSON payload with details about the database. To connect to the database, we need the value of the `DBCluster.Endpoint` property of the payload, which represents the database's hostname. We'll use this value in the next sections to connect to the database.

14.7.2 Managing secrets in Kubernetes

To connect our services to the database, we need a secure way to pass the connection credentials. The native way to manage sensitive information in Kubernetes is using Kubernetes secrets. This way, we avoid having to expose sensitive information through the code or through our image builds. In this section, you'll learn how to manage Kubernetes secrets securely.

AWS EKS offers two secure ways to manage Kubernetes secrets: we can use the AWS Secrets & Configuration Provider for Kubernetes,[7] or we can use AWS Key Management Service (KMS) to secure our secrets with envelope encryption. In this section, we'll use envelope encryption to protect our secrets.[8]

As you can see in figure 14.11, envelope encryption is the practice of encrypting your data with a data encryption key (DEK) and encrypting the DEK with a key encryption key (KEK).[9] It sounds complicated, but it's simple to use since AWS does the heavy lifting for us.

---

[6] See the official documentation for more information on how Aurora Serverless works and the autoscaling configuration parameters: https://docs.aws.amazon.com/AmazonRDS/latest/AuroraUserGuide/aurora-serverless-v2.html.

[7] You can learn more about this option through Tracy Pierce's article "How to use AWS Secrets & Configuration Provider with Your Kubernetes Secrets Store CSI driver," https://aws.amazon.com/blogs/security/how-to-use-aws-secrets-configuration-provider-with-kubernetes-secrets-store-csi-driver/.

[8] Managing Kubernetes securely is a big and important topic, and to learn more about, it you can check out Alex Soto Bueno and Andrew Block's *Securing Kubernetes Secrets* (Manning, 2022), https://livebook.manning.com/book/securing-kubernetes-secrets/chapter-4/v-3/point-13495-119-134-1.

[9] Ibid.

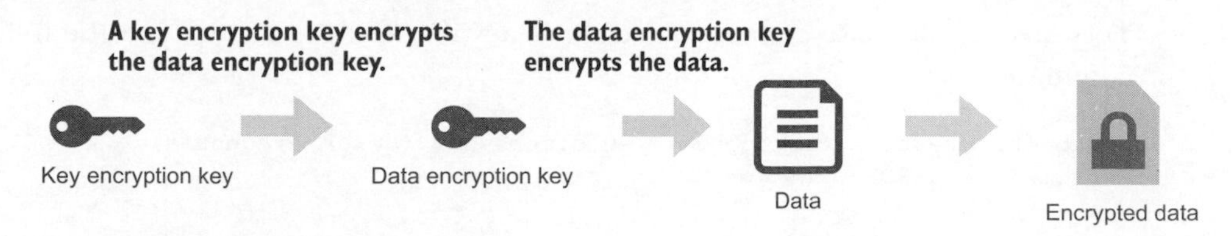
A key encryption key encrypts the data encryption key.
The data encryption key encrypts the data.
Key encryption key
Data encryption key
Data
Encrypted data

Figure 14.11 Envelope encryption is the practice of encrypting data with a data encryption key (DEK) and encrypting the DEK with a key encryption key.

To use envelope encryption, first we need to generate an AWS KMS key. You can use the following command to create the key:

```
$ aws kms create-key
```

The output of this command is a payload with metadata about the newly created key. From this payload, we want to use the `KeyMetadata.Arn` property, which represents the key's ARN, or Amazon Resource Name. The next step is to enable secrets encryption in our Kubernetes cluster using eksctl:

```
$ eksctl utils enable-secrets-encryption --cluster coffeemesh \
--key-arn=<key_arn> --region <aws_region>
```

Make sure you replace `<key_arn>` with the ARN of your KMS key and `<aws_region>` with the region where you deployed the Kubernetes cluster. The operation triggered by the previous command can take up to 45 minutes to complete. The command runs until the cluster is created, so just wait until it finishes. Once it's done, we can create Kubernetes secrets. Let's create a secret that represents the database connection string. A database connection string has the following structure:

```
<engine>://<username>:<password>@<hostname>:<port>/<database_name>
```

Let's look at each component of the connection string:

- `engine`—The database engine, for example, `postgresql`.
- `username`—The username we chose earlier when creating the database.
- `password`—The password we chose earlier when creating the database.
- `hostname`—The database's hostname, which we obtained in the previous section from the `DBCluster.Endpoint` property of the payload returned by the `aws rds create-db-cluster` command.
- `port`—The port on which the database is running. Each database has its own default port, such as 5432 for PostgreSQL and 3306 for MySQL.
- `database_name`—The name of the database we're connecting to. In PostgreSQL, the default database is called `postgres`.

For example, for a PostgreSQL database, a typical connection string looks like this:

```
postgresql://username:password@localhost:5432/postgres
```

To store the database connection string as a Kubernetes secret, we run the following command:

```
$ kubectl create secret generic -n orders-service db-credentials \
--from-literal=DB_URL=<connection_string>
```

The previous command creates a secret object named `db-credentials` within the `orders-service` namespace. To get the details of this secret object, you can run the following command:

```
$ kubectl get secret db-credentials -n orders-service -o json
# output:
{
    "apiVersion": "v1",
    "data": {
        "DB_URL": "cG9zdGdyZXNxbDovL3VzZXJuYW1lOnBhc3N3b3JkQGNvZmZlZW1lc2gtZG
     IuY2x1c3RlciljYn
➥ Y0YWhnc2JjZWcuZXUtd2VzdC0xLnJkcy5hbWF6b25hd3MuY29tOjU0MzIvcG9zdGdyZXM="
    },
    "kind": "Secret",
    "metadata": {
        "creationTimestamp": "2021-11-19T15:21:42Z",
        "name": "db-credentials",
        "namespace": "orders-service",
        "resourceVersion": "599258",
        "uid": "d2c210e7-c61c-46b7-9f43-9407766e147c"
    },
    "type": "Opaque"
}
```

The secrets are listed under the `data` property of the payload, and they're Base64 encoded. To obtain their values, you can run the following command:

```
$ echo <DB_URL> | base64 --decode
```

where `<DB_URL>` is the Base64 encoded value of the `DB_URL` key.

To make the secret available to the orders service, we need to update the order service deployment to consume the secret and expose it as an environment variable.

Listing 14.4 Consuming secrets as environment variables in a deployment

```
# file: orders-service-deployment.yaml

apiVersion: apps/v1
kind: Deployment
metadata:
  name: orders-service
  namespace: orders-service
  labels:
    app: orders-service
spec:
  replicas: 1
```

```
  selector:
    matchLabels:
      app: orders-service
  template:
    metadata:
      labels:
        app: orders-service
    spec:
      containers:
      - name: orders-service
        image:
➥ <aws_account_id>.dkr.ecr.<aws_region>.amazonaws.com/coffeemesh-orders:1.0
        ports:
          - containerPort: 8000
        imagePullPolicy: Always
        envFrom:
          - secretRef:
              name: db-credentials
```

Environment configuration for the pods

Configuration for identifying the secret

Environment must be loaded from the secret named db-credentials.

Let's apply the changes by running the following command:

```
$ kubectl apply -f orders-service-deployment.yaml
```

Our service can now connect to the database! We're almost done. The final step is to apply the database migrations, which we'll accomplish in the next section.

14.7.3 Running the database migrations and connecting our service to the database

Our database is up and running, and now we can connect the orders service with it. However, before we can create records and run queries, we must ensure the database has the expected schemas. As we saw in chapter 7, the process of creating the database schemas is called migration. Our application's migrations are available under the migrations folder. In this section, we'll run the migrations against the Aurora Serverless database.

In the previous section, we deployed the Aurora database to our private subnets, which means we can't access our database directly to run the migrations. We have two main options to connect to the database: connect through a bastion server or create a Kubernetes Job that applies the migrations. Since we're working with Kubernetes and our cluster is already up and running, using a Kubernetes Job is a suitable option for us.

> **DEFINITION** A *bastion server* is a server that allows you to establish a secure connection with a private network. By connecting to the bastion server, you are able to access other servers within the private network.

To create the Kubernetes job, we first need to create a Docker image for running the database migrations. Create a file named migrations.dockerfile, and copy the contents of listing 14.5 into it. This Dockerfile installs both the production and the development dependencies and copies over the migrations and the Alembic configuration into the container. As we saw in chapter 7, we use Alembic to manage our database migrations. The command for this container is a one-off `alembic upgrade`.

Listing 14.5 Dockerfile for the database migrations job

```
# file: migrations.dockerfile

FROM python:3.9-slim

RUN mkdir -p /orders/orders

WORKDIR /orders

RUN pip install -U pip && pip install pipenv

COPY Pipfile Pipfile.lock /orders/

RUN pipenv install --dev --system --deploy

COPY orders/repository /orders/orders/repository/
COPY migrations /orders/migrations
COPY alembic.ini /orders/alembic.ini

ENV PYTHONPATH=/orders          <-- We set the PYTHONPATH environment variable.

CMD ["alembic", "upgrade", "heads"]
```

To build the Docker image, run the following command:

```
$ docker build -t
➥ <aws_account_number>.dkr.ecr.<aws_region>.amazonaws.com/coffeemesh-
➥ orders-migrations:1.0 -f migrations.dockerfile .
```

We're naming the image `coffeemesh-orders-migrations` and tagging it with version 1.0. Make sure you replace `<aws_account_id>` with your AWS account ID and `<aws_region>` with the region where you want to store your Docker builds. Before we push the image to the container registry, we need to create a repository:

```
$ aws ecr create-repository --repository-name coffeemesh-orders-migrations
```

Now let's push the image to the container registry:

```
$ docker push
➥ <aws_account_id>.dkr.ecr.<aws_region>.amazonaws.com/coffeemesh-orders-
➥ migrations:1.0
```

If your ECR credentials have expired, you can refresh them by running the following command again:

```
$ aws ecr get-login-password --region <aws_region> | docker login \
--username AWS --password-stdin \
<aws_account_id>.dkr.ecr.<aws_region>.amazonaws.com
```

Now that our image is ready, we need to create a Kubernetes Job object. We use a manifest file to create the Job. Create a file named orders-migrations-job.yaml and copy the contents of listing 14.6 into it. Listing 14.6 defines a Kubernetes object of type `Job` using the batch/v1 API. Just as we did in the previous section for the orders service, we expose the database connection string in the environment by loading the `db-credentials` secret using the `envFrom` property of the container's definition. We also set the `ttlSecondsAfterFinished` parameter to 30 seconds, which controls how long the pod will last in the `orders-service` namespace once it's finished the job.

Listing 14.6 Creating a database migrations job

```
# file: orders-migrations-job.yaml

apiVersion: batch/v1
kind: Job
metadata:
  name: orders-service-migrations
  namespace: orders-service
  labels:
    app: orders-service
spec:
  ttlSecondsAfterFinished: 30    <-- The pod must be deleted 30 seconds after completing.
  template:
    spec:
      containers:
      - name: orders-service-migrations
        image:
➥ <aws_account_id>.dkr.ecr.<aws_region>.amazonaws.com/coffeemesh-orders-
➥ migrations:1.0
        imagePullPolicy: Always
        envFrom:
          - secretRef:
              name: db-credentials
      restartPolicy: Never
```

Let's create the Job by running the following command:

```
$ kubectl apply -f orders-migrations-job.yaml
```

It'll take a few seconds until the `job`'s pod is up and running. You can check its status by running the following command:

```
$ kubectl get pods -n orders-service
```

Once the pod's status is `Running` or `Completed`, you can check the `job`'s logs by running the following command:

```
$ kubectl logs -f jobs/orders-service-migrations -n orders-service
```

Watching the pod's logs in this way is useful to check how the process is going and to spot any issues raised in its execution. Since the migration job is ephemeral and will be deleted after completion, make sure you check the logs while the process is running. Once the migrations job has completed, the database is finally ready to be used! We can finally interact with the orders service—the moment we've been waiting for! Our service is now ready for use. The next section explains one more change we need to make to finalize the deployment.

14.8 Updating the OpenAPI specification with the ALB's hostname

Now that our service is ready and the database is deployed and configured, it's time to play around with the application! In chapters 2 and 6, we learned to interact with our APIs using a Swagger UI. To use the Swagger UI in our deployment, we need to update the API specification with the hostname of our Kubernetes cluster's ALB. In this section, we update the order's API specification, make a new deployment, and test it.

Listing 14.7 Adding the ALB's hostname as a server

```
# file: oas.yaml

openapi: 3.0.0

info:
  title: Orders API
  description: API that allows you to manage orders for CoffeeMesh
  version: 1.0.0

servers:
  - url: <alb-hostname>
    description: ALB's hostname
  - url: https://coffeemesh.com
    description: main production server
  - url: https://coffeemesh-staging.com
    description: staging server for testing purposes only
  - url: http://localhost:8000
    description: URL for local testing

...
```

In listing 14.8, replace `<alb-hostname>` with the hostname of your own ALB. As we learned in section 14.6, you obtain the ALB's hostname by running the following command:

```
$ kubectl get ingress/orders-service-ingress -n orders-service -o json | \
jq '.status.loadBalancer.ingress[0].hostname'
# output:
# "k8s-ordersse-ordersse-8cf837ce7a-1036161040.<aws_region>.elb.amazonaws.com"
```

Now we need to rebuild our Docker image:

```
$ docker build -t
<aws_account_number>.dkr.ecr.<aws_region>.amazonaws.com/coffeemesh-
➥ orders:1.1 .
```

Then, we publish the new build to AWS ECR:

```
$ docker push
<aws_account_number>.dkr.ecr.<aws_region>.amazonaws.com/coffeemesh-
➥ orders:1.1
```

Next, we need to update the orders service deployment manifest.

Listing 14.8 Declaring a deployment manifest

```
# file: orders-service-deployment.yaml

apiVersion: apps/v1
kind: Deployment
metadata:
  name: orders-service
  namespace: orders-service
  labels:
    app: orders-service
spec:
  replicas: 1
  selector:
    matchLabels:
      app: orders-service
  template:
    metadata:
      labels:
        app: orders-service
    spec:
      containers:
      - name: orders-service
        image:
➥ <aws_account_id>.dkr.ecr.<aws_region>.amazonaws.com/coffeemesh-orders:1.1
        ports:
          - containerPort: 8000
        imagePullPolicy: Always
```

Finally, we apply the new deployment configuration by running the following command:

```
$ kubectl apply -f orders-service-deployment.yaml
```

Monitor the rollout by running the following command:

```
kubectl get pods -n orders-service
```

Once the old pod is terminated and the new one is up and running, load the order's service Swagger UI by pasting the ALB's hostname in a browser and visiting the /docs/orders page. You can play around with the API using the same approach you learned in chapters 2 and 6: creating orders, modifying them, and fetching their details from the server.

And the journey is finally complete! If you've been able to follow up to this point and managed to get your Kubernetes cluster up and running, please accept my most sincere congratulations! You've made it! Figure 14.12 shows a high-level overview of the architecture you've deployed in this chapter.

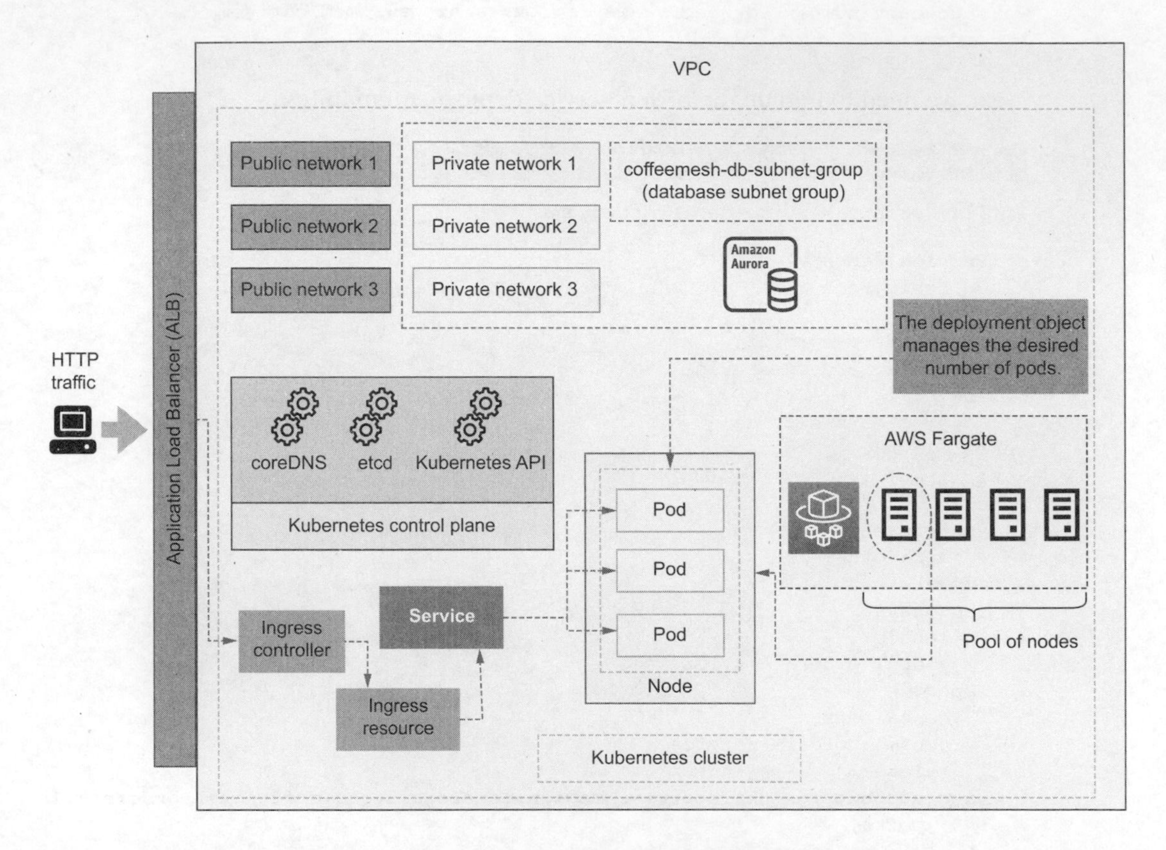

Figure 14.12 High-level overview of the architecture deployed in this chapter

The overview of Kubernetes in this chapter is a brief one, but it's enough to get an understanding of how Kubernetes works, and it's sufficient to get a cluster up and running in your production environment. If you work or intend to work with Kubernetes, I strongly encourage you to continue reading about this technology. You can check all the references I've cited in this chapter, to which I'd like to add Marko Lukša's fundamental *Kubernetes in Action* (2nd ed., Manning, expected 2023).

In the next section, we'll delete all the resources we created during this chapter. Don't miss it if you don't want to be charged more than needed!

14.9 Deleting the Kubernetes cluster

This section explains how to delete all the resources we created in this chapter. This step is crucial to make sure you don't get billed for the Kubernetes cluster once you've finished working through the examples. As you can see in figure 14.13, we have dependency relationships among some of our resources. To successfully delete all resources, we must delete them in reverse order of their dependencies. For example, the database cluster depends on the database subnet group, which depends on the VPC subnets, which depend on the VPC. In this case, we'll start by deleting the database cluster, and in the last step we'll delete the VPC.

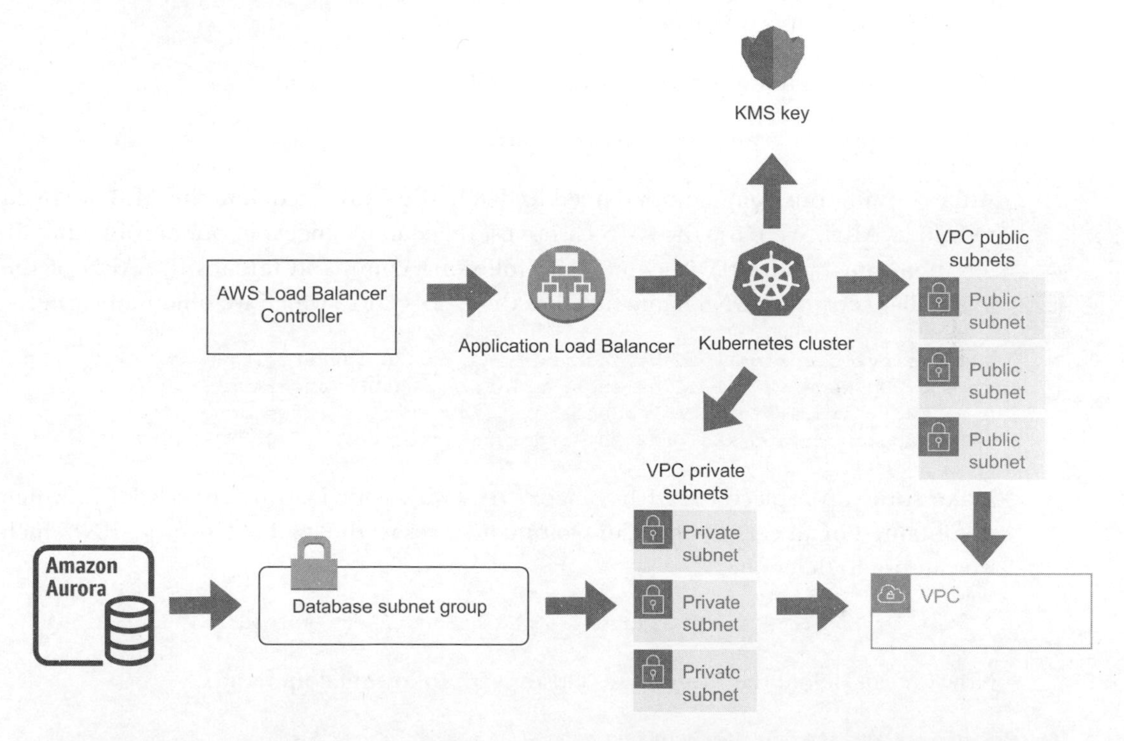

Figure 14.13 The resources in our stack have relationships of dependency. The direction of dependency is indicated by the direction of the arrows. To delete the resources, we start by deleting those that have no arrows pointing to them.

Let's delete the database cluster with the following command:

```
$ aws rds delete-db-cluster --db-cluster-identifier coffeemesh-db \
--skip-final-snapshot
```

The `--skip-final-snapshot` flag instructs the command not to create a snapshot of the database before deletion. It takes a few minutes for the database to be deleted. Once it's deleted, we can delete the database subnet group with the following command:

```
$ aws rds delete-db-subnet-group --db-subnet-group-name \
coffeemesh-db-subnet-group
```

Next, let's delete the AWS Load Balancer Controller. Deleting the AWS Load Balancer Controller is a two-step process: first we uninstall the controller using `helm`, and then we delete the ALB that was created when we installed the controller. To delete the ALB we need its URL, so let's fetch that value first (make sure you run this step before uninstalling with `helm`):

```
$ kubectl get ingress/orders-service-ingress -n orders-service -o json | \
jq '.status.loadBalancer.ingress[0].hostname'
# output: "k8s-ordersse-ordersse-8cf837ce7a-
➥ 1036161040.<aws_region>.elb.amazonaws.com"
```

Now let's uninstall the controller with the following command:

```
$ helm uninstall aws-load-balancer-controller -n kube-system
```

After running this command, we need to delete the ALB. To delete the ALB, we need to find its ARN. We'll use the AWS CLI to list the load balancers in our account and filter them out by their DNS name. The following command fetches the ARN of the load balancer whose DNS name matches the ALB's URL, which we obtained earlier:

```
$ aws elbv2 describe-load-balancers | jq '.LoadBalancers[] | \
select(.DNSName == "<load_balancer_url>") | .LoadBalancerArn'
# output: "arn:aws:elasticloadbalancing:<aws_region>:<aws_account_id>:
➥ loadbalancer/app/k8s-ordersse-ordersse-8cf837ce7a/cf708f97c2485719"
```

Make sure you replace `<load_balancer_url>` with your load balancer's URL, which we obtained in an earlier step. This command gives us the load balancer's ARN, which we can use to delete it:

```
$ aws elbv2 delete-load-balancer --load-balancer-arn "<load_balancer_arn>"
```

Now we can delete the Kubernetes cluster with following command:

```
$ eksctl delete cluster coffeemesh
```

Finally, let's delete the KMS key we created earlier to encrypt our Kubernetes secrets. To delete the key, we run the following command:

```
$ aws kms schedule-key-deletion --key-id <key_id>
```

where `<key_id>` is the ID of the key we created earlier.

Summary

- Kubernetes is a container orchestration tool that's becoming a standard for deploying microservices at scale. Using Kubernetes helps us to move across cloud providers while keeping a consistent interface to our services.
- The three major managed Kubernetes services are Google's Kubernetes Engine (GKE), Azure's Kubernetes Service (AKS), and AWS's Elastic Kubernetes Service (EKS). In this chapter, we learned to deploy a Kubernetes cluster with EKS, which is the most widely adopted Kubernetes managed service.

- We can deploy a Kubernetes cluster in AWS using the console, CloudFormation, or the eksctl command-line tool. In this chapter, we used the eksctl CLI since it's the AWS recommended way to manage a Kubernetes cluster.
- To make our Kubernetes cluster reachable from the internet, we use an ingress controller such as the AWS Load Balancer Controller.
- To deploy a microservice to a Kubernetes cluster, we create the following resources:
  - A `Deployment`, which manages the desired state of the pods, processes that run the Docker build
  - A `Service` that allows us to expose our application as a web service
  - An `Ingress` object bound to the ingress controller (the AWS Load Balancer Controller) that forwards traffic to the service
- Aurora Serverless is a powerful database engine and a convenient choice for microservices. With Aurora Serverless, you only pay for what you use, and you don't need to worry about scaling the database, thereby reducing your costs and the time you spend managing it.
- To securely feed sensitive configuration details to your applications in Kubernetes, we use Kubernetes secrets. With EKS, we have two strategies for managing Kubernetes secrets securely:
  - Using the AWS Secrets & Configuration Provider for Kubernetes
  - Using Kubernetes secrets in combination with the AWS Key Managed Service

appendix A
Types of web APIs and protocols

In this appendix, we study the API protocols we can use to implement application interfaces. Each of these protocols evolved to address specific problems in the integration between API consumers and producers. We discuss the benefits and the limitations of each protocol so that we can make the best choice when designing and building our own APIs. We will discuss the following protocols:

- RPC and its variants, JSON-RPC and XML-RPC
- SOAP
- gRPC
- REST
- GraphQL

Choosing the right type of API is fundamental for the performance and integration strategy of our microservices. The factors that will condition our choice of API protocol include these:

- Whether the API is public or private
- Type of API consumer: small devices, mobile applications, browsers, or other microservices
- The capabilities and resources we wish to expose; for example, whether it is a hierarchical data model that can be organized around endpoints or a highly interconnected net of resources with cross-references among them

We take these factors into consideration when discussing the benefits and constraints of each protocol in the following sections to assess their suitability for different scenarios.

A.1 The dawn of APIs: RPC, XML-RPC, and JSON-RPC

Let's begin by explaining a remote procedure call and its two most common implementations, namely, XML-RPC and JSON-RPC. As you can see in figure A.1, a *remote procedure call* (RPC) is a protocol that allows a client to invoke a procedure or subroutine in a different machine. The origins of this form of communication go back to the 1980s, with the emergence of distributed computing systems, and over time it has evolved into standard implementations.[1] Two popular implementations are XML-RPC and JSON-RPC.

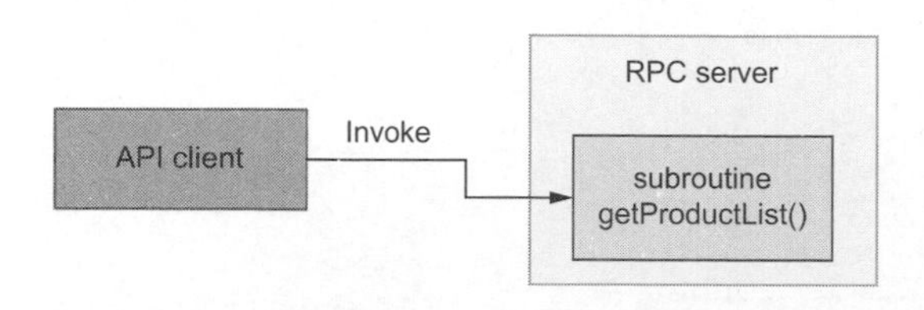

Figure A.1 Using RPC, a program invokes a function or subroutine from the API server.

XML-RPC is an RPC protocol that uses Extensible Markup Language (XML) over HTTP to exchange data between a client and a server. It was created by Dave Winer in 1998, and it eventually grew into what later came to be known as SOAP (see section A.2).

With the increasing popularity of JavaScript Object Notation (JSON) as a data serialization format, an alternative implementation of RPC came in the form of JSON-RPC. It was introduced in 2005 and offers a simplified way for exchanging data between an API client and the server. As you can see in figure A.2, JSON-RPC payloads usually include three properties:

- `method`—The method or function that the client wishes to invoke in the remote server
- `params`—The parameters that must be passed to the method or function on invocation
- `id`—A value to identify the request

In turn, JSON-RPC response payloads include the following parameters:

- `result`—The value returned by the invoked method or function
- `error`—An error code raised during the invocation, if any
- `id`—The ID of the request which is being handled

RPC is a lightweight protocol that allows you to drive API integrations without having to implement complex interfaces. An RPC client only needs to know the name of the

[1] Bruce Jay Nelson is credited with the introduction of the term *remote procedure call* in his doctoral dissertation (Technical Report CSL-81-9, Xero Palo Alto Research Center, Palo Alto CA, 1981). For a more formal description of the implementation requirements of RPC, see Andrew B. Birrell and Bruce Jay Nelson, "Implementing Remote Procedure Calls," *ACM Transactions on Computer Systems*, vol. 2, no. 1, 1984, pp. 39–59.

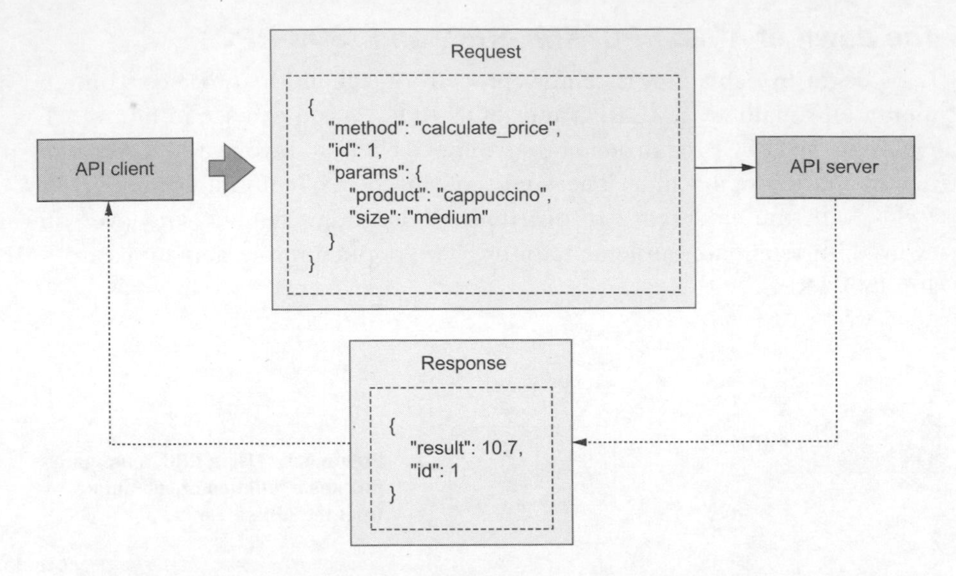

Figure A.2 Using JSON-RPC, an API client sends a request to an API server invoking the `calculate_price()` function to get the price of a medium cup of cappuccino. The server responds with the result of the invocation: $10.70.

function it needs to invoke in the remote server, with its signature. It doesn't need to look for different endpoints and comply with their schemas as in REST. However, the lack of a proper interface layer between the API consumer and the producer inevitably tends to create tight coupling between the client and the implementation details of the server. As a consequence, a small change in implementation details risks breaking the integration. For this reason, RPC is recommended mostly for internal API integrations, where you're in full control of both the client and the server.

A.2 SOAP and the emergence of API standards

This section discusses the Simple Object Access Protocol (SOAP). SOAP enables communication with web services through the exchange of XML payloads. It was introduced in 1998 by Dave Winer, Don Box, Bob Atkisnon, and Mohsen Al-Ghosein for Microsoft, and after a number of iterations, it became a standard protocol for web applications in 2003. SOAP was conceived as a messaging protocol, and it runs on top of a data transport layer, such as HTTP.

SOAP was designed to meet three major goals:

- *Extensibility*—SOAP can be extended with capabilities found in other messaging systems.
- *Neutrality*—It can operate over any data transfer protocol of choice, including HTTP, or directly over TCP or UDP, among others.
- *Independence*—It enables communication between web applications regardless of their programming models.

The payloads exchanged with a SOAP endpoint are represented in XML, and as illustrated in figure A.3, they include the following properties:

- `Envelope` *(required)*—Identifies the XML document as a SOAP payload
- `Header` *(optional)*—Includes additional information about the data contained in the message, for example, the type of encoding
- `Body` *(required)*—Contains the payload (actual message being exchanged) of the request/response
- `Fault` *(optional)*—Contains errors that occurred while processing the request

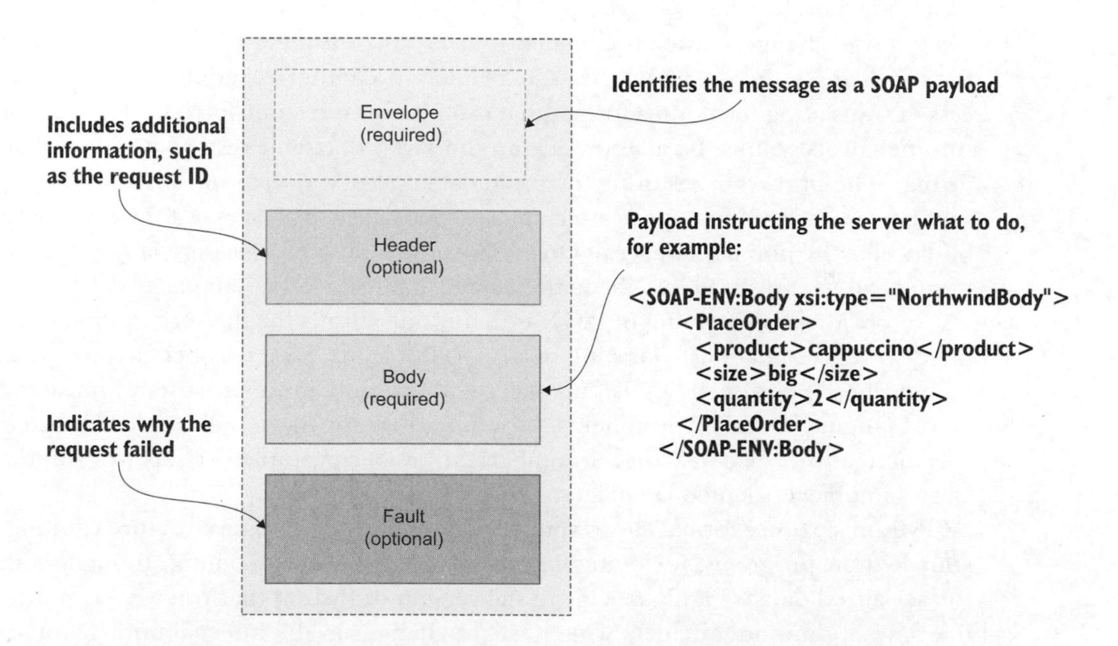

Figure A.3 At the top of a SOAP message, we find a section called `Envelope` that tells us that this is a SOAP payload. An optional `Header` section includes metadata about the message, such as the type of encoding. The `Body` section includes the actual payload of the message: the data being exchanged between the client and the server. Finally, a section called `Fault` includes details of any errors raised while processing the payload.

SOAP was a major contribution to the field of APIs. The availability of a standard protocol for communication across web applications led to the emergence of vendor APIs. Suddenly, it was possible to sell digital services by simply exposing an API that everybody could understand and consume.

In recent years, SOAP has been superseded by newer protocols and architectures. The factors that contributed to the decline of SOAP include these:

- The payloads exchanged through SOAP contain large XML documents, which consume a large amount of bandwidth.

- XML is difficult to read and maintain, and it requires careful parsing, which makes exchanging messages structured in XML less convenient.
- SOAP does not provide a clear framework for organizing the data and capabilities that we want to expose through an API. It provides a way of exchanging messages, and it is up to the agents involved on both sides of the API to decide how to make sense of such messages.

A.3 RPC strikes again: Fast exchanges over gRPC

This section discusses a specific implementation of the RPC protocol called gRPC,[2] which was developed by Google in 2015. This protocol uses HTTP/2 as a transport layer and exchanges payloads encoded with Protocol Buffers (Protobuf)—a method for serializing structured data. As we explained in chapter 2, serialization is the process of translating data into a format that can be stored or transferred over a network. Another process must be able to pick up the saved data and restore it to its original format. The process of restoring serialized data is also known as *unmarshalling*.

Some serialization methods are language specific, such as `pickle` for Python. Some others, like the popular JavaScript Object Notation (JSON) format, are language agnostic and can be translated into the native data structures of other languages.

An obvious shortcoming of JSON is that it only allows for the serialization of simple data representations consisting of strings, Booleans, arrays, associative arrays, and `null` values. Because JSON is language agnostic and must be strictly transferable across languages and environments, it cannot allow for the serialization of language-specific features, like `NaN` (not a number) in JavaScript, tuples or sets in Python, or classes in object-oriented languages.

Python's `pickle` format allows you to serialize any type of data structure running in your Python programs, including custom objects. The shortcoming, though, is that the serialized data is highly specific to the version of Python that you were running at the time of dumping the data. Due to slight changes in the internal implementation of Python between different releases, you cannot expect a different process to be able to reliably parse a pickled file.

Protobuf comes somewhere in between: it allows you to define more complex data structures than JSON, including enumerations, and it is able to generate native classes from the serialized data, which you can extend to add custom functionality. As you can see in figure A.4, in gRPC you must first define the schema for the data structures that you want to exchange over the API using the Protobuf specification format, and then use the Protubuf CLI to automatically generate code for both the client and the API server.

---

[2] You're surely wondering what the "g" in gRPC stands for. According to the official documentation, it stands for a different word in every release. For example, in version 1.1 it stands for "good," while in version 1.2 it stands for "green," and so on (https://grpc.github.io/grpc/core/md_doc_g_stands_for.html). Some people believe that the "g" stands for Google, as this protocol was invented by Google (see "Is gRPC the Future of Client-Server Communication?" by Bleeding Edge Press, *Medium*, July 19, 2018, https://medium.com/@EdgePress/is-grpc-the-future-of-client-server-communication-b112acf9f365).

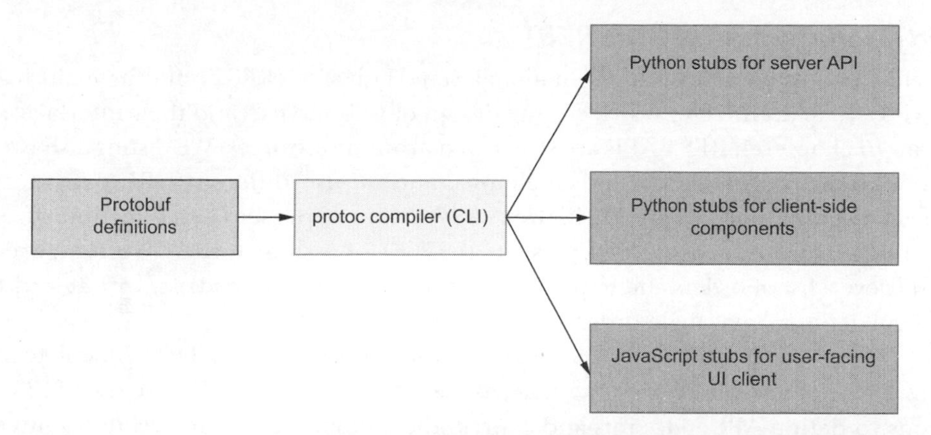

Figure A.4 gRPC uses Protobuf to encode the data exchanged through the API. Using the `protoc` CLI, we can generate code (stubs) for both the client and the server from a Protobuf specification.

The data structures generated from the Protobuf specifications are called *stubs*. The stubs are implemented in code native to the language we use to build the API client and the server. As you can see in figure A.5, the stubs take care of parsing and validating the data exchanged between client and server.

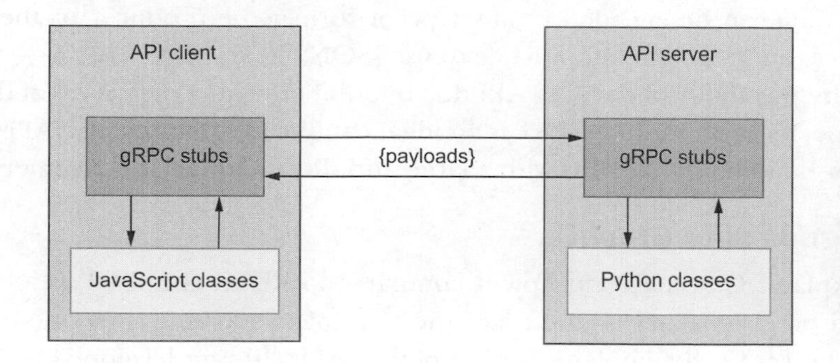

Figure A.5 The stubs generated with Protobuf take care of parsing the payloads exchanged between the API client and the API server and translating them into native code.

gRPC offers a more reliable approach for API integrations than plain RPC. The use of Protobuf serves as an enforcement mechanism that ensures the data exchanged between the client and the server comes in the expected format. It also helps to make sure that communication over the API is highly optimized, since the data is exchanged directly in binary format. For this reason, gRPC is an ideal candidate for the implementation of internal API integrations where performance is a relevant factor.[3]

[3] According to Postman's 2022 State of the API Report, 11% of the surveyed developers use gRPC (https://www.postman.com/state-of-api/api-technologies/#api-technologies).

A.4 HTTP-native APIs with REST

This section explains Representational State Transfer (REST) and its main features. REST is an architectural style for the design of web services and their interfaces. As we saw in chapter 4, REST APIs are structured around resources. We distinguish two types of resources, collections and singletons, and we use different URL paths to represent them. For example, in figure A.6, `/orders` represents a collection of orders, while `/orders/{order_id}` represents the URI of a single order. We use `/orders` to retrieve a list of orders and to place new orders, and we use `/orders/{order_id}` to perform actions on a single order.

Good REST API design leverages features from the HTTP protocol to deliver highly expressive APIs. For example, as you can see in figure A.7, we use HTTP methods to define API endpoints and express their intent (POST to create resources and GET to retrieve resources); we use HTTP status codes to signal the result of processing a request; and we use HTTP payloads to carry exchange data between the client and the server.

We document REST APIs using the OpenAPI standard, which was originally created in 2010 by Tony Tam under the name Swagger API. The project gained in popularity, and in 2015 the OpenAPI Initiative was launched to maintain the specification. In 2016, the specification was officially released under the name OpenAPI Specification (OAS).

The data exchanged through a REST API goes in the body of an HTTP request/response. This data can be encoded in any type of format the producer of the API wishes to enforce, but it is common practice to use JSON.

Thanks to the possibility of creating API documentation with a high level of detail in a standard specification format, REST is an ideal candidate for enterprise API integrations and for building public APIs with a large and diverse range of consumers.

A.5 Granular queries with GraphQL

This section explains GraphQL and how it compares to REST. GraphQL is a query language based on graphs and nodes. As of the time of this writing, it is one of the most popular choices for the implementation of web APIs.[4] It was developed by Facebook in 2012 and publicly released in 2015.

GraphQL is designed to address some of the limitations of REST APIs, such as the difficulty of representing certain operations through HTTP endpoints. For example, let's say you ordered a cup of coffee through the CoffeeMesh website, and later you change your mind and decide to cancel the order. Which HTTP method is most appropriate to represent this action? You can argue that cancelling an order is akin to deleting it, so you could use the DELETE method. But, is cancelling really the same as deleting? Are you going to delete the order from your records after cancellation?

[4] According to Postman's 2022 State of the API Report, 28% of the surveyed developers use GraphQL (https://www.postman.com/state-of-api/api-technologies/#api-technologies).

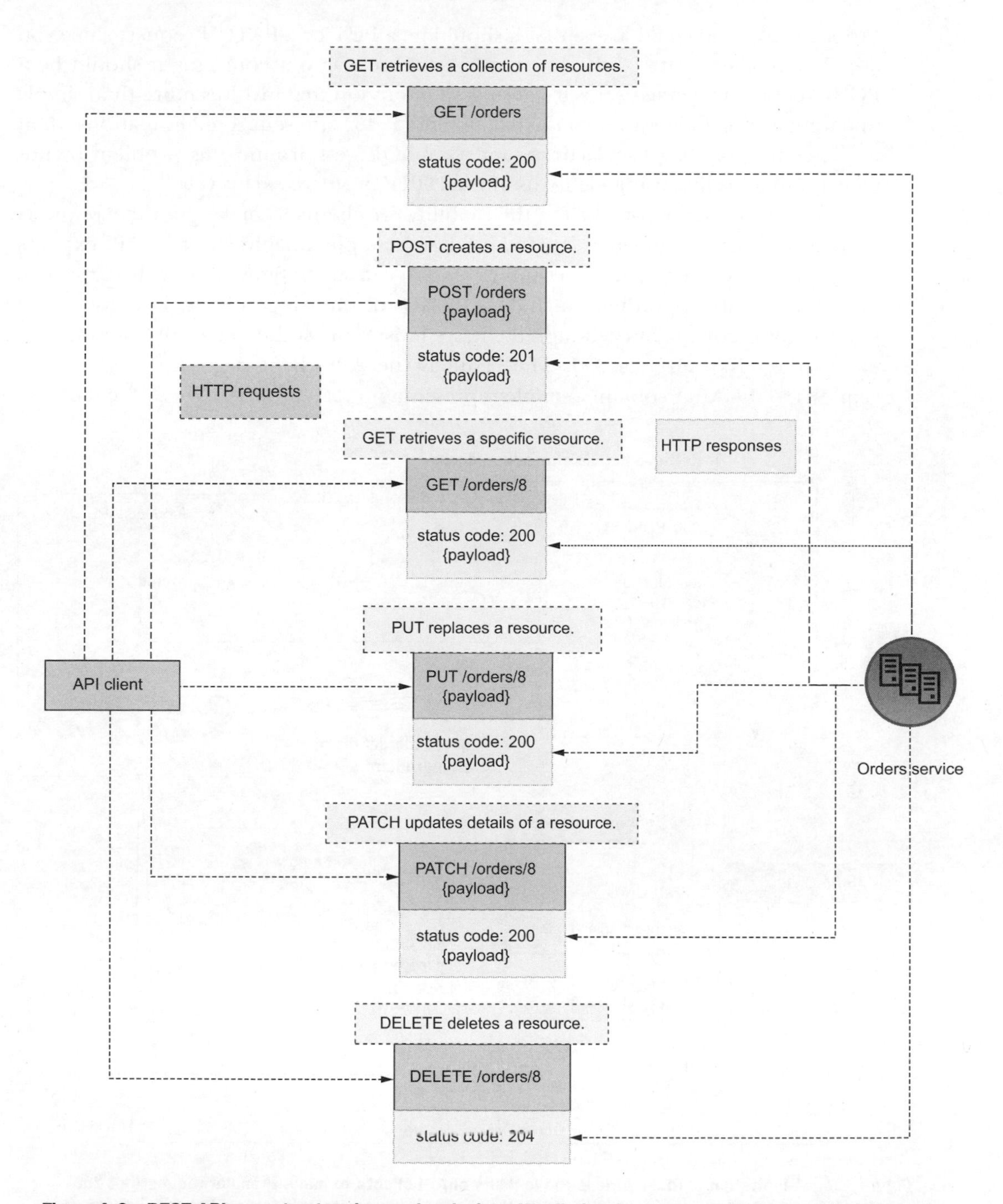

Figure A.6 REST APIs are structured around endpoints. We distinguish between singleton endpoints, such as GET `/orders/8`, and collection endpoints, such as GET `/orders`. Leveraging the semantics of HTTP methods, REST API responses include HTTP status codes that signal the result of processing the request.

Probably not. You could argue that it should be a PUT or a PATCH request since you are changing the state of the order to `cancelled`. Or you could say it should be a POST request since the user is triggering an operation that involves more than simply updating a record. However you look at it, HTTP does present some limitations when it comes to modeling user actions, and GraphQL gets around this problem by not constraining itself to using elements of the HTTP protocol exclusively.

Another limitation of REST is the inability for clients to make granular requests of data, technically known as *overfetching*. For example, imagine that an API exposes `/products` and `/ingredients` resources. As you can see in figure A.7, with `/products` we can get a list of products, including the IDs of their ingredients. However, if we want to get the name of each ingredient, we must request the details of each ingredient to the `/ingredients` API. The result is the API client needs to send various requests to the API to obtain a simple representation of a product. The API client also

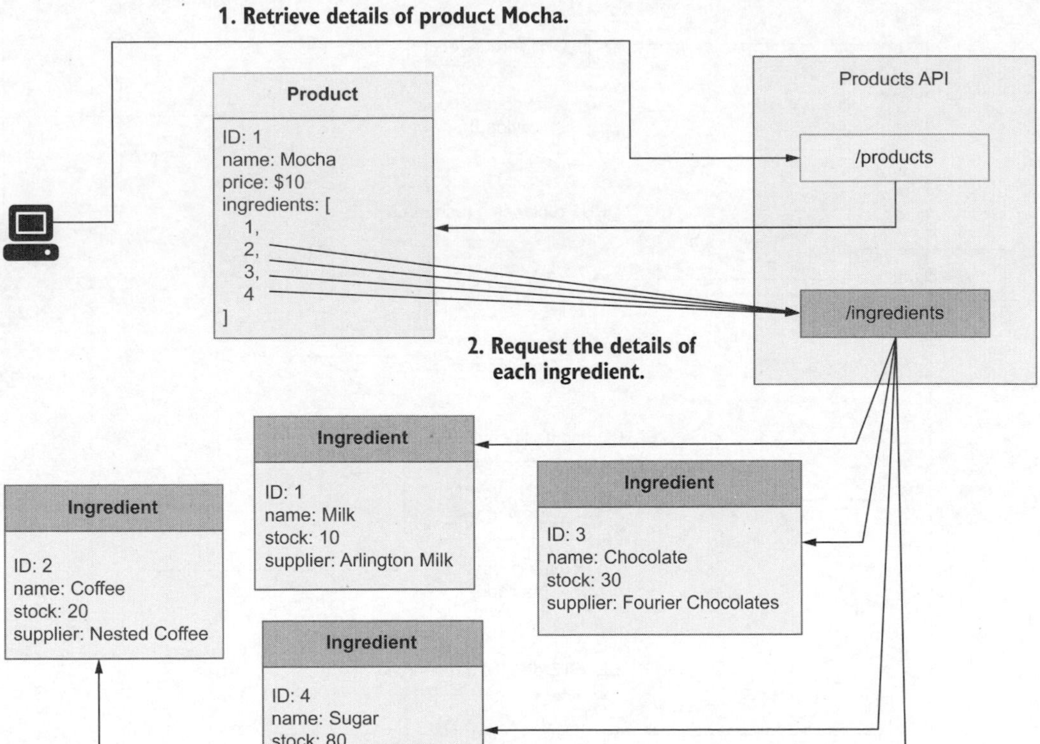

Figure A.7 A limitation of REST APIs is the inability of API clients to make granular requests of data, otherwise known as overfetching. In the figure, the `/products` endpoint returns a list of products with the IDs of their ingredients. To obtain the ingredients' names, the client must request the details of each ingredient from the `/ingredients` endpoint. As a result, the API client ends up making too many requests to the server and receiving more data than it needs.

receives more information than it needs: in each request against the `/ingredients` API, the client receives a full description of each ingredient, when it only needs the name. Overfetching is a challenge for small devices such as mobile phones, which may not be able to handle and store large amounts of data and may have more limited network access.

GraphQL avoids these problems by allowing clients to make granular queries on the server. With GraphQL, we can create relationships between different data models, allowing API clients to fetch data from related entities. For example, in figure A.8, an API client can request a list of products and the names of their ingredients in a single request. By allowing clients to retrieve the data they need from the server in a single request, GraphQL is an ideal candidate for APIs, which are consumed by clients with limited network access or limited storage capabilities, such as mobile devices. GraphQL is also a good choice for APIs with highly interconnected resources, in which users are likely to fetch data from related entities, such as products and ingredients in figure A.8.

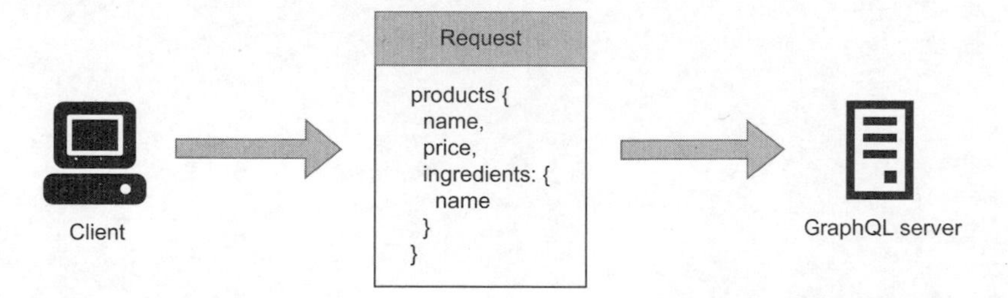

Figure A.8 Using a GraphQL API, we can query data from related entities, such as products and ingredients. In this figure, an API client requests a list of products with the names of their ingredients.

Despite its benefits, GraphQL also comes with constraints. A major limitation of GraphQL is that it doesn't provide great support for custom scalar types. GraphQL ships with a basic set of built-in scalars, such as integer (`Int`) and string (`String`). GraphQL allows you to declare your own custom scalars, but you can't document their shape or how they're validated using the SDL. In the words of GraphQL's official documentation, "It's up to our implementation to define how that type should be serialized, deserialized, and validated" (https://graphql.org/learn/schema/). Since one of the cornerstones of robust API integrations is great documentation, GraphQL is a challenging choice for public APIs that must be reliably consumed by external clients.

Another limitation of GraphQL is that all the queries are typically done with POST requests, which makes it more difficult to cache the responses. In my experience, most developers also find it more difficult to interact with a GraphQL API. In fact, Postman's 2022 State of the API Report found that only 28% of the surveyed developers use GraphQL, and up to 14% of them hadn't heard of it. While interacting with a

REST API may be as simple as hitting a GET endpoint, with GraphQL you must know how to build query documents and how to send them to the server. Since developers are less familiar with GraphQL, choosing this technology may make your APIs less likely to be consumed.

appendix B Managing an API's life cycle

APIs are very rarely static. As your product evolves, you need to expose new capabilities and features through your API, and this means that you will need to create new endpoints or change your schemas to introduce new entities or fields. Often, API changes are backward incompatible, which means clients who are unaware of the new changes will get failed responses to their requests. Part of managing an API is making sure that any changes you make don't break the integrations that already exist with other applications, and API versioning serves that purpose. In this appendix, we study API versioning strategies to manage API changes.

In addition to evolving and changing, APIs also sometimes come to an end. Perhaps you're migrating a REST API to GraphQL, or you're ceasing a product altogether. If you're planning to deprecate an API, you must let your clients know when and how it'll happen, and in the second part of this appendix, you'll learn to broadcast this information to your users.

B.1 Versioning strategies for evolving APIs

Let's see how we use versioning to manage API changes. We use two major types of versioning systems for APIs:

- *Semantic versioning* (SemVer, https://semver.org/)—This is the most common type of versioning, and it is widely used to manage software releases. It has the following format: MAJOR.MINOR.PATCH, for example, 1.1.0. The first number indicates the major version of the release, the second number indicates the minor version, and the third number indicates the patch version.

  The major version changes whenever you make a breaking change to the API, for example, when a new field is required in a request payload. Minor versions represent nonbreaking changes to the API, such as the introduction of a new optional query parameter. Your API consumers expect to be able to keep calling your endpoints in the same way on different minor versions and continue to obtain responses. Patch versions indicate bug fixes.

In the context of APIs, we typically only use the major version, so we may have v1 and v2 of an API. Minor changes and patches that improve the API can generally be rolled out without the risk of breaking existing integrations.

- Calendar versioning (CalVer, https://calver.org/)—Calendar versioning uses calendar dates to version releases. This system is useful when your APIs change very often, or when your releases are time sensitive. An increasing number of software products use calendar versioning, including Ubuntu (https://ubuntu.com/). AWS also uses calendar versioning in some of its products, such as CloudFormation (http://mng.bz/epQZ) and the S3 API (http://mng.bz/p6B0).

  CalVer does not provide a full specification about how to format your versions; it only emphasizes the use of dates. Some projects use the format YYYY.MM.DD, while others use YY.MM. If you make several releases per day, you can use an additional counter to keep track of each release, for example, 2022.12.01.3, which means this is the third release made on the 12th of December in 2022. (For more details on calendar versioning, see http://mng.bz/O6MO.)

Which type of versioning system is better? It depends on your specific needs and your overall API management strategy. SemVer is more commonly used since it's more intuitive. However, if your product rollouts are time sensitive, CalVer is a better fit. Your choice of versioning system will also be affected by your versioning management strategy, so let's take a look at the different methods we use to indicate the version of our APIs:

- *Versioning using the URL*—You can embed the API version in the URL, for example, https://coffeemesh.com/api/v1/coffee. This is very convenient because consumers of your API know that they will always be able to call the same endpoint and get the same results. If you release a new version of your API, that version will go into a different URL path (/api/v2) and therefore will not conflict with your previous releases. It also makes your API easier to explore, since, to discover and test different versions of it, API consumers only need to change the version field in the URL. On the downside, when working with REST APIs, using the URL to manage versions is considered a violation of the principles of REST since every resource should be represented by one and only one URI.
- *Versioning using the* `Accept Header` *field*—An API consumer uses the `Accept` HTTP request `Header` field to advertise the type of content they can parse. In the context of APIs, the typical value of the `Accept Header` is `application/json`, which means the client only accepts data in JSON format. Since the API version also influences the type of content we receive from the server, we can use the `Header` field to advertise which API version we want to use. An example

of a `Header` field that specifies the content type and API version is `Accept: application/json;v1`.

This approach is more harmonious with the principles of REST since it does not modify the resource endpoints, but it requires careful parsing. Introducing additional characters in the header's value, as in the following snippet, can cause errors at runtime:

```
Accept: application/json; v1  # note the additional space after the
➥ semicolon
```

Since we're using the `Accept` header, we respond with a 415 (Unsupported Media Type) to any errors in the API version declaration, or when the client requests an unavailable version of the API.

- *Versioning using custom* `Request Header` *fields*—In this approach, you use a custom `Request Header` field such as `Accept-version` to specify the version of the API you want to use. This approach is the least preferred, since some frameworks may not accept nonstandard `Header` fields, thus leading to integration issues with your clients.

Each versioning strategy comes with its own benefits and challenges. URL versioning is the most adopted strategy since it's intuitive and easy to use. However, indicating the API version in the URL also means that our resource URIs change depending on the version of the API, which may be confusing for some clients.

Using the `Accept` header is another popular option, but it couples the logic for handling our media types with the logic for handling our API versions. Also, using the same error status code for both media types and API versions may be confusing for our API clients. The best strategy is to carefully consider the needs of our application and to agree with your API clients on the most preferred solution.

B.2 Managing the life cycle of your APIs

In this section, we study strategies to gracefully deprecate our APIs. APIs don't last forever; as the products and services that you offer through APIs evolve and change, some of your APIs will become deprecated, and you will eventually retire them. However, you may have external consumers whose systems depend on your APIs, so you cannot just take them down without causing disruption to your clients. You must orchestrate your API deprecation process, and as you'll see, we use specific HTTP headers to give notice of API deprecation. Let's see how that works!

Before you retire an API, you should deprecate it first. A deprecated API is still in service, but it lacks maintenance, enhancements, and fixes. Once you deprecate your APIs, your users won't expect further changes to them. Deprecation serves as a grace period for your users to give them time to migrate their systems to a new API without disrupting their operations.

As soon as you decide to deprecate your API, you should announce it to your API consumers through a standard communication channel, such as by email or in a newsletter. At the same time, you should set the `Deprecation` header in your responses.[1] If the API is going to be deprecated in the future, we set the `Deprecation` header to the date when the API will be deprecated:

```
Deprecation: Friday, 22nd March 2025 23:59:59 GMT
```

Once the API is deprecated, we set the `Deprecation` header to `true`:

```
Deprecation: true
```

You can also use the `Link` header to provide additional information about your API deprecation process. For example, you can provide a link to your deprecation policy:

```
Link: <https://coffeemesh.com/deprecation>; rel="deprecation";
➥ type="text/html"
```

In this case, we are telling the user that they can follow the link https://coffeemesh.com/deprecation to find additional information about the deprecation of the API.

If you're deprecating an old version of your API, you can use the `Link` header to provide the URL that replaces or supersedes the current API version:

```
Link: <https://coffeemesh.com/v2.0.0/coffee>; rel="successor-version"
```

In addition to broadcasting the deprecation of your APIs, you should also announce when the API will be retired. We use the `Sunset` header to signal when the API will be retired:[2]

```
Sunset: Friday, 22nd June 2025 23:59:59 GMT
```

The date of the `Sunset` header must be later or the same as the date given in the `Deprecation` header. Once you've retired an API, you must let your API clients know that the old endpoints are no longer available. You may use any combination of 3xx and 4xx status codes when a user calls the old API. A good option is the 410 (Gone) status code. We use the 410 status code to signal that the requested resource no longer exists for a known reason. In some circumstances, 301 (Moved Permanently) might be useful. We use the 301 status code to signal that the requested resource has been assigned a new URI, and therefore it may be useful when you migrate your API to a new endpoint.

Proper management of API changes and deprecations is a crucial yet often overlooked ingredient necessary to deliver high-quality and reliable API integrations. By applying the recommendations from this appendix, you'll be able to evolve your APIs with confidence and without breaking integrations with your clients.

---

[1] Sanjay Dalal and Erik Wilde, "The Deprecation HTTP Header Field," https://datatracker.ietf.org/doc/html/draft-ietf-httpapi-deprecation-header-02.

[2] Erik Wilde, "The Sunset HTTP Header Field," RFC 8594, https://tools.ietf.org/html/rfc8594.

appendix C
API authorization using an identity provider

In chapter 11, you learned how the Open Authorization (OAuth) and the OpenID Connect (OIDC) protocols work. You also learned how to produce, inspect, and validate JSON Web Tokens (JWTs). Finally, you learned a pattern for adding authorization middleware to your APIs. The question we still need to answer is, how do we build an end-to-end authentication and authorization system?

You can use various strategies to handle authentication and authorization. You can build your own authentication service, or you can use an identity-as-a-service provider, such as Auth0, Okta, Azure Active Directory, or AWS Cognito. Unless you're an expert in web security and authentication protocols and have sufficient resources to build the system correctly, I recommend you use an identity service provider. In this appendix, you'll learn to add authentication to your APIs with Auth0, which is one of the most popular identity management systems.

We'll use Auth0's free plan. Auth0 takes care of managing user accounts and issuing secure tokens, and it also provides easy integrations for social login with identity providers such as Google, Facebook, Twitter, and others. Auth0's authentication system is built on standards, so everything you learn about authenticating with Auth0 applies to any other provider. If you use a different authentication system in your own projects or at work, you'll be able to take the lessons from this appendix and apply them to whichever other system you use.

The code for this appendix is available under the appendix_c folder in the GitHub repository for this book. I recommend you pull this code to follow along with the examples, in particular, the folder named appendix_c/ui since you'll need it to run the examples in section C.2.

C.1 Using an identity as a service provider

This section explains how to integrate our code with an identity-as-a-service (IDaaS) provider. An IDaaS provider is a service that takes care of handling user authentication and issuing access tokens for our users. Using an IDaaS provider is convenient, since it means we can focus our time and efforts on building our APIs. Good IDaaS providers are built on standards and with strong security protocols, which also reduces the security risks of our servers. In this section, you'll learn how to build an integration with Auth0, which is one of the most popular IDaaS providers.

To work with Auth0, first create an account, and then create a tenant following Auth0's documentation (https://auth0.com/docs/get-started). As a first step, go to your dashboard and create an API to represent the orders API. Configure it as shown in figure C.1,

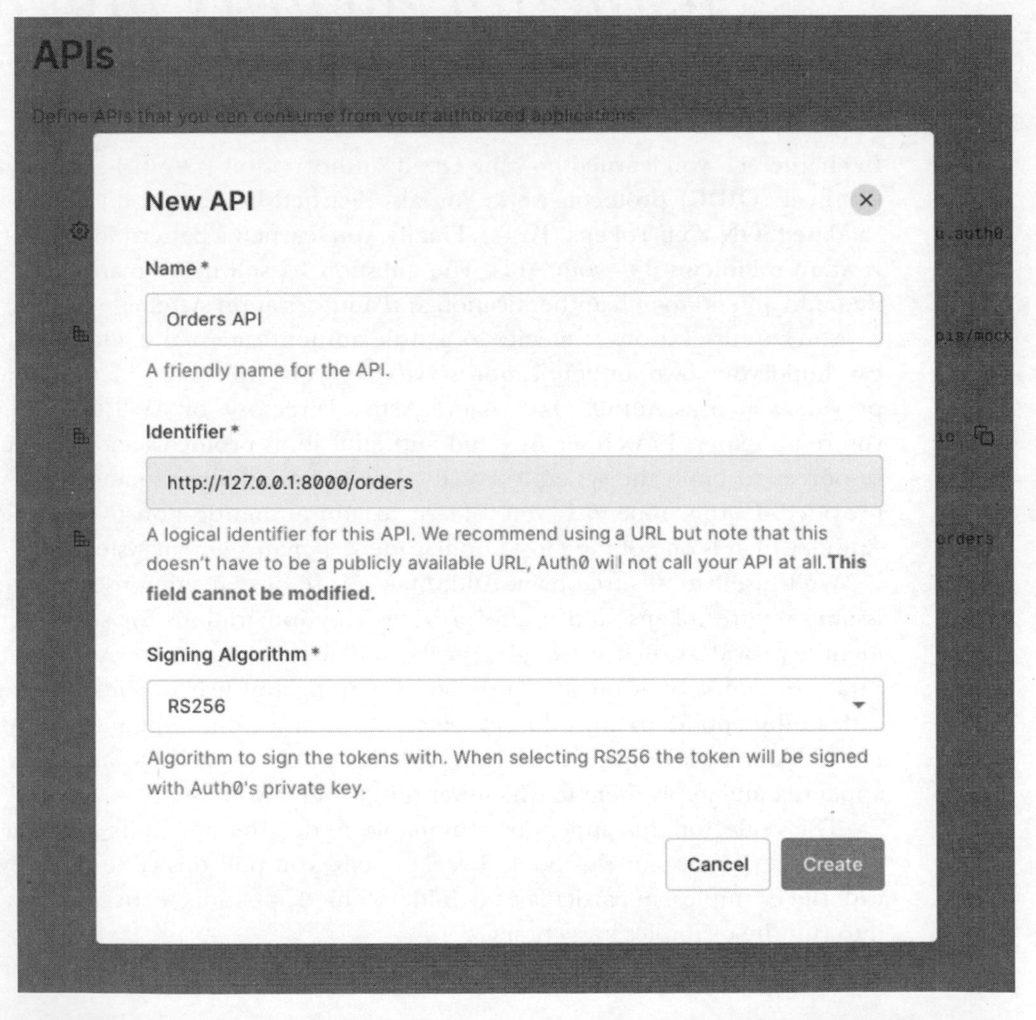

Figure C.1 To create a new API, click the Create API button, and fill in the form with the API's name, its URL identifier, and the signing algorithm you want to use for its access tokens.

giving it http://127.0.0.1:8000/orders as the identifier's value and selecting the RS256 signing algorithm.

Once you've created the API, go to Permissions and add a permission scope to the API, as shown in figure C.2.

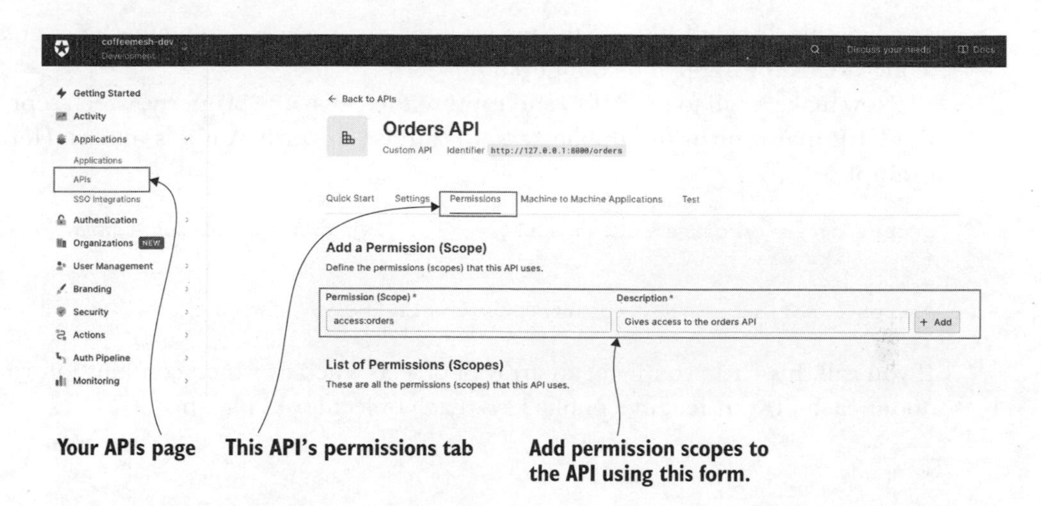

Figure C.2 To add permission scopes to the API, click on the Permissions tab, and fill in the Add a Permission (Scope) form.

Next, click Settings on the left-side bar, and then click the Custom Domains tab, as shown in figure C.3.

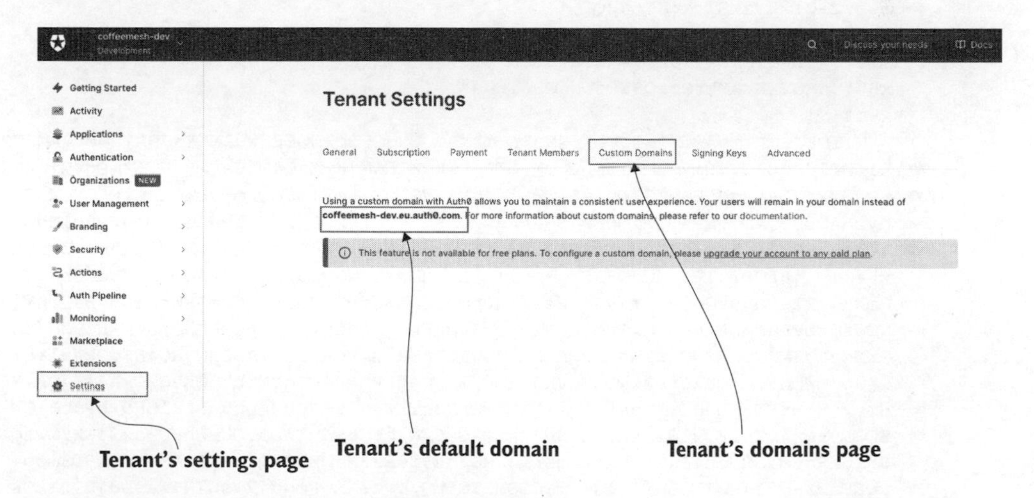

Figure C.3 To find out your tenant's default domain, go to the tenant's settings page and click the Custom Domains tab.

You can add a custom domain if you want, or you can use Auth0's default domain for your tenant. We use this domain to build the well-known URL of our authentication service:

```
https://<tenant>.<region>.auth0.com/.well-known/openid-configuration
```

For example, for CoffeeMesh, the tenant's domain is https://coffeemesh-dev.eu.auth0.com/.well-known/openid-configuration.

Now make a call to this URL, and capture the `jwks_uri` property, which represents the URL that returns the public keys we can use to verify Auth0's tokens. Here's an example:

```
$ curl https://coffeemesh.eu.auth0.com/.well-known/openid-configuration \
| jq .jwks_uri
# output:
"https://coffeemesh-dev.eu.auth0.com/.well-known/jwks.json"
```

If you call this URL, you'll get an array of objects, each of which contains information about each of your tenant's public keys. Each object looks like this:


```
{
  "alg": "RS256",
  "kty": "RSA",
  "use": "sig",
  "n": "sV2z9AApyKK-
➥ Zo9vrzHbonNsHTgYiIOx1dHx3U102fUhPFzUcdnjb7li960iTKyTbFlMRbsN2fFZOHa5_4Q
➥ 3C7UzjkVw__jK3AcPZ-0cCiLBS-HQzE_6ii-OPo84-
➥ W9Pp2ScKdAlJIqBimDtNv8vuOEMr5c5YbJz1HlppFY_hA71dgc101SHp0n9GZYqP5HV713m
➥ 6smE5b7abHLqrUSz9eVbSOrTUOcSd5_LUHvQqFb5Wt7kRalIiHnQFob-
➥ cyM1AmxDNsX1qR2cX_jqjWCRO2iK5DTG--ure8GQUTCMPZ0LkBKSDelTwHuEn_r4z-
➥ x30wf-2lA0yzMSlcxcJIojpQ",
  "e": "AQAB",
  "kid": "ZweIFRR4l1dJlVPHOoZqf",
  "x5t": "OJXBmAMkfObrQ9YkfUb4O20l_us",
  "x5c": [
    "MIIDETCCAfmgAwIBAgIJUbXpEMz8nlmXMA0GCSqGSIb3DQEBCwUAMCYxJDAiBgNVBAMTG2NvZm
➥ ZlZW1lc2gtZGV2LmV1LmF1dGgwLmNvbTAeFw0yMTEwMjkyMjQ4MjBaFw0zNTA3MDgyMjQ4M[
➥ jBaMCYxJDAiBgNVBAMTG2NvZmZlZW1lc2gtZGV2LmV1LmF1dGgwLmNvbTCCASIwDQYJKoZI
➥ hvcNAQEBBQADggEPADCCAQoCggEBALFds/QAKciivmaPb68x26JzbB04GIiDsdXR8d1NdNn
➥ 1ITxc1HHZ42+5YvetIkysk2xZTEW7DdnxWTh2uf+ENwu1M45FcP/4ytwHD2ftHAoiwUvh0M
➥ xP+oovjj6POPlvT6dknCnQJSSKgYpg7Tb/L7jhDK+XOWGyc9R5aaRWP4QO9XYHNdNUh6dJ/
➥ RmWKj+R1e9d5urJhOW+2mxy6q1Es/XlW0jq01DnEnefy1B70KhW+Vre5EWpSIh50BaG/nMj
➥ NQJsQzbF9akdnF/46o1gkTtoiuQ0xvvrq3vBkFEwjD2dC5ASkg3pU8B7hJ/6+M/sd9MH/tp
➥ QNMszEpXMXCSKI6UCAwEAAaNCMEAwDwYDVR0TAQH/BAUwAwEB/zAdBgNVHQ4EFgQUWrl+q/
➥ l4wp/MWDdYrhjxns0iP2wwDgYDVR0PAQH/BAQDAgKEMA0GCSqGSIb3DQEBCwUAA4IBAQA+Y
➥ H+sxcMlBzEOJ5hJgZw1upRroCgmeQzEh+Cx73sTKw+vi8u70bdkDt9sBLKlGK9xbPJt3+QW
➥ ZDJF9rwx4vXbfFvxZD+dthIvn4NH4/sLQXG20JN/b6GtHdVllbJIGUeWb8DBsx94wXYMwag
➥ 0gXUk5spgaGGdoc16uSrrbxt/rmzFk3VMQ8qG5i8E33N/DZb88P4u3WJMNMsmujw9Q8meg4
➥ ygEFadXBcfJPHuiriLWi0j1Gm+m6DZQM51OtpQ/cvcZXRNPogqj7wsZXH4za9DJjnQf8ZOK
➥ Q86WKl/9CE5AvHBTTTr810DviJIqv8sqC866+2t2euxcfOYMIw5E42o"
  ]
}
```

The two most important fields in this payload are `kid` and `x5c`. `kid` is the ID of the key, and we use it to match the `kid` field of the JWT's header section. It tells us which key we need to use to verify the token's signature. The `x5c` field contains an array of public keys in the form of X.509 certificates, the first of which we use to verify the JWT's signature.

This is all the information we need to integrate our code with Auth0. We'll implement our Auth0 integration in the orders/web/api/auth.py module, which we created in chapter 11 (section 11.4.1) to encapsulate our authorization code. Delete the contents of orders/web/api/auth.py, and replace them with the contents of listing C.1. We first import the necessary dependencies, create a template for the X.509 certificate, and load the public keys from the well-known endpoint. X.509 certificates are wrapped between `-----BEGIN CERTIFICATE-----` and `-----END CERTIFICATE-----` statements, so our template includes both statements with a template variable named `key`, which we'll replace with the actual key.

Since Auth0 uses several keys to sign the tokens, we load the public keys by calling the JWKS endpoint, and we dynamically load the right key for the given token. As you can see in figure C.4, the `kid` property in the token's headers tells us which key we need to use, and our custom function `_get_certificate_for_kid()` finds the X.509 certificate for the token's `kid`. To load the key, we use cryptography's `load_pem_x509_certificate()` function, passing in the public key formatted into our X.509 byte-encoded certificate.

Since tokens can be signed with different algorithms, we fetch the algorithms directly from the token's headers. Auth0 issues tokens that can access both our API and the user information API, so we include both services in the audience.

Listing C.1 Adding an authorization module to the API

```
# file: orders/web/api/auth.py

import jwt
import requests
from cryptography.x509 import load_pem_x509_certificate

X509_CERT_TEMPLATE = (
        "-----BEGIN CERTIFICATE-----\n{key}\n-----END CERTIFICATE-----"
   )


public_keys = requests.get(
    "https://coffeemesh-dev.eu.auth0.com/.well-known/jwks.json"
).json()["keys"]


def _get_certificate_for_kid(kid):
    """
    Return the public key whose ID matches the provided kid.
```

Template for a X509 certificate

We pull the list of signing keys from the tenant's well-known endpoint.

Function that returns the certificate for a given key ID

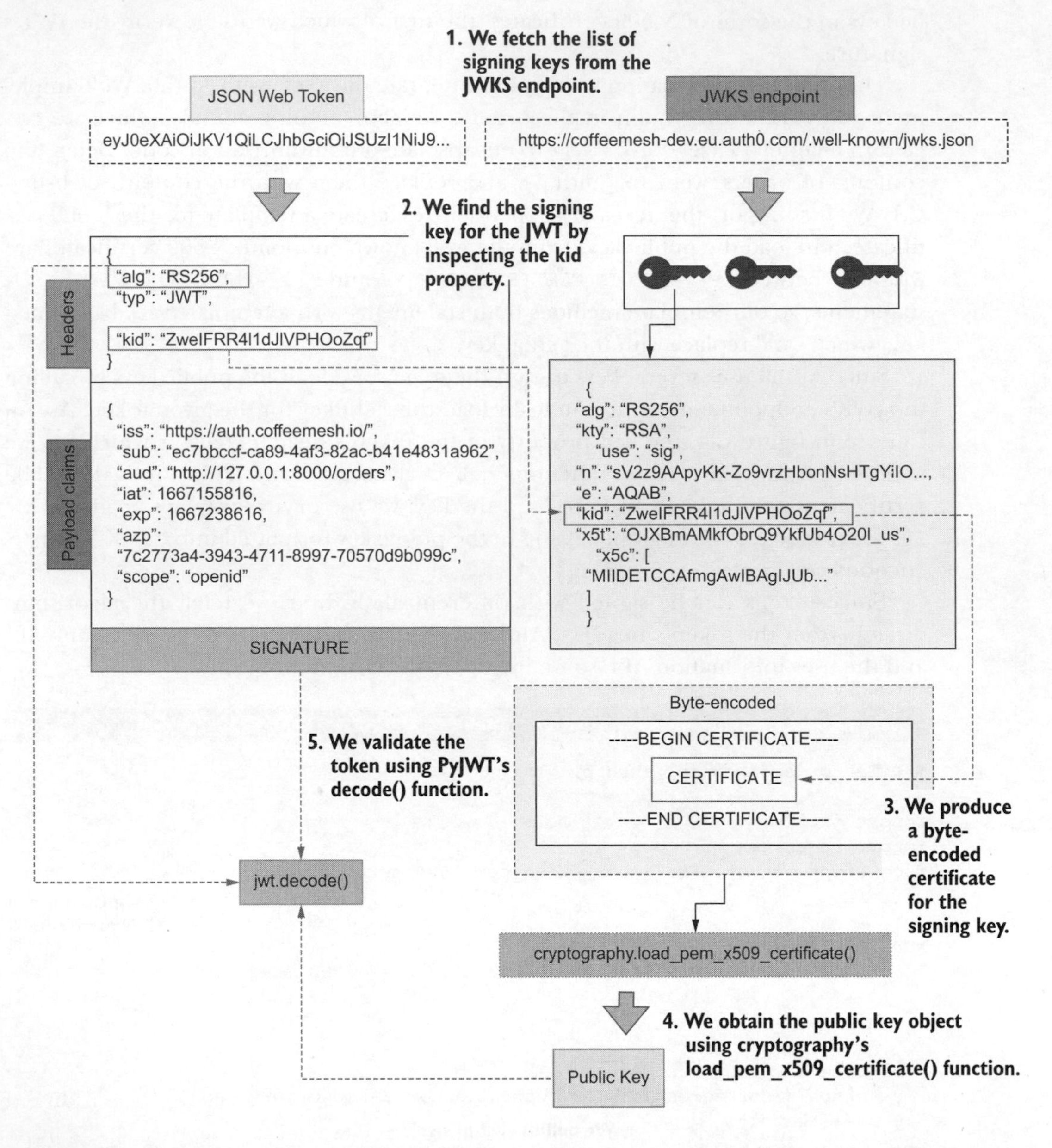

Figure C.4 To validate a JWT, we verify its signature using its corresponding signing key. The signing key is available in the JWKS endpoint.

```
    If no match is found, an exception is raised.
    """
    for key in public_keys:
        if key["kid"] == kid:
            return key["x5c"][0]
    raise Exception(f"Not matching key found for kid {kid}")


def load_public_key_from_x509_cert(certificate):
    """
    Loads the public signing key into a RSAPublicKey object. To do that,
    we first need to format the key into a PEM certificate and make sure
    it's utf-8 encoded. We can then load the key using cryptography's
    convenient `load_pem_x509_certificate` function.
    """
    return load_pem_x509_certificate(certificate).public_key()


def decode_and_validate_token(access_token):
    """
    Validates an access token. If the token is valid, it returns the token
    payload.
    """
    unverified_headers = jwt.get_unverified_header(access_token)
    x509_certificate = _get_certificate_for_kid(
        unverified_headers["kid"]
    )
    public_key = load_public_key_from_x509_cert(
        X509_CERT_TEMPLATE.format(key=x509_certificate).encode("utf-8")
    )
    return jwt.decode(
        access_token,
        key=public_key,
        algorithms=unverified_headers["alg"],
        audience=[
            "http://127.0.0.1:8000/orders",
            "https://coffeemesh-dev.eu.auth0.com/userinfo",
        ],
    )
```

- We look for the certificate that matches the supplied key ID.
- If a match isn't found, we raise an exception.
- Function that loads the public key object for a given certificate
- We load the public key.
- Function that decodes and validates a JWT
- We fetch the token's headers without verification.
- We fetch the certificate corresponding to the token's key ID.
- We load the certificate's public key object.
- We validate and decode the token.
- We verify the token's signature using the algorithm indicated in the token's header.
- We pass the list of expected audiences for the token.

We're ready to go! The orders service is now able to validate tokens issued by Auth0. The following sections illustrate how to leverage this integration to make our API server accessible to a single-page application (SPA) and to another microservice.

C.2 Using the PKCE authorization flow

In the PKCE flow, the API client requests an ID token and an access token directly from the authorization server. As we explained in chapter 11, we must use the access token to interact with the API server. The ID token can be used in the UI to show the details of the user, but it must never be sent to our API server.

To illustrate how this flow works, I've included an SPA under the appendix_c/ui directory in the GitHub repository for this book. The SPA is a simple application built with Vue.js that talks to the orders API, and it's configured to authenticate with an Auth0 server.

We'll first configure the application. Go to your Auth0 account, and create a new application. Select Single Page Web Applications, and give it a name, then click Create. In the application's settings page, under the Application URIs section, give the value of http://localhost:8000 to the Allowed Callback URLs, the Allowed Logout URLs, the Allowed Web Origins, and the Allowed Origins (CORS) fields. From the application's settings, we need two values to configure our application: the domain and the client ID. Open the ui/.env.local file, and replace the value for `VUE_APP_AUTH_CLIENT_ID` with the client ID and `VUE_APP_AUTH_DOMAIN` with the domain from your application's settings page in Auth0.

To run the UI, you need an up-to-date version of Node.js and npm, which you can download from the node.js website (https://nodejs.org/en/). Once you've installed these, you need to install yarn with the following command:

```
$ npm install -g yarn
```

Next, `cd` into the ui/ folder, and install the dependencies by running the following command:

```
$ yarn
```

Once the application is configured, you can run it by executing the following command:

```
$ yarn serve --mode local
```

The application will become available under the http://localhost:8080 address. Make sure the orders API is also running, since the Vue.js application talks to it. To run the orders API, run the following command from the orders folder:

```
$ AUTH_ON=True uvicorn orders.web.app:app --reload
```

Once you register a user through the UI, you'll be able to see your authorization token in the UI. You can use this token to call the API directly from the terminal. For example, you can get a list of orders for your user by calling the API with the following command:

```
$ curl http://localhost:8000/orders \
-H 'Authorization: Bearer <ACCESS_TOKEN>'
```

Through the Vue.js application, you can create new orders and display the orders placed by the user by clicking the Show My Orders button.

The PKCE flow works for users accessing your APIs through the browser. However, this flow isn't convenient for machine-to-machine communication. To allow more programmatic access to your APIs, you need to support the client credentials flow. In the next section, we explain how to enable that flow!

C.3 Using the client credentials flow

This section explains how to implement the client credentials flow for server-to-server communication. We use the server-to-server flow when we must authenticate our own services to access other APIs, or when we want to allow programmatic access to our APIs. In the client credentials flow, our services request an access token from the authentication service by providing a shared secret with the client ID and the desired audience. We can then use this access token to access the API of the target audience.

To use this authorization flow, you need to register a server-to-server client with your IDaaS provider. In your Auth0 dashboard's applications page, click Create Application and select Machine to Machine Applications. Give it a name, and click Create. On the next screen, where you're asked to select the API you want to authorize this client for, select the orders API, and then select the permission we created in chapter 11 (section 11.6). Once you've registered the client, you get a client ID and a client secret, which you can use to obtain access tokens.

Listing C.2 shows how to implement server-to-server authorization to obtain an access token and make a call to the orders API. The code in listing C.2 is available in the book's GitHub repository under the machine_to_machine_test.py file. We create a function to obtain the access token from the authorization server by calling the POST `https://coffeemesh-dev.eu.auth0.com/oauth/token` endpoint. In the payload, we provide the client ID and the client secret, and we specify the audience for which we want to generate the access token. We also declare that we want to use the client credentials flow under the `grant_type` property. If the client is correctly authenticated, we get back an access token, which we then use to call the orders API.

Listing C.2 Authorizing a client for machine-to-machine access to the orders API

```
# file: machine_to_machine_test.py

import requests


def get_access_token():
    payload = {
        "client_id": "<client_id>",
        "client_secret": "<client_secret>",
        "audience": "http://127.0.0.1:8000/orders",
        "grant_type": "client_credentials"
    }

    response = requests.post(
        "https://coffeemesh-dev.eu.auth0.com/oauth/token",
        json=payload,
        headers={'content-type': "application/json"}
    )

    return response.json()['access_token']
```

```
def create_order(token):
    order_payload = {
        'order': [{
            'product': 'cappuccino',
            'size': 'small',
            'quantity': 1
        }]
    }

    order = requests.post(
        'http://127.0.0.1:8000/orders',
        json=order_payload,
        headers={
            "content-type": "application/json",
            "authorization": f"Bearer {token}",
        }
    )

    return order.json()


access_token = get_access_token()
print(access_token)
order = create_order(access_token)
print(order)
```

That's all it takes to use the client credentials flow! In the next section, you'll learn to authenticate your requests using a Swagger UI so that you can test your API more easily.

C.4 Authorizing requests in the Swagger UI

Over the course of this book, you've learned to test your APIs using a Swagger UI. You can use the Swagger UI to test your API authorization as well, and in this section you'll learn how. First, `cd` into appendix_c/orders and up the API server with authorization on:

```
$ AUTH_ON=True uvicorn orders.web.app:app --reload
```

You can now access the Swagger UI on http://localhost:8000/docs/orders. As you can see in figure C.5, if you try any of the endpoints, you'll get a 401 response since we haven't authorized our requests.

To authorize a request, click the Authorize button on the top-right corner of the screen. You'll get a pop-up menu with the security schemes documented in the API specification: `openId` (authorization code and PKCE flows), `oauth2` (client credentials flow), and `bearerAuth`. The easiest way to test the API's authorization layer is using the `bearerAuth` security scheme, since it only requires you to feed the authorization token. You can produce a token with the Vue.js application under appendix_c/ui or using the

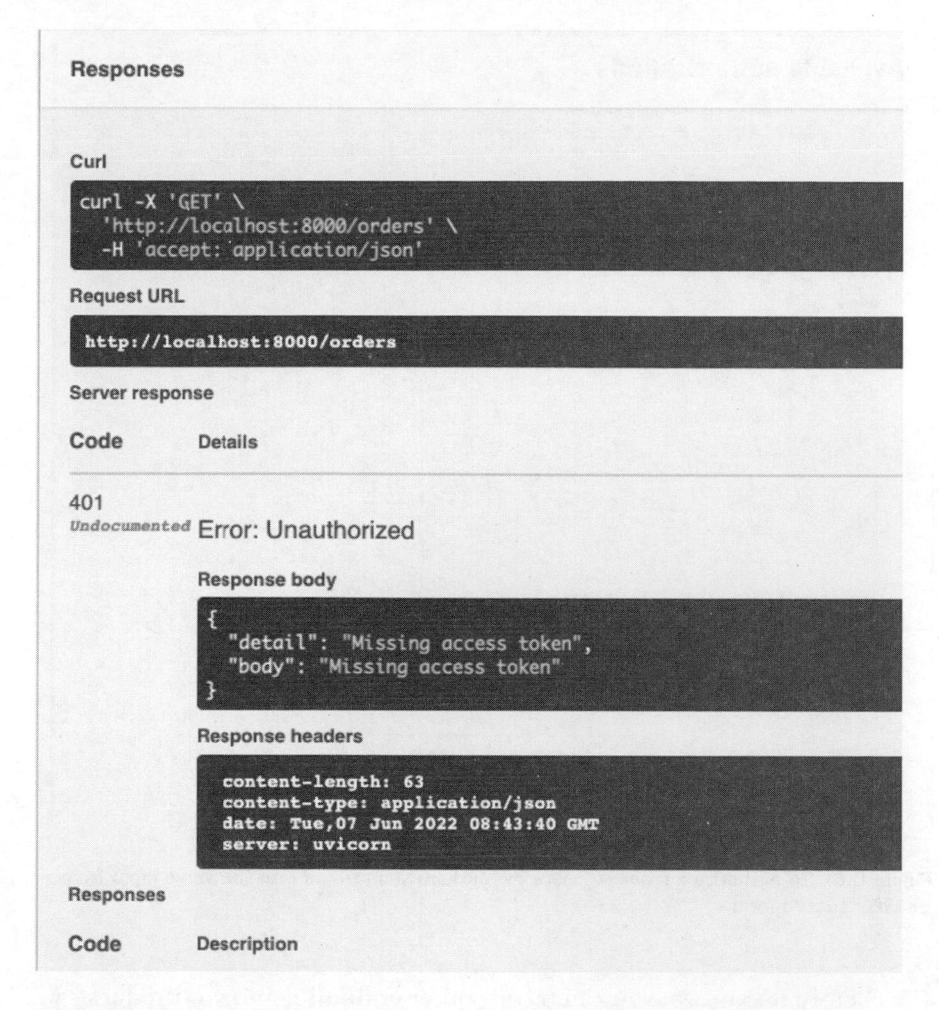

Figure C.5 If we make an unauthorized request with the Swagger UI, we'll get a 401 response.

machine_to_machine_test.py script. For example, if you run the machine_to_machine_test.py script, you'll get a token and the result of creating an order:

```
$ python machine_to_machine_test.py
# output:
eyJhbGciOiJSUzI1NiIsInR5cCI6IkpXVCIsImtpZCI6Ilp3ZUlGUlI0bDFkSmxWUEhPb1px...
➥ {'order': [{'product'. 'latte', 'size': 'small', 'quantity': 1}], 'id':
➥ '6e420d2e-b213-4d15-bc46-0c680e590154', 'created': '2022-06-
➥ 07T09:01:47.757223', 'status': 'created'}
```

Copy the token, and paste it into the value input field of the `bearerAuth`'s security scheme, as shown in figure C.6, and then click Authorize. If you send a request to the GET `/orders` endpoint now, you'll get a successful response. While the token is valid

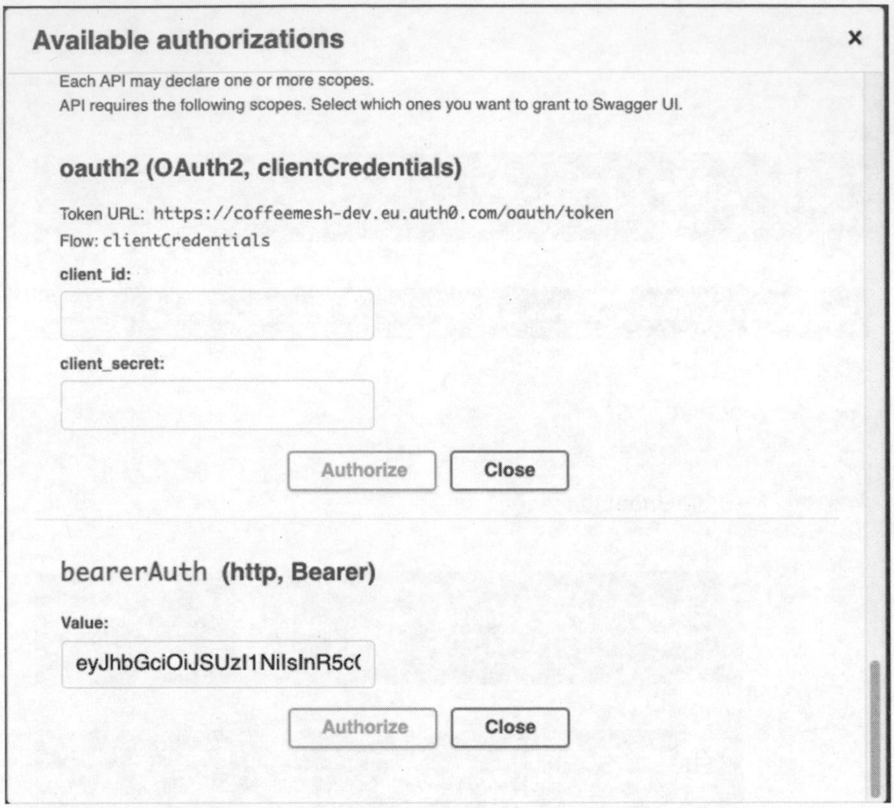

Figure C.6 To authorize a request, paste the authorization token into the value input from `bearerAuth`'s form.

(i.e., before it expires), you can try any other endpoint, and your requests will be successfully processed.

This is all it takes to test your API authorization with a Swagger UI. You just learned how to add a robust authentication and authorization layer by integrating with an external identity provider, how to test the PKCE and the client credentials flows, and how to test your API authorization implementation with Swagger. You're all set to go and build secure APIs!

index

Symbols

A

B

C

E

F

G

L

M

N

O

P

S

T

U

V

W

X

Y